Growth of Personal Awareness

Growth of Personal Awareness

A Reader in Psychology

Edited by
George Stricker and Michael Merbaum
Institute of Advanced Psychological Studies
Adelphi University

Holt, Rinehart and Winston, Inc.

New York   Chicago   San Francisco   Atlanta   Dallas   Montreal   Toronto   London   Sydney

The cover photograph and all photographs in text by
courtesy of Fred Weiss.

Preface

The readings in this supplementary textbook are designed to acquaint the student with a compelling and informative record of the activities of psychologists and of the findings of psychological inquiry. The vehicle we have chosen to accomplish this purpose is the popular press. Quality newspapers and magazines often carry articles discussing the results of psychological investigation. These articles, frequently written by or in collaboration with professional psychologists, are aimed at an audience of intelligent but untrained laymen who are unfamiliar with technical jargon. This target group, the intelligent lay reader, more closely resembles the college student than does the target group for professional journal articles. Thus as an educational technique, the presentation of good, solid research and theoretical material in this form should generate greater student enthusiasm and motivation to read the assigned material.

In selecting these articles, we used two basic criteria. First, the article had to contain psychologically sound and accurate information. Second, the article had to be interesting and readable. In almost every case, these two criteria were satisfied by material drawn from popular sources. In those few cases where articles were taken from journals, the journal material was selected to meet the above conditions.

Our readings are selected and organized to emphasize the main features of personal adjustment courses. There are sections dealing with basic psychological processes and with the developing human organism. There are also specialized sections on such subjects as therapeutic approaches to behavior and the impact and relevance of psychology in our time. A wide variety of groups—students in high schools, community colleges, junior colleges, and traditional four-year colleges—should find this collection appealing. In addition, introductory social science and educational courses could make significant use of these supplementary readings.

To aid the student in making effective use of this book we have included a number of study aids. Essays introduce each section and describe the major content and importance within the science of psychology. Bibliographies follow each introduction and include a list of pertinent books from the professional literature, along with a brief description of the content of each book. Finally, each chapter ends with a set of questions which can be used by the instructor to stimulate classroom discussion or by the individual student in thinking about the material.

A number of individuals have generously contributed their time and effort in the preparation of this volume. We acknowledge our debt and appreciation to Audrey Cunningham, Christine Price, Rhonda Warshaw, and Dale Grossmen for their secretarial help, and to Susan Aliman, Marie Oppedisano, Diana Ronell, Dale Grossmen for their assistance in preparing the test items which accompany this book.

At this point an explanation about authorship is in order. Each editor participated equally in all phases of the preparation of this book. The sequence of authorship, therefore, rested entirely on the outcome of a game of chance and skill, and is the reverse of the order in our previous book, *Seach for Human Understanding*.

And finally to our wives, Joan Stricker and Marta Merbaum, who gave continuing moral support to the project, we express our gratitude.

G. S.
M. M.

Garden City, New York
January 1973

Contents

Growth of
Personal
Awareness

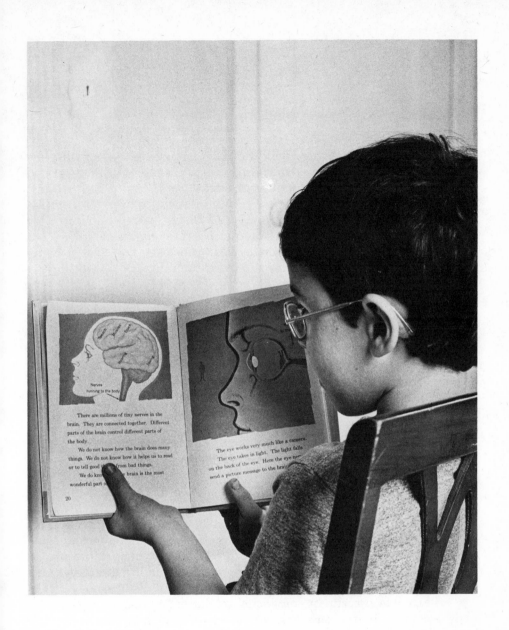

Chapter 1
Basic Processes

It is a common observation by most people that science and technology are expanding at a fantastically accelerated rate. New ideas, exciting research, and ingenious applications of knowledge are creating the kind of human possibilities today which only yesterday were generated by the fertile imagination of writers of fantasy and science fiction. Now, unlike earlier periods in history, we are effortlessly exposed to television and other information media that allow us to glimpse the future in the present and, either with pleasure or concern, to contemplate where our knowledge is leading us. One thing is clearly evident, however: it is unlikely that the pace of technological change will diminish. Two illustrations may be sufficient to convey this point effectively.

In 6000 B.C. the fastest people could travel was 8 miles per hour by camel and 20 miles per hour by horse. In 1800 A.D., nearly 8000 years later, people could go up to 100 miles per hour in a steam locomotive. In 1930 it was possible to go 400 miles in an airplane and in 1950 people were able to travel 800 miles per hour at 60,000 feet altitude. By 1960 people could travel 25,000 miles per hour by rocket and now even greater speeds are being reached. Now for another example.

One thousand years ago there were possibly 100 books and it took one scribe about five years to produce one book. In the fifteenth century the Guttenberg revolution increased the number to 1000 books a year. These were produce by monks who used hand presses. Moving ahead, in 1960 there were a thousand books produced in one day and in 1965 the government alone circulated about 60,000 pages. But in 1970 using laser and computer technology, it was possible to transmit and have instantaneous access to approximately two billion bits of information per second. And these data are even now conservative. The information technology is so sophisticated that it is possible to store 10,000,000 bits of information on an area the size of a postage stamp, and the limit has not yet been reached.

These data are surely convincing to the extent that men have not only gained a tremendous amount of knowledge about their physical world but, in the process, have also developed a huge technological base from which to create a gigantic assortment of products. Yet, an important point worth considering is whether our understanding of man himself has kept pace with this vast leap in technological know-how. To a great extent it probably has not, but the advancement currently being made in the study of man himself cannot be underestimated or dismissed as trivial. The purpose of this chapter is to provide the reader with a sample of studies that are important in the area of the science of psychology.

The first article in this section deals with the innovative work of José Delgado, a pioneer in the use of electrical stimulation of the brain.

The critical feature of Delgado's work lies in his efforts to decode the intricate nature of brain processes. The superiority of man over all species on this planet is directly attributable to a highly evolved brain structure. Delgado's radical experiments have begun to map those structures in our extraordinarily complex brain that are involved with pain, emotionality, pleasure, and higher areas of intellectual control. Delgado's intention is not simply to discover but to put to practical medical use these discoveries so that pain and stress might be eventually relieved. The implications of Delgado's work are just beginning to be felt in the scientific community, and these crude beginnings are becoming the foundation for a more sophisticated study of the human brain.

As you will see, much of Delgado's interest is in designing methods of influencing brain function through the use of electrical stimulation transmitted via micro-electrodes implanted into the cellular structure of the brain. In a real sense this represents control over the brain by an external agent. A fascinating series of experiments that run parallel but study the problems of brain control from a significantly different angle is the research area of bio-feedback and "self-control." Here, the individual is the agent for the control of his own bodily resources. What is bio-feedback training and how does it relate to our ability to control ourselves?

The article by Barnard Law Collier, summarizing recent studies, gives a superb picture of the experimental process and the research problems currently being tackled. The goal of bio-feedback training is to increase effective self-monitoring of physiological processes and through this information gathering to increase a person's voluntary capacity to consciously regulate his own bodily processes. We have all heard of yogis and mystics in various parts of the world who have developed the remarkable ability to control respiration, to lower heart rate, and to perform physical feats that on the surface seem truly phenomenal. However, recent studies suggest that training methods for the average person can be devised to facilitate the voluntary control over the autonomic nervous system and the viscera thereby approximating some of the yogi phenomenon. These methods of learning generally involve the systematic shaping up of a response through reinforcement and follow the principles of the operant conditioning model. Briefly, a great part of our learning occurs through the constant effect of sensory feedback. We act in a particular way to obtain consequences of our behavior from the environment. If the behavior is reinforced or rewarded, there is a high probability that similar behavior will be committed in the future. If our behavior is inappropriate and not reinforced, we will usually try different methods and modify our approach until we obtain the reinforcement we find so desirable. The same is true with feedback training in modifying our physiological processes. By amplifying our internal feedback system with electrical recording devices, we can observe our heart rate or alpha rhythm and, coupled with information, devise a variety of trial-and-error methods to achieve purposive control over the biological systems which regulate these functions. These notions are the foundation of the bio-feedback training programs that are currently being explored in many laboratories across the country.

The next article in this chapter explores the fascinating world of sexual differences. It is a scientific fact that much of our behavior is learned through varied experience in our social environment. In Western society the cultural heritage of women has for the most part been subordinate to men. It is not necessary to justify this conclusion since the evidence for social inequality in work, education, and so forth is well documented. In the United States, as in other Western countries, feminine demands for economic and social equality are vigorous and persistent, so much so that legislation is being enacted to ensure equality. Therefore, the scientific study of male and female differences is timely and relevant. The fascinating article by Tom Alexander examines a controversial feature of the feminist movement. It has been argued that men and women are biologically similar and behavioral distinctions are mainly a result of cultural influences which have defined and reinforced the roles of male and female in our society. Without minimizing the importance of social learning, scientific evidence also suggests that there are innate differences between men and women which significantly influence mood and temperament and other "behavioral differences between the sexes." The author of this article examines the evidence and comes up with some interesting findings, for example, the fact that the physiological effects of hormonal substances such as progesterone, a female hormone, and testosterone, a male hormone, appear to subtley influence many forms of behavior. The major conclusion from this article is that sex distinctions are based upon real biological differences and to deny these facts runs in the face of current scientific evidence. However, these differences cannot be the basis for exploitation or the perpetration of unequal opportunities. Differences must be respected and understood so that diverse but complementary behavior will stimulate the continuation and creative extension of human society.

A number of years ago Stanley Milgram, a social psychologist at Yale University, conducted a series of controversial experiments which attempted to demonstrate the power of social authority in generating blindly rigid obedience. Aside from the fact that obedience is a fascinating topic in its own right, the implications of excessive control have had frightening consequences in our recent past. This fact is easily illustrated by the Nazis' destruction of the Jewish community in western and eastern Europe and of the many murders of innocent people during the second world war. The violence of the American presence in Vietnam and the murder of innocent civilians in My Lai and so on also suggests that most individuals respond obediently to orders from above despite the fact that these orders may include demands which are morally repugnant to the persons performing these actions. The extraordinary power of authority in producing obedient behavior is well documented in Milgram's work. Milgram found that the pressure to conform to an order is both obvious and subtle. The coercion involved in creating conformance is usually not necessarily physical but subtly psychological. In his study, Milgram duped innocent subjects into believing that they were involved in a learning task for the betterment of a subject who was strapped into an electric-chair-type apparatus. The naive teacher was encouraged by an experimenter to present increasingly intense doses of electrcial shock to the hapless learner. While no shocks were actually given, the atmosphere of the experiment was so genuinely deceptive that the teacher was convinced he was giving shocks to his learning subject. The results were quite conclusive in showing that persons receiving orders from a respected authority frequently will engage in behavior which they regard as morally objectionable. Nonetheless, the pressures to conform are so powerful that obedience occurs despite the intervention of conscience. The societal implications of these findings perhaps are obvious and lead us to speculate on how to achieve a balance between an allegiance to responsible authority and the ability to make independent decisions in the face of pressures that are objectionable to personal moral principles.

Suggested Readings
Bardwick, Judith M. *Psychology of Women: A Study of Bio-Cultural Conflicts.* New York: Harper & Row, 1972. This book throws the many aspects of the psychology of women in bold relief.
Delgado, José M. R. *Physical Control of the Mind: Toward a Psychocivilized Society.* New York: Harper Colophon Books, Harper & Row, Publishers, 1969. A brilliant review of Delgado by Delgado written for the intelligent layman.
Goldfried, Marvin R., and Merbaum, Michael (Eds.) *Behavior Change through Self-Control.* New York: Holt, Rinehart and Winston, 1972. This volume presents classic articles in the area of self-control emphasizing theory and therapeutic applications.
Hilgard, Ernest R., and Bower, Gordon H. *Theories of Learning.* New York: Appleton-Century-Crofts, 1966. The most popular text in the learning area.

1. Brain Researcher José Delgado Asks—"What Kind of Humans Would We Like to Construct?"
Maggie Scarf

" 'The human race,' he says, 'is at an evolutionary turning point.' "

One of the most brilliantly innovative researchers in brain processes is José Delgado. His work on electrical brain stimulation has opened the way for greater understanding of the function and control of the brain.

"We are going to talk about love and war and hate," begins the professor, Dr. José M. R. Delgado of the Yale University School of Medicine. The class is an undergraduate course at Yale. Although registration was limited to 15, the seminar room is crowded; every chair around the long table is filled, and some students are sitting on packing cases stored at one end, and some are on extra chairs near the door. "But we shall consider these subjects in a novel way: from the inside of the thinking brain. What is going on there, what is happening in the *nerve cells* while we talk, while we behave, while we feel?"

Delgado, an emotional speaker, pauses. A spare man in his mid-50's, he leans forward on the table, resting his weight on both large hands. His eyes, restless and light in color, rove swiftly around the circle of staring faces. "We have a new way to study behavior, a new methodology which we have developed," he resumes in a voice that is low but as vibrant with promise as a preacher's. There is a stir, almost a sigh from the students; this is what they want to hear about, this "new methodology."

It is E. S. B.: electrical stimulation of the brain. Delgado is one of the leading pioneers in its refinement and development. He is also the impassioned prophet of a new "psychocivilized" society whose members would influence and alter their own mental functions to create a "happier, less destructive and better balanced man."

A few days earlier, just before the start of classes, *The New York Times* ran a front-page story on Dr. Delgado which was picked up by newspapers across the country. It described his most recent accomplishment: the establishment of direct nonsensory communication between the computer and the brain of a chimp. This study was the latest in a series of experiments involving two-way radio-wave contact with the brains of freely interacting animals. Because it clearly demonstrates that behavior can be influenced by remote radio command, this research has been seen by some as posing an ultimate threat to human freedom and integrity.

The morning that story appeared, it was raining mildly in New Haven. In Delgado's secretary's office, part of the cluttered wing his staff occupies on the second floor of the Sterling Hall of Medicine, the telephone started ringing early; it kept on and on. In the darkroom next door, Delgado was just finishing the photographing of some E.E.G. recordings, or "brain waves." He bustles back across the hall and into his own office, immaculate as a surgeon in his white laboratory coat. "What do you want me to tell you?" he asks shortly, sitting down at his desk. He runs an irritable hand over his short-cut, curly hair. "I don't want to talk about my wife, my family, my friends. That's not science." He glances, scowling, through the window at the large white square of the School of Public Health building next door, and his expression suddenly clears. He turns back, leans forward over his desk relaxedly in one of the rapid mood changes which one very quickly learns to expect.

"The human race," he says, "is at an evolutionary turning point. We're very close to having the power to construct our own mental functions, through a knowledge of genetics (which I think will be complete within the next 25 years); and through a knowledge of the cerebral mechanisms which underlie our behavior. The question is what sort of humans would we like, ideally, to construct?" He smiles. "Not only our cities are very badly planned; we as human beings are, too. The results in both cases are disastrous.

"I am an optimist," continues Delgado. "I don't accept Lorenz's 'cosmic slip.' I don't think we're condemned by our natural fate to violence and self-destruction. My thesis is that just as we've evolved in our understanding of material forces, so we can—through a combination of new technology and of intelligence —evolve in our understanding of the mind.

"Man once used his intelligence to achieve ecological liberation, so that he no longer had to be wet when it rained, or cold when the sun was hidden, or killed because predators were hungry. He can achieve mental liberation also. Through an understanding of the brain, the brain itself may act to reshape its own structures and functions intelligently. That we bring this about is most essential for the future of mankind."

Delgado glances at his watch: "Come, I will show you around; I must hurry; I'm leaving for Zurich in two days." He looks impatient and harried again.

We go across the hall, through the secretary's office, into a large room full of equipment. Here, the two electronics engineers on Delgado's staff are at work. "How are you coming along?" asks Delgado, falling into a rapid conversation about equipment that will be needed for an experiment going on in Bermuda, for a motion-recording study to be carried out in a psychiatric ward, for a monkey-colony investigation going on upstairs; also, he checks over drawings of an improved transdermal (under the skin) brain stimulator. The noise of the phone and the secretary's voice provide a constant backdrop: "Dr. Delgado?" she asks, hurrying in suddenly. "How would you like to be on television?"

"What?" he says distractedly, in his rapid Spanish accent. "I wouldn't like it at all."

"How would you like to be on the David Frost show?"

"What's that?" he taps his foot impatiently. She seems uncomfortable:

"He doesn't know," she says, looking at the two engineers helplessly. But they both shake their heads and shrug; they don't know either. "What shall I say?" she asks.

"Say no," Delgado answers curtly, but then more gently, adds: "Tell them I'm going to Zurich. Tell them to call me some other time. I'm sorry."

On the way up to the fourth-floor laboratory, he stops in his office to pick up a small plastic box which at first sight looks empty. "Here is something that's going to be fantastic, really exciting," he says, holding it up like a conjuror. "But I can't tell you what it is; it's too early, it wouldn't be scientific."

Wouldn't he be willing to explain what it is privately? He hesitates: "All right. . . ." But then he hurries off, at a pace only a little short of a run. Staring at the box in his hand, I see that it does contain something—two tiny chemitrodes, that is, arrays of electrodes and fine chemical tubes that can be inserted into the brain. "When we know the mechanisms by which the brain operates," resumes Delgado, "then we will be able to control our reality. The predicament of mankind is not too different from that of the dinosaurs, who flourished on earth for some 30 million years. They had very little intelligence; and 40 tons of flesh and bones. When the environment began to change, they lacked the intelligence to understand their situation, to adapt. Their fate—extinction."

"We, too, have developed disproportionate muscles and bones: missiles, guns, biological warfare. Our brains are not developed accordingly; they must become so or our own fate will be the same." We pass through a wide corridor. On either side are shining steel machines with bright plastic, electric leads coming out of them; it looks as cheery as a nursery school. In one room a monkey is calmly sitting in a plastic chair while his brain waves are recorded. He throws us a curious glance as we go by.

Delgado turns into a room at the left, the laboratory of his new young assistant, freshly arrived from Germany. They sit down together and the older man begins a careful explanation of how the chemitrodes are to be mounted. When he is finished, the new researcher blushes and stammers: "Please, I'm still not understanding too well . . . the English. Won't you repeat?" Delgado, very patiently goes over the instructions. Then he stands up and excuses himself for a moment.

While he is gone, I ask the assistant what the new experiment will be. He explains, haltingly, that they are going to infuse a radioactive substance through the monkey's brain very slowly—"Stop, don't say anything!" cries Delgado, rushing back into the laboratory. "You mustn't tell her, she's dangerous. She's a journalist!"

"What, what?" demands the assistant, jumping back frightened. And suddenly, inexplicably, the three of us burst out laughing.

In a small corridor off the end of the main hallway are the animal cages, full of rhesus monkeys and gibbons right now. Delgado goes into one room, opening the cage of a female rhesus named Linda (after his 8-year-old daughter). "Hello, hello, Linda," he says softly to the monkey, who scampers up on to the wire-mesh ceiling. "It's OK, it's OK, come down." He takes a piece of apple, holds it out to her. Linda comes down, grabs the apple; a moment later she throws it at Delgado. He laughs: "That's not nice Linda, come down." She consents at last, comes swiftly to sit in Delgado's arms and throws her own around his neck.

He parts the hair on her shoulder, revealing an almost invisible transdermal brain stimulator. "Linda has been wearing this for over a year now; it's very important in its implication for humans. One of the real difficulties with humans is the cosmetic one. This transdermal can be placed below the skin and sealed forever, so that there are no unsightly plugs or equipment showing. We're working now on another one that would be even smaller."

Delgado strokes Linda's fur, then he looks up: "I have a great respect for the human brain," he remarks with the air of a man who has had to reiterate the statement often. "It distressed me greatly when I first came to this country in the early fifties to see so many patients without frontal lobes. Of course, much psychosurgery has now been replaced by drug treatment, but there are still people with dangerous seizures which simply do not respond to medication. In these cases, rather extensive portions of the temporal lobe may be removed— and since brain tissue doesn't regenerate, those functions which are lost are lost.

"Intracerebral electrodes offer a more conservative approach. Instead of cutting down through cerebral tissue, we insert very fine stainless steel wires. Then we can record the activity of various brain areas; in this way it becomes possible to locate the disturbances with a good degree of precision. After that, damaged areas can be treated by cauterization, or by E.S.B. in a brain area which inhibits on-going activity. Or still another possibility would be inducing electrical excitement in a competing area. For instance, there is one epileptic patient who uses a self-stimulator each time he feels a seizure coming on. By activating another part of the brain, he stops the discharge from spreading; the fit never develops."

In the past several years, electrode implantation has been used in the diagnosis and treatment of involuntary movements and intractable pain, as well as in epilepsy, some cases of schizophrenia and of excessive anxiety. Delgado was one of a small group of brain researchers to pioneer their clinical application. Implantation of electrodes, although carried out only as an alternative to destructive surgery, is "like installing a magic window through which one may look at the activity of the conscious, behaving brain.

"We are," says Delgado, "only in the initial stages of our understanding of E.S.B., but we know that it can delay a heartbeat, move a finger, bring a word to memory, evoke a sensation."

Brain stimulation in humans has elicited diverse and curious responses. It has stirred long hallucinations, such as hearing a piece of music being played from beginning to end; it has produced peculiar illusions of *deja vu*—the intense feeling that the present moment has been experienced in the past. Patients have also described the vivid "reliving" of moments from their past, far more immediate than mere recollection. All the sensations of the former experience seem to spring to life—cars passing in the street outside, the sounds of children playing, words said and forgotten long ago.

"There are basic mechanisms inside the brain, I believe," says Delgado, "that are responsible for all mental activities, including emotion. I think we are now on the threshold of understanding them. We must do so—and soon—if the precarious race between unchained atoms and intelligent brains is to be won."

José Manuel Rodriguez Delgado was born in Ronda, Spain, in 1915. The town, which stands high on a rocky cliff to the southwest of Granada, was one of the last strongholds of the Moors. Dr. Delgado is the son of Rafael Rodriguez

Amerigo; on the paternal side he is directly descended from Amerigo Vespucci. (The name Delgado is his mother's maiden name: in Spain, where lineage is of paramount importance, a child takes the names of both grandparents as surname. Thus, Delgado's last name there is Rodriguez Delgado.)

José, the second of three boys (his older brother is a staff member of the United Nations), went directly from high school to the University of Madrid, taking his degree in medicine just before the outbreak of the Spanish Civil War. In 1938 he was drafted and joined the Spanish Republicans. "I fought with them until the triumph of France, then I was thrown in a concentration camp. Those few months had a great effect upon me; they shaped me."

In what way?

"Oh, well," he shrugs slightly, his brows beetling in annoyance; he dislikes direct questions. "That all has nothing to do with my work." After his release in 1939, Delgado returned to the University of Madrid to take his M.D. once again (the old one was no longer valid). Then he lingered to take a Ph.D. in science at the Cajal Institute in Madrid. In 1950, he was invited to Yale by the famed neurophysiologist John Fulton. "And I never have left here," he concludes in a pleased voice.

In 1956, Delgado, in his early 40's met Caroline Stoddard, the pretty, 22-year-old daughter of a Yale administrator; they were married within the year. They now have two children: Linda, 8, and José Carlos, 11. After 14 years of marriage, Caroline Delgado is quietly and passionately devoted to her husband's work, perhaps even a bit awed by it. (She sometimes refers to him, in a voice innocent of irony, as "the great Delgado.") "I go in to the lab with José pretty much every morning," she says cheerfully. She generally works in the same office, editing and typing papers. Does she mind the work? "Oh, no, I love it! It's nice being with someone who's always optimistic. And then it's a continuing circus; it's fun to see what's coming next. The brain is a relatively new field —there's a tremendous feeling of excitement."

The human brain—that most delicate, complex organ, the organ of selection and imagination—is a mass of about 10 billion neurons, or nerve cells, which are almost continually receiving, transmitting, and discharging electrical impulses. In the early nineteen-twenties, Hans Berger, a German psychiatrist, first recorded the electrical activity of the human brain. Berger's electroencephalograms (E.E.G.'s) were made by attaching electrodes to the outside of the scalp. They could convey only the crudest information, for the signals emanating from the "black box" of the brain were bewildering and manifold: It was like opening the door on a cocktail party where many conversations were going on at once. Some of the voices were persistent, some started and stopped; there was a great deal of background racket. Not for many years—and not until the advent of electronic computers—were researchers able to sort out the signals coming from various structures and areas of the brain.

Shortly after Berger first recorded brain waves, the Swiss neurophysiologist W. R. Hess implanted very fine, stainless-steel electrodes deep within the brain of a cat. The cat, once recovered from the anesthesia, could not feel the wires at all. For the brain, the most exquisite of sensory interpreters, actually has no receptors or nerve endings in its own tissue; it feels nothing. Hess introduced a mild electrical impulse, stimulating the central gray matter, and the cat suddenly behaved "as if threatened by a dog." Evidently, nerve cells associated with emotions of rage had been activated. "It spits, snorts or growls," wrote Hess, ". . . its pupils widen . . . its ears lie back, or move back and forth to frighten the nonexisting enemy."

Hess's experiment raised some excited speculations. It was known that certain areas of the brain controlled specific functions such as speech, sight, the flexing of arm and leg muscles. But emotions were not thought to be represented specifically—was it possible that there *were* areas or "centers" in the brain which corresponded to the different emotional states? E.S.B. seemed to offer a way to study the mechanisms of emotions experimentally, and yet, says Delgado: "When I came to this country some 20 years after Hess's early work, there were very few people—practically no one—working with brain stimulation."

Delgado had learned E.S.B. techniques while still in Spain, "mainly from reading about Hess's experiments. I was self-taught." Electrode implantation does not entail a large opening in the skull. Only a small burr hole is drilled, through which micromanipulators guide the electrode shafts—assemblies of very fine wires insulated with Teflon and scraped bare at the tips to permit the passage of current—down to their desired locations in the brain. The electrodes can be placed quite precisely with the aid of special (stereotaxic) maps of the brain and measuring instruments. Once they are in, the ends of the wires are soldered to a small exterior socket anchored to the skull.

After anesthesia wears off, plugging into the fully awake brain of cat, monkey or man is as simple as putting a lamp plug in a wall socket. There is no "awareness" of the electrodes, no ensuing damage to brain tissue. "There are chimps in our laboratory," Delgado says, "who have had up to 100 contacts implanted for more than four years; there seems to be no limit to how long they may safely be left in."

Delgado's early work at Yale was done with cats, and then increasingly with the far more intelligent and interesting monkey. Under the influence of E.S.B., the animals performed like electrical toys. "By pushing the right 'button' we could make a monkey open or shut his eyes, turn his head, move his tongue, flex his limbs. He could be made to yawn, sneeze, hop." During one experiment, a cat began the motions of licking each time it was stimulated at a certain point in the cortex. If the animal happened to be sleeping, it licked in its sleep; if awake, however, the cat looked around for a milk bowl to lap at; if there was no bowl, it began licking its own fur. "The cat seemed determined," smiles Delgado, "to make sense out of what he was doing."

E.S.B. can evoke not only simple but complicated behaviors which may be performed in sequence. One monkey, Ludy, each time she was stimulated in the red nucleus (in the posterior part of the brain) would stop what she was doing; change expression, turn her head to the right; stand up on two feet and circle to the right; climb a pole and then descend again; growl, threaten and often attack another monkey; then change attitude and approach the rest of the group in a friendly way. This "automatism" was repeated in the same order each time —through 20,000 stimulations!

"Interestingly enough," remarks Delgado, "when Ludy was stimulated at another point in the red nucleus only 3 millimeters away, she simply yawned."

Stimulation of certain brain areas has caused animals to increase the amount of food they eat by as much as 1,000 percent, while E.S.B. at hunger-inhibiting points will make starving monkeys and cats turn away from food. The tickling of a few electric volts can send a monkey into a deep sleep, or snap him awake. "By brain stimulations in the hypothalamic region we can adjust the size of a monkey's eye pupil, making it larger or smaller as easily as you would the lens of a camera," Delgado adds.

Sometimes it may happen that the voluntary impulse of an animal opposes an electrically evoked movement such as raising of a foreleg; in that case, the movement might not occur. "But," Delgado says, "by increasing the intensity of stimulation it is always possible to get the animal to respond as 'directed.' "

Similarly, human beings are unable to resist motor responses elicited by E.S.B.: Delgado describes a patient under treatment for psychomotor epilepsy who slowly clenched his hand into a fist each time he was stimulated through an electrode in the left parietal cortex. When asked to try to keep his fingers extended through the next stimulation, the man simply could not do it. "I guess, doctor," he commented ruefully, "that your electricity is stronger than my will."

One fascinating question, debated since the time of Hess, was whether the rage which could be induced in cats by E.S.B. was truly experienced by them emotionally. Were the hissing and spitting mere motor responses—or did the cat actually feel all the noxious sensations which accompany anger and fear? In 1954, Delgado, working with Warren Roberts and Neal Miller, the well-known psychologist, demonstrated that E.S.B. in certain brain areas which produce rage responses could act as a powerful punishment. Hungry cats who received E.S.B. at these points each time they began to eat quickly learned to avoid food. But cats being stimulated in other cerebral areas—though they might rear back from the bowl momentarily—never were motivated to learn to refuse food: they returned to eating as soon as the stimulation was over.

"The implication," explains Delgado, "was that there were places in the brain which corresponded to negative emotional states, to the cerebral perception of pain. If that were so, we could understand the mechanisms of suffering and block them at their source." Shortly after this experiment, doctors started to use brain stimulation for the relief of intractable pain.

A few months after the Delgado-Roberts-Miller study was published, a young Canadian, James Olds, began wondering . . . If there were "pain centers" in the brain, were there also areas devoted to the perception of pleasure? Olds, working at McGill University, implanted electrodes in the brains of a group of rats: He meant to probe an area just below the one that the Yale group had been studying, but in one rat an electrode went astray, landing a good deal above its target—it was an inspired mistake. For, as Olds soon realized, the rat found the stimulation rewarding; in fact it kept continually and dedicatedly returning for more.

Old's subsequent large-scale studies of rats with electrodes in this "pleasureful area" found that they preferred E.S.B. above all else—including water, sex and food. Even when famished, they would run toward a stimulating lever faster than they would run toward food. They would remove obstacles, run mazes and even cross electrified grids in order to press the wonderful lever that provided self-stimulation. Sometimes ravenously hungry rats, ignoring nearby food, would stimulate themselves up to 5,000 times an hour—persisting with manic singleness of purpose for more than a day running, until they keeled over on the floor in a faint!

Olds thought that the pleasure areas must contain nerve cells that would be excited by satisfaction of the basic drives—such as hunger and sex—but that somehow E.S.B. of them was even better. In a subsequent experiment he demonstrated that the delights of E.S.B. in certain brain areas could be abolished by castration; they could then be restored by injections of the sex hormone, testosterone.

Delgado, among others, later confirmed the existence of "reward areas" in the brain of the monkey. "In humans also, during diagnostic procedures, states of arousal and pleasure have been evoked. We have seen this in our own experience. One patient of ours was a rather reserved 30-year-old woman suffering from psychomotor epilepsy; she had electrodes implanted in her right temporal lobe. E.S.B. at one cerebral point made her suddenly confess her passionate regard for the therapist—whom she'd never seen before. She grabbed his hands and kissed them and told him how grateful she was for what he was doing for her.

"When stimulation was over, she was as poised and distant as ever; she remained so during E.S.B. through all other electrodes. But," one of Delgado's eyebrows rises slightly, "the same thing happened when she was stimulated at the same point on another day."

There have been several studies of humans with implanted electrodes. One carried out by Dr. C. Sem-Jacobsen in Norway with a group of patients suffering from schizophrenia and Parkinson's disease describes E.S.B. at different cerebral points as producing moods which ranged from "feeling good," to "slight euphoria," to where "the euphoria was beyond normal limits" and the patients laughed hilariously. During another study, a man being treated for narcolepsia (irresistible sleep attacks) was given a small self-stimulator. He kept pushing one particular button which, he declared, made him feel as if he were building up to a sexual climax.

"Pleasure is not in the skin being caressed or in a full stomach," remarks Delgado. "It is somewhere inside the cranial vault."

And so, also, are anxiety, fear, aggression. Early in the sixties, Delgado wanted to study problems of aggression—and its inhibition—among rhesus monkey colonies in which some members were receiving E.S.B. which increased or decreased levels of hostility. But there were practical problems: the monkeys tended to become curious about trailing wires, and their destructive capabilities were legendary. Most researchers had to keep them separated and restrained in little plastic chairs.

The nineteen-fifties, however, had brought advances in electronic technology and miniaturization of components. Delgado, who is, in the words of a colleague, "a kind of nineteenth-century mad inventor, a real technological wizard," developed an instrument called a stimoceiver. This was, as its name implies, both a brain stimulator and brain wave receiver; it could send stimulations by remote radio command on three channels and receive E.E.G. recordings on three channels. Weighing roughly just over an ounce, the stimoceiver was easily anchored to the animal's skull: it was monkey-proof.

A series of experiments was now carried out with monkeys who were freed of wires, interacting spontaneously and receiving E.S.B. by remote radio command. They demonstrated that while stimulation could increase the level of hostility experienced by an animal, whether or not he expressed his hostility against another monkey depended upon the social situation. Monkeys form hierarchical societies. If rage and aggression were evoked in a monkey at the bottom of the social scale, no threats would be directed against other monkeys. If, however, the animal were moved into another colony in which he held a higher rank, he would threaten or attack the animals below him. When the "boss monkey" of a colony was stimulated, his attacks were also carefully determined by the social situation: he attacked the male just below him in rank, never his favorite girl friend.

Thus, while E.S.B. could arouse aggressions in peaceful simian societies, these feelings were always expressed in socially intelligent ways. In one study a small female named Elsa learned to press a lever which activated a radio stimulator and inhibited the aggressiveness of the powerful, mean-tempered boss of the colony. "The old dream of an individual overpowering the strength of a dictator by remote control has come true," laughs Delgado. "At least, in our monkey colonies."

Two years after developing the stimoceiver he and his invention made world headlines when Delgado took part in a "bullfight" in Spain. Climbing into the ring at a farm near Cordova, this matador in sweater and slacks faced a brave bull—one of a species genetically bred for fierceness.

Delgado, standing in the sun, waved a heavy red cape in the air. The bull lowered his head and charged through the dust. But, as the animal bore down on him, Delgado pressed a small button on the radio transmitter in his hand: the bull braked to a halt.

When the professor pressed another button, the bull turned away and trotted docilely toward the high wooden barrier. The bull had, of course, had electrodes implanted shortly before. The radio stimulation had activated an inhibitory area deep in the bull's brain, thus halting it in mid-charge.

This disquieting demonstration of the power of brain stimulation aroused a flurry of speculation about the possibilities of remote-controlled behavior. "Since that time," Delgado says ruefully, "'I've received mail each year from people who think I'm controlling their thoughts."

Crank letters are not likely to stop arriving after Delgado's recent announcement that he has established two-way, nonsensory communication between the brain and the computer. In the experiment, a young chimp named Paddy (after an Irish research assistant) was equipped with 100 electrodes implanted in his brain and wired to a socket on top of his skull. Mounted over the socket was a stimoceiver, its tiny components encased in a Teflon box not much bigger than a cigarette lighter.

Paddy, in the company of three other chimpanzees, was left to roam about an artificial, moat-surrounded island at Holloman Air Force Base in New Mexico. As he ran, ate, sat and played, his brain waves and other activities were monitored 24 hours a day. During early testing, it was found that E.S.B. in the central gray—the emotionally "negative" area explored by Hess and then Delgado—was obnoxious and disturbing for Paddy.

In the meanwhile, a computer standing nearby was programed to receive radio signals which were broadcasts of electrical activity from the chimp's brain and to respond to certain waves called "spindles." The spindles, coming from the amygdala, a structure deep in the temporal lobe, are correlated with aggressiveness and excitement; they occur spontaneously about 1000 times an hour in the brain waves from the amygdala. In response to each spindle, the computer was instructed to deliver a radio stimulation to Paddy's central gray.

When the experiment began, each spindle produced by the amygdala was followed immediately by the punishing E.S.B. in the emotionally negative area—it was similar to the slapping of a child's hand each time he touches a forbidden object. Within two hours, spindling had diminished by 50 percent. A few days later, there were practically no spindles at all. One part of the brain (the central gray) had "talked to" the other: it had forced the amygdala to change its normally occurring electrical activity! Paddy's behavior changed also. He was less aggressive, his appetite waned, he sat around lazily with visitors or with the other chimps. "In this case, we were able to get one area of the brain to communicate with the other," Delgado says. "Soon, with the aid of the computer, we may have direct contact between two different brains—without the participation of the senses."

Paddy's changed behavior persisted for two weeks following the experiment. Then the amygdala resumed its spindling and the chimp returned to normal. "One of the implications of this study," explains Delgado, "is that unwanted patterns of brain activity—for instance those correlated with assaultive or antisocial activity—could be recognized by the computer before they ever reached consciousness in order to trigger pacification of the subject.

"Another speculation is that the onset of epileptic attacks could be recognized and avoided by feedback." (Feedback occurs when the activities of an organism or machine are modified continuously by the interaction between its signals or output and the environment; thus E.S.B. in the central gray made the amygdala suppress its spindling in much the same way that warmth rising in a room causes a thermostat to shut off the supply of heat.)

Delgado looks forward to a time "not very far in the future" when cerebral pacemakers, operating in much the same way that cardiac pacemakers now do, will treat illnesses such as Parkinson's disease, anxiety, fear, obsessions, violent behavior, by direct stimulation of the brain. The premise is that each of these illnesses has its own characteristic pattern of electrical activity. In the case of an epileptic, these would be the high voltage slow waves which represent the simultaneous "explosion" of groups of neurons. Long before the first muscle twitch of an epileptic fit is seen, the brain waves show this typical pattern. If they were being monitored by a computer, the machine could respond immediately by triggering radio stimulation to brain areas that would inhibit and contain the seizure.

This would all take place below the level of perception, without the person's conscious awareness. For instance, a man walking down a street, equipped with a subcutaneous stimulator, could avoid an epileptic seizure through interaction with a computer miles away—and never know it. Or, as seems quite feasible technologically, a minicomputer programed to respond to a specific type of electrical activity could be worn on the person's body. Thus, the "go-between" connecting two areas of the same brain might be situated either in the middle of a medical center or the middle of a shirt pocket.

Certain types of uncontrollably assaultive behavior might be treated without the computer, using carefully programed stimulation in inhibitory brain areas. According to Delgado, these could, over a period of time, cause a mellowing of aggressive reactions.

What is the choice? Does it lie on the one hand between spiraling violence and continuous outbreaks of aggression and war, and, on the other hand, the development of a race of electrical toys whose every antisocial impulse could be neatly nipped by the computer before it ever became realized in the form of behavior? In his intriguing, troubling book, *Physical Control of the Mind*, Delgado carefully explores the implications of E.S.B.

"The possibility of scientific annihilation of personal identity, or even worse, its purposeful control, has sometimes been considered a future threat more awful than atomic holocaust," he writes. "The prospect of any degree of physical control of the mind provokes a variety of objections: theological objections because it affects free will, moral objections because it affects individual responsibility, ethical objections because it may block self-defense mechanisms, philosophical objections because it threatens personal identity."

However: ". . . it is not knowledge itself but its improper use which should be regulated. A knife is neither good nor bad; but it may be used by a surgeon or an assassin. . . . Psychoanalysis, the use of drugs . . . insulin or electroshock . . . are all aimed at influencing the abnormal personality of the patient in order to change his undesirable mental characteristics."

Patients on drugs, he points out, are being controlled. Their behavior is modified, their systems are flooded and sometimes there are deleterious side effects; also, they are made lethargic and stupid. "And why? Because one little group of neurons keep misfiring. Is it destroying that patient's personal freedom to offer him precise, on-demand medication affecting only the area involved, so that none of his other mental processes are altered?

"Suppose that the onset of epileptic attacks could be recognized by the computer and avoided by feedback: would that threaten identity? Or if you think of patients displaying assaultive behavior due to abnormalities in brain functioning: do we preserve their individual integrity by keeping them locked up in wards for the criminally insane?"

E.S.B. is actually a rather crude technique based on the delivery of a monotonous train of messageless electrical pulses. Like the button which launches a rocket, it sets off a train of programed events, biochemical, thermal, enzymatic, electrical. "Nothing which is not already in the brain can be put there by E.S.B.," Delgado says. "It cannot be used as a teaching tool [to impart knowledge]. Since it doesn't carry specific thoughts it can certainly *not* be used to implant ideas or to order people about like robots—you couldn't use it to direct a person down to the mailbox to get the mail."

Brain stimulation does offer, however, an experimental method for the study of the neurophysiological basis of behavior. "True freedom," insists Delgado, "will come from an understanding of how the brain works; then we will be able to control our reality." A high-priority national goal ought to be an intensive study of cerebral processes for the purpose of establishing an educational system based on that knowledge: "We must first start with the realization that the mind, to all intents and purposes, does not exist at birth; in some brain areas as many as 80 to 90 percent of the neurons don't form until afterwards. Personal identity is not something we are born with. It is a combination of genetic bias, the sensory information we receive, our educational and cultural inheritance. In other words, the mind is not revealed as the child matures; it is constructed."

Genetic determination is like the blueprint of a beautiful house, Delgado contends: "But the house itself is not there; you can't sleep in a blueprint. The kind of building you eventually have will depend on the choice of which bricks, which wood, which glass are used—just as the virgin brain will be shaped by what is given to it from the environment. Now in order to give this newborn brain the best possible building materials, there are questions to which we need answers: What is the chronology of imprinting? At what ages are certain patterns fixed? What are the true sources of pleasure and accomplishment?—this question has not only a psychological but a neurophysiological component, since we know that pleasure is localized in certain areas of the brain."

Most important, according to Delgado, is the need to develop an educational system that is based on knowledge of our biological realities, an education that would attempt to: first, establish good "automatisms" in the child, and, second, as he matures, permit his thinking capability to evolve without being subjected to unknown forces and impulses which may overpower his rational intelligence.

Like many another prophet, Delgado is not always seen as such in his own country. Aside from the fantasy and fears aroused by his experiments, there are criticisms of the public stance he has adopted, as well as of his techniques and method. "There's something idiosyncratic about the way he works," remarks one Yale colleague. "He doesn't follow the ordinary rules. I mean one mustn't confuse technological elegance with methodological rigor: there must be the slow dogged part, the careful checking of observations, the randomization of experiments, the estimate of the probability that your findings weren't just due to chance . . . .

"Delgado doesn't seem to have the patience to fool around with that. If he stimulates a monkey's brain and gets an expected reaction he gets bored. He gets a lot of things started, and then leaves other people to clean up after him. But let's face it, technologically the man's incredible; he's a real genius in a practical way—a sort of Thomas Edison of the brain."

Questions about the brain, says a young neurophysiologist, are extremely complex: "People like Delgado can talk about breakthroughs in this and that, but progress in knowledge is slow. It may be several centuries before we have any real understanding of what is going on. . . . And besides there are different schools of thought. Some neurophysiologists think it's a waste of time to study groups of neurons and over-all behavior—that we'll learn more by figuring out what's happening in a single nerve cell. To a man with this approach, trying to understand the workings of the brain through gross stimulation appears silly—like using a hand lens to try and unlock the mysteries of the fine structure of a virus."

Nevertheless, if not the dogmatic experimentalist, Delgado, according to his research associates, more than makes up for it: "He's an inventor in the purest sense. You can't fault his creativity," says Dan Snyder, a Ph.D. in physiological psychology who has worked with Delgado for the past several years. "The man drops gems of ideas in his casual conversations the way some people shed bacteria. That's part of the problem: he hasn't time to beat an experiment to death because he's got so many good ideas that he more or less has to be in 10 places at once."

"The truth is," adds Snyder, "he's opened up enough research potentials to keep several laboratories busy for a lifetime.

Speculations about the future implications of E.S.B.—medical and social—

are still various and vague. According to Dr. Morton Reiser, chairman of the Yale department of psychiatry (in which Delgado holds his appointment as professor of physiology), there are "probably some frightening potentials" in Delgado's work. "If you can use computer technology to send an unmanned space satellite to the moon, then it doesn't seem utterly impossible that one day our computers will be sophisticated enough to be used to put thoughts into people's heads." He pauses doubtfully. "At any rate, one could possibly exert some influence on gross emotional behavior. Suppose, for instance, there were someone with uncontrollable rage reactions which were due to something detectable in the nervous system. The computer could send back a stimulus to inhibit that response. I don't think *that's* science fiction. . . ."

Professor David Hamburg, chairman of the psychiatry department at Stanford and an expert on brain and behavior, says: "The stronger our scientific base, the better our position for making rational choices. Brain stimulation could lead to the relief of much human suffering, to new treatments for mental and neurological disorders; it could possibly help to solve some human problems and it may ultimately affect man's understanding and conception of himself.

"Of course," adds Hamburg, "the utilization of knowledge always presents certain problems. Any increase in understanding can be used in ways that are harmful or helpful. As with atomic research, as with our investigation into the chemistry of behavior, E.S.B. does open up possibilities for exploitation and harm. Any new technique for understanding how the brain mediates behavior could affect our lives for better or worse."

Certainly, mistrust and doubt are aroused on many sides by the suggestion that thought process can be rerouted and the mind physically controlled. According to one psychoanalyst, "The danger of this being abused is, I think, tremendous."

"I suppose," remarks Delgado, aware of the controversy his work inevitably stirs, "that to primitive man the idea of diverting the course of a river would have seemed irreligious."

2. Brain Power: The Case for Bio-Feedback Training
Barnard Law Collier

"After a patient learns to speed his heart, he is then taught to slow it down."

Bio-feedback is currently an exciting area of study. The ability to exercise voluntary control over internal states is apparently capable of being learned. This article describes some of the fascinating possibilities.

Inside a darkened chamber in the laboratory of Dr. Lester Fehmi sits Ralph Press, a nineteen-year-old mathematics student at the State University of New York in Stony Brook, Long Island. Relaxed in an armchair with his eyes closed, Ralph is undergoing his eleventh session of bio-feedback training to help him learn to control his brain waves.

Four silver electrodes are pasted to Ralph's scalp, their orange lead wires plugged into an electroencephalograph that is tracing his brain-wave activity on thick ribbons of EEG paper in the next room. The silence in the sound-proofed chamber is broken only by the long and short beepings of a rather high-pitched tone: the key to Ralph's bio-feedback training.

Dr. Fehmi, a professor of psychology at Stony Brook, has told Ralph that he can learn to increase his brain's output of an eight-to-fourteen-cycle-per-second brain sine wave called alpha. Alpha waves are one of four known brain waves. They are generated, billions of them, by the tiny electrical pulses that surge through the brain as it does its complex chores. High production of alpha waves is often associated with the objective state of peak mental and physical performance, a relaxed yet extremely sensitive alertness.

Dr. Fehmi and George Sintchak, the Stony Brook psychology department's chief electronic engineer, have rigged the EEG machine and a computer so that each time Ralph's brain generates a burst of alpha activity the occurrence is recorded, timed, and almost instantly made known to Ralph by means of the beeping tone. The tone is Ralph's bio-feedback. It is an audible signal that lets Ralph be consciously aware of a visceral function, in this case the production of his alpha brain waves, which his mind ordinarily blocks out, ignores, or is unable to perceive without external assistance. When Ralph's brain generates only snippets of alpha radiation, the tone comes in staccato little blips. As he produces more and more alpha, the tone stays on longer and longer. Ralph, of course, wants to succeed by producing as much alpha as he can.

For nearly an hour, Ralph shows minute-by-minute improvement in his ability to keep the tone on. A computer read-out verifies that he is maintaining the tone for a cumulative average of twenty-eight seconds out of each minute. "He's one of our super-subjects," Dr. Fehmi remarks. "He's not the best, but he's getting pretty good."

Ralph's alpha waves are of high amplitude, very rhythmic and regular. . . .

"OK, Ralph," Dr. Fehmi says quietly over the intercom, "I want you to turn the tone off and keep it off."

The tone that Ralph has learned to sustain for upwards of three seconds now goes beep, beep, *blip*; within seconds, it has died away except for tiny random beeps. . . .

"Now turn the tone back on," Dr. Fehmi says.

A pause of a second or so and the tone beeps back to life and stays on for seconds at a time. Then on, off, on, off. The tests continue until it is clear that Ralph is in personal command of his brain's alpha-wave activity as evidenced by the EEG machine's record.

A steady flow of new scientific findings indicates that, with the aid of the teaching technique called bio-feedback training, man can learn to control willfully his body and his state of consciousness to a degree that traditionally has been dismissed in Western cultures as mere trickery or condemned as somehow wicked or blasphemous.

Projects in hospitals and research laboratories around the world are convincingly demonstrating that it may be possible to learn personal mastery over the functions of our visceral organs—the heart, liver, kidneys, intestines, glands, and blood vessels—in the same specific way that we learn to manipulate our fingers to play Chopin or our legs to kick a field goal. There is also highly intriguing research going on in laboratories like Dr. Fehmi's to demonstrate that with bio-feedback training we can learn self-control over the electrical activity of our brain. These studies indicate that man may possess the ability to will himself into whatever state of consciousness seems most appropriate to his environment, to accomplishing a task at hand, or to some special pursuit.

The implications of bio-feedback training are proving terribly easy to overstate, given the limited amount of solid experimental evidence that presently exists. People seem peculiarly ready nowadays to lunge at the adventurous prospect of employing new methods and modern technology to explore and conquer one's own brain and body instead of, say, the moon or Southeast Asia. The propensity for exaggeration about progress in this area frightens prudent scientists. Already they are encountering the con artists, the charlatans, and the quacks who are taking people's money by glibly mouthing the jargon associated with bio-feedback research and similar studies of the mind's control over internal organs. This caveat is offered early because it is difficult to keep one's imagination reined in unless one is warned that much of the data accumulated so far are limited to experiments with rats, monkeys, rabbits, or other lab animals. And the remarkable results with animals may not travel well from the laboratory to humans. Nevertheless, research teams are reporting an ever increasing number of cases in which human subjects have unquestionably gained conscious control over visceral organs once thought beyond the mastery of the mind.

In Baltimore, for example, Dr. Bernard T. Engel, a psychologist, and Dr. Eugene Bleecker, a cardiovascular specialist, have conducted bio-feedback training sessions with eight patients suffering from premature ventricular contractions, a dangerous irregularity of the heartbeat involving the heart's main pumping chamber. With significant success, these patients have learned to speed, slow, and narrowly regulate their heart by force of mental discipline alone.

At the Gerontology Research Center of the National Institute of Child Health and Human Development, Dr. Engel and Dr. Bleeker use a visual form of bio-feedback training to help patients control their heart. In a typical experiment, the patient lies quietly on a hospital bed in a small, windowless laboratory near Dr. Engel's office The electrodes of an electrocardiograph are attached to his chest and pulse points, and the EKG machine is hooked up with a specially programmed computer. On the bed table in front of the patient sits a small metal box fitted with a red, a yellow, and a green light in the same pattern as a regular traffic signal. The display is hooked into the computer, which almost instantly analyzes the EKG readings and provides bio-feedback information to the patient by means of the flashing colored lights.

The first phase of the training is speeding the heart rate. The patient may be told that when the yellow light goes on he will know that his heart is beating faster; the green light flashing on means it is slowing down. A small meter next to the light box indicates to the patient what percentage of the time he is succeeding in keeping the yellow light lit. The goal for the heart patient, of course, is to gain control over the lights and his heartbeat in the same way Ralph Press controlled the beeping tone and his alpha-wave production: by sheer mental effort, and without any muscular exertion—which amounts to cheating.

After a patient learns to speed his heart, he is then taught to slow it down with the red light and later to keep it beating within narrow normal limits, with the three lights acting as too fast, too slow, and normal signals. Some of Dr. Engel's patients have achieved a 20 percent speeding or slowing of their hearts —about sixteen beats a minute from an eighty-beat-per-minute base. This self-willed rate change in one direction or the other tends to even out the irregular beats. Why? Researchers are not quite sure, but it works.

But what happens when the patient goes home, away from Dr. Engel's bio-feedback light box? The final stage of the five-phase training program is the stepped withdrawal of the bio-feedback light signals. The patient, after extensive training, finds he can deliberately alter his heartbeats in the desired direction without artificial feedback. One of Dr. Engel's patients could still remember how to control his rate after two years. That Dr. Engel's patients retain what they have learned without the aid of an electronic device to provide feedback is what excites many researchers who feel that we may be capable of discovering unknown mechanisms, or "feedback loops," within ourselves that will allow us, after some basic training, to monitor our viscera and their functions at will throughout life.

In Boston and New York City, scientists are trying to see how people with hypertension can effectively lower their abnormally high blood pressure by thinking it down. Under the direction of Dr. Neal E. Miller, a professor of physiological psychology at Rockefeller University in New York and a pioneer in the brain sciences, experiments are now proceeding to discover if human subjects can learn to control the contractions of their intestinal tract. Laboratory can do as well, it could mean relief from much suffering for people with spastic colons and similar gastrointestinal ailments usually associated with stress and psychosomatic illness.

Dr. Miller was in the forefront of what seemed, just a decade or so ago, a vain and somewhat foolhardy challenge to the bedrock idea that the viscera and the autonomic nervous system that controls them operate entirely independently of an animal's deliberate control. Dr. Miller has traced back to Plato the dogma that the organs controlled by the autonomic nervous system function at a kind of cave-mannish level, learning only in classical Pavlovian fashion to react to such stimuli as sour lemons and growling bears. On the other hand, the somatic, or cerebrospinal, nervous system, which transmits nerve signals from the brain to the spinal cord and directly to the skeletal muscles, can learn by the sophisticated trial-and-error instrumental process. Perhaps the Greeks considered it an act of hubris to believe that they, not the gods, exercised command of their heart, brain, and guts. Dr. Engel, who also has studied the accumulated prejudices against the viscera, can recite a chain of erroneous proofs put forth until only a few years ago by scientists who, with a kind of religious fervor. had shunned anatomical facts and new information in order to steadfastly support Plato.

At the root of the research reports on bio-feedback training is what Dr. Miller describes as "an almost complete change in our way of thinking about our viscera and their ability to learn. We are now able to regard the activities of our internal organs as behavior in the same sense that the movements of our hands and fingers are behavior. This is the basic stem of it all, but just where this rather radical new orientation will lead, we can't be sure yet."

Some indications that we can possibly control our viscera have been around for centuries without anyone's grasping their import. Dr. Miller points out that actors and actresses can control their tear glands, which are visceral organs, to make themselves cry on cue. It is possible that some classical conditioning is involved: The actor recalls something sad and the sadness makes him cry. But many actors and actresses say they can cry without any recalling, that all they have to do is think "cry" and the tears flow.

Magicians and mystics and meditators have often gained mental control over visceral organs to a significant degree. Harry Houdini is said to have been able to swallow and regurgitate a key that would unlock him from some otherwise unopenable box. If he did this, it would mean he had gained mastery over the muscles of his esophagus and stomach, part of the viscera.

A few yogis, it would seem, can control their metabolism to some extent. But whether or not they "cheat" by using skeletal muscles instead of only their mind to perform their tricks is unknown. Scientists have found that some yogis who can "stop" their hearts so that no pulse or sound of beating can be detected are actually performing what is called the Valsalva maneuver. By taking a deep breath, closing their windpipe, and breathing hard to increase the pressure inside their chest and around their heart, they collapse the veins to the heart and clamp off the return of blood. This arrests heart sounds and the pulse, but an EKG shows that the heart is still beating and usually quite fast. "We must reexamine a lot of phenomena we may have dismissed as fakery before," Dr. Miller says.

The belief in a "superior" somatic nervous system and an "inferior" autonomic nervous system was so strong that, according to Dr. Miller, "for more than a dozen years I had extreme difficulty getting students or even paid assistants to conduct experiments on the control of internal organs." But Dr. Miller persisted, and his research has led many other scientists to abandon the old dogma. He has shown that the internal organs in animals and to a significant extent in man, as well, are capable of learning by trial and error—and with a startling degree of specificity and discrimination. In one experiment, which Dr. Miller particularly enjoys mentioning, he and his research colleague, Dr. Leo V. DiCara, tuned their instrumental conditioning process down so fine that a rat learned to blush one ear and blanch the other. In almost all of his animal experiments, Dr. Miller paralyzes the rats and other lab animals with curare, a powerful drug used by South American Indians to tip their poison darts. The curare interferes with all the nerve impulses that keep the skeletal muscles working—including respiration. The paralyzing of the skeletal muscles ensures that the animals do not "cheat" by somehow using their skeletal muscles to affect their visceral responses. (It is thus far a frustration for Dr. Miller and others that non-curarized animals are slower to learn viscerally than the curarized ones.)

The difference between the way the body learns by classical conditioning and by instrumental conditioning is crucial to understanding how bio-feedback training works. Classical conditioning, or learning, always demands a stimulus that elicits an innate response. For example, the first time you ever saw a lemon, nothing much happened with your saliva glands, which are visceral organs. But after you first tasted its sour juice, your saliva glands automatically secreted lots of saliva to dilute and wash away the puckering citric acid. You cannot control the response of your saliva glands to the lemon juice, and after you have tasted several lemons your mouth will start watering at the very sight of one. You have been classically conditioned to salivate at the sight of lemons. The same thing works for other such stimuli: a mad dog, for example. The sight of one will boost your heart rate, increase your adrenaline flow, and generally activate other innate fear responses.

The process of instrumental learning is much less limited since it requires no specific stimulus to provoke a response. If you want to sink a twelve-foot golf putt, for instance, there is nothing anyone can offer you, not a lemon or $5,000, that will get your body to hole the ball out with Pavlovian sureness. But by the process of trial and error, or instrumental conditioning, you can learn to coordinate your muscles and other responses. You stroke the ball toward the hole and it glides by. You try again and again. Each time you get closer. You are not aware of precisely what you are doing to improve; you cannot say which muscles are contracting or relaxing and in what order. But you get closer nonetheless, and each near success is a reward that is likely to keep you trying. At last you are in control of your muscles, your responses, and the golf ball. It plunks into the hole. This trial-and-error process is called instrumental learning.

Now imagine that you are trying to make the same putt blindfolded. Very difficult, if not impossible. Why? Because something essential is missing from the learning process: feedback. In this case, the feedback is the sight of the ball getting closer to the cup. Of course, you could learn to make the putt blindfolded if you substituted for the feedback of your visual perception the voice (feedback) of your caddy. He might, at the simplest level, say "yes" when your direction was right and say nothing or "no" when it wasn't. He might offer more guidance: "A little more to the right" or "A little to the left and harder." You would still be badly handicapped by the imprecision of your caddy's second-hand information, but eventually you would sink one and then perhaps quite a few.

Our mind is in some ways like the blindfolded golfer where the viscera are concerned. Scientists are trying to find new ways to remove the blindfold, which is enormously difficult indeed, or to substitute the guidance of the caddy-type feedback for sensory information about visceral organs that the mind for some reason dismisses or never perceives. Dr. Fehmi's beeping tone and the mini-volt currents of pleasurable brain stimulation that lab rats get are simple reward bio-feedback signals; Dr. Engel's colored lights represent more guidance. All are examples of bio-feedback used to instrumentally condition internal organs by letting the mind know, within predetermined limits, what those organs are up to.

One path of bio-feedback research has branched slightly away from the strictly therapeutic approach and is investigating the ability of human beings to exert purposeful control over their visceral functions, especially their brain functions, with the goal of making the essentially healthy person better able to cope with his world. At the United States Navy Medical Neuropsychiatric Research Unit in San Diego, California, Dr. Ardie Lubin and Dr. David Hord, both psychologists, are studying the relationship between the output of alpha waves and sleep. What they want to determine is whether or not a person deprived of sleep can be returned to a state of effectiveness and acceptable decision-making capacity by willing himself into an alpha state for a certain length of time. Some preliminary tests have shown that alpha states may be recuperative.

At the Langley Porter Neuropsychiatric Institute, part of the University of California Medical Center in San Francisco, a research group headed by Dr. Joe Kamiya is exploring the possibility that brain-wave control may have important effects on health, creativity, and such mental functions as perception and memory. Dr. Kamiya is regarded by most psychologists as the pioneer in the field of brain-wave control. Dr. Kamiya and his research team have found that subjects who do best at mastering their alpha-wave output are those who have had some training in meditation, as in Zen. At Stony Brook, Dr. Fehmi has noted that musicians, athletes, and artists are especially adept at control over their brain waves. Conversely, he has found that subjects who come into his chamber and slouch in their armchair in the spaced-out way associated with drug trips produce precious little alpha.

It is frustrating to researchers that the subjects who are most proficient in gaining brain-wave control are often strangely tongue-tied when it comes to telling just how they do it. Some say they relax and wipe everything from their mind. Others concentrate on some infinite point like a mystical third eye in the middle of their forehead. Some are unable to verbalize the experience at all.

"The best way I can describe the feeling of alpha," says Dr. Fehmi, "is a relaxed but alert and sensitive 'into-it-ness.'" Dr. Edgar E. Coons, a physiological psychologist at New York University and a musician, has been trained to produce alpha waves in Dr. Fehmi's lab; he says the alpha state "makes me feel as if I'm floating about half an inch above my seat." A talented young musician named David Rosenboom, who recently presented a bio-feedback brain-wave concert at Automation House in New York (brain-wave activity was fed into a computer and an ARP synthesizer; the result was a weird but not unpleasing effect), is the reigning champion brain-wave producer for Dr. Fehmi. When his alpha is really going strong in all parts of his brain, Rosenboom says he is plugged in to a "great energy source." Another musician named LaMonte Young, who keeps a forty-cycle "home" tone going in his Manhattan studio at all times, explained that he had no trouble generating alpha the first time he ever tried it, because his mind "is tuned to frequencies and intervals."

At the University of Colorado Medical School, Dr. Hans Stoyva has had notable success in teaching his patients how to relax specific muscles that tense up and cause certain kinds of tension headaches. The easing of pain has been swift and dramatic.

Dr. Martin Orne, director of experimental psychiatry at the University of Pennsylvania Medical School in Philadelphia, is studying the alpha-wave phenomenon with an eye toward finding out what exactly an alpha state does to or for an individual and how it might be beneficial to him. "It's not enough to know you can contemplate your navel," Dr. Orne says, "You then have to ask, 'What happens?'" Experiments conducted with subjects who have been trained to produce a reliably high alpha-wave output show, according to Dr. Orne, that critical thinking tends to interfere with alpha waves, but that alpha-wave production does not mean blunted intellectual capacity. What alpha production seems to do best for the alpha producer is relax him, insulate him from stressful critical thought, and rehabilitate his autonomic nervous system to some degree.

"What this may mean," Dr. Orne says, "is that alpha might be used to bring down the level of a person's anxiety to a point where he can function at his best. We all need a certain amount of anxiety to function. It is well accepted that we function best as anxiety rises to a certain point on a bell-shaped curve, and past that point we do increasingly worse as anxiety increases. If alpha can be used to knock down anxiety to the point on the curve where we work most effectively, it can be a most important development." However, Dr. Orne is quick to point out that "this is three levels or more from where we are now, but it is something to consider."

Another prospect for visceral learning is its use as a possible alternative to drugs. If, for example, a high alpha output can cause deep relaxation, or a specific focusing of bio-feedback training can loosen up a taut muscle, this could well substitute for the billions of transquilizers consumed to achieve essentially the same effect. The advantage over drugs might be considerable. For instance, while a tranquilizer acts in a general way on the whole body or an entire bodily system (perhaps with unwanted side effects), bio-feedback training might be specific enough to do the job required and let the rest of the body function undisturbed.

"There is also," says Dr. Orne, "the general question of personal control and how we might be able to bring our emotions under control. We want to know, of course, to what extent an individual can gain control with precision and reliability over the things he fears. A good part of fear is the fear of fear. If you know you are going to be hurt, you will hurt more with exactly the same degree of hurting stimulus. If we can break into some of the feedback loops that are part of the fear cycle, we may be able to control unpleasant and unproductive anxiety."

To Dr. Orne, the goal is clear. "We may be able to become actual masters of our destiny. As a psychiatrist, my purpose is to enable man to decide his own fate instead of his juices deciding for him."

At Rockefeller University, Dr. DiCara, a burly ex-football player, is attempting to unravel some of the whys and hows of visceral learning. In one recent experiment, he and Dr. Eric Stone found that rats trained to increase their heart rate had significantly more of a powerful group of chemicals called catecholamines in their brains and hearts than rats who learned to *lower* their heart rates. In humans, catecholamines are associated with hypertension and coronary artery disease. The possibility of learning to slow the heart rate to achieve beneficial effects on hypertension and heart ailments is intriguing; however, a major obstacle still to be overcome is the inability at present to measure catecholamines in the human brain.

An equally intriguing possibility has been raised by an experiment conducted by Dr. DiCara and Dr. Jay M. Weiss. Rats that had learned to slow their heart rates subsequently showed excellent ability to learn to move back and forth in a shuttle box to avoid an electric shock. Rats trained to speed their hearts learned very poorly and exhibited signs of extreme fearfulness by leaping into the air, squealing, and turning toward their tails with each pulse of shock instead of getting away from it. In contrast, the slow heart-rate rats took each shock in stride, with only "mild jerks," and slowly walked out of the electrified side of the box.

"It is crystal-clear," says Dr. Miller, with whom Dr. DiCara has worked as co-experimenter on many projects, "that heart rate training affects rats' learning. What is further indicated is that the training also affects their emotionality. We cannot jump from the laboratory to the clinic, but we may indeed find that in human subjects trained to lower their heart rates there could be an increased capacity to adapt to stressful situations and a corresponding decrease in emotionality."

The field of bio-feedback training and visceral learning is still only crudely charted. New research teams are forming to explore further; the mechanical and electronic spin-offs of the space age are providing the new tools and infinitely more sensitive measuring devices that are required for progress. But most of all there seems to be a new attitude.

"We have brought four to five thousand years of cultural myths into the laboratory to be investigated," says Dr. Miller, who, in just a few years, has seen the pendulum of interest swing from "great resistance to great readiness." Although he is understandably reluctant to speculate on what the future holds, he is nonetheless confident that the new knowledge about our internal organs will stimulate much more research into the astonishing ability of human beings to learn.

3. There Are Sex Differences in the Mind, Too
Tom Alexander

"Virtually all the ground-dwelling primates have some sort of social structure in which the leaders are male."

In this article Alexander summarizes a body of research evidence suggesting the biological nature of sexual differences. His conclusions may not sit well with the women's liberation movement, but are lively, controversial, and provocative nonetheless.

Few of the brickbats that have recently been sailing through the fragile greenhouses of our society have sprayed out more flinders of emotions and self-doubt than the women's liberation movement. With so many sharp edges flying about, it is understandable that some important distinctions have been generally overlooked. The many-faceted movement embraces a diversity of contentions, with very different implications for both women and men. The demands put forward by many of the feminists—probably the majority—seem quite reasonable: changes in male-oriented attitudes and arrangements so that women can enter upon and advance in a greater variety of careers and, if they wish, combine these careers with motherhood. Progress in these directions is not only possible but inevitable; and, to an extent that might surprise some of the fiercer soldiers of women's lib, a great many men will applaud.

But some of the more radical spokeswomen of the movement are asserting a much more questionable, and potentially much more momentous, set of contentions and claims. They maintain that innate differences in temperament and ability between men and women are nonexistent or insignificant, and that the differences in the roles performed by men and women in our society are *entirely* due to social indoctrination and discrimination. The solution proposed by many radical feminists is an "androgynous" society—one in which the treatment accorded to, and the performance expected from, males and females would be essentially identical, whether at home, at school, or at work. "For the sexes are inherently in everything alike," writes Kate Millett, one widely known philosopher of the movement, "save reproductive systems, secondary sexual characteristics, orgasmic capacity, and genetic and morphological structure."

As it happens, such assertions about fundamental alikeness are being advanced at the very time when research from many scientific fields has been converging to suggest quite the opposite—that there are some inborn differences

From *Fortune*. Reprinted by permission.

between the sexes in temperament and inclination. The most general finding of all, to be sure, is that aside from obvious differences in anatomy, physiology, and reproductive behavior, no characteristic belongs exclusively to one sex. Some differences are much more sex-specific than others, but in general, no matter what nominally male psychological trait is under consideration, some women exceed the male norm; and vice versa for nominally female traits. Some of the uncertainty in psychology is merely about the extent of these overlaps. More of the uncertainty is about the extent to which the traits have biological or social origins or some combination of both.

Differences in behavior are evident very early in life. Male infants are generally more active than females. They cry more, sleep less, and demand more attention. Female babies, while apparently more sensitive to cold, touch, and sounds, are more passive and content. They smile more often, appear to learn more rapidly, and generally seem more mature. At the age of only twelve weeks, according to some experiments, girls look longer at pictures of faces than at geometrical figures, while boys show no preference (but later they come to prefer the geometrical forms). On the average, however, boys look longer at *all* kinds of pictures than girls do.

At so early an age, it seems, females are already expressing the preferences and behavior that, for whatever reason, will develop more completely later. Girls, research predicts, will find their satisfactions in relationships with people to a greater extent than boys. They will learn to talk earlier and more fluently, and this superiority will persist through life. They will be more concerned with having companionship than boys. They will be more docile, will strive harder to please both at home and at school.

Later on, the work women select will usually involve close interaction with people. Social scientists apply the term "nurturant" to typical female professions such as child care, teaching, nursing, or social work. The feelings and the opinions of others matter more to women than to men; words of encouragement and praise often elicit more dogged effort than the prospect of promotion. One of the persistent problems of women in careers is that as they rise to high levels they often enter realms where competition is keener and praise is rare. An even more basic female handicap in the pursuit of careers is distraction: the single overriding preoccupation of most women, psychologists agree, is marriage.

A Negative Image of Success

Rightly or wrongly, women often come to suspect that too much intellectual achievement or success in male-dominated fields can impair their marriage prospects. An examination of the attitudes of Harvard law graduates by psychologist Matina Horner revealed that the women as a group had a considerably more negative image of a successful women lawyer than the men. Moreover, the present generation of students exhibits more, not less, of this attitude than former generations did. Horner has also found that even girls in elite colleges demonstrate a powerful "motive to avoid success" in careers. It appears to arise from what they perceive as a conflict between career success and feminine identity.

There is evidence, indeed, that women who do well in male specialties tend to be a good deal more masculine in other respects than most women—they show, for example, less interest in marriage and children. A set of experiments carried out by psychologist Brian Sutton-Smith (now at Columbia) revealed that girls who are able to work out successful strategies in ticktack-toe—which is usually a male specialty—also display personality traits of an aggressive and domineering sort, more so even than boys who quickly get the hang of ticktacktoe.

Stanford psychologist Eleanor Maccoby, who herself has combined mother-hood (three children) and top achievement in a male-dominated field, deplores the current low status accorded to motherhood. "We've had twenty-five years of derogating momism. While we ought to leave the doors open to those who don't choose motherhood, I would also like to see more respect for those who do." She also deplores the strains imposed upon women who enter intellectual fields. What they encounter "is something of a horror story," she says. "It would appear that even when a woman is suitably endowed intellectually and develops the right temperament and habits of thought to make use of her endowment, she must be fleet of foot indeed to scale the hurdles the society has erected for her and to remain a whole and happy person while continuing to follow her intellectual bent."

In contrast to girls, boys will maintain and develop their early dissatisfactions and quarrelsomeness and their greater interest in "things." They will give their teachers more trouble and get lower grades through high school. They will tumble and wrestle more; they will instigate catastrophes involving blocks and toy cars, and ultimately real automobiles and real implements of war. Economic considerations aside, males will work more often than females for victory over others, for power, or for achievement in workmanship or intellect. When they work for approval it will often be for those peculiar forms called prestige or fame or glory. And no matter what level they attain, males will be less content with it than their female counterparts. In short, their drive and persistence and self-motivation are likely to be greater; and, psychological experiments show, they are likely to be spurred by competition and difficulty rather than discouraged by it as females tend to be.

Tests of particular mental abilities sometimes show striking disparities between the sexes. Only about one girl in twenty, for example, demonstrates the boys' average level of ability at mechanical aptitude or certain kinds of spatial reasoning, such as is required for solving mazes. And only one male in five equals the average female in ability to perform certain kinds of perceptual tasks involving accuracy and rapid shifts of attention in the place of monotony.

Among characteristics in which the sexes show the *smallest* differences is intelligence, as measured by ordinary I.Q. tests. One thing often overlooked, however, is that this indistinguishability is a deliberate artifact of the tests themselves. The test compilers, from Alfred Binet on, found that males tended to score better on certain kinds of test items, such as those calling for a wide store of information or for arithmetical or spatial reasoning. Girls, on the other hand, consistently excelled on items involving symbol manipulation (as in encoding) and recognition of similarities between different things. On virtually all standard I.Q. tests in use today, the mix of such items is deliberately adjusted to equalize the average male and female scores.

Beyond Nature versus Nurture

Despite wide agreement that differences exist, the social and behavioral sciences have been sharply—often emotionally—divided over whether the differences are biological or social in origin. "Science really hasn't answered the question of nature versus nurture," comments University of California psychologist Frank Beach, a long-time investigator of sex differences. This probably means that the question has never been asked properly." But at least it is becoming clear that "nature versus nurture" is the wrong formulation. The current trend is away from contentions that sex differences are entirely attributable to nature or to nurture. What goes on, it appears, is a complex interaction between the two.

Until roughly a hundred years ago, scarcely anyone questioned the assumption that along with their obviously inherited bodily differences, the two sexes had inherited differences in temperament and intellect as well. But in the last decades of the nineteenth century there emerged a basic shift to the opposite view. Egalitarianism, coeducation, the feminist revolt, and the high achievements of women in male fields began chopping the ground out from under male claims to a God-given dominance and superiority. Pavlov's revealing experiments in the phenomenon of conditioning and the subsequent rise of the behavioral psychologists views of the child as *tabula rasa*—the "blank slate" upon which over time the environment writes–led psychologists, anthropologists, sociologists, and popular opinion to view innate sex differences as insignificant and to emphasize cultural influences.

For a long time these views amounted to dogma. Frank Beach sums up the way things were: "When I was a graduate student in the early Thirties the problem of sex differences was extremely sensitive, as it is today. At that time the psychologists were all environmentalists, and it was simply unthinkable to say that the sexes could differ psychologically for any reason except conditioning. Nobody argued that a woman's size, general body formation, or reproductive anatomy were not strongly influenced by genetic factors. But the curtain dropped when it got to psychology, as though the brain, which controls behavior, was totally unaffected. I can recall getting scolded when I even raised the issue, because if you said that boys and girls differed, it seemed automatically to mean that one was inferior and the other superior. Even then tests were coming out showing that boys did better in math and girls did better in English, but if you ever suggested that this kind of thing had genetic origins at all it somehow suggested that girls were inferior. Why English should be inferior to math, I don't know."

By now, however, most adherents of the environmental explanation of sex differences have shifted away from older behaviorist ideas that externally imposed reward and punishment—i.e., approval or disapproval by parents or society—were the principal shapers of male or female personality. Now widely held is the "role modeling" theory, which stresses some sort of motivation in the individual to shape himself accordingly to the society's prevailing stereotypes. Once a child begins to identify itself as male or female—that seldom happens before the age of eighteen months, psychologists think—it is driven to search the world around it for clues as to how to assemble a personality appropriate to its sex and culture. In effect, this need to establish an "identity" is akin to the innate and irrepressible drive to learn the culture's language.

Both science and common sense lead inescapably to the conclusion that some form of role modeling is a major shaper of personality. The roles of the sexes differ widely from one culture to another. Among the Tchambuli of New Guinea, the males are raised to be passive and emotionally dependent. Anthropologists who studied a large number of cultures found that in more than half of them the accepted role of women included doing practically all the heavy carrying. In some West African societies women control much of the commerce. Even modern nations show striking differences in the extent to which women do various kinds of work. In the U.S.S.R., for example, some 75 percent of the medical doctors are women.

The Best of Inner Drums

Even so, any simple version of the role-modeling hypothesis faces certain logical difficulties that clearly point to limits in the malleability of the sexes. One problem, for instance, is that traits such as male aggressiveness or female verbal superiority display themselves at a very early age, presumably long before the child knows which parent to imitate. Similarly, it seems unlikely that, for example, male children are able to discern subtle differences in their parents' intellectual styles by the early age at which males begin to evidence signs of their superiority at spatial reasoning. So, while males and females need to respond to their culture's peculiar orchestration, they hear the beat of inner drums as well.

Two developments in the 1950's helped to breed a new industry of speculative writing about innate components of behavior. One was the flowering of ethology, the study of animal behavior. The other was the discovery in Africa of fossil remains indicating that man is a direct descendant of weapon-wielding, tool-using, ground-living, hunting primates whose emergence may date as far back as twenty million years or more. Putting together findings from these two areas of research, a number of scientists have concluded that much more of human behavior may have genetic roots than was previously imagined.

For the closest living analogues to mankind's predecessors, scientists have looked to other primate species. Virtually all of the ground-dwelling primates have some sort of social structure in which the leaders are male. Because of their vulnerability to predators, baboons and rhesus and Japanese macaque monkeys appear to have evolved defensive cultures complete with intricate hierarchies of dominance and submission and considerable differentiation in sex roles and traits. In general, a groundling primate troop of whatever size has a single dominant leader (ethologists refer to him as the "alpha" male), with lesser males arrayed in a rank order beneath him. The male hierarchy favors organized action for the defense of the females and their young.

It is a notable aspect of these primate societies that the basic social format of each species is transmitted at least partly in the form of a genetic program, a program that permits a limited range of variations in behavior to accommodate changes in the environment. The definitive experiments have yet to be carried out, but there is suggestive evidence that if infant members of these "culture-forming" primates are placed together before they have had a chance to learn the society's norms, they will nevertheless eventually sort themselves into a fair copy of the social order characteristic of their species.

Primate young also display behavioral sex differences that appear to be innate. Males are more aggressive and indulge more in playful mounting. Females perform more "grooming" of other members and show more interest in still younger infants.

As a ground-dwelling primate, man must have received a good deal of genetic programming from many millions of years of hunting ancestors. Though wide variations in behavior patterns are evident in various cultures, there do appear to be quite a few cultural "universals" for the human species. The most obvious, probably, are male dominance and aggression and, of course, female nurturance, or maternalism. Despite much speculation in fable and feminist literature about matriarchal—i.e., female-governed—societies, there is no evidence that such have ever really existed. There have been, and are, quite a few "matrilineal" cultures, in which descent is reckoned by the blood line of the female, but even in these societies governance is largely or entirely a male domain.

Man, the Domesticated Animal

Those who emphasize innate sex differences often encounter the objection that it is useless or deluding to try to extrapolate from the ethological or fossil evidence to human behavior. "In general," cautions Frank Beach, "the higher you go on the evolutionary scale, the more behavior is determined by environmental factors and learning than by biological influence directly. Susceptibilities and predispositions may be genetic; complex behavior patterns are probably not."

The well-known ethologist, Konrad Lorenz, contends that humans are more closely analogous to domesticated animals than to wild animals. Usually, wild animals express their genetically transmitted behavior in direct, unambiguous ways. But in a state of domestication, those adaptations that were once necessary for survival in a perilous environment are gradually bred out or distorted or become dangerously inappropriate, as may be the case with the human will to violence.

Nevertheless, like many other ethologists, Lorenz believes that a large and perhaps dominant source of our behavior is genetic or instinctual. Even when it does not express itself in the complicated behavior patterns of lower species, it shows up in propensities, mainly as strong emotions—such as love, anger, maternalism, and probably yearnings to dominance or affiliation as well. Most of these propensities in humans, it is true, can be modified or overridden by cultural influences. But a persistent question keeps occurring to ethologists and psychiatrists: What are the costs—to the individual and to society—of overriding them? Do these costs, for example, include what in some instances we mean by neurosis?

Altered in the Womb

Major contributions to the understanding of sex differences have come from the field of endocrinology. Scientists have long known that sex hormones—the female hormones, such as progesterone and various estrogens, and the male hormones or androgens such as testosterone—must be involved in behavior. But prior to puberty, it is thought, roughly equal amounts of androgens and estrogens are present in the blood stream of male and female children alike, and this originally lent support to the role-modeling theorists' views that whatever differences in behavior were to be found in children must be due to learning.

Beginning in the 1950's, however, animal experiments have clearly shown that not only anatomical differences between males and females but also certain aspects of male and female behavior are determined prior to birth. In the late Fifties, for example, a group of University of Kansas scientists, including Charles Phoenix, Robert Goy, and the late William Young, injected female guinea pigs with small amounts of masculinizing hormone before birth and found that the animals' anatomical and behavioral futures could thereby be altered for all their lives. That is to say, these genetic females proceeded to develop not only the genitalia but also the mating behavior typical of males. Subsequent experiments have revealed that the same effects hold for animals higher than the guinea pig.

The fundamental organization of mammalian brains and bodies, it appears, is female first and only secondarily male, a reversal of the sequence assumed in the story of Adam and Eve. In human fetuses during the early stages of gestation, the brain of either sex possesses, in effect, the "blueprints" and latent neural circuits to develop and behave either as a female or a male. But if left hormonally alone, the fetus will always develop into a female. What happens in the case of males is that the male sex chromosome triggers a brief spurt of androgen from the fetal gonads. This spurt, in turn, somehow triggers a chain of chemical and organizational events that result in maleness. These include activating the neural circuits that will generate masculine behavioral propensities in the later presence of male hormones.

The female circuits, however, are not completely turned off; they continue to make a greater or lesser contribution to the behavior of even a "normal" male all through life. Experiments with rats, for instance, have shown that even a normal adult male rat can be induced to simulate female mating and maternal behavior by injections of hormones at certain sites in the brain. The reverse holds for females.

An Unhappy Bunch of Boys

Recent experiments reveal not only how the sex hormones influence the behavior of individual rhesus and macaque monkeys but also how the very composition of the monkey "culture" is partly subject to the hormonal balance of one or two individuals. These experiments were conducted at the Oregon Regional Primate Research Center near Portland, one of seven federally funded research centers set up in the U.S. to take experimental advantage of the kinship between monkeys and men. Psychologists Goy and Phoenix, who had taken part in the pioneering experiments at Kansas, are now at the Oregon center. They and several of their colleagues have altered the direction of development of fetal female monkeys by means of male hormone injections prior to birth. After birth these masculinized females behave more like males than females. That is to say, from infancy onward they indulge in much of the rough-and-tumble play and threatening grimaces of males of their species, as well as imitating the male-type infantile mating play.

It sometimes happens that by dint of sheer aggressiveness one of these

masculinized females will work her way up to become the "alpha" individual
in her troop. So far as human observers are able to judge, the members of these
troops are quite happy with their unorthodox leaders. But the results of some
other hormone experiments at the Oregon center have been less happy for the
monkey communities involved. In one study, instead of masculinizing the fetus,
a researcher has injected male hormones into normal females after birth but
prior to puberty. These monkeys too become aggressive, and sometimes one
emerges into alpha status. The day this happens is a dark one for the males;
from that time on she absolutely prohibits her male subjects from playing their
rough-and-tumble games or engaging in their mock-sexual play. "She makes the
boys sit quietly in the corners," says Goy, "and they're obviously a very
unhappy bunch of boys."

These experiments with guinea pigs, rats, and monkeys clearly signal that
temperament is related to sex hormones. Recent research reveals that this is
true of people too. At Johns Hopkins Hospital, for example, psychologists John
Money and Anke Ehrhardt have investigated several varieties of human
hermaphroditism—ambiguities in sexual development. Hermaphroditism occurs
in a fetus because of some congenital inability of the cells to respond to sex
hormones, or because of hormone therapy to the mother during pregnancy.
Occasionally, therefore, a genetic male is born indistinguishable in infantile
appearance from a female (though possessing no uterus and with internal testes
in place of ovaries). Naturally, parents often unknowingly raise these infants
as girls. Usually, these children grow up happily into women. They may like
dolls, they often date boys, and they frequently marry. Though sterile, of course,
they adopt children and display normal maternal affection.

Mysterious Programs

Initially, evidence of this kind was seen by some psychologists as support
for the view that social upbringing was the all-important shaper of behavior.
But later studies by Money and others now suggest a different interpretation:
in the feminized-male hermaphrodite, the brain as well as the body has failed to
receive the normal hormonal stimulation toward maleness. Support for this view
comes from investigation of another form of hermaphroditism. It involves
genetic females who because of therapy or a glandular malfunction are supplied
before birth with excessive amounts of androgen-like substances after their
ovaries and female internal reproductive organs are already formed, but before
the external genitalia have stopped developing. In many such cases, surgery
and hormone treatments can be employed early to bring about the development
of a completely normal-appearing fertile female. But this intervention apparently
comes too late to offset completely the effects on the brain. The girls often act
more like boys than girls. They tend to display an unusual degree of interest
in outdoor athletics, a preference for boys' toys instead of dolls, and even a
pattern, in Money's words, of "giving priority to career over marriage or at least
combining the two in future expectancies."

Very early in the development of any human being, the evidence suggests,
the presence of minute amounts of one hormone or the other activates some as
yet mysterious program that, together with later hormonal activity, will partly
determine what kinds of experiences and social molding a given individual will

tend to prefer, ignore, or reject. Some researchers go further and purpose that differences in cognitive "style" between males and females are traceable to hormonal influences upon the central nervous system. Psychologists Donald and Inge Broverman, a husband and wife team who work at Worcester State Hospital in Massachusetts, draw upon a great deal of psychological and biochemical research in arguing the controversial hypothesis that such intellectual differences are due to the differential stimulating effects of male and female hormones upon different nervous subsystems.

Why Women Feel Hurt

The Brovermans maintain that estrogen increases the acuteness of many sensory perceptions. This may account for the observations reported by various researchers that females tend to show more acute hearing, taste, and tactile sense than males. By the same token, according to Broverman, this lower sensory threshold may also cause most women to hurt more under punishment, and to have a greater need than most men to avoid stressful situations. From an evolutionary standpoint this would make sense, for lower levels of fear and sensitivity to pain would be of benefit to males engaged in the rigors of hunt or combat.

The greater sensitivity of women leads Broverman to speculate that females can be conditioned more quickly to respond to stimuli than males. This might help explain some of the male puzzlement at the feminist contentions that our patriarchal society will not "let" women practice male pursuits and occupations. The explanation may be that women tend to respond to the conditioning pressures of society more acutely than do men.

Better Living through Chemistry?

The large and growing body of evidence of the existence of inborn differences in temperament between men and women does not deny the validity of feminist demands for changes in existing social arrangements. All aspects of society should be subject to re-examination and readjustment to ensure that all citizens enjoy the right to optimal development of their human potentialities. But Kate Millett was much too dolorous when she wrote: "If human sexual temperament is inherent, there is really very little hope for us."

Indeed, innate differences need not stand in the way even of the homogenized androgyny that some radical feminists call for. If that were what society really wanted, it might one day be possible to use hormone pills to make males and females think and behave very much alike. (A side effect might be to suppress women's menstrual cycle, which has pervasive debilitating effects. A British study reports, for example, that schoolgirls' performance on written examinations declines by roughly 15 percent during the few days prior to menstruation.) A more efficient approach to androgyny would be to intervene in the early stages of pregnancy when the male or female neural circuits were being activated. By means of hormone implantations or deletions in this period, it should be perfectly feasible to masculinize the female fetus or feminize the male. The society thus created would be undeniably androgynous, and—most people would agree—awful.

Short of such measures, education and social pressures could undoubtedly bring about a considerable narrowing of the differences between the roles of the two sexes. Several educational researchers have demonstrated that special encouragement can offset much of women's lack of interest or ability in certain kinds of creative problem solving. It also seems clear that social influences can reduce overt male aggressiveness.

Competing at Men's Own Games

It is far from clear, however, that the use of training and indoctrination to make the sexes behave more alike would foster optimal satisfaction for either males or females. Edward Zigler, formerly a psychologist at Yale and now director of the federal Office of Child Development, puts the matter this way: "All that behavior geneticists have taught us suggests that genetic variation is an important component in many of the male-female behavioral differences we observe. Perhaps many of these genetically influenced behavioral differences could be overridden through training, but only at some considerable psychological cost. I think that such a thing as being true to one's self makes sense genetically as well as making for a much more interesting society."

What does seem clear is that deliberate blindness toward the evidence of innate differences is likely to lead to greater strains and dissatisfactions among women—and men as well. So long as feminists measure their progress in terms of how well they as a class compete with men at men's own games, their cause is likely to be damaging to women's self-esteem. For there will always be fewer high-ranking jobs than there are people who want them, and society has found no effective—or fair—way of filling them except through some kind of competition. Individual women, of course, should be free to decide which of these kinds of games they want to play, as well as how hard. But given the psychological evidence on male needs for achievement, together with the female distractions of marriage and maternity, it seems likely that there will always be more men than women at the top.

On the other hand, the importance of men's special traits may be on the decline. Aggression, preoccupation with technology, even competitive ambition itself, seem to be counting for less and less as our society matures. Conversely, the especially feminine qualities of nurturance and concern for people may be assuming more importance in a society threatened with disintegration. If in their quest for a more androgynous world, feminists lop off the feminine end of the behavioral spectrum, the operation could well be fatal.

4. If Hitler Asked You to Electrocute a Stranger, Would You? Probably
Philip Meyer

"We Americans are an obedient people: not blindly obedient, and not blissfully obedient, just obedient."

The social psychological studies described by Philip Meyer show how people can be influenced by authority to act in ways possibly contrary to their values. It is a chilling story that has to be studied, digested, and understood within the context of our society.

In the beginning, Stanley Milgram was worried about the Nazi problem. He doesn't worry much about the Nazis anymore. He worries about you and me, and, perhaps, himself a little bit too.

Stanley Milgram is a social psychologist, and when he began his career at Yale University in 1960 he had a plan to prove, scientifically, that Germans are different. The Germans-are-different hypothesis has been used by historians, such as William L. Shirer, to explain the systematic destruction of the Jews by the Third Reich. One madman could decide to destroy the Jews and even create a master plan for getting it done. But to implement it on the scale that Hitler did meant that thousands of other people had to go along with the scheme and help to do the work. The Shirer thesis, which Milgram set out to test, is that Germans have a basic character flaw which explains the whole thing, and this flaw is a readiness to obey authority without question, no matter what outrageous acts the authority commands.

The appealing thing about this theory is that it makes those of us who are not Germans feel better about the whole business. Obviously, you and I are not Hitler, and it seems equally obvious that we would never do Hitler's dirty work for him. But now, because of Stanley Milgram, we are compelled to wonder. Milgram developed a laboratory experiment which provided a systematic way to measure obedience. His plan was to try it out in New Haven on Americans and then go to Germany and try it out on Germans. He was strongly motivated by scientific curiosity, but there was also some moral content in his decision to pursue this line of research, which was, in turn, colored by his own Jewish background. If he could show that Germans are more obedient than Americans, he could then vary the conditions of the experiment and try to find out just what it is that makes some people more obedient than others. With this understanding, the world might, conceivably, be just a little bit better.

But he never took his experiment to Germany. He never took it any farther than Bridgeport. The first finding, also the most unexpected and disturbing finding, was that we Americans are an obedient people: not blindly obedient, and not blissfully obedient, just obedient. "I found so much obedience," says Milgram softly, a little sadly, "I hardly saw the need for taking the experiment to Germany."

There is something of the theatre director in Milgram, and his technique, which he learned from one of the old masters in experimental psychology, Solomon Asch, is to stage a play with every line rehearsed, every prop carefully selected, and everybody an actor except one person. That one person is the subject of the experiment. The subject, of course, does not know he is in a play. He thinks he is in real life. The value of this technique is that the experimenter, as though he were God, can change a prop here, vary a line there, and see how the subject responds. Milgram eventually had to change a lot of the script just to get people to stop obeying. They were obeying so much, the experiment wasn't working—it was like trying to measure oven temperature with a freezer thermometer.

The experiment worked like this: If you were an innocent subject in Milgram's melodrama, you read an ad in the newspaper or received one in the mail asking for volunteers for an educational experiment. The job would take about an hour and pay $4.50. So you make an appointment and go to an old Romanesque stone structure on High Street with the imposing name of The Yale Interaction Laboratory. It looks something like a broadcasting studio. Inside, you meet a young, crew-cut man in a laboratory coat who says he is Jack Williams, the experimenter. There is another citizen, fiftyish, Irish face, an accountant, a little overweight, and very mild and harmless-looking. This other citizen seems nervous and plays with his hat while the two of you sit in chairs side by side and are told that the $4.50 checks are yours no matter what happens. Then you listen to Jack Williams explain the experiment.

It is about learning, says Jack Williams in a quiet, knowledgeable way. Science does not know much about the conditions under which people learn and this experiment is to find out about negative reinforcement. Negative reinforcement is getting punished when you do something wrong, as opposed to positive reinforcement which is getting rewarded when you do something right. The negative reinforcement in this case is electric shock. You notice a book an the table, titled, *The Teaching-Learning Process,* and you assume that this has something to do with the experiment.

Then Jack Williams takes two pieces of paper, puts them in a hat, and shakes them up. One piece of paper is supposed to say, "Teacher" and the other, "Learner." Draw one and you will see which you will be. The mild-looking accountant draws one, holds it close to his vest like a poker player, looks at it, and says, "Learner," You look at yours. It says, "Teacher." You do not know that the drawing is rigged, and both slips say "Teacher." The experimenter beckons to the mild-mannered "learner."

"Want to step right in here and have a seat, please?" he says. "You can leave your coat on the back of that chair . . . roll up your right sleeve, please. Now what I want to do is strap down your arms to avoid excessive movement on your part during the experiment. This electrode is connected to the shock generator in the next room.

"And this electrode paste," he says, squeezing some stuff out of a plastic bottle and putting it on the man's arm, "is to provide a good contact and to avoid a blister or burn. Are there any questions now before we go into the next room?"

You don't have any, but the strapped-in "learner" does.

"I do think I should say this," says the learner. "About two years ago, I was at the veterans' hospital . . . they detected a heart condition. Nothing serious, but as long as I'm having these shocks, how strong are they—how dangerous are they?"

Williams, the experimenter, shakes his head casually. "Oh, no," he says. "Although they may be painful, they're not dangerous. Anything else?"

Nothing else. And so you play the game. The game is for you to read a series of word pairs: for example, blue-girl, nice-day, fat-neck. When you finish the list, you read just the first word in each pair and then a multiple-choice list of four other words, including the second word of the pair. The learner, from his remote, strapped-in position, pushes one of four switches to indicate which of the four answers he thinks is the right one. If he gets it right, nothing happens and you go on to the next one. If he gets it wrong, you push a switch that buzzes and gives him an electric shock. And then you go to the next word. You start with 15 volts and increase the number of volts by 15 for each wrong answer. The control board goes from 15 volts on one end to 450 volts on the other. So that you know what you are doing, you get a test shock yourself, at 45 volts. It hurts. To further keep you aware of what you are doing to that man in there, the board has verbal descriptions of the shock levels, ranging from "Slight Shock" at the left-hand side, through "Intense Shock" in the middle, to "Danger: Severe Shock" toward the far right. Finally, at the very end, under 435- and 450-volt switches, there are three ambiguous X's. If, at any point, you hesitate, Mr. Williams calmly tells you to go on. If you still hesitate, he tells you again.

Except for some terrifying details, which will be explained in a moment, this is the experiment. The object is to find the shock level at which you disobey the experimenter and refuse to pull the switch.

When Stanley Milgram first wrote this script, he took it to fourteen Yale psychology majors and asked them what they thought would happen. He put it this way: Out of one hundred persons in the teacher's predicament, how would their break-off points be distributed along the 15-to-450-volt scale? They thought a few would break off very early, most would quit someplace in the middle and a few would go all the way to the end. The highest estimate of the number out of one hundred who would go all the way to the end was three. Milgram then informally polled some of his fellow scholars in the psychology department. They agreed that very few would go to the end. Milgram thought so too.

"I'll tell you quite frankly," he says, "before I began this experiment, before any shock generator was built. I thought that most people would break off at 'Strong Shock' or 'Very Strong Shock.' You would get only a very, very small proportion of people going out to the end of the shock generator, and they would constitute a pathological fringe."

In his pilot experiments, Milgram used Yale students as subjects. Each of them pushed the shock switches one by one, all the way to the end of the board.

So he rewrote the script to include some protests from the learner. At first, they were mild, gentlemanly, Yalie protests, but "it didn't seem to have as much effect as I thought it would or should," Milgram recalls. "So we had more violent protestation on the part of the person getting the shock. All of the time, of course, what we were trying to do was not to create a macabre situation, but simply to generate disobedience. And that was one of the first findings. This was not only a technical deficiency of the experiment, that we didn't get disobedience. It really was the first finding: that obedience would be much greater than we had assumed it would be and disobedience would be much more difficult than we had assumed."

As it turned out, the situation did become rather macabre. The only meaningful way to generate disobedience was to have the victim protest with great anguish, noise, and vehemence. The protests were tape-recorded so that all the teachers ordinarily would hear the same sounds and nuances, and they started with a grunt at 75 volts, proceeded through a "Hey, that really hurts," at 125 volts, got desperate with, "I can't stand the pain, don't do that," at 180 volts, reached complaints of heart trouble at 195, an agonized scream at 285, a refusal to answer at 315, and only heartrendering, ominous silence after that.

Still, sixty-five percent of the subjects, twenty- to fifty-year-old American males, everyday, ordinary people, like you and me, obediently kept pushing those levers in the belief that they were shocking the mild-mannered learner, whose name was Mr. Wallace, and who was chosen for the role because of his innocent appearance, all the way up to 450 volts.

Milgram was now getting enough disobedience so that he had something he could measure. The next step was to vary the circumstances to see what would encourage or discourage obedience. There seemed very little left in the way of discouragement. The victim was already screaming at the top of his lungs and feigning a heart attack. So whatever new impediment to obedience reached the brain of the subject had to travel by some route other than the ear. Milgram thought of one.

He put the learner in the same room with the teacher. He stopped strapping the learner's hand down. He rewrote the script so that at 150 volts the learner took his hand off the shock plate and declared that he wanted out of the experiment. He rewrote the script some more so that the experimenter then told the teacher to grasp the learner's hand and physically force it down on the plate to give Mr. Wallace his unwanted electric shock.

"I had the feeling that very few people would go on at that point, if any," Milgram says. "I thought that would be the limit of obedience that you find in the laboratory."

It wasn't.

Although seven years have now gone by, Milgram still remembers the first person to walk into the laboratory in the newly rewritten script. He was a construction worker, a very short man. "He was so small," says Milgram, "that when he sat on the chair in front of the shock generator, his feet didn't reach the floor. When the experimenter told him to push the victim's hand down and give the shock, he turned to the experimenter, and he turned to the victim, his elbow went up, he fell down on the hand of the victim, his feet kind of tugged to one side, and he said, 'Like this, boss?' ZZUMPH!"

The experiment was played out to its bitter end. Milgram tried it with forty different subjects. And thirty percent of them obeyed the experimenter and kept on obeying.

"The protests of the victim were strong and vehement, he was screaming his guts out, he refused to participate, and you had to physically struggle with him in order to get his hand down on the shock generator," Milgram remembers. But twelve out of forty did it.

Milgram took his experiment out of New Haven. Not to Germany, just twenty miles down the road to Bridgeport. Maybe, he reasoned, the people obeyed because of the prestigious setting of Yale University. If they couldn't trust a center of learning that had been there for two centuries, whom could they trust? So he moved the experiment to an untrustworthy setting.

The new setting was a suite of three rooms in a run-down office building in Bridgeport. The only identification was a sign with a fictitious name: "Research Associates of Bridgeport." Questions about professional connections got only vague answers about "research for industry."

Obedience was less in Bridgeport. Forty-eight percent of the subjects stayed for the maximum shock, compared to sixty-five percent at Yale. But this was enough to prove that far more than Yale's prestige was behind the obedient behavior.

For more than seven years now, Stanley Milgram has been trying to figure out what makes ordinary American citizens so obedient. The most obvious answer—that people are mean, nasty, brutish and sadistic—won't do. The subjects who gave the shocks to Mr. Wallace to the end of the board did not enjoy it. They groaned, protested, fidgeted, argued, and in some cases, were seized by fits of nervous, agitated giggling.

"They even try to get out of it," says Milgram, "but they are somehow engaged in something from which they cannot liberate themselves. They are locked into a structure, and they do not have the skills or inner resources to disengage themselves."

Milgram, because he mistakenly had assumed that he would have trouble getting people to obey the orders to shock Mr. Wallace, went to a lot of trouble to create a realistic situation.

There was crew-cut Jack Williams and his grey laboratory coat. Not white, which might denote a medical technician, but ambiguously authoritative grey. Then there was the book on the table, and the other appurtenances of the laboratory which emitted the silent message that things were being performed here in the name of science, and were therefore great and good.

But the nicest touch of all was the shock generator. When Milgram started out, he had only a $300 grant from the Higgins Fund of Yale University. Later he got more ample support from the National Science Foundation, but in the beginning he had to create this authentic-looking mchine with very scarce resources except for his own imagination. So he went to New York and roamed around the electronic shops until he found some little black switches at Lafayette Radio for a dollar apiece. He bought thirty of them. The generator was a metal box, about the size of a small footlocker, and he drilled the thirty holes for the thirty switches himself in a Yale machine shop. But the fine detail was left to professional industrial engravers. So he ended up with a splendid-looking control panel dominated by the row of switches, each labeled with its voltage, and each having its own red light that flashed on when the switch was pulled. Other things happened when a switch was pushed. Besides the ZZUMPH-ing noise, a blue light labeled "voltage energizer" went on, and a needle on a dial labeled "voltage" flicked from left to right. Relays inside the box clicked. Finally, in the upper left-hand corner of the control panel was this inscription, engraved in precise block letters:

SHOCK GENERATOR TYPE ZLB
DYSON INSTRUMENT COMPANY
WALTHAM, MASS.
OUTPUT: 15 VOLTS—450 VOLTS

One day a man from the Lehigh Valley Electronics Company of Pennsylvania was passing through the laboratory, and he stopped to admire the shock generator.

"This is a very fine shock generator," he said. "But who is this Dyson Instrument Company?" Milgram felt proud at that, since Dyson Instrument Company existed only in the recesses of his imagination.

When you consider the seeming authenticity of the situation, you can appreciate the agony some of the subjects went through. It was pure conflict. As Milgram explains to his students. "When a parent says, 'Don't strike old ladies,' you are learning two things: the content, and, also, to obey authority. This experiment creates conflicts between the two elements."

Here is a partial transcription from one of the experiments. The naive "teacher" is a heavyset, worried-looking man with prematurely grey hair. He is wearing a polo shirt. He is very polite. He has just pushed the 180-volt lever. A hidden camera is recording the performance.

LEARNER (*who, from the teacher's point of view is heard but not seen, an offstage voice*): Ow, I can't stand the pain. Don't do that. . . .

TEACHER (*pivoting around in his chair and shaking his head*): I can't stand it. I'm not going to kill that man in there. You hear him hollering?

EXPERIMENTER: As I told you before, the shocks may be painful, but—

TEACHER: But he's hollering. He can't stand it. What's going to happen to him?

EXPERIMENTER (*his voice is patient, matter-of-fact*): The experiment requires that you continue, Teacher.

TEACHER: Aaah, but, unh, I'm not going to get that man sick in there . . . know what I mean?

EXPERIMENTER: Whether the learner likes it or not, we must go on, through all the word pairs.

TEACHER: I refuse to take the responsibility. He's in there hollering!

EXPERIMENTER: It's absolutely essential that you continue, Teacher.

TEACHER (*indicating the unused questions*): There's too many left here, I mean, Geez, if he gets them wrong, there's too many of them left. I mean who's going to take the responsibility if anything happens to that gentleman?

EXPERIMENTER: I'm responsible for anything that happens to him. Continue please.

TEACHER: All right. (*Consults list of words.*) The next one's "Slow— walk, truck, dance, music." Answer, please. (*A buzzing sound indicates the learner has signaled his answer.*) Wrong. A hundred and ninety-five volts. "Dance." (*Zzumph!*)

LEARNER: Let me out of here. My heart's bothering me! (*Teacher looks at experimenter.*)

EXPERIMENTER: Continue, please.

LEARNER (*screaming*): Let me out of here, you have no right to keep me here. Let's me out of here, let me out, my heart's bothering me, let me out! (*Teacher shakes head, pats the table nervously.*)

TEACHER: You see, he's hollering. Hear that? Gee, I don't know.

EXPERIMENTER: The experiment requires. . . .

TEACHER (*interrupting*): I know it does, sir, but I mean—hunh! He don't know what he's getting in for. He's up to 195 volts! (*Experiment continues, through 210 volts, 225 volts, 240 volts, 255 volts, 270 volts, delivered to the man in the electric chair, at which point the teacher, with evident relief, runs out of word-pair questions.*)

EXPERIMENTER: You'll have to go back to the beginning of that page and go through them again until he's learned them all correctly.

TEACHER: Aw, no. I'm not going to kill that man. You mean I've got to keep going up with the scale. No sir. He's hollering in there, I'm not going to give him 450 volts.

EXPERIMENTER: The experiment requires that you go on.

TEACHER: I know it does, but that man is hollering in there, sir.

EXPERIMENTER (*same matter-of-fact tone*): As I said before, although the shocks may be painful. . . .

TEACHER (*interrupting*): Awwww. He—he—he's yelling in there.

EXPERIMENTER: Start with "Blue," please, at the top of the page. Continue, please, Teacher. Just go ahead.

TEACHER (*concentrating intently on list of words in front of him, as if to shut everything else out*): "Blue—boy, girl, grass, hat." (*Buzz indicates answer.*) Correct. "Night—day, sky, job, chair. (*Buzz*) Wrong. The answer is "day." Two hundred and eighty-five volts. (*Zzumph!*)

LEARNER: Ohhhuhhoohhh!

EXPERIMENTER: Continue, please.

TEACHER: "Fat—man, lady, tub, neck." Answer, please. (*Buzz*) Wrong. The answer is "neck." Three hundred volts. (*Zzumph!*)

LEARNER: Ohhh. I absolutely refuse to answer any more. (*Shouting urgently, now*) Let me out of here. You can't hold me here. Get me out. Get—me—out—of—here.

EXPERIMENTER: Continue. The next word is "Green," please.

TEACHER: "Green—grass, hat, ink, apple." (*Nothing happens. No answering buzz. Just gloomy silence.*)

TEACHER: I don't think he is going to answer.

EXPERIMENTER: If the learner doesn't answer in a reasonable time, about four or five seconds, consider the answer wrong. And follow the same procedures you have been doing for wrong answers. Say "Wrong," tell him the number of volts, give him the punishment, read him the correct answer. Continue, please.

TEACHER: "Green—grass, hat, ink, apple." Answer, please. (*More silence. Teacher just sits there.*)

EXPERIMENTER: Go on with the procedure, please, Teacher.

TEACHER: Three hundred and fifteen volts. The answer is "ink." (*Zzumph!*)

LEARNER: Ohh. Ooohh.

TEACHER (*relieved to hear response*): Next one. . . .

LEARNER: I absolutely refuse to answer.

TEACHER: You got to. You get a shock if you don't answer. (*Experiment continues with learner refusing to answer, and, finally, failing even to grunt or groan. At 375 volts, the teacher stands up. Has he had enough? Will he break off the experiment? Will he disobey?*)

TEACHER: I think something's happened to that fellow in there. I don't get no answer. He was hollering at less voltage. Can't you check in and see if he's all right, please?

EXPERIMENTER (*same detached calm*): Not once we've started. Please continue, Teacher.

TEACHER (*sits down, sighs deeply*): "Cool—day, shade, water, paint." Answer, please. Are you all right in there? Are you all right?

EXPERIMENTER: Please continue, Teacher. Continue, please. (*Teacher pushes lever. Zzumph!*)

TEACHER (*swiveling around in his chair*): Something's happened to that man in there. (*Swiveling back*) Next one. "Low—dollar, necklace, moon, paint." (*Turning around again*) Something's happened to that man in there. You better check in on him, sir. He won't answer or nothing.

EXPERIMENTER: Continue. Go on, please.

TEACHER: You accept all responsibility.

EXPERIMENTER: The responsibility is mine. Correct. Please go on. (*Teacher returns to his list, starts running through words as rapidly as he can read them, works through to 450 volts.*)

TEACHER: That's that.

EXPERIMENTER: Continue using the last switch on the board, please. The four-fifty switch for each wrong answer. Continue, please.

TEACHER: But I don't get no anything!

EXPERIMENTER: Please continue. The next word is "White."

TEACHER: Don't you think you should look in on him, please.

EXPERIMENTER: Not once we've started the experiment.

TEACHER: But what if something has happened to the man?

EXPERIMENTER: The experiment requires that you continue. Go on, please.

TEACHER: Don't the man's health mean anything?

EXPERIMENTER: Whether the learner likes it or not. . . .

TEACHER: What if he's dead in there? (*Gestures toward the room with the electric chair.*) I mean, he told me he can't stand the shock, sir. I don't mean to be rude, but I think you should look in on him. All you have to do is look in the door. I don't get no answer, no noise. Something might have happened to the gentleman in there, sir.

EXPERIMENTER: We must continue. Go on, please.

TEACHER: You mean keep giving him what? Four hundred fifty volts, what's he got now?

EXPERIMENTER: That's correct. Continue. The next word is "White."

TEACHER (*now at a furious pace*): "White—cloud, horse, rock, house." Answer, please. The answer is "horse." Four hundred and fifty volts. (*Zzumph!*) Next word, "Bag—paint, music, clown, girl." The answer is "paint." Four hundred and fifty volts (*Zzumph!*) Next word is "Short—sentence, movie. . . ."

EXPERIMETER: Excuse me, Teacher. We'll have to discontinue the experiment.

(*Enter Milgram from camera's left. He has been watching from behind one-way glass.*)

MILGRAM: I'd like to ask you a few questions. (*Slowly, patiently, he dehoaxes the teacher, telling him that the shocks and screams were not real.*)

TEACHER: You mean he wasn't getting nothing? Well, I'm glad to hear that. I was getting upset there. I was getting ready to walk out.

(*Finally, to make sure there are no hard feelings, friendly, harmless Mr. Wallace comes out in coat and tie. Gives jovial greeting. Friendly reconciliation takes place. Experiment ends.*)*

Subjects in the experiment were not asked to give the 450-volt shock more than three times. By that time, it seemed evident that they would go on indefinitely. "No one," says Milgram, "who got within five shocks of the end ever broke off. By that point, he had resolved the conflict."

Why do so many people resolve the conflict in favor of obedience?

Milgram's theory assumes that people behave in two different operating modes as different as ice and water. He does not rely on Freud or sex or toilet-training hang-ups for this theory. All he says is that ordinarily we operate in a state of autonomy, which means we pretty much have and assert control over what we do. But in certain circumstances. we operate under what Milgram calls a state of agency (after agent, n . . . one who acts for or in the place of another by authority from him; a substitute; a deputy.—*Webster's Collegiate Dictionary*). A state of agency, to Milgram, is nothing more than a frame of mind.

"There's nothing bad about it, there's nothing good about it," he says. "It's a natural circumstance of living with other people. . . . I think of a state of agency as a real transformation of a person; if a person has different properties when he's in that state, just as water can turn to ice under certain conditions of temperature, a person can move to the state of mind that I call agency . . . the critical thing is that you see yourself as the instrument of the execution of another person's wishes. You do not see yourself as acting on your own. And there's a real transformation, a real change of properties of the person."

To achieve this change, you have to be in a situation where there seems to be a ruling authority whose commands are relevant to some legitimate purpose; the authority's power is not unlimited.

But situations can be and have been structured to make people do unusual things, and not just in Milgram's laboratory. The reason, says Milgram, is that no action, in and of itself, contains meaning.

"The meaning always depends on your definition of the situation. Take an action like killing another person. It sounds bad.

*© Stanley Milgram 1965.

"But then we say the other person was about to destroy a hundred children, and the only way to stop him was to kill him. Well, that sounds good.

"Or, you take destroying your own life. It sounds very bad. Yet, in the Second World War, thousands of persons thought it was a good thing to destroy your own life. It was set in the proper context. You sipped some saki from a whistling cup, recited a few haiku. You said, 'May my death be as clean and as quick as the shattering of crystal.' And it almost seemed like a good, noble thing to do, to crash your kamikaze plane into an aircraft carrier. But the main thing was, the definition of what a kamikaze pilot was doing had been determined by the relevant authority. Now, once you are in a state of agency, you allow the authority to determine, to define what the situation is. The meaning of your actions is altered."

So, for most subjects in Milgram's laboratory experiments, the act of giving Mr. Wallace his painful shock was necessary, even though unpleasant, and besides they were doing it on behalf of somebody else and it was for science. There was still strain and conflict, of course. Most people resolved it by grimly sticking to their task and obeying. But some broke out. Milgram tried varying the conditions of the experiment to see what would help break people out of their state of agency.

"The results, as seen and felt in the laboratory," he has written, "are disturbing. They raise the possibility that human nature, or more specifically the kind of character produced in American democratic society, cannot be counted on to insulate its citizens from brutality and inhumane treatment at the direction of malevolent authority. A substantial proportion of people do what they are told to do, irrespective of the content of the act and without limitations of conscience, so long as they perceive that the command comes from a legitimate authority. If in this study, an anonymous experimenter can successfully command adults to subdue a fifty-year-old man and force on him painful electric shocks against his protest, one can only wonder what government, with its vastly greater authority and prestige, can command of its subjects."

This is a nice statement, but it falls short of summing up the full meaning of Milgram's work. It leaves some questions still unanswered.

The first question is this: Should we really be surprised and alarmed that people obey? Wouldn't it be even more alarming if they all refused to obey? Without obedience to a relevant ruling authority there could not be a civil society. And without a civil society, as Thomas Hobbes pointed out in the seventeenth century, we would live in a condition of war, "of every man against every other man," and life would be "solitary, poor, nasty, brutish and short."

In the middle of one of Stanley Milgram's lectures of C.U.N.Y. recently, some mini-skirted undergraduates started whispering and giggling in the back of the room. He told them to cut it out. Since he was the relevant authority in that time and that place, they obeyed, and most people in the room were glad that they obeyed.

This was not, of course, a conflict situation. Nothing in the coeds' social upbringing made it a matter of conscience for them to whisper and giggle. But a case can be made that in a conflict situation it is all the more important to obey. Take the case of war, for example. Would we really want a situation in which every participant in a war, direct, or indirect—from front-line soldiers to the people who sell coffee and cigarettes to employees at the Concertina barbed-wire factory in Kansas—stops and consults his conscience before each action. It is asking for an awful lot of mental strain and anguish from an awful lot of people. The value of having civil order is that one can do his duty, or whatever interests him, or whatever seems to benefit him at the moment, and leave the agonizing to others. When Francis Gary Powers was being tried by a Soviet military tribunal after his U-2 spy plane was shot down, the presiding judge asked if he had thought about the possibility that his flight might have provoked a war. Powers replied with Hobbesian clarity: "The people who sent me should think of these things. My job was to carry out orders. I do not think it was my responsibility to make such decisions."

It was not his responsibility. And it is quite possible that if everyone felt responsible for each of the ultimate consequences of his own tiny contributions to complex chains of events, then society simply would not work. Milgram, fully conscious of the moral and social implications of his research, believes that people should feel responsible for their actions. If someone else had invented the experiment, and if he had been the naive subject, he feels certain that he would have been among the disobedient minority.

"There is no very good solution to this," he admits, thoughtfully. "To simply and categorically say that you won't obey authority may resolve your personal conflict, but it creates more problems for society which may be more serious in the long run. But I have no doubt that to disobey is the proper thing to do in this [the laboratory] situation. It is the only reasonable value judgment to make."

The conflict between the need to obey the relevant ruling authority and the need to follow your conscience becomes sharpest if you insist on living by an ethical system based on a rigid code—a code that seeks to answer all questions in advance of their being raised. Code ethics cannot solve the obedience problem. Stanley Milgram seems to be a situation ethicist, and situation ethics does offer a way out: When you feel conflict, you examine the situation and then make a choice among the competing evils. You may act with a presumption in favor of obedience, but reserve the possibility that you will disobey whenever obedience demands a flagrant and outrageous affront to conscience. This, by the way, is the philosophical position of many who resist the draft. In World War II, they would have fought. Vietnam is a different, an outrageously different, situation.

Life can be difficult for the situation ethicist, because he does not see the world in straight lines, while the social system too often assumes such a God-given, squared-off structure. If your moral code includes an injunction against all war, you may be deferred as a conscientious objector. If you merely oppose this particular war, you may not be deferred.

Stanley Milgram has his problems, too. He believes that in the laboratory situation, he would not have shocked Mr. Wallace. His professional critics reply that in his real-life situation he has done the equivalent. He has placed innocent and naive subjects under great emotional strain and pressure in selfish obedience to his quest for knowledge. When you raise this issue with Milgram, he has an answer ready. There is, he explains patiently, a critical difference between his naive subjects and the man in the electric chair. The man in the electric chair (in the mind of the naive subject) is helpless, strapped in. But the naive subject is free to go at any time.

Immediately after he offers this distinction, Milgrim anticipates the objection.

"It's quite true," he says, "that this is almost a philosophic position, because we have learned that some people are psychologically incapable of disengaging themselves. But that doesn't relieve them of the moral responsibility."

The parallel is exquisite. "The tension problem was unexpected," says Milgram in his defense. But he went on anyway. The naive subjects didn't expect the screaming protests from the strapped-in learner. But that went on.

"I had to make a judgment," says Milgram. "I had to ask myself, was this harming the person or not? My judgment is that it was not. Even in the extreme cases, I wouldn't say that permanent damage results."

Sound familiar? "The shocks may be painful," the experimeter kept saying, "but they're not dangerous."

After the series of experiments was completed, Milgram sent a report of the results to his subjects and a questionnaire, asking whether they were glad or sorry to have been in the experiment. Eighty-three and seven-tenths percent said they were glad and only 1.3 percent were sorry; 15 percent were neither sorry nor glad. However, Milgram could not be sure at the time of the experiment that only 1.3 percent would be sorry.

Kurt Vonnegut Jr. put one paragraph in the preface to *Mother Night,* in 1966, which pretty much says it for the people with their fingers on the shock-generator switches, for you and me, and maybe even for Milgram. "If I'd been born in Germany," Vonnegut said, "I suppose I would have *been* a Nazi, bopping Jews and gypsies and Poles around, leaving boots sticking out of snowbanks, warming myself with my sweetly virtuous insides. So it goes."

Just so. One thing that happened to Milgram back in New Haven during the days of the experiment was that he kept running into people he'd watched from behind the one-way glass. It gave him a funny feeling, seeing those people going about their everyday business in New Haven and knowing what they would do to Mr. Wallace if ordered to. Now that his research results are in and you've thought about it, you can get this funny feeling too. You don't need one-way glass. A glance in your own mirror may serve just as well.

Discussion Questions

1. Discuss the impact of culture and biology in understanding male and female differences.
2. What are the implications of electrical brain stimulation in the control of human behavior?
3. What makes people obedient to authority? Speculate on the variables that create this predisposition in our culture.
4. In what way may self-control be the basic foundation of our personal freedom? Discuss the implications of self-control.

Chapter 2
Group Identity

Group influence is one of the most powerful determiners of social behavior. Children learn very early to identify with people who have similarities with their own family experience. These affiliations are extremely durable especially when they are based on such potent forces as religion and racial or national background. As people get older, their group associations often enlarge dramatically. Furthermore, their relationships with other people take on multiple characteristics, so that it is not uncommon to have significant emotional contact with a variety of different groups. Although many of these group investments can be transient or persistent, the identity of each person tends to hinge on his relationships with others.

In this chapter we are particularly concerned with groups united on the basis of cultural and racial similarities. Most often these groups have not been created out of personal preference but are more likely to be accidents of nature. Furthermore, the individual may remain a group member as much out of external pressure as by personal choice. As a consequence, racial, religious, and national groups are usually more vulnerable to discrimination and vigorous attacks from various quarters than any other group categories. In most instances, members of these groups cannot easily lose themselves in the population at large. They are, for all intents and purposes, easily identifiable because of physical idiosyncrasies, a commitment to various ceremonial patterns, or simple determination to retain their special identity no matter what the cost may be.

The first article in this chapter "The Awakening of the Chicanos" by Arnold Hano is a poignant study of the tragic experience of the Mexican American. It is possibly surprising to learn that there are over six million Mexican Americans who live in tremendous poverty and who are as economically disadvantaged as any group in the United States. The large majority of the Mexican Americans are settled in California working as agricultural laborers. The Chicano is segregated from the white community and has a special problem in that he is often bilingual. Yet American schools pay little cognizance to the Spanish language and tend simply to ignore the colorful culture and tradition from which these people have emerged. Thus, the personal identity of the Mexican Americans is clearly ambiguous. Living in the United States as an American citizen, they are no longer Mexican; and because of their Spanish language, physical characteristics, and cultural heritage, they are labeled by Americans as Mexican but are not considered fully American by the in-group itself. This article beautifully captures the dilemma of Chicanos and the social problem that hopefully will some day be resolved.

To say that American Indians have been treated indecently in our society is an understatement. For years they have been forced to live on reservations, denied equal opportunity under law, excluded from social interaction with the rest of the country, and cheated economically by unscrupulous operators. The Indians have remained virtual prisoners in their own land. The article "Seminole Girl" by Merwyn S. Garbarino studies the experience of a Seminole girl who works her way off the reservation and who tries to find her identity within a larger American culture. However, her ties to the reservation are extremely strong and she returns to live with her own people. The story is told more or less in her own words and is a sensitive portrait of problems Indians must face in securing some degree of self-respect in a culture that has denied this possibility for many years.

In the field of psychology, one of the most significant developments of this century has been the definition and measurement of human intelligence. Beginning with the pioneering work of Binet at the turn of the century and continuing with the more recent work of Terman, Gilford and Wechsler, the fascinating study of human intelligence has continued to yield convincing evidence for its power in understanding and predicting varied aspects of human behavior. Over the years, the importance of psychological intelligence testing has become a powerfully loaded emotional issue in American psychology. This scientific issue, still being argued, revolves around the relative significance of biological versus environmental conditions in the understanding and prediction of human behavior. To many scientists there is considerable evidence that biological inheritance accounts for a great deal of what we call I.Q., and I.Q., in turn, appears highly related to occupational choice, achievement, and social mobility among other things. To other scientists, equally well versed in the psychological literature, the opinion is that, while genetic components are important in the I.Q., the most important variance is contributed by environmental variables which set the stage for biological traits to emerge.

The controversy about the relative importance of nature versus nurture has aroused a scientific furor that has taken on enormous social implications. This has developed around the socially loaded issue of black versus white intelligence. The general problem can be stated as follows: Given the undisputed fact that blacks score on the average lower than whites on I.Q. tests, does this evidence support an inference that blacks are therefore biologically inferior to whites with respect to intelligence? Pursuing this issue even further, which has been done by a number of authors, the problem becomes more involved. If blacks are considered intellectually inferior as a result of I.Q. tests, and if these differences are assumed to be a function of biological differences, does it then follow that learning programs based upon the manipulation of environmental conditions would be practically ineffectual in making up this biological deficit? A few years ago Arthur R. Jensen, a very reputable psychologist, developed a thesis that suggested certain biological deficits in the intellectual equipment of blacks and attributed the failure of governmental programs such as Head Start to this "fact." The article by Jensen was immediately subjected to severe and scathing criticism by many scientists around the country. One of the most scholarly rejoinders to the Jensen thesis was prepared by Richard C. Lewontin, an eminent geneticist at the University of Chicago. In this article Lewontin accused Jensen of taking presumptuous leaps and distorting genetic evidence. Lewontin argued that Jensen had not paid sufficient attention to the subtle interplay between genetics and the environment and had accepted conclusions which are basically unwarranted at this stage of our understanding.

Recently, the prominent psychoanalyst Bruno Bettelheim published a fascinating book entitled *The Children of the Dream.* Bettelheim spent seven weeks intensively studying a kibbutz in Israel and from this experience created a controversial portrait of kibbutz education and speculated on the kind of personality that kibbutz living produces. Furthermore, Bettelheim also extended the insights of kibbutz living to a solution for the psychological and educational problems faced by the black community in the United States. A scholarly discussion of Bettelheim's view is found in "The Dream of the Kibbutz" by Urie Bronfenbrenner. Bronfenbrenner disputes many of Bettelheim's conclusions and draws on other observations of kibbutz life that are not in accord with Bettelheim's findings. This paper is a fascinating account of kibbutz life, on the one hand, and a scholarly scientific argument by two eminent social scientists who have studied the same social psychological phenomenon, on the other.

Suggested Readings

Al-Issa, Ihson, and Dennis, Wayne. *Cross Cultural Studies of Behavior.* New York: Holt, Rinehart and Winston, 1970. Covers a broad spectrum of cross cultural phenomena such as child rearing, personality, mental health, and intellectual development.

Deutsch, Martin, Katz, Irwin, and Jensen, Arthur R. *Social Class, Race, and Psychological Development.* New York: Holt, Rinehart and Winston, 1968. A series of scholarly papers by experts studying the social and intellectual problems of race and social class differences.

Kiev, Ari. *Transcultural Psychiatry.* New York: The Free Press, 1971. Studies the cultural definitions of "normal" and "abnormal" in primitive and advanced societies.

Spiro, Melford E. *Kibbutz: Venture in Utopia.* New York: Schocken Paperback, 1963. This is the classic study of kibbutz life by an eminent anthropologist.

5. The Awakening of the Chicanos
Arnold Hano

"You are told that a Spanish word doesn't count. Only English words are words. You are told you don't know anything. You are taught you are dumb."

The Mexican American has experienced the worst discrimination America has to offer. Yet like blacks and Indians, the Chicano has begun to demand equal social and economic rights. Arnold Hano has intimately captured the tragedy and promise of the Chicano.

Sixteen-year-old Martie Hernandez—petite and spirited—remembers her first day in school, on Los Angeles' east side. A teacher asked for words beginning with the letter *c*. One child said, "Cat." Another offered, "Car." Then a girl sitting next to Martie murmured, "Chancla."

The teacher shook her head scornfully. There was no such word as "chancla." Next?

Martie Hernandez sat bewildered. She knew chancla was a word—a perfectly good word. It meant slipper, old shoe. Today, Martie Hernandez sums up the experience, the cry of Mexican American youth shut off from the American Dream.

"You are told that a Spanish word doesn't count. Only English words are words. You are told you don't know anything. You are taught you are dumb. You are taught there are two worlds, white and brown, and that white is better. Well, I am Chicano—I am brown—and I am proud of what I am!"

These past weeks, traveling in the Far West and in the Southwest, where nearly 90 percent of our country's six million Mexican Americans live, I have learned much about the Chicanos. A new feeling of personal worth, a surge of pride, has risen among Mexican American youth.

Once, Mexican Americans were a docile group, isolated, despised. The Mexican American—so the stereotype went—was a lazy, good-natured creature, sleeping off his wine-induced siesta beneath a huge sombrero.

Not so now. The siesta is over. Young Chicanos—the word seems to be a version of Mexicanos—are fully roused. They are demanding change. They are speaking out their grievances. The educational system, they will tell you, is unfair. It puts a terrible burden on youngsters who come from homes where only Spanish has been spoken and go to schools where only English will be spoken. They live in tumbling-down, overcrowded barrios, a word that means neighborhoods but just as easily could mean ghettos, slums.

Mexican American job seekers are shuffled off to perform manual labor in the cities or "stoop labor" in the fields. The police, a recent government report says, often single out Mexican Americans for arrest and harassment. It is a litany of woe familiar to other minority groups, particularly the Negro and the American Indian. More than a third of Mexican American families live in officially designated poverty, on incomes under $3,000 a year. In one county in New Mexico, the number is an appalling 68 percent. Unemployment is twice that of Anglo-Americans (white, English-speaking Americans as opposed to Mexican Americans). Those who are employed work with little hope of advancement. An Arizona employer admitted before the United States Commission on Civil Rights: "Yes, we discriminate. We always have. We have never permitted Mexican Americans to get higher than a certain level in this company."

Mexican Americans are seven times more likely to dwell in substandard housing than Anglo-Americans. They are seven times less likely to go to college. The high school dropout rate is twice as high. So is infant mortality. Adult males die ten years sooner. A seventeen-year-old peach picker in the San Joaquin Valley of California told me she had never seen a chemical toilet in the fields, though the law states there must be one nearby. "I hide in the bushes," she confessed.

"We are treated like animals," a New Mexico farm worker said. A California judge snarled, "Animal!" at a teen-aged Mexican American before him, and suggested Hitler had been right. "People like you ought to be destroyed!"

Let me tell you about Colonia Independencia—a barrio at the edge of Anaheim, California. Anaheim is the home of Disneyland, the nation's favorite tourist attraction. From Disneyland you drive west two and a half miles through Anaheim's residential sections with quiet, tree-shaded streets. There is a sturdy respectability to this part of the city.

You come on the barrio suddenly. You cross the railroad tracks of the Southern Pacific, and instantly it all changes. This is the wrong side of the tracks. This is the barrio: three short blocks by one long block of dingy shacks, some of them bravely painted to present a bright face to the street. But in back, you can see how shabbily constructed the houses are. Behind each house is a smaller house and behind that a still smaller house, each more dilapidated as you move down the alley away from the street front.

Many of the houses have been condemned by building and safety inspectors as unfit to live in. Yet nobody moves the families out. A Mexican American youth walking with me asks, "Where would we move to? Just another barrio."

On one street is a brand-new church, lovely and serene. But the church is closed all week except for a few hours on Sunday. The pastor does not live in the neighborhood. Across from the church is a parking lot, a harsh expanse of black asphalt. There was not a single parked automobile when I drove by at noon. But then, as my guide said, "Who visits the barrio?"

As barrios go, Colonia Independencia is not bad. The barrio of Santa Anita in Santa Ana, California, five miles distant, has been called by some the worst poverty area in southern California. Here there are no street lights, no sidewalks.

Just darkness and dirt. Garbage spills out of broken containers, waiting to be collected. It waits a long time. The smell is high, the flies a black cloud. The houses are a pitiful clutter of matchboxes. Yet, compared to the colonias of southern Texas, Santa Ana is sheer affluence.

Delinquency is high in the barrios. (Delinquents are known as *pachucos* or *cholos*.) Squalid surroundings offer up a spoiled harvest. Dorothy Herrera is a probation officer in Orange County, California with a case load of Mexican American youngsters. "The children feel cheated," Dorothy Herrera says. "They feel they have been let down, left out. Resentment grows. Anger grows. They turn to drugs, they sniff glue. They have little self-respect."

I sat with three of Dorothy Herrera's charges, three girls on probation. Bonnie Lopes is fourteen, one of five children. Her mother and father are separated. Her mother does not speak English. At home the family speaks Spanish. "I feel more comfortable speaking Spanish," Bonnie says. "I'm talking my own language." Bonnie is on probation for running away. She has smoked grass and popped pills. Once she got into a fight in school. "A white girl called me a dirty Mexican. I jumped her and beat her up. Once I wanted to beat up my teacher. She said, 'You Mexicans never do your work.' I cussed her out in Spanish."

Luisa Ortega, just seventeen, dropped out of school in the tenth grade. "I was using drugs. I started flunking." Now Luisa baby-sits for a married sister from six in the morning to 3:30 every afternoon, nine and a half hours a day. Luisa slumps in her chair and lets her hair fall over her face as though she does not wish to be seen.

Jan Andrade is one of nine children. Her parents also are separated. She has not seen her father "for years and years." Her mother is on welfare. Jan, who turned eighteen in January, has been arrested for possessing dangerous drugs and for assault and battery. I asked Jan to answer the question "Who am I?" in three different ways. "I'm Jan," she said. "I'm me. I'm a bum."

Though not all Chicano youngsters are like Bonnie, Luisa and Jan, the three girls symbolize the alienation many Mexican Americans feel.

Miguel Alvarado also remembers his first day in an American school. He had been born in Mexico. His family came to El Paso, Texas, when Miguel was nine. His mother said, "Learn English. But do not forget your Spanish. Spanish is a beautiful language." In class Miguel uttered a word in Spanish. His teacher stood over him. "You will not speak Spanish," she warned. "Not in class. Not on the playground. Not even when you go home." Then she struck him over the head with a ruler. When Miguel Alvarado got home, he sobbed to his mother, "You did not tell the truth. Spanish is not a beautiful language." His mother slapped him hard for calling her a liar. Says Miguel: "I was trapped between two cultures."

Trapped between two cultures, many Mexican Americans become confused as to who they are. I spoke with fifteen-year-old Virginia Dueñas, of Santa Ana, a girl with hair so shining and thickly black it shames the night. I listened as Virginia kept referring to herself as Mexican and to other people as American.

"But *you're* American," I said.

"I am?" she asked, puzzled. She did not know.

Nor is the problem solved by simply plunging across the nearby Mexican border. Mexican Americans often cross over, to visit family and friends, to realize again the heritage from which they have sprung. But it is no panacea.

Fidel Hernandez, last semester's student body president of Abraham Lincoln High in Los Angeles' Lincoln Heights barrio, says, "In Mexico, I am not considered a true Mexican. Here, I am not considered a true American. I am always seeking my identity."

The Chicano movement speaks to the problem of identity. The message is: "There is much to be proud of in your Mexican heritage. Find it and assert it." For all the broken homes of the barrio, family solidarity still characterizes the Mexican American. The home remains the rock against the hostility of an outside world.

Anthropologist William Madsen tells of sixteen-year-old Lolita, who was sent to a Texas reformatory for prostitution. After her release, her father barred her from the house, forbade his family to speak to her. Yet when Lolita's older brother overheard a friend making a lewd remark about Lolita, he beat up the friend so badly he sent him to the hospital. Family honor had been at stake. Family honor, family solidarity, religious faith, manliness, purity among the women, reverence of nature and of the land, a priority list that places spiritual concerns before material concerns—these are the values of the Mexican American.

Today the Chicano feels that those who want to be helped must help themselves. Mexican American youth is pressing its demands. Chicanos call for an end to punishment for speaking Spanish in Texas classrooms. Students in Redwood (California) High want Mexican food in the school cafeteria. Young people from all over the Southwest support Cesar Chavez and his farm workers' strike against the grape growers of California's central valley. The fiery Reies Lopez Tijerina of New Mexico—El Tigre, his followers call him—went all the way to the Supreme Court, demanding bilingual instruction in the schools of his state. When he lost the case, Robert Finch, then Secretary of the Department of Health, Education and Welfare, sent down a directive to a thousand school boards, establishing as "our first order of business" the need to overcome the English-language deficiencies among Spanish-speaking students.

Hector Aguiniga, eighteen, a freshman at UCLA, is critical of the history textbooks he read in grade school and high school. "All you learn is how the Pilgrims landed on Plymouth Rock and began to settle America. You never read that at that time the Southwest had already been settled."

Under pressure by Chicano spokesmen, the textbooks are now saying this. American students of all colors and backgrounds are learning that the Mexican American is not the immigrant to the Southwest. He was there first. The Spanish heritage of this vast sunbaked land is older than the American republic. Spanish explorers, under Cortés, came to central America in the sixteenth century. Spanish men married Indian women in Mexico and produced the blending of races known as *mestizo*, the ethnic fountainhead of today's Mexican. By 1609 the Spanish had already erected a series of missions along a rutted wagon trail up the California coast. That trail, today a modern highway, is still called by its old name—El Camino Real. The royal road. Long before the mountain men, Spaniards had explored the Rockies. They saw the river that notched a path through the Grand Canyon and because the river was stained with sandstone silt, they named it the Colorado. Colorado means reddish.

When the Anglo first came to the Southwest, the Mexican taught him to survive the rigors of desert life. The Mexicans were the first to cultivate the land we call Texas. But when Americans migrated in numbers and saw the unending land, they wanted it. Thus, the Mexican War, and its inevitable result in 1848, the ceding to the United States of all Mexican territory north of the Rio Grande. All or parts of what we today call Colorado, Utah, Nevada, New Mexico, Texas, Arizona and California became part of the United States, over five hundred thousand square miles of what once was Mexico.

The Mexicans who remained north of the Rio Grande saw much of their land stolen. The rest was lost to taxes. A century of despair set in. Uprooted and impoverished, they became an easy source of cheap labor. A landless people, they fitted neatly into the pattern of migrant farm labor, following the crops. Their children seldom attended school. How could they? Families trekked to one town to pick peaches and a week later moved to another town to chop cotton. They lived in sweltering corrugated metal shacks in squalid workers' camps. A Mexican American in Colorado describes the housing: "They just run out the chickens, and the migratory worker moves in. When he moves out, the chickens move back in."

Over the years a migration to the cities began. Today more than three-fourths of all Mexican Americans in the Southwest live in cities, huddled in segregated barrios. The men work as unskilled or semiskilled laborers.

Out of all this has grown an anger, mixed with the towering dignity that is the mark of the Mexican temperament. Anger gives spirit to the Chicano movement; dignity keeps it from exploding. In a Denver barrio, a college-bound youth tells a group of high schoolers: "By holding on to your heritage, you can still get what you want and keep what you have."

Phil Montez, western regional director of the United States Commission on Civil Rights, and before that a school psychologist (and before that a school dropout), rejects the notion that total assimilation into the American system is the answer. "In this country, we always want to make everyone over in the image of the American monolith—blond and blue-eyed. 'Assimilate and you will succeed.' Well, that is now past. Young people know it won't work. It destroys the personality. I know Mexican American youth. They want an identity as what they are, not what the rest of the country wants them to be."

What are they?

"An advantaged group. The Mexican American can communicate with 270 million people in the western hemisphere who live south of the border. Anglos can't. Since when is this a disadvantage?"

In some young people the anger itself is absent. Marisela Montes, seventeen, is one of eight children whose father was struck down by polio and is now training to be a TV technician. Marisela has just finished high school in one of the Los Angeles barrios, where she also worked at a nearby elementary school every afternoon as a teaching assistant, helping Mexican American youngsters with their English. Marisela has not missed a day of school in her life. "I see no conflict between the Anglo world and the Chicano world," she says softly. Marisela is no militant. "Anglos have been very kind to me." Yet she does not remove herself from her people. "What I want is to become a teacher in the Mexican American community. We don't have enough teachers who speak Spanish."

Javier Sandoval grew up in the same barrio. Now at eighteen he is a freshman at Yale, on a $4500 scholarship. He is the youngest of eleven children; his mother has been dead for six years. His father is an unemployed laborer. Javier likens the problem of Mexican American youth to one in nature.

"If you snuff the light from the plant, the plant will not live. If the Mexican American youth is constantly put down by teachers, if he is told he is just naturally an underachiever, he will be like the plant. His oxygen and light will be snuffed out. Inside, he will die."

No, some are not angry. But they will not permit the oxygen and light to be cut off. Meeting in a barrio in El Paso in October of 1967, a group of Chicano leaders formed an organization committed to the development of pride in the Mexican culture and the improvement of the lot of the people. Impatient youth made its imprint there. A Texas teen-ager said, "If nothing happens at this conference, you'll have to step aside. Or we'll walk over you." What happened was the forming of La Raza Unida—the united race—an independent party. Today the slogan of the Chicano movement is *Viva La Raza!* Not all barrio politicians, however, support La Raza Unida. One of the most influential, Congressman Henry Gonzales of Texas, has attacked it as "reverse racism."

Offshoots from La Raza Unida have sprung up throughout the Southwest. One organization trains Mexican Americans to become lawyers, to fight legal battles. Another group attacks TV advertising that depicts the Mexican American as either a shiftless ne'er-do-well or a bandit. Chicano spokesmen demand greater representation on juries. Chicano educators want to see an end to I.Q. and aptitude tests that are based on fluency in the English language.

Chicano clubs have sprouted in schools and barrios. In Los Angeles in March, 1968, fifteen thousand Chicano students walked out of five east-side high schools to protest the lack of quality education in the barrios. A typical placard read: "Education, not contempt." Similar walkouts—exuberant Chicanos call them "blow-outs"—have happened all through the Southwest. In Crystal City, Texas, a predominantly Mexican American community, high-schoolers began a blow-out in December of 1969 to protest unfair selection of cheerleaders, class representatives and the school homecoming queen. Money was collected to send two students to Washington, where they buttonholed congressmen to gain support for equal treatment.

In Webb City, outside of Laredo, Texas, a full bilingual program was installed after Chicano protest. Half of each class day is conducted in English, half in Spanish. Authorities call it the finest program in bilingual instruction in the nation. Chicanos say yes, it is excellent, but there should be more like it.

In the main, the movement has been nonviolent. But it may not always remain so. Some vocal Chicano activists are beginning to emulate the rhetoric of black militants. A University of California student at Berkeley, Manuel Madrid, twenty-three, says, "I hope we don't have to get as militant as the blacks." The daughter of a Texas farmer says, "How come other people get so much for rioting, and we don't get anything for being cool?"

Petite Martie Hernandez, who remembers how Spanish words did not count as words on her first day in school, is impatient with the progress of the movement. "The Chicanos are still not united. Not the way the Negroes are. They were united, and they were willing to shed their blood."

Not that Martie Hernandez is a violent girl. Impatient, yes. Violent, no. What Martie wants after she finishes her schooling is to be a doctor in the barrio where she lives. "I will have my office in my own house, so when my children come from school, I will be home to greet them. A woman should be there when her children need her."

Let's go back to Miguel Alvarado, whose story I have only half told. He too had a terrible first day in school.

Because his English was not good, Miguel was placed in a class for the mentally retarded. To compensate, he became the school tough guy. Once he knifed a boy; the boy nearly died. The boy's uncle came after Miguel. Miguel knifed the uncle. A sympathetic teacher tried to teach Miguel English. He stole money from her desk. He dropped out of school, joined the Marines and fought in Vietnam.

Today, at twenty-five, Miguel Alvarado is a school administrator in Anaheim, California, where he works with Mexican American youth. "I was lucky. I could have been killed. I could have spent years in prison." He goes into the barrios, finds boys or girls using drugs or committing acts of vandalism. He drags out a Bible and makes them swear on the spot not to break the law, not to drop out of school, to honor the flag and the Constitution. He has organized service clubs in the Anaheim schools for the underachievers. The members turn garbage-laden neighborhood lots into shaded green mini-parks. They paint the shabby houses of elderly residents of the barrio. They hold fund-raising dances to buy raincoats for children who do not own them. An abandoned church building has been turned into a community center; three- and four-year-olds are brought there each morning to learn English. Mothers of the youngsters must volunteer one or two mornings a week at the center. Education becomes a family concern. "Violence is no solution," says Miguel. "The only way to survive is through education." Miguel Alvarado has found himself. Other Chicanos are trying to do the same.

6. Seminole Girl
Merwyn S. Garbarino

"The old ways are changing...."

This is the story of a college-educated Indian woman struggling to retain her identity within the Indian culture. Her personal reflections create a poignant view of the life on an Indian reservation.

One hundred and thirty miles of circuitous road and 250 years of history separate the city of Miami from the four federal reservations that lock the

From *Transaction*, February 1970. Copyright © February, 1970 by Transaction, Inc., New Brunswick, New Jersey. Reprinted by permission.

Seminole Indians into the Florida swamplands known as Big Cypress Swamp. A new road is under construction that will trim in half the traveling distance between the city and the reservations scattered along the present winding U.S. Highway 41 or Tamiami Trail as it is called by the Indians. But the new road will only draw the two communities closer on the speedometer; it will not alter the vastly different lifeways it links; it may only make more apparent the historical inequities that brought the two areas into existence.

The Seminoles are harsh examples of what happened to American Indians caught in the expansion process that saw the United States swell from a federation of 13 colonies to a nation blanketing more than half a continent. The peoples who came to be known as "Seminole," which means "wild" or "undomesticated," were Indians who fled south from the guns and plows of the whites. Some were Yamassee who were driven from the Carolinas in 1715. Others were Hitchiti-speaking Oconee who moved down the Apalachicola River to settle in Spanish-held Florida. These two groups were joined by others escaping soldiers or settlers or other Indians demanding their lands.

The loose confederation of Seminoles was tripled by a large influx of Creeks after the Creek War of 1813–14. Although the Creeks were linguistically related to the Hitchiti, the primary factor uniting the diverse groups was the hatred and fear they felt toward their common foe, the young United States. But this common bond was enough to regroup the broken political units into a single body that absorbed not only Indians, but renegade whites and Negroes escaping slavery.

In 1817–18, the United States sent Andrew Jackson to Florida, ostensibly to recover runaway slaves. This resulted in the First Seminole War, one of the three Seminole Wars that were among the bloodiest ever fought by American forces against Indians. The war also led to the annexation of Florida by the U.S. in 1821 because Spain was in no position to fight for it.

At the time of annexation, the Indians held extensive farm and pasture lands that the Spaniards had not wanted for themselves. American settlers, however, wanted them very much. Insatiable, they forced the Seminoles ever southward, until finally they demanded that the Indians relocate to the area of the Louisiana Purchase which is now Oklahoma. Some Indians went westward, but a number under the leadership of Osceola fought bitterly. When Osceola was captured under a flag of truce, some of his warriors fled into the Everglades where they could not be flushed out. To this day they haven't recognized the treaty that drove their fellow tribesmen to the West.

In 1911, Florida reservation land was set aside by an executive order. The Seminoles, however, were not pressured at that time into moving on to the federal territory. South Florida was a real wilderness; Miami was little more than a town, and lavish coastal resorts were unforeseen. Literally no one but the alligators, snakes, birds and the Indians wanted the land they lived on. The climate is one of wet summers and dry winters, and the area is often struck by hurricanes from the Caribbean. Annual rainfall is in excess of 60 inches and without drainage, the prairie is almost always under water. Brush fires in the dry season destroy valuable hardwood trees on the hummocks which are the low-lying hills undulating through the swampland. Fire also destroys the highly flammable drained peat and for the same reason, there is an absence of pines in many areas suitable for their growth. Elsewhere however, there are moderately to heavily wooded places, and sometimes great flocks of white egrets alight in the branches of the trees, looking like puffs of white blossoms. Except for the hummocks, the horizon is flat, a vista of sky and water, broken only by the occasional wooded clumps.

Most inhabitants of this waste and water live on elevated platforms under thatched roofs held in place by poles. Unemployment is an ever-present problem helped somewhat by seasonal agricultural work or by crafts such as the gaily colored garments, dolls, basketry and carvings made for the tourists who are now visiting their homeland on a year 'round basis. Lands are leased to commercial vegetable farmers and deer can still be hunted. So subsistence living is still possible for the "wild" Seminoles.

Somewhere along the Tamaimi Trail, Nellie Greene—a pseudonym of course —was born a Seminole, raised in a chickee, and learned the ways of her people. Her father was a frog hunter and could neither read nor write; her mother was a good Seminole mother who later had troubles with tuberculosis and drinking. No one Nellie knew had much more education than her father and mother. Yet, despite the ignorance and illiteracy on the reservation, Nellie Greene wanted and was encouraged to get a good education. As it does for most Indians in the United States, this meant leaving her "backward" people, mixing with whites who at best patronized her.

I first met Nellie Greene when she had graduated from college and was living in an apartment in Miami where she worked as a bank clerk. I knew her background from having spent three summers in the middle sixties, thanks to the National Science Foundation, on the Seminole reservations of Florida. In September of 1966 Nellie wrote me that she had been offered a job as manager in the grocery store back on the reservation. If she didn't take it, a white person would, for she was the only native with the necessary knowledge of bookkeeping. She had accepted the job, she said, but since she had once told me (in Miami) that she could never give up the kind of life style she had grown accustomed to there, I was curious to find out why she had returned to the reservation.

She herself said that she took the job to help her people, but she added that it had not been an easy decision; in fact it had been quite a struggle. I could have guessed that this was so; many Indian tribes that offer educational grants to their younger members do so only with the stipulation that the recipients later return to the reservation. The stipulation is a measure of the difficulty in getting their educated members to come back to the tribe. In any event, I wanted to hear Nellie Greene tell her own story. I went to see her, and this is what she told me.

Nellie Greene's Story

I was born in a Miami hospital on February 6, 1943. At that time my parents were living on the (Tamiami) Trail, and my daddy was making his living frog hunting. He owned an air boat and everything that goes along with frog hunting. It was during the war, and at that time I guess it was hard to get gas. When it was time for me to be born, my father had to borrow gas from a farmer to get to Miami. But the tail light was broken, so my father took a flashlight and put a red cloth over it and tied it on to the truck and went to the hospital. My daddy often told me about that.

I had an older sister and an older brother. We lived in a chickee until 1961 when my daddy bought a CBS (a cement block structure, "hurricane proof" according to state standards) at Big Cypress, and we moved into it. When I was little, my daddy had to be out in the Everglades a lot, so he would take all of us out to a hummock, and we would make camp there and stay there while he went off to hunt for frogs. When he got back, he'd take the frog legs into the hotels and sell them. Then he would bring back something for each of us. When he would ask us what we wanted, I always asked for chocolate candy.

About all I remember of the Everglades is that it was a custom when you got up to take a bath or go swimming early in the morning. My mother says they always had to chase me because I didn't like to get wet in winter when it was cold. We were there four or five years, and then we moved near the Agency at Dania (renamed Hollywood in 1966). I had never been to school until then. We were taught at home, the traditional things: to share with each other and with children of other families, to eat after the others—father and grandfather first, then mothers and kids. But lots of times us kids would climb up on our father's knees while they were eating. They didn't say anything, and they'd give us something. It just wasn't the custom for families to eat the way we do today, everybody sitting together around the table.

Folktales, too, we learned; they were like education for us, you know. The stories told about someone doing something bad, and then something bad happened to him. That was the way of teaching right and wrong.

When we were growing up we broke away from some family customs. My parents spanked us, for instance, not my mother's brother, who would have been the right person to punish his sister's children—one of the old ways. But they were not close to my mother's family because my daddy was a frog hunter, and we wandered around with him. My parents were chosen for each other by their families. I guess they learned to love each other in some ways, but I have heard my mother say that it is not the same kind of love she would have had if she had chosen her own husband. It was respect, and that was the custom of the Indians.

Most parents here show so little affection. Even if they love their kids, maybe they don't think they should show love. I know a lot of parents who really care, but they don't tell their kids how they feel. We always knew how our parents felt about us. They showed us affection. Sometimes I hear kids say, "My mother doesn't care whether I go to school or not." These kids have seen how others get care from their parents, like the white children at school. And that kind of concern doesn't show up here. A lot of parents don't even think of telling their children that they want them to succeed. They don't communicate with their children. You never see an Indian mother here kiss and hug children going to school. But white parents do that, and when Indian children see this in town or on TV, it makes them think that Indian parents just don't care. Kids are just left to go to school or not as they wish. Often the mothers have already left to work in the fields before the school bus comes. So no one sees whether children even go to school.

I felt loved. My parents never neglected us. We have never gone without food or clothes or a home. I have always adored my mother. She has made her mistakes, but I still feel the same about her as when I was a child.

We moved to Big Cypress around 1951 or 1952. I had been in first grade at Dania. I remember I didn't understand English at all when I started first grade. I learned it then. We moved around between Big Cypress and Dania, visiting, or because my father was doing odd jobs here and there.

Both my parents wanted me to go to school because they had wanted to go to school when they were kids. I can remember my mother telling me that she and her sister wanted to go to school. But the clan elders—their uncles—wouldn't let them. The uncles said they would whip the two girls if they went.

One of my father's greatest desires was to go to school when he was a boy. He said that he used to sneak papers and pencils into the camp so that he could write the things he saw on the cardboard boxes that the groceries came in, and figures and words on canned goods. He thought he would learn to read and write by copying these things. My daddy adds columns of figures from left to right, and he subtracts the same way. His answers will be correct, but I don't know how. Almost everything he knows he learned on his own. He can understand English, but he stutters when he talks. He has a difficult time finding the right word when he speaks English, but he understands it.

When my parents said no, they meant no. That was important to me. They could be counted on. The other thing that was important in my childhood schooling was that my daddy always looked at my report card when I brought it home from school. He didn't really know what it meant, and he couldn't read, but he always looked at my report card and made me feel that he cared how I did in school. Other parents didn't do this. In fact, most of the kids never showed their parents their report cards. But my daddy made me feel that it was important to him. I told him what the marks stood for. It was rewarding for me because he took the time.

"Nothing for Me to Do"

Public school was hard compared to what I'd had before, day school on the reservation and a year at Sequoyah Government School. I almost flunked eighth grade at the public school, and it was a miracle that I passed. I just didn't know a lot of things, mathematics and stuff. I survived it somehow. I don't know how, but I did. The man who was head of the department of education at the Agency was the only person outside of my family who helped me and encouraged me to get an education. He understood and really helped me with many things I didn't know about. For a long time the white public school for the Big Cypress area would not let Indian children attend. A boy and I were the first Big Cypress Indians to graduate from that school. He is now in the armed forces.

After I graduated from high school I went to business college, because in high school I didn't take courses that would prepare me for the university. I realized that there was nothing for me to do. I had no training. All I could do was go back to the reservation. I thought maybe I'd go to Haskell Institute, but my mother was in a TB hospital, and I didn't want to go too far away. I did want to go on to school and find some job and work. So the director of education said maybe he could work something out for me so I could go to school down here. I thought bookkeeping would be good because I had had that in high school and loved it. So I enrolled in the business college, but my English was so bad that I had an awful time. I had to take three extra months of English courses. But that helped me. I never did understand why my English was so bad— whether it was my fault or the English I had in high school. I thought I got by in high school; they never told me that my English was so inferior, but it was not good enough for college. It was *terrible* having to attend special classes.

"I Learned How to Dress"

At college the hardest thing was not loneliness but schoolwork itself. I had a roommate from Brighton (one of the three reservations), so I had some- one to talk to. The landlady was awfully suspicious at first. We were Indians, you know. She would go through our apartment, and if we hadn't done the dishes, she washed them. We didn't like that. But then she learned to trust us.

College was so fast for me. Everyone knew so much more. It was as though I had never been to school before. As soon as I got home, I started studying. I read assignments both before and after the lectures. I read them before so I could understand what the professor was saying, and I read them again after- wards because he talked so fast. I was never sure I understood.

In college they dressed differently from high school, and I didn't know anything about that. I learned how to dress. For the first six weeks, though, I never went anywhere. I stayed home and studied. It was hard—real hard. (I can imagine what a real university would be like.) And it was so different. If you didn't turn in your work, that was just your tough luck. No one kept at me the way they did in high school. They didn't say, "OK, I'll give you another week."

Gradually I started making friends. I guess some of them thought I was different. One boy asked me what part of India I was from. He didn't even know there were Indians in Florida. I said, "I'm an American." Things like that are kind of hard. I couldn't see my family often, but in a way that was helpful because I had to learn to adjust to my new environment. Nobody could help me but myself.

Well, I graduated and went down to the bank. The president of the bank had called the agency and said he would like to employ a qualified Indian girl. So I went down there and they gave me a test, and I was interviewed. And then they told me to come in the following Monday. That's how I went to work. I finished college May 29, and I went to work June 1. I worked there for three years.

In the fall of 1966, my father and the president of the Tribal Board asked me to come back to Big Cypress to manage a new economic enterprise there. It seemed like a dream come true, because I could not go back to live at Big Cypress without a job there. But it was not an easy decision. I liked my bank work. You might say I had fallen in love with banking. But all my life I had wanted to do something to help my people, and I could do that only by leav- ing my bank job in Miami. Being the person I am, I had to go back. I would have felt guilty if I had a chance to help and I didn't. But I told my daddy that I couldn't give him an answer right away, and I knew he was upset because he had expected me to jump at the chance to come back. He did understand though, that I had to think about it. He knew when I went to live off the reservation that I had had a pretty hard time, getting used to a job, getting used to people. He knew I had accomplished a lot, and it wasn't easy for me to give it up. But that's how I felt. I had to think. At one time it seemed to me that I could never go back to reservation life.

But then really, through it all, I always wished there was something, even the smallest thing, that I could do for my people. Maybe I'm helping now. But I can see that I may get tired of it in a year, or even less. But right now I'm glad to help build up the store. If it didn't work out, if the store failed, and I thought I hadn't even tried, I would really feel bad. The basic thing about my feeling is that my brothers and sisters and nieces and nephews can build later on in the future only through the foundation their parents and I build. Maybe Indian parents don't always show their affection, but they have taught us that, even though we have a problem, we are still supposed to help one another. And that is what I am trying to do. Even when we were kids, if we had something and other kids didn't, we must share what we had with the others. Kids grow up the way their parents train them.

By the age of nine, girls were expected to take complete care of younger children. I too had to take care of my little brother and sister. I grew up fast. That's just what parents expected. Now teen-agers don't want to do that, so they get angry and take off. Headstart and nurseries help the working mothers because older children don't tend the little ones any more. The old ways are changing, and I hope to help some of the people, particularly girls about my age, change to something good.

There are people on the reservation who don't seem to like me. Maybe they are jealous, but I don't know why. I know they resent me somehow. When I used to come in from school or from work back to the reservation, I could tell some people felt like this. I don't think that I have ever, ever, even in the smallest way, tried to prove myself better or more knowing than other people. I have two close friends here, so I don't feel too lonely; but other people my age do not make friends with me. I miss my sister, and I miss my roommate from Miami. My two friends here are good friends. I can tell them anything I want. I can talk to them. That's important, that I can talk to them. That's what I look for in a friend, not their education, but for enjoyment of the same things, and understanding. But there are only two of them. I have not been able to find other friends.

The old people think I know everything because I've been to school. They think it is a good thing for us to go to school. But the old people don't have the kind of experience which allows them to understand our problems. They think that it is easy somehow to come back here. They think there is nothing else. They do not understand that there are things I miss on the outside. They do not understand enough to be friends. They are kind, and they are glad that I am educated, but they do not understand my problems. They do not understand loneliness.

It was hard for me to get used again to the way people talk. They have nothing interesting to talk about. They are satisfied to have a TV or radio, but they don't know anything about good books or good movies or the news. There is almost no one I have to talk to about things like that. Here people don't know what discussion is. That's something I found really hard. They gossip: they talk about people, not ideas.

And it was hard getting used to what people think about time. You know, when you live in the city and work, everything is according to time. You race yourself to death, really. But I got used to that and put myself on a schedule. But here, when you want something done, people take their time. They don't come to work when they should, and I just don't want to push them. I would expect it of the older people, but the younger generation should realize how important time is. When you go to school, you just eat and study and go to school, and not worry too much about time; but on a job, you must keep pace. You are being paid for a certain performance. If you do not do what you are supposed to, you do not get paid. But how do I get that across to my people?

"I Don't Know Why . . ."

I was lonely when I first came back here. I was ready to pack up and go back to Miami. People hardly talked to me—just a few words. I don't know why. I've known these people all my life. I don't know why they didn't know me after just three years. I couldn't carry on a conversation with anyone except my own family. I was working all day at the store, and then I had nothing to do but clean the house, or go fishing alone, or with someone from my family.

Coming back to the reservation to live did not seem to be physically hard. At first I lived in a house with a girl friend because I did not want to stay with my family. I wanted to be sure of my independence. I think this hurt my father. But later, when more of my friend's family moved back to the reservation, I decided it was too crowded with her and went back to live in my old home with my father and family. My father's CBS is clean and comfortable. It is as nice as an apartment in Miami.

My idea was that, being raised on the reservation and knowing the problems here, I could hope that the Indian girls would come to me and ask about what they could do after they finished high school: what they could do on the reservation, what jobs they could get off the reservation. I hoped they would discuss their problems with me, what their goals should be. I'd be more than happy to talk with them. But I can't go to them and tell them what to do. Just because I've worked outside for three years doesn't give me the right to plan for other people. But I thought I had something to offer the girls here, if only they would come for advice.

"They Say I'm Mean . . ."

I would like to see the financial records at the store so well kept that an accountant could come in at any time and check the books, and they would be in perfect order. It is difficult because only Louise and I can run the store, and if either of us gets sick, the other one has to be at the store from 7 A.M. to 9 P.M., or else close the store. At first I had to be very patient with Louise and explain everything to her. She had no training at all. Sometimes I started to get mad when I explained and explained, but then I'd remember that she can't help it. People do not know some of the things I know, and I must not get irritated. But if things go wrong, I am responsible, and it is a big responsibility. The younger people are not exactly lazy; they just don't know how to work. I want them to work and be on time. If they need time off, they should tell me, not just go away or not appear on some days.

So some of them start calling me bossy. But that is my responsibility. I tried to talk to them and tell them why I wanted them to come to work on time, but still they didn't. I want them to realize that they have to work to earn their money. It is not a gift. They were supposed to do something in return for their wages. They are interested in boys at their age, and that's why they aren't good workers. But still, the National Youth Corps, operating in Big Cypress, gives kids some idea of how it is to work, to have a job. If I don't make them do the job, they're really not earning their money. That is one thing I had to face. I know that they are going to say I'm mean and bossy. I expect that. But if I'm in charge, they're going to do what they're supposed to do. That's the way I look at it. Everybody talks here. I know that, but I've been away, and I can take it.

I think people my own age are jealous. It is not shyness. Before I left, they were all friendly to me. I came back, and they all look at me, but when I go to talk to them, they just turn around, and it is so hard for me. They answer me, but they don't answer like they used to, and talk to me. That has been my main problem. It is hard for someone to come back, but if he is strong enough, you know, he can go ahead and take that. Maybe some day people will understand. There is no reason to come back if you really think you are better than the people. They are wrong if that is what they believe about me. There is not enough money here, and if I didn't really care about the people, then I would have no reason to return.

I am worried about my mother, and I want to stay where I can help her (my parents are now divorced). It is best to come back and act like the other people, dress like they dress, try to be a part of them again. So even if a person didn't have kinfolk here, if he wanted to help, he could. But he must not show off or try to appear better.

If I didn't have a family here, it would be almost like going to live with strangers. I have to work now. It has become a part of my life. People here just don't understand that. I can't just sit around or visit and do nothing. If there were no work here, I could not live here. It would be so hard for me to live the way the women here do, sewing all the time or working in the fields, but if I had to take care of my family and there was nothing else to do, I guess I would stay here for that. My aunt has taught me to do the traditional sewing, and how to make the dolls, so I could earn money doing that; but I wouldn't do it unless I had to stay here to take care of my family.

I think the reason almost all the educated Indians are girls is because a woman's life here on the reservation is harder than the man's. The women have to take all the responsibility for everything. To go to school and get a job is really easier for a woman than staying on the reservation. The men on the reservation can just lay around all day and go hunting. They can work for a little while on the plantations if they need a little money. But the women have to worry about the children. If the women go away and get jobs, then the men have to take responsibility.

A woman and a man should have about the same amount of education when they marry. That means there is no one at Big Cypress I can marry. The boys my age here do not have anything in common with me. If a girl marries an outsider, she has to move away, because the Tribal Council has voted that no white man can live on the reservation. A woman probably would miss the closeness of her family on the reservation. I would want to come back and visit, but

I think I could marry out and make it successful. I would expect to meet and know his family. I would like to live near our families, if possible. I will always feel close to my family.

"I Think about the City . . ."

Sometimes I think about the city and all the things to do there. Then I remember my mother and how she is weak and needs someone who will watch over her and help her. You know my mother drinks a lot. She is sick, and the doctors want her to stop; but she herself cannot control her drinking. Well, I guess us kids have shut our eyes, hoping things will get better by themselves. I know you have not heard this before, and I wish I was not the one to tell you this sad story, but my move back to the reservation was partly brought on because of this. She has been to a sanitarium where they help people like her. It has helped her already to know that I want to see her get help and be a better person. I am having a chickee built for her, and I must stay here until she is well enough to manage alone.

Economic opportunity has been severely limited on the reservation until recently. Employment for field hands or driving farm machinery has been available on ranches in the area, but the income is seasonal. Both men and women work at crafts. The products are sold either privately or through the Arts and Crafts Store at the tribal agency on the coast but the income is inadequate by itself. Some of the men and one or two Indian women own cattle, but none of these sources of income would appeal to a person with higher education. Until the opening of the grocery store, there was no job on the reservation which really required literacy, let alone a diploma.

Examining these possibilities and the words of Nellie Greene, what would entice an educated Indian to come back to work and live on the reservation? A good paying job; a high status as an educated or skilled person; to be back in a familiar, friendly community; a desire to be with his family and to help them. Perhaps for the rare individual, an earnest wish to try to help his own people. But income from a job on the reservation must allow a standard of living not too much lower than that previously enjoyed as a member of outer society. Nellie never gave any consideration to returning to the reservation until there was the possibility of a job that challenged her skills and promised a comparable income. The salary she receives from managing the store is close to what she had made at the bank in Miami. In Miami, however, she worked 40 hours a week, while on the reservation she works nearly 60 hours a week for approximately the same pay, because there are no trained personnel to share the responsibility. Given the isolation of Big Cypress, there is not enough time, after she has put in her hours at the store, to go anywhere off the reservation. It is not merely a question of total pay; it is a problem of access to a way of life unattainable on the reservation. Economic opportunity alone is not sufficient.

It is quite apparent from Nellie's interviews and from observation of the interaction between Nellie and other Indians, both in the store and elsewhere on the reservation, that her status is very low. Her position appears to vary: from some slight recognition that her training places her in a category by herself, to distinct jealousy, to apparent puzzlement on the part of some of the old folks as to just what her place in the society is. Through the whole gamut of reaction to Nellie, only her proud family considers her status a high one.

The primary reason Nellie gave for returning to the reservation was to help her people, but the reservation inhabitants did not indicate that they viewed her activities or presence as beneficial to them. Older Indians, both male and female, stated that it was "right" that she returned because Indians should stay together, not because she might help her people or set an example to inspire young Indians who might otherwise be tempted to drop out of school. Younger people regard her as bossy and trying to act "white." She does not even have the status of a marriageable female. There is no Indian man on the reservation with the sort of background that would make him a desirable marriage partner, from her standpoint; in their traditional view of an ideal wife, she does not display the qualities preferred by the men. At the same time, there is a council ordinance which prohibits white men from living on the reservation, and therefore marriage to a white man would mean that she would have to leave the reservation to live. There is no recognized status of "career woman," educated Indian, or marriageable girl, or any traditional status for her.

Obviously, with an inferior status, it is unlikely that a person would perceive the community as a friendly, familiar environment. From the point of view of the reservation people, who have had contacts with her, she is no longer truly "Indian," but rather someone who has taken over so much of the Anglo-American ways as to have lost her identity as an Indian woman. Nearly all of Nellie's close acquaintances are living off the reservation. The only two girls she considers friends on the reservation are, like herself, young women with more than average contact with outside society, although with less formal education.

Nellie may have rationalized her decision to return by stressing her determination to help the people, but her personal concern for her mother probably influenced her decision to return more than she herself realized. Nellie was the only person in the family who had the ability, knowledge and willingness to see that her mother received the proper supervision and help.

The Bureau of Indian Affairs is attempting to increase the economic opportunities on the reservations, but I believe their efforts at holding back the "brain drain" of educated Indians will not be effective. Retraining the reservation people who do not have an education is certainly desirable. But, as the story of Nellie Greene points out, it takes more than good pay and rewarding work to keep the educated Indians down on the reservations. If the educated Indian expects to find status with his people, he is going to be disappointed. White people outside are apt to pay more attention to an educated Seminole than his own Indian society will. If the Indian returns from college and expects to find warm personal relationships with persons of his own or opposite sex, he is going to find little empathy, some distrust and jealousy because of his training and experiences outside the reservation. For Nellie Greene there was a personal goal, helping her sick mother. She was lucky to find a job that required her skills as an educated person, and which paid her as well as the bank at Miami. Her other goal, to help her own people, was thwarted rather than helped by her college education.

7. **Race and Intelligence**
Richard C. Lewontin

"... there's no evidence one way or the other about the genetics of inter-racial I.Q. differences."

A scholarly article by the well-known psychologist Arthur R. Jensen has raised a storm of controversy over his contention that higher I.Q. scores reflect the intellectual superiority of one racial group over another. Richard C. Lewontin, an equally eminent geneticist, challenges Jensen's conclusions in this provocative article.

In the Spring of 1653 Pope Innocent X condemned a pernicious heresy which espoused the doctrines of "total depravity, irresistible grace, lack of free will, predestination and limited atonement." That heresy was Jansenism and its author was Cornelius Jansen, Bishop of Ypres.

In the winter of 1968 the same doctrine appeared in the *Harvard Educational Review*. That doctrine is now called "jensenism" by the *New York Times Magazine* and its author is Arthur R. Jensen, professor of educational psychology at the University of California at Berkeley. It is a doctrine as erroneous in the twentieth century as it was in the seventeenth. I shall try to play the Innocent.

Jensen's article, "How Much Can We Boost I.Q. and Scholastic Achievement?" created such a furor that the *Review* reprinted it along with critiques by psychologists, theorists of education and a population geneticist under the title "Environment, Heredity and Intelligence." The article first came to my attention when, at no little expense, it was sent to every member of the National Academy of Sciences by the eminent white Anglo-Saxon inventor, William Shockley, as part of his continuing campaign to have the Academy study the effects of inter-racial mating. It is little wonder that the *New York Times* found the matter newsworthy, and that Professor Jensen has surely become the most discussed and least read essayist since Karl Marx. I shall try, in this article, to display Professor Jensen's argument, to show how the structure of his argument is designed to make his point and to reveal what appear to be deeply embedded assumptions derived from a particular world view, leading him to erroneous conclusions. I shall say little or nothing about the critiques of Jensen's article, which would require even more space to criticize than the original article itself.

From *Bulletin of the Atomic Scientists*, March 1970. Reprinted by permission of Science and Public Affairs, The Bulletin of Atomic Scientists. Copyright © 1970 by the Educational Foundation for Nuclear Science.

The Position

Jensen's argument consists essentially of an elaboration on two incontrovertible facts, a causative explanation and a programmatic conclusion. The two
facts are that black people perform, on the average, more poorly than whites
on standard I.Q. tests, and that special programs of compensatory education
so far tried have not had much success in removing this difference. His causative
explanation for these facts is that I.Q. is highly heritable, with most of the variation among individuals arising from genetic rather than environmental sources.
His programmatic conclusion is that there is no use in trying to remove the
difference in I.Q. by education since it arises chiefly from genetic causes and
the best thing that can be done for black children is to capitalize on those skills
for which they are biologically adapted. Such a conclusion is so clearly at
variance with the present egalitarian consensus and so clearly smacks of a racist
elitism, whatever its merit or motivation, that a very careful analysis of the
argument is in order.

The article begins with the pronouncement: "Compensatory education has
been tried and it apparently has failed." A documentation of that failure and a
definition of compensatory education are left to the end of the article for good
logical and pedagogical reasons. Having caught our attention by whacking us
over the head with a two-by-four, like that famous trainer of mules, Jensen
then asks:

> What has gone wrong? In other fields, when bridges do not stand, when
> aircraft do not fly, when machines do not work, when treatments do not
> cure, despite all the conscientious efforts on the part of many persons to
> make them do so, one begins to question the basic assumptions, principles,
> theories, and hypotheses that guide one's efforts. Is it time to follow suit
> in education?

Who can help but answer that last rhetorical question with a resounding
"Yes"? What thoughtful and intelligent person can avoid being struck by the
intellectual and empirical bankruptcy of educational psychology as it is practiced in our mass educational systems? The innocent reader will immediately
fall into close sympathy with Professor Jensen, who, it seems, is about to dissect
educational psychology and show it up as a pre-scientific jumble without theo-
retic coherence or prescriptive competence. But the innocent reader will be
wrong. For the rest of Jensen's article puts the blame for the failure of his
science not on the scientists but on the children. According to him, it is not
that his science and its practitioners have failed utterly to understand human
motivation, behavior and development but simply that the damn kids are
ineducable.

The unconscious irony of his metaphor of bridges, airplanes and machines
has apparently been lost on him. The fact is that in the twentieth century bridges
do stand, machines do work and airplanes do fly, because they are built on
clearly understood mechanical and hydrodynamic principles which even moderately careful and intelligent engineers can put into practice. In the seventeenth century that was not the case, and the general opinion was that men
would never succeed in their attempts to fly because flying was impossible.
Jensen proposes that we take the same view of education and that, in the terms
of his metaphor, fallen bridges be taken as evidence of the unbridgeability of

rivers. The alternative explanation, that educational psychology is still in the seventeenth century, is apparently not part of his philosophy.

This view of technological failure as arising from ontological rather than epistemological sources is a common form of apology at many levels of practice. Anyone who has dealt with plumbers will appreciate how many things "can't be fixed" or "weren't meant to be used like that." Physicists tell me that their failure to formulate an elegant general theory of fundamental particles is a result of there not being any underlying regularity to be discerned. How often men, in their overweening pride, blame nature for their own failures. This professionalist bias, that if a problem were soluble it would have been solved, lies at the basis of Jensen's thesis which can only be appreciated when seen in this light.

Having begun with the assumption that I.Q. cannot be equalized, Jensen now goes on to why not. He begins his investigation with a discussion of the "nature of intelligence," by which he means the way in which intelligence is defined by testing and the correlation of intelligence test scores with scholastic and occupational performance. A very strong point is made that I.Q. testing was developed in a Western industrialized society specifically as a prognostication of success in that society by the generally accepted criteria. He makes a special point of noting that psychologists' notions of status and success have a high correlation with those of the society at large, so that it is entirely reasonable that tests created by psychologists will correlate highly with conventional measures of success. One might think that this argument, that I.Q. testing is "culture bound," would militate against Jensen's general thesis of the biological and specifically genetical basis of I.Q. differences. Indeed, it is an argument often used against I.Q. testing for so-called "deprived" children, since it is supposed that they have developed in a subculture that does not prepare them for such tests. What role does this "environmentalist" argument play in Jensen's thesis? Is it simply evidence of his total fairness and objectivity? No. Jensen has seen, more clearly than most, that the argument of the specific cultural origins of I.Q. testing and especially the high correlation of these tests with occupational status cuts both ways. For if the poorer performance of blacks on I.Q. tests has largely genetic rather than environmental causes, then it follows that blacks are also genetically handicapped for other high status components of Western culture. That is, what Jensen is arguing is that differences between cultures are in large part genetically determined and that I.Q. testing is simply one manifestation of those differences.

In this light we can also understand his argument concerning the existence of "general intelligence" as measured by I.Q. tests. Jensen is at some pains to convince his readers that there is a single factor, g, which, in factor analysis of various intelligence tests, accounts for a large fraction of the variance of scores. The existence of such a factor, while not critical to the argument, obviously simplifies it, for then I.Q. tests would really be testing for "something" rather than just being correlated with scholastic and occupational performance. While Jensen denies that intelligence should be reified, he comes perilously close to doing so in his discussion of g.

Without going into factor analysis at any length, I will point out only that factor analysis does not give a unique result for any given set of data. Rather, it gives an infinity of possible results among which the investigator chooses according to his tastes and preconceptions of the models he is fitting. One strategy in factor analysis is to pack as much weight as possible into one factor, while another is to distribute the weights over as many factors as possible as equally as possible. Whether one chooses one of these or some other depends upon one's model, the numerical analysis only providing the weights appropriate for each model. Thus, the impression left by Jensen that factor analysis somehow naturally or ineluctably isolates one factor with high weight is wrong.

"True Merit?"

In the welter of psychological metaphysics involving concepts of "crystallized" as against "fluid" intelligence, "generalized" intelligence, "intelligence" as opposed to "mental ability," there is some danger of losing sight of Jensen's main point: I.Q. tests are culture bound and there is good reason that they should be, because they are predictors of culture bound activities and values. What is further implied, of course, is that those who do not perform well on these tests are less well suited for high status and must paint barns rather than pictures. We read that "We have to face it: the assortment of persons into occupational roles simply is not 'fair' in any absolute sense. The best we can hope for is that true merit, given equality of opportunity, act as a basis for the natural assorting process." What a world view is there revealed! The most rewarding places in society shall go to those with "true merit" and that is the best we can hope for. Of course, Professor Jensen is safe since, despite the abject failure of educational psychology to solve the problems it has set itself, that failure does not arise from lack of "true merit" on the part of psychologists but from the natural intransigence of their human subjects.

Having established that there are differences among men in the degree to which they are adapted to higher status and high satisfaction roles in Western society, and having stated that education has not succeeded in removing these differences, Jensen now moves on to their cause. He raises the question of "fixed" intelligence and quite rightly dismisses it as misleading. He introduces us here to what he regards as the two real issues. "The first issue concerns the genetic basis of individual differences in intelligence; the second concerns the stability of constancy of the I.Q. through the individual's lifetime." Jensen devotes some three-quarters of his essay to an attempt to demonstrate that I.Q. is developmentally rather stable, being to all intents and purposes fixed after the age of eight, and that most of the variation in I.Q. among individuals in the population has a genetic rather than environmental basis. Before looking in detail at some of these arguments, we must again ask where he is headed. While Jensen argues strongly that I.Q. is "culture bound," he wishes to argue that it is not environmentally determined. This is a vital distinction. I.Q. is "culture bound" in the sense that it is related to performance in a Western industrial society. But the determination of the ability to perform culturally defined tasks might itself be entirely genetic. For example, a person suffering from a genetically caused deaf-mutism is handicapped to different extents in cultures requiring different degrees of verbal performance, yet his disorder did not have an environmental origin.

Jensen first dispenses with the question of developmental stability of I.Q. Citing Benjamin Bloom's survey of the literature, he concludes that the correlation between test scores of an individual at different ages is close to unity after the age of eight. The inference to be drawn from this fact is, I suppose, that it is not worth trying to change I.Q. by training after that age. But such an inference cannot be made. All that can be said is that, given the usual progression of educational experience to which most children are exposed, there is sufficient consistency not to cause any remarkable changes in I.Q. That is, a child whose educational experience (in the broad sense) may have ruined his capacity to perform by the age of eight is not likely to experience an environment in his later years that will do much to alter those capacities. Indeed, given the present state of educational theory and practice, there is likely to be a considerable reinforcement of early performance. To say that children do not change their I.Q. is not the same as saying they cannot. Moreover, Jensen is curiously silent on the lower correlation and apparent plasticity of I.Q. at younger ages, which is after all the chief point of Bloom's work.

The Genetic Argument

The heart of Jensen's paper is contained in his long discussion of the distribution and inheritance of intelligence. Clearly he feels that here his main point is to be established. The failure of compensatory education, the developmental stability of I.Q., the obvious difference between the performance of blacks and whites can be best understood, he believes, when the full impact of the findings of genetics is felt. In his view, insufficient attention has been given by social scientists to the findings of geneticists, and I must agree with him. Although there are exceptions, there has been a strong professional bias toward the assumption that human behavior is infinitely plastic, a bias natural enough in men whose professional commitment is to changing behavior. It is as a reaction to this tradition, and as a natural outcome of his confrontation with the failure of educational psychology, that Jensen's own opposite bias flows, as I have already claimed.

The first step in his genetical argument is the demonstration that I.Q. scores are normally distributed or nearly so. I am unable to find in his paper any explicit statement of why he regards this point as so important. From repeated references to Sir Francis Galton, filial regression, mutant genes, a few major genes for exceptional ability and assortative mating, it gradually emerges that an underlying normality of the distribution appears to Jensen as an important consequence of genetic control of I.Q. He asks: ". . . is intelligence itself—not just our measurements of it—really normally distributed?" Apparently he believes that if intelligence, quite aside from measurement, were really normally distributed, this would demonstrate its biological and genetical status. Aside from a serious epistemological error involved in the question, the basis for his concern is itself erroneous. There is nothing in genetic theory that requires or even suggests that a phenotypic character should be normally distributed, even when it is completely determined genetically. Depending upon the degree of dominance of genes, interaction between them, frequencies of alternative alleles at the various gene loci in the population and allometric growth relations between various parts of the organism transforming primary gene effects, a character may have almost any uni-modal distribution and under some circumstances even a multi-modal one.

After establishing the near-normality of the curve of I.Q. scores, Jensen goes directly to a discussion of the genetics of continuously varying characters. He begins by quoting with approbation E. L. Thorndike's maxim: "In the actual race of life, which is not to get ahead, but to get ahead of somebody, the chief determining factor is heredity." This quotation along with many others used by Jensen shows a style of argument that is not congenial to natural scientists, however it may be a part of other disciplines. There is a great deal of appeal to authority and the acceptance of the empirically unsubstantiated opinions of eminent authorities as a kind of relevant evidence. We hear of "three eminent geneticists," or "the most distinguished exponent [of genetical methods], Sir Cyril Burt." The irrelevance of this kind of argument is illustrated precisely by the appeal to E. L. Thorndike, who, despite his eminence in the history of psychology, made the statement quoted by Jensen in 1905, when nothing was known about genetics outside of attempts to confirm Mendel's paper. Whatever the eventual truth of his statement turns out to be, Thorndike made it out of his utter ignorance of the genetics of human behavior, and it can only be ascribed to the sheer prejudice of a Methodist Yankee.

Heritability

To understand the main genetical argument of Jensen, we must dwell, as he does, on the concept of heritability. We cannot speak of a trait being molded by heredity, as opposed to environment. Every character of an organism is the result of a unique interaction between the inherited genetic information and the sequence of environments through which the organism has passed during its development. For some traits the variations in environment have little effect, so that once the genotype is known, the eventual form of the organism is pretty well specified. For other traits, specification of the genetic makeup may be a very poor predictor of the eventual phenotype because even the smallest environmental effects may affect the trait greatly. But for all traits there is a many-many relationship between gene and character and between environment and character. Only by a specification of both the genotype and the environmental sequence can the character be predicted. Nevertheless, traits do vary in the degree of their genetic determination and this degree can be expressed, among other ways, by their heritabilities.

The distribution of character values, say I.Q. scores, in a population arises from a mixture of a large number of genotypes. Each genotype in the population does not have a unique phenotype corresponding to it because the different individuals of that genotype have undergone somewhat different environmental sequences in their development. Thus, each genotype has a distribution of I.Q. scores associated with it. Some genotypes are more common in the population so their distributions contribute heavily to determining the overall distribution, while others are rare and make little contribution. The total variation in the population, as measured by the variance, results from the variation between the mean I.Q. scores of the different genotypes and the variation around each genotypic mean. The heritability of a measurement is defined as the ratio of the variance due to the differences between the genotypes to the total variance in the population. If this heritability were 1.0, it would mean that all the variation in the population resulted from differences between genotypes but that there was no environmentally caused variation around each genotype mean. On the other hand, a heritability of 0.0 would mean that there was no genetic variation because all individuals were effectively identical in their genes, and that all the variation in the population arose from environmental differences in the development of the different individuals.

Defined in this way, heritability is not a concept that can be applied to a trait in general, but only to a trait in a particular population, in a particular set of environments. Thus, different populations may have more or less genetic variation for the same character. Moreover, a character may be relatively insensitive to environment in a particular environmental range, but be extremely sensitive outside this range. Many such characters are known, and it is the commonest kind of relation between character and environment. Finally, some genotypes are more sensitive to environmental fluctuation than others so that two populations with the same genetic variance but different genotypes, and living in the same environments, may still have different heritabilities for a trait.

The estimation of heritability of a trait in a population depends on measuring individuals of known degrees of relationship to each other and comparing the observed correlation in the trait between relatives with the theoretical correlation from genetic theory. There are two difficulties that arise in such a procedure. First, the exact theoretical correlation between relatives, except for identical twins, cannot be specified unless there is detailed knowledge of the mode of inheritance of the character. A first order approximation is possible, however, based upon some simplifying assumptions, and it is unusual for this approximation to be badly off.

A much more serious difficulty arises because relatives are correlated not only in their heredities but also in their environments. Two sibs are much more alike in the sequence of environments in which they developed than are two cousins or two unrelated persons. As a result, there will be an overestimate of the heritability of a character, arising from the added correlation between relatives from environmental similarities. There is no easy way to get around this bias in general so that great weight must be put on peculiar situations in which the ordinary environmental correlations are disturbed. That is why so much emphasis is placed, in human genetics, on the handful of cases of identical twins raised apart from birth, and the much more numerous cases of totally unrelated children raised in the same family. Neither of these cases is completely reliable, however, since twins separated from birth are nevertheless likely to be raised in families belonging to the same socio-economic, racial, religious and ethnic categories, while unrelated children raised in the same family may easily be treated rather more differently than biological sibs. Despite these difficulties, the weight of evidence from a variety of correlations between relatives puts the heritability of I.Q. in various human populations between .6 and .8. For reasons of his argument, Jensen prefers the higher value but it is not worth quibbling over. Volumes could be written on the evaluation of heritability estimates for I.Q. and one can find a number of faults with Jensen's treatment of the published data. However, it is irrelevant to questions of race and intelligence, and to questions of the failure of compensatory education, whether the heritability of I.Q. is .4 or .8, so I shall accept Jensen's rather high estimate without serious argument.

The description I have given of heritability, its application to a specific population in a specific set of environments and the difficulties in its accurate estimation are all discussed by Jensen. While the emphasis he gives to various points differs from mine, and his estimate of heritability is on the high side, he appears to have said in one way or another just about everything that a judicious man can say. The very judiciousness of his argument has been disarming to geneticists especially, and they have failed to note the extraordinary conclusions that are drawn from these reasonable premises. Indeed, the logical and empirical hiatus between the conclusions and the premises is especially striking and thought-provoking in view of Jensen's apparent understanding of the technical issues.

The first conclusion concerns the cause of the difference between the I.Q. distributions of black and whites. On the average, over a number of studies, blacks have a distribution of I.Q. scores whose mean is about 15 points—about 1 standard deviation—below whites. Taking into account the lower variance of scores among blacks than among whites, this difference means that about 11 percent of blacks have I.Q. scores above the mean white score (as compared with 50 percent of whites) while 18 percent of whites score below the mean black score (again, as compared to 50 percent of blacks). If, according to Jensen, "gross socio-economic factors" are equalized between the tested groups, the difference in means is reduced to 11 points. It is hard to know what to say about overlap between the groups after this correction, since the standard deviations of such equalized populations will be lower. From these and related observations, and the estimate of .8 for the heritability of I.Q. (in white populations, no reliable estimate existing for blacks), Jensen concludes that:

> . . . all we are left with are various lines of evidence, no one of which is definitive alone, but which, viewed altogether, make it a not unreasonable hypothesis that genetic factors are strongly implicated in the average Negro-white intelligence difference. The preponderance of evidence is, in my opinion, less consistent with a strictly environmental hypothesis than with a genetic hypothesis, which, of course, does not exclude the influence of environment on its interaction with genetic factors.

Anyone not familiar with the standard litany of academic disclaimers ("not unreasonable hypothesis," "does not exclude," "in my opinion") will, taking this statement at face value, find nothing to disagree with since it says nothing. To contrast a "strictly environmental hypothesis" with "a genetic hypothesis which . . . does not exclude the influence of the environment" is to be guilty of the utmost triviality. If that is the only conclusion he means to come to, Jensen has just wasted a great deal of space in the *Harvard Educational Review*. But of course, like all cant, the special language of the social scientist needs to be translated into common English. What Jensen is saying is: "It is pretty clear, although not absolutely proved, that most of the difference in I.Q. between blacks and whites is genetical." This, at least, is not a trivial conclusion. Indeed, it may even be true. However, the evidence offered by Jensen is irrelevant.

Is It Likely?
How can that be? We have admitted the high heritability of I.Q. and the reality of the difference between the black and the white distributions. Moreover, we have seen that adjustment for gross socio-economic level still leaves a large difference. Is it not then likely that the difference is genetic? No. It is neither likely nor unlikely. There is no evidence. The fundamental error of Jensen's argument is to confuse heritability of a character within a population with heritability of the difference between two populations. Indeed, between two populations, the concept of heritability of their difference is meaningless.

This is because a variance based upon two measurements has only one degree of freedom and so cannot be partitioned into genetic and environmental components. The genetic basis of the difference between two populations bears no logical or empirical relation to the heritability within populations and cannot be inferred from it, as I will show in a simple but realistic example. In addition, the notion that eliminating what appear a priori to be major environmental variables will serve to eliminate a large part of the environmentally caused difference between the populations is biologically naive. In the context of I.Q. testing, it assumes that educational psychologists know what the major sources of environmental difference between black and white performance are. Thus, Jensen compares blacks with American Indians whom he regards as far more environmentally disadvantaged. But a priori judgments of the importance of different aspects of the environment are valueless, as every ecologist and plant physiologist knows. My example will speak to that point as well.

Let us take two completely inbred lines of corn. Because they are completely inbred by self-fertilization, there is no genetic variation in either line, but the two lines will be genetically different from each other. Let us now plant seeds of these two inbred lines in flower pots with ordinary potting soil, one seed of each line to a pot. After they have germinated and grown for a few weeks we will measure the height of each plant. We will discover variation in height from plant to plant. Because each line is completely inbred, the variation in height within lines must be entirely environmental, a result of variation in potting conditions from pot to pot. Then the heritability of plant height in both lines is 0.0. But there will be an average difference in plant height between lines that arises entirely from the fact that the two lines are genetically different. Thus the difference between lines is entirely genetical even though the heritability of height is 0!

Now let us do the opposite experiment. We will take two handsful from a sack containing seed of an open-pollinated variety of corn. Such a variety has lots of genetic variation in it. Instead of using potting soil, however, we will grow the seed in vermiculite watered with a carefully made up nutrient, Knop's solution, used by plant physiologists for controlled growth experiments. One batch of seed will be grown on complete Knop's solution, but the other will have the concentration of nitrates cut in half and, in addition, we will leave out the minute trace of zinc salt that is part of the necessary trace elements (30 parts per billion). After several weeks we will measure the plants. Now we will find variation within seed lots which is entirely genetical since no environmental variation within lots was allowed. Thus heritability will be 1.0. However, there will be a radical difference between seed lots which is ascribable entirely to the difference in nutrient levels. Thus, we have a case where heritability within populations is complete, yet the difference between populations is entirely environmental!

But let us carry our experiment to the end. Suppose we do not know about the difference in the nutrient solutions because it was really the carelessness of our assistant that was involved. We call in a friend who is a very careful chemist and ask him to look into the matter for us. He analyzes the nutrient solutions and discovers the obvious—only half as much nitrates in the case of the stunted plants. So we add the missing nitrates and do the experiment again. This time our second batch of plants will grow a little larger but not much, and we will conclude that the difference between the lots is genetic since equalizing the large difference in nitrate level had so little effect. But, of course, we would be wrong for it is the missing trace of zinc that is the real culprit. Finally, it should be pointed out that it took many years before the importance of minute trace elements in plant physiology was worked out because ordinary laboratory glassware will leach out enough of many trace elements to let plants grow normally. Should educational psychologists study plant physiology?

Having disposed, I hope, of Jensen's conclusion that the high heritability of I.Q. and the lack of effect of correction for gross socio-economic class are presumptive evidence for the genetic basis of the difference between blacks and whites, I will turn to his second erroneous conclusion. The article under discussion began with the observation, which he documents, that compensatory education for the disadvantaged (blacks, chiefly) has failed. The explanation offered for the failure is that I.Q. has a high heritability and that therefore the difference between the races is also mostly genetical. Given that the racial difference is genetical, then environmental change and educational effort cannot make much difference and cannot close the gap very much between blacks and whites. I have already argued that there is no evidence one way or the other about the genetics of inter-racial I.Q. differences. To understand Jensen's second error, however, we will suppose that the difference is indeed genetical. Let it be entirely genetical. Does this mean that compensatory education, having failed, must fail? The supposition that it must arises from a misapprehension about the fixity of genetically determined traits. It was thought at one time that genetic disorders, because they were genetic, were incurable. Yet we now know that inborn errors of metabolism are indeed curable if their biochemistry is sufficiently well understood and if deficient metabolic products can be supplied exogenously. Yet in the normal range of environments, these inborn errors manifest themselves irrespective of the usual environmental variables. That is, even though no environment in the normal range has an effect on the character, there may be special environments, created in response to our knowledge of the underlying biology of a character, which are effective in altering it.

But we do not need recourse to abnormalities of development to see this point. Jensen says that "there is no reason to believe that the I.Q.'s of deprived children, given an environment of abundance, would rise to a higher level than the already privileged children's I.Q.'s." It is empirically wrong to argue that if the richest environment experience we can conceive does not raise I.Q. substantially, that we have exhausted the environmental possibilities. In the seventeenth century the infant mortality rates were many times their present level at all socio-economic levels. Using what was then the normal range of environments, the infant mortality rate of the highest socio-economic class would have been regarded as the limit below which one could not reasonably expect to reduce the death rate. But changes in sanitation, public health and disease control—changes which are commonplace to us now but would have seemed incredible to a man of the seventeenth century—have reduced the infant mortality rates of "disadvantaged" urban Americans well below those of even the richest members of seventeenth-century society. The argument that compensatory education is hopeless is equivalent to saying that changing the form of the seventeenth century gutter would not have a pronounced effect on public sanitation. What compensatory education will be able to accomplish when the study of human behavior finally emerges from its pre-scientific era is anyone's guess. It will be most extraordinary if it stands as the sole exception to the rule that technological progress exceeds by manyfold what even the most optimistic might have imagined.

The real issue in compensatory education does not lie in the heritability of I.Q. or in the possible limits of educational technology. On the reasonable assumption that ways of significantly altering mental capacities can be developed if it is important enough to do so, the real issue is what the goals of our society will be. Do we want to foster a society in which the "race of life" is "to get ahead of somebody" and in which "true merit," be it genetically or environmentally determined, will be the criterion of men's earthly reward? Or do we want a society in which every man can aspire to the fullest measure of psychic and material fulfillment that social activity can produce? Professor Jensen has made it fairly clear to me what sort of society he wants.

I oppose him.

8. The Dream of the Kibbutz
Urie Bronfenbrenner

"The Israeli kibbutzim, some of them more than fifty years old, constitute what is probably the most significant social experiment in modern times."

The kibbutzim, communal settlements in Israel, have been extensively studied by many social scientists. The appeal of the kibbutz has led some to theorize how its educational structure might be applied in other cultural situations. Urie Bronfenbrenner in this paper examines the kibbutz method of child rearing and social structure.

The Israeli kibbutzim, some of them more than fifty years old, constitute what is probably the most significant social experiment in modern times on the "making of men." In these collective settlements, children are raised in group settings outside the home from shortly after birth until late adolescence. Reacting against existing studies of kibbutz upbringing for their "unwarranted assumption that child-rearing methods that are standard in our middle-class culture are therefore best in all cultures," Professor Bruno Bettelheim of the University of Chicago, a psychoanalyst and well-known authority on the emotional problems of children, has carried out what he calls "a study in depth" of kibbutz upbringing and its effects.

For this purpose, he journeyed to Israel and spent seven weeks living in a kibbutz, observing methods of child rearing and interviewing several hundred persons of all ages including parents, professional educators, and, above all, the young people who are the products of the system, many of them now adults raising their own families. The result is a book (*The Children of the Dream*, Macmillan, 363 pp., $6.95) which, because of the dramatic nature of its conclusions and the reputation of its author, is likely to become the most widely read and accepted account of what kibbutz education is and the kind of personality it produces. Moreover, Bettelheim contends that the child-rearing practices of the kibbutzim have implications which are of more than just academic interest for those concerned with education in the United States. Many advocates of change in American educational practices—those who are concerned with the inability of the school to educate poor black children, and with the often repressive and alienating effects of the schools and society on children of all colors and classes—see in the kibbutzim some potential answers to these problems.

What, then, are Professor Bettelheim's conclusions? To begin with, he sees his study as shedding light on a fundamental question: "Can children be reared successfully away from their mothers, as kibbutz children are?" The kibbutz situation, as Bettelheim views it, entails not only separation from the mother ("a daily occurrence"), but also lack of deep attachment between mother and child. The weakened maternal tie has different origins depending on whether or not the mother herself was brought up in a kibbutz. It is Bettelheim's thesis that adult women who came to live on a kibbutz were motivated to do so, in part, by an unconscious fear "about their own mothering abilities." For these women, the kibbutz way of life served "to quiet their guilt about refusing to personally care for their own children." The story is "entirely different" for kibbutz-born mothers. "Not having experienced intense mothering care as infants, they are emotionally somewhat detached from their own children and from mothering." Despite the difference in origin, both types of mother-child relations are seen as having the same effect. Kibbutz-reared children "wanted more from their mothers than they got, and they learned from infancy what no child brought up in a middle-class family learns—that only the peer group comes close to giving them all they would like to receive but do not get."

What kind of human being is produced by this pattern of child rearing? Bettelheim speaks to this question not once, but many times, and the answers are somewhat difficult to reconcile with each other. On the one hand, at the general level, he repeatedly asserts that the kibbutz experience confirms his fundamental thesis that children can be brought up quite satisfactorily away from their mothers (e.g., "My conclusion must be that despite published reports to the contrary, the kibbutz system seems quite successful in raising children by others than their mothers, and this from infancy on."). On the other hand, when one looks at his specifics, the "success" would seem to be rather seriously qualified in a number of respects.

According to Bettelheim, "the kibbutz-reared youngster seems unable to project himself into the feelings or deeply personal experience of others." This incapacity derives from the pallidness of his emotional attachments to parents, and, in later years, is manifested as an "only limited ability to accept any viewpoint as valid but one's own, which means a limited capacity to deal with hypothetical questions that put in question one's values or way of life."

Bettelheim sees the kibbutz adolescent as "depleted of energy because so much of it goes into keeping up repressions. . . . Again and again I saw groups of late adolescents lying on the grass or on their cots, totally exhausted. . . . They are easily tired out by inner and outer pressures. . . . Most of their vitality is drained by having so much to repress."

The source of repression in kibbutz-born adolescents is to be found, says Bettelheim, in the contrasting experience and reaction of the older generation:

> Their parents were spilling over with energy, because the kibbutz gave them leave, for the first time in their lives, to throw off old repressions. Much of their new and contagious joy of living came also of having suddenly thrown off their sexual repressions. . . . Eventually it turned out that what many had embraced as sexual freedom was a sexual acting out, that promiscuity did not give them the greater sexual satisfaction they had hoped it would bring. But this they did not realize till later in life, when the bloom of exuberance was already receding with age and with the need to come to terms with reality.
>
> It was this later experience with how a heedless promiscuity can breed disruption in the social life that led them to impose on their adolescent children a very high and depressive sex morality. And it is this that saps the youngsters of a great deal of libidinal energy. . . . These adolescents cannot throw off parental inhibitions, because it is not true for them as it was for their parents that their elders seemed puny figures, willing slaves of the ghetto. To them, their parents seem true giants. . . . To the kibbutz-born generation, their parents loom as the great figures who brought freedom to the Jews in the face of a whole doubting world. How can one throw off repressions that seem part of what put an end to two thousand years of bondage?

Kibbutz adolescents must conform not only to the imperious demands of a repressive conscience but also to the equally compelling pressures of the group. According to Bettelheim, "with very rare exceptions, they cannot buck the group, not for a moment; it is too threatening. This is where their emotional security resides. Without the peer group they are lost."

The combined influences of repression and group conformity result in a personality that finds it difficult to express strong, intimate emotions that cannot be shared by all members of the group. In Bettelheim's words:

> True intimacy finds no soil to grow on in the kibbutz. . . . Kibbutz generations grow up in a society that neither shows, nor approves, nor provides opportunities for strong private emotions, as powered by a sense of the two or three of us against all the rest. In addition, the community has provided them with such a puritanical background in their formative years

(as far as private emotions are concerned) that by adulthood their strong emotions do not press toward intimacy as a means to satisfaction.

Kibbutzniks, Bettelheim concludes, "cannot show deep personal feeling. They cannot commit themselves emotionally to each other." The kibbutznik's devotion to and dependence on the group brings with it both great strengths and liabilities. As an example, Bettelheim cites the performance of kibbutz-born soldiers. While acknowledging the superior record of this group, both in training and in battle, he maintains that "the reality is more complex." He further states:

> From the moment they join the army until the end of their service, they tend to stick together, feeling superior to the others, whom they accuse (and probably rightly) of being selfish, of not subordinating personal interest to the group. But their inner conviction of being superior does not make for good feelings among the rest of the peacetime army.

As for their performance under fire, Bettelheim concurs with the judgment of an unnamed "high-ranking officer" who told him:

> "They make wonderful soldiers in the sense of the Roman sentry at Pompei who would rather die than desert his post until ordered to. But modern war needs soldiers who try to survive the battle in order to fight in the next one."
>
> Despite great courage and devotion, he went on to imply, they are lacking in that immediate and flexible evaluation, a spontaneous adjustment to ever-changing situations that make for the most useful soldier today. Not for them . . . "the lonely deed, when it requires not heroism but unusually complex decisions. For that they are somehow not flexible enough. They are at their very best in the direct attack, in making direct decisions and in sticking with them. They have little taste for the back and forth vagaries of complex developments."

The number and nature of the personality deficiencies, which Bettelheim diagnoses as characteristic of the kibbutz-born generation, seem hardly consistent with his claim of success for the collective system of upbringing. In particular, it is difficult to reconcile his picture of a rigid, emotionally flat, highly repressed personality, limited in capacity for empathy and intimate relationships, with his repeated claim that the kibbutz-born show a "relative absence of emotional disturbance"—both in number of cases and severity.

In addition to internal inconsistencies, there are external ones as well. Although this reviewer's observations were admittedly much more limited than Bettelheim's, they clash sharply with his in a number of respects. For example, in the half-dozen or so kibbutzim which I had opportunity to visit earlier this year, I was struck by the intimacy and warmth of the parent-child relationship, particularly during the two hours in the later afternoon that parents reserve for spending with their children, and in the evening time when the parents put their children to bed. What I saw during these periods was a mutually rewarding experience involving a great deal of play, companionship, and expression of affection. Putting the children to bed, for example, entailed a good half-hour of animated talk, singing, cuddling, and kisses; the overall impression was of a lovers' parting protracted as long as possible on both sides.

Bettelheim viewed the same experience in an altogether different light:

> In theory, the policy of putting the children to bed was adopted . . . to make for more intimacy between parent and child. But how can intimacy deepen at a moment when both partners know it has to end by official decree?
>
> I found that most parents defend themselves by relating to it little. Most of them, from the moment they enter the children's house, feel very self-conscious, and so do the children.
>
> Most of all, the parents feel pressured and rushed; guilty as much about hurrying the child to bed as about keeping the other children waiting. It becomes an ordeal, even for the most loving and conscientious parent, and an empty routine for the parent less emotionally involved.
>
> Matters are even worse for the children. . . . During this time, the child must come to hate his mother and siblings, particularly since he has to watch two or three of his roommates being put to bed by their parents while he waits by himself in his loneliness—or he would come to hate them if he did not repress it. Finally, the mother (or father, or both) comes, for at best half an hour. This half-hour the child must now grab, because it's all he is going to get. That is why he cannot afford to hate the mother or to act out his emotions. Because if he does the half-hour will be gone, and nothing will be left.

On similar grounds, Bettelheim dismisses as essentially superficial, and even counter-productive, the two hours the child spends daily in the home:

> A place that offers a haven of closeness for a few discrete hours a day is not much of a physical or emotional haven. A warm hearth from 5 to 7 in the afternoon, even with a few minutes leeway, cannot offer much security, however nice a time and place the parents try to make it. Because a place that offers the kind of security that stops by the hand of the clock merely rubs in how precarious a haven it is.

Since Bettelheim's impressions contrasted so markedly with my own, I felt the need for additional evidence. Accordingly, on a recent trip to Israel in connection with some research on kibbutz upbringing, which my colleagues and I are now beginning there, I asked several leading educators and social scientists, both in and outside the kibbutz movement, to comment on the major theses of Bettelheim's book. In general, their reactions were highly critical. In particular, they took issue with Bettelheim's assumption that kibbutz children are being raised away from their mothers with "basic security provided not by their parents but the kibbutz."

Dr. Menachem Gerson, director of the Institute of Research on Kibbutz Education at Oranim and a founding member of Kibbutz Hasorea, writes that although "at an early stage of kibbutz development, the family was regarded as a potential danger . . . this stage did not last for long." Strong familistic tendencies soon became apparent as documented in systematic research by the late

Dr. Yonina Tolman (a highly respected Israeli sociologist). Additional support for Dr. Gerson's views comes from a recent study by two psychologists at Hebrew University (Kugelmass and Breznitz). Working with a sample of adolescents from seven kibbutz settlements, these investigators examined the young people's perceptions of their parents and found that "the pattern of the perception of parental sex roles had not changed radically" from that observed previously in a non-kibbutz group.

As for Bettelheim's diagnosis of "emotional shallowness," this conclusion, writes Gerson, "makes kibbutzniks laugh and cry at the same time." As evidence of "their capacity for emotional communication," Gerson calls attention to two recently published books. The first, *Children under Fire*, documents the reaction of youngsters in border kibbutzim during the Six Day War. The second is a collection (soon to be published in English) of informal conversations among kibbutz soldiers that "reveals a wealth of profound human emotions." Gerson acknowledges that the kibbutznik does not wear his heart on his sleeve. He puts it more eloquently with a quote from Nietzsche: *"Ich liebe die Scham Eurer Herzlichkeit."* ("I like the modesty of your affection.") But the *Herzlichkeit,* he insists, is there.

Regarding Bettelheim's conclusion that kibbutzniks are characterized by dogmatic self-righteousness and lack the capacity for "flexible evaluation," Dr. Joseph Marcus, a child psychiatrist with extensive clinical and research experience in the study of the kibbutzim, calls attention to recent research by Antonovsky and himself on soldiers in the Israeli Army. Kibbutz and city-raised youth were compared on a number of personality variables including dogmatism. "The results," writes Dr. Marcus, "showed that there was almost no difference in scores between the kibbutz and city samples." Both scored "low on dogmatism," were similar to a university group, and scored "much lower than a sample of Yeshiva students" (those preparing for the rabbinate).

Bettelheim's thesis that kibbutz children are conforming to pressures from both parents and peers is called directly into question by some results of experiments currently being conducted by this reviewer in cooperation with colleagues at the University of Tel Aviv. The experiments measure the readiness of twelve-year-old children to engage in adult-disapproved behavior under threat of exposure first to adults and then to peers. Although data are available as yet from only half a dozen kibbutzim, they indicate that kibbutz-born youngsters are much more ready to engage in misconduct than age mates, for example, brought up in Soviet boarding schools, or even German or American school children. Moreover, rather than exerting a repressive influence, the kibbutz peer group appears to encourage acting against adult-approved norms.

As for the presumed unfitness of the kibbutznik soldier for "the lonely deed when it requires not heroism but unusually complex decisions," Gerson calls attention to the unduly high proportion and superior performance— documented in the research of Yehuda Amir and others—of kibbutz youngsters in such often solitary and hardly simple assignments as fighter pilot, commando, and paratrooper.

In summary, it would seem that many of Bettelheim's conclusions are called into question by the results of other research. This in turn raises the issue of the nature of his own evidence. His findings are based on observations primarily at the one kibbutz in which he lived. In justification, he writes:

I was told again and again how different the various kibbutz movements are and how unique was each one of its settlements. I soon found that my worries were unjustified as to whether the study, principally, of one single kibbutz would invalidate my findings. . . . I found the more or less random sample of kibbutzim I visited, in all the other three movements, astonishingly similar to the one I studied intensively.

Bettelheim also found homogeneity among kibbutz members themselves: "Despite differences among them in regard to politics, and some economic and other arrangements, the inner attitudes of kibbutzniks are most similar."

This has not been my own experience, or that of any of the Israeli educators and social scientists I consulted. Data from our own research on effects of collective upbringing, limited as yet to half a dozen kibbutzim, show wide variation from one settlement to the next. Indeed, in the body of the text, Bettelheim himself, from time to time, acknowledges such differences: "There is, on the other hand, considerable variety among the various movements—and sometimes kibbutzim of the same movement—as to how parents separate from their children at bedtime, after their daily visits."

Another limitation of Dr. Bettelheim's study is the absence of a control group of non-kibbutz families. As a result, the question arises how Professor Bettelheim would have known whether the characteristics he saw in kibbutz families and personalities were not common to Israeli society in general. The issue is particularly relevant in view of the fact, pointed out in a penetrating review by Henry Near in the Jerusalem Post, that "the stereotypic image of the town-bred sabra (the native born Israeli) contains many of the traits which Dr. Bettelheim sees as characteristic of the kibbutznik."

So much for the experimental design. As to the evidence itself, there isn't much of it. The book is long on interpretation but short on data. What little there is, is anecdotal in character. Often, as in the case of the combat performance of kibbutzniks, a broad generalization is documented only by a quotation from a single interview. Yet, it turns out that Bettelheim had much more data at his disposal, a good deal of it of an objective nature, that he deliberately chose not to present. In a passage, which to this reviewer epitomizes the self-contradiction and bypassing of evidence so characteristic of this work, Bettelheim writes:

> The objective data consisted of interviews with several hundred persons, as recorded on tape, and other materials such as projective tests ("three wishes," "draw-a-person"). These tests were given to 191 children drawn from four different kibbutzim, and at all grade levels from the second to the highest. I do not report here on the results of these tests for the same reason that I was critical of the results of the academic tests. . . . Because these tests, too, are standardized for a culture that values different traits from the kibbutz. This qualification apart, the test findings strongly support the views presented in this book on the results of kibbutz education and the personality it produces.

Bettelheim would have his cake and eat it too, which leaves the rest of us little substantial to digest. It is all the more regrettable, since he is entirely correct in his view that both science and mankind have much to learn from the kibbutz experiment. But the learning must begin with an explicit and accurate description of the phenomenon, preferably on a comparative basis. How are children raised on a kibbutz? Do kibbutz parents in fact treat their children differently from Israeli parents generally? What part do upbringers and other adults actually play? How does the kibbutz peer group influence the individual child? What kind of personality emerges from the process, and what, if any, are its special weaknesses and strengths? All these are questions to which objective answers are obtainable. Regrettably, few of them are to be found in Bettelheim's book, and the consequent uncertainty of the effects of the kibbutzim prevents any judgment about the importance of their implications for change in American education.

All in all, *The Children of the Dream* comes closer to being a Dream of the Children, imbued with the qualities that Bettelheim's field of psychoanalysis has taught us are characteristic of dream work: logical inconsistencies, secondary elaborations, and the manifest and latent content that reveals less of objective reality than of the mind of the dreamer.

Discussion Questions
1. How would you compare the plight of the Chicano with black and Indian Americans?
2. What are some of the reasons behind social inequality practiced in the United States today?
3. What feeling for the Indian culture did you receive from the article "Seminole Girl"?
4. What are some of the arguments Lewontin presents in criticizing Jensen's article? What is your opinion of the issues raised in the article, "Race and Intelligence"?
5. What child-rearing practices are characteristic of kibbutz living? Do you think they might be applied in the United States with any success?

Chapter 3
Childhood

Centuries ago the stage of life referred to as "childhood" was unknown. Children were thought of as small adults, and no attention was given to ways in which they might differ from adults. This attitude was probably due in part to economic conditions that frequently necessitated children working at early ages, and in part to public health conditions which produced such high infant mortality rates that parents were reluctant to develop deep emotional attachments to their offspring. As health conditions improved, so that most infants could be expected to live, and compulsory education postponed the time when children would be expected to take their vocational position in the adult world, more and more attention was given to the time of life known as childhood. This has evolved to the point where childhood has practically become a cult, and children are seen not only as different, but as very special. In this same vein it should be noted that adolescence is also a relatively recently recognized stage of life, and our attention to what is unique about adolescence also reflects social conditions that have postponed the time when adolescents take their place in the adult world.

A general question that is often raised about children concerns how they get to be the way they are. Strict environmentalists see children as being a *tabula rasa,* or blank slate, upon birth, with everything that they learn written upon that slate as a result of their life experiences. On the other hand, strict hereditarians will see children as organisms whose future is clearly laid out for them by their genes at birth, with their innate potential merely unfolding in their environment. It is unlikely that either strict point of view is accurate. Further, it is increasingly difficult to see heredity and environment as separate forces brought to bear upon the organism. It is becoming clear that an individual's genetic makeup is influenced by the fetal environment, and after birth there is a constant interplay between the two forces so that it becomes almost impossible to separate one from the other. Thus, concerning intelligence, it is impossible to say whether heredity or environment is more important; but it is clear that an individual with very poor genetic inheritance will find it difficult to reach great intellectual heights in even the most stimulating environments, while individuals with excellent genetic potential will probably show signs of high intelligence despite the most oppressive environment. However, it is also clear that if there is little or no difference as far as genetic potential is concerned, the major intellectual differences in children will be related to the environment in which they are brought up.

The work of Dr. Jerome Bruner is not concerned as much with the absolute level of intelligence in children as with the way in which they approach intellectual tasks. He is more concerned with the techniques by which children approach intellectual problems than with individual differences among them. Here too, the question may be raised as to whether these intellectual styles or techniques are learned through experience or are innate. This is one concern of Dr. Bruner, and some of his work in this area is reported by Maya Pines.

Very young children do not have the ability to use language, and it is often many years before they learn to speak well enough to communicate clearly about their feelings. However, even infants have feelings, and sensations of comfort or discomfort are probably known from the day of birth. Infants learn to communicate about their feelings without speech by means of noises and physical gestures. As they grow older their vocabularies increase, but often they will continue to use nonverbal rather than verbal means of expressing these feelings. They also may learn to use indirect rather than direct verbal messages as a means of getting their points across. Parents are very attuned to reading the meaning of the gestures of their infants, since there is no other way that they can learn about their needs. However, when children master the art of speech parents often forget what they once knew about the meaning of nonverbal behavior and take the verbal message literally. Dr. Kempler points to the importance of looking behind the surface meaning of children's communications in order to interpret the feeling that is being masked. Not only is this helpful with young children, but masked messages probably persist throughout life, and a recognition that people do not always mean exactly what they say is a very important aid in understanding others.

As children grow they are learning by great leaps and bounds. The difference between what is known by infants and what is known five years later by pre-school children is staggering, and the amount that is learned in each year of childhood greatly exceeds the amount learned in any year of adulthood for most people. Children will learn from whatever source is available, and in our media-dominated society one of the most available sources of learning for children is the television set. Dr. Albert Bandura has conducted a great deal of research on the effects of visual media on the development of children's personality. This research is reviewed in the article by Clarissa Wittenberg.

The concern about the impact of popular culture upon children's personality is a long-standing one. A number of decades ago there was a great deal of attention given to whether or not violence in comic books was a breeding ground for violence in children. As comic books became replaced by television programs as a major source of input to children, the focus of this concern shifted, but adult society continued to wonder why children are as aggressive as they are. They did not spend as much time wondering why adults are as aggressive as they are. Recently a report was published by the United States Surgeon General's office concerning the effects of television on social behavior. That report drew upon the available experimental research, such as that of Dr. Bandura, and also upon surveys that had been conducted. The major point of the reports was the need for further research and the inadequate state of current knowledge. However, within these limitations, there were some conclusions that could be drawn. The commission saw a relationship between viewing violence on television and aggressive behavior, but saw that relationship as existing only in some children who were predisposed to be aggressive, and in some environmental contexts. They did not have good information about why certain types of children choose certain types of programs or why television in general is viewed as extensively as it is.

Up to this point we have noted the importance of heredity, parents, and social forces such as television upon the development of children. One other major influence upon the socialization and development of children is the school. Most children spend the majority of their waking hours in a schoolroom. School has always been seen as a vehicle through which information would be given to children, although many questions have been raised about the adequacy with which that is done. It is only recently that many people have come to realize the large role that the school plays in teaching children about the rules in their society, and thereby helping to develop the personality of young students. With this recognition an approach to education has developed that focuses on feelings as well as on facts. This approach is given a variety of different names, such as "affective education" or "moral education," and the names very often serve to antagonize the community at large. Despite the evidence that schools cannot help but teach personality and morality, many parents do not want their children exposed to such influence in a systematic way outside the home. Therefore, they oppose any attempt to convert the school from a place for learning information to a place for growing as a human being. Whether or not information effectively can be learned independent of development as a human being is a question that is raised by many proponents of the new method of teaching. Terry Borton describes his experiences with one such program in the Philadelphia school system.

The approach that Borton describes incorporates a number of aspects of sensitivity training within the classroom. Sensitivity training also is an area that has attracted a great deal of attention lately. Much more about this topic is presented later in this book, in both the chapters on therapeutic approaches and on the counter culture. The term is sufficiently frightening to many parents that they object to it being used in the school. Perhaps they would be more accepting if they were told that techniques would be used to motivate their children so that they could learn more relevant material in a more effective manner.

Suggested Readings
Borton, Terry. *Reach, Touch, and Teach*. New York: McGraw-Hill, 1971. The selection in this chapter also appeared in Borton's book describing an approach to affective education in the public schools.

Feshbach, Seymour, and Singer, Robert. *Television and Aggression*. San Francisco: Jossey-Bass, 1971. A field study reporting the effects of extended television viewing of violence on boy's overt aggressive behavior. Results were complex and it was necessary to take initial personality characteristics into account in order to explain them.

Ginott, Haim G. *Between Parent and Child*. New York: The Macmillan Company, 1965. A national best seller describing a method of understanding and communicating between parents and children. Techniques described in this book might be helpful in "uncovering masked messages."

Piaget, Jean. *The Origins of Intelligence in Children*. New York: W. W. Norton & Co., 1963. In this volume Jean Piaget, the world-famous Swiss developmental psychologist, describes his theories concerning the stages through which children go as they develop the ability to use intelligence in their functioning.

9. The Development of Intelligence in Babies
Maya Pines

"You can also be trained to be stupid."

Do babies enter the world as empty organisms who have to be taught everything they learn, or do they begin with innate predispositions which help them to order the world? This is the subject of Dr. Jerome Bruner's research, and Ms. Pines describes that research as well as many of Dr. Bruner's other intellectual interests.

For the past four years, Dr. Jerome S. Bruner has been concerned primarily with the cognitive development of babies: How does the human infant—so helpless and limited at birth—learn to control his environment and himself? How does he grow up intelligent?

Although human babies at first appear more stupid than chimpanzees of the same age, by the age of 2 or 3 the normal child has achieved one of the most difficult intellectual feats he may ever perform: he has reinvented the rules of grammar, all by himself, and he has learned to speak. He has also constructed a fairly complex mental model of the world, which allows him to manipulate various aspects of the world in his thoughts and fantasies. And he has learned to mobilize various skill patterns whenever he needs them. Under the guidance of Dr. Bruner, the Center for Cognitive Studies at Harvard is trying to unravel the sources of these formidable achievements.

There are various theories about how children acquire language. In his book, *Verbal Behavior* (1967), Dr. B. F. Skinner claimed that children learn to speak as a result of stimulus-response conditioning. All complicated behavior is learned, he argued; one learns to behave in ordered ways because there is order in the environment. Linguists such as Dr. Noam Chomsky disagreed, suggesting that human beings have an innate competence for language which sets them apart from all other creatures. This innate competence is what allows babies to learn language on the basis of relatively few encounters with words and sentences, they claimed, crediting babies—and mankind—with far more "mind" than most scientists were willing to accept at the time.

Innate Competence
Dr. Bruner and a number of other psychologists in the U.S. and abroad have now gone one step further than Chomsky in emphasizing the importance

From *The Mental Health of the Child*, June 1971. Public Health Service Publication No. 2168. Reprinted by permission.

and activity of the infant's own nervous system. By studying babies well before they learn to speak, these researchers have come to the conclusion that language competence is just one example of an even more significant ability with which infants enter the world: the basic ability to pick up logical rules from mere fragments of evidence, and then use these rules in a variety of combinations. There are programs of action in the human mind right after birth, they believe, not only for language but also for the intelligent use of hands, eyes and tools.

"It's a very different view of man," says Dr. Bruner, "and it's just beginning. People are starting to see that skills of this wide-ranging type couldn't possibly be learned element by element. There must be some kind of predisposition in man to allow babies to pick up so quickly rules that go for such a large number of situations."

Only a few years ago, it was generally believed that newborns could not see more than the differences between light and dark; that during their first three months of life they were so absorbed by their insides that they could hardly react to the outside world; and consequently, that their physical environment had little impact on them—all that mattered was the provision of food and comfort. It now turns out, however, that even on the day of their birth, infants can track a triangle with their eyes. By the time they are 1 month old, they can spot the identity of objects and know when something has been changed. Furthermore, they actively invent rules of theories to explain what they perceive. Even at 3 weeks of age, an infant will have fairly complex hypotheses about the world he has just been born into—and if he is proved wrong, he may burst into tears.

That was exactly what happened at the Center two years ago, during an experiment conducted by a Radcliffe undergraduate, Shelly Rosenbloom. Researchers there wondered whether babies of 3 to 8 weeks really understood that a person's voice should come from the spot where the person stood— whether babies had the idea of a locus. If so, did these babies also grasp the fact that when the person moved, the sound of his voice should travel along the same path? To what extent had they organized their experience at that age? To find out, it was decided to use stereo speakers that could separate the sound of a voice from its origin. In response to ads in the *Harvard Crimson*, there is always a procession of babies—mostly the offspring of graduate students —to the Center's lab, where they are made comfortable, given toys, and usually offered something interesting to see or do as part of a psychological experiment, while their mothers look on. This time, the infants were seated in front of a glass partition that separated them from their mothers, whom they could see just two feet away. As long as the speakers were balanced so that the mother's voice seemed to come directly from her, an infant would be quite content. But as soon as the phase relationship between the speakers was changed so that the voice seemed to come from a different spot, the baby would become agitated, look around, or cry—showing that his expectations were thwarted, and that there is powerful information-processing ability in the brains of infants even at that early age. "We now believe that infants have a notion not only of locus, but of path, right from the beginning," says Dr. Bruner. "Then, with experience, it becomes increasingly differentiated. But there is some notion of it right from the start."

The Study of Infancy

The Center's study of infancy has focused on five issues:

(1) How the infant achieves voluntary control behavior in a fashion governed by prediction and anticipation;

(2) How visually guided and intelligent manipulative behavior emerges, with emphasis on the transferability and generativeness of skills;

(3) How the infant progresses from being a "one-track" enterprise to being able to carry out several activities simultaneously and under the control of an over-rule;

(4) How attention develops and its control shifts from external constraints (novelty) to internal constraints (problem-solving); and

(5) How pre-linguistic codes develop, particularly in the interaction of the mother and infant.

("Our underlying assumption is that the codes of language, while they may indeed reflect innate patterns, are first primed by a great deal of interactive code-learning of a nonsyntactic type," writes Dr. Bruner. "When certain of these pre-linguistic manifestations are understood, perhaps light will be shed on the deeper question of the nature of language as such.")

In babies' hands, Dr. Bruner believes, lie clues to much of their later development, and he particularly wants to find out how babies learn the value of two-handedness. Nobody teaches infants this skill, just as nobody teaches them to talk. Yet around the age of 1, a baby will master the "two-handed obstacle box," a simple puzzle devised by the Center to study this process. Seated on his mother's lap, he will suddenly use one hand to push and hold a transparent cover, while the other hand reaches inside the box for a toy.

To Dr. Bruner this is extraordinary, for it shows that the baby has learned to distinguish between the two kinds of grip—the power or "holding" grip, which stabilizes an object, and the precision or "operating" grip, which does the work. Monkeys and apes have developed a precision grip, Dr. Bruner says, but "it is not until one comes to man with his asymmetry that the power grip migrates to one hand (usually the left) and the precision to the other." From then on, he emphasizes, many routines can be devised for holding an object with one hand while working it with the other, leading to the distinctively human use of tools and tool-making.

The experiments at the Center are essentially very simple, but their interpretations parallel Noam Chomsky's "transformation" approach to linguistics, which reduces language to basic kernel sentences, each one made up of a noun phrase and a verb phrase. Early in childhood every human being learns the logical rules which allow him to transform these kernels into any possible sentence. Dr. Bruner speculates that when a baby learns to differentiate between the two kinds of manual grip, this foreshadows "the development of topic and comment in human language"—the basic sentence form of subject/predicate, which may be found in all languages, with no exception whatsoever, and which a baby expresses when he combines a holophrase (a single word or a very short phrase that is used as one word) with another word. Thus, man may be uniquely predisposed, at birth, to reinvent the rules of grammar, to process information, and to develop "clever hands." He is born with a highly complex programing system, the result of millions of years of evolution.

What about disadvantaged children, then—why should they be different, if they are born with the same programing system? "Mind you, you can ruin a child's inheritance, too," warns Dr. Bruner, "with an environment where he acquires helplessness. You can also be trained to be stupid."

Before man's marvellous programing system can be activated for language, for instance, a baby must learn a series of primitive codes—and these require interaction with an adult. "What seems to get established very quickly between infant and parent is some sort of code of mutual expectancy," says Dr. Bruner, "when the adult responds to an initiative on the part of the child, thus converting some feature of the child's spontaneous behavior into a signal." Right from the start, parent and infant are busy communicating through eye-to-eye contact, smiles and sounds. As early as 4 months of age, an infant will smile more to a face that smiles back than to one that does not respond; and if the adult face then stops smiling back, the infant will look away. In some cases, he may even struggle bodily to look away. A child's other attempts at learning can similarly be brought to a halt when his expectancy is thwarted, and things stop making sense.

The Development of Strategies

The prolonged infancy of man has definite functional importance, Dr. Bruner concludes: During that time, the infant is basically developing the strategies that will later be combined for intelligent action—for thought and language, as well as for the manipulation of tools.

One such strategy is "place-holding." The earliest evidence of this can be seen in infants' sucking behavior. As everybody knows, a pacifier will calm a baby. But why? Earlier research had shown that sucking reduces hunger pangs and relieves muscle tension. "Well, but putting electrodes on the temples of babies as they were watching a movie here, we've begun to find out what a pacifier really does," says Dr. Bruner. "One of its principal effects is to cut down scanning eye movements, which cuts down the baby's information intake." At birth, and for a few days thereafter, babies can't cope with more than one activity at a time. When they wish to suck, they close their eyes tightly, to avoid taking in information from the outside. When their eyes are open, they stop sucking. By the age of 3 to 5 weeks, however, they can suck with their eyes open—but as soon as they become really interested in something, the sucking stops. Finally, between the ages of 2 and 4 months, a new strategy appears. Whenever something catches their attention while they are sucking, they stop their usual suctioning and shift to a sort of mouthing which keeps the nipple active, though at a reduced rate. This allows them to pick up where they left off with great ease, once their curiosity has been satisfied. A neat solution to an early problem, "place-holding" of this sort leads to many later skills, both manual and linguistic.

"As I got more into this work on skilled behavior, it became increasingly evident to what extent intention and hypothesis are central to the organization of knowledge and to the filtering of input," declares Dr. Bruner. In his most recent study, "Studies in the Growth of Manual Intelligence in Infancy," which he did with Karlen Lyons and Kenneth Kaye, Dr. Bruner emphasizes the importance of the infants' own programs of action. "When one observes the early behavior of infants—say at the onset of visually guided reaching at around 4 months of age—one is struck by the fact that arousal of intention is the initial reaction to an 'appropriate' stimulus," he writes. "The earliest overt expression of activated intention is not 'trial and error,' but an awkward but recognizable instrumental act that expresses a preadapted program of action."

His movie, "The Intention to Take—The Infancy of Object Capture," illustrates how babies begin with an intention, act out its intended results (or an approximation thereof) and then work backward to the components that will in fact make such results possible. "First, they look at the object," says Dr. Bruner, describing the movie. "They want to take it. It's an intense gazing. Then, as the child's intention gets organized, his lips come forward in what we call an 'A-frame mouth.' Later on, when he takes hold of the object, it will go into his mouth; but already, his whole system is activated, his mouth works. Then his arms come up in an antigravitational movement, and up comes that fist." The infants' actions are not yet in the right order for success. "Six weeks later, these actions will seem so well regulated that we'll forget the complexity of even so simple a task. Then they will leap forward to a fully orchestrated act. But the preparation is slow and demanding."

The infants' own intentions, then, are crucial. Of course, some goals can be imposed from outside, and babies can be taught, for instance, to respond to a buzzer in certain ways. Thus, Dr. Hanus Papousek, a Czech psychologist who is now spending a year at the Center, has conditioned newborns to turn their heads sharply to the side at the sound of a buzzer, in order to get milk from a buzzer. "It can be done," says Dr. Bruner, "but it's endless. The babies show so much aversion to this. They're so slow at learning it, you have to present the stimulus hundreds of times."

By contrast, when the infant uses his own initiative, learning often comes with lightning speed. In the Center's lab, a medium-sized room which might be called a baby theater, babies are placed in a well-padded seat facing a blank wall which serves as a screen. Then, with a pacifier in their mouth, they are shown a movie. "We didn't want to condition them to respond to a stimulus," Dr. Bruner explains. "Instead, we wanted to choose something the child does and give it some consequence. Then he is at the controls. So we chose sucking. Would they learn to suck at different speeds in order to produce changes in their environment? And, lo and behold, these little 4-, 5- and 6-week-old infants do learn to suck in longer bursts to produce a clear focus. Or else, if you reverse the conditions so that sucking blurs the picture, they learn to desist from sucking on this pacifier. They respond immediately, during the very first session, to changes produced by their own acts."

The movie that the babies watched so eagerly showed an Eskimo mother playing with her child. "It was shot in winter, indoors, and she was constantly involved in little games with him—string games and so on," explains Dr. Bruner. The experiment was devised by a graduate student, Mrs. Ilze Kalnins. When the babies discovered that sucking made the pictures clearer, they cut down their pauses between sucks, stopping only four seconds. On other visits to the lab, when they found that sucking blurred the image, they lengthened the pauses to about eight seconds.

The babies' performance was all the more remarkable because of their inexperience with "place-holding." To bring the picture into focus, they had to suck in longer bursts without looking at the film, then take a quick look before it blurred again.

Curiously, this experiment comes quite close to the kind of operant conditioning pioneered by Dr. Skinner, in which rewards are used to "shape" a child's activity. But Dr. Bruner interprets it quite differently, seeing the babies' rapid learning as the effect of fulfilling their own intentions. Sucking to produce a sharp focus involves quite complex strategies to coordinate looking and sucking. Such strategies come from the inside out, from an innate preadaptation, Dr. Bruner believes. Only after their appearance has been evoked by events can trial and error and reinforcements be of any use.

"What reinforcement is doing, in effect, is locking in that response in a set of alternative responses which in fact works," he writes. "It does not bring into being new responses. For the most part, the children do not *gradually* improve their strategies, but rather increase the skill with which they perform old routines. . . . Two-handed efforts make their appearance abruptly, rather than by some gradual route, and seem to be 'ready' for triggering."

He points to an experiment performed at the Center two years ago with three groups of babies of different ages. The babies were seated in front of a table on which a jingly toy was placed behind a small transparent screen, open at one end. The youngest babies, only 7 months old, simply reached for the toy with the nearest hand and bumped into the screen. After banging on and clawing at the screen for a while, they lost interest and gave up. The next group, the 1-year-olds, began in the same fashion, but then let their hands follow the edge of the screen and reached behind it in a sort of backhand grasp until they got the toy. Only the 18-month-old babies knew right away how to reach the toy efficiently, and did so. Over 16 trials each, none of the babies ever changed his initial strategy; this was the best he was capable of at that stage.

"Trial and error implies the capacity to hold an end constant while varying means," notes Dr. Bruner. "The segments in which this is possible are very short in duration for the child. What thwarts him is distraction, not error." This is why he is so interested in the development of the child's own intentions, and in the kind of "planning control" described by the Russian psychologist, Dr. A. R. Luria, as being located in the frontal lobes. He hopes to study the development of strategies and plans in primates and compare it to that of human infants, so as to gain further insight into this issue.

Studies of Perception and Thinking

The Center for Cognitive Studies came into being in 1960. During its first years of operation, it paid no attention to babies. For Dr. Bruner, too, infant development is a comparatively recent interest. Unlike many other psychologists, who study the same topic for their entire working lives, he has ranged all over the field. And before calling attention to the cognitive growth of infants, he had helped to create interest in four major movements: (1) the so-called "New Look" in perception in the late forties and early fifties; (2) the study of cognitive processes, mostly in adults; (3) educational reform, with emphasis on new curricula; and (4) the study of children's cognitive development. Throughout, he always came back to the same basic questions: How do human beings gather, categorize, store, use and communicate knowledge?

"You can never get a direct test on reality," he says. "You must take scraps and test them against your mental model of the world." In his work on perception, he wanted to learn how people register information through the filter of their own experience. He concluded that the same objects—for example, coins—are perceived differently by different people, in accordance with their values and needs. "Perceptions are highly regulated entry ports," he notes. "An experienced eye will pick up so much more!" In contrast to work that considered perception to be strictly passive, this approach was called "hot" perception, or "the New Look" in perception. It led him to the boundary line between perception and thinking.

Together with other members of the Harvard Cognition Project, he then spent five years studying cognitive processes—"the means whereby organisms achieve, retain and transform information." At the time, this was a major departure from the accepted approach to psychological problems, behaviorism. For roughly 30 years, most positions of prestige in American psychology had gone to people who studied stimuli and responses, bypassing anything that smacked of the "mental."

Spurred on by work in computer simulation and information theory, a few psychologists were beginning to worry about the mind again. Sometimes they called it "the black box." Clearly, the black box had to sort out all the inputs and outputs; but how did it do it? The behaviorists did not even attempt to answer this question, which they considered irrelevant. The members of the Harvard Cognition Project did, as described in Dr. Bruner's book, *A Study of Thinking* (1956). Specifically, they tried to deal with what Dr. Bruner called "one of the simplest and most ubiquitous phenomena of cognition: categorizing or conceptualizing. On closer inspection, it is not so simple. The spirit of the inquiry is descriptive. We have not sought 'explanation' in terms of learning theory, information theory, or personality theory. We have sought to describe and in a small measure to explain what happens when an intelligent human being seeks to sort the environment into significant classes of events so that he may end by treating discriminably different things as equivalents."

"There were some strategy theories I had picked up from John von Neumann," recalls Dr. Bruner. "I wanted to show how, in problem-solving, as in perception, people use strategy for choosing the instances they want to think about. I was arguing that strategy and systematic search efforts are characteristic of all living systems—that there are structures and hypotheses in the mind, and that you're constantly testing them against fragmentary evidence from the environment. You're locked—at the most tragic—you're locked into the structures that are species-specific to you, because that's the way the human nervous system is. But over and beyond that, there is a way in which, through the exercise of initiative on your part, you can turn on your own information, reorder it, and generate hypotheses. The structures in men's minds are productive, generative, just as grammar makes it possible for men to emit any number of utterances."

The Impact of Piaget

The emphasis on strategy in Bruner's work on perception and thought caught the interest of the famous Swiss psychologist, Dr. Jean Piaget. "It was the last thing he expected from an American psychologist," Dr. Bruner notes. "I guess I'm not a very typical American psychologist—at least my colleagues don't think so. I think I'm right in the tradition that started with William James, of pragmatism, and that they're very much in the tradition of Ivan Pavlov! You know—'we don't have to look inside the organism, there's no structure at all, all the order is outside, and all you do is mirror it.' Well, I take a drastically different view." Drs. Bruner and Piaget first met 16 years ago, when Dr. Piaget came to Boston to give a lecture. And Dr. Bruner was among the first Americans to appreciate the importance of Dr. Piaget's work.

Piaget's monumental studies of child development had been ignored in the U.S. for several decades, until the cognitive movement awakened to their value. In bold strokes, as well as painstaking detail, Piaget had described the growth of human intelligence, from the first day of life until adulthood. He had shown how children construct their own mental models of the world in successive stages, following an invariant sequence, though they may go through the stages at different rates. When a child has experienced enough conflict between reality and his image of it, he changes this image to make it more accurate. Thus, at first a child cannot understand that when water is poured out of a full glass into a wider glass which it fills only half way, the amount of water is unchanged. Being "centered" on only one aspect of reality at a time, he sees that the glass is half empty and says there is "less" water than before. Through a series of experiments, Piaget explored how children develop what he calls "conservation," the understanding that a quantity of water or clay will remain the same, regardless of the shape it takes. As children realize that objects and people have properties that do not depend on their immediate appearance, they become able to deal with symbols. Intelligence consists of such leaps into abstraction—but it depends on a large repertoire of images with which one can visualize certain sequences of cause and effect.

Dr. Bruner devotes considerable space to the contributions of "the Geneva school" in his book, *The Process of Education*. Many of his own papers show a strong Piagetian influence, particularly those in which he discusses the stages in cognitive growth. But eventually he developed differences of opinion with Piaget about how children acquire the notions of conservation and—much more fundamentally—about what produces intellectual growth.

"Mostly we argue about prefixedness," he says. "I found increasingly with Piaget that his notions of interior order were much more prefigured, prefixed than mine. I think this was the thing that caused something of an intellectual rift between us. I think that he misunderstands me more than I misunderstand him. He is too concerned with how the mind just processes things. I told him once, only half-jokingly, that his study of mollusks (conducted when he was only 15) was characteristic of him. His idea was that there was a mollusk, and no matter what that mollusk ate or what that mollusk did, it always turned out to have the same prefigured shell. Piaget's notion of intellectual development is a bit too much like his early conception of the way in which a mollusk grows. As one of his colleagues pointed out when he was here a few weeks ago: What does Piaget need a theory of education for? Either the child hasn't reached the right stage, and there's no point in trying to teach him anything; or he has already reached that stage, and why bother to teach, as he'll learn anyway."

In Dr. Bruner's view, evolution has given man a wide range of possibilities—

far wider than Piaget would allow—because man is a culture user, and his growth depends largely on the kinds of tools he uses. "I don't believe you can or should separate anthropology from psychology," he declares.

The Center of Cognitive Studies

By 1960, a number of converging trends made the study of cognition seem particularly promising. Some central place was needed to stimulate interdisciplinary research on the subject. With grants from the Carnegie Corporation of New York and other foundations, Dr. Bruner then founded the Center for Cognitive Studies, together with Dr. George A. Miller, a psychologist who was known for his work on psycholinguistics—the study of how cognition and language interact.

At first the Center focused on four areas: psycholinguistics, human memory, perception, and the cognitive growth of children. Among its many research fellows and visitors could be found psychologists, philosophers, physicians, linguists, anthropologists, sociologists and cyberneticists. Dr. Bruner was most involved in research on the cognitive growth of children, particularly those between the ages of 9 and 13. A Mobile Laboratory helped him and his associates to do experiments on the development of perception, attention, and judgment in children under controlled conditions, right next to the children's schools.

In the meantime, he had become famous in another field—education. This helped to make it respectable for psychologists to be concerned with the subject. His involvement began when he served as chairman of a conference of scientists, scholars, and educators at Woods Hole, Cape Cod, on better ways to teach science. His resulting report, *The Process of Education* (1960), was the clearest work on curriculum reform at the time, and won him instant fame. It has since been translated into 22 languages and is still being studied by teachers all over the world, particularly the ringing statement—which has been quoted over and over again—that "any subject can be taught effectively in some intellectually honest form to any child at any stage of development."

Although many of Dr. Bruner's ideas have changed since then, he stands by his famous statement, declaring that there is "absolutely no evidence against it." Another dominant theme persists: physics (or math, language, or any other subject) is not something that one "knows about," but something one "knows how to do." It is a way of thinking, rather than a series of facts. Thus, when Dr. Bruner devised a social studies curriculum for the fifth grade, "Man, A Course of Study," he gave 10-year-olds the raw materials with which to act like social scientists and three basic questions to start them off: What is human about human beings? How did they get that way? And how can they be made more so? The materials include films on the life cycle of the salmon, on free-ranging baboons, and on the Netsilik Eskimos, the purest surviving example of traditional Eskimo culture—the kind of authentic records previously available only to college or graduate students. The course has now been adopted by more than 1,500 schools. "Intellectual activity is the same whether at the frontiers of knowledge or in a third-grade classroom," Dr. Bruner wrote in *The Process of Education*. He still believes it passionately. And he is still involved in the creation of new curricula—right now, a new course for adolescents on principles of child development.

At the college level, he proposes a dual curriculum to take advantage of young people's drive to control their environment: On Mondays, Wednesdays and Fridays, students would continue with the essential basic course, such as mathematics or language, in which one step must be taken before another; and on Tuesdays and Thursdays, they would be let loose to govern their own learning in ways as experimental as possible. This would include taking part in budget decisions, teacher evaluation, and related matters—but more than that, it would mean that they could find their own problems to study. Preferably, these should be problems for which no answers yet exist.

Students are usually exposed to only two types of problems, Dr. Bruner points out: those which require analytical thought—e.g., dealing with abstract formulas—and those which require them to do some kind of laboratory exercise. "Both are formulated by the instructor or the text or the manual, and both are important in any science, art, or practical sphere," he says. "But neither is much like problem-finding. This requires the location of incompleteness, anomaly, trouble, inequity, contradiction. . . ."

The Growth Sciences

In the mid-sixties, as his studies on children's cognitive growth progressed, Dr. Bruner became increasingly dissatisfied with the age group he had been working with. "We were left with a sharp sense of incompleteness concerning the origins of what we had studied," he noted. He saw that by the age of 3, a repertory of skills is already well developed. Therefore, he began studying younger and younger children.

By 1967, when Dr. George Miller left the Center, the transformation was complete: nearly all the Center's research dealt with the cognitive development of babies, including infants only a few weeks or a few months old. Traditionally, this age period had been neglected because the child seemed so inaccessible between his fifth day of life when he left the maternity hospital, and his entry into nursery school at 3. Dr. Bruner urged his students to adopt the viewpoint of a naturalist exploring a new species, rather than try to test specific hypotheses derived from a general theory of infant development. "Assume that you are studying the great-chested Jabberwocky," he advised.

In this way, he took a lead in the development of what he calls "the growth sciences," a new composite discipline concentrating on the early years of life. "Just as medical research was organized around concepts of pathology, so today we would do well to organize our efforts anew around the concept of growth," he declared. "Those sciences that can help us understand and nurture human growth—biological, behavioral and social sciences alike—should find ways of joining forces as the growth sciences. Let them make their knowledge relevant to those who are practitioners of the nurturing of growth: parents, teachers, counselors. It is bizarre that no such organization has yet emerged, though it is plainly on its way."

"...learning to express oneself is a far cry from learning words."

When children are born they feel, but they do not speak. As they grow older they learn to speak, but often not about their feelings. Dr. Kempler discusses the importance of expressing and understanding the emotional meaning that accompanies many communications.

Four-year-old Adam had a vocabulary of several hundred words. Yet one bedtime Adam was speechless. His father had just tucked in the boy's younger brother and kissed him goodnight. Then he passed Adam with a friendly but cursory "G'night." Adam began to cry.

"What's the matter, Adam?" Father asked. Adam just turned toward the wall.

"Hey, fella, what's the trouble?" his father said. After a minute of silence, Adam said, "I'm cold."

"Pull up your blanket. You can do that." But Adam continued sobbing.

Getting annoyed, Father said, "Oh, c'mon now. Stop being such a helpless baby. Now stop that crying. Pull up your blanket and go to sleep!"

Father stalked out angrily, and Adam cried himself to sleep.

Adam's masked message was missed. He could not express in words his need for Father's goodnight kiss, and his parent could not decipher his behavior. Adam probably concluded, "Just as I feared. Daddy likes my brother better than me." The consequences, such as estrangement from father and increased jealousy toward brother, may injure Adam's developing personality. The injury is not serious when the occurrence is singular or infrequent, but it may emerge years later as a vague, nagging feeling of unworthiness.

A child's messages are not intentionally masked. The verbal art of self-expression must be learned.

Even a retarded child can learn words. Combine education with a youngster's natural desire to imitate his talking parents, and it would seem there is nothing left for parents to do about their offspring's use of language.

This is not so. Teaching a child the art of personal speech—a far cry from merely learning words—is, unfortunately, a lost talent in many families. If a child does not learn this when young, he is likely to have difficulty in his adult life. This may show up in endless ways, from simple communication problems to severe emotional disabilities.

From *Today's Health*, April 1970, published by the American Medical Association. Reprinted by permission.

Personal speaking means using language to reflect accurately to others not only what is on your mind but what is in your heart—conveying how you feel, what you want, what you need. It means learning to tune in to what you feel, to translate it, and to express it. It means changing the infant's feeding cry to "I'm hungry." In areas such as eating, this is not too difficult. But there are many other subtle yet equally important areas where the art is often overlooked.

Jeanie, age seven, frequently gets up in the morning and says she doesn't feel well enough to go to school. Mother has stopped asking for specifics as to what hurts, since Jeanie's answer is always vague: "I just don't feel good." Sometimes Jeanie cooperates with Mother's wish for details by rubbing her abdomen, saying, "Here." Mother investigates: no fever, no vomiting, no diarrhea, no localized pain. Mother remembers the last time she let Jeanie stay home. By nine A.M. she had recovered completely.

With exasperation, in spite of a slight nagging fear that maybe Jeanie really does have some low-grade disease, Mother takes a stand: "Jean, get dressed right now and go to school. I don't know what you're up to, but you aren't sick. Now get dressed while I fix your breakfast." Jeanie moves slowly and sullenly. After eating very little breakfast, she leaves for school.

Had Jeanie learned the art of personal speech, instead of feigning illness, she might have said, "Mom, I don't feel like going to school today. I'd rather stay home and do things with you. Sometimes it's hard to get up and go to school five days in a row."

If she were eloquent, Jeanie might add, "After all, six-sevenths of my life was spent playing near you, and all of a sudden I spend most of my day away from you. I can't even call you to say hello. I miss you!"

Had she been able to say this, or had Mother been able to hear through Jeanie's ill-contrived complaints, Mother could have sat down on her daughter's bed and replied with something like, "We don't share much time together since you're in school. I miss you, too. Suppose I pick you up after school today and we'll do something together till dinnertime."

The art of personal expression is not a natural consequence of learning words and phrases. It must be taught. In school it is resisted rather than appreciated and encouraged. I recall being taught in an English composition class: Don't start sentences with "I." That pseudo-modest directive may be sophisticated and appropriate for social intercourse and public speaking, but for personal messages it is a disaster. When speaking about yourself, it is sound and sensible to start sentences with "I."

However, teaching your child the art of personal speech is not resolved simply by training him to say "I" at the beginning of sentences. You must help him translate the messages he feels inside.

Some psychologists and psychiatrists accuse parents of not listening to children or of thwarting kids by preventing them from having their say. From my experience as a family psychiatrist, I've concluded this is not so. More often the problem is that parents, not having been taught by *their* parents, do not know how to teach their children the art of personal speech. It is simply overlooked.

Let's see how Adam's bedtime scene might have been enacted: After Father kisses younger brother, he passes Adam with a warm but casual "G'night, Adam," and is on his way out of the bedroom. Adam begins to cry.

"What's the matter, Adam?" Father asks.

Adam turns to the wall. Father walks over, sits down on the bed, and puts his hand on Adam.

"Hey fella, what's the trouble?" Adam moves as if he is annoyed at being touched.

"I must have done something terribly wrong, but I don't know what it is," Father says. Adam remains silent. They sit together a while without speaking.

"Okay, Adam, I'm going to leave now. I wish you could tell me what's the matter."

"I'm cold," the youngster whimpers.

Father, since he knows full well that Adam can pull up his blanket if he is cold, translates Adam's plea: "Oh, I see. Well, I'd like to tuck you in and kiss you goodnight if you don't mind. That's really what you wanted to tell me, wasn't it?"

Father pulls up the blanket and kisses the boy goodnight. He doesn't need Adam's answer. He knows he is right. He has, in addition to providing Adam with a satisfying experience, given him an important lesson in the art of personal speaking.

Infants and young children intuitively express their needs nonverbally, by crying, hitting, snuggling. To learn to translate and communicate their needs through words requires copious parental coaching. Particularly valuable are direct, personal experiences between parent and child.

Now that she and Mother are almost the same size, Sandy frequently borrows her mother's clothes. She takes them without asking, and Mother gets furious. "Leave my things alone," Mother yells. "If you want something of mine, ask for it. Don't just take it." Mother cannot hear Sandy's hidden message which says, "I like you and want to be like you. But I dare not be obvious about it."

Mother, of course, has a right to her privacy, and it would be well for Sandy to learn to be more open about her needs. But when Sandy cannot speak her personal message and Mother cannot detect it, who is to help them discover that the subject really is personal needs and feelings, not bits of cloth?

Then there are the countless schoolboys who wait for Dad to come home, ostensibly to get help with their homework. These boys are asking for a first-hand experience from their number one idol, but they cannot speak their message of love and admiration. Part of the message is "I'd like to do something with you, Dad, that is part of my world. I need you to be interested in me in order to build my confidence." Rarely, if ever, is the subject actually arithmetic or geography.

Or consider this case. It's 7:30 P.M., any night. Mary, age 14, is on the phone. Her mother calls, "Mary, time to do the dishes." No answer. Mother goes to Mary's room and repeats it. "In a minute, Mom." Thirty minutes later, Mother again goes to Mary, who is still on the phone, and says, "Mary, now!" Mary, with a look of disgust, tells her girl friend, "I gotta do the dishes *right now*. Like they'll *rot* if I don't do them this minute. You know. . . ."

She hangs up and loiters around her room until her mother comes in a third time saying, "Must we go through this every night? Can't you just do the dishes and be done with it so we don't have to hassle about them constantly?"

Mary replies angrily, "I'll get them done. I always do, don't I? Why must it always be *right now*?"

The typical teen-ager's most misunderstood masked message, expressed defiantly or with sullen, smoldering dawdling, is "I don't want to!"

Unfortunately, too many parents of adolescents take the message literally, The real message, hidden behind a thin covering of bravado, goes something like this: "Mom and Dad, I must oppose you. I must try you every way that I can. I do this not out of meanness or wantonness; I am neither bad nor incorrigible. It is the only way I know how to test my wings as I prepare for adulthood.

"Although it is a very difficult time for me, I must not ask your help. I do not expect you to like it or cater to it, but I would like you to remember all you have invested in me and have confidence in that. Stop me when you must, but don't ask me to stop. Oppose what I do whenever you must, but don't ask that I like you for it. Our love must be strong enough to let us be enemies for a while."

Can parents whose masked messages were not heard during their childhood learn to hear their own children now? It is not easy, but it is unquestionably worth the effort, for this understanding holds the promise of new and deeply satisfying experiences with your children.

Begin with the recognition that learning to express oneself is a far cry from learning words. Know that it is necessary to attach the appropriate words to the feelings within us. Know that once they are attached, it is still a slow and complex task to explain those words so that other people can plumb the full personal depth of their message. Finally, know that the task is a lifelong challenge for all of us, regardless of whether our masked messages are unveiled early or late in life.

When your child hits or cries or says something that seems a bit absurd, ask yourself, "what's the message?" before you label him "brat." If you can't figure out the message, try imagining what it would be like to be in his place right then. What would you be saying? If you come up with some answer, check it out by voicing it.

Suppose you can't figure or feel it out. Then tell your youngster that you'd like to know what he's trying to say. Ask him for help. Hold him for a moment at this point; it may bring the message into clear focus. But don't do it as a tactic; obvious falseness alienates.

What if you're just plain annoyed? If that's what you are at that moment, don't convert it to guilt feelings. Just tell him you're annoyed. It's only half a message, but it's better than none.

The whole message may be, "I want very much to be a good parent, and I wish I could always understand you. But right now I can't"; or "I don't want to bother right now, and as foolish as it may seem, I'm angry with you."

Sometimes we are so angry we only express the last four words. Sometimes we don't even use the words; we just act mad. That's the same dilemma the child faces. It's better for both of you to express exasperation verbally than to act it out silently or try to hide it.

Trying to hide frustration and anger is an added, unnecessary danger. It delays the time of reckoning. And when that time comes, the message will be badly distorted because it has been squeezed into your storehouse of unpleasant memories.

Wouldn't it be better, you might ask, to avoid anger toward children and choose an alternative such as expressing the exasperation to a spouse or neighbor?

No, absolutely not. That's depriving your child. He needs to learn from you how to express frustration as a healthy adult. Crying, without the accompanying verbal message, isn't enough, and hitting is socially unacceptable. He needs to observe your behavior as an example.

Speak—shout if necessary—your message of frustration to your child. How thoroughly and honestly it is expressed matters more than how carefully the message is presented or how well he is able to understand the words.

When you do not understand your child's message and you do not feel resentful, it is sufficient to tell him simply, "I don't understand what you are trying to say to me. I'm sorry." If his frustration continues, let it. Though he doesn't learn the art of expression on that particular occasion, access to crying or raging bathes the wound and diminishes psychological damage. If you can't bear to witness his anguish, send him to his room to finish.

Don't try to make up for your inability to understand your child's messages. Don't cater or be oversolicitous. Try to listen for messages, not words.

11. The Impact of Visual Media on Personality
Clarissa Wittenberg

"...filmed or televised images have tremendous power...."

Imitation is one of the most important ways that children learn, and with the number of hours children spend in front of a television set, real questions can be raised about how important an influence television programs are. Ms. Wittenberg reports on a series of research projects conducted by Dr. Albert Bandura that reflect on those questions.

One of the fundamental means by which human behavior is acquired and modified involves vicarious learning. Both children and adults learn modes and standards to a great extent by observing the behavior of others. A great deal of attention has been focused in this country upon the television industry as this fact has become more and more apparent. In addition to television, motion pictures, books, and other reading material are visual media effective in pro-

From *The Mental Health of the Child,* June 1971. Public Health Service Publication No. 2168. Reprinted by permission.

ducing vicarious, as opposed to directly experienced, learning. The variety represented by television alone demonstrates the difficulty of making simple judgments about the effect on the viewer. The variations in viewers and the surrounding circumstances in which they see the television again points out the complexity. The most insistent public focus on TV has been with regard to violence and its part in the violence observed in our society. An investigation of violence per se seems less likely to yield information on the underlying process of influence than is the study of the visual media with regard to its impact on learning in general. Dr. Albert Bandura has spent over ten years studying the effects of such media upon children and adults in a variety of situations. His work yields the definite finding that such media are powerful methods of teaching and important sources of influence, but that many lessons may be taught and they may not be the obvious ones. It becomes obvious that the environment in which the media is viewed is very important.

This research has demonstrated the stimulation of aggressive behavior by the viewing of aggressive acts on a screen. Variables have then been explored with attention given to the characteristics of the model and the attributes of the observer, and the consequences accompanying the demonstrated patterns of behavior. The difference between acquisition and spontaneous performance of aggressive acts has been examined. Further research has been done with the use of the visual media as therapeutic tools to relieve longstanding and serious phobias and to improve the social adjustment of withdrawn children. The common thread throughout the research of Doctor Bandura and his associates is the concept of observational learning and the effectivity of the modeling process.

Doctor Bandura states that research bearing on modeling processes demonstrates that, unlike the relatively slow process of trial-and-error learning, patterns of behavior are rapidly acquired observationally in large segments or in their entirety. The extent of this form of learning can be seen in children's play when they reproduce parental behavior, including the appropriate mannerisms, voice inflections, and attitudes. This process in a more general way is referred to as "identification."

Doctor Bandura became involved in this subject in 1958 when he conducted, with Richard Walters, research on the family conditions which gave rise to extreme aggression in children. The focus was the adolescent from the "good home" who became antisocial and delinquent. Although a great deal of research had been done about the effects of poor and adverse family and social conditions, not much had been done to explain the reasons why affluent young men were becoming delinquent and antisocial. Families were selected who looked well integrated and socially well adjusted, but whose children were being followed by the probation department in the San Francisco area. A matched control group was also interviewed. Two central factors emerged. Many parents of the delinquent boys were models for antisocial attitudes and aggressive behavior despite their smooth social exterior. A second pattern was that the parents, especially the fathers, often would not permit aggression towards themselves but would encourage and reward their son in fights outside the family or defend the boy's right to "raise—." In sharp contrast, the nondelinquent boys were encouraged more to defend themselves with their ideas or in the nonphysical spheres. Aggression of a physical type was consistently discouraged through nonpunitive means in these families. These boys, who were not on probation, had been taught through example and precept a different way of solving their interpersonal problems than the aggressive boys.

Another incident occurred that dramatized the influence of demonstration or modeling. In 1961 the San Francisco *Chronicle* reported that a boy had been seriously knifed during a reenactment of a switchblade fight the boys had seen the previous evening on a televised rerun of the James Dean movie, *Rebel Without a Cause.* This was a vivid illustration of the imitation of film stimulation and stirred considerable speculation. The form of the aggression had been so clearly shaped by the film that it gave rise to the idea that aggression viewed through pictorial media may be influential in shaping the form of aggression when the person is in a provocative situation. The importance of the visual media in stimulating or instigating aggression also became a focus on this research.

Transmission of Aggression

One set of experiments was designed in 1961 to determine the extent to which aggression could be transmitted to children through exposure to aggressive adult models. In this early experiment children observed an adult who exhibited relatively unusual forms of physical and verbal aggression towards a large inflated "Bobo" doll. A second group watched a very subdued and inhibited model. The control group saw no model at all. Half the children in each experimental condition saw models of the same sex and half observed the opposite sex. Later the children were mildly frustrated by having toys restricted for their use and then their behavior was recorded in a new situation where they could behave either aggressively or nonaggressively. The results showed that exposure to aggressive models heightened the children's aggressive responses to subsequent frustration in new settings in which the model was absent.

In 1963 this investigation was extended by Bandura, Ross and Ross. The effects of real life models and filmed models were compared. The children in this project, as well as in many of these studies, were drawn from the Stanford University Nursery School. In this study they ranged from 35 to 69 months of age, with a mean age of 52 months. There were 48 boys and 48 girls who took part. Two adults, a male and female, served as models. A female experimenter conducted the study with all of the children. A "Bobo" doll was again used as the subject of aggression.

One group of children observed real models in the room with them, behaving aggressively toward the doll. A second group saw a film of the same models performing the same acts. A third group saw a cartoon of an aggressive figure. The control group was not exposed to any of these stimulations. Again half of the children saw models of their same sex. These children had previously been rated in terms of their normal aggressive behavior by their nursery school teachers and they were matched to the control group on this basis.

The children who saw the real life aggression were asked into a room and invited to join a game. The child was shown a table with a variety of activities. The model also worked at a small table doing tinker toys. Then the model turned to the "Bobo" doll and kicked it about the room, sat on it and punched it in the head, pummeled it, and hit it with a mallet among other things. The sequence of acts was repeated three times and was accompanied by verbally aggressive comments such as "Sock him in the nose * * * ," "hit him down * * * ," "Pow." These acts were not those usually performed spontaneously by children with a "Bobo" doll. Although the doll is designed to be hit, the usual play involves poking it or trying to knock it over rather than "beating it up." The main interest of the research was not whether the children hit the doll but whether they adopted the unusual modes of aggression demonstrated by the adults.

The movie sequence was identical except it was presented on film.

The cartoon sequence was presented in a TV console and the experimenter introduced it as a color TV cartoon program. A film was then presented of a female model costumed as a cat performing against a brightly colored and fantastic setting. A title and a picture of a stage introduced the production. The cat figure then performed the same acts with the "Bobo" doll. Music was played accompanying the film.

Following the exposure, the children were tested for the amount of imitative and nonimitative aggression in a different experimental setting without the presence of models.

In order to clearly differentiate the exposure and test situations, subjects were tested for the amount of imitative learning in a different experimental room which was set off from the main nursery school building.

The children, both control and experimental groups, were mildly frustrated before they were brought to the test room by having the children begin to play with attractive toys and then being told that they were the experimenter's best toys and that she was saving them. The children were then taken to the testing room and the experimenter stayed with them, but did paperwork off to one side.

The testing room contained a variety of toys, some of which could be used for imitative or nonimitative aggressive acts, and others which tend to elicit predominantly nonaggressive forms of behavior. The aggressively oriented toys included a "Bobo" doll, a mallet and pegboard, dart guns, etc. The others included a tea set, crayons and paper, a ball, two dolls, etc. Play material was also arranged in such a way as to eliminate any variations in behavior due to mere placement.

The subject spent 20 minutes in the testing room during which time he was observed through a one-way mirror and his behavior was rated. The 20-minute session was divided into 5-second intervals, and so a subject was scored 240 times. The judges reached high levels of reliability in their scoring. The following response measures were obtained: imitative aggression; partially imitative responses; mallet aggression; sitting on "Bobo" doll; nonimitative aggression; aggressive gunplay.

Results

Exposure to aggressive models increased the probability that subjects will respond aggressively when instigated on later occasions. Further analysis shows that subjects who viewed the real life models do not differ from those who viewed the filmed or TV models in total aggressiveness, but all three experimental groups expressed significantly more nonimitative aggressive behavior than the control subjects.

The exposure to aggressive models is a highly effective method for shaping subjects' aggressive responses. Experimental subjects displayed a high level of imitative physical and verbally aggressive acts whereas control subjects rarely behaved in these novel aggressive ways. Thus exposure to aggressive models not only reduced children's inhibitions over aggressive behavior that they had previously learned, but also taught them new ways of aggressing.

A prediction had been made that imitation is positively related to the reality cues of the model and this was only partially supported. While subjects who observed the real-life aggressive models exhibited significantly more imitative aggression than subjects who viewed the cartoon model, the live and film, and the film and cartoon models increased nonimitative aggression in the children to the same degree. Data indicated that of the three experimental conditions, *exposure to humans on film portraying aggression was the most influential in eliciting and shaping aggressive behavior.*

The Effect of the Sex of the Model

The boys exhibited more total aggression than girls, more imitative aggression, more aggressive gunplay and more nonimitative aggressive behavior. The girls, for instance, were more likely to sit on a "Bobo" doll and refrain from punching it.

Subjects who were exposed to male models as compared to female models expressed significantly more aggressive gunplay. The most marked differences in aggressive gunplay were, however, found between the girls who had been exposed to the female model and males who had observed the male model. The girls who saw the female model tended to reproduce more partially imitative acts than the boys who saw the male model and were more likely to reproduce the larger actions.

The sex of the child and the sex of the model have an effect upon the degree of influence of the models, and this influence is determined in part by the sex appropriateness of the model's behavior.

Another section of this experiment dealt with the possibility of cathartic action upon the viewing of aggressive film material. The subjects were first frustrated and then provided with an opportunity to view an aggressive film following which their overt or fantasied aggression was measured. Many parents and educators encourage hyperaggressive children to participate in aggressive recreational activities, to view highly aggressive TV programs, and to be aggressive in therapeutic settings in order to "discharge" their aggression. Bandura's work and the work of other investigators demonstrate that the provision of aggressive models and the inadvertent reinforcement of aggression which occurs in these situations act to encourage aggressive tendencies rather than dissipating them. On the other hand, providing aggressive children with examples of alternative, constructive ways of coping with frustration can be very successful in helping them modify their destructive behavior patterns. Already frustrated children show more aggressive behavior after viewing live or filmed aggression than do frustrated children who are not shown a film. The filmed aggression *does not* fill their need, nor does it diminish their aggressive tendencies.

The view that social learning of aggression through exposure to aggressive film content is adopted by only deviant children, also finds little support in Doctor Bandura's research. The children who participated in the experiment were all considered normal; yet 88 percent of the subjects in the "Real-Life" and in the "Human Film" condition, and 79 percent of those in the "Cartoon" condition, exhibited varying degrees of imitative aggressive behavior. In assessing the possible influence of televised stimulation on behavior, it is important to distinguish between learning and overt performance. Although children may learn whole patterns of behavior by watching TV, they do not ordinarily perform indiscriminately the behavior of televised characters, even those who they regard as highly attractive. The responses of the parents appear to be very important in discouraging overt imitation. The investigators stress that the behavior is learned, however, even if parental disapproval inhibits it being performed and it may be elicited on future occasions. Indeed, recent research demonstrations show that children will not exhibit disapproved aggression in the presence of the prohibitive adult, but that they are inclined to perform such behavior when the disapproving adult is absent.

Children who had been previously rated as more aggressive than the others by their teachers did not differ in their aggressive reactions in the experimental setting.

The investigators have formulated a theory of social learning of aggression (Bandura and Walters, 1959) that would suggest that most of the responses utilized to hurt or injure others, such as kicking or hitting, were learned as exploratory asocial acts. For instance, the infant who learns to control his legs and kick is exercising and exploring his own movements, but not being aggressive. When frustrated, however, he may call on this response as one that can express his intense feelings, and then the kicking becomes involved in social interaction. On the basis of this theory, it would be predicted that the aggressive responses acquired imitatively, while not necessarily for aggressive goals in the experimental setting, would be utilized to serve such purposes in other social settings. It would also be predicted that children in the experimental settings would use this behavior aggressively more frequently than children in the control groups.

These previously mentioned experiments were primarily designed to measure the extent to which children learn by observing the aggressive action of adults. A second major question is whether exposure to aggressive models influences the harshness with which people treat others. To study interpersonal expression and aggressive behavior requires studies in which people are provided with opportunities to behave punitively toward another person after viewing aggressive or nonaggressive models. A study conducted in Doctor Bandura's laboratory by Donald Hartman reveals that aggressive models not only foster learning of aggressive behavior, but can also increase interpersonal aggression.

The catharsis hypothesis has generally assumed that viewing aggression reduces aggressive tendencies in observers if they experience anger at the time of exposure, but that it may increase aggression in nonangered viewers. To test this idea, Hartman conducted an experiment that proceeded in the following manner. One group of delinquent adolescents underwent an anger-arousing experience, while a second group had an essentially neutral experience. The boys then observed one of three movies. In the control film two boys engage in an active but cooperative basketball game, whereas in the other two films the boys get into an argument that develops into a fist fight. The instrumental-aggression film focuses on the behavior of the attacker, including his angry facial expressions, flying fists, foot thrusts, and hostile remarks. The pain-cues film focuses almost exclusively on the reactions of the victim as he is pummeled and kicked by his opponent.

Major obstacles arise in the study of interpersonal aggression because a socially significant measure would involve injurious behavior which cannot be used for humane and ethical reasons. This major obstacle has been overcome by several researchers by creating a situation in which one person can administer shocks of differing intensities and durations of his own choosing to another person. However, the electrodes are not connected to the victim so that he in fact does not suffer any pain. After viewing the films, the boys in Hartman's study were provided with opportunities to shock a victim. The intensity and the duration of the shocks administered were recorded.

Boys who had observed either the aggressive acts or the pain-cues films selected significantly higher shock levels, both under angered and nonangered conditions than boys who watched the control film. Moreover, angered viewers behaved more punitively than nonangered viewers following exposure to the aggressive films, a finding that is directly counter to the prediction of the usual catharsis hypothesis. Boys behaved most aggressively when they were angered and witnessed another person beaten severely.

Vicarious Reinforcement and Learning

In 1963 a study was reported by Bandura, Ross and Ross which explored the issue of vicarious reinforcement; that is, the changes in the behavior of observers resulting from witnessing the consequences experienced by others. In this study, nursery school children witnessed a variety of situations. The prime issue was whether or not they viewed an aggressive model being rewarded for his acts. The major finding was that children who witnessed the aggressive model rewarded showed more imitative aggression, and preferred to emulate the successful aggressor than children who observed the aggressive model who was punished. This last group failed to reproduce his behavior and rejected him as a model. Control over aggression was vicariously transmitted to the boys by the administration of negative responses to the model and to the girls by the presentation of socially incompatible examples of behavior.

Interviews with the children at the completion of the experiment disclosed that although children in the aggression-rewarded conditions voiced disapproval while they watched the acts that they nevertheless emulated his behavior on the basis of its success. The key issue was that they admired the power the model gained over reward resources through his reprehensible behavior. The investigators noted that the children stated that physical aggression and forceful confiscation of the property of others is wrong and they criticized the model for doing it. Therefore, when these same children later copied this type of behavior, they can be expected to experience considerable conflict and discomfort. They did not resolve this conflict by praising violence, but tended to do it by criticizing the victim. They viewed the victim as weak or provocative, ungenerous or unsharing, and thereby in a sense "bringing it on himself." In situations where the aggressive model was punished, even when the victim was quite provocative, the victim was not criticized and the aggressor was considered bad. Successful "pay off" of aggression rather than its intrinsic desirability served to stimulate imitation.

The implications of this finding in terms of the attitudinal and behavioral effects of television would indicate that successful hostile aggression would outweigh even the previously established values of right or wrong for the viewer. This study involves only a single aggressive incident that was rewarded or punished. In most televised programs the "bad guys" gain control over important resources and win considerable social and material rewards through aggressive acts, and punishment, if any, is delayed, as Dr. Bandura says, "until the last commercial." Many episodes which are antisocial and "pay off" are viewed before the punishment occurs.

Bandura and his associates find that fear of a punitive or aggressive model is not a necessary factor in identification and adoption of aggressive behavior. The success of the aggressive act rather than the fear of the aggressive agent is seen as more influential. This has relevance to the concept suggested by Freud of "identification with the aggressor," which postulates that a perceived threat by a punitive agent is the primary motivating force in the assumption of aggressive traits.

Social Power, Status and Identification

Although it is often assumed that social behavior is learned and modified through direct reward and punishment of responses, informal observation and studies suggest that the "power" of the individual involved may also be influential. A child who perceives his mother as a prime source of rewards in the family may identify with her rather than with the father who he may see as occupying a subordinate position, and even compete with him for rewards.

A study was devised to set up conditions with nursery school children and female and male models to reproduce possible family constellations of power and reward structures. One of the adults assumed the role of controller of a fabulous collection of toys and offered to go shopping for such highly desirable items as two-wheel bicycles for the children. The other adult served as a competitor, who monopolized the attractive play equipment and left the child out. In a second condition, the child was the recipient of rewards and attention. For half the boys and girls, the male controlled the reward resources simulating a husband-dominant home, and for the remaining children the female model controlled the positive resources as in a wife-dominant home. The two adults exhibited divergent patterns of behavior, and then the imitative behavior of the child was measured.

Models who were seen as having the power to reward elicited twice as much imitative behavior as models who were perceived by the children as possessing no control over the rewarding resources. Power inversions on the part of the male and female models produced cross-sex differences, particularly in girls. It was found a differential readiness existed between boys and girls in the willingness to imitate behavior by an opposite sex model. Boys showed a decided preference for the masculine role, whereas ambivalence and a masculine role preference were widespread among the girls. The investigators suggest that these findings probably reflect both the differential cultural tolerance for cross-sex behavior displayed by males and females, and the privileged status and relatively greater positive reinforcement of masculine role behavior in our society.

The research team further suggests that although failure to develop sex-appropriate behavior has received considerable attention and is often assumed to be established and maintained by concepts of dependency, psychosexual threat and anxiety, external social variables may also be important. For instance, the distribution of the rewarding power within a family may be very important. Although the small child has great contact with his mother, he also has ample time to observe his father's behavior. Also children do not adopt "wholesale" the traits of one model. A child exhibits a relatively novel mix of behavior in his own repertoire.

The makeup of the family constellation is also important. This research shows that in a three-person group, for instance, if one person is denied access to rewards, the others may experience negative evaluations of the rewarding model and thereby decrease his impact as a modeling stimulus. The introduction of each new person and his treatment at the hands of the model may produce new shifts in the relationships.

Reinforcement by Self-Approval

People tend to set for themselves certain standards of behavior and respond to their own actions in self-rewarding and self-punishing ways in accordance with their self-imposed demands. This is a major difference in human and animal learning studies. Even children can decide whether their own performance is creditable or not. Speculation about how children develop these internal standards was transformed into an experiment. The children were given the opportunity to observe models performing, and then permitted to evaluate their attainments according to high or low standards and reward themselves accordingly. It was predicted that children tend to adopt the standards of self-reward exhibited by the models they observed, but that children in the control group who saw no model would have no consistent pattern of self-reinforcement. It was also predicted that the subjects would adopt the self-reinforcement patterns of the same sex model to a greater degree than that of a model of the opposite sex. It was also predicted that children would match the self-reinforcement patterns of adult models more closely than those of peers.

This study reported by Bandura and Kupers had a group of boys and girls from a summer recreation program as subjects. It was designed to be an investigation of the transmission of standards of self-reward. The children ranged from 7 to 9 years in age. Adult and child models performed a bowling game in which they adopted either high achievement standards or a low standard for self-reward. On games in which the models attained their standard, they praised themselves and treated themselves to candy; but when their attainments fell short of their adopted standards, they appeared self-critical. Later, the children who had observed, played the same game alone and the scores for which they rewarded themselves were recorded. The control children saw no models at all.

Children who saw no models or who saw models with low standards tended to reward themselves generously following a mediocre attainment. Children, who saw models set high standards for self-rewards, rewarded themselves sparingly and only when they attained a superior performance. This suggests that the behavior of the models is influential in the development of self-control as well as in the transmission of standards for self-rewards. The children tended to match the patterns for rewards set by the adult models more closely than those set by peer models. The results showed that patterns of self-reinforcement can be acquired imitatively through exposure to models, without the subjects themselves being administered any direct differential reinforcement by external agents.

Another study was devised to further examine the formation of personal standards. In the experiment previously described, the children modeled their own standards after those of the model. It was thought that this was partly because the performance scores had little absolute value and therefore the evaluation of the model served as a primary basis for judging what might constitute an inadequate or superior performance. This study was also designed to see if observers would select models who were similar to themselves in ability and reject those who were markedly divergent. It was predicted that subjects would adopt the self-reinforcement standards of the model whose ability or competence was similar to their own. They would disregard the examples of those whose accomplishments were too different from their own and adopt a more reasonable standard for themselves. The investigators hypothesized that even low or merely adequate performances by adults would be highly regarded, and if a child matched or exceeded the performance of an adult that it would raise his own self-esteem. It was hypothesized that children attaining the achievement level of even an inadequate adult would tend to reward themselves highly.

In this study, groups of 80 boys and 80 girls ranging in age from 8 to 11 years were given a series of tasks and then they were either told that they were successful or not. Then they observed a model displaying competent, superior or inferior performance. The superior model adopted an exceedingly high standard for self-reward, and the inferior model set a low one. The children assigned to a control group saw no models at all.

Results showed that children who observed inferior models tended to adopt lower standards for themselves and rewarded themselves more generously than children who were exposed to more competent models with higher standards. Children tended to scale down the achievements of the adults to a lower standard more commensurate with their own abilities.

This experiment also examined whether children's willingness to adhere to high standards is affected by their prior success or failure experiences. Children who have had failure experiences tended to reward themselves less than their successful counterparts, a finding that was most noticeable among children exposed to the inferior model. Control subjects who had experienced failure displayed a higher rate of self-reinforcement at lower levels of performance than did children who experienced past success. The investigators suggest that under some circumstances self-gratification may primarily serve a therapeutic rather than a self-congratulatory function. The same principle is seen when a person "treats" himself to a play or a special dinner to help himself over a difficult experience.

Another finding was that boys and girls differed significantly in the frequency of verbal self-praise, but not in the incidence and magnitude of self-administered material rewards, such as candy. Boys were more generous in commending themselves for equivalent achievements.

Contiguity and Other Factors

It is often assumed that the occurrence of imitative or observational learning is based on the observer experiencing reinforcing consequences. This does not account for the learning of imitative behavior when the observer does not perform the model's responses during the process of acquisition, and where neither rewards nor punishments are given to either model or observer. It is suggested that in these cases a contiguity theory can best account for observational learning. Contiguity means that events or objects in a series or close to each other in time or space become associated. When an observer then witnesses a model exhibit a sequence of responses the observer acquires through the principle of contiguous association of sensory events certain perceptual and symbolic responses that cue other responses even after time has elapsed.

Bandura states that the acquisition of matching responses may take place through contiguity, whereas the reinforcements administered to a model exert their major influence on the performance of imitatively learned responses. Several of Bandura's studies have shown that even children who do not reproduce the aggressive behavior of models were able to describe the behavior in great and accurate detail. When these nonperformers were rewarded they would readily reproduce the modeled behavior. However, these children usually failed to reproduce the entire behavior pattern and this indicates that factors other than exposure to models or contiguity influence response acquisition. It appears that observers attend to models that are most relevant to them. Both prior experience and the distinctive qualities of the modeling example are important in determining the attention paid to it by the observer.

Social behavior is generally highly complex and composed of a large number of different behavior units combined in a particular manner. Bandura points out that such responses are produced by combinations of previously learned components which themselves may be intricate units. The rate of acquisition of new responses will then be partly determined by the extent to which the necessary components are contained in the repertoire of the observer. For instance, small children may be more able to reproduce motor behavior than verbal behavior.

Learning—Pain, Fear, and Other Emotional States

Studies of vicarious emotional learning show that people develop emotional reactions to certain places, people, or events through observing others undergoing emotional experiences. However, the findings reveal wide individual differences in the degree to which people are affected by the emotional arousal of others. Bandura and Rosenthal reasoned that observers who are easily susceptible to emotional reactions and who are emotionally aroused at the time of exposure to the affective expressions of others will show the strongest emotional learning. To test the hypotheses, adults observed a model performing a task when a buzzer sounds and then the model feigns an expression of pain as though he had been shocked. Throughout this period, the observers' physiological responses were measured to determine the degree to which the formerly neutral buzzer had taken on negative emotional value for the observers as a result of the other person's adverse experiences.

Prior to the emotional conditioning phase of the study, observers experienced different degrees of emotional arousal produced both physiologically
and psychologically through the administration of epinephrine, a sympathetic
stimulant. Before the study began all subjects completed the Taylor Manifest
Anxiety Scale to provide a measure of their general susceptibility to emotional
arousal.

The results show that the observer's level of emotional arousal is a significant determinant of vicarious emotional learning. Observers who experienced
either very low or very high arousal displayed the weakest vicarious learning of
emotional responses, whereas those who were under moderate arousal were
affected most. Interviews conducted with the adults after the experiment was
completed disclosed that those in the high arousal groups neutralized the emo-
tion-arousing situation by diverting their attention from the model's distressing
cues and by conjuring up positive or relaxing thoughts. Further study of these
cognitive activities may throw light on how people insulate themselves against
the distressing experiences of others. In this experiment some subjects felt extremely empathic with the model and others derived considerable satisfaction
from witnessing pain being inflicted upon the model.

Therapeutic Applications of Modeling Procedures

Research in this area has shown the potential of modeling influences for
changing people's attitudes, behavior, and even their personal standards of self-
evaluation. It is also a potent means of treating powerfully charged patterns
such as phobias and fears of long standing. One experiment, reported in 1967
by Bandura, Grusec, and Menlove, treated children who were extremely afraid
of dogs. During the course of treatment, the phobic children who observed a
bold peer-model handle dogs comfortably and appropriately, lost their fears.

After being referred by their parents, the children were given standardized
performance tests, on the basis of which 24 boys and 24 girls, ranging in ages
from 3 to 5 years, were selected.

The initial selection test included a graded sequence of tasks which involved
increasingly intimate interactions with a dog. Initially, the investigators brought
the children into a room where a cocker spaniel was confined in a modified
playpen. Later, tasks were required which ranged from walking up to and looking at the dog, to finally climbing into the pen with the dog, petting her,
scratching her, and then remaining alone with the dog in the room.

The children were then assigned to one of the following treatments: a
modeling-positive-context where a fearless peer model exhibited progressively
bold interaction with a dog in the midst of an enjoyable partylike atmosphere;
a modeling-neutral-context where the subjects observed the same type of brave
behavior modeled, but in a neutral atmosphere; an exposure-no-model condition
(here the children saw the dog, but with the model absent); a positive-context
group which participated in the party, but were never exposed to either the dog
or the model.

The day after the treatment series was completed the children were tested
with the experimental animal; then about 1½ hours later, with an unfamiliar
white mongrel. The dogs had been tested prior to the experiment, and it was

established that they were about the same in terms of activity level and attractiveness. Half the children were tested with the familiar animal first, and then with the unfamiliar white mongrel; for the remainder, the sequence was reversed.

A month later a followup evaluation was done, and the children were again tested to determine the stability of the treatment effects, as manifested by the children's willingness to interact fearlessly with the dogs. The two groups of children who observed the peer model interact fearlessly with the dog, achieved and retained substantial reduction in their fears of dogs. In an effort to minimize the cognitive aspects, all the children were informed that the test animals were harmless. After the experiment was over, the children were told that while most dogs were friendly, before petting an unfamiliar dog they should ask the owner. This was done to reduce indiscriminate acts by the children toward strange dogs.

The effect of the modeling was obvious; the atmosphere, whether partylike or not, had a minor effect, if any.

The investigators speculate that several factors are involved in the extinction or disappearance of the avoidant behavior. One is simply that as the child acquires more information about dogs and about contact with dogs, he becomes less fearful. The nonoccurrence of anticipated adverse consequences to the model, plus the pleasure the model has from contact with the dog, may help extinguish the fear reaction as well.

Treatment of Dog Phobia through Filmed Modeling

Another experiment was done (Bandura and Menlove, 1968) with children who were seriously fearful of dogs. One group was shown a movie which demonstrated how a single model would display progressively less fearful interactions with a dog, as in the preceding experiment. Another group observed a movie which showed boys and girls of varying ages interacting positively with a variety of dogs of different sizes and dispositions. Children in the control group were shown movies with no canine characters.

Results showed that children who observed approach behavior which resulted in no adverse effects to the model, displayed enduring and generalized reductions in their own concerns about dogs. Controls showed no change. Comparison of the final step achieved (i.e., staying with a dog alone) by children who had seen the single model and those who had seen the movie with many models showed that the latter approach was superior. However, although modeling was equally effective regardless of the severity of the children's phobic behavior, those who manifested a wide variety of fears benefited somewhat less from the multiple modeling technique than children who had fewer fears.

The control children were shown the multiple model film after the main experiment was completed. They were markedly more able to handle dogs after this.

The investigators found here that the symbolic portrayal is less powerful than live demonstrations. A single model seen live is more effective than a single model shown in a movie. However, a movie can be made more powerful by using multiple models and a wider variety of objects than it is usually practical to provide live.

Snake Phobia Project

This project, conducted by Bandura, Blanchard, and Ritter, was carried out with adolescent and adult subjects who were terrified of snakes. In the area of California where Stanford is located, snakes are prevalent enough to seriously limit the life choices of any adult who is severely frightened by snakes. For instance, it would mean he couldn't be in any job where he would be required to inspect houses, read meters, show real estate, do plumbing, or any activity where he might be out of doors or in basements. He would be limited as to the location of his home and be largely unable to participate in many popular local sports, such as hiking or camping.

Fear of snakes is considered by psychologists to be a relatively stable fear and for that reason is often used in laboratory experiments.

The subjects ranged in age from 14 to 60 years of age. Some of the phobias had existed for 15 to 20 years. In the initial phase of the experiment, the participants were administered a behavioral test that measured the strength of their avoidance of snakes. In addition, they completed a comprehensive fear inventory. This inventory was then available for determination later to determine if reduction in anxiety about snakes brought about other changes.

The cases were individually matched on the basis of their avoidance behavior and assigned to one of four conditions. One group participated in a symbolic modeling treatment where they would run for themselves a film depicting young children, adolescents, and adults engaging in progressively more threatening situations and interactions with a large (about 4-feet long) king snake. The subjects were taught to be relaxed during the film. They were told to stop the film when scenes made them anxious, reverse it to the beginning, and watch it over. They were asked to attempt to achieve deep relaxation at the same time. They were to view the threatening scene repeatedly until it was neutralized for them.

The second group, receiving live modeling with guided participation, watched a model handle a snake in increasing proximity until it was wrapped around him. The subjects were then aided in performing with the snake. The model held the snake and had the subject touch it, stroke it, and then gradually hold it until anxieties about contact were gone. Then the subject and the model performed the tasks together until the clients were able to hold the snake in their laps, to let it crawl around, and finally to retrieve it.

The third group received a form of desensitization treatment. Deep relaxation was paired with imagined scenes of interactions with snakes. As in other conditions, the treatment was continued until the clients' anxieties had disappeared or until the maximum time of 6 hours allotted had passed. This time limit was imposed upon all groups.

Subjects in the control condition participated in the behavioral and attitudinal assessments without receiving any intervening treatment.

In the assessment phase, all initial tests were readministered. In order to test the generality of extinction effects, half the clients in each of the conditions were tested with the now familiar brown-striped king snake and then with an unfamiliar crimson-splotched corn snake that appeared strikingly different. The rest of the groups saw the snakes in reverse order.

The subjects were asked to look at, touch, and hold a snake with bare and gloved hands; to remove the snake from its cage, let it loose in the room, and then replace it in the cage; to hold it within 5 inches of their faces, and finally to tolerate the snake in their laps while they held their hands passively at their sides. Before and during these tests clients rated the intensity of their anxiety on scales.

Control subjects remained unchanged in their ability to handle the snake. The subjects who had symbolic modeling and desensitization had substantial reductions in phobic behavior, and *live modeling combined with guided participation proved to be an unusually powerful treatment that eliminated snake phobias in virtually all subjects (92 percent)*. The modeling procedures not only extinguished avoidance responses of long standing, but they also neutralized the anxiety-arousing properties of the phobic objects. Both of the modeling treatments achieved marked decrements in anticipatory and performance anxiety. Although subjects who had received desensitization treatment also experienced less emotional arousal when approaching a snake, the magnitude of their fear reduction was significantly less than that shown by their counterparts in the modeling conditions.

It was found that attitude changes toward snakes occurred. The more potent the treatment and the more changed the subjects' ability to handle the snake, the greater the positive change in attitude.

In addition, other fears were affected by the removal of the snake phobias. Fear of other issues was relieved in proportion to the potency of the treatments employed. For instance, live modeling with subject participation effected widespread fear reductions, not only related to animal anxieties, but also in relation to a variety of threats involving both interpersonal and nonsocial events. The investigators note that this seems to involve two different processes. The first involves generalization of extinction effects from treated stimuli to related anxiety sources. In other words, being relieved of one serious fear makes a person generally less fearful and more able to cope realistically with other concerns. The second entails positive reinforcement of a sense of capability. Having successfully overcome a phobia that had plagued them for most of their lives, subjects reported new confidence that they could conquer other problems and successfully deal with other anxiety-arousing situations.

A 1-month followup assessment revealed that the beneficial changes produced in behavior, attitudes, and emotional responsiveness were effectively maintained. The clients also displayed evidence that the behavior improvements had been carried over from the therapeutic to the real-life situations. They were able to hike, garden, and even help frightened friends or children overcome fear of snakes.

It is the conviction of these investigators that any type of phobic disorder can be successfully treated by this method with considerable success. Subsequent experiments show that information alone does not contribute to therapeutic change. It was primarily through a combination of demonstration, information, guided performance, and the control over observational experiences that this success was achieved.

Other snake phobia treatment experiments have been done with children as subjects, and these have been equally successful.

A slightly different type of therapeutic program was developed by Robert O'Connor working with Doctor Bandura to improve the social behavior of withdrawn children in a nursery school setting. A group of withdrawn children was shown films of children playing together and having a very good time. Another group, as controls, was shown a movie about Marineland, instead. The group of withdrawn children, who had seen the movie designed to help them overcome their social inhibitions, showed demonstrable improvements in social interactions; those who had seen the other film showed no change in their behavior.

Conclusions

There is little doubt that filmed or televised images have tremendous power to shape attitudes and behavior. That this deserves investigation can hardly be questioned when we realize the almost universal contemporary exposure to TV. The complexity of the problem and the successful study of TV and movies are best approached by isolating factor after factor, and then painstakingly evaluating the results. These studies are even more striking when it is clear that they, for the most part, deal with the impact of single incidents with relatively little reinforcement, whereas the average commercial-viewing fare is repetitive and often highly glamorized. The multiple violent technique demonstrated by a wide variety of relatively unpunished people on TV can be expected to be highly effective in teaching, and even in eliciting violent and aggressive behavior in the viewers. On the other hand, there is the same potential for influencing viewers toward positive action and more constructive methods of problem solving. Unfortunately some of the problem-solving forums that are televised, such as the U.N. in critical debates, are repetitious, monotonous, lacking in the pace and focused force of the usual programming, even though there is no denying their importance. Television can contribute to the dissemination of information and be highly influential in developing awareness. However, this research points out that, at times, new information without some guide as to action can arouse increased anxiety. The stream of information about slums and racial tensions without constructive proposals may illustrate this phenomenon.

Since people can imitate more successfully acts that are within their own range, they may imitate the more direct acts rather than the more abstract ones. This is likely to be especially true of children who, for instance, are more likely to have extensive physical vocabularies than verbal ones.

Doctor Bandura's research has dealt with the simpler units of behavior, and he indicates that he feels that more research should be done in terms of subtle factors. Physical violence is not the only kind of destructive act and, perhaps, even more benign than some types of interactions between people. For example, the portrayal of racial prejudice, the dramatizing and romanticizing of poor marital interactions, lying, and cheating may be more important than the number of fist fights and murders that are seen. In addition, Dr. Bandura states:

All the laboratory studies that I have reported deal with the immediate impact of a single exposure to aggression on the viewer's attitude and conduct. While the questions about immediate effect have been clarified to some extent, we need much more research on the cumulative impact of television, and the way in which the medium combines with other beneficial or adverse influences in the shaping of people's thoughts and actions.

He also points out that results of recent studies of therapeutic applications of modeling show that such influences can produce generalized and enduring effects.

Another factor is the number of people exposed to essentially the same stimulation. The same visual images are seen by people who ordinarily would not come into contact with the same influences. The cultural spread is much larger than ever before in history. Certainly, an unprecedented audience all over the world witnessed the Apollo 11 walk on the moon.

This body of research points up the fallacies in several popular ideas. One is that violence only affects those who are already violent or deviant and involved in aggression. This has not been borne out. All viewers tend to be affected. Normal children also learn and are encouraged to perform aggressive acts by viewing them under certain circumstances. Another idea is that if parents instill in their children adequate standards of what is right or wrong, the violence they see will "wash over them." It was clearly demonstrated that even where children can label behavior as bad or wrong, if it was successful, they may imitate it and the conflicts would be resolved more often by a reevaluation downward of the worth or the role of the victim. Whether or not the observed aggressive acts are successful becomes more important than the moral value of these aggressive acts.

Perhaps the most prominent idea which has been questioned is that of catharsis. There is no evidence that viewing violence, at least in most forms, dissipates aggressive drives and makes a person more healthy. In fact, it has been demonstrated that a frustrated viewer watching violence would become less inhibited and more likely to act on violent impulses.

The difference of sex roles and the impact of male and female models have been briefly discussed and seem important. Clearly, our society works toward helping girls inhibit aggression and to enhance masculine roles at the same time. The boys are given more latitude towards aggressive expression and less toward the emulation of any feminine traits. Still the effects cannot be oversimplified, as can be seen in the new phenomenon of unisex clothes and the girls who picket, swear, and attack the police; and the boys who embrace nonviolence even to the point of choosing prison over the army. What part in this was played by TV is not fully understood. This is the generation, however, that is often referred to as the "TV generation" and one of the first groups to have been exposed to its influence during the entire span of their lives. Doctor Bandura points out:

> It is evident that observers do not function as passive videotape recorders which indiscriminately register and store all modeling stimuli encountered in everyday life.

The tremendous prices commanded by advertising time on TV would alone testify to the power that both the industry and the public attribute to it.

Learning often takes place in a neutral setting and even with strict prohibitions, and then acts are later effectively performed. The police recruit learns to shoot on a range, the army enlistee at a camp. Later they shoot people. Undoubtedly parents can have a considerable effect on their children's activities, either by monitoring what is seen or by encouraging or discouraging imitation. This research shows, too, that the learned behavior may still be retained. However, it will take more to break down a parental prohibition if it is firmly expressed on the part of the parent than if no intervention is attempted.

Many issues, such as moral and personal achievement standards, often considered the province of the parent, school, and church are now being directly and powerfully influenced by other sources, such as TV. Certainly, censorship seems a limited answer. It is doubtful, for instance, that merely banishing cigarette commercials from TV would have been as effective as the antismoking campaign has been. It may be that the key lies in the presentation of a broader variety of ideas and more objective information.

12. Reach, Touch, and Teach
Terry Borton

"Good teachers... have always responded to the emotional side of their students' lives...."

Students in school are expected to think, and teachers help them to do so. They also feel, but that is less frequently a source of concern to the teacher. Borton discusses a new approach in education that does focus on feelings.

There are two sections to almost every school's statement of educational objectives—one for real, and one for show. The first, the real one, talks about academic excellence, subject mastery, and getting into college or a job. The other discusses the human purpose of school—values, feelings, personal growth, the full and happy life. It is included because everyone knows that it is important, and it ought to be central to the life of every school. But it is only for show. Everyone knows how little schools have done about it.

In spite of this, the human objectives describe the things all of us cite when we try to remember what "made a difference" in our school careers: the teacher who touched us as persons, or the one who ground out our lives to polish our intellects; the class that moved with the strength and grace of an Olympic team, or the dozens of lessons when each of us slogged separately toward the freedom of 3 o'clock. What we learned, and what we became, depended to a significant degree on how we felt about ourselves, our classmates, and our teachers. The schools were right—the human purposes *were* important. But with the exception of those teachers who were so rare we never forgot them, the schools did little to put their philosophy into practice.

Recently, however, a variety of programs have begun to build curricula and teaching methodology that speak directly to the human objectives. These programs, stemming both from within the schools and from various branches of psychology, point the way to a school practice which not only recognizes the power of feelings, but also combines academic training with an education directly aimed at the student's most important concerns. Schools may soon be explicitly teaching students such things as how to sort out and guide their own psychological growth, or increase their desire to achieve, or handle their aggressive instincts in nonviolent forms.

The new impetus has a variety of names: "psychological education," "affective," "humanistic," "personological," "eupsychian," "synoetic." Some of these names are a bit bizarre, and none has yet gained wide acceptance. But taken together their presence indicates a growing recognition that in the world's present state of social and moral turmoil, the schools' traditional second objective can no longer be for show. Riots, poverty, war, student rebellion, swollen mental hospitals, and soaring crime rates have involved an enormous number of people. They have generated a broadening conviction that society is as responsible for the psychological well-being of each of its members as is each individual. And that conviction has created a receptive audience for new kinds of educational critics.

The new critics do not simply attack the schools for their academic incompetence, as did the Rickovers of a decade ago. They are equally concerned with the schools' basic lack of understanding that students are human beings with feelings as well as intellects. Jonathan Kozol has given a gripping sense of the "destruction of the hearts and minds of Negro children" in his *Death at an Early Age*. In *How Children Fail* John Holt has shown that even in the best "progressive" schools, children live in constant fear which inhibits their learning, and Paul Goodman's *Compulsory Mis-Education* has made a powerful case for his contention that "the present school system is leading straight to 1984." The intuitive warnings of these "romantic critics" have been backed up by statistical evidence from the largest survey of education ever conducted, James Coleman's *Equality of Educational Opportunity*. This survey correlates academic achievement with attitudes such as a student's self-concept, sense of control over his fate, and interest in school. The study concludes that these attitudes and feelings are more highly correlated with how well a student achieves academically than a combination of many of the factors which educators have usually thought were crucial, such as class size, salary of teachers, facilities, curriculum.

The pressure to deal more directly with student feelings (increasingly a pressure from students as well as critics) has given rise to dozens of different projects. None of the three examples which I will discuss here has yet reached the size or influence of the giant curriculum centers (such as the Educational Development Corporation) which grew up as a result of the post-Sputnik criticism. But in the long run they may be much more important. For the post-Sputnik curriculum reforms were essentially attempts to find better ways to teach the traditional disciplines of math, science, or social studies—often with the effect of moving the college curriculum into elementary and secondary school orientation toward practical and applied psychology. If expanded, they niques, but also begin to define and develop new curriculum subjects and a new school orientation toward practical and applied psychology. If expanded, they will mark a profound change in American education—hopefully a change toward a more humane educational process, and a more human student.

The project which I co-directed with Norman Newberg, the Philadelphia School Board's specialist in "affective education," is an example of such a curriculum. It is being developed from within the schools—in this case by a group of urban teachers trying to find a philosophy and method which would work with the students they were asked to teach. The program is based on the assumption that every person handles massive amounts of information, and needs to be taught both logical and psychological processes for handling it. Two semester-long courses, one in communications, and one in urban affairs, isolate such processes as symbolization, simulation, dreaming, and de-escalating pressure, and teach them in an explicit fashion. At the same time the classes are designed to tie these processes to the amorphous undercurrent of student concerns for self-identity, power, and relationship.

I dropped into a high school communications class one hot day during last summer's field testing, when the teacher was working on "taxonomy of process," or a way of looking at what, why, and how behavior occurs and changes. The purpose of the class was to show the students a simple technique for analyzing their own habitual forms of processing the world around them, and then to show them how they could develop new responses if they wanted to. The class was working in groups of twos, filling in "What Wheels" for each other. One boy in the back was without a partner, so I joined him, and we agreed that I would make a What Wheel for him, and he would make one for me. I drew a circle, filled in the spokes, and wrote down my first impressions of him: "strong, quick, Afro, shy, bright."

The teacher asked us to read each other our What Wheels, select one adjective which interested us most, and ask our partner to draw a "Why Wheel" to explain *why* that adjective was meaningful to him.

Charlie read me his What Wheel—he was perceptive, as students usually are about teachers. Then I read him mine.

"Why'd you write 'shy'? I ain't shy."

"Well, I just met you, so I can't fill out a whole Why Wheel about it. But when I first sat there, I noticed you looked down at your desk instead of up at me. So I just guessed you were shy with strangers—maybe just with strange teachers."

Charlie took his What Wheel from me and looked at it. "You know, that's the truth. I thought nobody, except maybe my mother, knew that about me, but well, it's the truth anyhow."

The murmur of the class's conversation quieted while the teacher told us how to make up "How Wheels" with our partners. We were supposed to write down the range of actions which would either increase or decrease the trait we had been discussing.

"Aw, man, it would be easy to increase being shy," laughed Charlie. "I just wouldn't look at nobody."

"And decreasing it?"

"I'd look at you like I'm looking at you right now," he said, looking me straight in the eye. "And more than that, I'd look at you like that when you first came in here, Teacher, or white man, I wasn't afraid of you; no reason why I should act like I was."

We talked for a while—about my wheels, about the effectiveness of the what, why, how process questions for looking at behavior, and about school. When the bell rang, we shook hands. "See ya around," he said.

"See ya around," I said.

While many teachers have been experimenting with techniques similar to ours, research psychologists usually have been rather disdainful of the messy problems in the schools. Increasingly, however, psychologists such as David McClelland of Harvard are beginning to work on problems of motivation and attitude in schools. The progression of McClelland's study is a good example of how basic research may be applied to problems in education. McClelland began working on problems of measuring the motivation of rats deprived of food, performed a series of experiments to measure hunger motivation in humans, and then devised a system for measuring "achievement motivation" in men by counting the frequency of its appearance in fantasy images. He defined the need for achievement (n-Ach) as a pattern of thought and fantasy about doing things well, and discovered that those people who had such a pattern were characterized by a preference for moderate risk goals, a desire for immediate feedback on their performance, and a liking for personal responsibility. McClelland reasoned that if a society had a great number of such individuals, the society itself should show outstanding achievement. Twenty years were spent in a mammoth research effort to substantiate his claim that achievement research provided a "factual basis for evaluating theories that explain the rise and fall of civilizations." The next step was to devise educational methods for increasing the achievement motive in people who did not have much of it, and to test out these methods in this country and abroad.

Dr. Alfred Alschuler, director of the Harvard Achievement Motivation Development Project, which is one result of McClelland's research, is in charge of a federally funded five-year research project to assess what factors lead to effective achievement training. The project has devised many classroom techniques for increasing achievement motivation in students, most of them involving experiential learning that takes place in a game situation. I visited one training program for teachers in a nearby city, and sat in on a session that used a contest in making paper airplanes to demonstrate to the teachers how achievement motivation affects their students.

There was a lot of joking around the table, as everyone was a little nervous.

"Now they're going to use the old carrot on us," cracked a little physics teacher sitting on my right.

The head of the math department, an enormous man, smiled broadly, first at the physics teacher, and then at me. "Feeling cut-throat?" he asked.

I didn't say so, but I was, and he knew it. My "n-Ach" was way up. We eyed each other while we set our own quotas for the number of planes we would make.

Dr. Alschuler gave us the start sign. I was making planes feverishly; out of the corner of my eye, I could see the math department head moving more slowly, but doing a better job—the quality control check at the end of the game might go in his favor. The physics teacher was using mass production techniques, making one fold at a time.

At the end of five minutes the game was up, and we were all laughing at the tension it had produced. The physics teacher had more planes than any of us, but his mass production assembly had failed—all the planes were missing one wing. I had the second largest number of planes, but several had sloppy folds and were disqualified.

"Nuts to this," said the physics teacher, "I'm not going to get another heart attack over a bunch of paper airplanes. Next time I'm dropping my quota in half, I'm only going to make six."

I was swearing at myself—I should have been more careful. Next time through the game I would set a slightly lower quota and do a better job.

The math teacher was smiling broadly. He had won.

Later we all talked about our experience in the game and how our own behavior did or did not reflect the characteristics of a high achiever. Did we set moderate risk goals? Did we utilize information on our success or failure? Then we began to dig into the more fundamental value issues that were involved. Suppose that we could use games like the paper plane construction to teach students the characteristics of a high achiever, and through a variety of such exercises could actually train him to think and act as one. Was that a good thing? Did we want to subject our students to the pressure that we had felt? Could we decide that achievement training was good for some students who were not achieving up to our standards and bad for those who were too competitive? On what basis?

Just as researchers are becoming involved in the practical questions of education, so clinical psychotherapy is getting up off its couch and finding ways to add its skill to solving school problems. Dr. Carl Rogers, founder of client-centered therapy, is presently working with Western Behavioral Sciences Institute and a group of Catholic schools to devise ways to use "sensitivity groups" in the schools. (A "sensitivity group" or "T-group" is composed of about a dozen people who meet for the purpose of giving feedback on how each person's behavior affects the other people in the group.) The National Training Laboratory, an associate of the National Education Association, is now running a year-round series of T-groups and related experiences for teachers and administrators. And in San Diego, child psychiatrist Dr. Harold Bissell and educator Dr. Uvalo Palomares have set up the Human Development Training Institute which has written a two-year sequence of lesson plans to improve a primary school child's self-confidence and awareness, and has trained 1000 teachers to use it.

One of the most eclectic approaches in the clinical tradition is the project run by Dr. George Brown of the University of California at Santa Barbara. Brown's project, sponsored by the Ford Foundation through the ebullient Esalen Institute, utilizes many different approaches, but particularly the theories of Gestalt therapy which attempt to get youth in touch with how they are feeling in the "here and now." With such theoretical orientations in their background, the teachers in Brown's project are encouraged to devise their own techniques to integrate academic with affective or emotional learning in order to achieve a more "humanistic education."

I joined the teachers at one of the monthly meetings where they learn about new ideas and share with each other the techniques they have developed.

Gloria Siemons, a pretty first-grade teacher, was describing an exercise that she had first conducted with the entire class, and then used when one child became angry at another. She lined the class up in two rows on the playground, had them find a partner, put their hands up facing each other, and push.

Push they did, laughing all over the field, especially at their teacher, who was being pushed around in a circle by several of the bigger kids.

Later, when two kids got into an argument at recess, Mrs. Siemons simply asked them: "Are you angry now? Would you like to push?"

"Yes, I'm angry. I'm angry at him."

Both agreed to the contest, pushed for a minute as hard as they could, and then collapsed into each other's arms giggling. Their anger was worked out, but without hurting each other.

"What would happen," I asked Mrs. Siemons, "if one kid pushed another hard enough to hurt him?"

"We have a rule about that. 'It's OK to be angry with someone, and it's OK to push, but it's not OK to push him into the rosebush.' "

Good teachers, particularly good first-grade teachers such as Mrs. Siemons, have always responded to the emotional side of their students' lives, and it is precisely this intuitive gift which Dr. Brown is capitalizing on. By systematizing such techniques and relating them to a general theoretical framework, he and the teachers of his staff have begun to generate hundreds of ways to integrate the feelings of students with the regular curriculum taught from kindergarten to high school.

The techniques being developed, the dozens of programs, and the various theories differ in many respects, but they have several features in common. First, and most important, all of them deal in a very explicit and direct way with the student's feelings, interpersonal relations, or values. It is the fact that they are so explicit and direct which sets them apart from the vague protestations that schools have usually made about this area. While schools were concentrating on math, science, or English, they often ignored or actively suppressed feelings. The new programs make what was covert behavior the subject of overt discussion; they make the implicit explicit. They legitimize feelings, clarify them for the student, and suggest a variety of behaviors which he can use to express them. They do so on the assumption that these feelings exert a powerful effect on a student's behavior, both in the present and in the future. If schools want to influence behavior, then it makes sense to deal directly with its major sources, not just with the binomial theorem, the gerund, or the Seventeenth Amendment.

A factor in the new field which often causes misunderstanding is that most of the programs use non-verbal experiences, either through physical expression and involvement, or through art, sculpture, or music. For the most part, this involvement with the non-verbal is not anti-verbal or anti-intellectual. Non-verbal educational techniques are based on the obvious but little-utilized fact that a child learns most of his emotional response patterns at a very young age—before he can talk. His knowledge of love, rejection, anger, and need does not come through words, but through his physical senses—touch, a flushed face, a gnawing in his stomach. Even later, when he begins to talk, the words he learns are "Mama," "doggie," "see"—words for things and actions, not feelings. Indeed, many children seem entirely unable to give a name to their current feelings—they have been taught how to say "I am bad," but not "I feel bad." Education that deals with feelings is often facilitated by skipping over the verbal labels which have been learned relatively late in life, regaining the other senses, and then reintegrating them with verbal thought and new behaviors.

Another common technique which causes confusion is the reliance of many of the programs on games, dramatic improvisations, and role-playing. Again, though those utilizing the techniques believe in fun and use games, few of them are simply advocating "fun and games." Their interest stems from an insight into the learning process of small children. By playing games—house, fireman, office, war—little children learn what it will be like to be an adult, and begin to develop their own style in that role. But our culture provides few such opportunities for older children or adolescents, even though the society is changing so fast that many of the response patterns they learned as a three-year-old may be no longer relevant, or even dangerous. Games and improvisation allow a simulation of the self. While they are real and produce real emotions, their tightly defined limits provide a way to try out new behavior without taking the full consequences which might occur if the same action were performed in ordinary relationships.

There are answers for questions about non-verbal and gaming emphasis, but there are many other questions which the programs raise for which there are no answers. At best, solutions will come slowly, and that is bound to produce tremendous strain in a time when events wait for no one. Many of these problems are already developing. Though Dr. Alschuler at Harvard and Dr. Willis Harmon at the Stanford Research Institute are both engaged in large surveys to find out what techniques and philosophies are presently being employed in the field, there is still no common theoretical base for the programs, and very little research on their effectiveness. The Achievement Motivation Development Project has by far the most extensive research program, and Dr. Alschuler's experience with it has made him feel strongly about the need for additional evidence before program expansion:

> We have very little hard evidence that programs in this new field accomplish much more than natural maturation. We have claims, promises, and fascinating anecdotes. But we should not institute these programs without first using the most sophisticated research techniques we have to improve them and explore their consequences.

In addition to unanswered questions about effectiveness, there are practical limitations to all of the programs. Few have done an adequate job of integrating their material with the usual skills and knowledge that everyone recognizes the schools must continue to teach. No attempt has yet been made to work together with the free-flowing academic programs (such as the Leicestershire movement) which seem natural complements. Though all of the projects I have discussed here stress their responsiveness to student concerns, it is not yet clear how they can do that and yet not be heavily dependent on the skills and personalities of a few teachers like Mrs. Siemons who can both legitimize anger and make the rosebush out of bounds.

Politically, programs with both the potential and the liabilities of these are obvious hot potatoes. It is unclear as yet how projects designed by psychologists will fit in with current efforts toward more community control and what seems to be the resulting concentration on "teaching the basics." Even a mode of politics that is in consonance with the ideals and methods of the new programs is unknown, for the vision they present is often as utopian as that in George Leonard's exciting new book, *Education and Ecstasy*. How to get from here to there without waiting until 2001 is a complex political problem. Suppose, for instance, that a school district decided to adopt an entirely new curriculum and school organization based on the concepts I have been discussing. Would the teachers be able to change? Great care would have to be taken with their feelings and concerns, for not only are they as human as the children, but—as recent events in New York have indicated—they will strike if they feel they are being treated unfairly.

The most fundamental problem, and the one which is likely to get people the most upset, is the ethical question caused by changing the expectations of what schools are for. At present, students go to school to "learn stuff," and though they may expect schools to provide information, they do not expect schools to change them in any fundamental way, or even to offer that opportunity. As long as schools continue to have relatively little explicitly acknowledged impact on the students' values, attitudes, and behaviors, no one is likely to worry much about ethical issues. If schools consciously begin to make important changes in students' lives, people will suddenly become very concerned about what is happening to immature minds that are forced to accept this kind of education for twelve years. They will begin to ask whether there should be compulsory education, or whether students should be free to accept or reject schooling. And they will begin to ask hard questions about what should be taught, and how it should be presented.

If, for instance, all children should be motivated, should they also be "achievement motivated"? At what age? Who decides? And who teaches? What is to stop teachers from working out of their own needs rather than for those of their pupils? Should teachers who share an important confidence have the same legal privilege which a lawyer or a minister has? How can parents and children be assured of the privacy which is their right?

The ethical problems are likely to be compounded by the reporting of the mass media. The new field is peculiarly open to parody ("HARVARD PROF TEACHES AIRPLANE CONSTRUCTION") and to easy association with the exotic and erotic. (*Life* recently stuck a single misleading paragraph on Brown's project into a long article on Esalen Institute. By far the most arresting thing in the article was a two-page picture spread on a nude sensitivity group that had nothing to do with either Brown's project or Esalen.) Sensational publicity is not what the new field needs. It does need the time, the careful research and planning, and the critical reporting which will allow it to grow or decline on its merits. The alternative is a series of fads, created by ignorance and publicity, and death—after a short and enthusiastic life—in disillusionment.

The new programs are too important to allow that to happen. They are delicate, and they are moving into an area which is fundamentally new, so they can be expected to suffer from the attention they attract, to make mistakes and to run into blind alleys. If it takes the big curriculum development corporations a million dollars and three years to build a single course in science or social studies, it will be even more difficult to build a fully developed curriculum in a new field. But the effort should be encouraged. For while it may not be novel to assert that a man's feelings are a crucial determinant of his public behavior and private well-being, there is no question about the novelty and significance of school programs that explicitly educate both the feelings and the intellect. Such programs raise many of society's basic questions about purpose and meaning— tough questions which will not be easy to answer. But they also offer a possibility for building a saner world—a world where people are more open about their feelings, careful in their thinking, and responsible in their actions.

Discussion Questions
1. What are the relative effects of heredity and environment on children's behavior?
2. Should laws be passed to regulate the amount of violence shown on television?
3. How would Bruner and Bandura differ in their conception of how children learn?
4. How can you tell when somebody means what he says and when you are getting a "masked message"?
5. What, in your opinion, is the best way of teaching children?
6. What are schools for anyway?

Chapter 4
Adolescence

To social scientists and laymen alike adolescence is generally viewed as a critical developmental period. In the United States as well as in other advanced technological societies the years of eleven to approximately eighteen seem to carry stresses and strains that tax the adjustive capacities for most persons in this age group. Why this period of growth appears to set off the amount of personal and social turmoil it does is not entirely clear. Biological explanations have emphasized the importance of physiological changes in body structure and function. Certainly, sexual maturity begins to emerge full blown at this time and such drives are particularly powerful. While physiological changes are obviously important, it is principally the interaction of the physiology with the environment that brings about the dramatic social adjustments which are the hallmarks of adolescence.

The interaction between physiology and culture is, however, a complex matter that involves many serious considerations. During adolescence, for example, there are sudden spurts in height and weight as well as changes in hormonal functions. But these physiological changes are common everywhere to all persons who are in the midst of adolescence. What matters though is how the environment or the culture accommodates to these changes and provides the outlets for resolving or satisfying the growth changes that are taking place. Interestingly enough, anthropologists have found that adolescence is not as stressful in some other societies as it is in our own. For example, in Samoa this period is considered a time of happiness and personal satisfaction. One of the reasons for this relative calm in the Samoan culture is that sexual expressions are not restricted and inhibitions in this area are not so clearly manifest. On the contrary, in our culture, sexual desires are met with confusion, indecision, and excessive stimulation that can only be satisfied in illicit and often highly censured relationships. It is not only in terms of sexual behavior that adolescents meet confusion. In many respects they are suspended between the desire for independence and their naturally dependent status within the family setting. In the process of disengaging themselves from the family, adolescents face life problems that they have had little preparation in dealing with. Setting up a household, experiencing sexual intimacy, surviving vocationally and even educationally are reality issues about which most people in our culture have not had sufficient instruction, either in the schools or the family. Thus, the transition from adolescence to young adulthood is often fraught with chaos and indecision.

Intensive and well-designed studies of the mental health of adolescence are few and far between. One notable exception is the work by Daniel Offer which is summarized by Herbert Yahraes in his article "Young People of Normal Mental Health." Studies dealing with the psychological difficulties experienced by adolescents must often focus on youth going through serious emotional crisis or who are classified as emotionally disturbed. Offer's approach, on the other hand, was to study normal adolescent boys through a series of intensive interviews, projective tests, teachers' ratings, school performance, and other procedures. Furthermore, Offer selected his subjects in such a way as to have an average group representing boys of normal mental health. In selecting from a much larger sample, he eliminated those boys who were extremely well adjusted and those that scored lowest, the maladjusted part of the distribution. His intention was to try and obtain the "average or modal adolescent." In general, the results indicate that the average adolescent experiences the same problems as the disturbed adolescent but to a somewhat lesser degree. Feelings of shame, guilt, depression, and anxiety are considerable and these concerns center around issues such as sex, religion, and money. Studies like Dr. Offer's are beginning to yield the kinds of information that will allow us to talk in terms of fact rather than broad and untested generalizations.

Of deep concern to all people in our culture is the word "love." The dimensions of love are difficult to conceptualize because of the highly personal and intimate quality of love for each person. The article "The Many Faces of Love" by Daniel Sugarman and Rollie Hochstein deals with love, self-love, friendship, and the negative qualities of emotional deprivation and self-pity. The authors clearly point out the ways love can be overly sentimentalized or glorified to the extent that it loses all reason and meaning. Love can become an excuse for many behaviors that produce despair and unhappiness in others. The honest expression of love in our culture can be a great virtue and is the foundation of many honest and true relationships. However, because love is such an involved and complex process, its good features can be distorted and used as self-justification for acts of cruelty and insensitivity.

It may seem unusual to include an article that discusses techniques of studying. Since you have already progressed so far in school, obviously you must know something about studying. But it is surprising how many students in college or even graduate school use sloppy and inefficient approaches to their assignments. The techniques described by Walter Pauk may help you to organize your time and effort better and to get more out of your assignments. It is a system called the OK4R approach, and it is based on an approach developed by Francis Robinson and called the SQ3R method. In SQ3R the student first *surveys* the material, glancing over the headings to pick out the ideas and get some orientation toward the assignment. Then, for each subsection, the Q and two of the R's come into play. Each subsection heading is turned into a *question,* and then the student *reads* the subsection in order to find the answers to the question, and finally *recites* the answer without looking at the book. After this process is completed for the entire assignment, it is time for the third R, *review.* At this point the student should have a firm grasp on the essentials of the assignment, and also be prepared for examination questions on it.

Pauk's method is very similar. In his system OK refers to getting an *overview* and determining the *key ideas,* and this is akin to Robinson's survey. The four R's are *read, recall, reflect,* and *review.* While the initial questioning built into Robinson's system is omitted, the addition of time to reflect allows relationships among the material to be developed. With either system the student is provided with a coherent approach to what seems like an overwhelming mass of information.

In our society a college degree carries with it definite social and economic advantages. College graduates are supposed to live better, make more money, and have a general edge on those people who have not completed a college degree. Today a college education is an experience that hundreds of thousands of students participate in each year. At one time a college education was reserved for the wealthy. It was a special experience for the few with either considerable economic means or unique intellectual qualifications. But now a college education is available to almost anybody who wants it. The economic factor is not nearly as restrictive as before, and the intellectual qualifications for entry are so diverse that it is now possible for students to find a college on the basis of interest alone rather than on previous academic achievement. In many ways the college phenomenon is truly a uniquely American condition. In very few places is there a society which can remove hundreds of thousands of its young people from the economic sector and place them in a protective and secure environment during their "gestation" period. The article by Arthur W. Chickering entitled "The Best Colleges Have the Least Effect" takes a hard look at some general issues in college education and attempts to compare three different colleges and the classes of colleges they represent, on both educational and social variables. In this interesting study the focus is placed on students who remain at least two years after admittance and those who drop out or transfer or work or travel for various reasons. These leavers and stayers were compared on many different assessment measures. One of the most provocative findings was that the dropouts seemed to be more creative, more impulsive, and more independent-minded than their peers staying in college. In addition, the type of college one goes to seems to facilitate the phenomenon of stayers or leavers more than others. Thus, students who stay at one college may be quite different in personality from those students who stay at a different college. This article attempts to study some of the fascinating variables which are a part of the broad panorama of a college experience.

After finishing college most students enter the world of work. Wise students have prepared for this through the courses they have taken and the activities in which they have participated. It is usually helpful to anticipate a major turning point in life, so that you are ready to make a satisfying choice. However, it is also important not to commit yourself prematurely by ruling out alternatives which would be rewarding. In the paper by Alva C. Cooper, many of the considerations that students should keep in mind are reviewed, with several examples from the experience of both employers and students quoted. Not only does the article consider what you should look for when seeking a career, but it also discusses what employers are looking for when they review your application and decide whether or not to employ you. All of this information can be helpful to you in reaching a very important life decision, but ultimately it is a decision that each person must make by himself and for himself.

Suggested Readings

Blaine, G. B., McArthur, C. C., and others. *Emotional Problems of the Student.* New York: Anchor, 1966. Discussion of personality problems as seen in a university clinic. Actual cases are used as illustrations.

Erikson, Erik H. *Childhood and Society,* 2d ed. New York: W. W. Norton & Co., 1963. A fascinating theoretical study of personality development with case studies and cross-cultural material.

Grinder, Robert E. *Studies in Adolescence.* New York: The Macmillan Company, 1969. A group of interesting research papers and clinical reports of adolescent behavior.

Stone, L. Joseph, and Church, Joseph. *Childhood and Adolescence,* 2d ed. New York: Random House, 1968. An insightful journey into the world of the developing person.

13. Young People of Normal Mental Health
Herbert Yahraes

"The normal adolescent, like the disturbed one, has feelings of shame, guilt, depression, or anxiety."

Exploring the mental health of normal young people is a study in similarity and contrast. Mental health is a continuum. Therefore, being disturbed is in many instances an exaggeration of what we all feel from time to time. This paper discusses normal young people in this context.

Psychiatrists try to help sick people become well, but what is *well? What* do we mean by *normal mental health?*

Psychiatry has too long neglected this question, says Dr. Roy R. Grinker, Sr., an eminent psychiatrist and director of the Institute for Psychosomatic and Psychiatric Research and Training, Michael Reese Hospital and Medical Center, Chicago. Hence, as one part of a broad research program, members of the Institute's staff have been trying to find some of the answers. Their work is supported by the National Institute of Mental Health.

This report presents highlights of three studies: *First,* a continuing investigation of normal high school students, the work of a team headed by Dr. Daniel Offer, the institute's assistant director; *second,* a study, nearing completion, by Dr. David Marcus and several associates, including Dr. Offer, of what seems to be an important difference between families that do not have a disturbed adolescent child and families that do; *third,* a completed study by Dr. Grinker of a group of normal college students.

I. Psychiatry Views the Normal Adolescent

After some years of daily contact with adolescents who were disturbed or delinquent, or both, Dr. Offer decided to take a good look at the other kind, the normal ones—their backgrounds, personalities, viewpoints, worries, and behavior.

In adolescents, he points out, it has been unusually difficult to distinguish health from illness, normal turmoil from pathological process. Even in the case of psychotherapists, ideas about the characteristics making for normality in teenagers have been generally based on memories of a person's own adolescence and observations of his own children. With the understanding to be gained by

From *The Mental Health of the Child,* June 1971. Public Health Service Publication No. 2168. Reprinted by permission.

a systematic study, Dr. Offer reasoned, psychotherapists would have a more valid baseline for judging disturbed teenagers, and families, schools and society in general would be better able to handle problems presented by teenagers and to recognize, prevent, and cope with abnormal behavior.

Dr. Offer is now halfway through as intensive 3-year study of 84 normal adolescents—boys from middle-class families in the Chicago metropolitan area selected from two public high schools during their freshman year.

Among the findings to date:

1. The normal adolescent, like the disturbed one, has feelings of shame, guilt, depression, or anxiety. But he is less afraid to look at himself and to admit his feelings. Psychiatrists would be happy, Dr. Offer remarks, if patients even at the end of therapy were as aware of their problems as these normal boys are of theirs.

2. Many of these atomic-age boys are worried about the same things that boys have worried about for generations—including sex, religion, and money. Only a few are worried about the state of the world. A teenager's three most difficult problems, these boys say, are to do as well educationally and vocationally as his family expects, to control his impulses, and to get along with other people.

3. The boys have a conservative sexual code and, through the sophomore year at least, they behave conservatively. Many of them daydream about a specific girl but do not readily admit it. Five percent go steady; 35 percent group-date only; 35 percent do not date at all. Typically the boys are concerned with how to behave when out with a girl. Most are interested in sports as a means of displaying masculinity and of sublimating, Dr. Offer believes, both aggressive and sexual impulses.

4. About 20 percent smoke. A few drink.

5. Many of these normal boys—generally when they were only 12 or 13— have performed minor delinquent acts and have associated with delinquents. Twenty-five percent of them, in fact, have been involved with the police over such incidents as stealing from a drugstore, fighting, throwing bottles on highways, or overturning garbage cans. After a boy has been in trouble once or twice, though, he seems to have learned his lesson. He does not make delinquency a pattern. Nevertheless he sympathizes with juvenile delinquents and ascribes their troubles entirely to their parents and to society.

6. These normal teenagers are not inclined to rebel against either their parents or their parents' generation. They see clearly what values their parents hold, and they tend to hold the same ones themselves. When adolescents and parents disagree, it is on such matters as the use of the car and the time to come home at night. The boys find their fathers reliable, their mothers understanding. They feel closer to their mothers and can more easily discuss emotional problems with them.

7. Members of the group express definite ideas about what they are going to do when they have finished school. But they tend to change these ideas as time goes by.

For the most part these findings stem from four 40-minute psychiatric interviews with each boy, spread over a period of a year and a half. Four more such interviews are planned, as are less intensive interviews with the parents. The complete description of these normal adolescents will also take into account teacher ratings, school performance records, and the results of projective testing as other means of getting information about hopes, fears, and anxieties.

How does one pick a normal adolescent? Dr. Offer and his associates did it by going to two high schools in the fall of 1962, one in a suburb just north of Chicago and the other in a suburb just south, and giving several hundred freshmen boys two tests. One was the Self-Image Questionnaire for Adolescent Boys, developed by Dr. Offer and an associate, Dr. Melvin Sabshin, now head of the Department of Psychiatry of the University of Illinois College of Medicine; the other, the Bell Adjustment Inventory. Each comprised a number of scales, or subtests, and each scale was intended to measure one aspect of how the boy regarded himself or his world. Taken all together, the grantee believes, they provided a good picture of a boy's ability—in terms of his emotional adjustment —to meet his problems.

Of the boys tested, Dr. Offer selected the 114—about a third of the total— whose scores on all the subtests had been closest to the average. Thus he eliminated the boys who scored highest (and were, presumably, extremely well adjusted) and those who scored lowest. He also eliminated those who scored much higher than average in some areas and much lower than average in others. So in this study the normal adolescent is what Dr. Offer calls the *modal*, or average, adolescent.

After making his selections, the investigator checked with the school authorities and found that 3 of the boys were serious behavior problems (in a randomly chosen group of the same size, 15 would have been). These were dropped from the study. A few boys declined to participate and a number moved.

Dr. Offer emphasizes that most of the boys being studied come from families at one or another level of the middle class. About 10 percent come from stable, working-class families, as would be expected from the proportion of such families in the population represented, and about 7 percent are Negroes, as again would be expected. Presumably the study's findings would hold true for middle-class communities in any metropolitan area.

None of these well-adjusted boys has lost a parent because of divorce, only three because of separation, only two because of death: in sum, only 6 percent come from disrupted homes. This compares with 9 percent of the general population of teenagers (aged 18) in the two communities studied and with 45 percent of the delinquent adolescents studied by another investigator.

More than half of the selected group are either the oldest or the only child in the family—a striking statistic, says Dr. Offer, but one that may only reflect the tendency of families to move to the suburbs when the first child is ready for school.

It developed also that the group had its share of honor students—12 percent —during the freshman year, but no failures.

When Dr. Offer was organizing his project, some of his associates doubted that it could succeed. Normal teenagers, they argued, would never show up for appointments with a psychiatrist—they'd feel disgraced. As a matter of fact, more than half of the group did miss their appointments during the early months and had to be scheduled again. This proportion has now dropped to one-fifth, which the investigator considers good, because the interviews are held after school hours and frequently involve two round trips for the parent who does the driving.

Teenagers are extremely egotistical, Dr. Offer notes. They participate in the project because someone is interested in learning what they—and not adults—think about teenagers and the world. Teenagers are also extremely altruistic. They participate because they have been told that in the long run the project will help other teenagers.

What does he think of these normal youngsters? "Oh my!" the psychiatrist says, "They're tremendous!"

II. Teen-Agers in Trouble: A Communications Breakdown?

Parents requesting psychiatric help for an adolescent child, psychiatrists at Michael Reese observed over a 3-year period, complain most frequently about:

1. Delinquent behavior, ranging from assault and major theft to isolated incidences of vandalism in school.
2. Difficulty in making and keeping friends.
3. Inability to adjust to school situations.
4. Inability on the part of the parents to "manage" the adolescent.

The adolescents, on the other hand, most frequently complain that their parents do not understand them; hence their problems. Their second most frequent complaint is that they do not understand their parents.

The investigators asked themselves: In a family where the teenagers are apparently normal, have the parents and youngsters been understanding each other better than in a family where a teenager is disturbed?

Twenty middle-class families were studied, each intact and each including at least two adolescents ranging in age from 14 to 19 and in good physical health. Half the families were classified as normal, or non-disturbed: no member had, or had had, any obvious emotional trouble. The other half were classified as disturbed: one of the adolescents had been hospitalized for psychiatric reasons, the diagnosis in five cases was schizophrenia and in five cases character disorders that had led to such actions as car stealing, assaulting parents, and, in the case of one girl, becoming pregnant.

Then the Q-sort technique was used to obtain from each adolescent both a description of himself and an account of how he thought his mother would describe him. Similarly, each mother described her son both as she would have liked him to be and as she thought he would describe himself.

Analysis of the data leads to these principal findings:

1. In normal families, mothers and children were in good communication. An adolescent understood his mother's expectations for him and was able in turn to convey his own viewpoints to his mother.
2. In disturbed families, the patient and the mother were in poor communication. The lines between the other disturbed adolescent and the mother were open but not to the same extent as in undisturbed families.

In general, it has been the experience at Michael Reese that the mother of a disturbed child explains that the child is rebellious toward her ideas—an explanation that the Michael Reese psychiatrists are inclined to disbelieve. In describing behavior as rebellious, they suggest, perhaps a mother is excessively suspicious or distrustful. Or perhaps she has been making inappropriate demands on the adolescent. Or perhaps, as in this study, the lines of communications have broken down: the adolescent has not known where the parent stood and the parent has not known where the adolescent stood.

Lack of communication, the investigators report, may apply particularly to adolescents who are delinquent but not psychotic. In the present study, in any event, such teenagers said they had been trying through their behavior to force open the communications at home, particularly with their mothers.

III. Normality in Young College Men

Several years ago, as part of a research project on how the body responds when emotions are repressed, Dr. Grinker had occasion to study 65 normal young men. They were freshmen at George Williams College in Chicago where the basic goal is "to provide professional education for Christian leadership, primarily for Young Men's Christian Associations," but where "men and women of all faiths and races who seek to prepare themselves in a Christian atmosphere . . ." are welcomed.

About half the group had been selected as normal on the basis of various personality tests; the others were judged normal on the basis of a psychiatric interview and answers to an extensive questionnaire.

After interviewing the selected students, Dr. Grinker's findings were startling. "Here was a type of young man I had not met before in my role of psychiatrist and rarely in my personal life," he reported. "On the surface they were free from psychotic, neurotic, or disabling personality traits. It seemed that I had encountered some mentally 'healthy' men who presented a unique opportunity for study." As the investigation continued he came to feel that the entire student body enjoyed unusual health.

Typically the healthy young men in the study came from small- or medium-sized Midwestern cities. Their fathers were semiskilled or white-collar workers earning a little more than $5,000. The parents had been loving but strict. Family quarrels, if any, had been generally over money. The boys had gone to work early. They had loved sports. They had had rigorous training in religion.

Factors emphasized by Dr. Grinker as having contributed to the boy's mental health include:

1. Sound physical health from birth onward.
2. Average rather than high intelligence.
3. Warm relationship with both parents.
4. Parental agreement about bringing up children—including the setting of definite and understood limitations on behavior.
5. Reasonable and consistent punishment.
6. Sound early religious training.
7. Part-time jobs when young.
8. Strong identification with the father.

9. A viewpoint (picked up at home, at church, in boys' clubs, at the Y.M.C.A.) that sees the world as calling for action, not introspection: a person *does* something about problems.

10. Ideals centered on doing the job well, doing good, being liked, achieving contentment and sociability, and succeeding at what one chooses to do rather than striving for either social or economic prestige.

The investigator divided his healthy young men into three groups—the very well adjusted, the fairly well adjusted, and the marginally adjusted—and then studied differences in their background and behavior. In general, the parents of the very well adjusted group had more often been in agreement about their children's upbringing, had more openly expressed their affection for each other, and had shown a less rigid concern over such problems as dating, smoking, and drinking. The mothers had been warmer, closer, and more relaxed, and more of the fathers had given all the love the students recalled having wanted. The very well adjusted individuals had done better in school and had been more active socially during adolescence. They were more specific than the others about what they wanted to do—go into Y.M.C.A. work, most of them—after college. They were less frequently anxious, embarrassed, or depressed. When they were angered they tended to speak out—the marginally adjusted ones, to keep quiet.

Even members of the very well adjusted group have had and do have problems. Dr. Grinker reports, "Like anyone living, they have had conflicts, established defenses, and have had to sacrifice potential assets in the process of adjustment." He notes in particular a narrowed range of interests and a tendency toward some anxiety about failing. But in general they and the others who were studied work and play well, cope realistically with experiences that rouse them emotionally, and have had warm, human relationships with parents, teachers, friends, and girls. They also feel good, and have hopes for the future—among them, "doing the best I can."

When he describes these young men to social and professional groups, Dr. Grinker is often told, "Those boys are sick; they have no ambition," He disagrees because he thinks "doing the best I can" *is* an ambition.

Intense commitment to change, the investigator says, may in itself be one of the elements in neurosis-building. Neither the men in this study nor their parents have shown much interest in moving fast; they go ahead at a pace that does not overstrain. They are not creative, nor explorative; to many persons they might appear dull. But Dr. Grinker believes that they and people like them give our society "a solid steady core of stability."

The investigator observes that what he considers mental health or normality in these young men is of one type and that research among many kinds of populations is necessary to delineate other types and find what they have in common.

14. The Many Faces of Love
Daniel A. Sugarman and Rollie Hochstein

"The way your parents love you influences the way you love others."

Love is close to all of us. How we love and the motives behind loving are insightfully explored by Sugarman and Hochstein.

We are a pro-love society. The heart is our love symbol. But love is a matter for the mind as well as the heart. While it is true that love can be beautiful, that's not the whole story. Misused or misunderstood, it can be crippling, life-defeating. To learn how to use love's power both wisely and well, it is important to understand all sides of its nature.

The *positive* action of love is familiar and obvious. Love brings people close, creates a sense of well-being, strengthens and inspires. It influences human development even more than most people imagine. In the past forty years, scientists have begun to measure the effects of love—and the lack of it—on all living things. They have learned, for one thing, that mother love is vital for the normal development of children. Institutionalized infants—fed and cleaned regularly but with only minimal physical contact—tend to be underweight, apathetic and abnormally slow in muscular development. (In related studies, Dr. Harry Harlow, a prominent psychologist at the University of Wisconsin, found that monkeys deprived of soft, warm touch—though otherwise well cared for—developed bizarre, antisocial behavior patterns and in maturity were often incapable of mating.)

The way your parents loved you influences the way you love others. Your personality takes shape after the image of those who care for you. In a recent study a group of nursery school children were placed under the supervision of two adults: one openly affectionate, the other intentionally aloof. In little time almost all the youngsters had begun to imitate the behavior of the attentive, loving supervisor. Evidently, love is an attraction and an inspiration as well as a source of nourishment. Whether it comes from a parent or a substitute mother seems to be less important than the fact of its consistent presence.

In later childhood the love of friends builds upon the foundation laid by parental love. The reciprocal nature of friendship—mutual enjoyment, confidence, obligations—adds to the sense of self you have already developed as a reflection of your parents' attitude toward you. The support of friends is probably essential for a calm crossing from childhood to maturity. One of the first questions a counselor asks a troubled teen-ager is, "Do you have friends?" Even if there is only one close friend, the problem generally takes on a less serious aspect.

The ability to love others is contingent on self-love. Without a strong sense of your own worth as an individual, it is hard to be generous in your feelings for others. A distillation of all your previous experience in giving and taking love determines your behavior when romantic love occurs.

Being "in love" is unlike any other experience. Mutual love between a man and woman can bring out the best in both. The feeling of good health, of being "more alive," has a real physiological basis. Your body chemistry changes when you are with someone sexually attractive: skin temperature rises, blood pressure drops, the pupils of the eyes dilate. As a result of this general activation, you feel as if you could climb the highest mountain—equal to achievements beyond your ordinary limits.

There are also specifically psychological benefits that stem from having a boy friend's wholehearted approval and support. Self-confidence raises your spirits. Pleased with yourself, you find it easier to be generous and friendly. "All the world loves a lover" is a fairly accurate assessment of the general reaction to your expansive mood. Loving makes you lovable.

History and legend provide numerous examples of the curative powers of love. One of the most famous is Elizabeth Barrett, who was a chronic invalid until she fell in love with poet Robert Browning and recovered—almost miraculously—her appetite for life. Sleeping Beauty's awakening by a princely kiss is one of many fairy tales that tell a psychological truth.

Love works similar magic in everyday life. I worked recently with a young girl who had fallen into a deep depression. Joylessness showed in her shabby appearance: skin dull as putty, gross obesity, no interest in grooming. Therapy was difficult because she had little desire to change. After several weeks of fruitless consultation, she happened to meet a boy new in town and also lonely. Soon my patient was in love. It became important for her to lose weight; her entire appearance improved. For this girl, too, love seemed to be a miracle cure.

Of course it was not. Romance is not an automatic solution to poor health or any other problem. But once alive to the possibilities in her, my patient was able to work through the conflicts that had generated her depression.

Love often acts as a key to the hidden treasures of a personality. Its benefits enrich every phase of life. Mature love adds depth and shadings, operates as a bulwark against the stresses of responsibility and is a comfort in time of trouble. As it ripens and mellows, love in a variety of forms can provide life's deepest meaning.

While we recognize, however, that love is paramount as a human, humanizing emotion, it is a mistake to see it as an all-powerful force that works solely for good. Love is neither as pure nor as potent as sentimentalists would have it. Its negative application sometimes can do a great deal of damage. In some of its forms it can be a tool for control and domination, a crutch to evade the responsibility of standing on one's own feet, an instrument of self-punishment and a weapon.

It seems almost blasphemous to criticize the revered quality called mother love. Yet the love of many mothers contains a harmful amount of domination.

The woman who "needs to be needed" may unconsciously attempt to turn her children into lifetime dependents. If the instinct for control outweighs her desire to see her offspring strong and self-reliant, she may use the name of love to keep a tight rein on her family, thus retarding her children's development and saddling them with guilt feelings for wanting to break loose.

It is not uncommon for younger women, too, to use love as a control over their boy friends. When Bill wants to attend a superior college and his girl friend Peg begs him to choose a lesser school close to home, is it love for Bill or security for Peg that motivates her? When Jan interrupts Ernie's studies several nights a week, telephoning him to come and see her, what is her chief concern? When love must be proved, time after time, by the submission of one partner, there is an unlovely flavor of domination in the blend.

Conversely, a girl who is invariably on the giving end may be acting from emotional needs far from the unselfish love she claims to feel. The pliant female who makes continual sacrifices for her parents and boy friend is likely to be acting more from fear or guilt than from simple sweetness.

One example is Sally—who used love to avoid finding herself. She fell in love with a man whose authoritarian nature absorbed her weaker personality. At the time, she was drifting. Should she go to college or look for a job? Meeting Mark was like catching hold of a life preserver. In his late twenties, professionally established, strong and dynamic, Mark had all the answers. He even determined how Sally should wear her hair. When he decided to marry her, she discarded all her doubts and concentrated on being a good wife.

For a few years Mark and Sally were comfortable as leader and follower, protector and protected. But problems eventually arose. Mark had broad interests; he grew with his career. Sally stayed child-like, narrowly confined to her house and family. Bored, she imagined—and perhaps rightly—that Mark was bored with her. Headaches, restlessness, "nerves" were indications that she lacked outlets for her energy. The hope is that Sally may learn that even undeveloped abilities demand expression, that marriage is not meant to be an escape from the world of challenge and competition.

Then there are girls who fall in love with one boy after another and are hurt every time. Others are attracted only to boys who are unavailable or uninterested. It becomes clear, after a long run of bad deals, that such girls find an inverse satisfaction in painful relationships.

Sometimes love functions as a weapon of punishment. The classic case is the girl who manages to find boy friends who are living refutations of her parents' standards. She may not dare to criticize her mother's habits or argue against her father's ideas. But when a daughter presents to conservative, security-minded parents a long-haired fiancé provocatively dressed in beads and bluejeans, who flaunts his irresponsibility and proclaims his radical politics, she is making some solid strikes against them. Or she may choose companions whose supercilious or hostile attitudes produce a subtle put-down that she herself would never articulate. Occasionally, the choice of a boy friend is a tactic in a private war between the sexes, a girl responding to a boy only long enough to captivate him. Once he is caught, the interest of the huntress fades. When such situations repeat themselves, love is seldom more than a mask to cover hostility.

Often, too, the name of love is used to disguise a game of self-enhancement.

Almost everybody needs some form of recognition. A top-of-the-class mark, a pretty new ensemble, compliments, invitations all provide pats of support that keep us buoyant. But some girls, shaky in their self-esteem, need more than ordinary doses of ego boost. They try to associate themselves with successful, popular contemporaries. Their unconscious notion is that success is contagious. When a girl is drawn by superficial attributes—wardrobe, car, status—she acts more from self-love than from the outgoing feelings of real love.

If you want to give and receive love, it is important to understand the dynamics of your ties. Asking yourself some questions will help you make sure you are not using love to disguise other emotions:

1. *Does love bring out the best in me?* Even today, many families reserve a special set of limited objectives for female children. Some parents still assume that education, career training, intellectual development are not important for girls, whose talents will inevitably be turned to kitchen and nursery.

While there are women whose needs are completely fulfilled by caring for others, girls have about the same variety of talents and capacities that boys have. Conditioned to a narrow outlet, many fail to develop their abilities. They expect to find satisfaction through their husband's achievements.

Vicarious living, though, is seldom satisfying. Lacking outlets, a bright, sensitive girl is apt to harbor feelings of boredom and self-contempt. Commonly, she becomes envious of her husband's opportunities. It is better for you and better for your love to refuse to settle in somebody else's shadow. Let love be a catalyst for activating the best that's in you.

2. *Do I feel lost without my friends?* Sometimes a girl attaches herself to people who seem to possess qualities she lacks. A process called *identification* operates to give the weaker partner a share in the other's aura. Healthy relationships tend to be symbiotic, each partner taking and giving pleasure, comfort, support. When they become parasitic—one figuratively feeding off the other—the dependant grows steadily weaker.

If a girl's sense of personal value rests in her associations rather than in herself, she is in danger of becoming a parasite. The reserved girl who depends on an extroverted boy friend to make her comfortable with people, cultivate friends and keep up the conversation isn't giving herself a chance to develop her own social abilities.

3. *If I weren't really in love, would I feel guilty?* Most girls in our society are reluctant to enjoy sex without love. Teen-age boys usually find it easier to separate sexual desire from other attachments. They do not need to delude themselves that physical attraction includes deeper feelings.

Many girls, however, are unable to admit that their romantic feelings sometimes emanate from a simple sex drive. So they set up love as a standard of behavior: "If we are really in love, nothing we do together is wrong." And this rationale can work backwards: "If we were physically intimate, I must have loved him."

This kind of double-think may lead a girl to marry a man whose attractions are primarily physical and not necessarily the qualities conducive to a satisfying, durable relationship.

4. *Am I making great sacrifices for those I love?* Of course, we go out of our way to please people we love. When we "do for" parents or friends, we don't consider it a sacrifice. It is a choice we make willingly.

If you feel you are sacrificing a great deal in the name of love, some questions are in order. Would you really want to do otherwise? Is there an alternative which would not put you out so much? If so, why don't you take it?

In cases of clear need, there is no question. But when you find yourself in a chronic state of ignoring your own wishes and needs, you may find that you have "chosen" to make sacrifice a way of life.

A girl who gives up college "because one of us needs to work," who defers marriage "because my parents need me at home" may be using other people to excuse her from facing challenges. Often the perpetual martyr is working off feelings of guilt or unconsciously trying to tie people to her with unpayable debts of gratitude.

One thing is clear: great sacrifices are costly, to both giver and taker. When you override self-interest for a friend, boy friend, parent, be sure it is a free-will offering, gladly given and without an IOU. In any other spirit, gifts create resentment on both sides and have little to do with love.

5. *Am I playing a role?* Many girls play at romance like children playing house. If a girl has learned from her mother to associate love with domination or martyrdom, she is likely to play her role with a similar accent. When a fifteen-year-old uses such phrases as "I'm only telling you this for your own good," one suspects the influence of a parental author in the wings.

With some experience and self-knowledge, most girls soon outgrow this imitative stage. They develop the confidence to behave spontaneously, to respond to people and situations without referring to old scripts. Take a cool look at your relationships. If you seem consistently to play "boss" or "victim" or "serving maid," perhaps you can work toward more independent behavior.

6. *Do I always agree?* Some believe in peace at any price. Some are afraid they'll lose the love of anybody they oppose. Some have had the spark of controversy rubbed out of them. Others are playing the role of a "good little girl," docile and obedient.

The fact is that a good, strong argument seldom jeopardizes a solid relationship. Those who love you will continue to love you when you defend a conviction or stand up for your rights. In the long run, love weathers controversy better than it withstands the resentment that grows out of unexpressed feelings. If your boy friend really loves you, he'll continue to do so even if he knows that you dislike the smell of his pipe, disagree with his choice for state senator and are not particularly fond of his best friend. Honest communication can do more for mutual respect than a bland diet of submissiveness.

7. *Do I love him more since we broke up?* After a romance dies, the best move is forward. But some girls prefer to indulge themselves in melodramatic mournings. In retrospect, the lost lover rises to a status he never attained in reality. In love with a distorted memory, the sentimental girl hovers over the souvenirs of her romance, misted in self-pity.

Even if the breakup was not your idea and you really would like to have your boy friend back, mourning won't reclaim him. If you accept the fact of your separation and concentrate on full-time living, you have a better chance of meeting somebody who will return your love.

Real love is more concerned with today and tomorrow than with lost yesterdays.

8. *Do I believe that love can save the world?* "If only everybody loved

everybody else, everything would be groovy." It's fashionable these days to say that. But it's not true. It's only a wishful maxim.

The right kind of love with the right person at the right time is indeed a precious commodity. But however precious, love is not the answer to all the problems of living. Even the figure of Cupid, that blindfolded baby, suggests some of the limitations of love. Unseeing, immature love causes deep wounds when it flings its arrows in the wrong direction.

It is pleasant to idealize love. But the fullness of individual lives and the making of a better world depend on a good deal more. Honesty, generosity, respect, compassion, consideration and a healthy acceptance of self-interest are qualities that the world needs now and has, truly, too little of.

15. How to Read a Textbook
Walter Pauk

"Read for facts, ideas and relationships."

Perhaps this article should have been the first one in the book, since it includes many helpful hints about the proper way to read a book. It is one chapter taken from a volume that gives an extended series of hints about studying, and should be useful in organizing and approaching the material in this book and in many others.

Textbooks serve several purposes. They may provide a framework for the course; enforce learning by stating again much that is said in class; clarify by saying the same thing in a different way; amplify by introducing other material; and they may sometimes interpret by presenting a point of view different from the instructor's. A textbook should therefore not be studied by itself or simply memorized. It should at every step be related to what is being done in class.

Understanding the Aims of a Textbook
The first step in using a textbook efficiently is to understand its methods. Read the preface, the introduction, if there is one, and the table of contents.

Walter Pauk: *How to Study in College.* Houghton Mifflin Company, 1962. Reprinted by permission of the publisher.

These parts of a book give you valuable insights into an author's ideas about his book. Here, within a very few pages, you can grasp his central theme or prime objective, stated simply and directly.

The following, from the preface of a textbook on economics, states the author's point of view and admits his bias, and then gives you his "approach" to the subject.

> In addition to the importance of historical and institutional materials, I am convinced that a deliberate role should be given to *controversy* in introductory economics. All too often this is done, if at all, by presenting "both sides" to a question, and letting it go at that, leaving the student unstrung. I have not followed that procedure, but have allowed my own critical and positive views to emerge without inhibition. The reader may dispute my viewpoint at every turn, but I am convinced that the questions raised are important and that they merit serious examination. The good student of economics will learn something through honest and thorough dispute, even, perhaps particularly, with views he finds untenable. And he may thereby become more interested in the subject.[1]

The following paragraph, from the introduction to the same book, illustrates the author's use of "pre-outlining" to clarify the first chapter.

> In the following pages, we will examine the general features of capitalism, and go on to discuss some of the specific manifestations of American capitalism—something of its origins. the manner in which it has changed over time, and some of the leading tendencies now at work. We will examine, through the eyes of Karl Marx, how capitalism originated and developed; through the eyes of Adam Smith, we will examine the means by which a capitalist society is supposed to accomplish the end of social well-being.[2]

Mental Preparation

Effective reading takes concentration, and this may require some mental warming up. First, you might reflect on the importance and relation of the assignment to the whole pattern of the course. Make sure you know just what the assignment is, and review any comments your instructor may have made about it. (Form the habit in class of writing the assignment down exactly as the instructor gives it, together with full notes on anything he says about it.) If you are clear about the exact nature and purpose of the assignment, you will know what main points to look for as you read, and may be able to skip paragraphs or pages which are not relevant. In biology, for instance, you may be asked to learn the structure and life processes of an amoeba; in philosophy, the differences between the pragmatism of James and that of Peirce. Having these problems clearly in mind before you start reading makes it a good deal easier to find the answers.

[1] Reprinted by permission of the publisher, from Douglas F. Dowd: *Modern Economic Problems in Historical Perspective* (Lexington, Mass.: D. C. Heath and Company, 1965).
[2] *Ibid.*, p. 2.

Finally, before reading, ask yourself what you already know about the subject. The many landmarks already familiar to you will make it easier to get "the lay of the land."

Systematic Reading

Thorough, critical reading is easier if you develop the habit of reading systematically. Based in part on the SQ3R method developed by Professor F. P. Robinson,[3] the OK4R method described in the following pages employs some of the most effective techniques developed by psychologists of learning. The steps in this method are:

1. Get an Overview;
2. Determine Key Ideas;
3. Read;
4. Recall;
5. Reflect;
6. Review.

The OK4R Method of Reading

O 1. *Overview.* Take about five minutes to read introductory and summary paragraphs of the assignment. Then read center and side headings, to determine general content and sequence of topics. Locate the main divisions.

K 2. *Key Ideas.* Distinguish key ideas from secondary ideas and supporting materials. Convert headings or topic sentences into questions—a sure way to become involved in the author's ideas.

R¹ 3. *Read.* Read the sections or paragraphs consecutively to answer the questions you have formulated and to see how supporting materials reinforce key points. Pay close attention to transitional words and phrases. Keep asking yourself: What is the evidence? Does it prove the point? Is there enough support? Do I believe this? Why or why not?

R² 4. *Recall.* After reading, test your memory and understanding. Without looking at the book, try to say or write the main points and supporting materials in your own words. If you cannot do this immediately after reading, you cannot hope to tomorrow in class or next week in an examination.

R³ 5. *Reflect.* Step 4, Recall, will help fix the material in your mind. To make it really yours, go further: think about it. Relating new facts and ideas to others you already know gives added meaning to new and old knowledge and establishes both more firmly in your mind. This is the essence of creative thinking: the discovery of new relationships and new significance.

R⁴ 6. *Review.* To keep material fresh in mind, review it periodically. Re-read your notes and say over the sequence of main ideas and supporting materials until you have them once more firmly in mind. Mastery is a never-ending process.

[3] *Effective Study* (rev. ed.; New York: Harper and Brothers, 1961), pp. 29–30.

Using the OK4R System

1. *Overview.* Much can be learned in five minutes of overview. Reading introductory and concluding paragraphs, center and side headings, and topic sentences yields a quick impression of aim, coverage, and specific ideas. Note how much can be gleaned by reading only the first sentence of the paragraph in Figure 6–2. Getting an overview is like climbing a hill from which you can view the forest before starting to pick your way through the trees. It also helps you to concentrate better on a thorough reading.

2. *Key ideas.* Headings, such as "Mental Differences among Races" and "The Concept of Pure Races," tell you what the author is writing about, but not what he has to say. Ideas are the topics *plus* what the author says about them: e.g., "The concept of pure races *is not scientifically defensible*," or "The concept of pure races *was used by the Nazis as a brutal political weapon*." It is as important to know what the author says about his topic as to know what the topic is.

> Harlem, physically at least, has changed very little in my parents' lifetime or in mine. Now as then the buildings are old and in desperate need of repair, the streets are crowded and dirty, there are too many human beings per square block. Rents are 10 to 58 per cent higher than anywhere else in the city; food, expensive everywhere, is more expensive here and of an inferior quality; and now that the war is over and money is dwindling, clothes are carefully shopped for and seldom bought. Negroes, traditionally the last to be hired and the first to be fired, are finding jobs harder to get, and, while prices are rising implacably, wages are going down. All over Harlem now there is felt the same bitter expectancy with which, in my childhood, we awaited winter: it is coming and it will be hard; there is nothing anyone can do about it.[4]

Figure 6–2

The Function of a Topic Sentence

In this paragraph from James Baldwin, Notes of a Native Son *(Boston: Beacon Press, 1955), p. 57, notice particularly the following: (1) the topic sentence— here, the opening sentence—which states the subject of the paragraph; (2) the examples which support the topic sentence; (3) the final sentence, which rounds off the paragraph by referring back to the topic sentence.*

3. *Read.* It is not enough to grasp key ideas; it is necessary also to discover what supporting ideas and facts are used to develop them. As you read, you should continually ask, "Why—or how—is this true?" For example, the topic sentence (main idea) of the paragraph in Figure 6–2 is, "Harlem, physically at least, has changed very little in my parents' lifetime or in mine." With this idea firmly in mind you should ask, "What is the evidence for this statement?" Asking questions and finding answers is a stimulating intellectual exercise and an aid to understanding.

Read for facts, ideas, and relationships—in short, for *sense.* Make full use of organizational clues. If a sentence or paragraph begins "On the one hand," watch for the inevitable "On the other hand," which introduces the other side of the argument. Innocent little everyday words like "as," "since," "because,"

---

[4] From *Notes of a Native Son* by James Baldwin by permission of the publisher, Beacon Press.

and "although" are as important in relating parts of a thought as a plus, minus, or square root sign is in a math problem. Ignoring or misreading them can get you in serious trouble.

In following an author's development of his thought, keep his aim in mind. If you lose the thread, turn back to his introduction or his statement of his thesis, or look ahead to his conclusion, to get a better idea of where you are.

If you get bogged down in a really difficult sentence or paragraph, here is a method which some students find helpful. Read the material without the appositives and other modifying phrases, to avoid getting lost in a maze of language. When the framework shows clearly through, so that you can grasp the main idea or fact, then you can go back and read the material with all its "trimmings" to get the full sense.

If you are taking notes on your reading, you are ready to do so only when you have thoroughly assimilated the material and can condense the essence of it in your own words.

4. *Recall.* When you have finished reading, you are ready for the second R—Recall. Recalling what you have read forces you to test your understanding. It spotlights not only what you failed to remember, but what you failed to grasp.

As an aid to recall, you may want to mark your textbook for key ideas and other important information. . . . Or if you have been taking notes on your reading, now is the time to reinforce them with recall clues.

Another way to assist recall is to picture in your mind's eye concepts and facts which can be visualized—e.g., diagrammed mathematical, physical, or sociological relationships; a subtle color change during a chemical reaction; a dramatic moment in history.

If you will test yourself with the techniques of recall when you complete a reading assignment, you will know what you know—and what you don't know—while you still have time to do something about it.

5. *Reflect.* Professor Alfred North Whitehead, philosopher and mathematician, spoke about the knowledge which grows out of throwing ideas "into fresh combination." He was referring to speculation, projecting one's thoughts beyond familiar experience, considering new knowledge and ideas in the light of old, and old in the light of new. Reflection means investigating the implications of ideas, following up insights, asking questions, noting reservations. Reflections should not be left vague, but should be pursued until ideas take definite shape. If you need more information, an encyclopedia or a standard book on the subject will often give you what you need to bring fuzzy ideas into focus.

Students who do not think about what they have read miss the opportunity to gain real grasp of principles. Many students who can spout facts find it hard to apply these facts to unfamiliar situations or use them in new combinations. Manipulating facts—reflecting upon them—makes them yours as nothing else can. When different authors hold diverging opinions try to see why each believes as he does. Think through the problem from the viewpoint of each, and be alert to see where one or the other departs from the facts, overemphasizes some facts at the expense of others, or places a different interpretation on the facts. What do you think is the proper balance?

Reflection is a skill that you can take with you wherever you go and make use of in spare moments. It can be carried on while walking from one building to another, standing in line, waiting for a friend, or riding a bus. Men who have made great discoveries have reported that some of their best insights came in unlikely places and at odd times.

The subconscious plays an important role in creative thinking and discovery. We have all had an exciting idea or even the solution to a problem suddenly flash upon us at a moment when we have apparently not been thinking about it. The subconscious continues to work on concepts introduced deeply enough into the mind through reflection.

6. *Review.* Reviewing is the final step in effective reading. True reviewing is not just "looking over" lecture and reading notes. It is an active process of trying to remember, without prompting, what has already been learned. From time to time, go back over a section of your textbook or your reading notes, practice recalling as much as you can, then look again at book or notes to see where you were right, where you made mistakes, and what you left out. Continue recalling and verifying until you master the material.

To vary the process, put yourself in the instructor's place. What would you ask if you were given a test? Write out three or four questions which you believe cover the main issues, then answer them. You will be surprised how often these same questions come up in quizzes and exams. This is not out-guessing the instructor; this is studying to learn.

16. The Best Colleges Have the Least Effect
Arthur W. Chickering

"College drop outs may be more creative, more complex, more impulsive, and more autonomous than their peers who stay."

What makes a good college? What are the qualities of an involved student? How does the college and the student interact to produce a creative learning experience? These questions and many others are studied in the article by Arthur W. Chickering.

Although many undergraduate colleges no longer act *in loco parentis,* for many of their students they still act *in loco uteri.* Like wombs, most colleges offer a warm and cozy setting where the organism can exist protected from out-side influences until parturition sends him or her screaming into the world. Such colleges strive mightily to attract, recruit, and select students who at entrance display the characteristics desired of graduates. In large universities, students fashion their own wombs. They quickly seek our others like themselves and, as best they can, build their own symbiotic social systems.

The basic steps are familiar. Prospective students hear about the college from alumni, students currently enrolled, faculty members, and other college representatives. These communications are an early warning system that en-courages those students whose values, attitudes, life-styles, purposes, and aspira-tions are similar to those of persons already associated with the college to apply for admission. Other students are not encouraged, and often they are actively discouraged from applying. Admissions personnel then tackle the inquiries and applications and by using experience, intuition, prediction equa-tions, and other devices try to select those students who already seem to dem-onstrate the characteristics most valued by the institution.

Thus, a college that wants to graduate students with high intellectual com-petence and that takes large numbers of Rhodes Scholars and Woodrow Wilson Fellows as a mark of success selects students with high aptitude and achieve-ment test scores. When average scores on these measures move higher for enter-ing students, the college is pleased; if averages drop, dismay soon follows. Similarly, a church-related college that wants to graduate students who hold particular religious beliefs, young adults committed to tackling the evils of materialistic hedonism, works hard to encourage self-selection among prospec-tive students and then takes religious orientations and life-style into account at the point of admission. A liberal college with strong concerns that rest on humanistic rather than theological grounds takes another set of values, purposes, and motivations into account for admission.

When this process works, as it does for substantial numbers of entrants, it creates a comfortable fit between college and student. Students don't upset the college; the college doesn't upset the student. Students ride out the four-year gestation period in a comfortable womb, bathed by a continual flow of self-appreciation and self-gratification, nourished by the illusion of achievement resulting from a regular diet of grades, and well-insulated from disrupting out-side influences. A kick now and then is no cause for concern; it simply indi-cates that the infant is alive and presumably well.

A five-year Project on Student Development in Small Colleges attempted to discover what impact, if any, different kinds of colleges had on their students in the course of their undergraduate years. Findings from three of the thirteen participating institutions help to illustrate the variations among institutions and environments they offer. (See p. 159.)

First, consider the differences in institutional objectives. Savior's religious orientation is clearly expressed by the characteristics most desired and least desired of graduates. Elder's objectives reflect its concern for intellectual devel-opment, breadth of information, and social responsibility. Kildew's objectives reflect its student-centered, personal-social orientation. Note that Elder, along with Kildew, ranks lowest some of the objectives ranked highest by Savior. So these colleges differ substantially in their objectives, at least at the verbal level.

Teams of three professionals visited each campus for two or three days of observation during 1966, and their reports indicated that differing programs, practices, and operating principles accompanied these differences in objectives. At Savior, for example, they found these rules in the student handbook:

For men, sport clothes (slacks, sweaters, and sport jackets) "are usually worn" to classes. "Coats are expected for the evening dinner except during extremely hot weather." Shorts may be worn in recreation areas, but are not permitted for general campus wear. For women students: "Standards of modesty, femininity, and good taste, and neatness are expected of all." Coeds are warned to avoid the excesses of modern fashions and tight-fitting apparel. Sleeveless dresses, low necklines, open backs, and excessively short or tight skirts are prohibited, and "hose are expected for the evening dinner except during extremely hot weather." Concerning socializing between the sexes, the handbook said, "Couples spending an inordinate amount of time together on or off campus will be given counseling or discipline. Freshmen should refrain from socializing before 3:30 P.M. Monday through Friday."

In contrast, the rules at Kildew are few and fuzzy: (a) no unmannerly drinking (but this is not explicitly defined); (b) no drinking under the age of twenty-one; (c) sign out at the switchboard when leaving campus for more than twenty-four hours; (d) men and women permitted in each other's rooms only between 4:00 and 10:00 P.M. on weekdays and 2:00 and 10:00 P.M. on Sundays. Now these were the conditions as of 1966–67. Since then, both colleges have changed somewhat. Kildew has moved to twenty-four hours of intervisitation and Savior freshmen can socialize on weekdays before 3:30 P.M. But the relative positions of the two colleges have stayed about the same. Elder has the typical array of rules concerning gambling, drinking, dormitory curfews, etc., and they, too, have been moving toward greater freedom, maintaining their relative position.

The colleges also differ in other areas. Savior and Elder require that each student take at least one or two courses in the humanities, natural sciences, and social sciences. Evaluation is through quizzes, mid-terms, finals, and papers. In addition, Savior requires daily chapel attendance and a minimum of twelve credit hours in religion, theology, or Bible study. At Kildew, on the other hand, there are no required courses. Independent study is open to all students from the second year onward. Courses arise out of the interests of the students and the interests and capabilities of the faculty members. The usual system of examinations and grades is replaced by a system of written self-evaluations and instructors' comments. During a three-day registration period, students confer with teachers about courses and independent studies; during the last four or five days of each semester, students and teachers prepare written evaluations and confer about the work of the term.

The basic point then is this: These colleges differ dramatically—in objectives, in rules, regulations, and expectations concerning student behavior, and in educational philosophy and practice.

The students who are attracted and admitted also differ from college to college. Average scores on several personality scales for entering students at these different colleges range from very high to very low. Savior students are religious and political conservatives, authoritarians who give evidence of relatively little concern for social problems and for the welfare of others. They are oriented to practical achievement and express little interest in the arts and humanities or in reflective thought and academic activities. Kildew students

INSTITUTIONAL OBJECTIVES EXPRESSED AS MOST AND LEAST DESIRED CHARACTERISTICS OF GRADUATES

Four Most Desired	Four Least Desired
Savior	
Educated in the liberal arts within the context of a Christian world view	Independent member of society
	Recognizes and accepts feelings as relevant to decisions
Committed to Christ	Chooses friends carefully
Guided by God's will	Educated in the traditional liberal arts
Activated by Christian ideals in the various pursuits of life	
Elder	
Capable of effective judgment based on sound analysis of relevant information	Chooses friends carefully
	Committed to Christ
	Guided by God's will
Activated by the intellectual, cultural, moral, and spiritual values of our civilization	Mixes easily but chooses friends carefully
Constructive and creative member of interdependent society	
Socially responsible and a participating citizen	
Kildew	
Has understanding of self as an individual and as a member of society	Committed to Christ
	Guided by God's will
Constructive and creative member of interpendent society	Dedicated to Christian service
Capable of effective judgment based on sound analysis of relevant information	Educated in the liberal arts within the context of a Christian world view
Able to recognize and develop own creative potentials	

are at the opposite pole. With diverse interests in the arts and strong appreciation for literature, music, and dramatics, they are sensitive and emotional, ready to express feelings and to gratify impulses. Anti-authoritarian, skeptical of conventional beliefs and values, they are experimentally oriented; novel situations and ideas attract them. Between these two poles lies Elder, whose image and selectivity bring students above average in intellectual interests in both the arts and the sciences, more altruistically oriented than most, and less concerned with material possessions and practical achievement.

The differences among these groups of entrants are sufficiently large, and the groups themselves are sufficiently homogeneous, that at Savior there are no Kildew types and at Kildew no Savior types. At Elder a few Savior and Kildew types may be found, but most Elder students do not share their distinctive views. Thus, in these colleges—and the other ten project colleges can be placed along the continuum these three represent—the processes of self-selection and admission have effectively sorted high school graduates into discrete groups and have moved them into very different college environments and social systems. As these diverse students encounter these different colleges, what developmental outcomes follow?

Students who entered in September 1965 were "re-tested" at the ends of their first, second, and fourth years. When, for each college, average scores at entrance were compared with the average scores at the end of the freshman and sophomore years, the findings were astonishing. The areas of change, the directions of change, and even the amounts of change were very similar at all the diverse project colleges.

At all the colleges, scores after one or two years reflected increased autonomy, greater awareness of emotions and impulses and increased readiness to express them, stronger interest in the arts and humanities, and decreased concern for material possessions and practical achievement. Autonomy, for instance, increased among "authoritarian" students at highly structured institutions with numerous regulations and close adult supervision. It also occurred among "anti-authoritarians" attending a college with little overt structure, few regulations, and minimal adult supervision. Even on measures where stastistically significant change seldom occurred, similarity of direction was still highly consistent in the different colleges.

That, then, is what *in loco uteri* means. In each of these colleges students are developing along vectors of change set by the general cultural and genetic forces at work in our society. The colleges neither accelerate nor retard that development. They simply provide a safe haven where it can occur. Not that such outcomes and such a process are necessarily bad. Trent and Medsker's follow-up study of 10,000 high school graduates (*Beyond High School*, Jossey-Bass, Inc.) found that students who had four uninterrupted years of college changed more than their peers who spent four years in jobs or marriage, and the changes were similar to those reported above. Those who attended college became more autonomous, more flexible, complex, and tolerant of ambiguity, less dogmatic, more intellectually curious. So, wombs are good things. But it is important to recognize what is going on, because the womb as a model for college impact applies to a substantial number of students and their institutions.

There is, however, another model. Not all students fit comfortably into the womb; every college has its quota of misfits. And at every institution there are two kinds of misfits: those whose development has not yet proceeded to the general level at which the college operates, and those whose development has gone beyond the operating level of the college. Misfitting can also occur along many dimensions. A student's intellectual competence may be so limited that he finds it difficult to cope with the academic program, or his competence may be so high that course demands, classes, and other students contribute little. Students may be more liberal than most others at the college, or more conservative, more culturally sophisticated or less, more autonomous or more dependent. The proportions of misfits in any college, and their distinguishing characteristics, will vary depending upon how selective the college is, and upon its criteria for selection.

If these groups that deviate from the norm within different colleges are examined, then not only do they turn out to change in different ways but the changes that occur are related to differences in educational practices, student-faculty relationships, general atmosphere and student characteristics, and the nature of relationships among friends and acquaintances.

Various special studies of student development among misfits in college suggest two quite different patterns of college influence that depend upon the particular characteristics of the students as each encounters the special campus culture of his own college. When randomly selected groups of students are considered together, the *direction* and the *degree of change* that take place during the first year or two are similar for each group, even though the groups were dramatically different when they entered college and the colleges they entered were likewise different. Thus, in general, each college operates *in loco uteri*. But when subgroups of misfits are selected, both the direction and magnitude of change differ within individual colleges and among colleges. Thus, at each college development is accelerated or retarded for certain kinds of misfits.

Note that we have been studying students who stay, at least for the first two years. What about the dropouts—those who leave to transfer, to go to work, to travel, to loaf? Those who, we might say, experience premature parturition? We know they differ significantly from the typical student who stays. But they have much in common with some of the misfits who do not drop out.

Leavers and stayers were compared on numerous measures from several test instruments. Twenty-six different groups of students were examined. The characteristics that most sharply distinguished the leavers from the stayers were just those in which most change occurs; at entrance leavers consistently had scored higher on such measures than stayers. On a measure of impulse expression, for instance, students who left during the first or second year scored higher than their persisting peers in twenty-two of the twenty-six groups; they were more autonomous in eighteen of the twenty-six groups and more complex, innovative, and tolerant of ambiguity in nineteen of the groups.

These findings are consistent with other studies, which indicate that college dropouts tend to be more creative, more complex, more impulsive, and more autonomous than their peers who stay. But the important thing is that "higher" or "lower" in such areas depends entirely upon the college and upon a student's position in relation to it. For example, at WJB, which is a small college much like Savior, the leavers scored significantly higher than the stayers on such measures, but the leavers' scores were still lower than 70 percent of a representative national sample of freshmen. Therefore, compared with students at other colleges across the country, these leavers are relatively cautious, conservative, conforming, and dependent. But compared with their peers who stayed at WJB, they are outstanding in their impulsiveness, complexity, and autonomy. At the other end of the spectrum, the scores of Kildew girls who *stayed* were higher than 85 percent of the norms group. These girls, by any standard, are highly creative, impulsive, complex, autonomous. Yet, the girls who left scored significantly higher.

Thus, it is the fit between the student and his institution that makes a difference in his leaving or staying, not his general level in relation to the total population. And it is probably no coincidence that those characteristics which most distinguish leavers from stayers are also the characteristics where greatest change occurs among college students in general—the basic areas of development pursued by young adults in our society. Continued growth for these misfits may often require premature departure. Such moves toward more challenging and fruitful environments are healthy steps; such initiative in taking charge of one's own existence and future development is to be valued and fostered, not decried and curtailed.

These findings alter the way we must think about the dynamics of college influences on student development. Colleges and universities have usually treated students as though they were billiard balls, all alike in shape, size, and density, all stationary until struck. Administrators wield the cues, sending predominantly white, cue balls at such students, assuming that if just the right angle is found, students will behave in proper fashion and inexorably be propelled in the desired direction. Skilled administrators recognize that the force, the angle, and the English on the part of the faculty members as they encounter the students also determine the subsequent position of the faculty. One problem, of course, is that only some of the students are smooth and well rounded. Others are square or egg-shaped, flat or curvy. Some are Ping-pong balls, some are bowling balls. Some look symmetrical, but inside weight is concentrated in peculiar spots so they roll along in irregular and unpredictable fashion. Another problem, of course, is that some of the cues are badly twisted and some of the cue balls pretty peculiar themselves. So the game is frustrating and full of surprises.

But this way of thinking no longer makes sense. Students are not stationary at entrance or while at college. Each is flying his own vectors of change, each is actively pursuing his own development in several major areas. The pool table is tilted, and the balls are rolling. Some students enter at the end where they have plenty of room to roll and where they have space to accelerate and the stimulation to do so. Many students enter near the middle and have sufficient room to coast along while there. Students who enter at the far end, beyond the central location of the college, however, have little room to move. Those who stay frequently may bounce back closer to the middle of the table. But many of these misfits leave, challenged to find a roomier location where their own development can proceed more effectively.

If these conceptions are sound, they lead also to criteria for college effectiveness that contrast sharply with the usual view.

The most important index of college success and of its social contribution may be the quality of its dropouts, not the quality of its graduates. If it helps those misfits who enter near its upper limits to use the experiences that accompany such misfitting to clarify their own purposes and potentials, and if it then helps them to move on to more developmentally powerful or roomy settings, then its contribution both to the individuals and to the nation will be substantial. If, on the other hand, it confirms in such students suspicions of idiosyncrasy, instability, or illness, and if it will neither recognize their condition nor respond to it, then the potential for damage is great.

The second most important index of success rests on the changes that occur among those who stay. Those students most affected will be the other group of misfits whose development at entrance had not yet reached that at which the college operates. The college that helps such students survive and that helps them accelerate their own development through that struggle to survive makes a significant contribution.

The characteristics of the graduates per se is the least important index of college success and contribution. Indeed, it is often more spurious than accurate. For the numbers of fellowship winners, the numbers of graduates who become great men in the arts and humanities, in the social and natural sciences, in business and politics, is much more a function of student self-selection and institutional selection at entrance than of any contribution made by the college. The evidence, in fact, indicates that when the characteristics and qualifications of the students at entrance are taken into account, highly selective men's colleges reduce self-esteem and aspirations for such achievement, and underproduce such scholars and national leaders.

Finally, we are led to realize that under current patterns of recruitment and admission, and in the context of current practices in higher education, the most productive educational outcomes for individuals and for the country take place in those non-selective colleges where proportions of misfits are high and where they are recognized and helped. Selective colleges, which by their selectivity can function in loco uteri for most of their students and which remain content to do so, contribute least.

17. Facing Facts about Choosing Your Life's Work
Alva C. Cooper

"Above all,
be as realistic about yourself
as possible."

Before reading this paper, you should decide whether you are in a position to consider a career or if you are only looking for a job. If you are looking for a job you will probably think of the money or location and take what you can get. If a career is your concern many other factors become important, and they are discussed in this article.

Your Career is a Big Part of Your Future

The renowned automobile magnate and inventor, Charles Kettering, once said: "The future is what we all are interested in, because all of us are going to spend the rest of our lives there. And the future begins two seconds from now."

Such an attitude is most helpful in choosing your career. Somebody figured

From a brochure published by The Prudential Insurance Co. of America, 1968. Reprinted by permission.

out that you will spend 100,000 hours of your life working. Anything at which you are going to spend that amount of time should be worthwhile and enjoyable.

When Charles Kettering was born in 1876, the usual means of transportation was the horse. By the time he died in 1958, the average person was driving his own car and taking trips by jet plane, while astronauts were preparing for the first journey into outer space. One of Mr. Kettering's chief contributions was the self-starter on automobiles, an imaginative invention that revolutionized the auto industry and made him a fortune. His career achievements showed that he was a man with the talent, education, and flexibility to change with the times.

In your lifetime, you will undoubtedly see changes as sweeping as Charles Kettering saw. There are 30,000 different occupations today, more than half of them nonexistent when your father was born. By the time your children are ready to start thinking about a career, there will be thousands more new occupations for them to consider.

Dr. C. R. Voigtel, Director of Placement and Student Aid, Stephen F. Austin State College, Texas, feels that the biggest mistake made in trying to decide on a career is that students "limit their scope to long-established vocational areas." He adds, "Students need to be made aware of the job potentials being created each day by advancing technology."

And Newell Brown, Director of Counseling and Career Services, Princeton University, says: "The principal problem that confronts professionals in the field of career advising is the difficulty they have in persuading students to acquaint themselves with all of the many alternatives before them and with the relevant facts about each of these alternatives. Considering the stakes involved, one might think that students would be at least as painstaking in planning for the next 40 years of their lives as they are in researching a term paper. But not at all. The career decision is usually influenced by unsupportable stereotypes, misinformation and lack of information—indeed, even by lack of any thought until the chips are down."

More than a Job

A career is a great deal different from a job. If you are thinking only about "getting a job" when you finish school, you are saying that all you are interested in is some kind of work with regular pay.

A career has larger implications. It implies a life work in which you have interest and for which you have received some training and general education. But within any one career field, there may be many individual choices.

For instance, you may be thinking of becoming a teacher. Education, then, is the career field you have tentatively selected. Teaching is the largest profession in the United States, with nearly three million men and women teaching full time. As a teacher, you could work in the public or private schools, at home or abroad, or in private industry which trains tens of thousands of employees. You could teach any one of hundreds of subjects in the curriculum. You could specialize in guidance counseling or work in other special services that schools and colleges provide.

It is possible that another interest you have could be combined for a shift in career in your middle years. For example, many educators join book publishing companies where they work as editors, as salesmen, or as developers of new textbook programs. Educators sometimes transfer to foundations or other non-profit organizations to work on programs that especially interest them, such as education of the blind, urban development, or encouraging new methods in education.

Since education itself changes with the times in order to make use of new technologies and to meet the changing challenges of the world, an educator must remain flexible and be willing to spend his life learning as well as teaching.

These two characteristics—flexibility and an openness for lifelong learning —are necessary for any career if you want to keep growing. Nowhere is this more true than in the world of business. Just as typewriters and electronic data processing equipment have replaced the quill pen and the abacus, so has the world of business changed with the times. There are more than four-and-a-half million salaried workers in business. They range from accountants to zoologists. Not only is a company interested in the products or services it has to sell, but business today is a community partner, taking a wide-ranging interest in the problems of the community, state, and nation. Today's businessman is quite likely to devote a substantial part of his time and energy to educational and philanthropic matters. An appropriate career in business is open to young men and women from nearly every field of interest.

Public and Private Sectors

The two examples of career fields given above—education and business— represent two different elements or sectors in America. Generally speaking, education is a career in the public sector and business in the private sector. But they often overlap and, even more often, people move back and forth between them.

Many businessmen are tapped by government, either for unpaid, part-time duty or for full-time employment in the service of their country. A business executive may serve on an advisory board, or may do a tour as, say, Assistant Secretary of Defense. Or he may turn to elective office. Senator Charles Percy is one example of a successful businessman who turned to public office.

There are also many people who shift jobs within the public sector in the course of their careers. Walter Heller, for instance, left his post at the University of Minnesota to become Chairman, Council of Economic Advisers to the President.

In numberless cases, educators, businessmen, economists, psychologists, and others pursue their careers in both the public and private sectors of the economy.

Basic Characteristics Needed

There are four basic characteristics needed to make a wise career choice and then to go on to make a success of that career.

The most important characteristic is *flexibility.*

A recent college graduate who helped contribute the information for this booklet said: "Go to college with a clear head and be willing to change your plans at any time if you realize that what you are doing is not what you want to do for 40 years."

Another said: "I think that no one should enter or continue through school with his mind dead set on a particular goal or career. Though a student may feel strongly about a particular career, I do not feel that an early choice should block or prevent the student from investigating other possibilities."

Still another put it this way: "It is better to be unsure of your future than it is to be falsely certain and find out too late that you have pursued the wrong studies."

Here is a true story about a girl now in college who provides a good demonstration of flexibility. Janet decided to be a nurse when she was still in elementary school, and stuck to that decision until her senior year in high school. Then she was made editor of her school paper and began to attend conferences with other student editors in her state. After high school, she went to a state university, enrolled in a liberal arts course, and got a job on the student newspaper. Her idea was that she would need two years of a liberal arts course whether she majored in nursing or in journalism. Meanwhile, she was getting some practical experience in journalism to see if she liked it. At the end of her sophomore year, she decided that journalism was what she liked best, so she majored in it. But she had taken many science courses to keep open her option of going into nursing. Now she feels that she can combine her twin interests in science and journalism. When she graduates from college, she hopes to become a science writer for a newspaper. Janet displays the flexibility needed to find the career right for her.

The second ingredient for a desirable career is a *good general background*. Like flexibility, this is something you do not have to postpone developing. You have a full-time job right now: you're a student. Doing well at that job will prove to be important to you in many ways:

- you are now laying the foundation of your knowledge which can be used in many fields.
- you are now developing the work habits that will accompany you through life
- while you are exploring various fields of knowledge, you are also finding out about yourself—who you are, what interests you most, what you do best.

There are many employees who will not even give you an employment interview if your school record shows that you have done poorly. Such an attitude may seem unfair, but employers presume that if you have ability and did not use it in school, you are not serious about your future. They have found that success in school is the best predictor of success on the job.

College placement officers, when asked about the importance of a person's school record in getting satisfactory employment, gave these answers:

"For most jobs, the applicant's record—academic and extracurricular—is the deciding factor in his job acceptance. This is true because the record reflects the person."

"Scholastic success is significant; however, the total person and his attitude toward the working world are also of great significance."

"Grades are important, but work experience related to jobs is also important. Extracurricular activities take on importance *after* grades and work experience."

Among the answers given to this question by young people on their first big job, this one sums up what many said: "Studying is an essential, but employers are also looking for participation in social and professional organizations. Join in *worthwhile* organizations and try to develop your leadership abilities by holding office."

Another experience you have while you are still in school is learning to do your work as well as you can, even if it does not interest you or if you do not feel like doing it. Every job, including the most glamorous ones in television or government or business, has a large component of dull, repetitive routine. Thet habit of tending to the less interesting things can be developed early.

One reason many students do poorly in school is that they do not have general goals. Even though you may still be years away from a specific career choice, it is well to establish as early as you can what general fields you feel you would like to work in and what those fields demand.

This leads to the third general characteristic needed for an effective career: *the strength to follow your own lead.*

When young college graduates were asked about their experiences in choosing a career, one wrote, "I have problems!" One of his problems was not knowing himself and his interests, and then, when he found out what they were, not following them. He studied chemistry and found out only after starting graduate school that he was neither interested in nor suited for chemistry. His advice to high school students and college undergraduates is this: "Do what interests you and not necessarily what your parents suggest as a good field to enter." (Don't reject *all* parental career advice, however. Some of it may be very good.)

Dr. Alva C. Cooper, Director of Career Counseling and Placement at Hunter College, New York City, tells freshmen students: "Think about: Who am I? Who do I want to be? Where am I going? What are my abilities? What temperament do I have? What attitudes do I have? How do I get where I want to go?" Dr. Cooper calls a vocational choice "the implementation of a self-concept."

Dorothy Arnold, Director of Vocational Guidance, Goucher College, Maryland, calls "letting parents or faculty friends decide for them" the greatest mistake students make in deciding on a career.

Many young people let their parents select a college for them, plan their course of study, and map out their career. Some of them would be saved the pain of failure if they followed more closely their own interests and abilities. If your parents want you to be a doctor, it would be foolish to seek a medical career when you know in your heart that you are not suited for the profession and would be happier in something that might not even require a college education. On the other hand, you are selling yourself short if you have an aptitude for a particular field but choose another career because it takes less preparation.

The fourth characteristic needed for a worthwhile experience in a career is the *willingness to continue learning.*

You should find out enough about the field that interests you to know what preparation it entails. Is college a prerequisite? Will a bachelor's degree be enough or is graduate work now needed as well? Will it be better to work for a year or two after your first degree before getting a graduate degree? What education do the younger people in the field you have chosen usually have?

Even after your formal schooling is finished, there is no cutoff to your learning. There will be training on the job—sometimes very formal, long-term training.

For instance, some brokerage houses give a two-year course to college graduates, representing an investment in each trainee of many thousands of dollars. In addition, these companies expect their brokers to keep constantly informed about stock market trends, about world-wide economic trends, and about other factors that could affect investments. In different degrees this is true in any occupation. The chemist or physicist who has learned nothing for five years is almost hopelessly out-of-date. The television repairman has to keep up-to-date on new equipment. The doctor who has learned nothing since medical school might even be dangerous. The businessman who is operating with last year's knowledge is not advancing his company. The teacher who fails to keep up with trends and changes in the profession is short-changing students.

As with the other basic characteristics needed for a successful career, willingness to learn is an attitude that can be adopted right now. One young person wrote, when asked what advice he would give high school students on making a career choice: "Don't procrastinate. Begin reading books, pamphlets and brochures on career opportunities at your earliest convenience. Strive to become a well-rounded individual."

Interrupted Careers

The above characteristics are important for any career, and are especially important if your career is likely to be interrupted.

Many young men face military service after high school or college graduation. They will be serving themselves best if they are flexible (training in the service may even change your mind about your career choice), have a good general background (it might help get you a better assignment in the service), have the strength to follow themselves and learn more about themselves (in a service assignment you may find traits you did not know existed in yourself), and have a willingness to keep learning (so that you will be up-to-date in your career field when you return to civilian life).

Many young women will have a longer interruption, switching careers early in their twenties to become wives and mothers. Then, when the children are old enough for the mother to be away part of the day, many will return to the world of work. Those who have kept up with their skills and careers will be in a much better position to get back into their careers when the time comes.

What You Should Look for in a Career

Why do people work? One obvious reason is to make money. People also work to satisfy their physical needs, to meet their social needs, to meet such psychological needs as a sense of personal adequacy, and out of a need to be productive in something of intrinsic worth.

It is important to think of *your* needs, not those of your parents or your friends. Your parents, for instance, may have always wanted to go to college but never had the opportunity. They may now try to fulfill this need in themselves through you. Many parents, too, have unfulfilled professional ambitions— to be a doctor or a writer, for example; you may have neither the interests nor the abilities necessary to fulfill such ambitions.

Everyone has his own hierarchy of needs. Usually, when one need is

satisfied—such as making enough money to satisfy your needs and desires—
then other needs come to the fore.

We asked recent college graduates what factors they looked for in deciding
on a career. Surprisingly, salary ranked far from the top.

"Salary was not influential," one summed up for many. "Rather, the type
of work I would be doing and the possibilities for development and growth
within the position appealed greatly to me."

A young male graduate said his choice for a first position was "a growing
industry with a future where advancement seemed likely if one did his best."

Location turned out to be an important factor for many of these young
graduates. Some wanted to stay in the part of the country where they grew up.
Others wanted to move to a different region, or to a highly industrialized area
with more job opportunities.

Working conditions ranked high. Having a pleasant place to work, with
good facilities, proved to be important. Those who chose to go into teaching
mentioned the summers off as an important factor to them.

Salary, of course, *is* a factor. One insurance company personnel manager
said: "We can offer all the benefits in the world, including insurance, 12 paid
holidays a year, good possibilities for advancement, pleasant working conditions, a liberal educational policy. But if we didn't offer competitive salaries,
we simply wouldn't get the employees we need for an expanding business."

Your Own Checklist

Based on what *you* need—intellectually, socially, psychologically, financially
—the best thing to do is to make your own checklist when you are investigating
careers and, later, when you will be weighing possible job offers.

In your reading, talking with others, and actual looks at various professions in action, look for these factors:

Type of Work   On a day-to-day basis, what kind of work is actually done
by the people in this field?

Is it work that would continue to interest you or would it soon prove too
routine and boring.

Is it the kind of work that would make the fullest possible use of your
interests and abilities.

Is it the kind of work for which there will be a growing demand or it is a
diminishing field? (The classic story is told of the sales manager who says to
his board of directors, "I can't understand why we're not doing well. We make
the best buggy whips in the world.") Avoid the buggy whip industry.

Is the work done in a location that pleases you? (A word of advice on this
point: Many starting jobs are in field offices or in out-of-the-way locations.
Don't turn down a good job just because it is not in a metropolitan area. You
may find your best opportunity for good experience in an electronics plant in
the country or in a school system in a small town. If you prove yourself, your
next step could be a move to the big city.)

Advancement   Is the field in which you're interested one in which advancement comes if you prove yourself?

Is the company in which you're interested one that promotes people from
within the organization rather than looking outside to fill openings?

What does the United States Department of Labor say about the growth

possibilities of this industry or profession? What does the professional association for this career field indicate is its trend? What do the company publications
show on this point?

Training   Are there training and educational opportunities in this field and
in the specific companies?

Is the training paid for as a rule?

Have others in the field found it worthwhile to take further training?

Salary   Dr. Harold E. Mazyck, Jr., counselor at the Agricultural and Technical College of North Carolina, says that his most difficult counseling problem
is "convincing students that jobs with low salaries are as important as the more
highly paid jobs, and letting them know all jobs will require additional training
of some type in order to make the worker proficient." Yet you should be realistic
about financial needs.

Can you live on the salary paid in this field?

If you marry soon, will the salary be adequate?

Is there likelihood of more money for better performance?

Do the earnings depend heavily on day-to-day results, as they would for a
commission salesman? If so, are you the kind of self-starter who can work
that way, or do you need the security of a regular pay check?

What fringe benefits are offered that, in effect, increase the salary?

Where might you be financially in this field five or ten years from now?

What is the cost of living in the kind of community you would be living in
if you worked in this field?

Work Satisfaction   It is very hard to generalize about work satisfaction,
because so much depends on your personal needs.

Perhaps you are the kind of person who, for one reason or another, needs
a prestige job. This could be a handicap to you when you are just starting out.
But there are fields that, by their very nature, carry prestige. Just being in
television, even though you have a lowly job, carries an aura about it. Newspaper reporters have a certain prestige. In most communities and on most
college campuses, teachers and professors have status. Professional people such
as attorneys and physicians assume the prestige of the profession, even though
the starting job in law is as a law clerk, and in medicine as an intern in a
hospital.

If you are the kind of person who needs prestige, admit it. Otherwise you
will be miserable in an anonymous job with little status. But don't let prestige
get in your way. One college counselor says her most difficult problem is dealing
with the student "who unrealistically wants to start at the top or high middle of
the career ladder."

Some people derive satisfaction from the sense of a job well done, but
others must have their efforts recognized. Many Peace Cops workers find their
greatest satisfaction comes from knowing that they are helping someone,
although they may not receive any glory for it. This leads to the question of
whether you feel that what you do is important to the world. If this kind of
satisfaction is necessary to you, then you may be able to sacrifice other factors
for it. For example, social workers indicate that their greatest satisfaction comes
from the sense of helping others. This does not mean that you have to go into a
noncommercial field in order to have a sense of helping others. Many products

and services are designed to make life pleasanter, more secure, and easier, and the people working on or selling those products derive great personal satisfaction from their roles. Also, . . . more and more business organizations are addressing themselves to the solution of social problems, from which the employees derive great satisfaction.

Another source of work satisfaction comes to many from work in which they are continually learning. Although nearly every job teachers as it is performed, obviously some present greater opportunities for learning and growth. If continual growth is important to you, then choose a field where such growth is likely.

Above all, be as realistic about yourself as possible. Don't be afraid to aim high, but do select a career target that is in keeping with your own talents and abilities.

When and How to Make a Career Decision

Some people seem to know what they want to do in life almost from the time they are born. But such people are rare. Most students do not make a clear decision until quite late in their school lives.

The biggest handicap in making a career decision is lack of information about possible careers. The information exists but you have to dig it out.

Vocational guidance tests can help you discover where your abilities lie. Your guidance counselor can tell you where you could take such tests.

When Do You Know?

We asked some college seniors if and when they had made their career decisions. Almost all of them knew by their senior year what they wanted to do. But it was equally divided as to whether they knew while they were still in high school, or whether they made up their minds in their freshman, sophomore, or junior year of college.

Newly-graduated college people were asked these questions: Do you think it is important to have a specific career in mind when you enter college? How long do you think you can wait before making a decision?

Their answers show differing points of view on the subject.

One said, "You can wait until the very end of your senior year."

Another said, "I think that a student should be more interested in obtaining an education than in going to school for the purpose of job training. There can be no time limit set on such a decision. It depends entirely on the individual."

A third more or less agreed. "A student should have a general idea after two years of college so as to prepare himself. I feel he can wait as long as three years before choosing a specific career."

Others advised against making a hasty, wrong decision, saying it is better to take your time and be right.

Many advised flexibility. As one young man put it, "Even if you have a specific career in mind when entering college, you can change if another field interests you more."

Some felt it depends on your field. They said that a liberal arts major may not need to make an early career choice since his general education would fit him for many kinds of work. But they cautioned the student who may want to specialize in mathematics or science since he might not have the courses he needed to graduate if he postponed his career decision too long.

Still others felt that making your career decision early helps you make the best use of college. As one person stated: "College is a long enough road without taking time and effort that does not benefit you in your final goal." He felt that the decision should be made in the freshman year because, if it is made later, "the student may find it will take too long to graduate because of the many requirements he lacks."

When the answers were all thoroughly analyzed, however, they seemed to agree more than had at first appeared. The young graduates seemed to say that a *general* idea is good to have early, perhaps as early as high school. Then the *specific* career decisions can be made later.

For example, you may know from high school courses that the field of business seems right for you. But it is not until you actually begin to know more about the world of business that a specific aspect of the business world is selected. You may choose to go into public relations or advertising, once you know more about that aspect of business. Or you may find that your proficiency in mathematics suits you for a career as an actuary in an insurance company. Or you may choose retailing and begin work as an assistant buyer in a department store.

Professor Emily Chervenik, Coordinator of the University of Wisconsin Placement Services, says, "The choice of a college major should not be looked upon as a specific career commitment. Rather, it should be appreciated as the route by which the student can best achieve intellectual satisfaction and growth, and develop the tools of thinking, expression, discrimination, and problem-solving—techniques needed in every vocation."

If you do not know specifically what career you want for yourself, the advice seems to be, "Don't panic." Many people make their specific decisions late, even though they know their general fields early. On the other hand, don't wait too long or you will find that your courses have not been chosen appropriately, and you will need extra time to prepare yourself for your career.

College counselors warn against trying to force early choices. "Encourage students to look broadly," they say. But they also note that the goal-directed student is the one who ordinarily does better in both high school and college.

What Decides You?

How do people come to know what they want to do in life? We asked college seniors and recent graduates what influenced them in their choice of career.

In general, there were four factors:

* *high school courses in which they did well*
  ("Accounting came easy to me so it seemed logical to pursue this as a career.")
* *reading*
  ("I read all the available literature on careers that I could lay my hands on.")

- *friends and teachers*
  ("My advice is to rely on people in the field that interests you.")
- *work experience*
  (Many stated that summer or part-time jobs gave them a better idea of a field than anything else could have.)

Courses   One of the basic purposes of going to school is to be introduced to new and different areas of knowledge. Many students taking a foreign language for the first time in high school find that they learn it easily and enjoy it. This could lead to a career decision to teach a foreign language, to become a translator, or perhaps to combine the proficiency with another interest leading to work overseas for a corporation or for the government.

There are opportunities to take courses outside of school, too. Many cities now have an educational television station, and many of these give courses from time to time or on a regular basis. Some of the commercial networks offer courses in the early morning hours which might give you a better idea of the scope of the field in which you are interested.

Don't be afraid to register for a course in which you think you might not do well. Some students make the mistake of taking courses in too few fields, so that they never learn about possible interests and aptitudes in other fields. Although grades are important, they are not the real reason for an education.

Reading   The written sources of information about careers are many and varied.

Newspapers and magazines often carry stories about people in interesting careers, describing their preparation, the kind of work they do, and the rewards they get from their work.

Professional associations are another source of information. Nearly every profession has an association or society which publishes a magazine or newsletter, as well as separate pamphlets on various aspects of the profession. For example, the National Education Association has a student membership group which brings printed information on teaching to those who are considering a career in teaching. There is a society or association which publishes information of interest to those thinking about going into accounting, medicine, dentistry, nursing, advertising, radio and television, insurance, oceanography, the armed forces, scientific farming, forestry, sales, journalism, library science—almost anything you could name.

In addition to that, many high schools and nearly all colleges have collections of pamphlets and brochures on various careers. Many also have publications issued by specific companies to describe the kinds of jobs available at the company, as well as the company's activities.

Guidance and counseling are available in most high schools and all colleges. Recent graduates cited such services as extremely helpful. One University of Wisconsin graduate said, "The high school I attended had a counseling bureau. The services such bureaus offer, I feel, are the best guide to the student." Speaking of his college placement and counseling services, he added, "They are staffed by people who are intelligent, resourceful, and most important, understanding."

The United States government publishes many books and pamphlets on careers, telling the opportunities, the training needed, the outlook for the future, the range of salary paid and so on. One such book, *Occupational Outlook Handbook,* is issued every two years by the Department of Labor. The current edition is over 850 pages long, which gives you some idea of its comprehensiveness. In addition, the same department issues hundreds of separate pamphlets on various fields—dental hygiene, electronic computing, home economics, advertising, earth science, the FBI, psychology, watch repairing, biological science, just to mention a few.

Most of the pamphlets are sold for five or ten cents; the *Handbook* is five dollars. If you have no clear idea of the various occupations open to someone with your interests, you should browse through the *Handbook* and read descriptions of the kinds of work done by people in the fields that interest you. Most high schools and colleges have a copy. If you can't borrow a copy, you can purchase one from the Superintendent of Documents, Washington, D.C. 20402.

In addition, any company that interests you would be glad to send you whatever information it publishes on what it does and the kinds of work done by its employees.

Other People   Most students reported that they talked with just everybody they could buttonhole, including friends, their parents, teachers, counselors, older people working in their fields. One boy chose teaching when he saw "the close rapport my sister had been able to establish with her classes."

Many said that they "hung around" places where they thought they might like to work. A boy who chose medicine spent a great deal of time around hospitals. Another, who chose journalism, liked to drop in at a print shop and the local newspaper office to talk with the men and women working there.

Other opportunities for hearing people talk about their work come when career representatives visit the schools and colleges for Career Days. This is not only a chance to listen but a chance to ask questions about a field that may be right for you. John L. Munschauer, Director of Cornell University's Career Center, advises students to "develop a technique for interviewing people who work to learn about the world of work."

Work Experience   By far the greatest influence in deciding on a career comes from previous work experience.

"There's nothing like it," said one college girl, "to give you the inside picture of what actually goes on in the world of work."

Dr. Norman Frisbey, Director of the University Placement Service, The Pennsylvania State University, says that the greatest mistake students make in trying to decide on a career is "not gaining a realistic picture of what a particular career offers." Then he adds, "The student has to take the initiative in this respect."

When asked, "Have you done anything while in college to give you pre-career experience in your field?", college seniors were almost unanimous in answering "yes." They used summer and part-time work to get a good picture of what they were getting into and also to help them make up their minds about whether they had chosen correctly.

A senior who is majoring in statistics spent a summer working in the actuarial department of an insurance company. One who wants to be a magazine editor has worked in the university printing shop, written articles for newspapers and magazines, worked on the yearbook, and worked as a research assistant. A boy who wants to go into range management has been working for the Soil Conservation Service. A girl who wants to teach has participated in a student observation program with the Student National Education Association. A young man who intends to be a technical draftsman worked part time in a local shop while in college. A college senior who plans a career in public affairs spent two summers in Washington as a government intern, worked in some political campaigns, and took part in a work-study program in New York City in lieu of one senior course.

College seniors and those who have recently graduated warn against taking a job just for the money. In their opinion, summer and part-time work should be used as a means to explore fields and find out if you are suited to them. A summer as a hospital orderly or nurse's aide may convince you—one way or another—about a career in the health field.

More and more companies now have training programs for young men and women still in college. If you qualify, you work for the company during the summer in a training program that is partly classwork and partly on-the-job training. The hope is that you will join the company after you graduate from college. Because of the large amount of time and money invested in you, some companies ask that you work at least two years for them following graduation. The societies and professional associations in your field can tell you which companies have such summer training programs and whether you would qualify.

There are also internships now available in education and in government. Your placement counselor will have information on such jobs, many of which involve teaching young children, doing research, working with older people who need retraining or basic education, and so forth. Many Head Start programs for preschool youngsters need paid workers as well as volunteers during the summer months or part time during the regular school year.

There are also opportunities for studying abroad during the summer. Such study may not be precisely work-oriented, unless you plan to specialize in a foreign language or work in another country after graduation, but it contributes greatly to your general education. Some study is arranged on the basis of exchange followships, with all expenses paid except for travel to a port of embarkation, such as New York City or San Francisco. Information can be obtained from the Institute of International Education, 809 United Nations Plaza, New York, New York 10017.

The sum of all this occupational research—taking courses, reading, talking with others, work experience—is to get the "feel" of the occupation in which you are interested.

What Employers Are Looking for

You may have heard your parents or other adults talk about conditions at the time they finished school. If they happened to enter the job market during the depression of the 1930's, the lucky break was to get a job—any kind of job.

Today the situation is much different. There is a shortage of capable people in nearly every field. Although business and industry and government need people as never before for an expanding economy and growing population, they are not able to hire as many qualified people as they need. Despite the fact that the number of graduates is higher each year, the demand for them has recently exceeded the supply.

But do not be lulled into a false sense of security by such a situation. You still have to have appreciable qualifications to land a career-type job.

The Negative Side of the Coin

Not long ago, Dr. Frank S. Endicott, Director of Placement, Northwestern University, Evanston, Illinois, queried 153 companies and asked them to list the reasons they had rejected college graduate applicants. The 50 reasons listed by the companies point up the kinds of personal traits employers are not looking for. The same would apply in general to high school graduates and in nonprofit fields.

The number one reason for rejection was poor personal appearance. This may seem trivial, but every employee represents his company or organization in the eyes of the public and an unkempt appearance creates an unnecessary handicap. Moreover, if you are careless about your personal appearance, you are probably careless about your work.

Another reason why employment was refused was "inability to express himself clearly—poor voice, diction, grammar." Good speech has always been the mark of an educated person. Perhaps you have been handicapped by growing up in a family or community that lacked either the means for developing good speech habits or the interest in it. But you have the opportunity, through education, of developing good speech. There are very few jobs where it is not important. Certainly, if you are going to be a teacher or a salesperson, or will meet the public in any way, you must be able to express yourself effectively. In your dealings with your employers and fellow employees, communicating your ideas accurately and well is important. If your present speech would make a poor impression in a job interview or in your chosen career field, by all means do something about it now while you have the opportunities that school or college provides.

Also high on the list was "lack of planning for career—no purposes or goals." Closely following that was "lack of interest and enthusiasm—passive, indifferent."

Another reason for rejection was "failure to participate in activities." Earlier, we noted the advice of a college graduate to participate in *worthwhile* extracurricular activities. There is no need to join *everything,* but the failure to participate in *anything* indicates that you may not mix well with others on the job.

"Overemphasis on money" was next, and it was followed by "poor scholastic record—just got by." Next was "unwilling to start at the bottom—expects too much too soon."

If any of these reasons for rejection could apply to you, you might—with attention on your part and with help from teachers—be able to do something about them now, while you are still in school.

The Positive Side of the Coin

If you reverse the reasons why employers turn down applicants, you get some clues to what they are looking for. There is no standard packaged personality that employers want, but there are general characteristics that make a prospective employee appealing.

Your field, of course, determines to a certain extent the background and characteristics that will stand you in good stead. If you are bent on becoming a research scientist, you do not require the kind of outgoing personality that a salesman would need. If you intend to become an engineer, you need a different preparation than if you would like to become a textbook editor. Those seeking employment in the Peace Corps have either different personalities or different needs than those who want to begin in a long-range profession immediately after graduation.

But, in general, there are some qualities that are helpful in any kind of work.

All employers are looking for people who *show initiative.* Contrary to popular opinion about large organizations, nobody seeks the "yes man." Although a certain amount of conformity is needed in any organization—including nonconformist organizations—the better employees are those who find creative and new ways of doing things.

Employers expect a *basic background preparation.* The number of applicants among college graduates who cannot express themselves in writing or speaking is shocking to most employers. The employer also feels he has a right to expect that you have learned the fundamentals in your field. Every employer, including school systems, government, and business, expects to train you on the job for your specific duties. But you will be further ahead if you bring to this training basic knowledge of the general field on which you can build.

Employers expect you to be *interested in the job,* and in the field that it represents. If it's "just a job" to you, this general lack of interest in the goals of the company or organization will soon be reflected by your doing slipshod work.

Interest will be expressed by the good employee in *trying to learn more.* Opportunities frequently are offered for further training on the job, but most of the work will have to be done by you. This quality of eagerness to learn more is readily apparent to future employers if you have it and very difficult to fake if it is lacking.

Employers are also extremely interested in what you have accomplished to date because they believe in *patterns of behavior.* One personnel manager of a large corporation said, "The best indicator of future success is past performance." This does not mean that people cannot change. It does mean that people tend to follow general patterns of behavior and that these patterns are usually set at a very early age. Although everyone can cite examples of poor students who became great leaders in government or business, those examples are the exceptions. The ordinary pattern is for the student who does poorly in school to do poorly at work. Other patterns of behavior also seem to hold true. The student who participated in almost nothing in school will tend to be a loner on the job. If the job in which he is interested is one that is best done in isolation, then his lack of participation is almost an asset. But if he is seeking a job that requires team effort, as most jobs do, then a previous pattern of isolation is not a strong selling point to a prospective employer.

When you are doing your research on employment possibilities within your field, you will have an opportunity to observe the kinds of people who are recognized for doing an effective job. Although they will have different kinds of personalities and different strengths and weaknesses, they will probably display some of the positive characteristics we have just been discussing.

It would be well, too, to ask recruiters about the kinds of people they are most interested in hiring. You will find that they will emphasize attitudes more than they will emphasize present abilities, for they realize that abilities can be developed and learned while attitudes are fairly well established by the time a person is ready for his life's work.

A Final Word

In the writing of this booklet, we are indebted to the many college seniors, recent college graduates, and college placement directors who took the time and trouble to fully answer questions about choosing a career.

We were impressed with the effort that many students put into the task of selecting a career. Nearly every student and recent graduate queried had shown great enterprise and initiative in gathering information about careers and then looking further into those that interested them to gain more information and first-hand knowledge. The moral seems to be that nobody is going to walk up to you and hand you a career. You have to locate it for yourself, find out as much about it as you can for yourself, and then prepare yourself—academically and personally—for it.

This does not mean that you won't get help. It is there—in the placement and counseling offices, among people already in the world of work, among teachers and professors, in the thousands of publications that are written each year with you in mind.

The world of work needs you—if you are willing to work, and if you have something to offer a prospective employer. Now is the time for you to apply yourself to your full-time job of being a student so that you will enter the world of work with the equipment needed for a career in which you will find satisfaction.

Good luck!

Discussion Questions
1. What are some of the psychological characteristics of normal male adolescents?
2. In what ways can "love" be used to exploit rather than to enhance a relationship?
3. What are some of the behavioral differences between "stayers" and "leavers" in college?
4. What are some of the tricks you have developed to make studying easier and more effective for you?
5. What is the difference between a career and a job?

Chapter 5
Adulthood

In each culture, the standards for adulthood vary according to the social and economic conditions of that society. However, in our culture the term "adulthood" is not easy to define especially since, depending on various political or legal considerations, the criteria may shift dramatically from one decade to the next. For example, one of the legal standards for adulthood is whether or not an individual is allowed the right to vote. Traditionally, the voting age has been twenty-one but recent legal rulings have lowered the voting age to eighteen. This in itself represents a dramatic change in what society defines as the legal competence necessary to make an important political choice. Does it follow, however, that the simple definition of a voting age is a sufficiently clear reason to expect that adulthood has been reached? Probably not, but as you can see the concept of adulthood, as well as other terms that imply complex relationships between cultural, biological, and psychological variables, can become quite arbitrary. Most psychologists would probably evaluate each person's case for adulthood on its own individual merits. For example, a sixteen-year-old might show unusual responsibility and self-reliance, while another person, considerably older, might show immature dependency and lack of self-reliance. If, however, the second individual were twenty-one and the first sixteen, the legal code in most states would automatically confer adulthood on the twenty-one-year-old. This chapter examines a diverse group of adult experiences and may offer some insights into the complicated process of "adulthood."

The first article, "On Being a Scientist," is a penetrating description of the distinctive qualities that go into being a scientist. Many of us have developed interesting stereotypes about the kinds of intelligence and personal qualities which in our own minds define the term "scientist." Mitchell Wilson in this article carefully and insightfully penetrates beneath the outer coverings of science and tries to reach the uniquely creative qualities of the individual scientist. What emerges is a picture of individuals who are not only unusually intelligent but also capable of great emotion, temperament, and commitment. Like all people, scientists are idiosyncratic. They have their peculiar likes, dislikes, and quirks of personality that make them especially human. The picture one gets from Mitchell Wilson's writing is that scientists are not very much different from other people. An interesting point brought out in this paper is that the intended humanistic goal of a scientist may not necessarily turn out as originally anticipated. Alfred Nobel developed high explosives to make warfare so terrible that it would never be inflicted upon others again. How wrong he was; yet the Nobel prizes in many fields, as well as peace, are a memorial to his life. The Wright Brothers assumed that the airplane could act as an air scout to investigate enemy positions and detect movement of armaments to the front. Thus, military surprise would be impossible and large-scale warfare would be a thing of the past. How naive this assumption was. Still, science and technology are the foundations of our civilization and a remarkably important area of endeavor in any age of history.

The creativity found in science, art, literature, and so on is expressed quite differently in the acting profession. Acting is an unusual creative experience in that it requires the interpretation of other people's work through various mediums of communication. Actors do not personally or totally invent their characters but rather are tools that are molded by an author and director into a desired form.

The article by William Henry and John Sims portrays actors as people whose job it is to play other identities and whose quality as actors hinges upon how well they suppress their own identity so as not to blur the vividness of the role they are playing. These authors, psychologists, studied a group of acting professionals from the New York theater and younger actors in training. They interviewed and tested thirty-two professional actors and attempted to develop a profile of the personalities of actors, using Erikson's developmental stages as a psychological structure from which to conceptualize this information. Erik Erikson, of course, is a famous psychoanalyst who has offered a number of creative extensions of psychoanalytic theory and whose model of the person is an especially appropriate basis from which to study personality. How actors achieve a balance between the identity of the role and the identity of their person is interestingly studied in this article.

In the first chapter of this book on basic processes is found Tom Alexander's article entitled "There Are Sex Differences in the Mind, Too." His thesis is that there are crucial biological differences between males and females and that these biological differences are powerful enough to create temperamental variations between the sexes that cannot be accounted for by cultural factors. Diana Trilling in her article "Female Biology in a Male Culture" produces the view that psychoanalytic theory and social conditions have put women down in such a denigrating way that the identity of women has become completely submerged in a male-dominated culture. One of the many interesting points Diana Trilling makes is that female sexual differences which are biologically unique have been labeled by male commentators as having negative cultural values. For example, the appropriate biological distinction that Freud made between the activity of the male and the passivity of the female has assumed value connotations which are positive to the male but quite negative and blaming to the female. The cultural definition of passivity as bad has served to put down a variety of potentially rewarding interests of women and instead has created a psychological atmosphere of guilt and blame shared by many women in our society. Trilling would like to see cultural values revised to generate more appreciation of those meaningful biological functions of women which have been demeaned and devalued in our society.

Perhaps one of the most taboo subjects for discussion in our society is death. While all people learn that death is inevitable, our folkways and traditions always treat the prospect of death as an untouchable topic. Recently, for a variety of reasons, the medical and psychological communities have begun to study the phenomena of dying so as to develop a more humane understanding of the processes involved. The article "Learning to Die" by Thomas Powers is a powerful and significant review of what is being done in this area through a poignant description of a remarkable person going through the final stages of a terminal illness. Powers details some of the psychological stages the dying person experiences and the kind of behavior often expected under these circumstances. First denial, then anger, followed by a desperate bargaining for life, and finally in the fourth stage a sense of depression and grief breaks through. A fifth stage, referred to as acceptance, is to some a final realistic appraisal of an inevitable event. What is quite clear from this article is that people have different styles of facing and contending with perhaps the most threatening of all human concerns. While not mentioned in this article, there are other studies going on in which hallucinogenic drugs such as LSD are administered under medical and psychiatric supervision to relieve some of the fearful agonies of dying. These studies, incomplete as they are, also suggest that psychotherapy and other procedures which induce psychological understanding and acceptance are humane and decent treatments for people who are in the twilight of their lives.

Suggested Readings

Jourard, Sidney M. *Self-Disclosure: An Experimental Analysis of the Transparent Self.* New York: John Wiley & Sons, 1971. The experience of self-disclosure is examined by an eminent psychologist.

Lieberman, Bernhardt (Ed.) *Human Sexual Behavior.* New York: John Wiley & Sons, 1971. A series of readings covering material on the sexual revolution, marital and extramarital sex, and other topics.

Skinner, B. F. *Beyond Freedom and Dignity.* New York: Alfred A. Knopf, 1971. An exciting and controversial study of man by a prominent psychologist.

Southwell, Eugene A., and Merbaum, Michael (Eds.) *Personality: Readings in Theory and Research.* Belmont, Calif.: Brooks-Cole Publishing Co., 1971. Surveys the field of personality and presents classic theory, research, and critical articles by important personality theorists.

"In the end, among themselves, scientists respect only one quality —excellence."

The scientist has often been the object of both respect and awe by many people. In this paper, Mitchell Wilson attempts to humanize the scientist and allows us to glimpse the real figure behind the label.

To the outside world, the word *scientist* refers to a jumble of strange bed-fellows—physicists, chemists, biologists, and at least thirty other clans—who spend their lives among the riddles and realities of nature. Each man is convinced that his particular science is more important than the others—and totally different in the intellectual and temperamental qualities it requires. Physicists speak of organic chemistry as being as boring as bookkeeping. Biologists retort that the intellectual austerity of physics is as airless and soul-numbing as the inside of an ether cone. Lord Todd, white-haired Nobel laureate in organic chemistry, once while telling how he had taken over a problem from biochemistry, assured me that the two chemistries were totally different disciplines, even though to a non-scientist they seem to be concerned with almost identical material.

With preferences so passionately defended, and distinctions so finely drawn, one would assume that a man ought to be able to tell you why he made his particular choice. I. I. Rabi at Columbia said flatly: "Because physics is the only basic science there is. Everything else is to the right of it and depends on it. Nothing is to the left of it."

Max Perutz in Cambridge said just as flatly: "Molecular biology is the basic science of life; it is now the only way one knows what one is talking about."

Allan Sandage at Mount Palomar says: "Astronomy and cosmogony—that's where the great questions still have to be answered."

Jacques Monod of the Pasteur Institute says: "Why biology? Well, because I felt that was where the most work was to be done."

Picasso, when asked why he chose to be an artist, lost his temper and retorted that when a man finds himself asking why he is doing what he is doing, it is time for him to give it up. The men of science whom I questioned kept their tempers; still, what they gave me were not reasons at all but only statements of preference. These highly analytical men were no more able to describe precisely what had captured their minds than is any young lover to explain why he is deeply in love with a particular girl and not her sister. They knew there would never be wealth as the world measures it, nor even success in the popular sense. Why, then, do they do what they do? They don't know.

I had assumed, too, that the scientist's objectivity would enable him to discern not only new ideas but the men who generate new ideas. Among physicists, the saying goes that "there are really only two categories of men who become theoreticians: the geniuses, and the men who are merely brilliant. Those less than brilliant needn't bother to come around." Scientists themselves, of course, know their ranks include a great many who are far from brilliant, and some who are incompetent. They know, too, that among them are science snobs and climbers who want to be—and be seen—in the presence of famous and accomplished scientists. There are also the science politicians and influence brokers. But no matter how contemptible, foolish, fatuous, or venal a man may be, the work he does and has done weighs more with his fellow scientists than the ugliness which is all the outside world may see.

In the end, among themselves, scientists respect only one quality—excellence. No scientist cares that Newton could be meanly vindictive, that Michelson compulsively chased girls, that Pauli's wit could be malevolent and destructive. The scientist reveres talent when it exists, but the men whose careers are dedicated to increasing man's perception of the universe are not always able to perceive among themselves those who will emerge and tower over everyone else.

Albert Einstein was thought to have so little promise at graduation that no school or university bothered to offer him a job. Five years later, in 1905, at the age of twenty-six, the still supposedly untalented man working as an obscure patent clerk in Bern published three original papers in a single year, each of which was destined to become a classic of scientific thought. The response from the world of science to this unprecedented performance was total indifference. That silence persisted for another five years.

When Niels Bohr in 1913—also in his twenties—worked out the bizarre conditions under which an atom could have the planetary structure which experiment seemed to call for, it was only one of dozens of alternative atomic theories that had been appearing in the journals month after month for decades. No one paid very much attention even though, a few months after publication, Einstein confided to a friend that Bohr's ideas, however radical, were of the greatest importance. "I once had similar ideas but I didn't dare publish them!" was his amazing confession. Albert Szent-Gyorgyi, who has ranged over half a dozen fields in the life sciences with brilliance and Hungarian wit, admits that he once so despaired of any recognition in his early years in biochemistry that he actually determined on suicide.

There are instances of overlooked talent far worse than these—cases where true ability went unacknowledged until ten, twenty, thirty years after the man's death. The monk Mendel, for example, founded the science of genetics in a monastery garden; the physician Semmelweis was hounded out of Vienna for pioneering prophylaxis; and even Sadi Carnot's membership in one of France's more eminent families did not keep his work on thermodynamics from being totally ignored during his lifetime and for twenty years after his death.

Currently an attempt is being made to soften the latent but growing hostility to technology and science by insisting that the scientist *is* really quite human. Just like everyone else, he likes tennis, sports cars, cookouts, his family. The DuPont Corporation assures you that their scientists are just as active in local and community affairs as their neighbors—if not more so. A recent book stated that its "main aim is to present to the reader the American scientist just as he is—a person who happens to enjoy science as much as a lawyer enjoys law, or a doctor enjoys the practice of medicine, or a business-man enjoys the daily hassle of business."

Well, "enjoy" is a pretty pale word for what goes on. The scientist is like everyone else only if "everyone else" is restricted to that infinitely small number of fortunate men who manage to find in life precisely that one pursuit that engages their best abilities, their minds and passions, with more felicity than most wives ever do.

There is pleasure—profound pleasure, both of touch and mind—to the experimentalist in the manipulation of apparatus. If he has designed it himself, there is the added pleasure of seeing it perform its delicate intricacies exactly as he conceived it, under his direct control. The theorist, in addition, has the overwhelming satisfaction of feeling that he has been intuitively attuned to the subtlest nuances of nature when one of his hypotheses turns out to be true.

Richard Feynman at fifty wears his Nobel Prize like an open-collared shirt. Twenty-five years ago at Los Alamos, he was an *enfant terrible*, bubbling with quick brilliance on the theoretical problems of bomb-building that came his way. "It was a succession of successes—but easy successes. After the war, I moved over to the kind of problems [like the self-energy of the electron] that men spend years thinking about. On that level there are no easy successes; and the satisfaction you get when you're proved right is so great that even if it occurs only twice in a lifetime, everything else is worth it!"

Recently, Jack Peter Green, who does pharmacology in terms of quantum chemistry, was polishing a research paper during a country weekend. He had spent more than a year working over the molecular structure of a number of chemically diverse hallucinogens—LSD, mescaline, and others—and was finally able to prove that one specific atomic configuration can be discerned somewhere in the molecular structure of each. I was amazed to hear sounds of private satisfaction come from his room; but later when he was discussing his results, it was clear that his delight had nothing to do with pride in his own performance or with the prestige that would be coming to him for his discovery. It was purely aesthetic pleasure in the exquisite way nature ordered things. "How elegant it is!" he kept saying. "And so simple!"

A young Italian scientist's English was slow and meticulous. "I feel guilty about coming back to the lab after hours to get a little more done, and still I always come back," he said to me. "I know very well that whether I come in or not on Sunday, there will be no great change in science. I neglect my wife and my little daughter for those few extra hours—yet I keep coming. Why? Is it really only curiosity? Because if that's all that's driving me, then it's wrong for me to come for that additional time." "Then why *do* you come in?" I persisted. "Because it is my happiness," he said simply. "This is where I want most in the world to be—this is what I want most in the world to be doing."

Only young artists, actors, musicians, and writers know the same immersion, because what is involved is the deep engagement of a talent; and only a talent at work allows the hours, days, and years of a life to roll by without being counted. That is why, in such lives, there is a far more dangerous risk than failure—there is the terrifying possibility that some day the love affair may stop. Then, tragically, all that is left is the pain of disillusion and the stunned sense of all those wasted years. A scientist, like the artist, is not only different from other men; he had better go on being different!

Whatever is different about the scientist must begin with the particular kind of intelligence such a man possesses. It is said that the scientist must have an inquiring mind—which is true; and that he must also be one of those people who take deep pleasure in learning—which is also true, and also superficial; because both these qualities are demanded also by any number of other disciplines. The particular kind of sensibilities required by a scientist are more complicated.

Begin with his intense awareness of words and their meanings. While the poet's affinity for words makes him sensitive to their sound, emotion, and rhythm, the scientist uses them as instruments of precision. He must be capable of inventing new words to express new physical concepts. He must be able to reason verbally by analogy—to explain "how this thing is like that thing," and to be able to fit the many resemblances into one single generalization that covers them all.

The scientist must also think graphically, in terms of dynamical models, three-dimensional arrangements in space. The dynamical model of a bacterial cell, for example, is a hollow rigid capsule that may be either spherical or tubular, containing an otherwise shapeless living cell enclosed within a soft sac, the plasma membrane. Niels Bohr's dynamical model of an atom is a miniature solar system with relatively enormous electrons orbiting about an almost inconceivably small sun—the atomic nucleus—a tremendous distance away. Scientists keep these three-dimensional pictures in mind as vividly as if they were actually seeing them. Formulas and equations printed on a two-dimensional page have three-dimensional meanings, and the scientist must be able to read in three dimensions to "see the picture" at once. There is nothing "abstract" about a scientist's thinking.

This visualization is so vivid that a scientist examining a theoretical problem is really like a jeweler peering through his loupe at a gem which he holds close to his eye, turning it over and over in his fingers. To Einstein, there was nothing abstract about his theory of relativity. Even the slightest apparent deviation from the hard world of physical reality made him intellectually uncomfortable. For more than a decade, meeting at international science conferences, he and Bohr, by then both in middle age, had monumental arguments over the meaning of the uncertainty principle, with Einstein the one who stuck stolidly to the basic mechanistic principle of cause and effect. "I cannot believe that God throws dice," he said.

The split between the so-called "Two Cultures" is much more than a matter of humanists learning more about science, and the scientists spending more time on aesthetics. Unless a man has some kind of spatial imagination along with his verbal sensibility he will always be—as far as understanding science goes—in the role of the tone-deaf struggling with a course in music appreciation. On the other hand, the possessor of both verbal and spatial sensibility will rather quickly be bored if asked to limit his imagination to only the verbal domain, in the case of the humanities; or to only the spatial domain, in the case of the graphic arts.

A man accustomed to working at the peak of his powers has no patience with anything that calls on him to work at only half-load. With this dual sensibility then, the true scientist would find it difficult "to be like everyone else" even if he wanted to.

Not only is there a split between scientists and other people, there is also a sharp split among scientists themselves. Within specializations, a division runs across every field—a sort of trans-science geological fault, which results from the fact that there are two kinds of scientific knowledge. Claude Bernard, the founder of experimental medicine, pointed out that there is the knowledge we already possess, and there is the knowledge we still have to discover. One type of scientist—the man with encyclopedic knowledge of past and current thought in science—can make an inspiring teacher or a brilliant research administrator, but he is not necessarily the man who is most creative. The other type of scientist—a beachcomber on the edge of the sea of the unknown—may be so haphazardly versed in the literature of his own field that he sometimes invents and discovers things that have been invented and discovered before.

Szent-Gyorgyi says he feels embarrassed, isolated, and ignorant at meetings in the presence of these highly articulate scientists who seem to have all knowledge at their fingertips, even though he is the one with the Nobel Prize and they are not. The Polaroid inventor, Edwin Land, feels that discoveries are made by those scientists who have freed themselves "from a way of thinking that is held by friends and associates who may be more intelligent, better educated, better disciplined, but who have not mastered the art of the fresh clean look at the old, old knowledge."

In the main it is these intellectual ragamuffins who are responsible for the great advances; just as the great novels and poems are not written by men of the widest erudition and critical ability. History is a cruel bookkeeper and carries on its ledgers only the names of those who create what is enduring; it drops forever the men who appear to scintillate in their own times with the knowledge only of their own time. J. Robert Oppenheimer was a billiant administrator of other men's work, and a judge who could make piercing evaluations of other men's work. But when it came time—figuratively speaking— to write his own poetry in science, his work was sparse, angular, and limited, particularly when judged by the standards he himself set for everyone else. He knew the major problems of his time; he attacked them with style; but he apparently lacked that intuition—that faculty beyond logic which logic needs— in order to make great advances. If one were speaking not of science but of religion, one could say that Oppenheimer's religiosity was the kind that could make him a bishop but never a saint.

This particular quality which is so essential to the scientist is almost indefinable. Years ago, as a graduate student, I was present at a three-way argument between Rabi, Szilard, and Fermi. Szilard took a position and mathematically stated it on the blackboard. Rabi disagreed and rearranged the equations to the form he would accept. All the while Fermi was shaking his head. "You're both wrong," he said. They demanded proof. Smiling a little, he shrugged his shoulders as if proof weren't needed. "My intuition tells me so," he said.

I had never heard a scientist refer to his intuition, and I expected Rabi and Szilard to laugh. They didn't. The man of science, I soon found, works with the procedures of logic so much more than anyone else that he, more than anyone else, is aware of logic's limitations. Beyond logic there is intuition, and the creative scientist often is out there, rather than within the exquisitely arranged landscapes of rigorous logic.

For eighteen years before Newton wrote down the general law of gravitational attraction, he had an intuitive perception that the earth's gravitational force extended at least as far as the moon and was responsible for the moon's motion. Even then, another year passed before it became clear that an assumption basic to the whole idea had still not been proven—and the matter was brought to Newton's attention. He went to work on it at once. The next day he handed over a few sheets of paper containing the mathematical proof that a spherical mass, no matter how large—earth, moon, or sun—behaves gravitationally as if all its mass were concentrated into a single point at its center. Newton had assumed intuitively for years that something like this might be the case, and for all those years had never for a moment thought that everyone else did not share his perception.

A composer looked at me with surprise when I happened to mention that the scientist experienced creativity in exactly the same way as the artist. "But what does he create?" he asked. "I thought he dealt only with logical processes —deductions from experiment."

Creativity for the scientist does have certain characteristics that are unique. To begin with, the scientist picks his problem because he knows enough about it to know that no one knows very much about it—except that there are unanswered questions there. Out of insight or inspiration, he suggests a possible answer to one of the questions: for example, What *is* a possible structure for the atom? What *does* bind the atoms together to form molecules? By *what* means does the living cell store the chemical energy released within its walls? The creative moment occurs when the suggested answer is being formed. Naturally, the scientist would like to be proved right, and so the performance of the deciding experiment can never be the dispassionate exercise it is popularly thought to be. Experiment carries all the emotion of a contest. Objectivity lies in the scientist's willingness to accept, however reluctantly, evidence that his brilliant conception is wrong. Once Nature gives its decision, there is no appeal. In fairly short order then, the scientist is ruthlessly informed whether his creation is valid or not. The artist, on the other hand, has no such objective standard. He can always find, or invent, an aesthetic system to justify his creation.

There are several other important differences between creativity for the artist and for the scientist. If Shakespeare had never written *Hamlet,* if Beethoven had not lived to create *Eroica,* no one else would have brought these works into existence. Other artists would have created other works. In science, though, if Einstein had never lived to work out relativity, if Maarten Schmidt hadn't recognized the nature of the quasars in the sky, or if Crick and Watson had not solved the structure of DNA, other scientists would have done so. The world of art is infinite in creative possibilities, the world of science is restricted: there is only one Nature to be discovered.

Again, no work of art has ever had—even can have—the revolutionary impact on man and his society the way the introduction of a new technology can. With the artist, a moment of history comes to an end when he finishes his particular work and the act of creation is completed. With the scientist, it is that precise moment that a new phase of history begins; even though he himself cannot possibly foresee what future generations will add to his contribution or choose to do with it. This is where he is the prisoner of his own time.

Faraday couldn't conceivably guess that dropping a small bar magnet down the center of a coil of wire would mean that a hundred years later millions of miles of electric power lines would flash billions of kilowatt-hours back and forth across the earth. Nor could Semmelweis know that his campaign to save women from death by puerperal fever was one of the several steps that would help lead—five generations later—to the threat of such world overpopulation that mass starvation looms as one of man's possible fates.

Not long ago, I asked Otto Robert Frisch, who, with his aunt, Lise Meitner, had actually been the first to realize that uranium atoms were indeed undergoing nuclear fission with enormous emissions of energy, whether at that point (1939) he had any sense of what his work was to lead to. He had been a young man then, a refugee from Hitler Austria.

"My aunt and I spent the weekend together in the Swedish countryside," he said. "She told me what she had just heard from Hahn in Berlin. We discussed it over and over as we walked through the woods; and the more we talked, the more we became convinced that the uranium nuclei were indeed breaking up—*fission* was *her* word for it. We wrote up a short joint paper on this completely unsuspected nuclear process before we separated. She went back to Stockholm, and I went back to Copenhagen to the Bohr Institute. I had a vague sense that we were onto something that might be important, but I couldn't say how. I remember writing to my parents that we might have a tiger by the tail, but believe it or not I couldn't think of an experiment to do until Plazcek—do you remember him; the most skeptical man in the world?— Plazcek said he didn't believe any part of it, and that made me so angry that I said I'd prove it to him, and I did. But you see, that was all still months before Joliot in Paris detected the emission neutrons ejected during each fission which meant that a chain reaction was possible. I had no way of guessing that this would be so."

The inventors of radically new machines always judge the value of what they create, but their judgment is embedded in the standards and needs of their own times. Dr. Richard Gatling, a Union Army surgeon, appalled by the bloody cost of the American Civil War, reasoned that he could reduce the number of losses by reducing the size of armies. He developed a gun with a tenfold firing power so that one man could do the work of ten. The Gatling gun—the first modern machine gun—turned out to have a very different effect.

The Wright brothers seriously weighed the possible future effects of their invention. They saw their airplane as a sort of air scout able to fly over enemy lines and detect every movement. Military surprise would be impossible, and from then on wars would be useless.

When Einstein's work on relativity led him to the historic discovery of the convertibility of mass and energy, he did not foresee how this principle would act as a guide to the release of nuclear energy. Is he to be held responsible for the deaths at Hiroshima? Does history hold Newton guilty for every artillery barrage laid down by all the armies of the world in every war of the past three hundred years because one of the outcomes of Newton's laws of dynamics was the artillerist's science of ballistics?

Yet because of the scientist's inability to look over the walls of history and foresee what subsequent generations will do with the fruits of his discovery, society today blames the scientist for what it wrenched from his hand and turned into engines of evil, poisoning the earth's atmosphere, crust, and waters. The scientist is bewildered to find himself considered the villain. It is as if Prometheus were chained to the rock—not by the gods from whom he stole the fire, but by the men he tried to help, because, as they claim, he had now made it possible for them to burn one another to death. Nevertheless, the very scientists who are being considered the bogeymen are the ones who must still be called upon to use their ingenuity to help undo the damage which society has done to itself. They are more than anxious to meet the challenge.

19. Actor's Search for a Self
William E. Henry and John H. Sims

"His life is given over to portraying the identity of others."

The actor is a fascinating topic. We associate acting with glamour and a world of exciting fantasy. This study of the personality of the actor makes for interesting research and helps to shed some light on this group of talented people.

We seem to be of two minds in our thinking about creativity. Almost everyone agrees that creativity is desirable—we all like to think we are creative in our work as architects, social scientists, executives or chemists. And yet, simultaneously, we preserve an older, more exclusive meaning, one that supposes that there is a terrible price to be paid for being creative, a necessary correlation between it and personal disorder and intense unhappiness. This definition tends to be restricted to artists and writers, who in a sense suffer for us as *poetes maudits* and produce their work out of a life informed by the pain of infantile and violent behavior. Writing about Charles Baudelaire, Jean-Paul Sartre sets forth a slightly modified version of the myth:

He made up his mind that at any rate he would explore himself as the knife explores the wound in the hope of reaching the lonely depths which constitute his real nature . . . the tortures which he inflicted on himself . . . made his flesh grow beneath his fingers so that in the throes of its own sufferings it would recognize that it was his own flesh.

Suffering is conceived as a means of self-exploration. As well as incapacitating the artist, the wounds uncover his essential being, and the process of writing is one of progressively intense self-induced pain. To put the matter slightly differently, in John Berryman's words, "We are using our skins as wallpaper and we cannot win."

There is undeniably something archaic about this notion. The blandly efficient creator is decidedly more the man of our time. The word's reference has become so broad as to be synonymous with such qualities as inventive, even intelligent. According to this formulation, the creative man is the one who performs his job notably, a model of propriety who can find energy for unusually stringent work without backsliding and losing out in the business of ordinary life. The term has become a form of reward offered to the man who most clearly and unequivocally adopts the values of a production economy, someone who yields more of whatever function he performs without breaking the self-imposed restrictions in which his role has involved him.

Private Energy

Yet there remains something meretricious about the second of these definitions. We are not all "truly" creative. Fundamentally, the quality involves using the imagination in order to make new things, books, poems, pictures and so forth. The other creators are necessarily of secondary intensity, since they merely use the imagination as a surrogate in a situation where most of their work is actually routine, a manipulation of objects and persons in sustained collaboration with other people. The "real" creator works alone, sustained by his own resources. He has recourse to history, to tradition, to outside events; but for the most part he is concerned with himself, his private energies. And it is reasonable to assume that his relative independence, his self-concern and freedom of personal conduct will create a character structure that is distinguishable from the one imposed by work in complex interaction with other people in a large or small organization.

The actor's circumstances of work set him somewhat between these two definitions of creativity. His rehearsals bring him into a situation where interaction is possibly more crucial than in any other. It is, after all, what makes the finished play a success or a failure. And yet this interaction is only periodic—actors presumably learn their parts by themselves, and they spend time between roles in an environment where there is no external organization for them whatsoever. Also, although we conceive their function as one where the self is in constant use as a means of self-expression, the actor does not precisely, as creative writers are supposed to, work out of himself.

On the contrary, the actor normally works with other people's material—the script of the play—and his work demands that he make overt behavioral acts characteristic of one or another role model, those presented in the script. He gives to that role from his inner resource of talent, creating the atmosphere of reality that constitutes the play. As a result, he is living someone else's life; he is enacting a role that he did not invent. No matter how much personal style he may give to a particular role, it is not his own. And, furthermore, depending upon a series of events over which he seldom has control, he will shortly be playing the role of still a different person. His life is given over to portraying the identity of others, and his professional success may well depend upon how vividly he enlivens these other identities and, correlatively, how well he suppresses any self-identity that may blur the image of the other currently being played.

But what of the actor himself? What of his personality? We all tend to think of "mature" people as having a personality constellation of some degree of clarity, consistency and integrity. In Erik Erikson's terms we anticipate that the individual will resolve the conflicts and polar choices of earlier phases of life and by late adolescence develop a sense of identity—an identity that articulates inner life with outer social events and provides for the person a clear image of a single, if complex, self.

Is Acting Enough?

Yet what happens to the individual whose job consists of being different people and whose identity, if it exists, cannot benefit from a clarity and consistency of job behavior? Is "being an actor" sufficient? Is acting a role enough, when each of those roles requires different behavior and the portrayal of different feelings? To start from a different point, what must be the characteristics of the person who chooses and finds rewarding an occupation and a life style that demand the portrayal of the identities of other people—other people, furthermore, who are invented by still different people, the playwright and the director?

This study of the professional actor is an effort to explore the latter question. We began with the assumption that one prominent characteristic of the professional actor is his failure to develop the identity of which Erikson speaks. We also hypothesized that one of the things that sustains the creative life of the actor is his hope that the repeated portrayal of the lives of others will provide for him that very identity, the absence of which motivates him in this search. At the least, we would propose that long-running plays provide a temporary and fleeting identity sufficiently powerful or occurring too late in life to provide the initial basic trust necessary for the sense of confidence that comes with having a firm identity.

Cards of Identity

To test these propositions, we studied a group of professionals from the New York theater and a number of young actors in training. Our sample runs the full range in terms of employment—from actors who have steady work in the theater, who, while performing in one play, are deluged with scripts and offers for the following season, to actors whose economic existence is at best precarious, but who somehow manage to survive on an erratic combination of short-lived bit parts, occasional seasons of summer stock and unemployment compensation. Technically, all our subjects met three basic requirements: they belonged to an actors' union; they derived at least 50 percent of their income from acting; they had been employed as actors within the year previous to being interviewed.

Our actors are similarly varied regarding fame. The names of several would be recognized in most households; others are known widely in the trade; still others are known only by those with whom they have worked. The rough groupings below provide an approximation of the status of our sample of 32 professional actors:

"stars"	3
publicly well known	4
well known in the profession	9
less well known in the profession	7
virtually unknown	9

The term professional actor is used in a wide variety of theatrical enterprises, such as the legitimate theater, movies, television and night clubs, to cover a wide variety of entertainers—actors, comedians, TV panelists, M.C.'s and so forth. Though most of our subjects had experience in several media, all but one, an Academy Award winner, were primarily legitimate stage actors, both in terms of self-definition and in terms of actual professional experience. Sex is split fairly evenly; there is considerable spread regarding both age and success; different schools of acting are quite evenly represented.

Actors, at least highly successful ones, have often been burned by the glare of publicity. As a result, they are realistically cautious about disclosing their private lives. Considering the intimate nature of the data we were requesting, an impersonal method of contacting them was impracticable. Fortunately, we knew several persons prominent in Broadway theater—a playwright, an acting teacher and an actress. Through their influence our first subjects were contacted, and our discretion was guaranteed by them. These first actors, satisfied, even pleased with the testing and interviewing experience, were generous in personally referring us to others. Thus, an ever-widening network of contacts was developed. This method of personal referral did not, as we feared initially, restrict us to a limited number of cliques but led us to actors unknown to any of our other contacts. How representative our sample is, on the basis of this mode of selection, in an open question. However, we can discover no obvious biases.

Even the busiest of actors were generous with their time; the combined testing and interviewing sessions ranged in length from a minimum of four to a maximum of 20 hours. Often this involved tight scheduling and not inconsiderable sacrifice on their part, such as fitting in a couple of hours between their matinee and evening performances, rising early in the morning (rare for an actor) or giving up their day off. With few exceptions, the interviews took place in the actors' homes.

Their enthusiastic cooperation is probably attributable to several factors. First, actors, like many other people like to talk about themselves. Second, actors are fascinated with the process of acting itself, and with the problems involved in using one's self as the artistic medium. Third, we found actors generally to be relatively sophisticated in psychology. They didn't have to be convinced of the relevance of an area of inquiry before answering. Regardless of what we asked, we were never met with the attitude "What has this got to do with anything?" Finally, we found them to be utterly convinced of the value of research; sometimes they expressed envy of what was, for them, the unquestionable worth of the interviewer's profession.

As a framework for the study, we utilized the logic of Erikson's developmental stages. The eight stages of man which compose Erikson's theory of personality development are a formalization of the nature and consequences of a sequence of what he terms "decisive encounters" between the predetermined biological and psychological capacities of the individual and his social environment. These stages are designated by polar terms, such as trust versus mistrust, autonomy versus shame and doubt, intimacy versus isolation, which define the positive and negative extremes of their developmental alternatives. While the issues defining each stage have lifelong relevance, they are normally critical at a particular period in the life cycle because of the human organism's genetic timetable and the impact of social institutions coordinated to it. Each stage exists in some form both before and after its critical moment; all depends on the proper development of each in a correct sequence. Resolution of a stage is defined as a ratio between the positive and negative which remains in dynamic equilibrium throughout life and is either more or less vulnerable to new inner conflict and outer change.

We were primarily interested in Erikson's fifth stage, identity versus identity diffusion. While identity formation is a lifelong process, a constantly evolving configuration of successive ego syntheses and resyntheses, it reaches its normative developmental crisis during adolescence, a time when the physiological changes of puberty, in conjunction with the advent of major social demands, disrupt and challenge the samenesses and continuities of experience upon which the individual had previously based his psychosocial self-definition. The adolescent is threatened by unfamiliar inner experiences and bewildered by the variety of conflicting role possibilities now available to him.

Self-Shopping

Erikson postulates that society meets the individual's needs during this stage of identity crisis and supports his progress through it by granting an institutionalized period of delay between childhood and adulthood. This "psychosocial moratorium" provides the time required for the transition from child to adult, for the operation of the processes of becoming. New models appropriate to the different tasks facing the individual are found for identification, and childhood identifications are reviewed and accepted or repudiated. Most important, the neophyte-adult has the opportunity to establish patterns of consistent and continuous experience in the new roles he has assumed, roles through which his society is able to identify him. In this way, his inner certainty grows, affirmed by outer recognition.

When the individual cannot use the moratorium to find his place in society and fails to establish an identity, he suffers from identity diffusion. Sexually, occupationally, socially, both he and his society are unsure as to who he is or what he wants to become. Acute identity diffusion usually makes its appearance when the individual is faced with urgent and simultaneous demands for physical intimacy, occupational choice and psychosocial self-definition. In such a situation desperate and imprudent decisions and choices contract the range of further alternatives and entrap the individual in a binding, though unwanted, self-definition. At the same time, frightened abstention from making choices leads to isolation and a sense of emptiness. This can lead to psychological paralysis as the individual attempts vainly to reconcile his terror of committing himself with his desire to create and control his future.

Among the many and complex symptoms that characterize identity diffusion, the main features are:

A lack of intimacy; an inability for true engagement with others; a tenseness in interpersonal relations that leads to isolation and lonely stereotypic interaction or to frenetic and unsatisfactory attempts at intimacy with inappropriate partners.

Time diffusion; the inability to maintain perspective and expectancy; a distrust of waiting, hoping, planning, of one's relationship to the future; a disregard for time as a dimension for organizing one's life.

Diffusion industry; a disruption of the sense of workmanship which manifests itself in an incapacity for concentration and an inability to complete tasks or in an excessive preoccupation with one-sided activities.

Identity consciousness; extreme self-consciousness; an ashamed recognition of one's incomplete, inadequate identity; a sense of being exposed and vulnerable and the consequent wish to hide, either within some group uniformity or behind some false self-definition.

The choice of a negative identity; a hostile and snobbish rejection of those roles that society offers as proper and desirable and the contrary vengeful choice to become, as Erikson puts it, "nobody or somebody bad." This choice is manifested either in the adoption of a personally defined negative identity based on those roles which in the individual's history have been presented as undesirable and yet real or by membership in groups defying society's values, such as delinquent gangs or homosexual cliques.

The measurement of the continuum identity-identity diffusion presented the difficult problem of translating an imprecisely defined, abstract concept into concrete operational terms. We developed several techniques that approached this task in different ways. A series of Henry Murray's thematic apperception cards was used to explore the fantasies of our actors in order to acquire some insight into their general psychodynamics and, more specifically, to ascertain the appearance of identity problems. We took interviews exploring both contemporary life and past history to investigate current manifestations of identity diffusion and to provide materials relevant to their genesis.

To test the hypothesis—that the actor's creative life was somehow sustained by his search for an identity in his roles—required an instrument that could be administered twice to the same group of actors over a relatively short period and which, at the same time, would be sensitive enough to register the changes in identity anticipated as resulting from the rehearsal experience. Both of these considerations dictated the need for a short, easily administered instrument which would measure quantitative differences along the continuum of identity-identity diffusion.

To fill this need we devised the Identity Scale, an instrument similar to the seven-point polar choice semantic differential. It is composed of 56 pairs of words or phrases designed to elicit responses relevant to the issue of identity. One item of each pair denotes the negative possibility of a developmental issue, the other, the positive. All eight of Erikson's stages constitute sources of items relevant to the question of identity, for, as he makes clear, the derivatives of precursors of the issues defining each stage "are part and parcel of the struggle for identity." The scale also contains items based upon Erikson's clinical description of the symptoms of identity diffusion already discussed.

Before using the Identity Scale to test the study's hypotheses, we compared subjects' scores on it with another independent measure of identity. By categorizing the symptoms of identity diffusion, we designed an Index of Identity Diffusion on which we rated the current behavior of the actors as reported in the interviews. Scores on the Identity Scale were compared with ratings on the index for 14 male actors and were found significantly related.

For the purpose of exploring the two central hypotheses, we discuss the behavior of actors and criterion groups on the Identity Scale only. Scores referred to as high must be taken as an indication of a well-integrated identity, low scores as a reflection of identity diffusion. For comparison's sake we administered the scale to some 500 men and women in substantially different occupations—nurses, executives, civil servants, schoolteachers, housewives. The instrument was administered to all with the instructions to use the items to describe themselves as honestly as they could.

For the purpose of our first hypothesis, it may be noted that the average scores for groups of professional actors are in all cases lower—more on the identity diffusion side—than any single or all combined comparison groups and are significant in the statistical sense.

The identity instrument produces six fairly distinct factors. The largest is the identity factor mentioned above, and it is here that the major differences between actor and non-actor occur. However, since the symptoms of identity or of identity diffusion inherent in Erikson's theory contain elements of previous polar conflicts, it is not surprising that three of the remaining five factors appear to be echoes of Erikson's basic trust, autonomy and integrity. Elements of intimacy also appear, but these are included in the identity factor as we have defined it. On these three other factors, actors are lower than comparison groups —significantly so on integrity and trust.

One of the remaining factors appears to be a constellation of items relating to highly individualistic expressiveness. It has no social or interpersonal items in it, and hence we are inclined to think of it as a portrayal of ready changeability or adaptability of emotion in spontaneous and nonsocial forms. It has a ready appeal as a correlative to the stereotype of the "emotional" actor. That it may have some basis in reality is suggested by the fact that this is the only factor in which actors and actresses alike are significantly higher than comparison groups.

"Frenetic Search for Intimacy"

In other words, the actors do indeed appear lower, more identity diffuse, than comparison groups. And, further, they also appear lower on several elements which in theory are related to identity diffusion.

Evidence from our interviews can be summarized by saying that the symptoms of aimlessness, of distortion of time perspective, or frenetic search for intimacy are amply displayed. One fact that became apparent during these interviews is relevant and can be simply illustrated. The frenetic search for intimacy is crucial to Erikson's idea of diffused identity, as well as being a commonplace of public portrayals of actors and actresses. To test the truth of this stereotype we constructed an Index of Sexual Modes, with the assumption that sexual behavior was a partial but crucial factor in the intimacy concept. We based this index upon frequency, recentness and mode of sexual experience, taking as its logic the simple moral and psychodynamic view of good and bad sexual acts. Exclusive sexual intercourse with the same partner of the opposite sex scored zero, not as a comment on its worth but in order to emphasize divergences from this supposed norm. To variations in sexual mode, sex of partner, frequent changes of partner, we gave scores of 1, 2, and 3 respectively. This produced some high scores which unfortunately we were unable to compare with other groups for lack of comparable data. However, we made internal comparisons by dividing our actors into two groups, those with more and less identity diffusion. Again, the high group is the less identity-diffused, the one with better-integrated identity; the low group is the one with lower identity scores, more diffused. We gave the sex index additional reference to Erikson's concept of identity diffusion by making different tests for the successive stages of our subject's lives, thus evaluating their sexual behavior at preschool age, at grammar school, high school, young adult, and adult and present.

The test produced some striking results. The index relates to the evaluation of identity diffusion at a highly significant level. When comparisons were made separately on the basis of age, there were similar relations. The high school period produced least relations to the Identity Scale results, but this too supports our hypothesis, since this stage is precisely the one where, according to Erikson's theories, everyone should be chaotically experiencing the "psycho-social moratorium" or role experimentation.

We have proposed that the life of an actor is in part determined by the effort to create a sense of identity through the portrayal of the varieties of models available in scripts. Our evidence on this point lies partly in what we may generally infer from our long series of interviews. But some is available in readily reportable form. One group of data resides in the administration of the same identity diffusion instrument to actors-in-training with the instructions to describe themselves as they would feel when rehearsal for a role was going particularly well, as compared with scores under the original instructions. On these two administrations actors in training systematically "improve," significantly moving in the direction of identity. This is not unexpected, perhaps, since anyone might do this when things are ideally imagined as going well. And indeed a group of junior executives of similar age does the same. However, actors change more, and the difference between the amount of their change and that of the executives is significant.

We were also able to administer the identity instrument to the cast of a play during rehearsals and under the original instructions to describe themselves as honestly as they could. This was done at two different points in time—two days after the start of a play rehearsal and three weeks later but still during rehearsal periods. The scores move significantly in the direction of firm identity as the actors progressively settle into their roles during the course of their rehearsals. Conclusions to be drawn from these two tests are inescapable; not only do actors believe that they will possess coherent identities under conditions of intense identification with their roles, they also bear out their opinions in practice. The closer they come to total identification with a role utterly alien to their habitual, "real" one, the more identity they seem to possess.

The interviews with experienced actors more than amply documented their

own conviction of the vital importance to them personally of acting—an importance far outweighing that which anyone else might be expected to attach to
his means of livelihood. The words of two famous actors, in interviews published in the *New Yorker* in 1961, testify to the intensity of the need to act:

Ingrid Bergman: "I hate to make an entrance. It is difficult for me to get
up on a dance floor, because I feel everybody is watching. But if I played somebody else walking into a restaurant or getting up on a dance floor, I could do
it. I couldn't be blamed. It wouldn't be me."

Henry Fonda: "Acting is putting on a mask. The worst torture that can
happen to me is not having a mask to get in back of."

Our professionals are, of course, not our actors in training grown up, but
the symptoms of identity diffusion seen in the professionals are, if anything,
more marked in the students, and the contrast between those students and
comparison groups of the same age are similarly highly significant. If we draw
the cross-sectional conclusion, in part from these student data and in part from
the retrospective reports of professionals, it is that actors are people whose
early lives have been marked by disjunctive experiences, especially experiences
calling attention to role differences in intimate family members, to distinctions
between inner feelings and overt behavior in such figures, leaving each of our
actors with the sense of a quest, a search for the one life style appropriate to
them. We think that the role experimentation so begun, and subsequently institutionalized in acting, becomes the modus vivendi that has meaning for them.
Especially interesting is the fact that our professionals report that once they had
done some acting, commonly in high school, they never subsequently had any
doubt as to their future profession. In the unstructured and hectic work world
of the actor, the fight necessary to establish oneself is perhaps further evidence
of the deeply rooted impulse of that ambition.

This article has suggested that actors are one sort of creative person for
whom the inner personality meaning of work is extremely vital to an understanding of their adult lives and to an understanding of their creative work.
This is a consequence of their ability to isolate emotional spontaneity from
personal interactions, while searching endlessly for an outer form which will
have meaning. The real function of their work is indeed internal, residing in
the sense of personal identity that it provides. To some extent then, this study
moves toward an explanation, to quote Rod Steiger's *New Yorker* interview, of "the way a man can live so beautifully in the fantasy of his art even
when he can hardly live at all in the reality of his own life."

20. Female Biology in a Male Culture
Diana Trilling

"Freud's condescension toward women is rooted in his castration theory...."

This paper is an intimately female view of the role of women in our society. Diana Trilling is thoroughly committed to the crusade for securing women's rights. Here she attacks many misconceptions about female biology and psychology.

As a subject of conversation, women's liberation is certainly unequaled for putting everyone, women as well as men, in the happy state of mind that results from establishing one's superiority to whatever is benighted and ridiculous in human activity. In fact, I can think of only one other topic that matches it as a provoker of ignorant mirth among the presumably well-educated, and that is psychoanalysis—not psychiatry, which people have always recognized as a serious subject, but Freudian analysis.

The parallel should not surprise us. In both situations the derisive response represents embarrassment at being caught in a deception, and a defense against being confronted with an unwanted truth. The amusement with which, even at this late date, the mention of psychoanalysis can be met is confirmation that we do indeed have a life of the unconscious that we are fearful of bringing to consciousness. And, just so, the ready mockery of women's liberation is confirmation that women are indeed regarded in our society as of a second order of being, and that we are afraid of having the falseness of this assumption revealed to us. By us, of course, I mean women no less than men.

It is both appropriate and ironic that in undertaking to speak of the present movement for women's rights I bring it into such immediate conjunction with Freudian thought. The appropriateness lies in the fact that for many years my own view of the relation of the sexes was rather substantially shaped by Freud's perception of the differing biological natures of the sexes and of the consequent differences in their psychological lives and their social roles. Recently, this influence has been modified: I tend now to give more weight than I once did to the cultural, as opposed to the biological, determinism in sexual attitudes. For example, I am not as convinced as I might once have been that a woman's willingness to cede power to men necessarily represents a wholesome acceptance of her female role; now I might see it as a not very laudable cultural conformity or even an expediency of laziness. The irony of bringing

Freud into immediate connection with the subject of women's liberation lies in Freud's having had such an invidious view of the female sex. I am afraid that the man who sought to liberate the psyche from the hindrances imposed upon it in our human infancy was interested not at all in liberating women from the special handicaps imposed upon them in our society. Nowhere in his writings does Freud express sympathy for the problems that pertain to the female sex alone. On the contrary, his misogyny is now taken for granted even by his most admiring students.

Freud's condescension toward women is rooted in his castration theory, which plays a vital part in his whole theory of neurosis. According to Freud, it is the male sexual organ that constitutes what might be called the natural, or ideal, endowment from which stems the genital envy particular to women and the anxiety shared by both sexes. And no doubt it is as an extension of this view of woman's basic biological inferiority that Freud makes his forthright statement in *Civilization and Its Discontents* that it is men who are the makers and carriers of culture. He adjures women not to interfere with man's life in culture.

The adjuration could scarcely be more irritating, especially when we contemplate some of the activities that men regard as a proper life in culture, like inventing hydrogen bombs or claiming the moon for their own country. Such being man's impulses in culture, one might have hoped that Freud would have encouraged women to tell their husbands to stay home and be sensible. On the other hand, there is nothing either in Freud's formulation of the castration fear or in his general statement of the different relation of men and women to culture that I would be prepared to fault or that people far more competent than I have succeeded in refuting. It would be pleasant, for instance, to accept the idea proposed by Dr. Karen Horney, the mother of Freudian revisionism, and so widely propagated by Margaret Mead, that womb-envy, man's envy of woman because she can have babies and he cannot, plays as much a part in the life of men as penis-envy plays in the life of women. Such an appealing reassignment of biological advantage is supported, however, neither by men's dreams nor their free associations during psychoanalytical treatment.

As to the relative roles of men and women in culture, it would seem to be indisputable, at least historically, that for better or worse men have forged the ideas and provided the chief energies by which cultures develop, while women have devoted themselves to the conservation of what they have found valuable in the efforts of men. We may protest that there is no work in culture that is as valuable as woman's child-bearing and child-nurturing activities; that the ability to create and conserve the human race overshadows any other conceivable accomplishment in culture. But this, of course, begs the question of why women have not made even a small fraction of the intellectual, scientific, or artistic contributions to culture that men have made.

Finally, we may protest that women's small contribution to culture is not an indication of their capacities but simply reflects the way that men have contrived things to be—that is, we can blame women's small place in culture on culture—except that this leaves unanswered the question of why it is that over the long years women have been willing that culture should follow the male dictate. It also leaves unanswered the even more fundamental question of why it is that in every society that has ever been studied—so Margaret Mead tells us—whatever it is that is the occupation of men has the greater prestige: If the men do the hunting and fighting, hunting and fighting are the status-giving occupations of that society; if the men do the weaving and baby-tending, then weaving and baby-tending are the superior activities. We may think of this value system as something that men impose upon women. But then we are forced to explain why it is that even where the women bear arms they have not imposed a different system of values.

The reference back to biology would seem to be unavoidable, and we are returned to Freud's use of the words "passivity" and "activity"—female passivity, male activity. The words themselves almost inevitably imply a judgment, especially in a culture like ours where passivity connotes unattractive attributes: inertness, laxness, the uncritical acceptance of whatever happens to be given. Even as a concept in the purely sexual relation of men and women it suggests that man is the seeker and that woman yields to man's importunities, a description of the sexual roles that is not particularly congruent with our modern sense of the sexual realities. But actually this distinction between the active and the passive sexual roles is an irrefutable fact in nature: The most active seduction or participation on the part of a woman cannot relieve the male partner of his primary physical responsibility in their sexual union. To put the matter at its crudest, the male has the biological capacity to rape; the female has not. We may, if we wish, accuse Freud of drawing too many, or mistaken, emotional and social inferences from this fundamental biological difference between the sexes, but to try to ignore the difference, as some of the women's liberation groups do, is to narrow rather than widen the prospects opened up to us in refusing the tyrannies of biology.

It is reported that Freud would be rather bitterly amused when accused of being dirty-minded because he wrote about infant sexuality; he would point out that it was not he who had created the condition, he had merely recognized it. And obviously he didn't create the different sexual endowments of men and women nor even the emotional consequences of the difference; he only recognized them, and attached these words "active" and "passive" to the differing sexual roles. After centuries of female subjugation, however, it was perhaps expectable that the essential lack of sympathy for women in orthodox psychoanalysis, and in particular its emphasis on women's envy of men with its implication of hostility, would be one of the aspects of Freud's thought that would be most readily received by our society. I think there is small doubt that Freudian doctrine, often scarcely understood or even misunderstood, has enormously powered the development in recent decades of what amounts to virtually an anti-female movement in American culture.

The informing sentiment of this movement is that women are out to destroy men: Women are the natural destroyers of the male species, at least in America. As statistics have been gathering on the appalling numbers of men who die from heart disease in this country, increasingly, the blame has been put on the American wife for the killing demands she makes upon her husband for houses, cars, washing machines, and clothes. She has been pictured as the ruthless exploiter of her male partner, a sort of prototypical domestic statement of the national imperialism. And as Freud's views on the childhood source of mental disorder have percolated into the culture, there has been mounted a growing campaign of mother-suspicion and mother-discreditation. From Sidney Howard's play *The Silver Cord*, in the mid-Twenties, to Philip Roth's still current *Portnoy's*

Complaint, our literature has lent its traditional dignity to the idea that American women alternate a diet of husbands with a diet of sons.

Nor is it solely on the ground of her inordinate appetites that the American mother is chivvied and mocked: If she cannot be blamed for devouring her young, she is blamed for rejecting them. For some fifty years now, it has been impossible for a woman, especially a mother, to be anything but wrong in our culture; and the more supposedly enlightened her community, the more varied and virulent the attacks, to the point where one often has the impression that the prestige of our best and most progressive private schools is built on the humiliations of young mothers. Moreover, this pernicious assault on women's minds and spirits comes not alone from men. Perhaps even more of the time, it comes from other women.

Any adequate statement of woman's inhumanity to woman might perhaps suggest that what eventually is wrong with women is that there are other women in the world, and that women are to be condemned out of hand for their betrayals, overt and covert, of their own sex. But such harsh judgments of women minimize the range and subtlety of the difficulties by which they are beset. It may not be very edifying to contemplate the spectacle of women acceding in whatever is the form that the disparagement of their own sex may at the moment be taking just so that men will be reassured that they deserve the status conferred upon them by their superior biological endowment, but if it is on a man's sexual confidence that a woman's sexual and maternal satisfactions depend, and if, too, the male in our society is willing to pay for his biological advantage by assuming the financial support of his wife and family, it is more than understandable, it is plainest reason, that a woman should place the male interest, whether real or only fancied, above that of other women.

In particular it is understandable that women should come to feel that they are not defeated but fulfilled in accepting the passivity that is implied by acknowledging man's primary sexual-social role. For living by one's reference to the needs of those one loves is one of the pleasanter modes of existence—as well as, I might add, one of the most taxing. It is a grave fault of modern culture that it trains us in the belief that whatever defers to others is an *inaction* and therefore of only secondary social value.

And yet, even while we record the appeal on behalf of passivity, the question presses upon us whether our female-ists, who stress their satisfaction in devoting their lives to being good wives and mothers, would settle for this domestication of their capacities if they lived in a society where different requirements were made of women than are made in our culture. We are told that the women in the Israeli kibbutzim who serve side by side with their men in the army and in the fields and who give up the larger part of the rearing of their children to communal nurseries show no sign of being unfulfilled as women. Nor, apparently, are their men castrated by this sexual equality. It would also seem clear from Solzhenitsyn's remarkable novel *Cancer Ward* that, although a woman surgeon in the Soviet Union may return from a grueling day in the cancer hospital and, like working wives everywhere in our servantless world, still accept it as her job to do the marketing, cooking, cleaning, and laundry, it is not in her home and family but in her "real" work, her man's work if you will, that she invests her pride of being, including her peculiarly feminine pride of being. It is undoubtedly one of the significant revelations of this book that in a situation where the women carry equal responsibilities with men it is still the men who fill the top hospital posts; but no less fascinating is its revelation of the many wholly unself-conscious ways in which the women physicians manage to irradiate their grim hospital routines with a sexually distinguishing gentleness and delicacy. From evidences like these I think we must conclude that women are considerably more flexible in the matter of how they can derive their fulfill-ment than most American women are yet prepared to recognize, and that it is perhaps only because our culture prefers that its women find their best satisfac-tion in the activities of home and family that the women themselves obediently discover it there.

In other words, we are all of us, men and women both, the creatures of culture: We do and feel what our societies want us to do and feel, and the de-mands that they put upon us are not always either very consistent or very precisely correlated with biology. In wartime, for instance, when men are away and women not only take jobs in factories and on farms but make all the financial and practical decisions usually made by the male head of the family, no one thinks of accusing them of conduct unbecoming a woman. Or if a woman is forced through widowhood to earn her own living, no one is moved to put a brake on her competitiveness with men; she is thought a castrating woman only if she now switches the dependence she once had on her husband to her grown children.

And in a similar reversal of values, I can imagine a moment—and perhaps a not very distant moment—when the conserving instinct of women will become the most active force (and I emphasize the word "active") in the continuing life of society. I have in mind the active role that women may soon be called upon to play in rescuing the modern world from pollution; and when I say called upon, I mean called upon not by men but by themselves, by their own intelli-gence and appreciation of the extent of the emergency. Since so far it seems to be impossible for men to mobilize the energies they use for the conquest of other planets for the preservation of life on Earth, women may well have to take over the job. This is one kind of activity in culture, one form of competitiveness beyond the limits of home and family, in which the female sex would surely excel: the competition to perpetuate life. It is a program to which women's liberation could, and should, rally all women.

But when I say that women are the creatures of culture, while I obviously mean the prevailing culture, I do not necessarily mean only the dominant cul-ture of the society. It may well be that among those who most dramatically dissent from our dominant culture, and in particular among the young, there are being forged attitudes that will importantly alter the relation of the sexes in the dominant culture of the future.

I suppose it is natural enough that in the matter of renovating the relations of men and women it is on the score of women's professional and legal rights that the voice of contemporary protest is making itself most readily heard. This is perhaps the area in which men are finally the least challenged; it is, of course, the area that is sanctioned by the historical efforts on behalf of sexual equality. It is nevertheless possible, I think, that the cause of women's professional rights —the demand that women receive equal pay for equal work and similar ad-vancement for similar merit—may be becoming our newest middle-class liberal ritualism, to be embraced as a way of avoiding the need to look more closely at less crude but more troubling manifestations of the lack of parity between the sexes. I myself happen to think for instance, that, although it will indeed be a great day for women when they are appointed to full professorships at our leading universities on the same basis as men, it will be an even greater day for women when right in their own living rooms they are given as much serious attention and credence as men now receive when they pass judgment, especially adverse judgment, on an idea or a person.

It is not, however, the overt agitations on behalf of women that I actually have in mind when I speculate upon the possible effect our present-day dissent may eventually have upon the dominant culture. I am not closely enough acquainted with the dissident young to know exactly what decorousnesses, rules, and formalities pertain to their sexual relations, or what constitute their criteria of sexual worth and loyalty. What is nevertheless apparent even at my distance is the pervasive devaluation of those appurtenances of masculinity and femininity that our culture—by which I chiefly mean our competitive economy— sanctified for an earlier generation. I was myself of a generation in which any deviation from the specifications for female charm, as set down by Madison Avenue and the movies, was thought seriously to reduce a girl's sexual bargaining power. While intellectually we knew that the models by which we presumably were judged and by which we judged ourselves were the exceptions in any race of mortals, we suffered the private anguishes of living under the sexual dictates not of nature but of commerce. One recalls the father in Dostoevsky's *The Brothers Karamazov* who said there was no such thing as an ugly woman: The possibility that an opinion like this would one day infiltrate large sections of our society was beyond our wildest dreams, strained as we were by the demands for an ideal femininity put upon us by advertising and by Hollywood. This strain would happily seem to be gone, having disappeared in the radical effort to disavow the dominant capitalist culture. And as a woman, even though not a revolutionary, I can hope it is gone forever.

And gone—or going—with it, through the same effort, is the social-sexual differentiation between men and women in terms of dress and hairstyle. While I confess to having no love for the shared slovenliness of so many young men and women, since I see in it a depreciation of their pride in themselves as persons, I welcome the unisexual appearance of the sexes if only for its criticism of a culture in which sexually differentiated styles of hair and dress, designed not by God but by man, were treated as if they were biological actualities. As I see it, or at least as I hope it, whatever reduces the false separations between men and women is bound to reduce their suspicions and hostilities, and thus permit them a fuller expression of their human potentiality. Free of the cultural detritus of our sexual differences, perhaps we can come to a sounder and happier knowledge of our distinctive maleness and femaleness than is now permitted us.

**Children's old skip-rope song:
"Doctor, doctor, will I die?
Yes, my child, and so will I."**

Death is an uncomfortable topic for most people to even consider. However, as the restrictions on thought give way to honest reflection, all phenomena are open to consideration. This paper by Thomas Powers deals insightfully with this ever-present reality for all of us.

On November 8, 1970, Barbara B., a woman in her middle sixties, was admitted to New York Hospital with an unexplained intestinal blockage. Because it was a Sunday and her own doctor was unavailable, the doctor of a friend took over. He had never met Mrs. B. and knew nothing of her medical history. When he asked what was wrong she described her symptoms during the preceding few days but volunteered nothing else. Dr. C. began making arrangements for an exploratory operation in the next day or two if the situation did not correct itself.

A friend had accompanied Mrs. B. to the hospital. Later that day her daughter and son-in-law came up to see her. Mrs. B. was in considerable pain so there was not much conversation. When they did talk, it was about matters of little consequence. Not knowing exactly what Mrs. B.'s condition was they all hoped that an operation would not be necessary, but they did not speculate as to what might have caused the blockage. Each of the four had a pretty good idea of the cause: none of them mentioned it that first day.

On Monday Dr. C. contacted Mrs. B.'s regular doctor and was told she had had a cancerous breast removed in the summer of 1968, that malignant skin nodules had reappeared in the summer of 1970, and that laboratory tests showed spreading cancer. It was obvious to Dr. C. that Mrs. B.'s cancer had reached her abdomen and that she did not have long to live. When he spoke to Mrs. B.'s family, however, he was somewhat more tentative. He said he was not sure (which was true; he was not *absolutely certain*) what was causing the blockage, that the blockage might disappear, that he advised waiting for a few days to see how things developed. He admitted, in response to direct questions, that Mrs. B. was suffering from a serious case of cancer and that serious in her case probably meant fatal. He muted only the probable (but not yet *certain*) fact that Mrs. B. had already begun to die.

During the following few days Mrs. B. was in continual discomfort but nevertheless remained the same person her family had always known: witty,

unsentimental, interested in gossip, a passionate reader, a stern critic of everything about President Nixon except the good looks of his daughters, in all things
a woman determined to be strong. When friends or family came to visit she
talked about politics, life on Tenth Street, what she was reading, and so on.
Everyone asked how she was feeling. She always answered, "Oh, all right," with a
look of disgust. Once or twice she said she hoped she would not need an operation. A kind of unspoken agreement was in effect: cancer was not to be
mentioned. The reasons for the agreement varied. Mrs. B. felt it was weak to
discuss bodily ills, and wanted to spare her daughter. Her daughter wanted to
spare her mother. Mrs. B. and her family all knew her cancer had reappeared,
but discussion of the possible operation was based on the unstated assumption
that the cancer and the intestinal blockage were two entirely separate conditions. In other words, everyone knew the end was coming, but resisted the
notion that it was coming *now*.

When the blockage persisted into the middle of the next week, however,
it became increasingly difficult to ignore the seriousness of Mrs. B.'s condition.
Mrs. B. had nothing but contempt for people who complained and was inclined
to think that any mention of her own condition was a kind of complaining. In
spite of this, she began to refer to it elliptically.

One evening, as her son-in-law was just leaving, she abruptly mentioned a
Kingsley Amis novel she had once read in which a character visits a hospitalized
friend who is dying with cancer (Mrs. B. winced at the word) of the stomach. In
the novel, the dying friend makes little pretense of interest in the conversation;
he is simply trying to hold on until his next pain shot.

"I'm beginning to feel that way myself," Mrs. B. said with a bitter smile,
apologizing for her failure to keep up her end of the conversation and ashamed
of herself for bringing it up. "When something really hurts, all you live for is
that pain shot."

A couple of days later Mrs. B.'s son-in-law arrived just as Mrs. B.'s roommate was coming out of anesthesia following an operation to determine if
she had breast cancer. The son-in-law asked what the verdict had been. "She
had two tumors but neither was malignant," Mrs. B. said. "Some people have all
the luck."

Mrs. B. refrained from talking about her feelings directly on all but one or
two occasions. Once she told her daughter, "I've got so little to look forward to,"
but then regained her composure. "Sometimes I can't help feeling blue," she
explained. There were other slips, but generally she refused to talk about what
she was going through, or to let anyone else talk about it. Neither she nor anyone else had yet admitted fully what was now the one great fact in her life:
she was dying.

Dying is not a subject to which doctors have traditionally paid much attention. Their first purpose is to preserve life, and once life can no longer be
decently extended they tend to lose interest. Until fairly recently, the medical
profession reacted to death as if the subject were adequately covered by the
children's old skip-rope song:

Doctor, doctor, will I die?
Yes, my child, and so will I.

Since death was inevitable, discussion was restricted to secondary matters, centering on three main questions. The first was how to determine when the patient was really dead. Before the twentieth century, people were occasionally buried while still alive, and wills sometimes included a stipulation that the deceased remain above ground until his body actually began to smell. The second question, still much discussed, was whether or not to tell the patient he was dying. The third question, of more interest to doctors of divinity than of medicine, concerned the individual after the process of dying was complete: specifically, did the soul survive, and if so, in what form? All three questions are still open to dispute, and the first has attracted considerable scientific attention since the advent of organ transplants. Laws that require embalming before burial preclude the possibility of being buried alive, but there is still plenty of contention about identifying the precise moment at which a patient becomes sufficiently dead to justify the removal of vital organs.

The question of dying itself has been ignored. In 1912 a Boston doctor, Roswell Park, suggested that nothing was known about the subject and coined a word for its study—thanatology. No one remembered the word or undertook the study. With the exception of books on death as a religious event, almost nothing was published on the subject. The few books that were often had a cultist flavor, like *Death: Its Causes and Phenomena*, also published in 1912, which included a chapter on "Photographing and Weighing the Soul." Medical scientists acted as if Woodrow Wilson had adequately described death and dying in his last words before slipping into unconsciousness: "I am a broken machine. I am ready to go." Scientists were interested in the machine during, not after, its breakdown. They described dying exclusively in terms of the specific diseases or conditions which accompanied it, almost as if dying would not occur if there were no disease.

Since the second world war the subject has begun to receive some attention. In 1956, the American Psychological Association held a major symposium on death at its annual convention. In 1965, Dr. Elisabeth Kübler-Ross began a prolonged study of dying patients at the University of Chicago's Billings Hospital. Other organizations, institutes, and centers, usually with a highly specialized focus, have been established in Cleveland, Boston, Durham, North Carolina, and elsewhere. In 1967, a number of doctors in New York created the Foundation of Thanatology (the coincidental use of Dr. Park's word was not discovered until later) to encourage the study of death and dying from a broad perspective. They chose the word thanatology to make it easier to raise funds, figuring that philanthropists, like others, would find the word death so disturbing they would prefer to have nothing to do with it. La Rochefoucauld, the seventeenth-century French writer, said, "One can no more look steadily at death than at the sun." The Foundation of Thanatology has found that the attention span of those they approach for funds is generally just long enough to say no. Independent researchers have experienced similar difficulties and disappointments, including outright hostility on the part of doctors, nurses, and hospital administrators. Nevertheless, some important work has been done, and dying as a biological and psychological event is beginning to be understood.

The biological aspects of death have received the most attention. In most, but not all, cases an autopsy will reveal exactly how an individual died, by which doctors now usually mean what caused his brain to cease functioning.

Since respirators and other machines can keep the heart beating and other organs functioning virtually indefinitely, doctors have begun to accept "brain death" as adequate confirmation that the patient is actually "dead." The brain is considered to be dead when an electroencephalogram (EEG) is flat, which means that it detects no electromagnetic activity within the brain. It is a useful definition, compromised to some degree by the fact that patients have, if only rarely, recovered completely following two or even three days with an absolutely flat EEG. Brain death is generally (but not always) caused by a lack of oxygen, which is generally (but not always) caused by failure of the heart or lungs. The number of exact ways in which a human can die are, however, vast. Medical scientists are successful in describing how the body breaks down, not quite so successful in explaining why it breaks down; they admit that in a significant number of cases death occurs for no apparent medical reason whatever.

Dying as a psychological event, as an experience, is even more elusive. The principal obstacle to its study has been the fear of death on the part of patients, relatives, doctors, nurses, and the dispensers of funds for research. Since no one can say convincingly what death is, it is not easy to say why people fear it. In general, the fear of death has been broken down into the specific fears of pain, loneliness, abandonment, mutilation, and, somewhat more difficult to define, fear of the loss of self. This is not just another way of saying fear of death, but a kind of disassociation of the self as a conscious entity (the sense of me-ness one feels) from the self as a particular individual, with his particular history in the everyday world. That individual is one's closest associate and one fears his loss.

The fear of death also has a primitive, nonrational dimension, like fear of the dark and fear of the unknown. Conscious effort can bring such fear under control but cannot suppress it entirely. One doctor in New York uses complaints about the food in hospitals as a rule of thumb for gauging the fear of death: the more passionate and unreasonable the complaint, he has found, the greater the fear of dying. Everyone apparently experiences the fear of death in some degree, but reacts to it in his own way. People tend to die as they have lived, as suggested in the saying, "Death is terrible to Cicero, desirable to Cato, and indifferent to Socrates."

The experience of death is obviously related to its immediate cause. Heart disease and stroke are the conditions most likely to grant the widespread wish for death to occur in sleep. Heart patients who have been saved by modern techniques report they felt only a sudden pain and the beginning of mingled alarm and surprise. In earlier times, those sensations would have been death (as they presumably still are for those not saved). Patients who have suffered severe heart attacks often regain consciousness in some hospital's intensive-care unit with the words, "I'm dying, I'm dying." suggesting that awareness of death can be almost, but not quite, instantaneous. Nurses then find themselves in the awkward position of having to explain that the patient is not dying, without making clear the fact he still might at any moment. Diseases which do not attack vital centers directly and massively, and especially the forms of breakdown associated with old age, allow considerable warning before death actually arrives.

When an individual begins to die, much of what he suffers is the result of the fear of death on his own part and on the part of those around him. He reminds people that they, too, are going to die, which they naturally are not eager to consider. As a result, the first problem faced by the dying individual is to discover the truth about his condition.

In some rare instances doctors make a practice of telling patients the truth immediately, but in most cases the patient has to find out by himself. In their book, *Awareness of Dying*, Barney G. Glaser and Anselm L. Strauss describe a struggle for the truth which is sometimes Byzantine in its complexity, with patients trying to pick up clues while doctors, nurses, and relatives join in a conspiracy to conceal the patient's actual condition. The reason for withholding the truth, doctor's say, is that the patient would find it too upsetting, that he needs hope in order to keep on fighting for life, that one can never be absolutely certain of a diagnosis, that patients really do not want to know.

A number of studies have shown, however, that 80 percent (more or less, depending on the study) of doctors oppose telling dying patients the truth, while 80 percent of their patients want to be told. Doctors apparently shy from the subject because death represents a defeat and because, like everybody else, they find death upsetting to talk about. The psychological stratagems of medical students confronting death for the first time are notorious. The atmosphere of autopsy rooms is one of macabre humor, a degree or two short of hysteria. Doctors generally end up suppressing awareness of death so thoroughly some researchers speculate that that is why they are drawn to medicine in the first place.

Even while doctors and nurses do everything in their power to withhold the truth, resorting with a smile to outright lies, they customarily believe that the majority of their patients know the truth anyway. Relatives of the dying have the same mixture of feelings, trying to suppress the truth and yet assuming that eventually the patient will realize what is happening. Husbands and wives, each knowing the truth, often tell a third party that *they* know, but not to let the *other* know because he (or she) "couldn't stand it." The pretense naturally grows harder to sustain as the dying patient approaches a final decline. Nevertheless, the pretense is often maintained by sheer will until the end, even when all parties know the truth, and know the others know it too.

In rare instances patients refuse to recognize the truth, ignoring the most obvious clues (such as the visit of a relative who lives thousands of miles away) and insisting up until the end that they will be better in no time. For such patients almost any explanation will suffice. One woman dying of cancer, for example, believed (or pretended to believe) that she was only the victim of a slightly new strain of flu. Dr. Kübler-Ross describes a woman Christian Scientist who insisted until the end that faith in God was sufficient physic for an open cancer which was clearly killing her. As the woman declined she put on ever more garish makeup, until finally she was painting her white and withered cheeks a deep red, suppressing the distinctive smell of cancer with perfume and using false eyelashes and deep green eye shadow to insist she was still alive and even attractive. In most cases, however, patients eventually sense they are not getting better and either ask their doctors directly (by no means always getting an honest answer) or set verbal traps for nurses, relatives, and other patients, checking their responses for every discrepancy. One woman fatally ill with a rare disease discovered her condition when she casually ran across an article in *Newsweek* which described every symptom in exact detail. Nurses believe that "way deep down" patients sense when they are dying, and there is some evidence this is true. Patients who know they are dying will often tell a nurse,

"I'm going to die tonight," and then do so. Occasionally, however, patients feel they are going to die when, in fact, they are going to live. Persuading such a patient he's going to recover can be a frustrating experience, particularly when he has watched doctors and nurses deliberately deceive other patients who really were dying.

When patients finally do realize they are dying, a pattern of behavior often follows which was first described in detail by Dr. Kübler-Ross. Based on interviews with hundreds of dying patients over the past five years, she divides the reaction to knowledge of impending death into five distinctive stages.

The first stage is one of denial, even when a patient has suspected the worst and fought to determine the truth. All his life he has casually accepted the fact that "we all have to go." He is stunned to realize that now he has to go. After the discovery, patients often retreat into a self-imposed isolation, remaining silent with friends or relatives or even refusing to see them, while they get used to the fact that no mistake has been made, that they are now in the process of dying. Dr. Kübler-Ross believes that the dying never completely lose hope that a cure for their disease will be discovered at the last minute or that an outright miracle will occur ("the Scripture says that nothing is impossible with God"). This hope remains a deep-seated thing, and for practical purposes, such as writing wills and settling their affairs, the dying generally accept the fact they are dying once they have been told, directly or indirectly, that it is truly so.

The second stage is one of anger, especially when the dying individual is young. The anger can be released in any direction: at the doctors for doing nothing, at relatives because they are going to live, at other patients for not being quite so ill, at nurses for being young and healthy, at God for being unjust. In 1603, when Queen Elizabeth was told by her physician, Sir Robert Cecil, that she was seriously ill and must go to bed, she flared back, "*Must!* Is *must* a word to be addressed to princes? Little man, little man! Thy father, were he alive, durst not have used that word." Her mood quickly shifted to gloomy self-pity. "Thou are so presumptuous," she said, "because thou knowest that I shall die."

Eventually the anger subsides and the dying patient enters a curious stage in which he tries to bargain for his life. He begins to talk about all the things he has failed to do but will undertake if he recovers. He laments the fact he spent so much time earning a living and so little with his family, promising to alter his priorities if he gets home again. The most explicit bargains, generally proposed to God, are usually kept in secret. They are often legally precise, offering regular church attendance and sincere belief in return for a few more years. The bargains tend to be selfless, for the dying person knows he is about to lose himself altogether. Bargains can be offered for almost anything, for the chance to attend a son's wedding or to see another spring, but they all have one element in common: they are never kept. If the dying person actually does live until spring he immediately proposes another bargain.

Religious individuals often insist they submit themselves happily to God's pleasure ("Thy will be done") but are prepared to propose a reasonable compromise. St. Anselm, the Archbishop of Canterbury, dying in 1109, told fellow clerics gathered about his deathbed, "I shall gladly obey His call. Yet I should also feel grateful if He would grant me a little longer time with you, and if I could be permitted to solve a question—the origin of the soul." God did not accept the offer, and St. Anselm shortly died, but if He had, Dr. Kübler-Ross suggests that St. Anselm would quickly have proposed another bargain.

The fourth stage is one of altogether reasonable depression, part of the process doctors refer to as "anticipatory grief." In effect, the dying patient is grieving for himself before the fact of death, since he is about to lose everything he loves. It is this grieving which is probably most feared by doctors and relatives. It is painful to witness a death, and doubly painful when the dying person reacts in a fearful or hysterical manner. This is exceedingly rare, and yet doctors and relatives, perhaps unsure what their own reactions would be, fear the possibility so greatly that they put off discussion of death as long as possible and sometimes, as mentioned above, deny the truth until the end. In every other circumstance of life, no matter how bleak, some consolation can be genuinely offered; with those who know they are dying, there is nothing to say. Dr. Kübler-Ross has found, however, that the grieving patient will often come out of his depression and face the prospect of death more calmly for having been through it.

The final stage, not always reached, is one of acceptance.

When Mrs. B. woke up one afternoon following a nap, she saw her daughter standing by her bed with tears streaming down her cheeks. "Now, we're not going to have any tears," Mrs. B. said.

Nevertheless, she, too, had recognized the seriousness of her condition. During the first week she was in the hospital she made a point of telling her daily visitors they really didn't have to come so often. Now she admitted to looking forward to every visit. "It's nice to wake up and find somebody there," she confessed. Her last roommate had remained only a day before moving into a single room, so Mrs. B. was entirely alone between visits. The roommate, a woman in her forties who had also had a cancerous breast removed, had been shifted by her husband when he learned of Mrs. B.'s medical history. He said he wanted to protect the feelings of his wife, but she was acutely embarrassed by the move and came to see Mrs. B. every day. When the woman left the hospital she stopped by to say goodbye and suggested that she and Mrs. B. meet in New York for lunch someday. "Or," she said, "we have a place near you in the country. Maybe we can get together next spring." Mrs. B. said that would be fine and then added, "Good luck."

By the second week it was obvious Mrs. B.'s intestinal blockage was not going to clear by itself. Her doctors told her family the cancer had reached her liver and had probably affected her entire abdominal area. The sole remaining question was how long it would take Mrs. B. to die and whether or not she would be able to go home again in the time remaining. The only way she could leave the hospital, the doctors said, would be to undergo an operation in order to remove whatever was obstructing her intestine. They warned that she was in a weakened condition and might die during the operation, or that cancer might have affected so much of her intestine nothing could be done. The alternatives were also presented to Mrs. B., although in less detail and more tentatively. Both she and her family decided it would be better to go ahead.

Mrs. B.'s eldest daughter, living in California, already had made plans to come East for Thanksgiving, knowing it would probably be her last chance to see her mother. When she was told about the operation she asked over the phone, "Shall I wait until next week or should I come now?"

"I think you'd better come now," her brother-in-law said. She arranged for someone to take care of her three children and made a plane reservation for the day after the operation. Mrs. B.'s two brothers were also called, but they decided to wait until after the operation before coming to New York. "If I came now it would scare her to death," said the brother who lived in Washington.

The operation was scheduled for the morning of Thursday, November 19. Her family remained by the phone throughout the day. At 6 P.M. the surgeon finally called and said Mrs. B.'s intestine was blocked by cancer every two or three inches. There was nothing he could do. He was asked how long Mrs. B. might live. "Perhaps a week," he said.

Later that evening Mrs. B.'s family visited her briefly after she came up from the recovery room. She was pale and drawn and barely able to speak. The operation had obviously been an ordeal. "Never again," she whispered. "Never again."

The next day Mrs. B.'s eldest daughter flew to New York and went to see her mother, already beginning to regain her strength after the operation. Before the family went to see her on Saturday they tried to decide what to say if she should ask about her condition. The hard thing was finding out what Mrs. B. already had been told by her doctors. Until they reached Dr. C., they decided, they would tell Mrs. B. everyone was worried but didn't yet know the full results of the operation. They feared she would press them, and they knew that if she asked directly whether or not the cancer had been cut out, the only possible answers would be the truth or an outright lie. They did not want to lie, knowing how much Mrs. B. would hate being lied to, but they dreaded equally talking about the true situation. They could not have explained why.

As things turned out they need not have worried. Mrs. B. had cross-examined her doctors on a number of occasions since Thursday night, when she had found the strength to say, "It was my cancer, wasn't it?" Dr. C. later explained that Mrs. B. kept after him until she had the truth. His practice was to answer all questions truthfully, leaving it up to the patient to decide which questions to ask. Some patients asked nothing. Others stopped as soon as Dr. C. indicated their condition was serious. Mrs. B. had been unusual, he said, in questioning him precisely about her condition.

On Sunday Mrs. B. began to weaken again. When her son-in-law arrived about 11 A.M., she shooed the nurse out of the room. "I want to be alone with my son-in-law," she said. As soon as the door was closed she said, "I'm dying. There's no use kidding ourselves."

She told her son-in-law where all her papers were and what was in her will, asking him to make sure his mother got the red leather box which Mrs. B. had bought for her in Czechoslovakia the previous summer, and then had liked so much she kept it. "I've been feeling guilty about that," she said.

She also asked her son-in-law to get her lawyer on the phone so she could give him "a pep talk." When she reached him she said, "Now listen, you take care of the kids and try and keep the government from getting it all." She gave her best to his wife and said goodbye.

Finally Mrs. B. asked her son-in-law to make sure her eyes went to the eye bank and that her body was given to "science." (Mrs. B.'s surgeon told her son-in-law he wanted to do an autopsy, but that cancer had destroyed her body's usefulness as far as "science" was concerned. Mrs. B.'s second choice had been cremation without any service, and that wish was carried out.)

After Mrs. B. had straightened out her affairs to her own satisfaction, she relaxed and began to chat and even joke about her situation. A few minutes later she suddenly weakened and seemed to doze off. After awhile she started awake, staring intently at the ceiling. "Is there anything up there, right over my bed?" she asked her son-in-law. He said there was not. A look of resigned disgust came over Mrs. B.'s face. "I'm afraid I'm going to have hallucinations," she said.

During the following days her decline was obvious to herself and her family. She spent more time dozing, was coherent for shorter periods which came farther apart. During one such moment she told her daughter, "I hadn't believed it would happen so fast."

In most American hospitals the experience of death is clouded by drugs. When drugs are necessary to relieve pain there is no alternative, but heavy sedatives, tranquilizers, and pain-killing drugs are also used for purposes of "patient management." In the final stages of dying the greatest fear of patients is abandonment, with good reason. When possible, hospitals will try to send patients home to die. Doctors often cut back their visits, overworked nurses save most of their attention for "those who can be helped," and even the families of the dying frequently begin to detach themselves. The belief that life must go on can be carried to brutal limits, with relatives and even husbands or wives acting as if the dying individual were already dead. When dying patients pester the nursing staff for attention, they are often simply trying to alleviate their loneliness; if the pestering becomes irksome there is a tendency to respond with drugs.

The abandonment which dying patients fear can be as much emotional as literal. Nurses say they do not become hardened to death and often dream about the death of their patients. As a result they attempt to distance themselves from the dying by thinking of them as no longer quite there, referring to the care of unconscious patients, for example, as "watering the vegetables." The terrible moment which demands that life-sustaining equipment be turned off is emotionally masked by the phrase, "pulling the plug."

The impulse to abandon the dying can become overwhelming. It is policy in most hospitals to move dying patients into single rooms as death approaches. Doctors, nurses, and even relatives tend to find good reasons to stay out of the dying patient's room. The pretense is that no one wants to "disturb" the dying person while he is "resting," but nurses say they have seen too many clusters of relatives outside hospital rooms at the moment of death to consider it a coincidence.

As death approaches, the world of the dying gradually shrinks. They talk less of their disease and more about their exact symptoms, how they feel, what they plan to do tomorrow, or this afternoon, or in the next hour. Hope generally remains until the final moments, but its focus tends to shift. The Rev. Robert Reeves, Jr., the chaplain of Columbia-Presbyterian Hospital in New York, tells of one middle-aged man who hoped to get back to his business up until five weeks before his death. During the first week after that he talked about getting home for Thanksgiving. During the second week he hoped to be able to get out of bed again. In the third week he hoped to regain the ability to swallow food. At the beginning of his final week of life he hoped for a good night's sleep. A day later he hoped his pain medicine would work. The day before he died he hoped he would die in his sleep. He was denied every hope except the last, and yet each had eased his way toward death.

When the layman speaks of death he is referring to *somatic* death, or the death of the entire organism. The traditional signs of somatic death are *rigor mortis* (the stiffening of certain muscles), *algor mortis* (the cooling of the body) and *liver mortis* (the purplish-red discoloration of the skin caused by the settling of the blood). Somatic death includes the death of all bodily tissues, but an individual is commonly said to be "dead" long before all his tissues have died. The death of the "person," then, is only one stage in what an increasing number of doctors tend to think of as a distinct physiological process.

One doctor likens the process of death to menopause, which has long been known to include profound biological changes in women going far beyond the simple cessation of ovulation. The fact of putrefaction can also be cited as evidence that dying is a coherent biological event, and not simply the exact condition which precipitates death (heart failure, say, or kidney shutdown). When the body dies, organisms escape the gastrointestinal tract and begin the process of general decomposition by which the body is returned to Biblical ashes and dust. Built into the body, in other words, is the biological mechanism of its own dissolution, a fact which hardly can be dismissed as a coincidence. In arguing for an expanded notion of death, doctors also mention the characteristic return of the dying to infancy. Gradually they sleep longer each day, until they wake for only minutes at a time. Emotionally, the dying become increasingly dependent. Waking in the night they may cry if they discover they are alone, or sink back to sleep if someone is there.

Given a choice, the vast majority of people would prefer to die in their sleep. The next best, they say, would be a "peaceful" death, a consummation largely under the control of doctors. "Dear gentlemen," said the eighteenth-century English doctor, Sir Samuel Garth, to physicians whispering together at the foot of his bed, "let me die a natural death." The ability of doctors to extend the process of dying, if not life, is incomparably greater now. Medical "heroics" can keep the heart beating, the lungs breathing, the kidneys functioning, the brain flickering long after death would normally have arrived. The deterioration of the body from disease, and especially from cancer, proceeds further than it would without medical intervention. The result is that patients often lose consciousness long before they die because doctors, or relatives, refuse to give up when the body does. One nurse with years of experience in an intensive-care unit says she finds it increasingly difficult to tell when a patient has died, since machines sustain his vital signs.

Once the process of dying has begun, death can arrive at any time. Some patients die quickly; some linger for months with conditions that ought to have been quickly fatal. Doctors are still exceedingly cautious about predicting when someone will die, since they are so often surprised. Thomas Lupton, a sixteenth-century English writer, made the following attempt to list sure signs of imminent death:

If the forehead of the sick wax red, and his brows fall down, and his nose wax sharp and cold, and his left eye becomes little, and the corner of his eye runs, if he turns to the wall, if his ears be cold, or if he may suffer no brightness, and if his womb fall, if he pulls straws or the clothes of his bed, or if he pick often his nostrils with his fingers, and if he wake much, these are almost certain tokens of death.

Signs which modern nurses look for are dilated nostrils, sagging of the tongue to one side of the mouth, and a tendency for the thumbs to tuck in toward the palms of the dying patient's hands. Just as dying people frequently sense the imminence of their own death and predict it accurately, nurses develop a sense which tells them (but not always correctly) when a patient is going to die.

In the early stages of dying, the patient remains essentially himself, afflicted only by the knowledge of impending death and the effect of that knowledge on himself and those around him. In the final stages, consciousness in the dying sometimes undergoes qualitative changes. This experience is the least well understood of all, since the nearer a patient approaches to death, the less he can describe what he feels. The crisis for the dying patient characteristically arrives when he stops "fighting" to live. Doctors cannot say just how patients "fight," but they are unanimous in saying that patients do so, and that "fighting" can make all the difference in situations which can go either way. A man fighting to stay alive apparently duplicates the experience of a man fighting to stay awake, i.e., alternating flashes of lucidity and delirium. Patients often signal the approach of death by simply saying, "I can't fight any longer." The period that follows is unlike any other experienced in life.

Until the twentieth century, this final period was often called "the dying hour," although it can last considerably longer than an hour. Physicians described it as being a peaceful period in which the dying person, accepting the lost struggle and the inevitable end, is relaxed and ready to depart. The patient may gradually distance himself from life, actually turning away close friends and relatives, literally turning to the wall (as suggested by Lupton) as he prepares himself to die. Accepting the fact of their own death, the dying frequently turn their attention to those who will live, who are sometimes aggrieved by the readiness of the dying to leave them behind. At the end it is often the dying who comfort the living. Even so self-centered a figure as Louis XIV said to those around his deathbed, "Why weep ye? Did you think I should live forever?" After a pause he reflected with equanimity, "I thought dying had been harder."

Dying patients who remain fully conscious, or nearly so, say they are tired, feel a growing calm, are ready to go, are perhaps even happy. When Stephen Crane died of tuberculosis in England in 1900, only twenty-nine years old, he tried to describe the sensation to a friend: "Robert—when you come to the hedge—that we must all go over. It isn't so bad. You feel sleepy—and you don't care. Just a little dreamy anxiety—which world you're really in—that's all."

Dr. Austin Kutscher, one of the creators of the Foundation of Thanatology, has been studying death and related questions since the death of his wife in 1966. He emphasizes that in some ways the living tyrannize over the dying, studying the experience of the latter for the sake of those who remain. An example is the effort of medical scientists to narrow the definition of death in order to allow the organs of the dying to be used for transplants. The decision to accept brain death as death itself may be valid, Kutscher says, but it can hardly be argued that the definition was framed for the benefit of the dying. As a result of this natural bias on the part of the living, the study of death and dying has tended to ignore the nature of the event, and of its experience.

"Isn't there something rather magical about life that defies measurement by a piece of apparatus?" Dr. Kutscher says. "We are begging the issue by trying to define death when we can't even define life."

The scientific study of dying is relatively recent, but there exists a vast literature, amounting to case studies, of the approach of death. The final moments of great men have always been minutely recorded, these accounts ranging from those in the *Lives of the Saints,* which tend to a dull predictability, to the moment-by-moment narratives of death as experienced by generals, poets, and kings. Again and again the last words of the dying concede their readiness to depart; an unfeigned peace seems to ease the final flickering out. History and modern research agree that, for unknown reasons, the dying do not find it hard to die.

The very last moments are, of course, the least accessible. Some doctors have found evidence that the experience of patients still conscious has an element of the mystical. The doctors are quick to say that they are not talking about God and religion and parapsychological cultism; also they admit that such experiences might be the result of anoxia, or oxygen starvation in the brain. Nevertheless, they say, there is reason to believe the dying can experience a sense of surrender which borders on ecstasy. In a secular age, as practitioners of a science which tends toward mechanism, doctors reluctantly speak of "soul" or "spirit." But, in the safety of anonymity, they return again and again to the puzzle of what it is that dies when the body ceases to function. One doctor, attempting to describe the mystery he had sensed in dying patients, quoted the dying words attributed to the ancient philosopher Plotinus: "I am making my last effort to return that which is divine in me to that which is divine in the universe."

During her final five days of life, Mrs. B. was rarely conscious. The hospital left the second bed in her room empty. Her doctors and family decided not to attempt extreme efforts which could only prolong her dying, but Mrs. B. continued to receive intravenous feeding and was regularly turned by the nurses as a precaution against pneumonia.

On two occasions Mrs. B. started violently awake and insisted, "Something is terribly wrong." She did not know her daughters and believed her doctors were conspiring against her. She was given heavy sedation, and her daughters felt that, in effect, she had already died. Nevertheless, on a few last occasions she regained consciousness and knew her family, if only briefly. Two days before she died, as her surgeon was examining her, she suddenly asked, "Why don't I die?"

"Because you're tough," the surgeon said.

"I dont want to be tough that way,'" Mrs. B. said.

Because one test of a patient's grip on life is the ability to respond, the doctors and nurses would call her name loudly from time to time to ask if she wanted anything. "Mrs. B.?" one of the nurses nearly shouted one night, "Mrs. B.?"

"I'm gone," said Mrs. B. in a faint whisper.

"No, you're still with us," the nurse said.

Mrs. B grew steadily weaker. Her kidneys began to fail. She began to breathe rapidly and heavily, then stopped altogether, and after a moment began again. A nurse called this "Cheyne-Stokes breathing" and said it was probably a sign that the end was approaching. Some of the nurses thought Mrs. B. was completely unconscious; others felt she had only lost the ability to respond. Not knowing who was right, her family spoke as if she could hear and understand everything said in the room.

When Mrs. B.'s youngest daughter arrived about 11 A.M. the morning of Thanksgiving Day, November 26, she found her mother breathing slowly and regularly. Her body was completely relaxed over onto one side. It was a bright sunlit day. Mrs. B.'s daughter sat down by the large bank of windows overlooking Manhattan to the south and tried to read, but found herself thinking of her mother. After a while she looked up and saw that her mother had stopped breathing. So long expected, death had arrived unnoticed. For eighteen days Mrs. B.'s daughter had restrained her tears. Now, finally, when her mother was no longer there to comfort or be comforted, she began to cry.

Discussion Questions
1. In what way does the scientist resemble the layman? How is he different?
2. Describe Erikson's developmental stages. How relevant do you think these stages are to the study of personality?
3. What do you think Freud's reaction would have been to the women's rights movement?
4. What are the various stages of dying described in "Learning to Die"? Can you think of other possible stages which might be relevant to this experience?

Chapter 6
Family
and Marriage

Both the structure and purpose of family life have recently generated serious critical evaluation on many counts. The family has been taken for granted for so long that searching questions about its place in a continuously accelerating technological culture are perhaps overdue. The questions being raised about the family as a viable social institution are not meaningless nor remote from powerful social and emotional upheavals that are occurring today in society. Among the social problems which are directly or indirectly related to the quality of family life are the extremely high divorce rate, the prevalence of violence in our country, the striking incidents of child abuse, the drastic changes in patterns of sexual morality, the ever-increasing use of drugs, and a sharply profound sense of alienation by our adolescents and young adults. In many ways the quality of family life is a mirror by which most of our social changes are in some way reflected.

People who have studied family life have discovered that it is an extremely complex social arrangement which defies most standard definitions. The family is a product of many cultural forces that are both traditional and contemporary in origin. The first paper in this chapter, entitled "Marriage on the Rocks," by James A. Peterson, delves into the family process and examines marriage, divorce, and other aspects of the family as a small social system. In his studies, Davis isolated four conditions that have produced significant emotional strain on the family and marriage. Briefly, the first has to do with the social and geographic mobility found in our culture. The second area of strain appears because of the changing role of men and women in our society so that even the most common roles are being altered by our rapidly changing technology. The third conflict area appears between the family and nonfamily roles. Nonfamily roles are gaining a more dominant interest in people's lives and considerably less attention and emotional investment are being committed to the family area. The final area of marital strain highlights the many cultural changes that have occurred within the last decade. Two aspects here are crucial. One is that divorce is becoming much easier to obtain, and thus emotional commitments can be legally terminated without long drawn-out procedures. A second point is that the marriage contract has been secularized so that sexual attitudes are not tied to a specific standard of religious morality. With secularization, sexual experience is opened up and experimentation occurs much earlier than before. Peterson feels that this probably contributes significantly to sexual maladjustment and creates important conflicts in marital life.

The changes in the family and married life obviously have many complex causes. One of the most important causes, described briefly in the Peterson article, is the changing role of women in our society. Women in all levels of society are demanding equal opportunity for advancement within the economic sector. A major social and economic problem for women is how to care for children, especially preschoolers, and still obtain employment. This is a tremendous problem because once there are children to care for, it is extremely difficult and costly to arrange for child care during the working hours. This problem has been particularly acute with lower socioeconomic income families, where it is even more important for the women to share the burden of finances so as to maintain a decent economic condition. The article by Bettye M. Caldwell titled "A Timid Giant Grows Bolder" surveys the effect of day-care centers on family life. The author points out that at one time the idea of day care services was essentially to protect young children from the hazards of inadequate supervision and poor food as well as physical abuse and lack of shelter. This was essentially a custodial arrangement in which children were merely covered by the service without any special educational advantages built in. Currently, however, there is a great deal of interest in producing a day-care arrangement that will provide a positive growth experience for children. Furthermore, the entire atmosphere surrounding the day-care concept has changed radically. Rather than being a depot for unwanted children, day-care services are now extremely respectable and run the gamut from church-inspired organizations, to federally sponsored day-care centers, to industries providing services, and to private corporations who are now franchising day care arrangements. If day care becomes an accepted concept and is provided on a massive scale, it cannot help but significantly alter the economic condition of women in our society. Furthermore, once women can become independent by choice of the burden of early child rearing, their relationship with men, their own sense of importance in society, and their role with children in the family is likely to take on new dimensions. This article throws the issue of day-care center services into bold relief.

Many of the changes which are reflected in our styles of family living are best represented in the widespread growth of the commune movement in the United States. Contrary to most stereotypes, the commune movement is not entirely composed of disgruntled youths or dope fiend fanatics but of mature and responsible persons in their mid-twenties to late thirties. To some extent the stimulus for communes was set off by the deterioration of traditional family bonds, a feeling of alienation by youth, and despair and helplessness about an ecological crisis of gigantic proportions that is now just beginning to be realized. What the commune has to offer is essentially a framework for people to reintroduce themselves to others and perhaps to counter the dehumanization process that is so prevalent in our society today. Like many communal organizations in the past, group life is regarded as a joyous experience, and work, especially on the land, is seen as the most basic means of self-expression. The article, "Communes: The Alternative Life Style," by Herbert A. Otto, is an extensive survey of the commune movement. Otto's impression is that communes now have grown to the extent that they are no longer simple social peculiarities but are taking on a measure of social significance that cannot be ignored. Communes of all sorts are being created. Agricultural communes, spiritual communes, church-sponsored communes, political communes, homosexual communes, and the list goes on. This is not to say that all communes succeed, but the movement is so broad that some varieties of group experimentation eventually will take hold and perhaps radically change many of our values into new forms and directions. Revolutions in sexual values, the rights of women, the rearing of children, and marital arrangements are all basically reflected in the commune movement and in many ways may represent a wave of the future.

Suggested Readings

Framo, James L. *Family Interaction: A Dialogue between Family Researchers and Family Therapists*. New York: Springer Publishing Co. 1971. An unusual conference with many well-known scholars interested in family development and process.

Fromm, Erich. *The Art of Loving*. New York: Harper & Row, 1956. A renowned work which examines many of the different meanings and expressions of love.

Murstein, Bernard I. *Theories of Attraction and Love*. New York: Springer Publishing Co., 1971. A series of papers, theory and research, on interpersonal behavior.

Patterson, Gerald R. *Families*. Champaign, Ill.: Research Press, 1971. A coverage of family intervention techniques inspired by behavior modification theory and practice.

"... many girls are not only not virgins at marriage but come to marriage with as much or more experience than their mates."

Marriage is suffering from the same instability affecting many areas of modern society. This is clearly documented by the extremely high divorce rate. This paper details a number of conflict areas in marriage which seriously undermine its success.

The paradox of a high level of marital dissolution combined with the highest marriage rate in any country at any period poses very complex problems of interpretation. Although in 1965 ten percent of the women who are now over 55 had never married, the prospect for those now in their late twenties is that only three percent would not marry. Yet divorces per one thousand population grew from .9 in 1900, to 1.6 in 1920, to 2.0 in 1940, to 2.2 in 1960. How can one explain this increasing popularity of an institution that shows an increasing failure rate?

Problems of Explanation

Much of the study of the family process that results in divorce has suffered from simplistic and unilateral causal explanation. Earlier analyses limited the discussion to deviance from normative standards and explained divorces as a failure of moral commitment. Later analyses, following Sigmund Freud, showed that in every divorce there were four persons involved, identifying the extra two persons as the "unconscious persons" who were the "efficient" board of directors controlling marriage and divorce. Still later, other sociologists concentrated on "a wide variety of items" in order to differentiate successful and unsuccessful marital unions. They believed that, by factoring out a series of disparate personality characteristics and historical marital events, they could eventually explain and predict marital success or failure. But such explanations never comprehend the dynamic processes involved in marital function.

Only recently has it been pointed out that Freud's emphasis on heredity and the predetermined unfolding of biological patterns neglected the profound impact of systemic and cultural considerations. Talcott Parsons has shown additionally that the small group characteristics of the family need emphasis if a

This article first appeared in *The Humanist*, May/June 1970, and is reprinted by permission.

scientific explanandum is to be inclusive enough to account for variance in the integration of the contemporary family.

The family system is extraordinarily complex. Therefore, no single explanatory variable, such as neurosis or heterogamous cultural marital origin, is sufficient to account for the paradoxes of contemporary marriage. The mere fact of a neurotic marital partner is no explanation of marital failure. It fails to account for the needs of a partner who would choose a neurotic mate, and it fails to describe the dysfunctional interactive processes between the partners. There are also many examples of highly integrated couples where the members represent every type of cultural disparity. Cultural dissonance, therefore, cannot offer a sufficient causal explanation for marital stress any more than neurosis.

The truth about studies describing with scaled precision individual symptoms of system failure is that they contribute little to either a theoretical or empirical understanding of the strains which could illumine marital integrative or disintegrative functions. Both the psychoanalytically-oriented and adjustment-trait-oriented explanations are powerless in explaining why in a period of high marital failure marriage grows more popular.

Direction of Future Analysis

The family is a small social system made up of the personal systems of individuals and integrated into the larger social systems of society. It exists and has existed in every known social system in history because it is structured to meet elemental needs of individuals and the systemic needs of the larger social systems. The normative role prescriptions of the social systems are so patterned as to meet the basic affect and maintenance needs of the personality-systems at the same time it socializes these for participation in non-family roles in other institutions. In the analysis of marital stress, three points of inquiry have to be pursued simultaneously. First, to what degree does the marital process meet the basic needs of its members? Second, how is the marital system kept in balance when new members are added? Third, how does the marital pair interact with larger social systems?

In a relatively stable social system, role behavior is firmly anchored in the cultural tradition. Modern marriage, however, occurs in a social system undergoing cultural and structural transition.

Four basic changes have occurred in the marital pair. First, the family has lost a great deal of primary interaction with kin. It has become, as Kingsley Davis described it, an introverted institution. In the second place, the century-old process of the democratization of sexual status has upset the reciprocal role expectations of the male and the female in the area of both power and function. The third change is that of role strain with relation to the balance of investment between family and non-family roles in the occupational or social system. The fourth change is connected with the changes in the normative values of the larger social system. Religious prescriptions decline in influence, and an element of hedonism subtracts power from the role aspects of role socialization both for those who are being socialized and for those doing the socialization. As a result, state statutes regarding divorce are tending toward abandonment of the adversary procedure with its inference of guilt. Another effect is the rapid shift in attitudes toward both pre-marital and post-marital sexual experimentation.

All of these changes operate to cause strain in a family which has rapidly changed its structure and which shows significant losses of many of its previous functions in the areas of education, religion, protection, recreation and work. These have increasingly been consigned to governmental or private sector systems.

The family used to be rich and full in the variety of the interactions which were located in the home. These were directed by the family leader in ways which made the output of the family significant both for the maintenance of the family and the economic and cultural systems. Today the transactions within the family are minimized, while those with non-family systems are maximized. The family has shrunk not only in size but in the number and scope of its inner transactions. The bonds of the family shrivel as its members work and plan and worship in specialized age and sex-graded systems away from the home.

While the increased traffic with nonfamily systems occasions opportunities for intra-family conflict, this traffic also imposes on the family increased responsibility in its socialization function. Furthermore, the social system with its mobility, isolation and competitive status system involves for people such anxiety and trauma that the small contemporary family becomes more and more essential for its members in terms of emotional support and therapy. Consequently, the family, while losing previously held functions, must function with considerably more expertise and emotional expenditure on the functions that remain.

All of these changes and many others have occurred very rapidly in the last fifty years. The result for the family system has been some cultural lag in maintaining its equilibrium in the face of functional losses, structural changes and differential role expectations. The really surprising aspect of the family's response to these changes has been its great stability and not its disorganization. Nevertheless, there is divorce, and divorce is indicative of the strain in the marital system due to these changes.

Areas of Marital Strain

The small contemporary family has lost much of its primary interaction with kin. Both social and geographical mobility result in the separation of kin to the extent that if there is to be daily emotional nourishment for family members it must come from within the small isolated family. Marital strain arises from the inability of husband and wife to function fully in meeting each other's psychological needs. When there were a dozen significant kin close by in the extended family to give the mother emotional support, it did not matter much if the father was a martinet and harsh. But there are now no dozen significant others either in the form of kin or neighbors. Consequently, where either one or the other of the actors in the marital system is rigid, schizoid, intemperate or non-responsive, the vacuum created is difficult to fill. By way of illustration, a study by one of my students indicated that only one-third of the men and sixteen percent of the women engaged in the extramarital affairs he studied were involved because of inadequate sexual lives; rather, they were there because of profound love relationships or companionship with the other party. In some cases the marriages have declined in meaning to that state in which there is little companionship or affection left. In such cases the tendency to turn children into adult companions for emotional support often distorts childhood. A woman who had grown up in such a home stated it very simply. She said, "I was never a child, only a very small and inadequate adult for my mother."

Sally Kotlar, under the direction of the author, has done some research into the more basic question of role congruity and marital adjustment. She generalizes from her data to say that if an individual perceives his mate as closely approximating his ideal for that marital role, this is significant for adaptive marital relations. Where the disparity is great, however, the frustration of role expectations leads to disruptive interpersonal transactions in the marital system.

What we have added here to this study is the inference that the critical nature of emotional role support is an emergent condition reflecting the isolation of the modern urban family. When role fulfillment is dependent on the narrow base of small family interaction rather than on a large network of kin and neighbor relationships, that fulfillment becomes much more difficult and makes the relationship both more demanding and more fragile.

Roles in Transition

A second area of strain stems from the transition from the roles of men and women associated with the traditional patriarchal family to new roles associated with the democratic equalitarian family. This transition has been well documented. What has not been so well documented is the mischief that is done to the marital system by the different rates at which the male and female make the transition. Every marital counselor in the country is well aware of the irony of the situation where a wife has moved into new personal freedom and with new personal opportunities with the result that she is so locked into role conflict with her husband that divorce is inevitable. In a sense this represents another case of cultural lag.

Studies of marriage and divorce indicate that for some persons the wife's employment is a primary factor in the divorce. As a woman's income increases, her power in the home increases. Husbands exercise less dominance over working wives than over nonworking wives. About one-half of all women are in the labor force at any given time and about 75 percent of these are married. The employment of a particular wife gives her a lever to demand more adequate treatment at home. Her grandmother had nowhere to go if she left her husband unless it was back to her old home. The modern wife has another alternative. She can move closer to the office or factory. That this new freedom has not made marriage any happier is evident from the findings that the passage of time in modern marriage is "corrosive," and that only seven out of every one hundred wives are "very satisfied" with their marriage. This is disenchantment!

A far more serious case can be made for the assumption of new emotional roles by the male. If the husband does not support his wife emotionally, if he does not comfort her, encourage her, love her, who will? What we have said about the isolation of the family from kin and neighbors indicates that if the husband cannot give emotional support to his wife the marital union will suffer disruption.

Role Conflicts Between Family and Non-family Roles

A third area of strain stems from conflicts between family and non-family roles. It is not surprising, in a system where status is not ascribed but achieved, that some individuals give almost all their energy and commitment to that system in which they can achieve status. In such cases the energy investment necessary to make sufficient role commitment in the marriage is lacking and the marriage fails.

This is precisely what happens in the case of many executives and lower echelon management personnel. Their point of view in terms of this role conflict is adequately stated by an executive from one of the companies of the country who said to the author:

> You're not doing very much for us, doctor. I think I've got a better handle on this thing than you have. There is only one issue and it's really very simple. I'm now secretary of my company. The vice-president of that company is now sixty years old and I'm forty. When I'm forty-five, he's going to retire. That's my only chance of being vice-president of such a company and I'm going to be vice-president! That means that I have to work every night to prove I'm worthy and I have to spend my weekend playing golf or entertaining the board. I tell you it's simple. All my wife has to do to have a good marriage is to quit bitching about seeing me and my seeing those bratty kids and everything will be all right. If she doesn't want that she can quit. I can't get another opportunity like this, but I can always get another wife.

She quit and he got another wife . . . and another wife.

If it is true that *companionship* has emerged as the most valued aspect of marriage today, it follows that where another role deprives the marriage of companionship, the marriage fails.

Other non-family role systems may take more energy and affect away from the marital system than the work role. Sally Kotlar found that the most serious marital difficulties encountered by her group of adjusted and unadjusted couples was the "interference of in-laws." The interference of the business secretary assumes a major place in many cases. The interference of in-laws generally represents a failure of one or both marital partners to ever establish a marital system. The expenditure of energy on a secretary more often reflects the earlier failure of the marital system to meet primary needs of the partner.

Cultural Changes

A fourth area of the marital strain differs from the others. It results from changes in the norms of the cultural system which influence the character and power of the normative aspect of role prescriptions. Two illustrations suffice. The first is the growing ease with which divorce is viewed as a solution to marital conflict, thus reducing the punishment associated with marital dissolution. The fear of social ostracism or inner guilt no longer constrains the individual who is contemplating divorce. In this sense the relaxation of social controls over divorce merely facilitates the rapidity with which one caught in any of the previously described strains may terminate the painful relationship.

If one is committed to the importance of healthy family life and a rewarding marital system, divorce may be viewed as a contribution to the larger social system by enhancing the breaking of inadequate relationships and the initiation of more adequate unions. There is some empirical justification for this view insofar as over one-half of the second marriages studied seem to have achieved as good an adjustment as intact first marriages. In this sense, divorce is functional to a more satisfactory marital system in terms of long-run considerations.

The second aspect of the secularization of cultural attitudes toward marriage and divorce that is having some impact has to do both with pre-marital socializing experiences and with dissatisfaction with marriage itself. Two diverse clinical interviews will illustrate both of these cases. There is little question but what the old double standard is disappearing in our society and that many girls are not only not virgins at marriage but come to marriage with as much or more experience than their mates. This can cause conflict. A recent case illustrates one result of this new freedom.

> Twenty-two year old Marjorie appeared at the clinic a year and a half after her marriage. Her complaint about her marriage centered on the sexual stupidity of her young husband. She related a long history of a very active sexual life which began when she was fifteen and involved a great many older men. She was used to all kinds of erotic arousal and sexual play. Her husband, who tended temperamentally to be somewhat deliberate and unimaginative, was relatively sexually inexperienced. She quickly became aware of his ineptness and scolded him for his awkwardness. This scolding was quite a blow to his male ego and for several months he was impotent. While she learned her lesson and was quiet after that, she became increasingly discontented with his lack of excitement and dullness. She was ready to divorce her husband because she found him "hopelessly inadequate in bed."

In all of the discussions about new sexual attitudes, very few individuals except clinicians have inquired as to the congruity of training for variety before marriage as adequate preparation for fidelity after marriage. The following case reports on this problem:

> James Smith was a 38-year-old, attractive, Caucasian male who came along for the first interview at the clinic. He told of having a beautiful wife and three children whom he now wanted to leave. He stated that he came to make the most reasonable settlement he could and to work out some therapeutic way of leaving his wife which would not hurt her, because he "loved" her. When the therapist asked then why he was leaving her, he said, "Jeannie is perhaps the most gorgeous female I know. She is also the most conscientious mother I know. She has fulfilled her role beautifully. If I wanted a wife I'd stick with her or I'd marry her if I were single. The fact is I don't want a wife. I have been married fifteen years and I've had

marriage. I've made it in business and I can set my wife and kids up so they'll never want for anything. As for me, I want now to have fun. I've worked hard for 18 years and that's enough. I've got an assistant who I've trained to carry on and run the business. I'm going to travel and laugh and play. Your job is to help adjust my wife to my leaving her. . . . The kids? They don't need me. My wife does a swell job with them.

It was possible to interview both husband and wife in this case. The possibility of a divorce came as a monstrous surprise to the wife, who protested her ignorance of any strain at all in the marriage. What is sobering in cases like this is the somewhat callous indifference to the needs of relatively young children for a father. In the case of male children, such a divorce deprives them of a male model and, in the case of the female child, it deprives them of the opportunity to learn the female role vis-à-vis the father.

To whatever extent these cases are representative of a type of emancipated and secularized men and women, their emerging cultural norms do not seem to fit with present marital systems. We suspect that if we were to make a systematic search we would find many other forms of marital deviance, such as the "cocktail type" of relationships described by Dr. Jessie Bernard or the "swingers" groups extant in all of our major metropolitan communities, which would illustrate in other ways the secularized and hedonistic cultural norm described here only in terms of divorce. In an ironic way the presence, or perhaps the threat, of such deviance may have a salutary effect on marriage partners insofar as they may be more alert to make their own partnership viable.

Conclusion

So, why is marriage more popular than ever when it is failing at such a high rate?

The reason for its popularity appears to stem from the increasing need in our lonely and isolated world for a small group system assuring companionship and intimacy. The reasons for failure seem to flow from monumental social changes, which result in demands upon the marital couple that are more severe in terms of emotional maturity and sharing than ever before in history.

The social need for a strong marital partnership stems from the specialized task of socialization of the next generation in highly complex role tasks. Yet this demand on parents comes at a time when normative changes associated with role expectations as to the meaning of masculinity and femininity make cultural transmission confused and irritating. When a couple is struggling with their own individual and couple identity, it is difficult to model clearly for the next generation.

In the face of both structural and cultural changes, the family is remarkably stable even though strain and tension must inevitably be its lot during these decades of social transition. The level of divorce is surprisingly low in view of the structural changes, social innovations, and normative shifts that characterize the social environment for contemporary marriage.

23. A Timid Giant Grows Bolder
Bettye M. Caldwell

"One of the reasons many persons have resisted day care on a large scale has been the fear that, no matter which generation it focused on, it would weaken the bond between children and their families."

Day care is a controversial topic in many parts of the country. It is tied to a variety of social changes that are currently altering the patterns of women's civil rights. This paper describes the issues and analyzes the fears being generated by these programs.

In recent months "day care"—an awkward and somewhat insulting term that few people used in either professional or personal vocabularies as recently as five years ago—has become a household term. Widely heralded by its advocates as a near panacea for many public ills, demanded by women as a civil right, offered as an employment lure by companies hiring large numbers of women, requested by city planners and boards of anti-poverty organizations, and recommended as an essential first step in reducing the large numbers of persons receiving welfare—how could the field have more status? But this pleasurable situation is very new.

Until recently, day care was but a poor relation of both social service and education. Neither field seemed disposed to embrace it fully or to recognize its legitimacy. But, historically speaking, day care has been much closer to the field of social welfare than to education. In fact, it is from the field of social service (child welfare, in particular) that day care received its definition as *care and protection* for children from *families with some type of social pathology.*

Early literature on day care generally took special pains to differentiate day care from education. For example, in the 1960 edition of the Child Welfare League of America's *Standards for Day Care Service* (which sets the standards for all agencies in the field), one finds day care delimited as follows:

> Day-care service has to be differentiated from the nursery school or kindergarten, and from extended school services and other programs for school-age children offered as part of elementary school systems. These have

education of young children as their main purpose. The primary purpose of a day-care service is the care and protection of children. This purpose, the reasons for which a child and family may need it, and the responsibility shared with parents distinguish a day-care service from education programs.

At the time the day-care movement gained adherents and momentum in America we wanted to protect young children from such hazards as inadequate supervision, insufficient food, lack of shelter, and physical abuse. As today's knowledge about the importance of early experience for child development was only faintly limned in our consciousness at that time, it is not surprising that the prevailing concept of quality day care failed to recognize education as an integral part of "care and protection."

A second factor that undoubtedly kept the day-care field slightly outside the bounds of general respectability was the designation of the family with problems as the primary group for whom the service was appropriate. To quote once again from the Child Welfare League's influential *Standards*:

> Day care, as a child welfare service, is an expression of the community's concern for the welfare and protection of *children whose parents need help* in providing the care, protection, and experiences essential for their healthy development [emphasis added].

The pamphlet goes on to identify such children as those whose mothers work, whose fathers might not be in the home, who are ill or have emotional problems, or who live in poor housing conditions. Certainly if families must see themselves as exemplifying social pathology in order to use day-care services, the field is not likely to be embraced by those who could give it status in the larger society.

Suddenly, however, day care is "in," and the groups that once neglected it now claim it as their own. Money that cannot be obtained for "early childhood education" may possibly be found for day care. Fundamental child welfare programs that cannot be launched independently can possibly be made available as riders on day-care appropriations. How do we explain the sudden popularity?

One reason that the number of day-care centers did not increase substantially for many years was the implicit fear that, if more such facilities were available, more mothers would be tempted to work outside the home. Yet more mothers *have* gone to work outside the home, including mothers with children younger than six. And these are generally conscientious mothers who want good child care during their working hours. Although relatives and neighbors still constitute by far the most frequently used child-care resources, more and more women have learned about day care, especially educational day care, and have come to request or demand such facilities for their own children. Furthermore, whereas national social policy formerly endorsed financial subsidies to keep mothers with young children at home (the Aid to Families with Dependent Children program), this policy is currently being re-examined. Training and employment of mothers are being urged, and quality day care is recognized as essential to this policy.

Employers also are turning to day-care programs as a way of attracting female workers and reducing absenteeism from the job. The best-known modern program exemplifying this is the day-care program operated in conjunction with the KLH factory in Cambridge, Massachusetts. Similar programs were funded under the Lanham Act during World War II, only to be discontinued at the end of the war when returning veterans dramatically changed the employment picture and displaced large numbers of women from their jobs.

Today, that pattern is being reversed by advocates of civil and personal rights for women. It has taken this group to strip day care of its social-pathology orientation. Stressing that personal fulfillment is a right to be shared by men and women alike and that child care is not the only valid avenue through which women may gain fulfillment, proponents of the Women's Liberation movement have demanded quality day care as a means to that personal fulfillment. At the 1970 White House Conference on Children last December, delegates representing various women's groups were among the most vocal in their demands that child care be made available around the clock throughout the year for all who want it, not just for indigent or minority groups. Such delegates also vehemently urged that federally supported day care be completely divorced from public assistance—thus officially removing the taint of social pathology from day-care services.

Despite the importance of these developments, however, the most fundamental influence has been the steady flow of information about the importance of the early childhood years. Evidence has gradually accumulated that certain kinds of experiences during the early years greatly influence how a child grows up in this society. Although the data are based on only about five years of research, the results have filtered out from scientific laboratories to popular magazines and thence to parents of all social classes, and the result is that parents are clamoring for more such programs for their children. As many of these same parents need child care, the request is generally for day care rather than "early education" per se.

The professionals who give semantic shape to social trends have not been indifferent to the new demands and conceptual changes. In 1969, the Child Welfare League's Standards was revised:

> At present, a wide range of resources and facilities, including informal arrangements and organized programs under various auspices, is used for the care of children outside of their homes during some part of the day. These resources and facilities have been established to serve many different purposes. They place differing emphases, reflected in their programs and the children whom they serve, on the responsibility for care, protection, child development, education, or treatment.

This new statement recognizes that care and protection involve an inherent developmental and educational component. Day care can no more be separated from education than it can from welfare or health. In breaking away from the earlier narrow concept that artificially tried to separate the two patterns of service, the day-care movement in this current definition has now given itself a new chapter.

In a second radical departure from the earlier concept, the new Standards suggests that day-care services may be offered more as a service to the mother than to the child. The pamphlet states:

> Day-care programs are promoted and used for purposes in which the interests of the child may be a secondary consideration. Day care is provided to allow mothers, particularly those who are unmarried, to complete their schooling or to train for new careers; to help financially dependent mothers attain self-support and to reduce public assistance expenditures; and to recruit women for, and retain them in, the labor force.

The league is not an organization that can lightly take the subordination of the needs of children, however, and the report goes on to caution:

> Under these circumstances, it is necessary to ensure that day care is in the best interests of the individual children, and that the daily experiences are of benefit to them, or at least not detrimental.

In a subsequent section of the new *Standards,* a third subtle but major conceptual shift is encountered. While the old *Standards* declared, "The primary purpose of a day-care service is the care and protection of children," the new version states, "The primary purpose of a day-care service is to *supplement* the care and protection that the child receives *from his parents* [emphasis added]." It seems as if the field were more willing to share the responsibility at this time, or else were more aware that care and protection for the young child attempted *in loco parentis* has little chance of providing much of either. The implication is that the family carries the major burden and the day-care service only supplements the family's endeavors.

The varied purposes of day care are reflected in a healthy diversity of programs. They include care provided by family members or baby-sitters, day-care centers operated as demonstration and research agencies, centers controlled by parents or offered as a public service by a church or secular organization or provided as a lure by industry, and centers run for profit by a private operator or as a franchise unit of a national corporation. Still relatively scarce are programs that involve a complete blending of day care with education.

The subtle changes in the day-care concept reflect a shift in orientation that is at once both honest and refreshing and yet just a little alarming. The new *Standards* has the audacity to suggest that day care is more than a noble service to the next generation, being in addition an important service and convenience for the present generation. The league is to be credited with recognizing the validity of that orientation. Day-care people *do* tend to get just a bit sugar-coated in talking about what the experience will do for the children—all the social, affective, and cognitive gains that will accrue as a result—that we tend to forget about the families of the children. And often, when we remember them, it has been in terms of concern with modifying their behavior in order to facilitate *our* goals for *their* children.

One of the reasons many persons have resisted day care on a large scale has been the fear that, no matter which generation it focused on, it would weaken the bond between children and their families. This fear has been more presumptive than factual and has been built upon an irrational equation of day care with institutional care. Day care—daily separation followed by nightly reunion in the context of social relationships that permit a sense of identity to be formed—appears to have none of the socially toxic effects of prolonged institutional care, or even of temporary separations (such as hospitalization) during which family contacts might be terminated for a given time. My colleagues and I in Syracuse recently published data that demonstrated rather persuasively that two-and-a-half-year-olds who had been in day care since around one year of age were as attached to their mothers as were comparable control children who had never had such a day-care experience.

Whatever the source of the fear, it appears to be a strong one. And some of the parent groups advocating more day-care facilities are also reminding the professionals that they, the parents, have a right to share in the planning and decision-making. During the summer of 1970, a workshop was held in Airlie House, Virginia, to prepare a number of pamphlets that could be used as guides by inexperienced groups wishing to initiate and operate day-care programs. A set of principles was prepared that went considerably beyond the league's position in recognizing that day care could sometimes be structured to meet the needs of the parents. Although the document is not now in its final version, the early draft proposed that the primary focus of any day-care program should be the *individual child and his family*—not the child alone or the parents alone. Furthermore, day care was described as a program that could either bring parents and children together or else drive a wedge between them. The statement of principles supported the former goal and stressed that quality day care should never do anything to reduce the family's commitment and responsibility. One suggestion was to supply parents with the information needed to make informed judgments and then to have them participate fully in decisions about what would be desirable for their children in day care as well as in the home.

Thus day care, formerly an advocate for the child, then for the parent (especially the mother), seems now to speak for the family. The policy implications of these different orientations are profound and far-reaching.

Because of its importance in the lives of children, one can imagine day care becoming a bold instrument of social policy. In fact, day care has not made policy; it has followed along when policy has been made. It has grown somewhat haphazardly, changing its own definition every ten years or so. At present it does not know whether it should serve the child, the parent, or the family. It cannot make up its mind whether it is a service for families with social pathology or for all families, whether it should be limited to children from economically underprivileged families or be offered to all children, whether it wants to change children or preserve cultural styles from one generation to the next. It does not know where to obtain its official identity. This confusion can be seen in state licensing patterns. The welfare department handles licensing in thirty-six states, the health department in five, and some different agency or combination of agencies in the remainder. The department of education is the licensing body in only one state, although it shares the task with welfare in one other and makes recommendations in many.

Thus, it is precisely in this area of planning for our children, except in the grossest sense, that we are most timid in this country. With our tradition of valuing rugged individualism, we have been reluctant to say much about the kinds of children we want. Do we want obedient children? Happy children?

Adaptive children? Children who remain faithful to the values of their families? Militant children? Bright children? Group-oriented children? Woodstock and Maypole youth or Peace Corps youth? Eventual adults who can slip from one type to another? Professor Urie Bronfenbrenner has commented on the extent to which child rearing in the U.S.S.R. has a clear objective to train children as responsible citizens of the Soviet state, in contrast to the lack of objectives and belief in autonomy in the U.S. In our concern for individuality we occasionally find license for evasion of the responsibility for guidance.

What the day-care field needs in order to be a powerful instrument of social policy is a forum from which to advertise its potential and a willingness to proclaim its importance. To this author that forum ought to be public education—albeit education defined more flexibly and comprehensively than it is today. Actually there is little justification for a conceptual separation between public education and public day care, for most schools are "day schools" and represent "day education" with or without the supportive family services generally offered under the rubric of day care. The significant difference, however, is that day care generally enters the lives of children at an earlier age, and, as infant day care becomes more respectable, the age of entry will become even lower. Any experience that enters the lives of children at a time when they are impressionable, when basic patterns of expressing, thinking, feeling, and problemsolving are being developed and value systems are being assimilated, has no need to feel apologetic.

The suggestion that day care find a forum in education may sound like a partisan recommendation. But I am talking more about a conceptual model for program design than about professional auspices for program operation. This orientation need not close out any of the diverse models now being tried. Essentially the same suggestion has been made by others, including Florence Ruderman in her book *Child Care and Working Mothers*:

> Day care, regardless of the auspices under which it is offered, should be developed as a child-care program: a program directed to optimum social and psychological health of the young child whose mother cannot care for him for some part of the day. . . . But a given family's need for social casework or other forms of help should no more define day care, nor determine eligibility for it, than the existence of social service departments in schools and hospitals now defines these facilities as social work services. For organized child-care service in this country to develop and meet adequately a growing social need, it must be recognized as a positive social institution and enabled to stand in its own right as an essential child-care program.

The challenge becomes one of having comprehensive child care embraced as a legitimate endeavor of that behemoth of public policy, public education, without having it consumed in the fire of an encrusted bureaucracy and without any loss of concern for "care and protection." Public education would do well to stop and reflect occasionally that one of its concerns should be with the care and protection of the children and youth who come within its sphere of influence!

At this moment in history, when we are on the threshold of embarking on a nationwide program of social intervention offered through comprehensive child care, we let ourselves prattle about such things as cost per child, physical facilities, or even community control. And when we begin to think big about what kinds of children we want to have in the next generation, about which human characteristics will stand them in good stead in a world changing so rapidly, we fall back on generalities such as care and protection. Yet any social institution that can shape behavior and help instill values and competencies and life-styles should also shape policy. Early child care is a powerful instrument for influencing patterns of development and the quality of life for children and adults. Because of its power, those who give it direction must not think or act with timidity.

24. Communes: The Alternative Life-Style
Herbert A. Otto

"Communes widely accept the idea that life is meant to be fundamentally joyous...."

The commune movement is currently expanding all over the country. The group experience is taking many forms and people seem to be looking for a way to find greater intimacy with each other. This article gives a provocative overview of communes and the people they appeal to.

Angelina is a tall, striking blonde in her mid-forties, with a husky voice and a motherly, forthright air about her. She had been a successful interior decorator in a well-known college town in Oregon. Following her divorce, Angelina decided to rent some of the extra bedrooms in her house to students.

"I was shocked seeing people dirty and with unwashed hair—until I got to know them better and saw their soul reflected in their eyes. They wanted country life and animals. They wanted to be creative and to be themselves. At that time, I was attending a Unitarian church. I talked to the minister about starting a commune. He said it wouldn't work."

Angelina felt she needed new ideas and viewpoints, and she went to the Esalen Institute at Big Sur, California. She stayed three months. "I could see so much, feel so much. I thought I was really called."

Upon returning to her business, which she had left in competent hands,

Angelina decided to sell out and was able to do so at a favorable price. "I made up my mind I wanted the family feeling. At this point, it was like Providence when I heard about the hundred and fifty acres. The price was so reasonable, I thought there was something wrong with the place. But when I saw it—with the half-dozen springs, three streams, and mixed timber—I knew this was the spot for a nature commune."

Angelina started the commune two-and-a-half years ago with a young couple she had met at Esalen. Today, there are thirty young people and eight children in the community. Twelve of this group are called "stable"; they have made a commitment to the commune. Median age within the commune is in the mid-twenties. Sixty-five percent of the group are young men. There are many high school and college dropouts, but also a number of successful former businessmen and professionals, several teachers, and two engineers.

This commune, with Angelina as its prime mover and guiding spirit, is just one of many such living arrangements that have mushroomed around the country. Over the past few years, the commune movement has grown at an unprecedented and explosive rate, and there is every indication that this is only the initial phase of a trend that is bound to have far-reaching implications for the function and structure of our contemporary society. Some traditional institutions are already beginning to feel the impact of this explosive growth.

The commune movement has passed far beyond its contemporary origins in hippie tribalism and can no longer be described as a movement for youth exclusively. There are a rapidly growing number of communes composed of persons in their mid-twenties to upper thirties. A source at the National Institute of Health has estimated that more than 3,000 urban communes are now in operation. This figure closely corresponds to a recent *New York Times* inquiry that uncovered 2,000 communes in thirty-four states.

Certain common viewpoints, almost a *Weltanschauung*, are shared by members of the contemporary commune movement. First, there is a deep respect and reverence for nature and the ecological system. There is a clear awareness that 70 percent of the population lives on 1 percent of the land and that this 1 percent is severely polluted, depressingly ugly, and psychologically overcrowded. Commune members generally believe that a very small but politically influential minority with no respect for the ecological system or the beauty of nature exploits all of the land for its own gain. Surpassing the credo of conservationist organizations, most commune members stress the rehabilitation of *all* lands and the conservation of *all* natural resources for the benefit of *all* the people.

Anti-Establishment sentiment is widespread, as is the conviction that a change in social and institutional structures is needed to halt man's dehumanization and to give him an opportunity to develop his potential. Considerable divergence of opinion exists on how social change is to be brought about, but there is general agreement that the commune movement contributes to change by bringing man closer to himself and to his fellow man through love and understanding.

Communes widely accept the idea that life is meant to be fundamentally joyous and that this is of the essence in doing, and enjoying, what you want to do—"doing your thing." Work in this context becomes a form of joyous self-expression and self-realization. Many commune members believe that existence

can be an almost continuous source of joyous affirmation. They usually trace
the absence of authentic joy in contemporary society to the confining nature
of many of our social institutions, the stifling of spontaneity, and the pre-
ponderance of game-playing and of devitalized artificial ways of relating socially.

A strong inner search for the meaning of one's own life, an openness and
willingness to communicate and encounter, coupled with a compelling desire for
personal growth and development, are hallmarks of the movement. A strong
anti-materialistic emphasis prevails; it decries a consumption-oriented society.
In many communes, what does not fit into a room becomes commune property.
A considerable number of communes aim for the type of self-sufficiency through
which they can exist independently of "the system."

There is a strong trend toward ownership of land and houses by communes,
Leasing arrangements have not proved satisfactory; in too many instances,
landlords have canceled leases when community pressures were exerted. The
non-urban communes I have visited are strongly aware of ecological factors,
and, because of this, members usually had consulted with local health authorities concerning the construction and placement of sanitary facilities. Among the
urban communes, toilet and bath facilities were in most cases short of the
demand.

Marked preferences for vegetarianism and for organically grown food are
noticeable in the commune movement. Many individual members also experiment with different health diets. Roughly 40 percent of the communes I visited
were vegetarian; 20 percent served both vegetarian and non-vegetarian meals.
The remainder served meat when available—usually two to six times a week.
This third group, although not vegetarian by choice, liked their vegetarian meals
and expressed very little craving for meat. Whenever possible, communes concentrate on growing and raising their own food. An estimated 60 percent of the
urban communes are now purchasing some or most of their supplies from health-
food stores or similar sources.

Not surprisingly, the commune has become the repository of repressed
man's erotic fantasy. I was continuously told that visitors who came not to
learn and understand but to peek and ogle invariably ask two questions: "Who
sleeps with whom?" And, "Do you have group sex?" There appears to be much
fantasizing by outsiders about the sex life in communes.

Although there is considerable sexual permissiveness, I found a high
degree of pairing with a strong tendency toward interpersonal commitment in a
continuing relationship. Nudism is casual and accepted, as is the development
of a healthy sensuality, and natural childbirth, preferably within the commune,
is encouraged. Group sex involving the whole commune occurs quite rarely,
although there may be sexual experimentation involving two or more couples
or combinations.

The research team of Larry and Joan Constantine has studied multilateral
(group) marriage for the past three years. They have written and published
more studies in this area than other behavioral scientists, but have found only
one commune practicing group marriage. Most likely, there are others. About
two dozen independent families are known to be engaged in multilateral marriage, taking as their model Bob Rimmer's novel *Proposition 31,* which presents
a case for group marriage. Many others prefer to keep their arrangement totally
secret for fear of reprisals. According to an article by the Constantines, entitled

"Personal Growth in Multiple Marriages," failure rate is better than one out of two, because "group marriage is a marathon that does not end—it takes a real commitment to genuine, substantial, and unrelenting personal growth to really make it function and work."

Interest in spiritual development is a dominant theme in most communes. Study of and acquaintance with Eastern and Western mystics and religious philosophies is widespread. Religiosity and denominationalism were seldom encountered. On the other hand, I was struck by the deep commitment to spiritual search of so many members in all the communes I visited. Many members were trying different forms of meditation, and books on Eastern religions and mysticism were prominent on shelves.

I find that although there is some overlapping of functions and categories, a number of distinct types of communes can be recognized and are found in operation.

- The Agricultural Subsistence Commune: The main thrust is to farm or till the soil (mostly organic farming) so that the land will provide most, if not all, needs and make the commune independent and self-supporting. Many of these communes cultivate such specialized crops as organically grown grain, vegetables, and other produce, which are then sold to health-food stores, health-food wholesalers, or supermarkets.
- The Nature Commune: Emphasis is on supporting the ecological system and on the enjoyment of nature. Buildings and gardening or farming plots are designed to fit into the landscape to preserve its natural beauty. Everyone "does his own thing," and economic support for subsistence usually comes from such varied sources as sale of produce and handicrafts, wages from part-time work, welfare support, etc.
- The Craft Commune: One or several crafts, such as weaving, pottery making, or carpentry (including construction or work on buildings outside the commune), occupy the interest of members. They often spend considerable blocks of time enjoying the exercise of their craft with the income contributed to the commune. Many of the craft communes sell directly to the consumer as a result of local, regional, or sometimes national advertisement and publicity. Profit margins vary since the vast majority of such communes do not subscribe to the amassing of profits as the primary aim of their enterprise. Included in this category are the multimedia communes that specialize in light shows, video tape, and film-making.
- The Spiritual/Mystical Commune: The ongoing spiritual development of members is recognized to be of primary importance. There may be adherence to a religious system, such as Buddhism, Sufism, or Zen, and a teacher or guru may be involved. Studies of various texts and mystical works, use of rituals, a number of forms of meditation (such as transcendental or Zen meditation), and spontaneous spiritual celebrations play key roles in the life of the commune. Several of these communes also describe themselves as Christian and have a strong spiritual, but not denominational, emphasis.
- The Denominational Commune: There is a religious emphasis with membership restricted to those of a particular denomination. Examples are the Episcopalian Order of St. Michael, in Crown Point, Indiana, and the Catholic Worker Farm, in Tivoli, New York.

• The Church-sponsored Commune: Such a commune may be originated or sponsored by a church. There is usually a religious emphasis, but denominationalism is not stressed.

• The Political Commune: Members subscribe to or share a common ideology. They may identify themselves as anarchists, socialists, pacifists, etc. Emphasis is on the communal living experience with others sharing the same viewpoint. This is seen as fostering the individuals' political development. The commune is rarely engaged in direct social action in opposition to the Establishment.

• The Political Action Commune: Members are committed and practicing political activists (or activists-in-training) for the purpose of changing the social system. Classes are conducted, strategy formulated and carried out. The commune may be identified with a minority cause or be interested in organizing an industry, community, or ghetto neighborhood. It often identifies itself by the single word "revolutionary."

• The Service Commune: The main goal is social service. Emphasis is on organizing communities, helping people to plan and carry out community projects, offering professional or case-aide services, etc. Some of these communes include members from the helping professions. There are several such communes in the Philadelphia and New York ghettos; another example is the Federation of Communities, which services several locations in the Appalachians.

• The Art Commune: Artists from different fields or the same field come together to share in the stimulating climate of communal artistic creativity. As compared with the craft commune, members of the art commune are often painters, sculptors, or poets, who usually sell their art works independently rather than collectively. There are poetry and street theater communes in Berkeley and San Francisco.

• The Teaching Commune: Emphasis is on training and developing people who are able both to live and to teach others according to a particular system of techniques and methods. Communes whose purpose or mainstay is to conduct a school or schools also fall into this category.

• The Group Marriage Commune: Although members may be given the freedom to join in the group marriage or not, the practice of group marriage plays an important and often central role in the life of the commune. All adults are considered to be parents of the members' children.

• The Homosexual Commune: Currently found in large urban areas, with admission restricted to homophiles. The aim of these communes is to afford individuals who share a common way of life an opportunity to live and communicate together and to benefit from the economies of a communal living arrangement. Some of the communes subscribe to the principles of the homophile liberation movement. From a recent ad in *Kaliflower,* the bi-weekly information journal for communes in the San Francisco Bay Area: "OUR GAY COMMUNE HAS ROOM FOR TWO MORE. CALL AND RAP."

• The Growth-centered Commune: The main focus is on helping members to grow as persons, to actualize their potential. There are ongoing group sessions; sometimes professionals are asked to lead these. The commune continues to seek out new experiences and methods designed to develop the potentialities of its members.

• The Mobile, or Gypsy, Commune: This is a caravan, usually on the move.

Cars, buses, and trucks provide both transportation and living quarters. Members usually include artists, a rock group, or a light-show staff. The mobile commune often obtains contributions from "happenings" or performances given in communities or on college campuses.

• The Street, or Neighborhood, Commune: Several of these communes often are on the same street, or in the same neighborhood. Ownership of property is in the hands of commune members or friendly and sympathetic neighbors. Basically the idea is of a free enclave or free community. For example, in a recent *New York Times* article, Albert Solnit, chief of advance planning for California's Marin County, was reported at work "on a city of 20,000 for those who wish to live communally." Several neighborhood or city communes are in the planning stage, but none to my knowledge has as yet been established.

Among the major problems faced by all communes are those involving authority and structure. Ideally, there is no one telling anyone else what to do; directions are given by those best qualified to do a job. In practice, strong personalities in the communes assume responsibility for what happens, and there is a tendency toward the emergence of mother and father figures. There are, however, a clear awareness of this problem and continuing efforts toward resolution. At present, opposition to any form of structure, is still so strong that communes have found it almost impossible to cooperate with each other in joint undertakings of a major nature. Interestingly enough, communes with transcendent or spiritual values are the most stable and have the highest survival quotient. It is my conclusion that the weekly or periodic meetings of all commune members, which are often run as encounter groups, have a limited effectiveness in the resolution of interpersonal problems and issues. Although trained encounter leaders may be present as facilitators, their effectiveness is often considerably curtailed due to their own deep involvement in the issues that are the subject of confrontation. One answer to this dilemma might be to bring in a trained facilitator or for communes to exchange facilitators.

It is difficult to determine to what extent narcotics represent a problem for communes precisely because their consumption is as casual, widespread, and accepted as is the downing of alcoholic beverages in the business community. Marijuana and hashish are widely enjoyed, while use of such hard drugs as heroin is seldom encountered, especially in the non-urban communes. In a number of communes where drug use was extensive, I noticed a general air of lassitude and a lack of vitality. I also had the distinct impression that "dropping acid" (LSD) was on the decline; among commune members there seemed to be a general awareness of the danger of "speed," or methedrine. A number of communes are totally opposed to the use of narcotics, especially those with members who were former drug addicts. In most communes the subject of drugs periodically comes up for discussion so that changes in the viewpoint of the commune flow from the experience of the members. Similarly, problems of sexual possessiveness and jealousy appear to be less critical and are also handled by open group discussion. I noticed a tendency toward the maintenance of traditional sex roles, with the women doing the cooking and sewing, the men cutting lumber, etc. Upon questioning this, I repeatedly received the same answer: "Everyone does what they enjoy doing."

Another major problem in most communes is overcrowding and the con-

sequent lack of privacy and alone-time. Rarely does a member enjoy the opportunity of having a room to himself for any length of time. The common practice
is to walk off into the woods or fields, but this is an inadequate substitute for
real privacy.

Community relations remains a major and critical problem since many
communes are "hassled" by authorities or are located amid unfriendly neighbors.
As one member described it, the emotional climate in a hassled commune is
"full of not so good vibes—you don't know what they will try next, and you
keep looking over your shoulder. That takes energy." Today's commune members generally have a clear awareness of the importance of establishing good
community relations.

Many of the communes that have got under way this past year or are now
being organized are beginning on a sound financial basis. This trend appears
to be related to the strong influx of people in their mid-twenties, early or mid-
thirties, and beyond. These individuals have financial reserves or savings and
are, for the most part, successful professionals and businessmen with families.

One example is the Morehouse Commune, which now consists of thirteen
houses in the San Francisco Bay Area, two in Hawaii, and another in Los
Angeles; total assets are in excess of $2-million. Morehouse was founded a
year and a half ago by Victor Baranco, a former attorney who is now head of
the Institute of Human Abilities, in Oakland, California. There are several
categories of membership or involvement in this commune. Members who
belong to "the family" give all their assets to the commune, which then "takes
care of them," although family members are expected to continue to make a
productive contribution within their chosen fields. All income from family
members goes into a general fund, but if a family member wishes to withdraw,
his assets are returned, including a standard rate of interest for their having
been used. Each Morehouse commune in effect makes its own arrangements with
members, who may be paid a salary or placed on an allowance system. All communes have a house manager, who assigns tasks or work on a rotating basis.
In some Morehouse communes, certain categories of members pay in a fixed
monthly sum (as much as $200) toward expenses.

About a third of the Morehouse couples are married and have children.
According to one member, "There is no pressure to be married or unmarried.
Nobody cares who lives with whom." Morehouse is a teaching commune built
around a philosophy and way of life often described by group members as
"responsible hedonism." The commune trains its own teachers and offers a
considerable number of courses, such as Basic Sensuality, Advanced Sensuality,
and Basic Communication.

The aim and credo of this group are taken from a description of the Institute of Human Abilities published in the commune journal *Aquarius*: "We offer
the tools of deliberate living; we offer the techniques of successful communication on any level. We offer the knowledge of the human body and its sensual
potential. And we offer love to a world that holds love to be suspect."

The rapid growth of the Morehouse communes is by no means an isolated
example. A minister in Los Angeles founded a social-service and action-type
commune that within a year grew to seven houses. Other instances can be cited.
An unprecedented number of people want to join communes. In all but a few
instances I was asked to conceal the name and location of the commune to

make identification impossible. "We don't know what to do with all the people who come knocking on our door now," I was told repeatedly. In every commune, I heard of people who had recently left either to start a new commune or to join in the founding of one.

There is considerable mobility in communes, which is symptomatic of an endemic wanderlust and search. If people have to leave for any reason, once they have been exposed to communal living, they tend to return. They like the deep involvement with others in a climate of freedom, openness, and commitment. This feeling of belonging has been described as both a "new tribalism" and "a new sense of brotherhood." One young woman with whom I spoke had this to say about her commune experience: "When a white man walks into a room full of other whites, he doesn't feel he is among brothers like the black man does. In the communes, we are now beginning to feel that man has many brothers. . . . There is a new sense of honesty. You can say things to each other and share things like you never could in the family. I never had so much love in my whole life—not even in my own family." She also indicated, however, that commune living is highly intense and possibly not for everyone: "In the commune, there is nothing you can hide. Some people can't take it. They get sick or they leave."

Alvin Toffler in his recent book *Future Shock* notes that "most of today's 'intentional communities' reveal a powerful preference for the past, . . . but society as a whole would be better served by utopian experiments based on super- rather than pre-industrial forms. . . . In short, we can use utopianism as a tool rather than as an escape, if we base our experiments on the technology and society of tomorrow rather than of the past."

Although Toffler's observation is relevant, we must recognize that the commune movement, as with most other movements, is passing through certain developmental stages. As this stage, there is little readiness for communes to define themselves as laboratories for the exploration of alternative models that might benefit the society of the future. Disenchantment with and opposition to science and technology are other impediments to the adoption of the laboratory concept. With today's communes, faith in the future of mankind appears to be at too low an ebb to produce any sustained interest in what Toffler calls "scientific future-sensing and the techniques of scientific futurism."

Although David Cooper, a colleague and disciple of British psychiatrist Ronald Laing, has sounded a death knell in his new book *The Death of the Family*, I believe we are far from writing the epitaph. The traditional nuclear family will continue, although its form, to some extent, may change; in the years to come, possibly as high as 20 percent of the population will explore alternative models of social living.

It would be a mistake to characterize the commune movement as a collection of dropouts who are content to exist like lilies in the field. A considerable number of successful people from all walks of life are now involved; they have merely shifted their sphere of interest and the nature of their creative contributon. We are dealing with a massive awakening of the awareness that life holds multiple options other than going from school to job to retirement. The commune movement has opened a new and wide range of alternative life-styles and offers another frontier to those who have the courage for adventure. It is the test tube for the growth of a new type of social relatedness, for the development of an organization having a structure that appears, disappears, and reappears as it chooses and as it is needed. Communes may well serve as a laboratory for the study of the processes involved in the regeneration of our social institutions. They have become the symbol of man's new freedom to explore alternative life-styles and to develop deep and fulfilling human relationships through the rebirth and extension of our capacity for familial togetherness.

The nature commune that Angelina started two years ago has a reputation as one of the oldest and best run among the eight communes located within a twenty-five-mile radius of a small town in southern Oregon. This is a hilly farm and lumber region where in winter it sometimes rains for weeks on end, after which the appearance of the sun is greeted with festivity.

I had arranged to first meet Angelina at a local coffee shop one afternoon. She was wearing a colorful dress, which, she explained, she had designed and sewn herself. She also explained that the couple she had met at Esalen and with whom she had founded the commune had since left. And that among the thirty-eight members presently living in the commune there are five individuals with exceptional skills as plumbers, mechanics, electricians, and carpenters. A stone-mason is also in residence. Financial support of the commune derives from a number of sources, including member contributions, with Angelina—as owner of the property—playing a major role. Of the dozen members considered "stable," Angelina also explained: "They all have to split every once in a while, but they feel it's their home." We talked for about an hour over coffee, and then Angelina invited me to come to the commune for supper.

Located fifteen miles from town on a blacktop road, the commune is flanked by well-kept small farms. An elaborately carved and painted sign close to the road announces "The Good Earth Commune." Immediately behind the sign is an improvised parking field. It was filled with about two dozen cars and trucks and a bus, which obviously served as living quarters. Some of the cars had thick layers of dust and either were abandoned or had not been used for a long time. As we drove past, five boys and two girls, all deeply suntanned, were gathered around a pickup truck and were talking leisurely while watching two of their number work on the motor. They seemed like high school or college kids on a summer vacation.

Over a slight rise, hidden from the road and surrounded by old oak trees, stands the barn. This was the only building on the property when Angelina bought it and it now serves as the main gathering place of the commune. The interior of the barn has been rebuilt and there is a large kitchen with a long, well-scrubbed wooden table; this area also serves as the dining room. Next to this room is a communal quarter, with an improvised fireplace in the center of the dirt floor and barrels and pieces of logs or wooden blocks to sit on. Further construction is under way, but a well-stocked library can be reached by climbing a ladder. In the middle of the library's floor squats an old-fashioned wood-burning iron stove. There are pillows scattered around to sit on and a few old easy chairs that show signs of having been repaired with care.

Hal, who is one of the four left from the original group of fifteen that started the commune with Angelina, volunteered to act as guide. He is a slender, blond-haired man in his middle or upper twenties; he was dressed in clean, faded bluejeans, sandals, and a multihued shirt he had dyed himself. He was also wearing an ankh suspended from a deceptively crude-looking, handmade brass chain around his neck. A drop-out from a social science doctoral program at

Yale, Hal has a habit of carefully forming his sentences. While dusk drew near, we walked together along paths through the wooden hillsides. More than a dozen single-room buildings have been so neatly fitted into the landscape that they are hard to distinguish from their surroundings. Each is different and has been constructed by the people who live in it from materials found on the land —old lumber and odds and ends. Some are built into the hillside and overlook the valley, and each structure is totally isolated, with no other neighbor visible. Only the sounds of birds could be heard; it was very peaceful.

Hal and I looked into several houses whose owners were away on trips. Most of these houses had one room dominated by a fireplace or an iron stove. There were mattresses on the floor, and chairs for the most part were improvised from lumber or were hand-hewn from logs. Navajo rugs and colorful madras cloth and prints from India provided decorative touches. Everything appeared neat and clean, and I was reminded of the outdoor shower and washing facilities near the barn, which we had investigated earlier and which had been shown with much pride.

On a different path back to the barn, we passed a tepee and a tent. A good-sized, intensively cultivated garden grows next to the barn; it furnishes the commune with most of the vegetables needed. Two nude girls with beautiful uniform tans were busy weeding. Hal explained that those who want to, go nude whenever they feel like it. As we passed the garden, we noticed Angelina walking along another path trying to join us. Although we slowed our pace so she could catch up with us, she had difficulty doing so, because out of nowhere would appear members who engaged her in intense conversations.

As we strolled on, I noticed several other people hovering in the background waiting. I asked Hal if Angelina functioned as guru or leader and if she were directing the course of the commune. He was emphatic—as were several others to whom I put the same question later—that Angelina is not in charge: "We all decide what we want to do."

Earlier, both Angelina and two of the other older members of the commune had made almost identical remarks: "We have lots of ideas and very little energy." Hal felt the reason was: "There is a lot of grass around and people drop acid." Although he did add, philosophically, "Everybody is into his own thing— each person is free to follow his own needs and interests. No one is forced to do anything. Everyone knows what needs to be done, and finally it gets done."

The commune has meetings once a week "to discuss everything that bothers us." There are seldom any major problems. Hal felt that the commune's only significant problem was the lack of energy. Other neighboring communes have factional disputes, hostile neighbors, suffer from lack of food and shelter, or are unable to pay their taxes. The Good Earth Commune's relations with neighbors are friendly. As Angelina had put it at the coffee shop, "We live a very honest life." She had related a story of how one of the commune members had stolen a pump from a lumber company. This was discussed at one of the weekly meetings, and although the community had definite strong feelings about lumber companies, the pump was returned.

During the weekly meetings, the group discusses what projects have priority; those members who want to, then volunteer for a particular project. To feed the commune, there is a kitchen list. Two members are chosen daily to provide the food and help prepare it. Farmers bring fruits and vegetables, which they barter for home-baked bread.

Eventually, Angelina caught up with us and led the way to her house. The second largest building on the grounds, it is almost circular in shape; members of the commune built it for her of field stones, hand-hewn timber, and used lumber. The large bedroom in the two-room dwelling has a fireplace and a double bed; placed here and there are many healthy-looking green plants in pots and on stands. An antique desk, a chest of drawers, a candelabra, and antique paintings and prints add richness to the room. The combination kitchen-living room was filled with young people reading, talking quietly, or playing the guitar and singing. Here also is the only phone in the commune. A young blonde girl was talking to her father. I could overhear snatches of her conversation: "No, Dad, I don't need any money. Just send me the plane ticket to Santa Barbara and I'll see you there at the house." Later, Angelina casually mentioned that the seventeen-year-old daughter of a two-star general is at the commune with the consent of her father. (She was not the girl using the telephone.)

The clanging of an old school bell called us to the barn for supper. Everyone formed a huge circle around the dinner table on which candles and kerosene lamps flickered. The room slowly grew quiet as the children scampered to their places in the circle. We all held hands. There was a long moment of silent communion, with heads bowed and eyes closed. The only sound was a dog barking in the distance. With no word spoken, the circle was broken. Conversation resumed, and we served ourselves buffet-style. The vegetarian meal consisted of a pea soup spiced with garden herbs; a combination entree of brown rice with onions, green peppers, and squash; a mixed green salad; freshly baked bread; and, for dessert, bran muffins with nuts and dried fruit. Following supper, a fire was lighted in the large unfinished room next door and there was chanting, singing, and dancing.

As the evening progressed, Angelina told me that she would like to meet a warm, loving, sensitive type of man, maybe a minister—someone who knows how to counsel and work with young people. She said, "I haven't had a vacation for two years. I want to live in my house and get uninvolved. I want to travel. Older people point their finger at the commune instead of helping. I want some people with money to get involved. Where are the parents of these kids? Many of them come from well-to-do homes. Why am I so alone in this?"

As I prepared to leave, a phone call came from another commune asking for advice. Going out the door, I could hear Angelina's husky voice as she offered sympathy and suggestions. She was obviously very much involved and perhaps not really as alone as she thought.

Discussion Questions
1. What are the major conflict areas described in "Marriage on the Rocks"? Can you think of any solutions?
2. What are the common goals of commune living? What are some of the major problems faced by all communes?
3. How is the day-care center tied to the movement for greater civil rights for women?
4. In what way would you think day-care programs might affect child-rearing practices in the United States?

Chapter 7
Therapeutic
Approaches
to Behavior

While psychology is quite properly defined as the science of behavior, which encompasses a wide variety of behaviors by a wide variety of organisms, the popular picture of the discipline still involves abnormal behavior. To most people, however incorrect they may be, the psychologist is one who studies abnormalities of behavior and participates in their treatment. While this area, in actuality, only represents a minority of individuals who are involved in psychology, it does form the dominant public image of the field. This chapter looks at a number of different approaches that have been used by psychologists and other mental health professionals in their attempts to deal with the problems created by abnormal behavior.

The most common approach in the attempt to change abnormal behavior is through psychotherapy. Psychotherapy is a procedure by which one individual, referred to as the "therapist," attempts to influence the behavior of another individual, referred to as the "patient," and to produce changes in behavior in the direction that both will agree is more healthy. There are many variations in the approach of therapists, many variations in the problems brought by patients, and many variations in the types of behavior change which are attempted and achieved. It is impossible to review all these variations in detail, but some of the highlights are portrayed in this chapter.

The most dominant early approach to psychotherapy was the technique referred to as "psychoanalysis" and developed by Sigmund Freud and his followers. This is a lengthy and intensive procedure in which the patient is seen as often as four or five times a week for sessions of one hour apiece, and treatment often lasts at least two or three years. Dr. Donald Kaplan describes the major procedures involved in an orthodox psychoanalysis and regrets the passing of this approach as it is traditionally formulated. Perhaps because of the time and expense that are involved for the patient, or perhaps because of some of the frustrations that are attendant for the therapist, or even perhaps because the behavioral change has not been as striking as might have been hoped, innumerable variations upon this central theme have been developed. It is further testimony to the genius of Freud that many of the revisions still incorporate the key aspects of his approach to treatment. It can clearly be stated that the field of psychotherapy owes its existence to Sigmund Freud regardless of whether his theories are strictly followed or not.

Perhaps the most radical departure from psychoanalytic therapy among the mental health professions is the approach known as "behavior modification," and this is an approach which appears most clearly to spring from psychological theory. While psychoanalysis would consider troublesome behavior as symptomatic of underlying problems and seek, through intensive inquiry, to discover these early causes, behavior modification sees these "symptoms" as no more than habits which are subject to elimination through the judicious application of principles of learning. These principles have been applied to various behaviors of both in-patients and out-patients. Herbert Yahraes describes one program that has been developed in a hospital setting for use with young schizophrenic children. This is one of the most difficult patient populations to work with; it is a group that has provided virtually no response to traditional psychoanalytic approaches.

The specific technique described by Yahraes in this article is based on the principles of operant conditioning. In this approach, desired behaviors are followed by a reward so that the individual is inclined to repeat them. Behaviors that are not desired are followed by punishment so that the individual is inclined to forsake them. Gradually, through the judicious management of rewards and punishments, behavior can be shaped so as to conform to more desirable and less pathological forms. An alternate approach to behavior modification is based on the principles of classical conditioning. In this approach, behavior that typically makes an individual anxious, such as thoughts about a feared object, is associated with relaxation through a specific relaxation training procedure. Eventually the patient comes to associate his relaxed state with the thought of the formerly feared object and his behavior undergoes change. Recently there has been a great emphasis on a number of behavior modification approaches. These approaches share a foundation in principles of learning and a focus on changes in overt behavior rather than on unconscious processes.

Sigmund Freud was trained in medicine and developed an approach to abnormal behavior which involved an analysis of the patient's conflicts. Behavior modifiers form a radical departure from this approach in that they attempt to modify behavior through principles that were developed in psychology. They see problem behaviors as being products of faulty learning rather than as symptomatic of mental illness. There is an approach to abnormal behavior which is also radically different from that of Freud but which goes in the other direction. This is the approach described by Dr. Henry Miller, and its claim is that abnormal behavior truly belongs in the province of medicine so that any attempts to study psychological rather than physical causes of dysfunction are misguided.

Miller describes a number of situations in which abnormal behavior clearly is the product of some underlying physical problem. Because of the clarity with which some diseases, such as syphilis, can be associated with abnormal behavior, he feels that we should investigate all other abnormal behaviors by looking for the underlying physical causes. He also applauds the development of drug therapy and cites this as further evidence for the physical causation of abnormal behavior.

This point of view is a radical statement of what has come to be known as the medical model of abnormal behavior. In this model, mental illness is seen as the end product of a disease process and therefore is as much an illness as a broken leg or the mumps. When we view mental illness in this framework, we are inclined to look for underlying physical causes and to seek treatment through the use of medication. In contrast to the medical model is the learning model adopted by behavior modifiers who see the problem as arising from faulty learning rather than in a faulty organism and who see the treatment as being through relearning rather than through medication. Midway between these points are the psychoanalysts who see the problem as one of psychological origin to be treated through therapeutic interventions aimed at modifying feelings and attitudes.

Questions may well be asked as to which of these approaches is the correct one and which has been the most productive in changing behavior. Unfortunately, the answer is not easily forthcoming. There is no clear evidence as to the superiority of any single approach, although the proponents of each would claim that their method is the superior one. There are some mental problems of unquestionable physical origin. Other problems appear to be rooted in problems with learning, while still others appear to be based on psychological experiences. Pills have been of help to some patients, behavior modification to others, and psychoanalysis to still another group. The issue before psychotherapy at the present time is not the selection of the one best approach but rather a wiser system of referrals so that patients can be treated by the method of choice for their own particular problems.

Although Freud worked on an individual basis with his patients—and this has also tended to be the model of most doctor-patient relationships and of most behavior modifiers—there has been a movement, based on both economy and effectiveness, toward the incorporation of group techniques in the treatment of abnormal behavior. Sam Blum reviews a number of different approaches that have been adopted in group therapy, and these run a fairly wide gamut. The psychoanalytic influence is keenly felt in some areas of group therapy, but it is renounced as overly intellectual by other groups.

Group methods of treatment have given rise to a popularization in the form of a widespread set of encounter groups that can be seen throughout the country. Encounter groups have come to be known as a form of behavior change for the healthy individual. Participants are not known as patients and leaders are not known as therapists; the goal is to increase positive behaviors rather than to reduce abnormal behaviors. It is likely that most students have either participated in such groups or have been given the opportunity to do so. In order to answer many of the questions about these groups that no doubt occur to students, we asked Dr. George Goldman to respond to these questions as they had been formulated for him by his son, Ira. Questions were raised about the history of encounter groups, the various types of groups, the circumstances in which they are to be recommended and the contraindications. The questions are answered in a professional manner and should provide valuable information to any student who is contemplating attendance at such a group. Further information about encounter groups is included in an article by Henry Resnick in a later chapter.

Suggested Readings

Brenner, Charles. *Elementary Textbook of Psychoanalysis.* New York: Doubleday, 1957. A very readable paperback book that outlines the essentials of psychoanalytic theory in an accurate but not overly technical manner.

Lazarus, Arnold A. *Behavior Therapy and Beyond.* New York: McGraw-Hill, 1971. A recent statement about the orientation and methods of behavior therapy by one of its founders. This is particularly instructive because of its relatively eclectic approach.

Zax, Melvin, and Cowen, Emory. *Abnormal Psychology: Changing Conceptions.* New York: Holt, Rinehart and Winston, 1972. An excellent new textbook that reviews the entire field of abnormal psychology with particular emphasis on the new developments such as community psychology.

Zax, Melvin, and Stricker, George (Eds.) *Study of Abnormal Behavior,* 2d ed. New York: The Macmillan Company, 1969. This is a collection of readings in abnormal psychology, with selections covering theoretical issues, diagnostic groups, therapeutic procedures, and community psychology.

25. Psychoanalysis: The Decline of a Golden Craft
Donald M. Kaplan

"...the orthodox analyst is pedantic, the liberal is simpleminded."

When we think of psychotherapy, we most often think first of psychoanalysis. Yet, psychoanalysis in its traditional form is growing increasingly rare. Dr. Kaplan describes some of the central tenets of psychoanalysis and some of the most common deviations.

From its beginnings, psychoanalysis has figured in a paradox; it has been at once the most talked about but least practiced of modern psychotherapies. Thus Freud remains the most widely recognized name in the flourishing mental-health movement and the couch its leading symbol; but while there is now a stupendous amount of psychotherapy going on of all kinds, the kind going on least of all—indeed, in vanishing proportion to all the others—is psychoanalysis.

Psychoanalysis is vanishing for several reasons. It is a very expensive procedure, which attracts patients with economic qualifications rather than those most likely to be helped. Many who can benefit from it cannot afford it, and analysis is almost never subsidized, as are other forms of therapy. Thus the science is at present troubled by its elite clientele. Also, the practice itself is arduous and often frustrating for the therapist. In fact, most of the men and women currently admitted to the field are unequal to the austere discipline it requires.

To understand why this is so, one must first understand what goes on in the analytic situation. Freud perceived that the very way in which a patient solicits help from a therapist reveals a crucial aspect of the patient's neurosis. To Freud, the symptoms which drove a patient into treatment were merely the epilogue to a complicated story, obscuring a larger and more painful failure in the patient's life. Freud glimpsed the nature of this failure in the patient's attitudes and unwitting strategies concerning the therapist.

For example, Freud became more interested in the style with which a patient registered a complaint about a sexual difficulty than in the fact that there was a complaint. Was the style meant to solicit pity, reassurance that the symptom was trivial, arbitration between the patient and his sexual partner, patronizing laughter? Each would reveal a different meaning.

Every analyst has also had the experience of interviewing a prospective patient whose exceedingly cooperative recital of his problems conveyed an underlying sense that the patient was actually saying, "I'm really here to help *you*, doctor." One patient reassured his analyst toward the end of an initial interview, "Look, I have always made an excellent patient—you can ask my dentist. Also, I am very interested in psychoanalysis. So don't worry. In my case, you won't have to work too hard." This patient went on to attend every appointment with an almost merciless punctuality and reliability. On the other hand, there are patients who immediately request shifts in appointments. The pretexts vary with the patient, from funerals to beauty-parlor appointments, but each pretext is embraced with equal fervor.

These attitudes toward the analyst are initially quite apart from the conscious problem that brought the patient to treatment. To them Freud assigned the term *transference* and created a unique procedure for employing the patient's transference in his therapy.

The transference is the only way the patient has for getting along with the analyst, and it is, in fact, a model for the way the patient gets along in life generally. But it should be understood that it has nothing to do with the conscious thoughts a patient has about the analyst. The transference is unwitting, the most thoughtless and spontaneous component of the patient's presentation of himself. The analyst's task is to demonstrate the patient's transference to him so that he will experience it, revise it, and thereby alter the circumstances of his neurosis.

The method Freud devised for demonstrating a transference to a patient is called free association. It is disarmingly simple, surpassingly elegant, and, in the popular mind, one of the most misunderstood features of the psychoanalytic situation. The rationale of the method might be expressed this way: if you want to convince a patient that there is something operating within him that he has no knowledge of, assign him a seemingly easy task which cannot be fulfilled precisely because of what is operating within him. The patient will undertake the task with full assurance that he can fulfill it; when he discovers that he cannot, he will then be able to understand what the obstacle is.

The task is for the patient to appear for appointments of a specified length of time and to report the thoughts that are occurring to him without regard to their logic, significance, or social acceptability. The patient is asked to speak his mind with complete candor. Since the analyst guarantees that he will only listen and try to understand what the patient reports—that is, he will not hold the patient accountable in any way for what occurs to the patient to say—the patient knows no reason for not speaking freely. Furthermore, since the patient regards the task as a therapeutic venture, he has every reason to try to fulfill it as compliantly as possible.

Yet, in all good faith, the patient does not succeed. Sooner or later, the patient's remarks betray a selectivity, often a frank censorship. They are regulated by unavoidable intentions. Even the very wish to be an especially cooperative patient conditions the patient's verbal freedom.

A patient, for example, may narrate an incident in considerable detail at certain points and conspicuously less detail as others. This shifting narrative style may be a subtle effort to regulate the reactions of the analyst. Too much detail, the patient may feel, will bore the analyst and arouse his impatience; too little will mislead him. Silence may ensue, anxiety set in. The patient has temporarily lost his freedom of expression, and it can be restored only by a clarification of how the patient's transference worked.

Now, the analyst not only listens to what the patient is saying; he also listens for the influence of his listening upon what the patient is saying. This particular attention is the brunt of the analyst's labor. What is gleaned through this labor decides his every communication to the patient, from dream interpretations to common courtesies.

Throughout the transference a very painful emotional repercussion is incessantly at work. The patient created his style of relating to the analyst in the first place in the hope of getting rid of anxiety. Any attempt then to disrupt this style will precipitate anxiety. In point of fact, this anxiety becomes the patient's chief symptom, replacing the original ones.

Obviously, anxiety is very unpleasant. Its presence always activates defenses aimed at extinguishing it. Yet the analyst must concentrate on maintaining an undefended gateway through which he can experience his patient's anxiety. Despite his analytic training, clinical experience, and professional role, the exposure requires no small determination. It is like picking up an invisible wire attached to the patient, thus completing a circuit, and holding onto it without relenting. To drop the wire would mean the end of the analytic dialogue, and the beginning of ordinary conversation.

A most important feature of this circuit is the way the analyst controls it; this technique is called "the rule of abstinence." The analyst's application of this rule regulates the anxiety and reveals the analyst's own emotional and intellectual suitability for conducting a psychoanalysis.

How is the word "abstinence" meant in the analytic situation? An example might occur at the end of a session. Since the analyst is watching the time, he will notify the patient that the session is over. Most often a cordial "Good afternoon," or a variation of it, is exchanged as the patient leaves the consulting room. However, if the session has been an especially upsetting one for the patient, the analyst may feel the impulse to add, "I'll see you tomorrow." He knows the patient understands this anyway but he senses—and usually quite rightly—that simply saying it out loud will reduce some of the patient's apprehension about the session. If the analyst withholds the impulse, he has "abstained."

The rule is that abstinence should be no more nor less than the patient can tolerate, for the goal of analysis is to increase the abstinence until the basis of the relationship between analyst and patient is extinguished. This is merely another way of saying that the analyst will have finally lost his value when his abstinences no longer produce intolerable anxiety in the patient. The dosing of this abstinence—how little, how much—is a matter of the analyst's humanity and courage.

The cruel truth is that there is no certainty about abstinence. Each day is a fresh struggle to reduce the error in the analyst's estimation of what the patient is able to stand; and the struggle goes on in an emotional climate of the patient's protests and maneuvers—obstinacy, ingratiation, adoration, abuse, rage, withdrawal, fear, discouragement. The struggle also goes on in a climate of the analyst's civility, restraint, human warmth, and availability. Abstinence is not punishment.

Too much abstinence can traumatize the patient and motivate emergency defenses, usually flight. Typical abuses can include answering a question with a question too often. The patient might be sent away in the middle of a sentence, as not a minute longer than the agreed-upon time for the session is conceded. None of the patient's jokes are responded to. A slip of the tongue becomes an occasion for ruthless probing, as though a butterfly is about to be assaulted with a sledgehammer.

Too little abstinence, on the other hand, turns the patient into a child. Gross instances of this usually indicate a hopelessly defective concept of psychoanalysis. I am thinking of practitioners who attend their patients' weddings, for example, or who obtain seats to a theater performance the patient is giving. I know of no patient so disturbed as to require this kind of gratification. One such magnanimous exploitation of the patient is enough to ruin the treatment situation irreparably.

There are other, more subtle erosions of the treatment process, but all originating in a retreat from the tiring burdens of analyzing the transference.

Currently, for example, there has been the tendency to provoke the patient by active interventions. A common ploy is to do something unexpected—to agree when the patient complains of hopelessness, to ape the patient's neurotic strategies, to side with the patient's paranoid ideas. Of course, if there is no indication that this is being done for his welfare, the patient will, in some way or other, break off treatment. Patients have an uncanny sensitivity to the spirit in which an analyst practices. They will put up with all kinds of buffoonery if they sense the analyst means well. But self-preservation rescues them from a completely hostile analyst.

The analyst's talking too much is another common sign of erosion. A pedantic overexplanation postpones the labor of retiring to a passive listening position to pick up the reaction of the patient to the interpretation. This soon leads to the ritual of one overly long interpretation per session, usually at the end.

Then there is the business of explaining the process rather than creating it. The analyst simply tells the patient what should happen. Often jargon creeps into the analyst's vocabulary, and while nothing therapeutic may be happening, the patient does acquire an extraordinary terminology for his own use.

"Philosophizing" is still another evasion of the analytic labor. Here the analyst responds to the patient's presentations with some truism or other about the human condition. Where the analyst has gotten involved personally in an elaborate philosophy—Existentialism is a vogue at present—he may succumb entirely to the temptation to indoctrinate the patient.

Most practitioners today are bright, earnest, ambitious professionals. They are also typical products of professional schooling and hence miseducated in matters of science and culture. By previous training, the candidate for a psychoanalytic certificate is usually a clinician (most often, a medical doctor)—that is, neither scientist nor humanist, but an often pallid mixture of both.

The leadership within the profession, moreover, shows signs of decadence and cynicism. I am reminded of the contradiction in the medieval Vatican between celibate vows and papal concubines. Lately, for example, an alarming number of celebrated analysts have been known to marry or have affairs with patients (usually half their age); each incident developed into a bewildering scandal because the basic tenets of analytic procedure prohibit even a social luncheon with a patient. Were it not so bizarre it would be amusing to note that some of these very same analytic leaders have acted brutally to students in training at the merest sign of their becoming caught up personally in a patient's neurosis.

Now this is said by way of complaint, indeed, of outrage. For the only stronghold psychoanalysis has ever counted upon was the responsibility of its own practitioners.

An added threat to the future of psychoanalysis comes from the division between the orthodox and liberal styles of analytic practice. How do they differ?

The transference relationship between patient and analyst is always ambiguous. There is nothing to be done for it. Nor does anything need to be done for it. The ambiguity is the mercurial variable which keeps the analytic situation alive. But neither the orthodox nor liberal analyst can tolerate leaving this alone.

The orthodox analyst sees the ambiguity as a threat to the certainty which he feels psychoanalysis should by now possess (a rather peculiar notion for a scientist to have about his science). His attitude toward his colleagues is not so much critical as captious, and he is forever preserving the doctrine against the profanities of his liberal opponents.

Many orthodox analysts also make a big thing about the patient's "analyzability." This is their great escape clause from the trials of the transference. Given their strict position about analytic procedure, orthodox analysts are always in a position to disqualify patients on grounds that the patient cannot produce an authentic analytic situation. That is, certain patients are too preoccupied with their symptoms to learn anything from the transference; or they are too anxious to "free-associate"; or they cannot sustain a long-standing relationship in which the frustrations of abstinence are a significant part of the experience; they simply need the sort of concessions which the orthodox analyst regards as pampering.

This can turn into a license for the analyst not to do what he knows to be analysis. At the first sign of trouble, the orthodox analyst can reach for the dictum: This patient can't be analyzed. The paradox here is that the orthodox analyst is apt to do very little analysis and a lot of pampering precisely because he cannot find a patient sufficiently "qualified" to be analyzed.

On the other hand, the liberal analyst sees the transference ambiguity as an opportunity for a self-indulgence which masquerades as experimentation. If the orthodox analyst is pedantic, the liberal is simpleminded. The liberal's emphasis on "feelings," "spontaneity," "creativity" disguises a hysterical anti-intellectualism.

For example, the liberal is always discovering the "evils of society" and complaining that his orthodox colleague is an archconservative who neglects the environment in which the patient lives. So-called "social neurosis" is "repressing" the patient. What good is it, then, to analyze the patient, only to return him to the "sick society"? (This is the liberal's license not to do analysis.) A liberal colleague once told me how a patient got his most "creative" ideas smoking marihuana, on which he was high for days on end. The patient was then dismissed from graduate school for failing to complete assignments. "You see how decadent institutions cannot accommodate the boldness of new creative mediums!" the analyst said.

In the end, both positions refer to the analyst's wholly human impulse to make a difficult thing easier. In psychoanalysis, there is a core of irreducible difficulty, and any attempt to diminish that core transforms the identity of the practice. Yet, a continuous, painstaking attention to the vicissitudes of the transference seems too much to expect of a human being.

The future of psychoanalysis depends upon a sufficient number of analysts who will continue to choose to do analysis wherever the chance arises. Obviously, these analysts must love an idea of craftsmanship and scientific enterprise with a passion transcending the personal temptations of easy communion with the patient.

What about the problem of future recruitment and education?

The psychoanalytic profession consists of psychiatrists and a small number of nonmedical clinicians. In America the clinician is trained in the backyards of science and is deprived of intensive training in the humanities. Medical training, too, turns out physicians who are preponderantly pragmatic, scarcely versed in experimental method and the philosophy of science, and practically illiterate about the broad issues of the Western cultural tradition. Today, the average physician is Neanderthal compared to his nineteenth-century forebears. (The increasingly longer personal analysis of analytic candidates may well be a misguided effort to rectify the defects in the human raw material; however, if you analyze a small-minded person for eight or nine years, you end up with a well-analyzed small-minded person.)

Yet, over the past decades, the physician has been generally the best recruit psychoanalysis has had. To have overcome so many hurdles strung out over so many years—medical school, psychiatry, psychoanalysis, in that order—is a test of no trivial stamina.

It was undoubtedly good for the science, when it was young and of doubtful repute, for established professionals to have to submit to the further training of psychoanalysis. Psychoanalysis needed this respectability. But the training situation grew unrealistic.

A long-standing proposal, advocated by physicians and nonphysicians alike (see, for example, Kurt Eissler's recent *Medical Orthodoxy and the Future of Psychoanalysis*), is an institute or graduate faculty which would eliminate the medical degree, or any advanced degree, as a requirement. Such an institute would offer a course of analytic training to college graduates, leading to a doctorate in psychoanalysis. Its graduates would not be psychiatrists or clinical psychologists but psychoanalysts. The program would be, of necessity, a very long one, for it would have to include a clinical, biological, and humanistic curriculum along with the special requirements of analytic training—personal analysis and supervision. But it would be less arbitrary than the present obstacle course, and a greater range of applicants would become available. Psychoanalysis would enjoy a transfusion of varied personnel—clinicians, researchers, experimentalists, and humanists.

At present, psychoanalysis is almost entirely a private-practice activity. This is another concern among those who love the science at least as much as their immediate gains from it.

While psychoanalysis is not geared for multitudes, it does not follow that it should be restricted to those patients qualified only by an unusual capacity to pay. But there are virtually no clinics where a prospective patient of less-than-average, or even average, means can obtain psychoanalysis. This tends to exclude as analytic subjects the large population of young adults, whose prognosis is likely to be favorable. The few clinics attached to the analytic institutes are serviced by trainees on their way to private practice, where the fees have been climbing by leaps and bounds (the routine twenty-five-dollars-per-session fee in New York City is already on its way up to thirty-five dollars). But what is also lost is the *esprit de corps* which the analyst experiences in an institutional setting. The handling of even one case under the auspices of an institution enlivens the ideals of analytic procedure and carries over into private practice. Yet, there are too few analytic clinics. Analysts don't want to staff them.

There are other problems and other proposals. But the outlook for actual change is not encouraging. Since psychoanalysis is not a guns-or-butter issue, there is no public pressure and little interest. Nor are the monetary grants, which analysts can get their share of, equivalent to the kind of moral virtue needed to sustain psychoanalysis.

It may be that the particular trial of intelligence, skill, nerve, and stamina which the analytic situation poses for the practitioner is becoming anachronistic in a society rapidly developing less sedulous values. I wish I could say I think not. But I can surely say I hope not. The disappearance of psychoanalysis would only augur a future of increased dehumanization. While it is a small institution, psychoanalysis is nevertheless both a scientific theory of the human condition and a certain ethical property which we shall miss if psychoanalysts abdicate their responsibility.

26. New Approaches to the Treatment of Very Young Schizophrenic Children
Herbert Yahraes

"... they are very adept at learning how *not* to learn...."

Herbert Yahraes has prepared this summary of a research project being conducted by Dr. Marian K. DeMyer. The techniques of operant conditioning, as they are applied to the treatment of schizophrenic children, are very well described. In addition, provocative issues concerning the relationship between organic and psychological factors are raised.

In a broad-front research attack on early childhood schizophrenia, the Indiana University School of Medicine is searching for causes, collecting information to facilitate diagnosis, and experimenting with promising new ways of treatment.

The program is headed by Dr. Marian K. DeMyer, a children's psychiatrist and director of the medical school's Clinical Research Center for Early Childhood Schizophrenia, housed in the La Rue D. Carter Memorial Hospital, Indianapolis. This hospital contains the State's residential treatment institution for disturbed children.

The children most intensively studied are inpatients at the Center. When admitted they are between 2 and 5 years old. In general, they cannot get along with adults or other children, fly easily into rage, either do not speak at all or else use language in odd and incomprehensible ways, do not listen to directions, find little pleasure in play, and show a remarkably narrow range of interests. Some of them twirl or rock themselves for long periods: others bite or hit themselves. They often seem unsure of who or what they are.

Some of these children have been diagnosed as *autistic*, a type of childhood schizophrenia marked by a withdrawal from other people; others as *symbiotic*, a type in which the child physically clings to his mother. Because some of the children display, at different times, each of these characteristics, Dr. DeMyer classes them as *symbiotic-autistic*. Still other patients suffer from what Dr. DeMyer labels *chronic undifferentiated schizophrenia*. Their behavior is less abysmally abnormal than that of the autistic and symbiotic children; they have some conversational ability and usually show some conformance to social amenities.

Investigations under way are directed toward:

From *The Mental Health of the Child*, June 1971. Public Health Service Publication No. 2168. Reprinted by permission.

- presenting detailed descriptions of the behavior of various types of schizophrenic children and of other children with psychiatric disorders;
- learning how, if at all, the preschool schizophrenic child differs biologically from normal children and whether or not the differences are responsible for his illness;
- learning whether or not certain influences in the home, notably the personalities of the parents and the way the parents treat the child, contribute to the onset of childhood schizophrenia;
- determining the value of several new approaches to treatment.

So far the Center's research program has led to two results of major importance.

First, out of a group of 149 young psychiatric patients, 51 percent were found to have clearly abnormal electroencephalograms and 15 percent had experienced at least one epileptic-like seizure.

In each instance the proportion would have been higher had borderline cases been counted. The abnormalities would be found in less than 1 percent of any randomly selected normal population.

The patients included neurotics, childhood schizophrenics of all types, and children with a severe but nonpsychotic behavior disorder, marked by such activities as stealing, setting fires, attacking other children and adults, and refusing to get along in school. A high proportion of abnormal EEG's was found among all the patients except the neurotics.

The results are important because they indicate that many children who are mentally ill have a physical impairment of the brain. The possibility that the impairment signals an effect of the illness rather than a cause, Dr. DeMyer observes, cannot yet be ruled out. Current studies of schizophrenic and nonschizophrenic children may turn up clues to the origin of the impairment.

Before the EEG study, Dr. DeMyer had leaned to the psychogenic explanation of most psychiatric illness and had given only superficial consideration to organic factors. "As the result of this study, done in a careful way and using the severest criteria for EEG dysrhythmias," she notes, "I knew that our research program would have to include a careful study of the central nervous system and other biological matters."

Second, conditioning principles similar to those used in training animals— and to those often used, unknowingly, by parents in training their children —have been successfully applied to improving the behavior of severely schizophrenic children and broadening the activities of which they are capable.

Under the Center's new treatment program, called the *semester system*, the child goes through cycles of 5 months at the center and 7 months at home, and the staff works first of all to make him easier to live with. It tries to correct those behaviors the parents have found most disruptive of family life and it instructs the parents how to handle him. In accordance with conditioning theory, desired behavior is rewarded, both with food and with a "social reinforcer" such as praise, and undesired behavior is ignored or is associated with an "aversion stimulus" such as physical restraint.

Proposed by Dr. Don Churchill, children's psychiatrist and the Center's assistant director, the semester system was introduced in the fall of 1965 with the admission of four new patients. In all these cases, after the children had gone home for a 7-month stay, the parents reported they were having much less, if any, difficulty with the particular kinds of behavior they had identified as the most troublesome. The system is now being used with all the Center's inpatients —11 at present.

How many times a child will return for the 5-month hospital cycle remains uncertain. But Dr. Churchill observes that he is not interested merely in improving behavior and has not thrown overboard the psychoanalytic concepts in which he was trained; he just doesn't find these concepts very useful in working with extremely sick children. According to psychoanalytic theory, the therapist establishes a relationship with a mentally ill person and uses this relationship to induce normal behavior. But with most children like those at the Center, Dr. Churchill notes, it has been extremely difficult both to establish a relationship and to effect much improvement. If a certain amount of normal behavior is first trained into such severely ill children, the investigator suggests, they may show more interest in the adults about them, and the therapeutic relationship will follow and be fruitful. In any event, the trained-in normal activities may crowd out at least some of the customary abnormal ones.

As one promising way of training in normal behavior, the Center has been experimenting with a technique for inducing a schizophrenic youngster to imitate specific actions of the therapist. The first results are exciting: two of the most severely sick children have been trained to imitate several hundred simple activities and to say a few dozen words. To Dr. Joseph N. Hingtgen, the psychologist in charge of this work, the preliminary outcome suggests that the schizophrenic process is not completely irreversible—that perhaps even terribly withdrawn children can be brought up to something approaching the normal level.

Dr. Hingtgen emphasizes that he is speaking on the basis of only a few cases—two of his own, and several reported by another psychologist, Dr. O. Ivar Lovaas, who works at the University of California, Los Angeles, and whose ideas have influenced the Indianapolis group. Further, the technique requires such an immense amount of work that only a relatively few children could be helped if it had to be administered professionally. But Dr. Hingtgen finds that it can easily be taught to parents. The basic idea is that normal children, to a great extent, learn by imitating adults. Gravely psychotic children, however, pay no attention to adults, and, therefore, fail to imitate. They have to be *trained* to imitate so that they can learn to behave normally. The training can be accomplished through many long and laborious sessions in which the child is rewarded for doing what the therapist—or the parent—does, beginning with such simple activities as holding up a finger. Eventually the child begins to imitate the adult spontaneously, and even to do what the adult requests.

This imitative learning technique fits in nicely with the ideas and practices of the new semester system and, depending on the results of current work, may eventually be tried with all the children at the Center.

More information about the findings noted, together with a brief report of some of the other research of the Indianapolis group, follows.

Abnormal EEG's in Young Psychiatric Patients

The EEG study was part of the research seeking to describe the anatomical, biochemical, and physiological makeup of the preschool schizophrenic child. Among the children tested were 58 diagnosed as autistic, symbiotic, or symbiotic-autistic, 44 with chronic undifferentiated schizophrenia, 37 with a nonpsychotic behavior disorder, 10 as neurotics, and 13 with normal controls. They were from 4 to 10 years old. Since most of the psychiatric patients fought against the test, the EEG's in virtually all the cases were taken after the children had been calmed by a tranquilizer, promazine—given in too small a dose, Dr. DeMyer reports, to affect the pattern of electrical discharges.

As noted earlier, 51 percent of the psychiatric patients were found to have abnormal EEG's, a proportion that would have been slightly higher had the neurotics, only one of whom showed an abnormality, been omitted. All of the normal children had normal EEG's. Among the children with nonpsychotic behavior disorders of the acting-out type and among those with the various types of schizophrenia, there were no significant differences in the proportion of abnormalities; also, the types of abnormalities were the same and were present to about the same extent. Most characteristic was the type of activity described as paroxysmal spike and wave (PSW), which consists of a mixture of synchronous spikes and slow waves. This type appeared in almost two-thirds of the children with abnormal EEG's.

The EEG study, which was directed by two neurologists—Drs. Philip T. White and William DeMyer—in cooperation with the investigator, opens several important questions, including:

1. *What relationship has the central nervous system disorder, demonstrated in half of the psychiatric patients, to the abnormal behavior of these children?*

On the basis of this and previous studies, the investigators answer, it seems established that at least the EEG abnormality labeled PSW has more than a chance relationship to disturbed behavior. This means that in seeking the causes of childhood schizophrenia and other psychiatric disorders, the role of cerebral dysfunction cannot be ignored. But the exact relationship between abnormality and behavior remains to be discovered. One puzzling fact is that most children with epilepsy, who have EEG abnormalities similar to those found in this study, have normal social and intellectual skills and behave normally except during a seizure. In the children with schizophrenia and behavior disorders the EEG abnormalities presumably could be the result of biochemical changes caused by the stress associated with psychiatric illness. But they could also be one aspect of an organized disturbance, congenital or acquired very early in life, directly responsible for the illness.

2. *Why did only about half of the psychiatric patients show abnormal brain waves?*

One possible answer, says the investigator, has to do with the electroencephalographic technique itself, which cannot pick up all abnormalities. Another possibility has to do with the way abnormalities are defined. The

Indianapolis study counted only those variations in the EEG that were distinctly different from normal; now the records are being reexamined to determine the effect of taking borderline changes into account. Previous EEG studies of psychiatrically disturbed children, Dr. DeMyer recalls, reported abnormalities in as low as 2 percent of the patients, and in as high as 90 percent. She thinks that biases both in psychiatric diagnosis and in EEG diagnosis explain part of this wide range.

As still another possibility, the sampling may have been inadequate, meaning that many of the records which were normal for the particular hour when they were made might have been abnormal if made at some other time. The investigator points out that even persons with epilepsy often have normal records except when seizures are occurring; perhaps, she reasons, the records of most psychiatric patients would show abnormalities if taken at times of intense anxiety or shortly afterward. A study in which brain waves would be picked up and telemetered to a recording station, by an apparatus worn by the child, throughout a day of usual activity is being planned.

There is the possibility, too, that a number of the children with normal records will show abnormal ones a little later in life.

The Center is preparing a laboratory to get further information about the brain's electrical activity in psychiatric patients by recording cerebral-evoked potentials, meaning the brain's electrical responses to external stimuli—a light, a touch, a sound. The subjects will be schizophrenic children whose EEG's are normal. Normal and retarded children will be tested the same way.

3. *Do the families of patients who show no EEG abnormalities differ significantly from the families of those who do?*

In the EEG study, no attempt was made to evaluate the families. However, a study nearing completion, in which families with a schizophrenic child are being compared with one another and with matched families whose children are normal, should provide an answer. The subject bears upon the genesis of childhood schizophrenia. Another investigator, working with somewhat older children, found that children showing no organic impairment came from more deeply disturbed families than the others, the implication being that in some cases an organic impairment contributes to the onset of schizophrenia, but in other cases—where the family is seriously disturbed—schizophrenia can develop whether or not something is organically wrong.

Dr. DeMyer and her associates have also used the EEG to study the sleep and dream patterns of seven schizophrenic children hospitalized at the Center. Their sleep habits at home, the parents reported, had been extremely erratic. At the Center, though, the staff considered their sleep to be remarkably regular, and the records of brain waves and eye movements during sleep showed that these children spent the same proportion of time in the dreaming stage as normal children. This study, then, finds no evidence to back up the suggestion that patients may hallucinate in the waking state because they have been unable to hallucinate as much as other persons during sleep.

Earlier Experiments in Conditioning

The Center's use of conditioning techniques—with promising results— follows a series of experiments to find ways of getting very sick youngsters to come out of their shells and act more normally toward people and things.

In one of the earlier experiments, directed by Dr. C. B. Ferster, an autistic child would spend an hour or two, every day, in a room containing such fascinating equipment as a pinball machine, an electric train set, a phonograph, a picture viewer, a telephone set, a trained monkey in a cage, and vending machines. Each device could be operated by the child if he put a coin in the proper slot (in the case of the monkey, the coin turned on a light in the cage and the animal went into his act); and the child could get the coins by pressing a key that operated a coin-dispensing machine.

Rats and cats will learn to keep pressing a bar, and pigeons to keep pecking at a disc, if such activity occasionally brings them food. This learning process is known as operant conditioning because it gets the subject to work, or operate, in a desired manner. The same principle held good with the schizophrenic children. They learned that by pressing the key often enough, they would get a coin good for any of the devices, and soon they spent most of their time working for coins and spending them. The most popular devices by far were the candy vending machines.

Dr. Ferster's next question was whether or not the same technique could be used to help the child understand more difficult situations and engage in more complex behavior—an important question because one of the most marked characteristics of schizophrenic children is their extremely narrow range of activity.

In one of the new situations, coins were delivered only when a panel on the dispensing machine was lighted. In another, a device could be operated only if a coin was placed in a slot when the slot was lighted. A more difficult task required the child, if he were to get a coin, to compare two colors or figures or pictures and touch the one that matched a third, which he had been previously trained to touch. Dr. Ferster's question was answered in the affirmative, even the autistic children came to understand and master the new situations, though more slowly than normal children.

To sum up, the study found that children who rarely had taken any account of their environment could soon begin, through the use of conditioning techniques, not only to notice the environment but also—by pressing keys, matching pictures, and dropping coins—to manipulate it. True, the environment was artificial and the behavior needed to control it a little out of the ordinary. But the results were taken to indicate, in these schizophrenic children, "at least the existence of normal processes at a very basic level," with no suggestion of an underlying deficit except in the rate at which the children learned.

The next question was whether or not a similar laboratory situation could be used to teach socially adaptive behavior—specifically, interaction with other children. Normal youngsters in a preschool group are almost constantly interacting: by playing together, for example, grabbing each other's toys, and fighting. But schizophrenic children hold themselves aloof.

In research directed by Dr. Hingtgen, the Center tried to develop cooperative behavior in some of its children. Only two machines were used—the coin dispenser, set to deliver one coin for every 15 presses of the key, and a vending machine offering candy, crackers, and cereal. Six children participated. After each had been trained to operate the machines, they were paired, and for the rest of the experiment both membrs of a pair went to the laboratory room together.

For a while, each member of a pair, A and B, was free to operate the coin lever at any time. When it was operated by A, a panel behind the lever showed red; when it was operated by B the panel showed green.

Step 2 required a little cooperation because A could operate the lever only when the panel showed red, and B only when it showed green. After one child received a coin, the other child's light was presented. The children learned by trial and error that they had to take turns.

In step 3, the children had to use a two-key panel in another part of the room. One key could be illuminated by a red light; the other by a green. When the red light was on and A pressed the corresponding key, the coin lever showed red; then A could go to work to get a coin.

In the final step, when A pressed the red-light key, the coin lever showed green, and B could operate the machine; when B pressed the green-light key, the light on the coin machine went red for A. Thus A and B had to work for each other by providing the appropriate coin-lever light.

Starting with step 2, the children learned to work for each other in an average of 23 sessions.

To the investigators' surprise, in view of earlier observations of schizophrenic children at play, the youngsters in this particular situation frequently made physical contact with each other. One would lead the other to the correct lever, or one would operate the correct lever by manipulating the other youngster's hand, or one would pull the other away from the coin lever or from the vending machine.

In one session a 4-year-old boy was working at a very low rate. He had to press the coin lever 15 times in order to be rewarded, but he often stopped and began twirling. Since his partner, a 6-year-old girl, could not go to work for her coin until he received his, she began pulling him back to the lever whenever he wandered off. Once she slapped him, and his response rate went up. Another time, a slap set him to crying and he refused to use the machine at all. After a long period, she went over to him, hugged him around the neck and led him back to the lever; his response rate went up. In later sessions, she slapped him at times, hugged him at others.

All the children appeared to be communicating with their partners through vocal and facial expressions, and two of the less seriously disturbed used words—"That's the red light." "That's enough." "Get the coin."

This social interaction, however, did not carry over from the experimental room to life outside. Evidently young schizophrenic children were capable of modifying their usual behavior, but how could the modifications be made to stick?

The next experiment tested the effect of directly rewarding the children for making physical contact with each other. The mechanical devices were not used: an observer simply handed the children a small piece of candy or a bit of a cookie or cracker whenever they performed the desired behavior. In the first stage the children were rewarded whenever one touched the other. The required behavior was made gradually more complex until, in the end, the reward was given only when the child touched the other with both hands and said something, whether comprehensible or not.

This time there was a little more carryover. Parents and ward personnel reported that the children would come up to them once in a while, touch them, and make a sound or two. But this social behavior died out in a few weeks, presumably because it no longer brought the kind of reward that had been used in developing it.

The research group then tackled one phase of an old and basic problem: why the severely schizophrenic child does not respond like a normal child to what he hears and sees. Clinicians are satisfied that he *can* hear and see, in spite of the many indications he may give to the contrary, particularly in the matter of hearing. But sometimes, apparently, he shuts out his perceptions, and other times, apparently, he fails to organize them—as least he does not act upon them in normal fashion. Part of the trouble, some investigators have thought, may be an inability to discriminate among stimuli.

Dr. Hingtgen used an auditory discrimination test with six of the children. First a child would learn that by pressing a lever often enough he would get a coin, which he could use to obtain candy from a vending machine. Then the experimenter fixed the dispenser so that it would drop coins only when music was playing. Like rats, pigeons, and normal children in earlier experiments, the schizophrenics soon learned to work at the dispenser only during periods of music; in other words, they learned to discriminate between music and silence.

The children also showed they could discriminate between speech (the voice of someone reading a story) and silence, and between speech and music. Then the investigators tried single words, in pairs. When a voice said *chalk*, for example, the machine was operating; when the voice said *ball*, it wasn't. Of the six children being tested, all except one learned to distinguish even between words, like *mama* and *apple*, that are rather similar phonetically. Again, though, the learning took longer than with normal children.

If schizophrenic children have this power of auditory discrimination, why don't they use it all the time? Maybe, Dr. Hingtgen ventures, it's a matter of paying attention, and perhaps they pay attention only when they are going to get something—and when that something meets such a basic need as for food.

The researchers were discussing ways of testing this and other possibilities, and of putting the findings to practical use, when Dr. Lovaas, the University of California psychologist mentioned earlier, came to the school of medicine and described some of his work with young schizophrenics. He, too, was using rewards—and punishments, also—but in a nonautomated situation, and with just one adult and a child working together, intensively. He theorized that a schizophrenic child fails to learn because he fails to imitate, and he fails to imitate because he doesn't associate paying attention with reward. Once the child has been taught to pay attention and to imitate, he can start learning on his own.

What was new here was not the general learning-by-imitation concept but its systematic and intensive application to schizophrenic children. One of the aspects that impressed the Indianapolis group was the comparative simplicity of the technique. You present the child with a model, or example, of the type of thing you want him to do. He imitates you. You reward his imitation. This is easier than waiting for the child to perform, more or less accidentally, the behavior you have in mind, then rewarding him for it and going on to shape that behavior by rewarding him for increasingly complex variations. Getting two children to the point where they were touching one another with both hands and saying something required as many as 30 daily sessions of at least an hour each.

But the most hopeful aspect of the learning-by-imitation concept was the possibility that eventually the schizophrenic child would come to imitate spontaneously. As Dr. Churchill puts it: "To teach a child separately every little thing he has to learn in the course of his growing up is patently impossible. But if we can teach a child to imitate others, there is the hope that the learning process will become more automatic—will not stop at the end of the learning session, but continue through the day."

The Indianapolis investigators decided to test the new technique—modified, though, to omit punishment—with some of the children at the Center.

Tommy was first. He was six-and-a-half, a mute child with a very narrow range of behavior. He had been subjected to every available type of therapy, but in 3 years at the Center had shown no significant improvement.

He was taken off the ward, given his own room, and kept there for 20 days. Every morning about 8 o'clock Dr. Hingtgen and Mrs. Susan Coulter, his research assistant, would come in when Tommy got up, and every evening about 8 o'clock they would put him to bed. They were there at least eight of the intervening hours and—so that he would come to associate food and drink with the adults who were asking him to imitate them—gave him all his meals.

The investigators aimed to get three types of imitation. One was imitation in use of body parts—touching two fingers together, for example. Another was imitation in use of objects—from so simple an activity as picking up a pencil to so complicated a one as using scissors to cut out a picture. The third, since Tommy was mute, was imitation of sounds and speech.

Like other seriously schizophrenic children, Tommy generally avoided looking at adults, so the first sessions were rather wearing. The procedure went like this. One of the teachers—Dr. Hingtgen and Mrs. Coulter alternated—would seat Tommy in a chair directly in front of him and say "Tommy, look here. Clap your hands." And the teacher would clap his own hands. At the beginning, Tommy would not clap his hands. So the teacher would clap his hands for him, to demonstrate what was wanted, and give him a piece of candy or sugar-coated cereal or some other food. The idea was that Tommy could not get out of his chair—he was held in by the teacher's legs if necessary—until he had done what his teacher wanted him to do. Fussing and crying did no good. After 20 minutes or so, Tommy clapped his hands.

When the boy had learned 15 or 20 imitative responses through such a grueling process, he began imitating immediately. For example, Dr. Hingtgen folded his hands in a rather complex fashion, and Tommy, though he had never before seen him do this, did it himself right away.

Sometimes the boy would try doing the same thing over and over, only to find that repetitive responses were not rewarded; so he would stop making them. For the sake of the reward, he learned to watch his teachers very carefully.

Tommy's use of objects had been limited and bizarre. He would busy himself for hours with ritualistic-like activities, such as moving a piece of string back and forth in front of his eyes or tearing paper to bits. Consequently, getting him to imitate the investigators' use of objects was especially difficult. He got around to picking up a pencil and drawing a straight line on a piece of paper only after 3 hours of work—spread over several days, for the sake of everyone's nervous system. But once he drew the straight line, it was easier to get him to draw X's, squares, and circles.

Learning to fold a piece of paper once and then to fold it again took 5 hours.

Geting him to use scissors was a traumatic experience, too. He watched Mrs. Coulter use them and he wanted to hold them but had no idea how. Eventually she used tape to help keep them in place, and in 2 hours she got him to make one little cut in paper. After a number of additional sessions, he was cutting out circles and squares.

Working like that 7 days a week, the investigators would go home "a bit edgy," Dr. Hingtgen recalls, but once the behavior started coming, a session with Tommy was rewarding as well as exhausting.

Getting this mute youngster to make sounds and say words proved to be, as expected, the most difficult part of the process. Since Tommy had no idea what to do with his mouth in order to voice a word, the teachers began by having him imitate the position of the mouth necessary for forming a given sound. In the case of the "ah" sound, for example, Tommy was rewarded at first merely for pointing to his chin and opening his mouth; later he had to make the sound.

To teach him the "P" sound, the teachers brought in a harmonica, which Tommy knew how to use. As he blew it, they would take it away and reward him for continuing to blow. After a long session, he finally came to voice the required sound every time the investigators offered it.

At the end of the 3 weeks, Tommy would say 18 words, imitatively. Some words were very clear—*baby, mama, daddy, puppy.* Some were approximations *feer* instead of *finger.* He also had more than 150 imitative responses, including standing, running, and jumping, that required him to make use of his body. And he had more than 100 uses of objects.

He was doing all these things only imitatively. But he was imitating consistently and paying consistent attention to the two adults closest to him. At this point, Tommy was returned to the ward, and Dr. Hingtgen and Mrs. Coulter began teaching the learning-by-imitation technique to the nurses and other personnel and to Tommy's parents. The emphasis now was not merely on increasing his imitative repertoire, but also on getting him to attach meaning to his various responses, particularly the vocal ones. After 2 more months of morning and afternoon sessions—in the hospital 5 days a week, at home on weekends— Tommy had about 30 words to which he attached meaning. For example, when a teacher pointed to her nose, Tommy said *nose*; when she held up a picture of a puppy, he said *puppy.*

Whatever the original cause of early childhood schizophrenia, Dr. Hingtgen believes a youngster persists in his withdrawn attitude and bizarre behavior because he has learned that he can get by without doing anything his parents want. "As home," the investigator points out, "the parents have never been able to command as much from the child as we have because they have not been able to invest so much time. Also, they never think of spending 3 hours trying to get him to hold a pair of scissors, for example, because no normal child requires that long.

"Some authorities have thought that these children really cannot learn, but our idea is that they are very adept at learning how *not* to learn—how not to have to do something." At the beginning of Tommy's training, for example, the boy would giggle or laugh instead of trying to do what had been requested.

Then he'd act as if he were going to cry. Then he'd try to fight his way out of the chair, and he might break into real tears. But the investigators would not go away, and they would not cease making their demand, so eventually Tommy would come out with the behavior they wanted. Since Tommy's avoidance behavior, as psychologists call it, was never successful, within 3 weeks he stopped using it.

The same technique has brought similar results in another autistic child, 5-year-old Peggy, who had been even more withdrawn at the beginning than Tommy.

Don't the children get tired of the rewards—become literally fed up? Tommy and Peggy did not, although they were eating almost continuously during the 3 weeks of intensive treatment, and each gained about a pound a week. But the rewards were very small; one potato chip would be broken into six or eight pieces.

Then, too, the food reward was coupled with two other reinforcement measures. One was the easing of physical restraint if such restraint had been necessary, as at first it generally had been. The other was *social reinforcement*. Whenever Tommy made the appropriate response, the investigator would say, "Good boy, Tommy"—or hug him, or give him a ride around the room, or just touch him. In an earlier study, the Indianapolis team had tried using social reinforcers alone to improve the behavior of children like Tommy, and the gains had been neither very large nor consistent. But when Tommy and Peggy had finished their intensive treatment, the investigators found it possible to reduce the frequency of the food rewards and count more and more on the social reinforcers alone. "One theory of learning," Dr. Hingtgen observes, "is that all social reinforcers gain their strength by having been initially paired with food and warmth. Hopefully, at some point in the training of these children, social reinforcers—paired only occasionally with food—will be sufficient."

Because only certain behaviors are rewarded—those the adults request and demonstrate—the children do not become automatons, doing everything they see their teachers do. Eventually, it is hoped, the habits they are learning, of paying attention and of doing what is asked and demonstrated, will take hold to such an extent that the children will spontaneously imitate behavior—including speech, play activities, use of household equipment—that normal children imitate. Tommy and Peggy do a little of this now. They also obey some simple instructions even when no demonstration is given.

Dr. Hingtgen throws in a cautioner. Both Tommy and Peggy have been significantly improved but are still a long way from where they should be, considering their ages. So the question is: How far can you take such children through the use of this technique? On the basis of Dr. Lovaas's work, Dr. Hingtgen notes, there is evidence that at least some severely schizophrenic children can be brought into a classroom situation. Whether or not they will ever be normal, no one can say.

Further, this investigator emphasizes, the technique has been used with probably not more than half a dozen children. "So we don't know yet whether this is a valid technique for all early child schizophrenics," he observes, "or whether those six just happened to be ones that it worked with."

The Indianapolis group, though, has made headway in answering some other questions about the technique. For one thing, its application can be made less strenuous for the teacher than Tommy's case may suggest. Tommy was isolated for 3 weeks and all the shaping of his behavior was done by two persons. Peggy, too, was isolated, but half a dozen persons guided the conditioning process. Dr. Hingtgen now suspects, and will try to confirm, that the same results can be obtained if the child continues to live on the ward instead of being isolated when the conditioning process begins. The investigator also plans to test his idea that the technique, after the intensive preliminary treatment, can be used with two or three children at a time. As he sees it, hospital care might then consist mainly of a series of classes in which the children would learn to imitate various kinds of responses. Sometimes the child would be with a small group; sometimes alone with a therapist or another adult.

In many cases, this investigator believes, it will be good for the parents to come right into the hospital and work with the child on a regular basis, as Tommy's and Peggy's mothers have been doing. "This is a very simple technique," he points out, "and can be taught to anybody: simply rewarding the child at the appropriate time and withholding reward at the appropriate time."

Among the basic questions still to be answered is how many models of behavior a schizophrenic child must be trained to imitate before he begins imitating on his own.

The Semester Program

As noted earlier, the Center now uses conditioning techniques with all its patients in an effort to correct those behaviors in a child that have most upset the family. Though the application is less intensive than the process used with Tommy and Peggy, the techniques are basically the same. While the children are in the hospital, the parents, individually and in groups, are instructed how to take care of them when they come home, as they do for 7 months of the year.

"The predominate experience everywhere in trying to help a young, severely ill child," Dr. Churchill remarks in explaining these rather revolutionary innovations, "has been of working hard and for a long time and then, more often than not, of seeing him transferred to a State institution for the mentally ill or the retarded."

After a child has been a patient at the Center or some comparable place for 2 or 3 years, the psychiatrist continues, the parents "have sort of fallen out of love with him." It is then extremely difficult to get him back into the family again, and this is partly because not very much has been done with either the child or the parents to enable him to live in the home.

"In other words," Dr. Churchill observes, "the emphasis has been on what might be called an all-or-nothing proposition—on curing." A psychoanalytically oriented therapist like himself, he goes on, "has been trained to establish a relationship with a patient and to consider, in line with psychoanalytic theory, what may be going on inside the patient, and why. Even with a very sick youngster it is possible to establish this relationship, to get him attached to you—though this may take a couple of years—and sometimes to work a little improvement. But generally the child still is psychotic."

At the Center, where the experience has been typical, he believes, the instances in which these young children have improved sufficiently to return home and to enter a public school have been so few and far between that "we're not sure whether they improved to this extent because of what we did or in spite of what we did."

Now, under the new semester system, the Center has a dual objective: to cure the children, "if they can be cured," and meanwhile to make them easier to live with and to help the families get along with them.

"Family morbidity in these cases is very high," Dr. Churchill notes. "These are families who haven't gone to a restaurant or even out on a family picnic for several years because they cannot manage the sick child. The parents may never go out together because babysitters won't come in. Often the house is stripped, with everything of value kept behind locked doors, and the family is living within bare walls."

In working with the parents, the therapists focus not so much on the emotional conflicts that may have led or contributed to the child's illness but on specific methods of dealing with his most disruptive types of behaviors—methods used by the Center itself while the child is an inpatient. For example, if the child is sitting at the table and throwing food, the parents are instructed to give him a warning. If he throws food again, that's the end of the meal for him and he doesn't eat until the next meal.

This, too, is operant conditioning. It pairs an undesirable behavior, throwing food, with an unpleasant result, removal of food. In the case of a child who begins to wreck a room or a grocery store, the unpleasant result may be simply physical restraint.

Many times, though, the best way to handle unwanted behavior is simply to ignore it. It was failure to do this when the behavior first appeared, Dr. Churchill believes, that may have helped perpetuate it. In other words, even if disturbed behavior has a physiological basis, the first adult response to it may have had a rewarding and thus a strengthening effect.

Sometimes, notably in the case of temper tantrums, there is more than one way of ignoring a behavior, and choosing the effective way requires the parent to consider why the child is acting as he is. For instance, if the child has been using tantrums as a means of compelling an adult to come and do something for him that he should be doing for himself, the effective form of ignoring the tantrum is to stay away. But if the child has been using tantrums to hold off an adult and prevent necessary ministrations, the effective form of ignoring the tantrum is to plow ahead and do what is needed.

Usually it is extremely difficult or impossible to learn whether the abnormal behavior of these young children had its roots in organic trouble or in childhood experiences or, as the psychiatrists and psychologists at the Center are inclined to think, in both.

As an example of the difficulty in tracing the origin of abnormal behaviors, Dr. Churchill tells about 5-year-old Jimmy who socks himself on the head and jaw until he is bruised and his knuckles have calluses. During some 20-minute periods he has been observed to hit himself more than 2,000 times.

After studying Jimmy's history, the psychiatrist first thought that the behavior probably had been *learned*, in the sense that Jimmy had received a lot of attention for it. Adults would step in and hold his hands. Jimmy would hit himself while eating, too, so his parents would hold his hands and feed him. Things got to the point where he was being held most of the time and was refusing to feed himself.

Under treatment at the Center, everything that might be considered to reinforce or reward the hitting behavior was withdrawn, but instead of dying out, as learning theory says should be the case, the behavior continued. There was some improvement, in that Jimmy began feeding himself, but Dr. Churchill noticed a strange correlation: the more the boy ate, the more he also used himself as a punching bag.

Recently the staff tried a different approach—the administration of painful but harmless electric shock, paired with the word *shock*, whenever Jimmy began hitting himself. Within 3 days his hitting behavior, which had been essentially unaltered for 3 years, practically stopped. Further, the investigator reports, this behavior can now be controlled by the word *shock* alone. The boy has become more approachable and is playing with toys, which he had ignored for months.

Some physiological factor is believed to be at least partly involved in Jimmy's trouble.

Sally, another child at the Center, typically withdraws to a corner of the playroom, sits on the floor, and rocks endlessly. All children do a little rocking, Dr. Churchill notes: they find pleasure in the rhythm. Why some schizophrenic children keep it up for hours is not known.

In this connection, Dr. Gerald D. Alpern, a psychologist, calls attention to *blindisms*, the term applied to the repetitive behavior—such as rocking, swaying, and passing the hands back and forth in front of the eyes—seen in many blind children. With much of their external stimulation cut off, these children have turned to themselves for stimulation. Blind youngsters are not mentally ill, but they do obviously have an organic defect: they cannot see. There is a possibility, then, that schizophrenic children who engage in behavior similar to blindisms also have an organic defect. There is also a possibility that blind children who engage most strongly in such behavior have an emotional disturbance as well as an organic defect. This second possibility is now being studied at the University of Indiana Medical School as part of a different research program.

Some of the Center's Other Research Projects

To help pin down the factors contributing to early childhood psychosis, Dr. DeMyer and her associates are comparing in great detail 30 schizophrenic children and their families with 30 normal children and their families. The children are given physical and neurological examinations and are tested psychologically. Samples of blood and urine are analyzed for the presence of abnormal metabolic products. Information about their behavior and growth from birth onward— including eating, sleeping, physical and mental development, and social skills— and about the attitudes, personalities, and life histories of their parents is obtained from an exhaustive series of interviews, covering 13 schedules, with the fathers and mothers.

The investigator points out that the study, like other research on the causes of schizophrenia, looks backward and therefore has to rely for much of its information on what the parents remember and choose to tell. However, it carefully checks the account of one parent against that of the other and it carefully compares all the data about a family in which a child is schizophrenic with all the data about a family that is similar to it except for the absence of schizophrenia.

Besides having to make its observations after the fact, research on the causes of schizophrenia is frequently hampered also by the fallibility of clinical judgment. Drawing upon her own experience, Dr. DeMyer says an investigator is likely to get quite definite impressions about the first families he sees in a study like this and then, unless he is very careful, he tends to see the rest of the families in the light of his early impressions. Dr. DeMyer, trying to be very careful, found that the more schizophrenic children she studied, the wider the range of characteristics she saw in their families.

To minimize the problem of clinical judgment and to permit hundreds of facts about each family to be considered, all data in the current research are given numerical ratings, and the comparisons will be made by a computer.

Tying in with this work on the antecedents of childhood schizophrenia is a recently completed survey of the families of 99 schizophrenic children and 146 disturbed but not psychotic children. These children had been seen at the La Rue Carter Hospital between 1955 and 1963, and the data about their families came from the files. The parents of schizophrenic children, no matter what the type of schizophrenia, were found to be significantly better educated than the other parents (who had about the same amount of schooling as the average Indiana adult) and the fathers held much better jobs.

These findings (a) support the early observation by another investigator that parents of autistic children tend to be well educated and successful, and (b) extend this observation to include the parents of schizophrenic children in general. Another interesting and unexplained finding: among the disturbed but nonpsychotic children, broken homes were common; among the schizophrenic children, they were not.

Other research underway by the Indianapolis group includes:

• Observations to test Dr. Churchill's hunch that autistic children at times pay considerably more attention to adults when the adults seem to be paying no attention to the children. In terms of conditioning theory, this would mean that the attention of adults had become negatively reinforcing, and it would have important implications for therapy.

• A variety of studies intended to learn more about, and to describe systematically, the behavior of schizophrenic children. In one of these, a moving picture is made of each child's "behavior day" by filming him for 10 seconds every 5 minutes, from the time he wakes up to the time he goes to sleep. The films will be used to compare the dominant behavioral characteristics of the different types of schizophrenic children and also to study changes in the children from one year to the next. Another study of behavior is concerned with the way autistic children use toys. The first findings show that autistic children, as compared with groups of normal and retarded children, (a) make fewer different uses of a given toy, and (b) spend less time using one toy in combination with another.

• An attempt to develop a quantitative means of measuring the abilities of young schizophrenic children who cannot be tested on standard intelligence tests. In one test being used by the investigator, Dr. Alpern, the youngster is scored on the basis of his failure to carry out certain activities of which he is known to be capable. The reasoning here is that it may be less important to know what a schizophrenic child can do than to know what he won't do. The variability in his "failure score" over time, it is hoped, may be a useful indicator of how well he will respond to treatment.

"The latest fashion in psychiatry... is to divorce the subject entirely from medicine...."

Whether or not all of psychiatry is a branch of medicine is a question of immense importance to the fields of psychiatry and psychology, and ultimately to the patient. Dr. Miller, in contrast to the other authors in this chapter, clearly believes it should be, and sees true psychiatric problems as being symptomatic of organic dysfunction.

I must begin with a qualification introduced by any writer about to discuss a persecuted minority. Many of my best friends are psychiatrists. This statement is more than a formality in the present context, because as a clinical neurologist I have had the good fortune over the years to work with and learn from a team of eclectic psychiatrists of outstanding calibre. They are the sort of hard-headed psychiatrists who would send the patient back to me with the polite suggestion that I have another look for the cerebral tumour—and they had an infuriating habit of being right. This is certainly one of his important functions, and the psychiatrist whose knowledge and experience of the many disguises of serious organic disease are too insecurely based for its exercise is a danger to his patient.

A few years ago a senior psychiatric colleague and I founded the "Society for the Abolition of Psychiatrists." Before I am overwhelmed with applications to join—and they have already come from some of Britain's most eminent psychiatrists—as well as, predictably, from a number of patients—I must point out that the society has not yet received its charter, and does no more than epitomise our conviction that the psychiatrist must be first and foremost and all the time a physician, expert certainly in unravelling the complexities of mental symptomatology, but also at least as adept in general medicine as his cardiological or neurological colleagues. In fact psychiatry is neurology without physical signs, a difficult branch of medicine that calls for diagnostic virtuosity of the highest order. Indeed, since the psychiatrist is concerned with disorders that carry a considerable mortality and a serious morbidity it is truly alarming that his is the only one of its branches that can be practised at a responsible level without a thorough training in internal medicine—without such a background of general clinical experience as is demanded, for example, of the skin specialist.

From *Encounter*, May 1970. Reprinted by permission.

The pattern of British psychiatry has its roots in history, and especially in the traditional isolation of psychiatrists in mental asylums, physically removed from the stimulating environment of the great general hospitals where the most advanced clinical medicine was developed and practised. On the continent of Europe this situation was tempered by the close association between psychiatry and neurology. Most universities had combined departments, and indeed many of the great figures of the nineteenth and early twentieth centuries were equally expert in both disciplines. The same applied initially in the United States, and the separation of the two disciplines is fairly recent. The association with neurology gave psychiatry an academic foothold, and ensured that the best of continental and American psychiatry retained a firm basis in medicine and neurology. The isolation of the British psychiatrist was partly due to the historical accident that clinical neurology developed in Britain as a branch of internal medicine rather than as a close associate of psychiatry.

In 1939 Britain could boast no more than a handful of physicians fully trained in psychiatry as well as in medicine, and they were mostly either in London or in Scotland. The war-time realisation of the magnitude of psychiatric illness and disability, and the coincidental therapeutic revolution in psychiatry, effected a radical change in this situation. The mental hospital psychiatrist was translated to wider fields of activity especially in the Armed Forces, improving his old skills and developing new ones, while the years immediately following the War saw the invasion of psychiatry by a regiment of well-trained young men. But the supply of high-grade recruits to the subject remained far short of meeting requirements, and the need to employ a large body of mental hospital medical officers for routine clinical duties has sustained a double standard of psychiatric practice. At one end of the scale is the consultant who has had a basic training in scientific medicine and probably several years of work in a general medical clinic before taking up psychiatry, already a Member of the Royal College of Physicians. At the other end is the mental hospital psychiatrist who has acquired a specialist diploma in psychiatry, but who has often had little training or practical experience in internal medicine, and whose professional life has been spent almost entirely in mental hospital practice. Doctors of the latter group are often highly skilled in the institutional management of severe mental illness; but they are less equipped for the extra-mural functions of the psychiatrist, whose consultative and out-patient practice comprises an enormous range of clinical problems, poses extremely difficult diagnostic issues, and demands immediate clinical decisions of great urgency and importance.

The problems raised by this double standard are very much in the minds of all psychiatrists. The higher examinations in internal medicine are searching. They require considerable and extended practical experience of clinical work in a variety of fields, as well as a grasp of basic medical science and fairly high intellectual capacity. They are often beyond the reach of the less outstanding recruits to psychiatry, and the Royal Colleges have been reluctant to make the minor concessions in the examination for psychiatrists that could have ensured at least a general improvement in the specialty's standards. The characteristic inertia of the established bodies has led to the impending establishment of a separate college. Although this has been delayed by internecine strife, it now seems virtually certain. Such a development will consolidate and perpetuate the double standard. The best physicians will continue to seek the status of physicians, and will undertake the arduous clinical apprenticeship that leads first to a higher qualification in medicine. The remainder will acquire a qualification orientated towards psychiatry as an autonomous discipline, superior certainly to the present Diploma in Psychological Medicine, but short of furnishing any kind of guarantee that the psychiatrist will also really be a physician. It is hard today to evoke great enthusiasm for either Royal Colleges or examinations, but when one considers the psychiatric disguises in which liver failure, brain tumour or inflammation, and lung cancer may present themselves to the psychiatrist, he is perhaps the best of all possible excuses for the continued existence of the searching higher examination in internal medicine.

I hope I have already made it clear that I have a high respect for psychiatry and that I regard it beyond doubt as the most important as well as the most fascinating branch of medicine. Unfortunately it is also the most abused, and there is little consolation in the reflection that much of the abuse of psychiatry is self-abuse: many psychiatrists lend it their whole-hearted collaboration.

In a nutshell, most of the abuses of the psychiatrist arise from his reluctance to restrict his activities to the field in which he is genuinely qualified to operate. The Oxford Dictionary definition of a psychiatrist is "one who treats mental disease." Not, you will observe, one who prevents wars, cures anti-Semitism, offers to transform the normally abrasive relations between men into a tedium of stultifying harmony, is the ultimate authority on bringing up children or selecting managing directors—or misuses his jargon to pronounce on every issue of the day in an incessant series of television appearances.

If we look again at the dictionary definition we must consider the term "mental disease." What does it mean? It means *disease with mental symptoms.* Mental disease is no more exclusively a disease of the mind that rheumatoid disease is exclusively a disease of the joints. In both there may be widespread disturbances of other body systems—and both are conveniently categorised on the basis of their most conspicuous symptoms. To the lay public, mental illness used to mean (and perhaps to some extent still means) *insanity,* a social rather than a medical term, suspect because of its spurious definitiveness, but on reflection perhaps still better defined than its successor "mental illness"—which is used to cover everything from shop-lifting to the psychological signs of a brain tumour. What mental illness means to the physician, of course, is illness with mental symptoms, illness that presents as a psychological disturbance. To practically all novelists and playwrights, to many laymen, and to a mercifully shrinking band of metaphysical psychiatrists, this means illness due to "emotional causes." But the experienced physician knows that illness with mental symptoms often results from physical causes, and indeed that nearly everything we know *with certainty* about the causes of mental disease has been gleaned from information at this level.

1. When, for example, the spirochaete of syphilis invades the brain tissues it evokes an indolent inflammatory and degenerative response, with gradual loss of function and ultimate disappearance of thousands of brain cells. The clinical picture is fairly characteristic, though it begins mildly and innocently enough and more often than not is at first misinterpreted and treated as "neurotic." In the fully developed case this progresses through insidious decline in intellect and behaviour to a deteriorated, often expansive and over-cheerful mental state

in which the patient endows himself with the physical prowess of Cassius Clay, the intellect of Einstein, and the amorous virtuosity of Casanova.

Following a minor surgical operation in hospital a middle-aged commercial traveller became wildly confused and held prolonged conversations with non-existent visitors. Enquiry revealed a history of personality change and a deterioration in occupational efficiency during the preceding six months.

Before this time he had been highly successful in his business activities and he had in fact won several annual national awards in his line of business. About nine months before this unimportant operation he began to complain of easy fatigue and three months later consulted his doctor with a vaguely neurasthenic syndrome. He was given simple medical treatment and some psychotherapy by his practitioner, without improvement. Neither the patient's family nor his medical practitioner appreciated the serious significance of an insidious decline in his personality and habits. Previously a highly respected figure, grave and dignified, he outraged his wife and neighbours by telling dubious stories in mixed company. He appeared late for work, and on more than one occasion exploited his complaint of fatigue to spend the day in bed. His business efficiency had declined so seriously that his employers were considering his dismissal.

All this was attributed to psychological causes, but routine tests in hospital confirmed the presence of active cerebral syphilis. He showed a rapid response to penicillin and made an excellent recovery. Had the correct diagnosis not been reached accidentally because of his hospital admission in another connection, his mental deterioration would soon have become irreversible.

2. *Porphyria,* on the other hand, is an inborn error of metabolism in which the periodic overproduction of a pigment in the blood-stream causes acute episodic mental illness of alarming degree, possibly by provoking intermittent spasm of blood vessels in various parts of the nervous system, and often in association with very severe abdominal pain. This was almost certainly the disease that caused George III's intermittent madness. At that time the condition was unrecognized, and the sometimes brutal mismanagement of the royal illness makes gloomy and pathetic reading.

An intelligent young professional woman went on a summer cruise. She had a rough crossing and was given some tablets by a fellow passenger to settle her vomiting and dizziness. The next morning she suffered severe abdominal pain and became very emotional and mentally confused. The ship's doctor gave her further sedatives which made matters worse rather than better. She saw a doctor at each of several ports of call. Each administered a sedative, and after each such treatment her condition became worse again.

Arriving back in England the history was repeated. Intermittent abdominal pain continued, while she was still very agitated and occasionally seemed to be hearing voices. She was intermittently and violently emotional, which was quite out of keeping with her normal personality.

This was the story, and apart from her abnormal emotional condition there was nothing to find on examination. Like most of those who had previously seen her, her own doctor considered the whole situation "hysterical." This diagnosis seemed quite incompatible with her previously resilient and effective personality, but I could think of no convincing alternative.

Halfway home the penny dropped: I turned my car round and returned to the house, where examination of her urine clinched the presence of porphyria. She was a mild case, though careful enquiry disclosed previous episodes of pain and mental disorder, sometimes one and sometimes the other predominating. As in many such cases her condition was activated by a number of drugs, amongst which barbiturates are conspicuous. The amytal and phenobarbitone administered for sedation during her sea trip intensified the biochemical abnormality and provoked symptoms of the latent disorder.

The diagnosis of an inborn anomaly was clinched when examination revealed a similar condition in her mother, who had several times been briefly admitted to a mental hospital. With careful avoidance of drugs known to exacerbate the biochemical fault the patient has subsequently avoided serious trouble.

3. The presence of a tumour in the pancreas intermittently secreting large amounts of insulin not only causes occasional fits quite indistinguishable from those due to epilepsy, but also leads to bizarre psychiatric illness, initially intermittent but ultimately persistent and irreversible. Confusion and excitement often alternate with periods of stupor or coma, and this is ultimately followed by intellectual deterioration of severe degree in untreated cases.

A middle-aged workman watched a popular medical television programme based on the history of a case of this kind. His wife had been in a neighbouring mental hospital for nearly a year. As the programme unfolded he was dumbfounded by the similarity of the television dramatisation to the course of his wife's illness.

The next morning he presented himself at the gates of the mental hospital, asked to see the medical superintendent, and told him the story. The superintendent was a shrewd and percipient man. Within a week the husband's diagnosis was confirmed, the pancreatic tumour was successfully removed at operation, and the woman made a perfect recovery.

To quote such cases is not to maintain the untenable claim that gross structural disease will be found in every patient with serious mental illness, though a scrupulous search will reveal significant physical abnormalities much more often than might be suspected. What these cases demonstrate is the order of the main causal factor in these psychoses, which are clearly accessible to physical rather than to psychological investigation and manipulation.

Everything we have learned from the last three decades of rigorous psychiatric research favours the view that the important mental illnesses—e.g.. depression and schizophrenia—originate in disturbances of biochemistry and metabolism. The illness is coloured and its symptomatology to some extent determined by the patient's personality and previous experiences, but the patient has become ill for physical reasons and his symptoms can be controlled only by manipulation of the physical component of his illness. The layman often objects that to treat the psychiatric patient with drugs is merely to treat symptoms and not to deal with "the root cause" of the illness. Such fundamentalism is foreign to medicine. It is the symptoms that are troubling the patient, not the latent vulnerability—which he bore with cheerful insouciance until it impinged on his consciousness—and, in any case, treatment in *every* field of medicine is more often directed to relief of symptoms than to the unrealistic aim of rebuilding the organism.

Even our prevailing mood depends on the level of certain identifiable chemical substances deep in the brain. A drug such as amphetamine (Benzedrine), which increases the concentration of cerebral catecholamines, excites an all-too-transient elation; one that destroys or blocks these chemical compounds may evoke gloom to the point of suicidal rumination. Indeed, models of some types of mental disease can be induced with reasonable predictability by the use of certain drugs. Especially in patients with a strong family history of depression, the drug reserpine, occasionally used for the control of high blood pressure, quite often produces a classical depressive illness. Prolonged and excessive dosage with amphetamine on the other hand evokes an illness that approximates to an experimental and reversible schizophrenia. The patient may well believe himself "spied on" and "persecuted." Although clearly conscious he may suffer fluctuating and variable delusions and be tortured by auditory hallucinations which terrify or threaten him. Furthermore, although the amphetamine addicts susceptible to such illnesses are often emotionally unstable, there is no evidence that this rapidly reversible schizophrenic-type illness itself has any constitutional component. It appears to be entirely due to the drug, and fades when it is withdrawn.

We know that both general diseases (such as lung cancer) and neurological illnesses (such as multiple sclerosis) may evoke serious psychiatric disturbances even before they have become evident in physical disability.

We know that certain drugs like sodium amytal, Librium, and Tofranil have specific and predictable effects on certain psychiatric symptoms such as insomnia, tension, and depression, respectively.

As a matter of fact this is really about all we know. Since the flight into so-called "dynamic psychiatry," with its speculative and entirely affirmative basis in psychological determinism, psychiatry has suffered from a surfeit of complex and unprovable theory and a dearth of simple testable hypotheses. Not unnaturally, the psychiatrist who believes that the phenomena of mental illness can be explained on the basis of *a universal prefabricated theory,* rather than by building a growing structure of certain knowledge on the basis of controlled observation and experiment, finds little difficulty in blowing up his theory to explain not only mental disease but also normal human behaviour, interpersonal relations, and ultimately world affairs. The results of such exercises are not impressive.

The psychiatrist is, of course, encouraged in his universal pontification by the inexplicable veneration with which his views are regarded by many who ought to know better. Socially, this surely springs in part from the priest's loss of prestige and from the collapse of religious values. Certainly the highly wrought and arcane structure of psycho-analysis betrays its man-made origin as transparently as does that of any religion. Nor is it fanciful to note the similarity that obtains in the wordy battles so full-bloodedly enjoyed by adherents of competing faiths whether religious or psychiatric.

But at a simpler level the popular endowment of the psychiatrist with universal omniscience also arises from a basic lay fallacy that few psychiatrists make any attempt to dispel. There are many quite well-educated people who really believe that psychiatrists have special and mysterious methods of finding out what is going on in their patients' minds that are denied to the rest of the profession and indeed to the rest of humanity. Such people do not appreciate—because they have never been told—the simple fact that a psychiatrist is *a physician who takes a longer history,* partly because he sees fewer patients. Does the psychiatrist know more about the roots of normal behavior than anyone else? His claim to do so arises from the fact that he studies the caricatures of normal human behaviour that present as psychoses or neuroses. He can certainly theorise about normal behaviour, but when he moves outside his strictly professional field there is little evidence that his views are any more interesting or his conclusions any more reliable than those of the rest of us. They are certainly less illuminating and less convincing than those of the novelist.

One curious phenomenon concerns "insight." This is the subject of so much discussion in psychiatric circles, in clinical formulations, and especially amongst those psychiatrists who lay great store on introspective data, that one might imagine it would be a quality carefully cultivated as well as highly valued by psychiatrists themselves. I have no hesitation in saying quite categorically that this is not so. Personal experience confirms the rather unexpected finding that the practice of psychiatry in any of its forms does not necessarily confer any insight whatever. Whether mechanist or psycho-analyst, there are many psychiatrists who manifest that insightless insensitivity to audience reaction that is the hallmark of the bore.

I have emphasised the psychiatrist's eagerness to account for psychological phenomena on the basis of some universal theory as evidence of his rejection of the methods of science; and indeed lack of objectivity is probably the main reason for the reluctance with which the typical psychiatrist is accepted into the scientific community. An eminent British professor of psychiatry recently went so far as to explain to an audience of lawyers, judges, and doctors that since the taking of a phychiatric history and the making of a psychiatric formulation involve the psychiatrist so intimately with the patient at an emotional level it was quite impossible for him ever to act as an objective expert witness in a court of law. He must always, according to this authority, be "on the side of" the person examined—a sort of perpetual prisoner's friend. Needless to say, this remark was greeted with alarm by one group of lawyers and with hilarious relief by others (who felt it fully confirmed everything they had long felt about psychiatric evidence in court). There are, of course, many psychiatrists who do not share this view. It is perfectly possible for a clearheaded psychiatrist with some expertise in forensic work to give a balanced and indeed an absolutely invaluable clinical opinion in a court of law. However, one must admit that there is a tendency for the psychiatrist to regard as a patient any individual whose history he takes—under whatever circumstances.

The word "malingering" is conspicuously absent from the index of several standard textbooks on psychiatry, and we all know of appalling instances where the lying statements of criminals were given spurious authenticity by being incorporated in the text of a psychiatrist's report as though they were matters of fact.

Readers of Freud will recall that his theory of hysteria rested on the basis of accounts of sexual assaults in infancy, revealed during analysis, which were later shown to have been entirely fabricated by the rather curious patients concerned. However, psycho-analytic causistry enabled Freud to preserve the fabric of his theory intact—by the simple expedient of substituting the *fantasy* of assault for its *reality* as the prime cause of subsequent developments. Freudians have quoted this as an example of the master's genius, though there are of course alternative interpretations. At any rate it is hardly surprising that the judge in court has so often to point out that the psychiatric assessment is based in essence on what the person examined told the psychiatrist, and that if the subject of the examination is endeavouring to escape from the consequences of a criminal act, to avoid an unpalatable social responsibility, or even to elicit sympathy, it would be as stupid to regard his statements about himself and his feelings as necessarily valid evidence as it would be to accept without question a criminal's uncorroborated account of his crime. I have also observed that, even outside a medico-legal situation, quite sophisticated psychiatrists in search of a psychological basis for a mental illness will cheerfully accept the patient's (usually creditable) account of the origin of his troubles, even though the same doctor would contemptuously brush aside the patient's equally insupportable theories as to the origin of his gallstones or cerebral thrombosis. Unless one accepts that psychogenesis is a game for amateurs the two situations seem to be not absolutely different.

A further vexed issue concerns how far the psychiatrist should permit his subject to be used, loosely and sometimes cynically, to ensure the smooth working of society. The term "psychopathic personality" lost its meaning in the Hitler war because it was used as a medical label for ridding the armed forces of inadequate or uncontrollable soldiers. Whether we lost much thereby is another matter. The term shares with some other psychiatric categories all the vices of a circular definition; irresponsible behaviour is caused by psychopathy, which is a diagnosis based on the subject's irresponsible behaviour. In this context no great harm was done. It was more important to ensure the survival of civilisation than to worry about terminology. However, in peace-time, the psychiatrist should perhaps be less ready to act as a garbage can for the problems of society and the law in connection with anti-social behaviour. If the middle-aged shoplifter is genuinely suffering from an agitated depression, hospital treatment is more appropriate than prison; but this does not justify the speculative attribution of all stealing and swindling to mental disease. What society does is to make the most convenient common-sense disposal of such cases. If the blanket application of any particular theory were shown to yield a better pragmatic result it would no doubt be hailed with relief as the basis of forensic practice; but so far there is no such glow on the horizon.

Nevertheless, the psychiatrist's willingness to regard as a patient anyone from whom he takes a history leads to considerable abuse. His appearance in Court to give evidence in a case of marital conflict after having talked to only one member of the marriage deprives his opinion of any conceivable value. It is probably of little value anyway. The fact that two people decide that they do not wish to spend more time together does not prove they are mad or ill, even in the mildest way. But a psychiatrist who gives an opinion in such a case without seeing both partners brings ridicule on his subject. He has in any case nothing to offer in this situation unless mental illness is present.

I would draw special attention to three current fashions in psychiatry that may contribute to its abuse.

Medical thought is, of course, notoriously susceptible to fashion, even in the tangible realms of physical disease. Where focal sepsis and auto-intoxication once held sway, the more sophisticated concepts of auto-immunity now reign, and the idea that the patient has become sensitised to his own tissues is currently used to "explain" a wide range of diseases. Like all such explanations it is directed to elucidating the intermediate steps in the chain of events that constitutes the development of a disease, rather than to identifying prime causes; and like all such explanations it contains a hard kernel of truth. Psychiatry is at least as vulnerable to fashion as any other branch of medicine.

I would draw attention first to the concept of social psychiatry, to the vogue it enjoys here at some cost to the clinical approach, and to the way in which with characteristic American thoroughness it is tending in some circles to displace the rather tarnished image of psycho-analysis as the mascot of the American academic psychiatrist.

I would be the last person to discourage epidemiological research, to which I have devoted many years of effort. There can be no doubt that this can display trends in differential prevalence and incidence; it can reveal broadly operative contributory causal factors; and it can pinpoint sensitive areas suitable for more intensive and definitive investigation either in the clinic or the laboratory. It has, for example, fully confirmed the powerful influence of the cigarette in the causation of chronic bronchitis, arterial disease, and coronary thrombosis, as well as cancer of the lung. Occasionally, also, epidemiological serendipity will unveil a truly significant rather than a merely contributory aetiological causal agent; the relationship of maternal German measles to congenital deformity in the baby is an outstanding recent example. More than this, epidemiological studies sharpen precision in diagnosis and encourage the formulation of those operational classifications that are needed to establish real differences and similarities between clinical categories. However, it must be clearly kept in mind that valid studies of illness within a community can be carried out only where there is already a firm and widely agreed basis of clinical diagnosis and classification, which is far from the case in psychiatry at the present time. Even the best of such attempts have often had to place undue and sometimes ludicrous reliance on the empirical quantification of symptoms. To grade subjective sensations on a numerical scale represents an attempt to achieve some approach to objectivity, and an advance on simple diagnostic labelling; but it emphasises the credibility gap between clinical research in this and simpler fields of medical investigation. What sort of effective classification could the heart specialist, for example, have developed if he were solely and entirely dependent on his patient's story, without the evidence yielded by physical examination, to say nothing of the crucial assistance of radiological, electrical and other ancillary methods of diagnosis? Furthermore, while epidemiological study can certainly yield useful information it is naive to expect it often to yield final answers. To shift the basis of psychiatry from medicine to general sociology on present evidence is to move from the well-lit contours of hard knowledge and clear definition into the half-light of a subject that is in its infancy, that is imprecise, that is still desperately short of basic data, and that is itself still groping for its first principles and for a clearly defined role in the scientific galaxy.

The second equally dangerous trend is the deliberate inflation of psychiatry from its preoccupation with the study and treatment of mental illness to what has been euphemistically termed "the science of behaviour." I have already expressed reservations as to the extent to which the psychiatrist's experience of the abnormal can reasonably be used as a guide to general behaviour, and the description of psychiatry as comprising the "science of behaviour" can be described only as a piece of remarkable arrogance. Of course all human behaviour can be described in the psychiatrist's terminology. Equally it can be described in the terms and concepts of the anthropologist, the sociologist, the historian, the economist—or even the practical politician. In psychiatric terms Hitler was a hysterical psychopath; to the literary historian he epitomised the dark aggressive mysticism of the German soul; to the economist he was a front man for big business who unfortunately got out of hand; to the politician a potentially convenient but ultimately uncontrollable complication of the European balance of power. There is some truth in all these views and in others; but I see no conceivable reason why the psychiatrist's monarchy of the kingdom of the abnormal should endow his particular synthesis with any overriding virtue.

The latest fashion in psychiatry—or it might be safer to say the penultimate fashion, since fashions succeed one another so rapidly that I am probably already out of date—is to divorce the subject entirely from medicine and to regard mental illness as a matter exclusively of the individual personality and his inter-personal relations. This view, which in its more bizarre manifestations regards the schizophrenic's family as more abnormal than the schizophrenic, light-heartedly begs the question of psycho-genesis, and accepts disturbed inter-personal relations as the cause of mental illness on the basis of affirmation alone and without troubling to adduce the kind of evidence that would be demanded in any other field of medicine. It also comfortably absolves the investigator from the hard exercise of diagnostic classification, and the search for other aetiological agents. It converts therapy into a miasma of well-motivated and mostly bumbling interference with complex relationships subjectively assessed by a mind with no verifiable basis of authentic professionalism. Attributing everything to psycho-genesis, it ignores the enzyme and the toxic chemical, or any of the other agents by which mental disturbances can be predictably provoked.

If the rest of medicine had restricted its aetiological hypotheses to those based on "inter-personal relationships" it could also have built a precarious edifice of similar causation for gallstones, piles, and baldness. It would be characterised by a vast, sprawling and inconsequential literature and it would never have developed the sleeping tablet, to say nothing of the antibiotic.

You will observe that the real issue concerns the use of the term *mental illness*. As in the case of physical illness the definition has a social as well as a semantic importance. All of us have physical and mental disabilities and for all of us they increase with advancing years. Every one of us has psychiatric symptoms. We are all symptomatic neurotics, but for the most part we endure our symptoms and expect treatment only when interference with our work or social function transforms us from symptomatic to social neurotics. And all of us occasionally magnify disabilities of both kinds to obtain our own ends. Such exaggerations range from fabricating a sick headache or pleading normal fatigue to avoid an unattractive social engagement, to simulating more serious disability for more serious purposes—madness to escape imprisonment.

The practitioner of internal medicine is fallible, but probably more sparing than the psychiatrist in bestowing the accolade of illness with its consequent privileges. This, I believe, is where he is most abused. It is axiomatic that the depressive patient should not be told to pull himself together and get on with the job. However, there are many circumstances when the patient with less serious psychiatric symptoms needs to be told quite clearly that they are no more important than the low back pains that trouble so many of his contemporaries, or the bunions that worry the rest.

I am fortunate that the psychiatrists with whom I have worked have been prepared to say this, and to make the rarest of all psychiatric diagnoses—that there is nothing seriously wrong with the patient and nothing requiring psychiatric treatment. If such self-denying stringency were more widely cultivated, abuse of the psychiatrist at every level of society would be less conspicuous.

28. Group Therapy: A Special Report
Sam Blum

"These are feelings the person appears to treasure...."

The use of group techniques constitutes a growing source of influence in clinical work and a potential social revolution. There are a wide variety of approaches to group therapy, and many of them are described in this article by Blum.

A few years ago, group therapy might have been described as just one of many techniques for treating mental disturbance. Today it has grown to be an important social movement. Groups using therapylike techniques are found not only in their customary environment—hospitals, clinics, social agencies and psychologists' offices—but also increasingly in universities, government agencies and even private homes throughout the country. Many of these groups seem to be promoting not merely mental health but also a new way of life for American society.

Precisely why anyone joins such groups may not be immediately apparent, for group therapy as it is most commonly practiced bears a superficial resemblance to the worst party you've ever attended. If you could watch a typical session, you'd see eight to 12 men and women sitting for two hours in their therapist's office, needling one another, prying into one another's secrets and complaining about every psychological ache and pain imaginable.

Group-therapy meetings are not polite. Participants accuse one another of being boring and phony and of wasting the group's time. They argue about whose turn it is to talk. Often they seem not to be listening to one another, but simply to be holding back and waiting for a chance to wisecrack or to make a hostile remark. There is invariably a lot of anger in the room, and in time every bit of it is expressed.

Though you also will hear many expressoins of understanding, support, friendship and even love at a group-therapy session, the ordeal to which the participants subject themselves regularly on a once- or twice-a-week basis may well make you wonder how the process could possibly help anyone. But clearly the professionals involved in mental health are convinced that it does. This is hardly surprising, because the same process is utilized in everyday life.

Women in bridge clubs often are helpful to one another by frankly discussing problems they are having with their children and sharing highly practical advice. Bull sessions are therapeutic for college students, as they reveal that they *all* have fears about love, life and death. Men in fraternal organizations feel more secure simply because each accepts another as someone special, as belonging.

Individuals who enter therapy groups, however, appear to need a more intense experience with other people than ordinarily can be found in fraternal organizations, bull sessions and bridge clubs. Most people turn to the therapy groups, says psychologist Zanvel A. Liff, president of the Eastern Group Psychotherapy Society, "because of difficulties at their jobs, or because of problems in relating to other people, or because they may just feel horrible about themselves. Often they are in a pattern of self-defeat and are experiencing no pleasure in life."

Many group leaders attribute the current mushrooming of the group-therapy movement to the fact that more and more Americans are lonely. Many people live far away from their relatives and old friends. Sometimes they are separated by miles, sometimes by their emotions; they are lonely as families and lonely as individuals.

As one therapist put it: "In a family with only a husband, a wife and a couple of children . . . there is not always enough intimacy to keep everyone on an even keel. In order not to become ingrown we have to be involved in the lives of others, because when we are not able to compare our own experiences to those of other people, we distort the meaning of what is happening to us.

"We need the corrective of other people's reactions to what we're doing— approving here, disapproving there, supporting us, caring about us. In the past we got this from uncles, aunts, parents, brothers, sisters, but now it appears necessary to set up groups to get that weekly ration of intimacy that can keep us sane."

Consequently, therapy groups no longer are limited to helping neurotics who are trying to straighten out their conflicts; today's groups also help reasonably normal people who simply are searching for ways to live in a more self-fulfilling fashion or attempting to bridge the deep rifts that exist in American social institutions and in American society itself. But because the group movement is new and experiments abound, it is impossible to make an accurate breakdown that will show which types of groups are working toward which kinds of goals.

It is also difficult to define therapy groups in terms of the techniques they use. No professional organization has ever set standards for the training of group therapists—or "group leaders," as they are sometimes called—and there is no licensing required. A group therapist therefore may be a psychiatrist, a social worker or even someone with no professional experience in (and no talent for) working with human emotions. Furthermore, most group leaders feel free to use techniques borrowed from method acting, children's games, dance, physiotherapy, yogic meditation and a great deal else, and no two leaders run their groups in precisely the same way.

But one characteristic that all therapy groups share—and perhaps it is the only one—is the premium they place on expressing feelings as honestly as possible. And in sharing some goals and techniques, the groups can be loosely classified.

Supportive Groups

In their frank discussions of mutual problems, members of any kind of group can be of aid to one another, and the discussions need not be very deeply psychological in order to be effective. Just hearing the similar problems of others, airing a problem and having it understood by others provides, if nothing else, assurance that the problem is real—not imagined—and therefore possibly solvable. In addition, the group can be of tremendous value in providing emotional support—encouragement when one fails in problem solving, praise when one succeeds.

This sort of "problem-centered," supportive therapy does not attempt to bring about deep personality changes, but in general limits itself to dealing with day-to-day realities. Sometimes this involves solving the problem, sometimes learning to avoid it, sometimes learning to live with it.

Countless such groups are operating within social agencies, usually under the guidance of a social caseworker, at just about this calm and reasonable level. There are groups of teen-agers in trouble with teachers and parents with whom they cannot communicate; yet with one another they are able to be frank and helpful. There are groups composed of parents who have disturbed or retarded children and who not only understand one another's heartbreak, but also recognize in one another a sense of personal guilt that must be brought into the open if it is to be overcome. There are groups of squabbling couples attempting to learn how to solve family problems instead of continuing to bury them under layer upon layer of coldness and resentment.

Such groups also are being used effectively to improve the self-image and the social competence of the poor, the elderly and the lonely. People who were functioning inadequately or hardly functioning at all often draw new strengths from such groups so that they can deal with their families, their jobs, their loneliness and their society.

"Reconditioning" Groups

Group pressure can bring about tremendous changes in the way human beings act. For example, the young man, terrified though he may be, straps on his parachute and leaps from the airplane rather than have his buddies think him a coward. And soon he's a paratrooper.

Group pressure has led people to drugs, to crime, to conformity, to hypocrisy and to mental breakdowns. But group pressure also can be used to aid people in moving away from drugs, crime, conformity, hypocrisy and mental breakdowns.

Synanon, for example, is an organization of "therapeutic communities" founded 11 years ago to treat drug addicts. Those who live in one or another of Synanon's seven houses in various parts of the country play the "Synanon Game" several times a week. They sit in a group of about 12 and gang up on individual members, attacking the image each has of himself.

Alcoholics Anonymous, most weight-reduction groups and other groups use techniques that are much gentler but in basic theory not too far removed from the Synanon Game. They attempt to cut through the nonsense everyone tells himself to excuse his faults (typically, that he is not really at fault at all, just helplessly reacting to evils done to him by wife, parents, society) and to make him face up to the unpleasant reality that he alone is responsible for the way he acts.

"Reconditioning" is then used in an attempt to change behavior. The group itself becomes something of a parent, offering a great deal of disapproval to the individual whose behavior is out of hand and a great deal of approval to the individual who is disciplining himself. And it often works.

Analytic Therapy Groups

The method used by most analytic groups is a sort of guided "free association." People speak up when they want to and carry the conversation wherever the group permits.

Says group therapist Zanvel Liff: "The group is a sort of laboratory where people can make their problems real in the presence of other people. Whatever problems the members have eventually come forth, and they start getting into the same difficulties inside the group that they get into outside it. They feel that people don't like them, or they manipulate their relationships in such a way that they end up as 'martyred' or 'misunderstood.' Or someone in the group may become a parent figure—the bad mother with whom they are constantly at odds or the good mother they always wished they had. In analytic groups we try to work through the distortions from the past that are penetrating the present and disrupting the patient's life."

Most people have analytic group therapy in mind when they speak of group therapy, and if there can be said to be an Establishment in a field this young, it is the 2,300 members of the 27-year-old American Group Psychotherapy Association. Analytic group therapy is an outgrowth of one-to-one analysis (one patient talking with one therapist), which in itself is an offspring of classical Freudian psychoanalysis.

It was Sigmund Freud who first saw clearly that the individual is a mass of hidden desires and drives, many of which may be in conflict. Neurosis, Freud claimed, was a result of the individual's attempts to repress and hide from himself the drives he was afraid to face, and the best treatment of the neurosis was to bring to light the repressed material.

Essentially, Freudian psychoanalysis depends on the patient's curing himself. In re-examining his past, his dreams, his fantasies and his feelings about his analyst, the patient can slowly uncover his subconscious fears and arrive at insights about what makes him ill. But this kind of one-to-one analysis costs thousands of dollars, since it takes hundreds of hours of a well-trained analyst's time. Therefore analytic therapies making use of psychoanalytic concepts but costing less in time and money had to be developed.

Analytic group therapy proved to be the most practical of the new techniques. It is both inexpensive for the patient and well paid for the therapist. A typical fee is $10 to $15 a session for each patient, with one session a week; many groups also meet weekly without the therapist, for which there is no payment.

But even more important, analytic group therapy appears to bring out significant material that individual analysis often misses; in a group the patient has 12 or more very different people instead of only one to whom he can react. Furthermore, many therapists claim that the group experience not only leads the patient to insights about his childhood family, but also provides a new, more open and supportive family where he can express his feelings and once again be freed to grow.

Since analytic therapy involves getting to real feelings, it requires a difficult relearning process, because many people were trained in childhood to ignore their feelings. Boys are taught that "men don't cry"; children are punished for expressing their anger against authority and taught that some wishes are "selfish" and others "sinful."

For self-protection all children set up defenses against their own feelings. So that they won't feel evil or sinful or unlovable or in great danger, they learn to deny even to themselves their "bad" desires. As they become adults this self-denial of feelings leaves them somewhat out of control of their lives. To an extent, all of us, no matter how we were raised, are controlled by fears and guilts and repetitive patterns of behavior that we developed as childish responses to childhood problems that we've outgrown.

One of the techniques of analytic group therapy—as well as most other therapies that hope to effect deep personality changes—is to bring the patient to a point of anxiety and then not permit him to use his usual defenses against it. He is not permitted to laugh off the attacks that other group members may make on him or to pretend that he doesn't care that the therapist has been ignoring his attempts to speak.

The curative theory behind analytic therapy groups is that slowly stripping away the patient's defenses will help him to get to his real feelings; and once there, he can discover what lies behind them. Generally the hidden, frightening material is pretty mild and even conventional. In group therapy the patient can test the harmless nature of his secrets by expressing them, and it has been postulated that half the cure in any therapy comes when the patient repeatedly airs the "ugly" side of himself and discovers that neither God nor his therapist nor his peers strike him dead.

Analytic group therapy, however, is not the best treatment for all neuroses. Says therapist Jerome Kosseff, "There are a lot of people who can sit for years and not profit from the ordinary kind of group session. There are things in them that won't come out unless they are forced, and we analytic therapists don't force them. That's why I think we have something to learn from the new approaches that are being used to cut through defenses."

Experiential Groups

New approaches for "cutting through defenses" have multiplied in recent years as many group leaders have turned away from the psychoanalytic concept that patients must "intellectully" grasp what it is that has been making them ill. Experiential therapists believe that it is enough if a patient can be led to feel once again the painful moments in childhood that probably caused his trouble and to dare experience the feelings that he is blocking.

Dr. Leonard Schwartz, Director of the Institute for Sensitivity Training and Educational Programming, in Brightwaters, New York, who uses the experiential approach in conducting therapy groups, explains that "we focus less on why a patient is acting as he is and more on helping him really to get involved in his problems. We're saying, 'Right now live it out, act it out, feel it.' "

Many innovations for helping a patient experience his blocked feelings fall under the heading of "Gestalt techniques." In Gestalt groups the leader focuses the group's attention on one member at a time, helping him to act out and play out and cry out the "unfinished business" of the past—the grief, loss, fear and humiliation that caused him to cut off his feelings.

Some "new" techniques used by experiential therapists actually are old ones that are regaining popularity. About 35 years ago psychiatrist Wilhelm Reich developed many approaches that combined analysis with breathing exercises, massage, bodily awareness and a certain amount of controlled violence. For example, he would tell a patient to visualize the father or mother who frustrated him during childhood as lying on the couch, and then have the patient pound on the couch and shout out his anger. That technique is now being used in some groups.

Another seemingly new group-therapy technique was originally developed in the 1920s by J. L. Moreno and termed "psychodrama." The patient, aided by other role-playing members of the group, acts out in little, ad-libbed plays painful childhood scenes as they actually happened or as the patient wishes they had happened. He may scream, cry and express anger and grief, and in this way reexperience lost emotions, settle old scores and bring painful events to a close.

Literally hundreds of techniques force the participant to face his anxieties. If he is afraid of his feelings of aggression, he may be asked to wrestle another participant or the group leader. Someone who cannot trust other people enough to love them, a common symptom, may lie down on the floor and then be lifted by the entire group and very gently rocked. From most reports, the rocking creates a feeling of extraordinary sensual well-being, and almost invariably the person being rocked will cry and afterward report strong feelings ("I was actually in your hands. I felt like a baby"). These are feelings the person appears to treasure, feelings he wants not so much to understand as to hold on to and perhaps build on.

T-Groups

Several kinds of groups that use therapy techniques are not primarily therapeutic. Among them are T-Groups—the first of the type now referred to as "sensitivity training groups," "human-relations laboratories," "encounter groups." The T-Group (short for Laboratory Training Group) was developed in the mid-1940s by the National Training Laboratories, an organization founded for the purpose of applying the discoveries of the social sciences to community and organizational problems.

As our institutions grow larger and more complex they also grow more impersonal, and the individual often begins to feel that he is not really needed. He feels that if the bosses could replace him with a machine, they would; that the organization has no loyalty to him and there is no reason for him to have loyalty to it.

Huge institutions also become splintered. Frequently, for example, there is no understanding between a company's engineers and its salesmen, or between a large hospital's administrators and its staff. The result can be inefficiency, waste, resentment and a huge turnover of personnel. The T-Group is an "educational device" that is used to bring disruptive conflicts and feelings into the open, where they may perhaps be eased.

As T-Groups are most commonly conducted, 12 to 15 people get together with a leader (called by NTL a "trainer") in a place far removed from their daily lives, often somewhere in the country. There for many hours each day for a week or two they meet to talk, interrelate, communicate nonverbally (with their eyes or with their hands) and otherwise increase their ability to understand one another and themselves.

In the T-Group many techniques are used to help a participant face his ever-shifting needs: the need to take over, to be included, to disrupt, to be secretive or open, to be hostile or helpful, to be dependent, to touch and be touched. A man can present himself to the group as he generally behaves or he can experiment with acting differently.

Through it all, the most important educational aspect of the T-Group is that it provides clear "feedback"; a participant hears not what the others think of him, but rather how he makes them feel. ("You make me feel as if you're not hearing what I'm saying. You may think you're listening and making helpful suggestions, but it doesn't come across.")

Through feedback one can increase one's sensitivity to one's own feelings as well as to the feelings of others. The concept is fairly simple. Every person, to some extent, hides behind masks—his job title, his college degree, his way of dressing, his social or intellectual status. All these are real aspects of his personality, but they also are the aspects that say, "I am part of this group and not of that one."

And yet there are emotional levels on which almost all human beings can identify with one another. Both the atomic physicist and the cab driver need love, understanding and an appreciation of their worth. When a person cries because of loneliness, all know the feelings that underlie those tears.

Since human beings can understand one another at an emotional level, sensitivity training is used more and more often in searching for solutions to our most serious social problems, including labor-management disputes, police-community hostilities, campus disorders and black-white confrontations.

Encounter Groups

"Encounter group" is a label sometimes affixed to virtually any group that uses intense experiences between people as part of its technique. The term is used most often, however, when amalgamations of all the intense-experience techniques are put to the service of "humanistic psychology." A humanistic psychologist, unlike most psychotherapists, does not deal so much with emotional disturbances as with helping normal people to "grow."

The theory is that as a person extends his creative potential and becomes more "vividly alive"—more "fully human"—he creates a more deeply satisfying life. The secret, say humanistic psychologists, lies in loosening emotional blocks and bringing people in closer touch with their feelings. Then these people can become more spontaneous, loving, creative, "genuine."

In order to live as fully as possible, one must be able to feel hate as well as love, terror and panic as well as self-control. If, in an encounter group, a participant can experience for the first time several minutes of trust, of courage and resolution, a sense of belonging and empathy, then he has experienced living more deeply than before and can carry away the knowledge that these emotions are truly in his repertoire of feelings—waiting to be used.

The most dramatic of all the types of encounter groups currently probing the emotions of their members is the marathon. Fundamentally, this is a very long group session. A typical marathon may begin at noon on Saturday, run as long as 15 or 16 hours, break for a few hours of sleep and then continue for another six or seven hours on Sunday. Since every technique known is used to break through to emotions, the power of feelings generated is hardly to be believed.

In spite of the strength of the emotions that are released, the marathon is, according to psychoanalyst Elizabeth Mintz, one of the foremost marathon leaders on the East Coast, "one of the safest group situations, because whatever problems you bring up, you have time to work through. Marathons are in great danger of being abused, however," she adds. "You can pick up a copy of a Greenwich Village newspaper and see an ad that says, 'Are you lonely? Come to our marathon.' Such group sessions are extremely dangerous when inexperienced people run them. With weak leadership at a marathon, people can really blow their stacks."

There is little question that quacks abound in the entire group movement and that the easy money of the marathon is particularly attractive to them. A hundred dollars or more per person per weekend is a standard fee and not much need be given for it. With Gestalt techniques it is easy enough to drive virtually anyone into an emotional frenzy; and perhaps all that should be said on this score is that anyone wishing to remain in his right mind should not join any group that deals with strong emotions unless it is run by a qualified psychiatrist or psychologist who works in and is known in the community. He should have enough experience to know when someone is being pushed too far, and he will remain available after the marathon to "pick up the pieces" in the event that something goes wrong.

Although many marathons and encounter groups are little more than entertainments aimed at bringing men and women together, the purpose of legitimate groups, says Dr. Mintz, is to provide a "growth experience."

At a recent marathon conducted by psychologists Leonard and Roslyn Schwartz it became somewhat clearer what is meant by a "growth experience." None of the 12 people who attended were searching for a cure. Rather, they appeared to want to try out unfamiliar feelings or to let down the defenses used in their daily lives to cut off their awareness of others. Most participants were striving to feel love. Said one girl, "Frankly, I came here to fall in love—with myself." She'd come to the right place, for one of the commonest insights at a marathon's end is "I'm worth loving."

For most participants the emotion of love was reached only after working through layer upon layer of other feelings. The emotion was achieved by acting out the painful details of childhood illness, the resentment of parents long dead, the terror that one was in truth insane, the desire to destroy, the need to crawl on the floor and cry like a baby, the drive to touch and embrace and kiss and be frankly sexual, the temptation to proposition someone else's husband, the compulsion to bore everyone, monopolize conversation and give nothing. Somehow it all ended in love. The participants all had taken risks and permitted others to do the same, and most came out of it with feelings similar to those of shipwreck survivors who have helped one another through the crisis: that no one who hadn't been there could ever understand what they had meant to one another.

Emotions felt in encounter-group marathons are in many ways debatable, however. Analytic group therapist Helen Durkin points out: "A marathon can be fun, relieving, exciting, like a holiday from the conscience. But afterward almost everyone goes back to his old habits."

It can be argued, however, that nobody goes back to his old habits in exactly the same way. Says Dr. Marvin L. Aronson: "I've heard patients say that they've been told for years that they were too detached from other people; yet they never really understood what it meant until they experienced at a marathon what it felt like to truly contact another human being."

Psychiatrist Carl Rogers has argued that the encounter group is the "most important social invention of the century," and others have seen in the encounter-group movement signs of the "first important cultural revolution since the rise of classical liberalism." They see in it a shift from a competitive to a co-operative society in which spontaneity, empathy and love will repace egoism, fear and the wearing of emotional masks.

In the huge institutes devoted to the exploration of sensitivity training, such as Esalen Institute or Western Behavioral Sciences Institute, both in California, and in the many colleges and universities now offering credits for sensitivity training and for "mini-labs" in the behavioral sciences, it is indeed the hope that society can be changed in such a way that it will no longer pressure men to block their feelings, their spontaneity, their natural playfulness and outgoing love.

The goal is to improve the quality of human life. It is, many therapists insist, the coldness and hypocrisy of the groups in which men live that break them down. Why not, they ask, make the openness and warmth of the encounter group a model for everyday living?

It is possible that young people are asking similar questions, and that a group therapeutic encounter was held by 300,000 young people at the Woodstock Music Festival last summer. In other words, it is very difficult to say today where group therapy ends and a new form of group life begins. But the group experience appears to be one that increasingly large numbers of Americans crave merely because they want to feel alive.

29. Some Answers to Questions that College Freshmen and Sophomores Ask about the Encounter Movement
George D. Goldman and Ira S. Goldman

"...the movement hopes to increase the scope and joy of living."

Dr. George Goldman is a psychoanalyst and Ira Goldman, his son, is a student at the University of Rochester. They have collaborated on this specially prepared paper, with the latter surveying college students and then raising questions about the encounter-group movement which are answered by the former.

Each of the authors independently had become interested in the encounter movement (Goldman, 1970), talked about their interests and evolved the questionnaire design to find out what a typical group of college underclassmen wanted to know about this new social psychological phenomenon. To have a proper perspective on this paper, it should be noted that the senior author is a practicing psychoanalyst and group psychotherapist and therefore will lean towards both a more traditional and an analytic view of groups. It is hoped however that any biases will be minimized by adequate explanation.

The questions were obtained from a random sample of approximately twenty-five male and female, freshman and sophomore students at the University of Rochester. The students were asked, "Picture yourself immediately before your first group experience. If you could have an expert to answer all your questions, what would you ask?" Many of the responses obtained were repeated and definite categories of concern emerged. People seemed to be interested in the

This article was prepared especially for this volume.

effects of the groups, the types of people who go to encounter groups, the process, and the leader's qualifications. These and other questions follow with their respective answers.

Q: *What is some of the history behind the encounter movement or T-groups? When did it all get started and where did it come from?*

A: The encounter movement as we know it today actually started in 1946 when some large corporations hired the National Training Laboratories (NTL Inst. News, 1968) (now the Institute of Applied Behavioral Research) to develop methods to help their executives relax and conduct business in a more effective manner. In response, NTL developed highly structured activities to be used in a small group setting. Thus the origin and name T (training) group. That same year the Human Relations Conference in Bethel, Maine, was the first organization to give the movement formal recognition.

Q: *What is the theory behind encounter groups or sensitivity training? What are the different types of viewpoints?*

A: To be quite frank, the theory behind the encounter movement can be whatever one wishes it to be. The most commonly associated theories are those of Rogers (1967) and Lewin (1967). Whether one be a Freudian or a behaviorist, justification can be found for either view or any found in between. Of course, this means different goals and techniques, but the encounter movement has not generally been tied to any one psychological point of view.

Q: *What are the different types of groups? Is there any advantage to homogeneity?*

A: (1) The Bion (1961) or Tavistock Conference—The emphasis in this type of group is upon the learning experience which is translatable into action in work and community settings. Special attention is paid to covert processes which occur in groups and to the way such processes hinder or further the performance of a task. The functions of leadership and attitudes towards authority are emphasized. Concentration is upon the functioning of groups as wholes rather than upon the individual personality. Members are encouraged to explore their common experience as a member of a social unit.

(2) The Psychodrama Method—Started by J. L. Morene (1946), psychodrama is not exclusively a method of group training. The leader in a psychodrama, termed the "director," does just that. He guides the participants, or "actors," in an enactment of their physical and emotional behavior. This procedure is generally done in front of an audience who serve as actors in the drama or other significant figures in the protagonists's life. At other times the audience as community may be called upon to enact a social drama that has meaning outside of the specific situation previously initiated. In any case, psychodrama is one of the few forms of sensitivity training that has been incorporated into encounter and therapy technique.

(3) The Marathon Group—The marathon group is defined not by any specific theoretical orientation or technique, but rather by the fact that it is a group that spends an extended period of time isolated from participants' normal everyday activities. Marathon groups are usually more structured than groups lasting two or three hours.

(4) The Gestalt Group—The Gestalt group is mainly concerned with finding ways and means to create individual change in a group setting. More so than any other sensitivity training method, the Gestalt approach originated by Perls

(1969) is to disregard the group as an entity and concern itself with each individual in the group in relation. The techniques are aimed at quickly reaching the participants' feelings and then to help establish a new life style.

(5) The Encounter Group—An encounter group is minimally different from the marathon excepting the time factor. Most encounter groups are viewed as extensions or introductions to individual and group psychotherapy. Often encounter groups are theme centered; a group of leaderless people get together in the attempt to explore their feelings in a specified area.

(6) The T-Group—The name T-group stands for many types of groups, with many different methods and objectives. A T-group may be devoted to individual change or to group dynamics. One major area of concern is the development of techniques dealing with interpersonal conflict situations. Whatever its focus, the T-group is considered a learning experience and is studied as such. A basic premise which separates the T-group from other sensitivity training groups is that the individual and not the leader is responsible for his own learning. The leader becomes a facilitator of interaction.

(7) Discussion Groups—These can be made up of any specific interest group, ranging from junior high school or college students to adult groups. The leader can be either a trained professional or a member of this group. The format is the "rap session" where the members are allowed, with impunity, to express their feelings and points of view.

As far as any advantage to homogeneity, I do not think so. I try to strive for heterogeneity in a group. In this way it is sort of a microcosm of society, and it is as true to life as it can be under the circumstances.

Q: *Who is the encounter movement for?*

A: I think it particularly important to bring out the fact that the encounter movement, and by this I lump together sensitivity training, marathons, and such, is for healthy people, as opposed to the therapy group which is usually used for a patient population. But it is particularly for those people who want to experience their feelings more intensely, a result very much like being "turned on" in some way, who want to maximize their potential, who want to find out who they are. It is for people who want feedback about themselves. Maybe the individual wants to get to feelings he has not been able to reach on his own. Encounter groups are sought to increase sensory awareness, sensitivity and perceptiveness to and of others. It is a way of getting at your own humanness when you are so alienated from yourself that you cannot be you by just living. So you have to find an accepting environment where you can be whoever you are.

Q: *What makes a successful group?*

A: From a therapists's point of view, a successful group is one where the members are able to freely and with authenticity experience and express their feelings, emotions, and attitudes as they are aroused by group situations and group members. This brings about insight and awareness which gives more control and a greater ability to make choices. It is a success if people can get to the point of communicating honestly and expressively with other human beings. I guess what I am heading for is the attainment of an atmosphere created by the leaders and the members, of honesty, openness, and cooperation. But nonjudgmental! The biggest thing I felt as a group member was the attitude of good will that pervaded. People really wanted to help each other!

Q: *What are the effects on an individual who participates in a successful group?*

A: That can be very varied. But hopefully the person will see himself in some new perspective and he will get a chance to express his feelings. Possibly during the group the individual will "bounce" himself off others, and they will give him feedback about how his behavior affects them. But more than anything else, a self-exploratory process should take place by which a member gets to know himself a little bit better and understands his behavior and its effects on others. The results can be either to decide to change some aspect of behavior or simply the increased acceptance of self.

Q: *What are the hoped for results of the movement on a group level?*

A: Basically, the movement hopes to increase the scope and joy of living. It is called the human potential movement because it aims to expand the individual's use of his potential in every possible way, making him a more fully functioning human being. It is hoped that the person participating in an encounter group will end up more authentic and less inhibited, much more aware of himself and able to see himself in a more constructive manner. Another hope I myself have for the movement, from a more analytic viewpoint, is that groups might open the paths to a more intense type of ongoing individual treatment. I see it as an excellent adjunct to individual treatment or as an avenue for gaining the awareness of the need for further treatment. It is a good diagnostic tool and an excellent jumping off point for therapy. Besides, after a really good group session you feel good, safe, and a little better able to deal with life's problems.

Q: *What constitutes an unsuccessful group?*

A: What impresses me most is the possibility that because a group may exist in a vacuum far removed from the real world, it may leave an individual open, raw, and hurting. Just the fact that often it is a one-shot deal and can open you up so quickly can be hurtful. Besides this, if the leaders are poorly trained and members are not adequately screened, you might end up with some very sick, destructive group members who could possibly be physically or emotionally hurtful to other members. If the initial mistrust common to group process is not properly or completely worked through, that can add to an unsuccessful group. Or if the group is too intellectual, is not really reaching gut feelings, too much talk and too little group experiencing, then the group falls on its face. One of the basic tenets of the movement is the all-important feeling tone, how emotions are experienced right in the here and now, with constant emphasis on sensory awareness and stimulation. If this is not in some measure achieved, the group is considered a failure.

There are some additional effects that result from an unsuccessful group. For instance, in the "opening up process" a group member may reveal painful and meaningful components of his life which often need long-term treatment and cannot be dealt with effectively in a group. Or a group member may be scapegoated or thought badly of by other group members and consequently leave the group with an enhanced negative self-image. It is important to emphasize that these results are the responsibility of the leader and should be dealt with in group so that members leaving a session or a marathon are not left emotionally hanging.

Q: *What factors could control these effects on an individual?*

A: In terms of destructive effects, good training of leaders and an appropriate frame of reference could mediate some of the effects of frustration. Good technical control by the leader can also minimize the destructive acting out that often occurs. Another preventative measure might be to screen members more carefully and therefore have a "healthier" group. Further, these individuals with some therapy experience would be less likely to do or say things potentially harmful to other members.

Q: *Are there possible harmful effects that can result from participation in a group? Are these effects more a function of the individual or of the group?*

A: Yes. A person can be prematurely opened up. He can be forced to face things he is not ready to accept. As a result, insurmountable anxiety, pain, or depression can be released. There have been reported cases of suicide after encounter groups because the person had seen a side of himself he could not tolerate and felt totally unable to escape. So that yes, there are definitely possible harmful effects of participating in a one-time-only group experience where you can be opened up without getting closed up again! It is somewhat like a surgeon starting an operation and not sewing the wound back together again.

These techniques are tremendous diagnostic tools, but they are not necessarily always that therapeutic. My own feelings are that there is a great therapeutic advantage to belonging, hearing, and learning, and it honestly helps to broaden one's self-image. But analysis of behavior is the destructive aspect of the therapy experience; it is only the resynthesis that becomes constructive. The basic point is that confrontation takes place quite often and the free expression of hostility and anger can be devastating. Also there is always the possibility of physical violence. I think that these effects are more a function of the leaders' inadequacy and the atmosphere they propagate. The trainers structure the nature of the group, and although there may be individuals present that contribute to the general destructiveness, the primary responsibility lies with the leader or therapist.

Q: *Are group effects long- or short-term?*

A: As far as a weekend encounter or a marathon for instance, my own experience is that effectiveness is probably short term. With regard to myself and people I have known, the effects have not really lasted, a matter of a few days or weeks, sometimes even a few hours, and then people return to whatever their lives have been. It is not going to transform one's life into something that it is not or has not been! It can start you thinking, feeling, and doing something in a positive direction, but in and of itself it is just a tool.

Q: *What is the usual focus for a group? Is it group-oriented or person-oriented?*

A: This depends upon the group. For example, some of the NTL groups deal for the most part with group process, and Tavistock groups concern themselves only with group process. On the other side of the coin there are some groups which are poorly run, where people do individual therapy in a group setting. But even if individual therapy is not taking place, there are exercises where individuals are focused on and reacted to for various lengths of time because of their personalities. The focus depends upon the purpose of the group, the leaders, and the individual members. No set focus or goal is always predetermined.

Q: *What in a person makes him (her) want to participate in a group? How about the person who is a consistent group participant?*

A: In addition to those who are intellectually curious, who want to try something that is new and promising as a potential source of accelerated human growth, there are those who join for more neurotic reasons. I think it is a sense of loneliness, alienation—a sense of being apart, of emotional deadness. Maybe the same kind of things that motivate someone to join the drug culture. In a group such a person hopes to achieve some measure of contact with himself, the world and other people. They obviously feel they cannot do it alone, it is a way to expand the mind and the emotions without drugs. People who attend consistently seem to be those who are, or at least feel, very alienated and lonely and need the belonging, the group sense.

Q: *What really is this craze on groups and the encounter movement? Is it sincere, or is it just a good way for capitalizing on individuals to cash in on a fad?*

A: I do not think it is a craze or just being used to cash in on a fad. I think it is a social movement that is springing out of the discontent and alienation felt by the people of the times. In this day and age the depth of closeness and friendship no longer exists as it once did. We are an urban society, and we have gotten away from intimacy, and now people are trying to get it from any source they can. The drug culture is one and the encounter group is another. I do not think the encounter movement is going to die out but rather be integrated by professionals. These groups seem to have caught on in the general population. Many "leaderless" groups exist which help propagate the notion of a real social movement. These groups direct themselves and do their own thing. I think that that is where it is at now, and it is not necessarily constructive. Eventually groups will be fully integrated into professional psychology and into the organized structure of group and individual therapy.

I have been struck by how little the growth centers exploit the participants financially. The prices for weekend retreats are usually extremely fair and even low. Most of the so-called growth centers, for example, are not exploitative monetarily.

Q: *Who should (can) lead a group? What are the qualifications for a group leader? Should there be qualifications if there are not any existing ones?*

A: Ideally I think it should be a professionally trained leader; a mental-health worker, a social worker, a psychologist or a psychiatrist. Someone who has been trained in therapy, group therapy in particular. There are situations where I feel others are qualified to lead groups with specified populations. Former drug addicts and alcoholics have led peer groups with amazing success, and local clergy have led community groups with effectiveness.

But, my big emphasis is that I would prefer a professional. Someone who not only has theoretical knowledge, but who has participated in groups himself. Many of the people who have been leading groups up to now have been untrained and have used methods based on their own "looseness" and charisma. This sometimes results in some therapeutic movement, but I think it is too limited a help. If you do not know some theory, you cannot anticipate and direct the group adequately.

Q: *What is the optimum size of a group?*

A: I certainly think it should be between ten and fifteen, not more than fifteen and optimumly around twelve to thirteen.

Q: *How often should a group meet?*

A: Marathons, encounters, T-groups, and such seem in practice to be mostly oneshot deals, or a weekend retreat. Some growth centers have opportunities to attend groups that range from a week, to a month, to several months. My own feelings are, since my bias is that of an analyst in private practice, that I see all these types of groups as an adjunct to individual treatment. Therefore I see encounter groups as one-time only affairs with a follow-up of individual treatment of analytic group, or possibly as a supplement to individual therapy. From a less analytic point of view, a group should meet as often as necessary to deal effectively with those issues arising, including their resolution.

Q: *What are the procedures of a group (acknowledging different types of groups)?*

A: Many different procedures are used, entirely dependent upon the goals and composition of the particular group. Role playing may be used in a couples group, whereas sensory awareness may be used in a group of executives. There is no set criteria for the selection of method.

What is common to almost all groups is what is known as group process. What is meant by this is the progressive stages a group goes through over a period of time. Rogers (1967) felt that the general stages are: (1) milling around or confusion, (2) resistance to personal expression of ambivalence towards the purpose of and participation in the group, (3) description of past feelings, the onset of group trust, (4) the expression of negative feelings, the first expression of significant "here and now" feelings, (5) the expression and exploration of personally meaningful material, the cracking of façades and the expression of immediate interpersonal feelings in the group (6) self-acceptance and the beginnings of change, and finally, (7) the expression of positive feelings and closeness.

Q: *How about the sincerity of those involved in groups? Do they get caught up in the jargon and forget about really trying to do something worthwhile?*

A: It is really a good question, but far too general to answer adequately. There are those leaders who are sincere and those whose intentions are good but whose results are not. If most were really sincere, I would wonder why, since most are either nonprofessionals or para-professionals, they do not obtain more training. Compassion and understanding are prerequisites for a good therapist, but you cannot just do your own thing! In order to be a truly effective leader or therapist, one should know as much about group dynamics and human behavior as possible, and yet these well-intentioned people rarely do!

Q: *What is the purpose of some of the physical-tension-letting-out techniques?*

A: Catharsis is the letting out and discharge of pent up anger and emotion, which if left dormant could be diverted into far more destructive channels such as physical symptoms and tensions. I do not know how long-term the effects are, but at least if feelings are released it leaves the individual freer to experience and express positive feelings previously blocked by negative emotion.

Q: *Are the games accomplishing some goal, or are they just for fun?*

A: They obviously are intended to accomplish some goal and often are fun too. If you take a book like *Joy* (Shutz, 1967) and look at various games and exercises, they are used at different times for different ends. For example, trust games; I have experienced them and used them in my own therapy groups. I have seen them engender a sense of trust and give someone the feeling that they can trust other people. They can establish the atmosphere of acceptance I have talked about which enables people to open up and share their problems in a meaningful way.

Q: *Can you make any stereotypes about those who participate in groups?*

A: No. You have groups made up of high school dropouts and groups comprised of university professors. You can have young members or old members. What I am trying to say is that it is a phenomenon of our time, a method to treat people and because we live in a society, the group is an ideal vehicle to treat or deal with numbers of people. I guess you cannot safely pin down any stereotype, it just could not fit all the people who have joined, experienced, or sampled the encounter movement.

Q: *Do you feel any need for justifying some of the techniques used, whether on a psychological, philosophical, or moral scale?*

A: I feel that I cannot justify some of the sexual exhibitionism, sexual acting out, aggressive acting out, and other techniques that hurt people in some way. I cannot justify those on any grounds. But there are scientific, experiential, and empirical bases for many of the other techniques and I do not feel the need to justify them. What I am saying is that there are sound techniques which have been proven by theory and experience over time, and those do not need justification. I do not think all the justification in the world could get me to advocate the use of those that are destructive.

Q: *What are the effects of group techniques in the treatment of mentally ill patients?*

A: If you divide the process of therapy into diagnostic questions, such as, (a) What am I characteristically doing with people that gets me into difficulty? (b) Why am I doing it? and (c) What are the alternative behaviors I might adopt and how?—although my bias is that regular analytic group psychotherapy is much superior to a marathon or two for this purpose, group techniques are excellent. They are better than any other tool for answering the first question. Groups introduce at least some social reality to the mental patient where often there is a great need to do so. Groups enable the mentally ill and the healthy individual to see themselves in some true perspective. It gives people the opportunity to decide if they are discontent with what they see, and if so, to choose an avenue for change.

Q: *What are the effects of some intense group experiences on a borderline type of individual?*

A: The intensity of experience in a group setting can be very destructive. If an individual's defenses are inadequate, if his self-esteem is poorly developed, if he has guilt and conflicts which he is unable to handle, a group experience may be the final straw. If you have a leader who is not in tune with these kinds of factors, in such a situation there exists a great deal of potential harm. Groups can and do release anxiety, depression, pain, and conflict. In some extreme cases they have precipitated a suicide or psychotic break. But these effects can be mitigated by well-trained leadership and proper screening of applicants and therefore need not occur.

Q: *Should you participate in a group with someone you know well? What are the effects of this?*

A: I do not think that I have a general answer for this question. In some cases you might choose to go to a group with someone specifically because you are having difficulties in your relationship. Other times you would want to work it out without the other party present, or it could be a homogeneous group such as a group conducted through your business organization. Obviously in that case you would know everyone there.

If knowing a person inhibits you from expressing yourself freely in the group there can be problems. But it is the leaders' responsibility to respond to this and help work through the difficulty. Often it is not the "knowing" the person; it is how you react to that individual as part of the group. If knowing another person in the group gives you more security and therefore the ability to open up more easily, then that is great.

Q: *Can a person really get to know himself in the encounter or sensitivity training milieu?*

A: Obviously yes and no. It depends on what you call getting to know yourself. You will have a group of people who are hopefully behaving in ways that are fairly characteristic and you will be doing the same. To the extent that the others are observant and honest and open, they will tell you how they see you, how they experience you, and consequently show you how they act and react towards you. From this you should be able to glean some new information about yourself as a result of having participated in the group. Will it be a permanent, long-term, extensive knowledge of self? I doubt it, but you should gain some new insight into the way you work.

Q: *What really is sensitivity training? Can one be taught how to use his senses?*

A: Generally speaking, sensitivity training is a group experience emphasizing the here and now, where the members experience each other, experience new patterns of behavior and resultantly give each other feedback about what they have felt. Emphasis is placed upon the group as a learning experience. Not learning to use one's senses in the strictest definition of the word "learn," but rather to increase the awareness of self and others, and increase the acceptance of responsibility for one's actions and their effects on others. Sensitivity training is an attempt to achieve more authentic relationships with other human beings. It is hoped that as a result of the movement there will be an increase in self-esteem and a decrease in defensive behavior.

Q: *Should one be honest in a T-group?*

A: It is one of the essentials! If you are going to attempt to have some degree of authenticity, you have to begin by being honest, real, and direct. But there is always the danger of destructive honesty and hostility. There are so many things that one can be open and real about that you have to trust that most of what will come out in a group will be positive.

Q: *Is there any advantage or disadvantage in going into a group with knowledge of group process and encounter movement theory? Is it more effective with a naive individual?*

A: I doubt it, except that it might be helpful if it gives you more trust in the leader and in the process, but that is about the only advantage I can think of. A naive individual would be no better or worse off than one with a great deal of group experience and theoretical knowledge. Each group is different. I think that if a person strives to be honest, open, and direct he will be a good group member; it works the same in therapy. If the individual is willing to look at himself and he is really discontent and wants to change, these things will help to make the experience more effective.

Q: *Is there much validity to the picture that one gets of himself from the other members in the group?*

A: Harry S. Sullivan (1953), one of the major theorists of the American psychological scene, says that mental health is seeing yourself as others see you. To the extent that people in a group, as representative human beings, give their honest reactions to someone's behavior, you can get some very reliable information about how you come across. I cannot see how it would be invalid, because even if there were several disturbed individuals present, their view of you cannot be based only upon their distortions; it has to be based on some characteristic they perceive. The thing that gets to most people is not that what they learn about themselves is so invalid, but that someone had the guts to say it!

Q: *How superficial are the group contacts?*

A: The contacts are superficial in the sense that for the most part members never see each other again. Even though it is an intense shared experience, lasting anywhere from three hours to three weeks, and often close feelings are generated, if contact is not maintained with other participants, their importance has to diminish over time. If you wish to initiate a relationship through this shared experience, it might be a fine base from which to begin.

Q: *Relate the effectiveness of group encounters to that of a one-to-one therapy contact.*

A: There is no comparison. They are in different worlds! In one you are talking about interpersonal intimacy, and a good psychotherapist can make contact with another person of a very special nature. In a dyadic relationship the therapist deals with early life experiences, socialization, and so on. But there are many roles that a group gets at directly and a therapist never does because of his proscribed role. Therefore, group contact can be much more immediately powerful in its affective impact. The intensity of a group can be far greater sooner than that of a usual therapeutic relationship.

We have tried to put the encounter movement in a perspective that is fair and valid. It is a social movement that has gone from the occasional institutionalized and formal NTL groups to the informal, leaderless, omnipresent college dorm rap sessions in a twenty-five-year period. It is hoped that this paper stirs your curiosity to explore this new frontier further.

References

Bion, W. R. Experience in Groups. London: Tavistock Publication, 1961.

Goldman, G. D., and Brody, H. M. An analytic and a behavioristic view of an encounter weekend, Group Process, 1970, 3, 101–121.

Lewin, K., Lippett, T. R., and White, R. Leader behavior and member reaction in three social climates, in Cartwright, D., and Zander, A. (Eds.), Group Dynamics, third ed. New York: Harper & Row, 1967.

Moreno, J. L. Psychodrama. New York: Beacon House, 1946.

National Training Laboratories Institute News and Reports 2, No. 2, Washington, D.C., April 1968.

Perls, F. S. Gestalt Therapy Verbatim. Lafayette, California: Real People Press, 1969.

Rogers, C. R. The process of the basic encounter group, in Bugental, J. F. (Ed.), Challenges of Humanistic Psychology. New York: McGraw-Hill, 1967.

Shutz, W. D. Joy: Expanding Human Awareness. New York: Grove Press, 1967.

Sullivan, H. S. The Collected Works of Harry Stack Sullivan. New York: W. W. Norton, 1953.

Discussion Questions

1. Can psychotherapy be of benefit to everyone? to anyone?
2. Is behavior determined by past experiences? Or can we exercise free will in determining our fate?

3. What would you want to know before entering an encounter group?
4. Can you think of situations in which physical illness appeared to be produced by psychological problems?
5. How can principles of behavior modification be used to understand and deal with everyday problems such as inability to study or stop smoking or lose weight?
6. What problems should be taken to a therapist? And which ones should be worked out alone?
7. How would you define "abnormal behavior"?

Chapter 8
Sexual Behavior

Sex is one of the most widely discussed of all human behaviors. In light of this, it is interesting how little actually is known about sex and how taboo the topic can be. It is only recently that research in the area of sexual behavior has become socially acceptable, and the findings of the research projects still have not become common knowledge. Regarding a function as important as sex, it is critical that we have as much factual information as possible so that decisions can be made on the basis of information rather than fiction.

The first social scientist to approach the area of sexuality as a legitimate source of concern and to use scientific methodology rather than clinical or anecdotal approaches was Dr. Alfred Kinsey at the University of Indiana. His approach was mostly through survey techniques. Large numbers of individuals were interviewed about their sexual experiences and attitudes; the result was two large volumes about the sexual behavior of the American male and the American female. The institute that Kinsey formed has survived him and is still very active in sexual research. The major impact of Kinsey's findings was to make clear to the American public how widespread different sexual activities were, and by doing so to remove the stigma that might have been attached to them by individuals who thought that their own behavior was unique and perverted.

More recently a second major area of research in human sexuality has developed under the sponsorship of Dr. William Masters and Virginia Johnson. To date this project has also produced two volumes and promises to add a great deal to our knowledge of sexual behavior. While they share Kinsey's pioneering spirit and the philosophy that sexual behavior is a legitimate source of scientific concern, Masters' and Johnson's work differs in a number of dimensions. It is far more clinical in approach to the problem and deals with live instances of sexual behavior rather than survey questions about such behavior. The project has already resulted in the development of a treatment center which is concerned with problems in sexual adjustment; and the clinical techniques developed by Masters and Johnson have been remarkably successful in their approach to sexual problems such as impotence and frigidity.

In his article about the Masters and Johnson project, Paul Wilkes describes many of the approaches that are taken in their St. Louis laboratory. He also provides a personal glimpse of the two individuals who have instituted this remarkable new development in the important area of sexuality. It is of some importance to know that the techniques developed by Masters and Johnson have not been restricted to their own laboratory in St. Louis, but people whom they have trained are developing similar laboratories around the country so that their findings are likely to produce widespread effects.

Whether or not we are now in an era of increased sexual activity is open to question. There are some who would suggest that the frequency of sexual behavior has not been greatly altered but the willingness to discuss it has. This greater openness may give the impression of much more frequent sexual behavior. However, others would agree that there is a good deal more openness but would also hold that there is more frequent sexual activity outside the marriage relationship. This is an area where good data would be far more helpful than speculation. In any case a concern about increased premarital sexual activity should lead to a concern about an increase in illegitimate birth. A number of contraceptive devices have been developed which can be enormously effective in the prevention of illegitimate birth or unwanted pregnancy, but these apparently are not being used as widely as they might. Some people would have objections to the use of any contraceptive device on religious grounds, but these same religious convictions would prohibit premarital relationships. Where individuals feel morally comfortable in engaging in sexual relationships outside of marriage, it would appear that they would be well advised to take precautions that would reduce the possibility of unwanted pregnancy. Thomas and Alice Fleming discuss many of the issues which concern contraceptive devices and arguments that have been raised which reduce the likelihood of their use. It should also be noted that the most widespread technique for population control throughout the world is abortion; and most authorities would agree that contraception, either as a desirable choice or as the lesser of two evils, would be a preferable approach to population control.

The increased openness regarding sexual behavior has not been restricted to relationships between males and females. The frequency with which adult males engage in homosexual relationships has been well known by the general public at least since the time of Kinsey's surveys, and the willingness of individual homosexuals to discuss their behavior openly has increased markedly over the past few years. What was once considered a perversion and a personal stigma has become increasingly acceptable, so that more and more adult male homosexuals are willing to acknowledge their preference.

To think of the homosexual as a stereotyped individual is as erroneous as over-generalization with any of the other subjects discussed in this book. There are a number of types of homosexuals and as many reasons for their behavior. Laud Humphreys describes and classifies a variety of categories of homosexuals. These include the traditional stereotype of the ultra-feminine man, the individual who engages in both homosexual and heterosexual activity but prefers the former, and also individuals whose homosexual activity seems of secondary importance in his pattern of adjustment.

There have also been groups of women whose sexual behavior has provided topics for gossip and social stigma. One of these is the stripteaser, a woman whose activity places her alongside the prostitute in most public eyes. Marilyn Salutin has conducted some research with a group of women strippers and characterizes their motivations and behavior in her article. In addition to her discussion of the stripper, two interesting points emerge incidentally. One of these has to do with the method by which any group of individuals who find themselves placed in the position of social outcasts will deal with that problem. The techniques with which the stripper seeks to legitimize her activity and remove the stigma from her behavior are most interesting. In addition there is the question of why strippers have so little trouble finding an audience. In most of the self-righteous attempts to stigmatize these women, little attention is given to the men in their audience. The characteristics and needs of this group might make a research project that would be at least of equal interest and might place more perspective on our attitudes toward strippers.

Suggested Readings

Kinsey, Alfred C., Pomeroy, Wardell B., and Martin, Cylde E. *Sexual Behavior in the Human Male.* Philadelphia: W. B. Saunders, 1948. Kinsey, Alfred C., Pomeroy, Wardell B., Martin, Clyde E., and Gebhard, Paul H. *Sexual Behavior in the Human Female.* Philadelphia: W. B. Saunders, 1953. These two volumes present the essential findings of Kinsey's pioneering research efforts in the field of human sexuality. The second volume is also available in paperback form.
Masters, William H., and Johnson, Virginia E. *Human Sexual Response.* Boston: Little, Brown & Co., 1966. Masters, William H., and Johnson, Virginia E. *Human Sexual Inadequacy.* Boston: Little, Brown & Co., 1970. These two volumes are the current publications available from Masters' and Johnson's important current research project in sexual behavior. They are important both for their research findings and their clinical implications.

30. Sex and the Married Couple
Paul Wilkes

"... they tell
the nun to masturbate
to orgasm."

The most comprehensive and important current study of sexual behavior is in the research and therapeutic program of Masters and Johnson. In this article Paul Wilkes not only describes that program, he also gives an interesting portrayal of the two people who developed it.

"Hey, mister, what floor ya goin' to in there?" the cabdriver asked, straining his neck to gain a good look at his rider.

The cabbie's question finally registered with the rider, who was fumbling in his pocket, already moist with perspiration from the muggy St. Louis summer day.

"Uh, I think it's the first . . . no it's the third floor."

He smiled so knowingly. "Going in there alone, are ya, mister?"

"Yeh, you see, I'm going in there . . ."

"You don't have to explain to me, mister. You just have a good time, because if you can't make it that way, life ain't worth much."

The cabbie was still smiling, smiling sympathetically, which is not the way of most cabbies, as he slipped back into traffic in front of the building on Forest Park Boulevard. Made of prepoured marbled beige slabs supported by white pillars, and with all its venetian blinds closed, 4910 is as nondescript and conservative as its name: Central Medical Building. It is only when those who have been referred to 4910 for special difficulties—one of which the cabbie knew about—come into the lobby and look up at the directory that they know they are in the right building. There it is: Reproductive Biology Research Foundation. There they are: Masters, W. H., Johnson, V. E.

William Masters is a gynecologist by training who was well known for his work in steroid replacement and infertility before he went into what he always dreamed would be his life's work: human sexual functioning—how it happens, why some people have difficulties with it, how they can be helped, and how their difficulties can be prevented. Virginia Johnson studied psychology but never received a degree for it. She responded to Bill Master's request at the Washington University placement office for a female assistant who was good with people, able to talk openly with them, able to understand their problems. For the last fourteen years they have worked together. Their names, always in tandem and always in that order, have become synonymous with the scientific study of sex. This year they published a book that told what they did after they moved out of the laboratory and into their offices to work with men and women, most of them married and most already in pairs, who either could not function at all sexually or were doing so at an unacceptably low level of success or enjoyment. *Human Sexual Inadequacy* fulfilled the promise of *Human Sexual Response*, Masters and Johnson's first book, and also disarmed those critics who saw little reason to record the sexual act on film and by various sensing devices, a modus operandi for the first book. Whatever the critics thought, both books have been instantly successful. Combined hardcover sales now appear to have climbed beyond the half-million mark.

It is actually on the second floor that Masters and Johnson have their offices and do their work. In room 220 shortly after 8 A.M. the air conditioning is over-responding, creating a slightly drafty and cold reception area, where Muzak is already playing its prerecorded Siren's repertoire. A familiar song. An old song blends into the violinized rock: "My One and Only Love."

Bill Masters has been up for nearly three hours. Before six he rose, drove to a high school quarter-mile track, jogged six slow laps, walked one, and then finished off with one fast lap. For a fifty-four-year-old man, who is bald except for a ring of white hair left by hereditary tonsure and two shafts of white side-burns, Bill Masters is still an attractive man. Writers have searched for descriptions of him, and because of the nature of his work, have been charitable but incorrect in labeling his as the look of the concerned family physician or the involved marriage counselor. The Masters look is hard, penetrating, an X-ray look that discourages frivolity and commands immediate candor. It seems to say: "Of course, I'll help you, but let's get on with it." When he moves his eyes, the right one lags behind, temporarily giving him a double image. Anyone seeing him for the first time might rivet attention on his steel-blue eyes and try to figure out which one, if either, is training on him.

Gini Johnson, wearing a black and white patterned overblouse and white uniform pants, is now on her way to the Foundation in an open convertible. She is a attractive forty-five-year-old who could, if she dedicated time to her-self instead of her work, be ravishing. In the publicity shot for their second book, Gini was made up by George Masters (no relative) and benefited greatly by eyeliner, eyeshadow, false eyelashes that wisp up quickly at the end, and lipstick applied by brush; but she usually wears her hair swept back from her face into a ponytail or covered by a fall that is a shade off from her own auburn. She smiles more readily than Masters, but keeps her lower jaw set, which prevents her from making full-fledged cheek-wrinkling grins.

Since the beginning of this year, when word began to circulate that Masters and Johnson were ready to publish their second book, they have made themselves available, within reason, to the print media, particularly the women's magazine's, which they consider a vital conduit for their information. After the first book, they appeared on the *Today* show, were interviewed by NBC for Huntley-Brinkley, and whistle-stopped from medical convention to medical convention, in an effort to explain to the lay and professional public what they were trying to do. Television has been shortchanged this time around. Although they have refused all talk shows and interviews, they have standing offers from Merv Griffin, Dick Cavett, and David Frost asking for a visit, under any conditions or time limits that Masters and Johnson would like to impose—no trained seals before or after, no monologue, no music. None of these offers has been accepted.

Those who have come to talk with Masters and Johnson about their work find that conversations occur in small segments, crowded into their busy schedule. In addition to counseling couples and working in infertility, Masters and Johnson have a half-million-dollar Foundation to administer and are now beginning to structure a postgraduate course in their techniques. It will be run by Dr. Ray Waggoner, immediate past president of the American Psychiatric Association, and Emily H. Mudd, professor emeritus of family study in psychiatry at the University of Pennsylvania, who have just joined the staff. Some conversations occur during lunch in the library, where a stack of issues of *Hospital Practice* and *Playboy* are pushed aside to make room for cold cuts, rye bread, potato chips, and iced tea. The library is small; ten or twelve people can be squeezed in. The number of volumes is not impressive, but the field of sexology hasn't produced many scholarly or even peripherally useful books. One of man's most basic needs—Masters claims it ranks second only to self-preservation—hasn't been a proper area for study. Here it is, unashamedly. On Bill Masters' desk, a lucite cube with Picasso's erotic and mildly pornographic sketches. In Gini Johnson's office a carving of two nude bodies, man and woman, together. On a shelf below her assortment of reference books is a roughhewn wooden block, with the outlines of a man and woman, not touching but contemplative, emerging out of the side that has been partially carved.

Masters has said it so many times: "Our job is to put sex back into its natural context; it is a perfectly normal function—as normal as breathing. Why do we have all these prohibitions, why have we legislated against it?" Sex is OK at 4910 Forest Park Boulevard. It can even be joked about. A gentleman wrote to say he could help Masters and Johnson in their work, for he had found that prior to his climax, his stomach growled. Now a stomach growl from a staff member will be greeted by, "Do you want to be alone or can we watch?" They have seen so many tense couples go through the first days of the two-week therapy program that a tense look on the face of a staff member evokes a saccharine "How did it go last night?" Sex back in context.

By midmorning Masters has counseled two couples. The first is in the last days of a two-week stay and had come to the Foundation with a typical problem: premature ejaculation on the part of the male that had resulted in a nonorgasmic wife. Both problems have been overcome. In place of two people who barely spoke upon arrival, there are now chatty, hand-holding honeymooners. The second couple has not been able to conceive. After a ten-minute interview, they come out of an office and wait in the hallway while Masters goes into a small laboratory. He comes back with a plastic vial with a cork stopper. Masters needs to check the viability of the man's sperm, and as he could, or would, not produce some by masturbating in one of the many lavatories, he will go back to his hotel room and, with his wife's assistance, produce.

Over twenty pieces of mail await Masters' personal response. Others, which ask for general information on the therapy program, are answered by a secretary and a series of form letters that are personally addressed and then typed through an automatic typewriter. The cry of the sexually maladjusted resounds from the pages, contained in envelopes with post-marks from as close as Illinois or as far away as Italy or Malta. In March there were 102 written inquiries; *Human Sexual Inadequacy* was published on April 27. In May, 429 letters. In June, 606. A man with primary impotence and no money wants the Foundation to supply a surrogate partner, as it has done scores of times in the past. "Tell him we have already taken all the free-care cases we can afford to this year; in fact we're over 30 percent free care and only budgeted to do 25." "Next, tell this guy in Italy there is no known way to increase male sperm production.," "Here's a guy with troubles every place but in bed. Tell him to see a marriage counselor." One woman offers her services as a ghostwriter for a popularization of *Human Sexual Inadequacy*. That is a sensitive subject. The answer is no. Another writer wants permission to quote twenty-eight pages from the book. "So that he can wrap some drivel around it, put on a cover, and sell it for a couple of bucks. Tell him no." A man asks specific questions about his trouble with premature ejaculation. "Tell him to read the book." A woman goes into detail about the pain she experiences during thrusting in intercourse. Is it real or imagined, she asks. Bill Masters leans back for a moment and smiles. His abrupt manner in answering correspondence might leave the impression of high-handedness or lack of concern. There is neither. He is sympathetic to human need or else he wouldn't have given up a $100,000-a-year private practice sixteen years ago to work as a $27,000-a-year researcher. And, he *does* answer every inquiry. It is just that he is asked to give diagnoses and miracle cures for the price of a first-class stamp and some stationery. "Tell her, tell her kindly, tell her how the hell do I know and that she should consult her local doctor."

Since they began eleven years ago to help couples solve their sexual dysfunctions, Masters and Johnson have refined the total treatment package to assure that patients are as relaxed as possible, given the problems they will have to talk about and the interpersonal therapy they will be exposed to. Before couples arrive, they are booked into such elegant accommodations as a penthouse suite in the nearby Chase Park Plaza Hotel or into one of the two small apartments that the Foundation maintains at the Forest Park Hotel. Each has cooking facilities and rents for $100 a week. Even the poorest patients must provide for their own transportation and living expenses. Scheduling of couples is done four months in advance, and for those who can bear the full cost, it is $2500 for the two-week program and five years of follow-up.

Mrs. Lynn Strenkofski, a bubbly brunette whose name is on all correspondence with patients so they feel they already know her, greets the couple as soon as they arrive. But never by name if there is anyone else in the room. That is cardinal rule one, for many Masters and Johnson patients are supposed to be motoring through Mexico for two weeks, or camping in Canada, away from the telephone. In addition to the malady the couple has reported, a few things are known. The woman will not menstruate in the next two weeks, nor is she nursing a baby. The couple have probably made an attempt at intercourse the night before coming to St. Louis, a last valiant attempt to show each other that they are basically sound and do not really need the treatment. They are wrong.

Wanda Bowen, a thin, graying woman with a ready smile, awaits the new couple on the second floor. She is dressed in a white pants suit and beige scarf, which is standard attire for the staff. She is the office manager and also the chief of the psychological-warfare department. "Warm, friendly, but professional" are her bywords. "If a couple walks in and somebody giggles about somebody else spilling some coffee, that couple will automatically think, "They know about us. They've read the report. They know I can't make it. They know I'm a prude.' " When a dentist Mrs. Bowen knew at the time she lived in Jacksonville, Florida, came with his wife for treatment, she remained distant and impersonal At the end of their successful visit, Mrs. Bowen switched from a professional smile to a personal one, winked, and said, "If it fits into the scheme of things, say hello to some people back there for me; say that on your fishing trip to Wisconsin you met me in a restaurant." Keeping staff members has been a problem for the Foundation. Some never learn the decorum needed. Some relish the vicarious thrill of knowing what is going on behind the closed doors on the second floor. Some pull stupid acts like calling a hotel manager, identifying the Foundation, and telling him that a certain well-known person and his wife are going to stay at his establishment for the next two weeks.

Mrs. Bowen gives each couple an ominous-looking plain brown paper envelope that contains nothing more crucial than a restaurant guide, the schedule for the chimpanzee show at the St. Louis zoo, locations of laundromats, planetarium shows. The two weeks in St. Louis are not two weeks by the bed as some expect. Depending on their needs and degree of articulation, they will spend from twelve to twenty-five hours in therapy sessions at the Foundation offices. Many other hours will be taken up with application of the therapy guidelines.

Now, after all the years of agony and months of waiting, the couple is ready to begin. In their first interview, they are faced by both cotherapists. It could be Masters and Johnson or a second team, Dr. Richard Spitz and Sallie Schumacher, or any combination of one male and one female. Dual sex-therapy teams, a Masters and Johnson concept, give each member of the marital unit a friend in court, a person who knows what the first nocturnal emission was like, or who knows what happened during the first menstrual cycle. The couple tell of their problems and their hopes, and then each one pairs off with the member of the same sex on the therapy team to discuss family background, religious beliefs, sexual activity with this mate and others. "Did you ever watch anyone else, accidentally or otherwise, involved in sexual activity? Do you recall your reaction? Which parent did you feel closest to? Who usually chooses the time for lovemaking? Do you tell your husband [wife] what pleases you most?"

The picture that emerges could keep soap operas in material for years. Two Ph.D.'s, she in anthropology, he is physics, have a marriage unconsummated after four years. A nonorgasmic woman was traumatized at fifteen with her first sexual encounter—a homosexual one with an overzealous teacher. A husband, out of work, turns to drink and loses his potency. A frustrated woman from a Fundamentalist Protestant background, whose premarital physical contact consisted of three chaste kisses, who fought to keep herself covered during intercourse while her husband fumbled through the nightclothes to do the job. A man from a Fundamentalist background whose first sexual encounter was with a prostitute, *standing up*, is impotent. A man punishing his mother by denying her a grandchild is denying his wife any sexual activity.

On the second day, the male patient talks with the female therapist and his mate with the male, and each goes deeper into background and difficulties. The couple know they are not supposed to engage in any form of sexual activity, and for most, at this point in the program, this is not too tall an order. On the third day, there is a round-table discussion, stories are matched, glossed-over fabrications are confronted, righted, and the couple are ready to begin the practical-application phase. They are given instructions to go back to their room and on two occasions simply rub or touch the other person wherever they would like, except genitally, just to give them pleasure. It was Gini Johnson's idea eleven years ago that non-demanding touching, called "sensate focus," was the first step in re-establishing a physical relationship that could lead to successful sexual functioning.

From the fourth day on, couples in therapy are encouraged to proceed, at their own pace, toward a more complete appreciation of the sexual component in their lives. Wanda Bowen and her staff see the couples go in for their daily sessions with Masters and Johnson and then emerge. "I don't have to listen to the tapes [all sessions are recorded] or look at the progress sheet," Mrs. Bowen says. "It's all there in their faces. Some are crying. Some snap at each other. Some are holding hands and smiling. The anthropologist Ph.D. was a mess in dumpy clothes on the first day. When she came in one day with lipstick, her hair done, and earrings on, I didn't have to ask anybody. She was advertising to the world that they had made it."

The men who come to Masters and Johnson for help break down into two basic categories, those who cannot perform sexually (primary impotence if they have never been able to achieve an erection and have intercourse; secondary impotence if, once having been successful, they are no longer able) and those who can perform (but who have an orgasm before they are able to satisfy their mate—premature ejaculation—or those who are never able to achieve orgasm—ejaculatory incompetence). No women are considered frigid by Masters and Johnson. "The word means nothing," says Masters. They are victims of either primary orgasmic dysfunction (they have never experienced orgasm or situational orgasmic dysfunction (once successful, but not currently).

The therapy is carefully orchestrated, from the moment of first instructed touch to successful intercourse and orgasm, to keep both partners calm and undemanding of one another. "Fear of performance is the biggest factor in sexual dysfunction, and once there is no premium on performance, we can get a lot of work done," says Masters. That work was detailed in *Human Sexual Inadequacy,* where Masters and Johnson reported they had failed in only 20 percent of 790 cases of male and female dysfunction that had been treated for two weeks and then followed up for five years. They did not claim success in the other 80 percent, stating that success was too difficult to define, but that failure, either in the two-week program or during the five-year follow-up, was easy to identify. Masters and Johnson's most stunning success came in the area of premature ejaculation, where only 5 of the 186 men thus afflicted could not bring their problem under control. By use of a "squeeze technique" where the female grasps the penis when the man says he is ready to climax, thus removing his desire to do so, Masters and Johnson have virtually proven this sexual problem can be vanquished. Their highest failure rate (40 percent) occurred with primary impotent men, many of whom could not overcome religious strictures that have effectively castrated them.

Because their work is shrouded in secrecy, few firsthand examples of how Masters and Johnson operate have reached the general public. One such story appeared in the July, 1969, issue of *Ladies' Home Journal*, told by an anonymous woman who had been married for nine years and found little sexual fulfillment in her marriage to a man who suffered from premature ejaculation. The scenario is all too familiar: intercourse degenerates into release for her husband and frustration for herself . . . the wife finds herself less responsive . . . she avoids her husband . . . he accuses her of extramarital activity . . . she becomes even less responsive . . . the psychiatrist is consulted . . . "Don't fret my dear," he answers, "your husband has a low sexual-interest level and unfortunately his problem of premature orgasm cannot be helped. Forget your problem and get involved in hobbies, go to the theater; there is more in life than sex."

This woman knew that, but she still wanted her share. Under Masters and Johnson's care everything seemed to be going well until Dr. Masters asked her if she would stay with the marriage if the sexual aspects were improved. She answered that she didn't know. "Why did you come here?" he shot back at the woman. At that point she knew he wouldn't stand for any idle chitchat, and she replied that whether or not the marriage survived, she didn't want to deprive her husband of his chance to find his manhood. She was surprised when the stern-faced Dr. Masters promised that within a year her husband would again be confident—both sexually and in his everyday life—and it would be due to her.

The evening before the round-table discussion the nervous couple found themselves consoling one another, holding each other—something unique in their marriage. They were alone in a strange city with no one to resort to except each other. This is obviously not an accidental benefit of the program. On the third day, instructed to go back to their room and simply "pleasure" each other with no special goal in mind, they did so. The woman explained: "I had never before been able to touch my husband in an uninhibited way and he had never learned to caress me with love. But now, with our fears of sexual performance or nonperformance removed, we relaxed and enjoyed each other. I was not really able to be purely platonic about the experience; I found myself becoming aroused in ways I had not felt for years."

In their first attempt at intercourse two days later, the couple were mutually successful. "It was not difficult to accomplish these victories . . . we were supremely confident and, as a result, were able to drop all pretenses." Along with her new physical openness, the woman found herself extremely sensitive to her husband's slightest ill word or look. And, over a trivial matter, a fight occurred. To the couple's astonishment Masters and Johnson were unmoved. Arguments frequently happen at this stage of therapy, they explained, and after all, weren't the couple in St. Louis to make their mistakes? The argument and the ensuing makeup assured the couple that the therapy was applicable not only under idyllic circumstances, but could work in everyday life. When Mrs. Johnson took the woman aside to ask how things were going, the woman said, "I was amazed to hear myself rhapsodize about how deeply in love I was. I was not being a Pollyanna; I knew that all our problems had not been solved overnight. But I felt that just the fact that some doors had been opened, that we were enjoying each other so much, was a small miracle. To go from almost nothing to so much in a short time made me very optimistic about our future."

Now that work with heterosexual couples has been established and proved, Masters and Johnson are spending an increasing number of hours working with homosexual couples. Contrary to what the straight world thinks, Masters and Johnson have found there are many impotent male homosexuals and nonorgasmic lesbians whose sexual distress in the relationship they are drawn to makes life and the relationship miserable. In addition to treating those two dysfunctions, Masters and Johnson have been working with those homosexuals who want to return to a heterosexual life. The first homosexual couples to be treated went through the therapy program two years ago, and so far the failure rate is within tolerable limits. Research on the physiology of human homosexual response, which will be included in a book to be published in the mid-1970s, was finished in 1965. While heterosexual response took six and a half years and thousands of feet of color film to record, homosexual response was completed in eighteen months and without visual documentation. The homosexual report will show how similar, almost without variation, the orgasm of two homosexuals is to that of two heterosexuals. (The famed "green room," where heterosexual and homosexual arousals and orgasms were duly recorded, now is painted a restful beige. In place of the hospital bed, sensors, cameras, and lights is a series of couches that will be used for post-marital group counseling. Only a baseboard riddled with electrical outlets and a two-way mirror tell of the room's past—and illustrious—history.)

The work with homosexuals might appear to endanger Masters and Johnson's standing in the medical community, which is high, if recent, in origin. But in five years their next book will probably raise no more eyebrows than did *Human Sexual Inadequacy*, which was greeted as healing balm for one of the most persistent wounds of society, a difficulty that is said to afflict half the marriages in the United States. Masters and Johnson have consistently kicked over barriers, pushed their way through myth, mores, and misconception, to come up with undisputedly sound medical and therapeutic information. When a Roman Catholic nun comes to them with complaints of pelvic pain, a bloated feeling at other than "that time of the month," and they find massive congestion that can be relieved in only one way, they tell the nun to masturbate to orgasm.

They do their work in a conservative city, St. Louis, a city that seems to have a special tolerance for research in medicine and science. If the city wanted Missouri law enforced, officers could come to Masters and Johnson and demand that their program of providing surrogate partners for single, sexually dysfunctional males be stopped. It is against the law in the state of Missouri for a man and woman, not married, to engage in sexual intercourse. There has been no harassment. (One disgruntled husband, however, has brought a $750,000 suit against Masters and Johnson, charging that his wife was paid $750 to engage in sexual activities with two men. Masters and Johnson have made it no secret that they have supplied female partners for males, but have also been extremely careful to choose women who are willing, sympathetic mates for the two-week therapy program and not promiscuous fun-seekers. Masters and Johnson have dismissed the suit as "ridiculous.")

At first, under the auspices of Washington University, the work of Masters and Johnson was done secretly. Once they began telling professional groups of their concepts and early findings, the word leaked to the local press and national medical writers. But the press agreed voluntarily not to print fragmentary information about the work in St. Louis and to wait until the first book was ready. If it had been Bill Masters' decision alone, the two books and medical journal articles would have been the extent of communication between the Reproductive Biology Research Foundation and the outside world. It was Gini Johnson, experienced in the ways of advertising and radio, who saw both the value and opportunity of communicating with ordinary men and women so that they, in turn, would begin to demand the type of therapy Masters and Johnson offered for professional use.

While resisting offers from publishers for additional books, from cosmetic firms for endorsement of a lotion that patients have used successfully during the two-week therapy program, and from movie producers, one of whom was willing to pay $100,000 for the use of the title of their first book, Masters and Johnson have stayed in firm control of much of their press. They have demanded, and usually obtained, the right to see copy before it was published. When *McCall's* was ready to run an article about their work that Mrs. Johnson thought was "bits and pieces and took our work out of context," she had the magazine scrap it and wrote the article herself. *Time*, a subsidiary of Time Inc., the parent company of Masters and Johnson's publisher, Little, Brown and Company, wanted advance galleys of *Human Sexual Inadequacy* so they could prepare a cover story to run when the book appeared. They were turned down. Masters and Johnson have never cooperated in working with magazines that wanted to do first-person stories about couples who have been treated. One such couple, in fact, approached NET and was interviewed on TV. After reading the transcript, Gini Johnson had to admit that the interview was a good reflection on why the couple was having troubles. "The woman had all the answers; every time he'd start to say something, she'd correct it and go off on a tangent. I'd be impotent in the face of that."

For instance:

> MAN: There was something very interesting I think they missed. We were told, in other words, if my wife or myself got out of line with each other, we should try to make up some sort of a signal that it's a danger—
> WOMAN: This is later.
> MAN: Yeah, this is later, yeah.
> WOMAN: You're jumping the gun.
> MAN: OK, take it.

And yet, even this overbearing woman and her subdued husband were able to find each other physically under the guidance of Masters and Johnson. Some other excerpts from the interview with WNDT-TV's Sherrye Henry give a behind-the-scenes flavor:

> WOMAN: Incidentally, at the first session we were not allowed to touch any sexual parts of either body. This was most important. I guess it did lead to the sensuousness which they expected of us. The next part of the lesson consisted of allowing us to touch one another on our sexual parts. But we weren't allowed to indulge in any sexual intercourse. We became sensitized, and we jumped the gun, as we later found out they expected us to do, and we did have sex.
> INTERVIEWER: Well, was it good for you?
> MAN: Yes, great!

INTERVIEWER: How precise were their instructions to you? When they sent you back home to practice, what did they give you? Diagrams? Pictures?

WOMAN: Dr. Masters would sit in his chair behind his desk, and he would tell us exactly what he wanted us to do and would use his hands to explain to us what he wanted done.

INTERVIEWER: Well, let's go back then to what I asked about your attitudes toward each other. As the release came in sex, did also the release come in your private—?

WOMAN: Physically, yes. We then had a mental barrier we hadn't broken down. With all married couples, you have two animals; you have a body and you have a mind. Our minds weren't meeting, and the only way that the minds could meet was by us having a battle. Dr. Masters tantalized me and said that he was going to get my husband a blonde. He [Masters] wanted him [husband] to do anything to make me angry. He [Masters] had broken off sex between us. So finally we were riding down the street looking for a restaurant, and he wanted me to read the map of St. Louis and I knew nothing about St. Louis, and he started screaming and yelling at me, and as soon as he did that, my hair stood on end, and I told him to take me back to the hotel and I proceeded to cut him to bits. I did mental surgery on him. The next morning we went anxiously to see Dr. Masters and Mrs. Johnson, and when the girl saw me downstairs in the reception room, she wanted to know what happened. I just said that men weren't any good. Dr. Masters came to the door of the reception room and he looked at me and said, "You, I want you in my office immediately. You [husband] stay here." And so I went into his office and I broke down; I cried like a baby. I told him what happened, and then Mrs. Johnson came in, and she literally tore me apart. Told me exactly what I had been doing wrong. Which was the best thing she could have done. I didn't like what she said. But it had its effect. And two minutes later they came back after me again. I went inside and they were laughing. I was very upset by all this and I went home and I cried from 11 o'clock in the morning until 3 o'clock in the afternoon. And he [husband] was there, the first time he really saw me.

INTERVIEWER: As a person.

WOMAN: A person and a woman and I . . .

INTERVIEWER: Who needed him, I suppose.

WOMAN: Right.

Masters and Johnson, who will surely take their place in the lineage of Freud and Kinsey, have made personal sacrifices to accomplish their work. Bill Masters has not taken a day off from his work in sixteen years. But he is a devoted football fan and a season-ticket holder for all the home football games of the St. Louis Cardinals. His eighty- and ninety-hour workweeks have left many things in their wake, including his marriage. He lived apart from his wife for almost two years, and is now divorced. He has worked at this feverish pace because he believes he has much more work to do and, at fifty-four, not enough years to accomplish it all. He wants to train senior therapists from all over the country who can then teach the techniques in their own clinics and medical schools. He wants to assemble a statistically sound group of adolescents and aged to study their sexual difficulties. He wants to develop preventive means to keep people from sexual dysfunction. All this for a man who describes himself as "not a people person; I could be happy alone in a laboratory for the rest of my life."

Gini Johnson, born Eshelman, married bandleader George Johnson and sang with him for several years. She was never the gushy type ("I was raised in a Victorian family, but we were warm to each other with words, not touches") and is not one to indulge in the very medium of sensitivity she has developed. After the first book, the inevitable question was asked of her: Did your own marriage fail (she was divorced in 1956) because of sexual troubles? She was quick to answer no, and looking back today, she is more calm about it: "He was a bandleader, a night person. We had children; they were day people. The two just didn't mix." Now that she feels she can relax and once again begin to enjoy life, she is concerned. "I've been removed from society for so long, I really don't know what I liked before. I don't know what I'd go back to."

Masters and Johnson, if they have little else in their personal lives, have each other. They work together seven days a week, they socialize together, they spend evenings at Virginia Johnson's comfortable home in a St. Louis suburb. All of which has kept people speculating about the degree of their involvement. "After my divorce, you won't see us running off to Mexico or anything like that," Masters said last spring, with a perfectly straight face. "But I may take it upon myself to chase as many women, eighteen years and older, as a slightly fat, bald, fifty-four-year-old can catch."

The response is made late one afternoon as he soaks in the pool at Gini Johnson's home. It is his idea of relaxation just to sit on the steps of the pool with the water lazily lapping at the long, white hairs on his chest, and then to swim a dozen lengths before dinner. Inside the deceptively simple brick house, with a stunning bilevel addition done in exposed rough beams with vaulted ceiling, Gini Johnson is preparing wild rice and peas and loins of pork and beef. Dressed in a striped caftan, she pads barefoot around the kitchen.

The house, like the rest of their lives, has an aura of privacy. Bill Masters points to a stand of four reasonably mature trees, through which can barely be seen windows of the only house not sheltered from view by topography, or by the high fence encircling the property. Those trees were recently moved into place to provide protection from those who would like to see what goes on in the backyard of the famed sex-researchers. Some of the wealthy who have sought Masters and Johnson's care, and were willing to pay them anything to perform their function outside St. Louis, have been turned down. Masters and Johnson simply won't leave all their other work for two weeks.

For many male and female homosexuals, fear of detection is an almost paralyzing thought. One, a well-known member of local society, ostensibly happily married, is a lesbian and has come to Masters and Johnson for aid. Over the past decade, Masters and Johnson have used many apartments in and around St. Louis to protect the identity of their patients. And they have been successful in this game of cat and mouse; no one has broken security. Many have tried. Masters found that a physician in an adjoining suite was using the same lavatory an inordinate number of times daily. One day, Masters saw him go in and waited for him to come out. One hour, two, three, four hours passed, and finally the physician unlocked the door and walked out, the stethoscope he had pressed against the wall still in his hand. Photographs taken through Foundation windows from across the street have been sent anonymously to Masters and Johnson.

As he prepared for his work in sex research and therapy, Masters studied the life of the late Alfred Kinsey, to see what motivated him and to see what pitfalls he could avoid. Masters found that Kinsey developed an overpowering ego, would not train a qualified successor, and thus guaranteed that his work would end with his death. He never collaborated with a female researcher although he was studying both sexes. And in his last years, Kinsey was obsessed with the thought that everyone was trying to steal his data. Masters admits to a mild case of paranoia himself. "You have to get a little sick in the head to try to figure out what somebody who is really sick in the head will do to break out our security. It isn't pleasant to continually worry about what some goon is up to."

Those who have criticized Masters and Johnson for their work have found them unwilling to defend themselves. "Continued research and publication of findings is our response; we can't take time to strike back at our detractors," says Masters doggedly. Over the dinner at Gini Johnson's, they loosen up and let go with a barb or two. They fault Leslie Farber—whose article "I'm Sorry Dear" in a 1964 issue of *Commentary* condemned their approach as mechanistic —for writing from hearsay two years before *Human Sexual Response* appeared. That book was written eighteen months earlier than planned because questions that the Farber article posed within the professional community could be answered with nothing short of the entire report.

In answer to Rollo May, who says, "They put the emphasis on orgasm when it should be on love. They help some couples, and I congratulate them for that, but their total impact on society is to send us further down the road of misunderstanding ourselves and our need to love one another," they have but a short reply. Smiling serenely, Gini Johnson says, "Dr. May has the corner on the love market and we couldn't presume to know anything about it." Masters adds, "If our job were only to reorient people sexually, we could do that in a long weekend. We *are* treating the whole marriage, and we start with the most intimate and necessary of all communications."

Late in the evening, after weaving its way through Victorian hangups, the difficulties the children of Masters and Johnson have had to face ("I don't want you hanging around with that Masters girl; her father's a sex maniac," one mother told her daughter), the conversation moves to an odd subject: why Masters and Johnson consider *Playboy* a good outlet for sex information. "There are millions of men reading it, eighteen to twenty-eight years old, who parade as knowledgeable about sex but who have the same old misconceptions about mutual orgasms being a necessity and penis size being important," says Gini Johnson. "Men read the magazine predisposed to reading about sex, and we want them to have good information." Masters and Johnson serve as consultants to the magazine, and when sex questions are asked in the Playboy Advisor, they edit the answers. After Hugh Hefner learned of their work, and his editor in the behavioral sciences, Nat Lehrman, did a penetrating interview with them, Hefner's foundation donated $25,000 and continues to donate annually.

Still later in the evening, just before Bill Masters is ready to drive back into St. Louis, his partner muses. Lately she has found she is getting forgetful, absentminded, and one day panicked when she thought she had left office records in her convertible and returned to find the car empty. The records were sitting on a table at home where she had left them. "I have always valued my sense of color, of being able to put furnishings, clothes together and making them look good. But all the years of seclusion. I was in a store the other day, and I had to walk out—I couldn't make a choice of colors; I really couldn't *see* the colors."

In his Chevrolet Nova (bottom of the line, no radio) a half hour later, Bill Masters, still in his blue terry cloth après-pool slacks, is speeding along a highway. Blocks of light form slowly on his face, expand quickly, then disappear as cars approach and pass. His sentences are short and punctuated by long silences. "Of course, it is great to finally see results. . . . People don't know that with ninety hours of work each week there's not time for anything else. . . . Biologically I guess I'm eighty. . . . But I don't really know. . . . I don't really know if I'd do the whole thing over again or not."

31. What Kids Still Don't Know about Sex
Thomas and Alice Fleming

"...marriages in which the bride is already pregnant have the poorest survival rate...."

An increase in the frequency of premarital sexual relations increases the probability of unwanted pregnancies. Effective contraception is a method of avoiding this, but there are a number of problems complicating their use. The Flemings discuss some of the issues surrounding contraception and illegitimacy.

Young Americans—more than two million of them a year—get in serious trouble because they do not know or will not face one of life's fundamental facts, that sexual intercourse causes babies.

Over the last five years, there has been an explosion of illegitimate pregnancy among young people. In Portland, Ore., Dr. Harold Osterud, chairman of the Department of Public Health and Preventive Medicine at the University of

Oregon Medical School, reports that one out of every 12 babies born in that state is illegitimate. (In 1950, it was one out of 53; in 1960, it was one out of 30.) More than half these unwed mothers are teen-agers, and 20- to 24-year-olds are the next largest group.

New York state's illegitimate births have quadrupled since 1946. Nationwide, the Department of Health, Education, and Welfare reports, these personal disasters have topped 300,000 a year. A shocking 245,983 of these births are from mothers between the ages of 15 and 24. With the number of young adults in the population rising steadily, government experts are already predicting that by 1980, our annual deluge of unwanted babies will hit 400,000.

Then there are the unknown, but undoubtedly huge, numbers of young people who get abortions each year. (One estimate of total abortions in the United States puts the figure at a million.) A doctor on the staff of a major Eastern-university hospital told us matter-of-factly: "If you want to get an abortion in this country today, consult a college girl. She knows more about where to go than anyone else, including doctors."

A study in California reports that one out of every two teen-age girls married there is already pregnant. At that rate, more than 200,000 of these hasty and insecure marriages take place in the country each year.

When you add up these figures—not forgetting that young men as well as women go through mental and emotional agonies when they are involved in out-of-wedlock pregnancies—the estimated yearly toll of two million disturbed, unhappy, guilt-ridden young people becomes a conservative figure.

There are also a million Americans between 15 and 24 suffering from gonorrhea, which has been increasing at the alarming rate of 20 percent a year. But the illegitimacy epidemic is the least known, least discussed and most arresting fact about a generation that claims to be leading a sexual revolution in America—and in the world. Obviously, the first and most fundamental question is, why?

The answers that emerge from discussions with psychiatrists, gynecologists and social workers point up wide gaps in young people's knowledge about their sexual motives and even about the facts of reproduction. They also present a major moral challenge to older Americans. Parents cannot continue to sit back and haphazardly tell themselves "the kids know more about sex than we do." They can no longer assume that because pornography is sold openly, and I Am Curious (Yellow) and (Blue) play to capacity crowds, their children automatically know how to handle the new atmosphere of sexual freedom.

Perhaps the most surprising revelation is the amount of sheer sexual ignorance that still exists in this supposedly swinging, aware generation. Alan Wachtel, a medical student at New York's Mount Sinai Hospital, surveyed coeds at Oberlin College, Ohio, a school that draws most of its students from middle- and upper-middle-class homes. He found almost 40 percent of the unmarried girls had had sexual intercourse. More than half of them reported they had not used any birth-control method whatsoever. Even the girls who did attempt to use some form of contraception generally relied on techniques that had extremely high failure rates, such as foam, the rhythm method or the male condom. Seven percent of the girls had become pregnant, almost three percent during the use of one of the high-failure nonprescription methods of birth control.

Among the low-income members of the younger generation, knowledge of contraception is abysmal. A survey of unmarried pregnant teen-agers at Sinai Hospital in Baltimore found that 25 percent of the girls had not even thought about the possibility that they might become pregnant from having sexual intercourse. Only 30 percent of the girls used *any* form of birth control regularly. Among the answers to the surveyors' questions were such mournful comments as this one: "I thought you could only get birth control after you were married or had your first child."

The answer is not simply better education. Improved sex education is needed in our schools, but there is equally strong evidence that parents need to understand the powerful emotional factors preventing too many young people from using the theoretical knowledge about sex that they already possess.

Among some, there is a deep-seated fear of the simplest and most effective contraceptive, the pill. The rash of magazine and newspaper articles in recent years warning of the pill's sometimes dangerous side effects has made a strong impression on teen-agers, already suspicious of many aspects of the adult world. In the Baltimore survey of unwed teen-age mothers, 40 percent of the girls agreed with the statement: "The kind of birth control that a woman has to put inside of herself makes me feel a little sick." Another 30 percent were undecided.

A far larger group of young people do not use contraception because they feel it is "unromantic." Mrs. Mazy O. Yurdin, director of the New York consultation center of the National Council on Illegitimacy, says: "Let's face it, every form of contraception that the woman can control—and this is the only reliable kind—involves a good deal of deliberate planning. Even the pill has to be taken on a systematic schedule. A diaphragm can only be obtained by consulting a physician and must be inserted in the vagina in advance of the time when intercourse takes place. Too many young people simply don't want to admit to themselves that they are prepared in advance to have intercourse outside marriage. They feel less guilty about doing it—and they call it more romantic—if it takes place in an impromptu manner."

The Rev. Ronald Mazur, former chaplain of Salem State College in Massachusetts and the author of the book *Commonsense Sex*, condemns this tendency. "There exist widespread ideas among young people," he says, "that contraceptives are unromantic and that premeditation ruins sex. Other false notions also prevail: to have sex without safeguards is more pleasant; to plan beforehand is dirty."

A smaller minority of the young are philosophically hostile to contraceptives. This attitude is particularly prevalent among those who have been influenced by the hippie philosophy, with its emphasis on doing things naturally. But a far larger number of young people are driven by emotions that most of them do not understand. Dr. Philip M. Sarrel, a gynecologist at the Yale University School of Medicine, who runs a special clinic for pregnant teen-agers and has lectured on sex at a number of New England women's colleges, says. "Getting pregnant and having a baby are not the same thing in the minds of a tremendous number of young women. The desire to get pregnant is often an unconscious need which a girl may feel impelled to fulfill. So she neglects contraceptive precautions."

What are some of her unconscious motives? Dr. Ruth Lidz, a psychiatrist who works with Dr. Sarrel, says a very common one is guilt. "The girl may want to punish herself for having intercourse outside marriage. Equally common is a poor relationship with her mother. She wants to simultaneously prove that she is the equal of the mother, by becoming pregnant, and punish her by becoming pregnant out of wedlock."

Young people freely admit that some of these hang-ups exist among their generation and may partially explain the illegitimate-pregnancy epidemic. But they point to another factor—the unavailability of the means of contraception—especially the pill—for unmarried young people who want to use it. Stephanie Mills, who graduated last year from Mills College in California, says: "I am so angry about this, I would like to lead a crusade to make the pill available on every college campus in the nation."

Dr. Louis Barbato, director of health services at the University of Denver, conducted a survey of the nation's campuses in 1966 to find out if college health services were prescribing the pill to coeds. He found that 92 percent of the schools refused to give the pill to unmarried girls for contraceptive purposes. Since that time, a number of schools have altered this policy. The University of California's Berkeley campus, a special object of Stephanie Mills' wrath, has opened a birth-control clinic at the University's Cowell Hospital. Stanford, Michigan, Illinois, Chicago, Washington and Minnesota are among the big-name schools that are offering a similar service to both married and unmarried coeds.

At Yale University, which admitted coeds for the first time last year, there has been no statement of policy. But doctors who are part of the college health service treat students as private patients. If the individual doctor's moral code permits him to prescribe a contraceptive for an unmarried student, he is free to do so. Dr. Sarrel and his wife, Lorna, a psychiatric social worker, have been operating a sexual-counseling service at Yale since last fall. They are booked a month in advance.

The American College Health Association, for whom Dr. Barbato is completing another study on the same subject, says it expects a "significant" increase in the number of schools that have relaxed their rules on contraception. But many schools are still taking a very firm stand. Typical is the University of Pennsylvania's Health Center, which requires parental consent before it dispenses the pill or any other birth-control device to girls under 21. Dr. Paul Trickett, director of the University of Texas Health Service, doesn't think "any state university has a right to set up a policy that could be interpreted to encourage premarital or extramarital relations." At Denver, Dr. Barbato refers girls who seek contraceptive help to private physicians in the area.

Dr. Beatrix Hamburg, a psychiatrist at the Stanford University School of Medicine, thinks that "in effect, students who are urging free availability of the pill at university health services are also asking for implied administrative endorsement of the new morality. Universities are diverse. Some students are ready for sexual experimentation. Others are not. No policy should be adopted that would put undue social pressure on students to engage in behavior for which they are emotionally unprepared." Dr. Avram Goldstein, professor of pharmacology at the same school, thinks the pill should be available: "If an unmarried girl has established a sexual relationship and seeks contraceptive information, she is not asking for advice about morality, she is asking for medical help."

Even more controversial is the question of making contraceptive help available to teen-agers under 18. A debate is going on in both the legal and the medical professions. The general counsel of the University of California has warned that any physician who prescribes contraceptives for a minor without the parents' consent is open to court action for committing a "battery" against the teen-ager, who is, in the eyes of the law, still a child. But Harriet F. Pilpel, counsel to Planned Parenthood of New York City, argues that the legal climate has changed drastically on the subject of birth control in the last three years, and where the minor is "emancipated" or is a "mature minor" managing his own affairs, the law in most states now would seem to give him the power to consent to medical treatment and care.

For the last two years, Planned Parenthood in San Francisco has been running a clinic that gives contraceptive help to teen-agers under 18. A similar program is operating in Baltimore, and since last fall, in New York City. Quigg Newton, president of the Commonwealth Fund, which gave $145,700 to Planned Parenthood to start the program in New York, said the goal was to reach those young people "most vulnerable to unwanted pregnancy and therefore the group most urgently in need of help." The success of these programs—particularly in New York where over 1,500 largely ghetto youngsters have been counseled in the last nine months—has inspired Planned Parenthood to prepare a statement calling on the nation's doctors to give responsible minors contraceptive assistance. New laws in several states, notably California, Illinois and New Jersey, have given minors the right to receive medical treatment, which would include birth-control help, without the consent of their parents.

But doctors are no more in agreement on the wisdom of this policy than they are about giving contraceptives to college students. Dr. Daniel G. Morton, until recently chairman of the Department of Obstetrics and Gynecology at the University of California, says flatly: "I am opposed to offering birth-control information to unmarried adolescent girls under 18 years, in most circumstances."

There are, then, no clear-cut directions to be gotten from the experts. Perhaps the best—even the only solution—comes from New York psychiatrist Dr. Max Levin: "Girls should be taught the value of premarital chastity as the ideal to follow." But Dr. Levin also believes that girls should have contraceptive instruction. Refusing this kind of information to a young person, he feels, is tantamount to saying, "I don't trust you." Nothing is more likely to break down communication between the generations, and there is often a direct psychological link between this breakdown and the promiscuity that leads to an unwanted pregnancy. But Dr. Levin insists that both contraceptive instruction and instilling the ideal of chastity should be "primarily the responsibility of parents."

Both the younger and the older generations need to take a more profound look at sexual experience in our time. Young people must face up to this fact: sexual intercourse is an act of deep significance, which always carries with it the potentiality of bringing another human being into this world, for whom they must be responsible. To tell themselves this can be ignored at any time is proof positive of immaturity or a serious emotional problem. To paper it over with the romantic idea that if pregnancy comes marriage cannot be far behind, is equally foolish. Mazy O. Yurdin of the National Council on Illegitimacy has pointed out that marriages in which the bride is already pregnant have the poorest survival rate in America.

But if young people need to achieve a greater maturity about sex, the older generation must match this maturity with an awareness that the prohibitory approach of traditional morality may be contributing to our tragic annual toll of illegitimacy. Garrett Hardin, professor of biology at the University of California and a noted exponent of abortion reform, says that parents who place total stress on the value of virginity are taking an all-or-nothing gamble. "It is good girls who get pregnant," he says. "Genuinely promiscuous girls know better."

At the same time, parents are not being called upon to endorse wholesale promiscuity for their children. Perhaps the most encouraging fact about the sexual habits of the younger generation is the almost total lack of promiscuity among college-age people. The vast percentage of these unwanted pregnancies arise from long-term, deeply sincere relationships, in which sex becomes an expression of genuine affection.

Should parents act as if this physical expression of love is never going to happen, or frankly discuss the possibility in advance? If a young couple insist on the right to choose their own code of sexual morality, there is an honest answer suggested by Dr. Mary Calderone, executive director of SIECUS (Sex Information and Education Council of the United States). "Here are the risks involved," Dr. Calderone tells them. "You're going to run them anyway? All right. I'm going to cut your risks. I'm going to help you at least to avoid pregnancy. But in return for this, I ask you not to marry unless you're solidly ready to assume that responsibility. Finish your education before you decide. Don't be promiscuous. Behave as responsibly as if you were married. If you do marry, don't have a pregnancy until you're ready to assume full responsibility for earning your living."

Dr. Calderone believes that parents and physicians must offer equally strong and frank support to young people who are being blackmailed by social pressure into sexual experiences many of them don't really want. One teen-ager asked her, almost desperately, "What can I do about my steady? He won't talk or think about anything but sex, and he keeps wanting to go all the way." Dr. Calderone replied: "Tell him whatever is true for you—that you couldn't bear to disappoint your mother, that your religious convictions won't permit it, that you don't feel the long-term risks are worth the short-term pleasures, or whatever you really feel. Ten to one he'll respect you for it."

It seems to us that such frank talk is infinitely preferable to the disconsolate words of a college girl in Chicago, describing her reaction to the discovery that she was pregnant. "Outwardly, I was calm—I went to my doctor and had a pregnancy test, and I told my boyfriend and my roommate and made lots of jokes about it. Inside, I was sick. I felt I had lost everything I ever wanted."

It is time—and past time—that we established between the generations honest communication about the facts of life—and love.

32. New Styles in Homosexual Manliness
Laud Humphreys

"As with Coca-Cola, things go better with sex."

There is a tendency to view homosexuals as a stereotyped group of highly recognizable men. Humphreys describes the various types of men who engage in homosexual activity. It may be interesting to think of some of the heterosexual parallels for the patterns of relationships that are described.

Near the heart of a metropolis on the eastern seaboard, there is a historic park where homosexuals have been cruising for at least a hundred years. As an aging man told me:

> Back around 1930, when I was a very young man, I had sex with a really old fellow who was nearly 80. He told me that when he was a youngster—around the end of the Civil War—he would make spending money by hustling in that very park. Wealthy men would come down from the Hill in their carriages to pick up boys who waited in the shadows of the tree-lined walks at night.

In our motorized age, I have observed car drivers circling this park and adjoining residential blocks for the same sexual purposes. On a Friday night, unless the weather is bitter cold, a solid line of cars moves slowly along the one-way streets of this area, bumper to bumper, from 9:00 P.M. until 5:00 in the morning. The drivers pause in their rounds only long enough to exchange a few words with a young man on the sidewalk or to admit a willing passenger. There is no need to name this park. A knowledgeable person can find such pickup activity, both homosexual and heterosexual, in every major city of the Western world.

Cruising for "one-night-stands" is a major feature of the market economy in sex. In *The Wealth of Nations* Adam Smith postulated the ideal form of human relationship as being specific, depersonalized, short-term and contractual. This capitalist ideal is realized in the sex exchange of the homosexual underworld perhaps more fully than in any other social group, and the cruising scene of the gay world may continue for another hundred years or more. There are indications, however, that in the affluent, highly industrialized centers of our civilization the popularity of this sort of activity is declining. No one, of course, could make an up-to-date count of all the participants in even a single segment of the sexual market, and no base is available from which to estimate variations in such activity over time. One can only depend on careful observers of the scene, chief among whom are the participants themselves. I can report, then, what respondents tell me, checking their observations against my own of the past six years.

Decline of Cruising

Even with this limited source of data, it is still possible to discern a trend away from the traditional cruising for pickups as the major activity of the homosexual market. Men still make sexual contracts with other men along the curbstones of our cities and in the shadowy places of public parks, but at least three social factors are acting to alter and curtail those operations and to increase the popularity of other forms of sexual exchange .

The most obvious factor affecting the cruising scene along this nation's roadways is perhaps the least important: the matter of crime in the streets. As a criminologist, I am yet to be convinced that the streets are actually less safe than they were 10, 30 or 100 years ago. American streets have been the scenes of assaults and robberies for generations. Slums expand into certain areas, making some streets more dangerous than they were; but slums also contract, leaving once dangerous streets more safe. I doubt, however, that it is any more dangerous to pick up a hitchhiker in 1970 than it was in 1940.

Moreover, anyone seeking deviant sex is engaged in a risky activity, and usually knows it. Indeed, risk in the pursuit of sex simply increases the appeal of the homosexual markets for millions of American men. The chances they take add an element of adventure to the gaming encounters and, for many participants, serve as an aphrodisiac. In fact, of course, most of the moral risk— and much of the physical danger—encountered by homosexuals comes from vice squad operations. The mugger is no more to be feared than the violent policeman. When I interviewed him, the man I quoted above was still recuperating from a severe beating at the hands of a patrolman. Two years ago, an active member of the homophile movement was shot to death by a vice squad detective in a Berkeley, California, park. But such attacks by police and youthful toughs are nothing new in homosexual marketplaces.

Nevertheless, crime in the streets is of importance in curtailing homosexual cruising, if only because it is perceived and publicized as being on the increase. It thus becomes more an excuse than a deterrent. Since the man who cruises for sex has always been vulnerable to such victimization, that alone does not serve as a major factor in his decision to switch to another form of sexual exchange. But, if he is driven by other social forces to a new market place, he may use the widely perceived threat of violence as an excuse for changing.

Another factor in contemporary society that does effectively turn men away from this sort of sexual liaison is the growing scarcity of time. To cruise for sex requires leisure. The successful cruiser must have plenty of time to devote to his favorite sport. As with fishing, one dare not be hurried. It takes a great deal of time to size up a trick, to convince him that you are a legitimate score, for both parties to signal their intentions and to effect a contract. More time is required to find a safe locale for the sexual act—an out-of-the-way place to park, an apartment or hotel room, a *pied-a-terre* maintained for this purpose. For cruising, expressways and fast cars are scarcely more advantageous than cobblestone streets and carriages; in this as in so many things, technological advance represents no gain because it has not been accompanied by increased leisure. The plague of anomie, caused by a people with too much time on its hands, has yet to descend on us.

The Swedish economist Staffan B. Linder discusses the actual fate of *The Harried Leisure Class*:

> We had always expected one of the beneficient results of economic afflu- ence to be a tranquil and harmonious manner of life, a life in Arcadia. What has happened is the exact opposite. The pace is quickening, and our lives in fact are becoming steadily more hectic.

The clock on the cover of a paperback edition of Thorstein Veblen's *The Theory of Leisure Class* has no hands. But Veblen was careful to point out that he used the term "leisure" not to "connote indolence of quiscence. What it con- notes is non-productive consumption of time." As Veblen indicated, it is con- sumption, not production, that is inefficient and time wasting. Indeed, so much time is consumed in our society, Linder says, that there is an increasing scarcity of it. The upper stratum of society that Veblen defined as the Lesiure Class at the end of the nineteenth century must now be defined as the Jet Set: "Super- ficial people in the rich countries [who] are often in a greater hurry than anyone else. They are enormously busy, even if it is sometimes difficult to see with what."

There was a time when a man of means could dally with a maid in a Vic- torian attic room or spend a leisurely afternoon with his mistress. He could afford to cruise for a pickup or manage a tryst in some sylvan glade. As Linder states, "To court and love someone in a satisfactory manner is a game with many and time-consuming phases." The pleasures of the bed are declining, he continues, in three ways: "Affairs, which by their very nature occupy a great deal of time, become less attractive; the time spent on each occasion of love- making is being reduced; the total number of sexual encounters is declining."

Among the evidence that tends to support Linder's hypotheses is that gathered in a recent study of the sexual behavior of Frenchmen. Jacques Baroche notes that the fabled Gallic lover is leaving his mistress and turning to the fleeting sex act. One man interviewed in the research states that "only one thing counts in love—it is the brief encounter."

Impersonalization

Cruising operations may have led to the ideal type of relationship for a laissez faire capitalist of a century ago, but the market economy has since pro- duced social factors necessitating transformation of its own sexual adjunct. It is no longer sufficient for human relationships to be depersonalized, short-term and contractual, such as that which might be expected to result from a pickup on the streets. In the sexual sphere, at least, relationships must now be utterly impersonal, highly expedient, fleeting in nature. The capitalist criteria have become more demanding.

In my study of the impersonal sex that occurs in public rest rooms, *Tea- room Trade*, I wrote:

What the covert deviant needs is a sexual machine—collapsible to hip-pocket size, silent in operation—plus the excitement of a risk-taking encounter. In tearoom sex he has the closest thing to such a device. This encounter functions, for the sex market, as does the automat for the culinary, providing a low-cost, impersonal, democratic means of commodity distribution.

The sexual encounter in the tearoom constitutes the epitome of libidinal enterprise for the contemporary, consuming society. An old man on the toilet stool, serving as habitual insertee in fellatio with a succession of commuters, could better meet the standards of Madison Avenue only if he were an antiseptic machine with a coin slot in his forehead and stereo speakers for ears.

Approaching the phenomena of impersonal sex from a psychoanalytic standpoint rather than a socioeconomic one, Rollo May says in "Love and Will:" "The Victorian person sought to have love without falling into sex; the modern person seeks to have sex without falling into love." My objection to May's analysis (other than his apparent ignorance of Steven Marcus' "Other Victorians") is its implication that modern man knows what he seeks. We pursue what we have been conditioned to seek, what is expedient for members of the consuming society. We are subject to the subliminal suggestion that love and sex are essentially indistinguishable and any distinctions irrelevant. As with Coca-Cola, things go better with sex.

The increasing scarcity of time has differing effects upon the various segments of American society. As Linder suggests, some men simply find it more expedient to take their sex at home. Millions of others, however, limited or lacking in the conjugal exchange of goods and services, are turning to market places of impersonal sex, such as the tearooms. For instance, my data indicate that Roman Catholic religious affiliation is a causal factor in tearoom participation, because that church's prohibition of the use of artificial contraceptives limits the sexual outlet in marriage. Of the married men in my sample of tearoom participants, 50 percent are Roman Catholic or married to a Roman Catholic, as compared to 26 percent of married men in the control sample. For some single men, primarily those with higher educational levels, masturbation provides a sufficiently expedient sexual outlet. Others must turn to impersonal sexual exchanges to meet these needs.

The overall effect is the increasing impersonalization of the sexual markets. Prostitutes are now offering five-minute "blow jobs" in the parking garages of major cities, while the free service of tearooms increases in popularity. As more "straight" men, those lacking in homosexual identity and self-image, turn to impersonal sexual outlets provided by the gay world, others who seek homosexual relationships find the tearooms more rewarding than cruising the streets. America's sexual answer to the increasing scarcity of time, tearoom activity, seems to counter Linder's prediction that "the total number of sexual encounters is declining." Perhaps Sweden is lacking in such facilities.

Virilization

If the scarcity of time in our society were the only factor influencing homosexual market operations, why aren't all men with homosexual interests crowding into the nation's public toilets to satisfy their growing demand for what can be found there? There is, however, another social factor acting upon the gay world to produce a countertendency. The cruising scene, so familiar to those interested in the homosexual subculture, is yielding to attacks from two sides: it is not sufficiently impersonal and expedient for some, and too much so for others. Sexual exchanges in the gay underworld are experiencing a polarization, torn between a growing impersonalization on the one hand and increasing virilization on the other.

By virilization, I refer to the increasingly masculine image of the gay scene. Few gay bars are now distinguished by the presence of limp wrists and falsetto voices. Increasingly, these centers for the homosexual subculture are indistinguishable from other hangouts for youths of college age. Girls are now common among the patrons in gay bars. Beards, leather vests, letter jackets and boots have their place alongside the more traditional blue jeans and T-shirts. If any style predominates, it is that of the turned-on, hip generation.

As Tom Burke pointed out in *Esquire* a year ago, just when the public seemed ready to accept the sort of homosexual portrayal in *The Boys in the Band* that life style began to fade away: "That the public's information vis-a-vis the new deviate is now hopelessly outdated is not the public's fault. It cannot examine him on its own because, from a polite distance, he is indistinguishable from the heterosexual hippie." Although this "new homosexuality" is increasingly evident on both coasts, as well as on campuses across the country, it is just beginning to appear in the gay bars and coffeehouses of Denver, Omaha and St. Louis. The hip, masculine image for homosexuals is not yet as universal, the transformation not so dramatic, as Burke would have us believe. "The majority of contemporary homosexuals under forty," he claims, "are confirmed potheads and at least occasional acid-trippers." Such a statement makes good copy, but there is no evidence for it. My sample of tearoom participants included fewer drug users than the control samples indicates are in the nondeviant population. But my research subjects were, by definition, only those who seek the impersonal sex of tearooms. My current research in the homosexual ecology of a sample of cities throughout the nation indicates a far higher proportion of pot smokers, perhaps 20 percent, among the population who engage in homosexual activity than I encountered during my field research six years ago. Clearly, the youth counterculture with its attendant styles of dress and drug use has spawned a young, virile set to coexist with the effete martini sippers of the traditional gay world.

The new emphasis in the homosexual subculture, then, is upon virility: not the hypermasculinity of Muscle Beach and the motorcycle set, for these are part of the old gay world's parody on heterosexuality, but the youthful masculinity of bare chests and beads, long hair, mustaches and hip-hugging pants. The new generation in gay society is more apt to sleep with a girl than to mock her speech or mannerisms. Many of these young men (along with the older ones who imitate their style) frown upon an exclusive orientation to homosexual or heterosexual activity. The ideal is to be a "swinger," sensitive to ambisexual pleasures, capable of turning on sexually with both men and women.

In a crowded gay bar in Boston I recently watched this new facet of the subculture in action. Neither the young men nor the girls scattered throughout the room were at all distinguishable from any other college-age group in the taverns of that city. There were fewer women, to be sure, but the dress, appearance and conversations were typical of any campus quadrangle. A handsome youth in a denim jacket and pants introduced an attractive young girl to a group standing at the bar as his fiancee. One man remarked, with a grin, that he was jealous. The young man, whom I shall call Jack, placed an arm around the shoulders of his fiancee, and, pulling her head toward his, explained: "Tom here is an old lover of mine." "Aren't we all!" another member of the party added, upon which all within earshot laughed.

After the bar closed, I was invited, along with the young couple, to join a number of patrons for "some group action" in a nearby apartment. A rather common, two-room pad with little furniture but many pillows and posters, the apartment was illuminated by only a single lightbulb suspended from the kitchen ceiling. Once our eyes had adjusted to the darkness of the other room, we could see about a dozen men, stretched in a number of stages of undress and sexual activity over the mattress and floor at the far end of the room. Excusing himself, Jack joined the orgy. In a few minutes, I could discern that he was necking with one man while being fellated by another.

Having explained my research purposes on the way to the apartment, I sought to explore the girl's reactions to her lover's apparent infidelity. I asked whether it bothered her. "Does it arouse me sexually, do you mean?" she replied. "No. Like, does Jack's behavior upset you?" With a laugh, she answered, "No, not at all. Like, I love Jack for what he is. You know, like, he swings both ways. If that's his thing, I groove on it. He could have left me home, you know— that's what some guys do. They leave their chicks home and, like, feed them a lot of shit so they can slip out and get their kicks. One of the things I dig most about Jack is that he shares everything with me. Having secrets just leads to hangups." "But don't you feel even a bit jealous?" I probed. "Like, wouldn't you rather be making love to him than standing here rapping with me?" "Why should I?" she said. "Like, Jack and I'll go home and ball after this is over. He's a beautiful person. Being able to share himself with so many different people makes him more beautiful!"

Later, Jack and his fiancee left those of us who were bound for an all-night restaurant. Arm in arm, they headed for the subway and a pad in Cambridge. Their story, I think, is an accurate reflection of the morality of the youth counterculture, both in its easy acceptance of a variety of sexual expressions and its nondefensive trust that the deeper, personal relationships are the more important ones.

Subcultural Diversity

Like the scarcity of time, such norms of the counterculture have differing effects upon the sexual markets and life styles of the gay world, depending upon the permeability of various segments of the homosexual society. In order to outline and gauge these changes, it is necessary to construct a taxonomy of the homosexual community. Once we are able to consider its diverse segments in relation to each other, we can compare their reactions to some of the forces of contemporary society.

In my study of tearoom sex, I delineated four basic types of participants in these impersonal encounters: trade, ambisexuals, the gay and closet queens.

These men are differentiated most clearly by the relative autonomy afforded them by their marital and occupational statuses. When one engages in sexual behavior against which the society has erected strong negative sanctions, his resources for control of information carry a determining relationship to his life style, as well as to his self-image and the adaptations he makes to his own discreditable behavior. An example of this principle of classification would be that married men who are bound hand and foot to their jobs have more to fear—and less to enjoy—from their clandestine encounters because they have relatively fewer means of countering exposure than men of greater autonomy.

I have chosen the word "trade" from the argot of the homosexual community because it best describes that largest class of my respondents, the married men with little occupational autonomy. In its most inclusive sense in the gay vocabulary, this term refers to all men, married or single, who think they are heterosexual but who will take the insertor role in homosexual acts. Except for hustlers, who will be discussed later, most of these men are married. As participants in homosexual activity, they are nonsubcultural, lacking both the sources of information and the rationalization for their behavior that the gay circles provide. Generally, the trade are of lower-middle or upper-lower socioeconomic status. They are machinists, truck drivers, teachers, sales and clerical workers, invariably masculine in appearance, mannerisms and self-image. Single men, I have found, are generally less stable in sexual identification. Once they begin to participate in homosexual relations, therefore, their straight self-image is threatened, and they tend to drift into the less heterosexual world of the closet queens or gay bar crowd. Apart from an exclusive concern with tearoom operations, however, I think it preferable to allow for the inclusion of some single men in the trade classification.

Moving into the upper strata of society, it is difficult to find participants in homosexual activity who think of themselves as strictly heterosexual. Americans with the higher educational level of the upper-middle and upper classes tend to find literary justification for their ventures into deviant sexual activity. The greater occupational autonomy of these men enables them to join in friendship networks with others who share their sexual interests. If these men are married, they tend to define themselves as "ambisexual," identifying with a distinguished company of men (Alexander the Great, Julius Caesar, Shakespeare, Walt Whitman and a number of movie stars) who are said to have enjoyed the pleasures of both sexual worlds. In this classification are to be found business executives, salesmen with little direct supervision, doctors, lawyers and interior decorators.

College students join with artists, the self-employed and a few professional men to constitute the more autonomous, unmarried segment of the gay society. These men share enough resources for information control that they are unafraid to be active in the more visible portions of the homosexual subculture. In the tearoom study, I refer to them as "the gay," because they are the most clearly definable, in the sociological sense, as being homosexual. They are apt to have been labeled as such by their friends, associates and even families. Their self-identification is strongly homosexual. Because their subcultural life centers in the gay bars, coffeehouses and baths of the community, I will refer to them here as the "gay bar crowd."

The fourth type identified in my previous research are the "closet queens." In the homosexual argot this term has meanings with varying degrees of specificity. Occasionally, trade who fear their own homosexual tendencies are called closet queens. Again, the term may be used in referring to those in the subculture who feel that they are too good or proper to patronize the gay bars. In its most general sense, however, it is employed to designate those men who know they are gay but fear involvement in the more overt, bar-centered activities of the homosexual world. Because they avoid overt participation in the subculture, the married ambisexuals often receive the closet queen label from the gay bar crowd. I should like to maintain the distinctions I have outlined between ambisexuals and closet queens, however, because of the contrasting marital and socioeconomic statuses of the two groups. As I employ the term in my tearoom typology, the closet queens are unmarried teachers, clerks, salesmen and factory workers. Living in fear that their deviance might be discovered, they tend to patterns of self-hatred, social isolation and lone-wolf sexual forays.

There is a fifth type of man who is seldom found in tearooms, where money does not change hands, but who plays an important role in the homosexual markets. I mean the hustlers, homosexual prostitutes who operate from the streets, theaters and certain bars, coffeehouses and restaurants of the urban centers. The majority of these "midnight cowboys" share a heterosexual self-image. Indeed, since relatively few of them make a living from sexual activity, there is strong evidence that, for most hustlers, the exchange of money functions more to neutralize the societal norms, to justify the deviant sexual behavior, than to meet economic needs.

My observations suggest that there are at least three subdivisions among male prostitutes. One large, relatively amorphous group might properly be called "pseudo-hustlers." For them the amount of money received holds little importance, a pack of cigarettes or a handful of change sufficing to justify their involvement in the forbidden behavior, which is what they really wanted. Another large number of young men would be called "semiprofessionals." This type includes members of delinquent peer groups who hustle for money and thrills. Unlike the pseudo-hustlers, these young men receive support and training from other members of the hustling subculture. They are apt to frequent a particular set of bars and coffeehouses where a strict code of hustling standards is adhered to. Although a minority of these boys rely upon their earnings for support, the majority gain from their hustling only enough to supplement allowances, using their take to finance autos and heterosexual dates.

New to the sexual markets are the "call boys." Advertising in the underground papers of such cities as Los Angeles, San Francisco and New York as "models," these young men charge an average fee of $100 for a night or $25 an hour. I have seen a catalogue distributed by one agency for such hustlers that provides frontal nude, full-page photographs of the "models," complete with telephone numbers. In general, the call boys share a gay or ambisexual identity and take pride in their professional status. The appearance of these handsome, masculine youngsters on the gay scene is an important manifestation of the virilization of the homosexual market.

These five, basic types constitute the personnel of the gay world. The hustlers and trade, few of whom think of themselves as homosexual, are the straight world's contribution to the gay scene. Without their participation, the sex exchanges would atrophy, becoming stale and ingrown. The ambisexual enjoys the benefits of his status, with a well-shod foot firmly planted in each sexual world. He need not be as covert as either the closet queen or trade and, when out of town on a business trip, may become very overt indeed. The open, visible members of the homosexual community are the hustlers and those I have called, for the purposes of this taxonomy, the gay bar crowd. With this classification in mind, it is possible to see how the contemporary social forces are diffused and filtered through interaction with each class of persons in the gay community.

Polarization of Market Activity

As the growing scarcity of time drives an increasing number of American males from every walk of life into one-night-stand sexuality, the impersonalized sex exchange thrives. Rest stops along the expressways, older tearooms in transportation terminals, subways, parks and public buildings—all enjoy popularity as trysting places for "instant sex." The more expedient an encounter's structure and the greater the variety of participants, as is the case with tearoom sex, the less attractive are the time-demanding liaisons of the cruising grounds.

The trade and closet queens, in particular, find their needs met in the impersonal sex market of our consuming society. Here they can find sex without commitment, an activity sufficiently swift to fit into the lunch hour or a brief stop on the way home from work. The ambisexuals—many of them harried business executives—prefer the tea-rooms, not only for the speed and anonymity they offer, but also for the kicks they add to the daily routine.

Covert members of the gay society provide impetus to the impersonalization of the homosexual market. My study of tearoom participants revealed that trade, closet queens and ambisexuals share highly conservative social and political views, surrounding themselves with an aura or respectability that I call the breastplate of righteousness. In life style, they epitomize the consuming man of the affluent society. In tearooms, they fill the role of sexual consumers, exchanging goods and services in every spare moment they can wring from the demands of computerized offices and automated homes. At the same time, however, their conservatism makes them nearly impervious to the pressures of the youth counterculture.

On the overt side of the gay world, the virile influence of hip culture is having profound effects. Already poorly represented in the tearoom scene, the gay bar crowd is preconditioned to embrace some of the stronger norms of the flower people. At least in word, if not always in deed, these overt leaders of the gay community espouse the deeper, more personal type of relationship. Theirs is a search for lovers, for men with whom they may build abiding relationships. Moreover, like hippies, these men flaunt some of the more sacrosanct mores of the straight society. With the hustlers, they share a sense of being an oppressed minority. On the whole, they are happy to discard the effeminate mannerisms and vocabulary of low camp in return for the influx of the new blood, the turned-on generation.

Arrival of the new bold masculinity on the gay bar scene has made the bars more suitable for hustlers of drinking age. As recently as 1967, I have seen hustlers ejected from a midwestern bar that now plays host to many of them. In those days, they were too easily identified by their rough, masculine appearance that contrasted with the neat effeminacy of the other customers. On both coasts, and increasingly in other parts of the country, bars and coffeehouses are now replacing the streets as sexual markets for hustlers and their scores.

One might surmise that the meeting of hustlers and the gay bar crowd in the same branch of the sexual market would signify a countertendency to what I see as a personalization of sex on the more virile side of the sexual exchange. But this, I think, is to misunderstand prostitution, both heterosexual and homosexual. Hustling involves many deeply personal relationships, often accompanied by a sense of commitment. Admittedly with much futility, prostitutes generally seek love and hope for the lover who will keep them. Persons who lack knowledge of the tearooms and other scenes of thoroughly impersonal sex fall victim to the stereotype of the frigid prostitute who values the customer only for his money. In reality, prostitution is at the corner grocery end of the market economy spectrum. Tearoom sex ranks near the public utility extreme of the continuum.

The addition of the hip set with its virile, drug-using, ambisexual life style has transformed the gay bar into a swinging, far less inhibited setting for sexual contact. The old bar is familiar from gay novels: a florid, clannish milieu for high-pitched flirtation. Patrons of the new bars are justifiably suspicious of possible narcotics agents; but black, white, lesbian, straight women, heterosexual couples, old and young mix with an abandon unknown a decade ago.

Gay bathhouses, once little more than shabby shelters for group sex, although still active as sexual exchanges, are now becoming true centers for recreation. The underground press, along with homophile publications such as the *Los Angeles Advocate*, provide a medium for such facilities to compete in advertising their expanding services. Such advertisements, limited as they may be to underground newspapers, are distinctive marks of the new virilized sex exchanges. By advertising, bars, baths and even hustlers proclaim their openness. It is as if this overt portion of the homosexual community were announcing: "Look, we're really men! Mod men, to be sure, children of the Age of Aquarius; but we are real men, with all the proper equipment, looking for love." In the 1970s it will be very difficult for a society to put that down as deviant.

Radicalization

The new generation's counterculture has also had its impact on the homophile movement, a loose federation of civil rights organizations that reached adolescence about the same time as the flower children. Beginning with the Mattachine Foundation, established around 1950 in Los Angeles, the homophile movement has produced a history remarkably parallel to that of the black freedom movement. Frightened by the spirit of McCarthyism, its first decade was devoted primarily to sponsoring educational forums and publications, along with mutual encouragement for members of an oppressed minority.

During the sixties, with the leadership of attorneys and other professional men, it began to enlist the support of the American Civil Liberties Union in using the courts to assure and defend the civil rights of homosexuals. About the time ministers marched in Selma, clergymen (inspired, perhaps, by the stand of the Church of England in support of homosexual law reform in that nation) began to join the movement as "concerned outsiders." The National Council on Religion and the Homosexual was formed, and, with clergy as sponsors and spokesmen, members of the movement entered into dialogues with straights.

With the proliferation of organizations for the homosexual, a variety of social services were initiated for the gay community: bulletins announcing social events; referral services to counselors, lawyers and doctors; venereal disease clinics; legal guides for those who might suffer arrest; lonely hearts clubs. As they gained strength, the organizations began to foster changes in legislation and to organize gay bar owners for defense against pressures from both the police and organized crime.

In the mid-sixties, the first homosexual pickets began to appear, and the North American Conference of Homophile Organizations (NACHO) held its first national meeting. San Francisco's Society for Individual Rights (SIR), now the largest homophile group, was created and soon began to use picketing and techniques of applying political pressure. "Equal" signs in lavender and white appeared on lapels. But the new militancy began, significantly enough, with demonstrations by Columbia University's Student Homophile League in 1968. At that year's NACHO meetings, the movement's official slogan was adopted: "Gay is Good!"

Radicalization of the movement seems to have peaked in 1969. In that year, homosexuals rioted in New York, shouting "Gay Power!", and the Gay Liberation Front was organized. Student homophile organizations were recognized on half a dozen campuses. By the end of 1970, such groups were recognized on about 30 campuses.

The Backlash—Normalization

Meanwhile, older leaders who had felt the sting of public sanctions recoiled in fear. Not only did the shouts of "Gay Power!" threaten to unlease a backlash of negative sentiment from a puritanical society, but the militants began to disrupt meetings, such as that of NACHO in San Francisco in the fall of 1970. As one homophile leader states: "The youngsters are demanding too much, too fast, and threatening to destroy all that has been gained over 20 painful years." Countless closet queens, who had joined when the movement was safer and more respectable, began to pressure the old militants to return to the early principles and activities of the movement.

An example of such reaction took place in St. Louis early in 1970. The campus-activist founders of the newly formed but thriving Mandrake Society were voted out of office and replaced by a conservative slate. Pages of the Mandrake newsletter, formerly occupied with items of national news interest, warnings about police activity and exhortations for homosexuals to band together in self-defense, have since been filled with notices of forthcoming social events. A Gay Liberation front has been formed in that city during the past few months.

In his report to the membership on the year 1969, SIR's president criticized the "developing determined and very vocal viewpoint that the homosexual movement must be 'radicalized' " by aligning with the New Left on such issues as draft resistance, Vietnam, the Grape Boycott, student strikes and abortion. He replied to this demand: "SIR is a one issue organization limiting itself to a concern for the welfare and rights of the homosexual as a homosexual. The SIR position has to be more like the American Civil Liberties Union than to be like a political club." While SIR's members recovered from the St. Valentine's Sweetheart Dance, the Gay Liberation Front at San Francisco State College threatened to take over all men's rooms on campus unless the administration grant them a charter.

As the process of normalization, with its emphasis on respectable causes, like social events and educational programs, asserts itself in established organizations of the gay world, more closet queens may be expected to join the movement. At the same time, Gay Liberation groups, cheered on by others of the New Left, should be expected to form on all the larger campuses of the nation. This marks a distinct rift in the homophile movement. At present, one finds an alignment of loyalties, chiefly along the dimensions of age and occupational status. Younger homophiles who enjoy relatively high autonomy follow a red banner with "Gay Power!" emblazoned upon it. (The motto of the recent Gay Liberation Conference was "Blatant Is Beautiful!") Older men—and those whose occupations require a style of covert behavior—sit beneath a lavender standard, neatly lettered "Gay Is Good!"

Sensitive to the need for unity, some leaders of the older homophile organizations plead for the changes needed to keep the young "Gayrevs" within the established groups. One such appeal is found in the April, 1969, issue of *Vector.*

It's time that we took some long, hard looks. If we want a retreat for middle-aged bitchery. A television room for tired cock-suckers. An eating club and community theatre—then let us admit it and work toward that.

If we are, as we say we are, interested in social change—then let's get on the ball. Let's throw some youth into our midst. But I warn you . . . they don't want to live in 1956 (and neither do I).

Unity in Adversity

In August of 1970, SIR began picketing Macy's in San Francisco to protest the arrest of 40 men in that store's restrooms. Young men in sandals demonstrated alongside the middle-aged in business suits, together suffering the insults and threats of passersby. Recently, they have called for a nation-wide boycott of the Macy's chain by homosexuals. Resulting internal struggle brought the resignation of Tom Maurer, SIR's conservative president. Present indications are that this large organization is successfully maintaining communication with both sides of the activist rift.

Meanwhile, New York's Gay Activists Alliance, dedicated to nonviolent protest, has provided youthful leadership for homophiles of varying ideological persuasions in the campaign to reform that state's sodomy, fair employment and solicitation statutes. In both Albany and San Diego, organizations with reformist emphases have taken the name of Gay Liberation Front.

Although severe enough to confound social scientists who attempt to describe or analyze the homophile movement, the rift between homophile groups has yet to diminish their effectiveness. Much anger was generated when invading radicals disrupted the 1970 meetings of NACHO, but that organization has yet to enjoy what anyone would call a successful conference anyway. Meanwhile, the hotline maintained by the Homophile Union of Boston serves as a center of communication for the nine, varied homophile groups that have developed in that city during the past 18 months.

Three factors promote cooperation between the conservative, reform and radical branches of the homophile movement. First, instances of police brutality in such widely scattered cities as New York, Los Angeles, San Francisco, and New Orleans have brought thousands of homosexuals together in protest marches during the past year. Nothing heals an ailing movement like martyrs, and the police seem pleased to provide them. Because a vice squad crusade is apt to strike baths and bars, parks and tearooms, all sectors of the homosexual market are subject to victimization in the form of arrests, extortion, assaults and prosecution. There is a vice squad behind every active homophile group in America. With a common enemy in plain clothes, differences in ideology and life style become irrelevant.

Second, the *Los Angeles Advocate* has emerged as the homosexual grapevine in print. With up-to-date, thorough news coverage rivaling that of the *Christian Science Monitor* and a moderate-activist editorial policy, this biweekly is, as it claims, the "Newspaper of America's Homophile Community." With communication provided by the *Advocate* and inspiration gained from the successes of the Women's Liberation Movement, the larger homophile organizations appear to be moving into a position best described as moderately activist.

Finally, a truly charismatic leader has appeared on the homophile scene. The Rev. Troy Perry, founder of the Metropolitan Community Church, a congregation for homosexuals in Los Angeles, was arrested during a fast in front of that city's Federal Building in June of 1970. The fast coincided with "Gay Liberation Day" marches of 2,000 persons in New York and 1,200 in Los Angeles. An articulate, moving speaker, Perry began to tour the nation for his cause. I have seen him honored by a standing ovation from an audience of a hundred mainline Protestant and Catholic clergy in Boston. Because he commands general respect from both gay libs and liberals in the movement, it is impossible not to draw a parallel between this minister and Martin Luther King. When I suggested that he was "the Martin Luther King of the homophile movement," he countered that "Martin Luther Queen might be more appropriate." As an evangelical religious movement spreads from the West coast, replacing drugs as a source of enthusiasm for many in the youth counterculture, Perry's position of leadership should increase in importance.

Just as the world of female homosexuals should benefit from the trend towards liberation of women, so the male homosexual world of the 1970s should thrive. Divisions of the movement may provide the advantages of diversification. The new blood provided by the Gay Liberation Front, alarming as it may be to some traditionalists, is much healthier than the bad blood that has existed between a number of NACHO leaders.

Concurrently, the same social forces that are dividing and transforming the homophile movement have polarized and strengthened the homosexual markets. By now, the consuming American should know that diversification in places and styles of exchange is a healthy indicator in the market economy. Both virilization and impersonalization will attract more participants to the market places of the gay world. At the same time, traditionalists will continue to cruise the streets and patronize the remaining sedate and elegant bars. When threatened by the forces of social control, however, even the closet queens should profit from the movement's newly-found militance.

33. Stripper Morality
Marilyn Salutin

"... society needs strippers in the same way it needs teachers or doctors."

Have you ever wondered about why a woman would choose stripping as a way of life? Ms. Salutin describes the background and personality of a group of strippers, and in doing so also casts some light on the needs of the men who make up their appreciative audience.

The corner of Dundas and Spadina, at the center of downtown Toronto's garment district, is one of the dirtiest areas of town, a conglomeration of hot, smoky dress and pants factories, wholesale outlets, delicatessens, bargain houses, bookie joints, noise, dust, cigarette stands and outdoor food markets run by Portuguese, Chinese, Italian and Jewish shop owners. Showroom models and working women walk past cheap rooming houses and beer parlors. Tempers are apt to explode easily here. In summertime, soft music flows out of the upper-story apartments on top of the stores.

Dundas and Spadina is just the sort of area where one might expect to find a burlesque show. Conventional standards of middle-class public morality aren't always in play here. And, of course, the spectacle of nude women simulating intercourse and orgasm on-stage does not precisely conform to conventional mores either. Thus, there is a nice social symbiosis here between street and theater. On the street the casual passerby is not expected to adhere to any particular standard of dress or behavior, as would be the case, for example, in the highly stratified social landscape of the financial district. On the contrary, Dundas and Spadina is a salad of social identities and personality types. Here the individual can lose himself, so to speak, in the street. He can slip into the burlesque during the afternoon without being given a second glance by other passersby. His presence in the theater will go unnoticed, and for $2.25 he can sit there, if he so desires, from 1:30 in the afternoon until late in the evening.

The theater itself is called the Victory, and it stands across from Switzer's, the most famous delicatessen in Toronto, where the strippers traditionally grab their evening meal before they go onstage and frontstage. For the passerby, the Victory's big neon lights and bold posters promise sexual delights. Huge blowups of famous strippers such as Sexotica, Sintana, Busty Haze and Sinto-Lation—posed in the traditional floor positions or bumping and grinding with larger-than-life red lips and lunging torsos—entice the audience while it is still on the street. For the linear minded there are captions: "One Hot Woman," "Sexual Delights Never Before Experienced," "Bare-Breasted Beauties" and "We Go All the Way—No Strings Attached." It is the big sex thrill in a world where, as Norman Mailer says, sex is sin and sin is paradise. Sin is also good for business at the Victory.

From the bright marquee to the little old man taking tickets and promising you that you haven't missed too much if you come late, the Victory might appear a haunting relic of the days of Broadway and working-class vaudeville. Inside, the stage is flanked by two statuesque cardboard strippers who stand like pillars setting off an altar. Perhaps they are guarding the sacred ritual of the burlesque from contamination or invasion by outsiders, or perhaps they are the fading afterimages of the time when Gypsy Rose Lee might have come down the aisle to wow the audience with her bumps and grinds.

No Lilies and Roses

But this is not the scene for Gypsy Rose Lee or even Lili St. Cyr. It is the scene for some would-be Gypsy Rose Lee who doesn't have what it takes, or for some Gypsy Rose Lee who made it several years ago and has had it or for some Gypsy Rose Lee who just never made it at all.

Because this is not Las Vegas with its gorgeous show girls, nor New York and Paris with their Lidos and Copas—it is Toronto, and it is the Victory at Dundas and Spadina, and I call it "poor man's burlesque." Still, poor man's burlesque is probably better than no burlesque at all, and it certainly is for the thousands of men in Canada and the Midwest who go to hundreds of other Victorys in search of a kind of "satisfaction."

At any rate, the Victory is a fag end of the day gone by, of which some still say "When men were men," because the Victory is run-down and old, with sleazy seats and cigarette-smoking, hunched-up, shabbily dressed men waiting, it seems, for equally jaded strippers to come out and turn them on with their make-believe sexuality, learned perhaps in Libby Jones' book on How to Striptease.

Burlesque in Toronto today means the nude dramatization of the sex act, including the orgasm. As such, it is, of course, considered an affront to the public definition of sexual morality. It is considered obscene.

In our society the spoken or unspoken reference point of all discussions of sexual morality is the animal. Sexually man is not supposed to be an animal— he is expected to attach social meanings and purposes to the sex act. Sex is associated with marriage and procreation, the preservation of the family system and is, in essence, useful for the maintenance of the ritual ordering of our way of life. Sex is usually exchanged by women for the financial security and honorable social status of marriage. Sex is also shrouded in romantic mystique. An aura of sacredness and privacy is associated with it, as is emotion and affection between the two love partners. Now, obviously, burlesque destroys all that. It is an exhibition of sheer animalistic physical sex for the sake of sex. This is offensive. It is offensive to lovers because they want to feel secure with each other, with the feeling that they are wanted and needed. It is offensive to women because women like to feel that they are usually more admired by men (and by other women) if they do not appear too eager to engage in sex. Many women, as Kingsley Davis has noted, feign contempt, or really feel contempt for sex, unless the submission of their bodies to their husbands brings them some material rewards. Strippers demand nothing like this from their public. They demand to be accepted as erotic people, sexual experts who can meet the needs of all men, who can excite all men no matter who they are, where they are from or where they are at. The public nudity, the portrayal of orgasm and masturbation, the open and public enjoyment of eroticism is something most people have been trained to condemn, or even to fear. It represents a devaluation of their sex values and a threat to what Herbert Marcuse has called the repressive nature of Western civilization's sexual order.

Strippers are viewed as "bad," then, because they strip away all social decorum with their clothes. They taunt the public with their own mores by teasing them and turning them on. The privacy of the sex act disappears as does its personal quality, that is, the physical touching of one another and the sharing of affection. In burlesque theater and in the strip bars, open to the public for the price of admission, the sex act is made a packaged commercial deal, one of a variety of sex deals offered in a large sex market aimed at exploiting the contingencies in our society that make it hard for some people to get the sex they think they want.

One of the most important aspects of burlesque is that sex is made impersonal. It has to be impersonal because it has to be available to large numbers of people at the same time, and it has to offer anonymity to the participants, to the audiences and performers. It has to be impersonal because, as a salable, exchangeable commodity, it confers some semblance of normalcy and stability to the occasion. And it has to be impersonal because, when the participants don't know one another and yet understand each other's needs, the deviant act becomes much easier to perform, more acceptable; it becomes something that can be engaged in and then forgotten as soon as it is over.

Burlesque is also made more acceptable by going under the guise of "entertainment" and "show business." But its function as a sex outlet is there for all to see who will see. Says one stripper in this respect, "I am really a professional cockteaser." She would not say this to a stranger, however, and most of the performers stick (at least in public) to the show business definition of burlesque. Audiences don't; they are most likely to see burlesque for what it is and to treat it as such. This is because the performers have most at stake in trying to protect their identities and pass themselves off as normal. For they are considered to be the initiators of the deviant act and are therefore regarded with more social contempt. The audience is merely the witness.

Moreover, audiences have more protection from social condemnation in that they are fully clothed whereas the strippers are naked. They can make all kinds of excuses to rationalize their attendance. Even if they masturbate in their seats, which some do, members of the audience aren't nude and can't be accused of public exhibitionism, which, of course, the strippers are accused of all the time. Until very recently, indeed, the accusation was often legal: strippers were subject to arrest if they showed their pubic hair or "flashed." Now they "show everything" with "no strings attached," but the tolerance of the law has scarcely improved their esteem in the eyes of the public. (For audiences the rules are clearly defined: they aren't to undress or go onstage with the strippers; if they do, they can be arrested.)

Ned Polsky would call burlesque soft-core pornography done to music and designed to stimulate masturbation in the audience. It does this, as well as act as an occasion for public voyeurism. In keeping with these functions, strippers learn and professionalize special techniques and skills. They adopt gimmicks such as wearing a particular costume or do something unusual such as eating fire while they strip. They learn how to move their bodies so that the act becomes a kind of sexual extravaganza, and because of that available to everyone there. Just to make sure, strippers often ask the audience if they can see what they are doing and point to whatever part of their body they want to "feature" for that moment.

The girls, needless to say, show no inhibitions or shyness or modesty about the body or about sex generally. But at the same time, they show no affection or emotional response towards the audience either. Instead, there is either a blank look, a wink or contempt expressed on the face of the stripper. If strippers choose a face that is shy, it is because they want their "floor work" (crouching or lying on the floor and simulating intercourse) and "dirty work" ("flashing" and spreading their legs) to remind the audience of demure girls. They feel this is more erotic; it is supposed to be like seeing the girl next door up there stripping.

Burlesque serves a market mainly composed of men from all walks of life. To the strippers they become indistinguishable from one another. They are seen as a collectivity representing all men. Yet they play to lonely men, frustrated men, happy men and unhappy men. They play to men who go there a lot and to men who may go once a year or once a month. They are businessmen, traveling salesmen, high school and university students, office clerks, professionals, immigrants, truck drivers and transients. They are married and unmarried, and sometimes men and women go together.

There are five shows daily at the Victory every day of the week, and almost every performance is filled. Men pour in during the day, some on lunch breaks, some on out-of-town business, and some just come in off the street. Groups of students bring their sandwiches and drinks and eat their lunch while they watch the show. They laugh and heckle the stripper and reach out for her as she comes down the ramp. They never take their eyes off her whether they are laughing at her or with her. Businessmen, well dressed, hurry in and sit either alone or with one or two others. After the show, they rush out and go back to work. Others, such as transients and immigrants, stop and stare at the photographs of strippers in the lobby on their way out. They talk slowly and stand outside for long periods of time, go away and come back for a later show or for the show the next day.

Strippers note the full houses, the cheering and jeering and excitement in the audience. It tells them that no matter what the public says about them, they are needed. This is gratifying to them. Equally so, perhaps, is the knowledge, if they have it, that burlesque today is a take-off and put-down of most people's sexual fantasies, a burlesque in the true sense, in which the conventional sexual imagination is mirrored and mocked in the act.

Strippers: Frontstage and Backstage

Like all stigmatized people, strippers, offstage, try to negotiate a more favorable self-image. Briefly, they do this in two ways. First of all, they try to upgrade their occupation in a redefintion of stripping that says it is socially useful, constructive, good and generally all right to do. Secondly, strippers conceal backstage information about their own personal lives that would label them as sexual deviants if known publicly. Their public face is designed to demonstrate that they are sexually normal and therefore moral, and that they are really entertainers, that stripping and sex shows in general are true forms of entertainment that require an artistic talent and openness and honesty about sexual matters. When strippers claim to be "exotics" or "dancers," they are giving the job a face-lifting. But they are not denying the fact that they are strippers, merely describing what they do and who they are in a more flattering way, in a way to save themselves embarrassment, shame and degradation. Still, replacing the negative definition of stripping with a positive one does replace the negative definition of themselves with a more positive one. It says they are engaged in a moral enterprise and therefore must be regarded as moral people.

Strippers' self-concepts are integrally tied up with what they do onstage. Their definition of stripping as good, legitimate entertainment is based largely on the fact that they never saw themselves as anything but strippers, that is, they never were or intended to become real singers, dancers or Broadway stars. They admire famous strippers like Oneida Mann, Babette and Amber Haze. Offstage, they talk about them—about their acts and the problems they have in their personal lives. Strippers feel complimented and flattered if one tells them they were good onstage and especially if you tell them they remind you of a famous stripper. For example, one girl remarked: "When they see me and say it looks like her [Oneida Mann] I know I'm doing good." They are proud if you refer to them in a flattering way about being part of a good show doing good work, meaning highly sexy, erotic work. Their vested interest is in the job as it stands, and it is this they are trying to protect in their various encounters with members of the public.

Strippers are realistic in their interpretation of their job and admit they are "with it" or "in it," or at least are "trying to make the most of it." Because strippers never envisioned themselves as show business stars in the normal sense of the word, they naturally do not fall back on lost dreams in the ways, for example, that their fellow troupers, the comics, do. Whatever lost dreams strippers have in their private worlds aren't tied up with ambitions in show business but with ambitions in life as normal women. This is why their stress is on the morality of sex shows in the sense that they are justified in doing them because they are "socially useful."

In short, strippers take the stance of a deviant minority forming and adhering to subcultural values of its own. This means, among other things, that they attempt to normalize or neutralize their roles by downgrading the public, condemning them for being hypocrites, ignorant and dishonest. Strippers blame many of their problems on the repressive nature of the public sex order, especially as represented by the police. In the strip bars, for example, strippers resent the police coming in and busting hookers. They are afraid they, too, will be arrested, even if they are just stripping, or that the cops will find dope of one kind or another on them. One stripper declared: "I hate these guys. . . . I can smell them whenever they're near, and I hate them. . . . Why don't they just go away and leave us alone. They could never understand the problems of people." How can the public condemn what it has created a need for and which it supports not just privately in ideology but openly with money (admission fees)?

Skid rowers and prostitutes also blame the public for their problems in an attempt to normalize their role. Said one stripper: "We just want to be left alone without any hassles with the public. We aren't trying to make them be like us, just understand us and let us go our way . . . leave us alone."

The public face of strippers should be seen as a cooling-out trick. It is a difficult stance to take because it involves the denial of social attitudes that form the basis of real social facts. For example, strippers must negate or deny that sex for the sake of sex is bad or immoral behavior in public. They must also negate the public typification that all strippers are whores. Strippers, consequently, must be seen as very complex personalities, not simply the middle-class stereotypes of them. What they do in their relations with others is difficult; they are constantly engaged in conscious manipulation of behavior. in concealing and revealing what they deem to be situationally proper and what they believe will bring them the most respect. They are always involved in what Erving Goffman calls strategic interaction—putting their best foot forward.

To illustrate how complicated these self-cooling-out or "passing" devices are, think of what strippers, in dealing with outsiders, have to conceal about themselves: their often ambivalent sexual activities, the kinds of men they become emotionally involved with and the exact nature of their heterosexual relationships, why they went into stripping in the first place, what other work they do that is directly related to stripping, what they might be getting out of stripping in addition to money.

Strippers can never reveal, offstage or on, if they want to keep their self-esteem, that they aren't normal women—very sexy and desirable women to be sure, but normal nonetheless. Any kind of contrary information can be a threat to their posited conception of who they really are. Little things, such as saying who they live with and what their husband does for a living, become obstacles in interaction with others who aren't part of their subculture, either because they fully support their husband or lover by stripping and prostitution or because they are living with a girl in a lesbian relationship. Their habits, and their pasts, have to be concealed from strangers because they might incriminate them. Strippers often invent elaborate tales about why they began stripping as an excuse for their participation in the show. One girl said she is using stripping as a means to get to Hollywood where she wants to become a movie star in the style of Jayne Mansfield. The idea is that they are doing it temporarily as a means to an end. Another girl said she was "tricked into it" and really thought she was going to be a "go-go girl to back up the Feature [an out-of-town star]." Others claim to be doing it just "temporarily" until they earn enough money to go into business. One girl said she wants to buy a flower shop in Chicago where she was born. She also says she wants to raise a family with her husband and that she is only killing time and making lots of money until that day. In reality, the girl is a lesbian who is constantly searching for a female lover in every city she visits, claiming: "I'm just not satisfied with my husband. . . . I need a girl, one who is nice. . . . anyone can satisfy you sexually, but I need somebody I can talk to and have a deep emotional relationship with, just like most women want from men." All this came out after a long talk in which, for the first hour or so, she tried to create the impression that, "like every other girl," she loved her husband and desired no other kind of sexual or emotional relationship. Another girl claimed she was stripping only until she saved enough money to go into the rooming house business. She asserted that her husband loved her to strip "because he knows he can really have me when all those other guys want me but can't get me."

Strippers place a high value on money and believe it should be made in the easiest way possible—their way. But they don't hold on to it for very long. One reason is that they usually are totally supporting the man they live with. Some are also supporting children. They feel a sense of power handing over money to their man because they enjoy his financial dependency, but at the same time they are being exploited because the man usually spends most of the money on himself. One night I listened for hours as a stripper and her husband argued over how he had spent her paycheck. He claimed he had bought a radio and some liquor. The girl was upset because she told me she was broke and that she couldn't control the way he spent the money. She wanted to buy a new costume but wouldn't be able to now, and she also owed her agent some money but couldn't pay him. Her husband tried to joke about it to cool her off. He asked her what she would do without him. She laughed and smiled and explained that they were both bad with money, that they couldn't save a dime, owed money all over town and lived from day to day never knowing what tomorrow would bring. She also told me she spends some of her money on pills she takes to "keep her going" and that the main reason she dislikes being so broke all the time is that it prevents them from taking off whenever they like (traveling) and that money is a constant source of argument between them.

And so they say that stripping is fun and that they are sexy "artistic" performers who are better than most women because they are more honest and direct about sex. They also take the following lines, in general—that they are happily married and look forward to the day when they can quit and "settle down with a family," or that the kind of men they go with admire them because they are sexy and actually prefer them to other women. That they are financially or emotionally exploited in their personal relationships with men, or that men go with them for any reasons other than their being sexually desirable, these facts are hidden. Like most other people, they also try to create the impression in public that their living arrangements are normal. They are apt to say, for example, that they are married rather than that they are "living common-law," which is usually the truth. Such are the pressures of conventional morality on these women.

Strippers don't end up stripping because they have skidded downwards in their careers as have the burlesque comics. They chose stripping as an occupation, and their decision was based upon what they knew of the world. The experiences they have had in the world formulate themselves into a common-sense rationality of how best to put their bodies to use, how best to live their lives. In their own view, they haven't fallen in status. After all, one alternative would have been full-time prostitution, which has neither the social status nor the economic payoff (the prostitutes they know only get $5.00 to $10.00 a trick in Toronto).

To strippers, stripping is a good thing, and they do it as naturally as stenographers type. It earns them a minimum of $165 a week and offers what they call an "easy life." They can sleep late each day, watch soap operas on television, sit around backstage until it is time to work, work, repeat the same process four or five times a day and pick up their pay at the end of the week. If they work steadily, they earn a fair amount of money.

What strippers don't mention, initially, is that stripping also facilitates lesbian relationships. This is backstage information, the kind that would label them as "unnatural." Backstage, however, they joke around a lot about sex and show a playful affection for each other by touching each others' bodies. One stripper explained that the constant exposure and manipulation of the body and the body contact backstage are often the beginning of lesbian experiences for strippers. They maintain it is very easy for a stripper to become a lesbian because it is "all around." If you add to this a contemptuous feeling for the public, especially the "johns" and "marks" in the audience, lesbianism, as an occupational contingency, is quite understandable. Contempt for men is expressed in terms like this: "All they need is a cute ass and a pair of tits wiggling." Strippers themselves say that more than 75 percent of their colleagues are lesbians and that often their first experiences came as a direct result of stripping—which is not to deny that some lesbian strippers are also married to men and continue to have sex with them. One stripper explained this situation like this: "It's quite simple, you see . . . . I'll go out and meet a girl and go home with her—that's all—and he'll do whatever he likes . . . . he knows I'll come back again . . . . he doesn't mind if I pick up a girl . . . . he knows what I am . . . . he sometimes picks up women . . . . but we have a companionship, a kind of love." Nevertheless, it is common for strippers to be bisexual or lesbian, but not straight.

Another occupational contingency of stripping is prostitution. And yet, strippers very carefully, in public, differentiate themselves from full-time prostitutes, whom they perceive to be of a lower social status. They stress the fact that they strip and don't hook for a living, whereas prostitutes just hook. If they do hook, they make sure one understands that it is "just once in a while" and for a very good reason, like "eating and putting a roof over my head."

Once You Start . . .

Nevertheless, and for all that they take pains to deny it, prostitution is almost an inevitable consequence of stripping. One woman remarked, for example: "My girl friend just hooks because she is afraid to do what I do in public, and if I was afraid to strip, I'd be doing it all the time too [hooking]." In my sample, most of the strippers hooked part time to supplement their income. They also performed at stags. They often get their customers in strip bars. Having a career in commercial sex makes prostitution easy to do, even if one doesn't really want to do it. For one thing, the general public regards all strippers as prostitutes anyway, and for another, strippers are always being propositioned. One stripper recalled: "It's so easy to start hooking for some guy. . . . You think, well, I really could use the extra money . . . but once you start, you never stop. And most of them never even save any of this money." Nevertheless, strippers much resent being labeled a prostitute. One woman said: "I hate clubs, especially small ones in northern Ontario. They'll treat you like a prostitute whether you are one or not just because most of them have been who were here before you. . . . When you finish the show, you never know what drunk is going to be waiting for you at the top of the stairs."

The strippers in my sample are poorly educated. The average level of education of the 20 strippers in this sample was grade seven or eight. They have no office skills or any other kind of talent suitable for an urban labor market. They cannot sing, dance or act nor could they ever. They do not have bodies suitable for modeling; they are too large, in all dimensions. (Amber Haze, a current favorite, measures 52 inches around the bust.) Nearly all said they left home at an early age—by the time they were 14 or 15 years old. They learned early that they had to support themselves. Most had what they described as unhappy home lives, either because they didn't get along with their parents or because they had too much work to do at home or because their sexual experiences upset their parents. For example, one girl said she had to leave home because she was a lesbian and her mother wanted to have her committed to a mental hospital because of it.

Most developed early, that is, their bodies matured early. Sexuality (their own and others') came early, too, often in a violent form such as being beaten or raped; and for as long as they can remember, their bodies were objects of talk, staring and sexual passes. They were used to being cheered and jeered as they walked down the street. They were used to being whistled at and pawed over. Yet even as they were often humiliated by the nature of some of their sexual experiences, most strippers, by the time they reached their late teens, had come to the conclusion that the body, because it attracts men, can bring in money. This knowledge, plus the desire for attention, plus the exhibitionist tendencies they acknowledge, led them to stripping. One girl claimed, for example: "I like it because to me it seems glamorous, and I like attention. I'm an exhibitionist really." They were also encouraged by people they knew—other girls who were doing it and boy friends who urged them to do it.

Strippers like stripping because it makes them feel important, especially when the audience claps and cheers. They feel exhilarated. They also like the money. By the time they are "in the life" they have developed an exploitative attitude to men and people in general. They become harder and tougher in their attitudes to men, money and sex. However, they do not feel badly about this, merely smart, one-up on the world. Said one girl, "If I don't exploit them, they'll do it to me." Stripping becomes easy to do with this kind of attitude.

Being paid to display their bodies in public means they are beating the world at its own game. It is no more immoral in their eyes than getting a man to marry them in exchange for intercourse. Indeed, in their own eyes or at least in the face they turn to the public, they are no different from other women with regard to sex, just more blunt, honest, open and direct. Other women are hypocrites; they may not strip for money, but they ask a price just the same. It's usually marriage, but it could be just a dinner. Strippers also claim all women are exhibitionists. Said one stripper, "All women are in spirit exhibitionists and prostitutes." Said another, "All women are exhibitionists . . . haven't you ever seen a woman wearing an extra-tight sweater?"

Both onstage and off, strippers like to be referred to as erotic, sexy people, professional sex experts, skilled in ways others aren't. They pride themselves on their knowledge of eroticism, and unlike the average woman, they aren't ashamed of their sexual knowledge and expertise. In fact, strippers often say that one of their special roles is to teach people about sex, for most people, especially women and most men in their audiences, don't know anything about it. For example, they say college students come to the Victory to learn about sex in a sort of initiation ritual. One stripper told me: "They're still wet behind the ears and embarrassed. We have to show them a few things."

The line they take is that society needs strippers in the same way it needs teachers or doctors. Without sex shows, men would be lonely and frustrated and lacking a sex outlet. Thus, their work is actually as good and helpful and socially constructive as any other kind of work, and because the work is useful, they are moral. This, of course, is a "passing" device and a cooling-out trick. Another line is their claim that strip shows are really good entertainment, as are all sex shows from live stag exhibitions to stag movies. One stripper performs at stags with her husband. He encourages it, and they both maintain it is good entertainment as well as a good way to make money.

The line that "anybody will do anything for a buck anyway" is perhaps their principal legitimizing tactic. They feel generally that any dealings they have with members of the public should be of a contractual nature—and that they should be paid for whatever they do. One girl said, "I'm being stared at anyway, so why not be paid for it?" Said another, "I don't care what they say or do to me as long as they pay." They should be paid, then, for just being around, for being sexy. They should be paid also for showing people the "truth" when they strip, which is doing everybody a favor. The "truth" here means the truth about sex—actually, the truth about life.

Who Profits

At the same time, however, strippers also maintain that they really aren't being so terribly exploitative, especially if one remembers that "all men are sexually frustrated and in need of their services," as one of them put it. They claim that if they didn't exploit the public's need for a sex outlet, that is, making a profit on it, men would be making a profit on them—that is, they, as women, would be taken advantage of by men. They would be touched, screwed and not paid.

Strippers, offstage, also argue that stripping is just a job like any other and that what they do is done in a routinized way (this despite their open acknowledgement that they are exhibitionists). One stripper told me:

> I don't think anything about stripping. . . . I don't stand nude. . . . I always wear a G-string even though it looks like I don't. I do my act as a routine, automatically. . . . sometimes I don't even see the audience. . . . I can black them out. . . . lots of girls do that. . . . we just do our act and do it again the next night. . . . but other girls get orgasms right on the stage. . . . they get a charge out of turning the guys on right there in the club or in the theater. . . . I saw a guy finish once right in this girl's face, and she thought it was cute.

Needless to say, if a stripper does get a sexual thrill out of performing, she wouldn't say so in public; it would make her seem unnatural, and that would be to contradict all the legitimizing lines she may have developed. By the same token, strippers never admit that their boy friends are often pimps or addicts who would push them onto the street if they didn't strip.

Backstage, however, these facts do emerge. They also reveal that they are constantly broke, their money being spent mainly on liquor, debts, drugs, traveling expenses, costumes, props as well as the usual rent and food. Other backstage information would include the fact that in certain centers, strippers are controlled by the Mafia, and they must turn tricks in the bars in order to keep their jobs. Strippers complain about insults from drunk customers, unwanted propositions, depression due to fights with theater owners, club managers and other strippers, being lied to, cheated and stolen from. Bosses are divided into categories of "nice guys" and "bad guys" according to how they treat them. By the same token, audiences are divided into "nice squares" and "bad squares" according to how they react to their performances—as one girl put it, "according to how hypocritical they are about their need for us." Loneliness is also a constant problem, whether traveling the circuit including New York, Chicago, Montreal, Toronto, Los Angeles and San Francisco or traveling from one small town in Ontario to another (Peterborough, Timmins, Sudbury). One girl claims she "carries her husband with her everywhere she goes" just to avoid this loneliness. Sometimes they make friends when they visit a town, but they become depressed because they know the chances of ever seeing the person again are slim. So they talk of writing letters to one another and express the hope they will meet again sometime.

But it is what happens to old strippers, or, more precisely, what the aging process does to them, that is perhaps their worst problem. They fear getting old, and if they are getting old, they will work desperately to create the illusion that their bodies are firm and still sexy. Growing old is an incontrovertible denial of a future in terms of the lines they adhere to, and even the youngest stripper is aware of this. What happens to older strippers is that they can't get by anymore with the "sex is fun and I am very sexy" line, and as a result, they have to "spread themselves" more and act as the butt of the MC's dirty jokes. In fact, they become the joke itself, the source of all the dirty humor. They are no longer very persuasive sexually, but they are still usable, and perhaps this is the biggest difference between them and the younger women. Their usability is what keeps them working, not their desirability, and this is a difficult thing to rationalize to anybody, especially themselves.

Often older strippers become alcoholics and do what they do drunk. Younger strippers know about this, too, but they don't seem to have any way of stopping it from happening to them. They have no plans for the future. They live from day to day and plan only far enough ahead for tomorrow.

As suggested earlier, life to a stripper is a game of one-upmanship where everyone has the potential to be had. To be a winner, one must be on top of the situation at all times, whether onstage or off. If one lets one's defenses down, she becomes vulnerable to attack and shame.

When audiences clap for them at the end of performances at the Victory, strippers really feel they have put one over. They are being paid and applauded, but they have given nothing of themselves in return. Even their nudity is neutralized by becoming just a part of the job. Winning at the end of a performance lets them see themselves as successful not only as strippers but in life itself.

Strippers expect one another to adhere to the same line in normal interaction with the public. They attempt to reinforce their definition of the situation within the ranks of their own group. They need solidarity in order for the definition of their situation to have any kind of social reality. For this reason, strippers rarely downgrade each other in the presence of strangers. Only if a stripper disobeys norms does she come under public attack. A stripper who "flashes" too easily, who doesn't demand a higher price for doing it, is immensely disliked by the others and is not considered to be a "good stripper," meaning a loyal member of the group. They also avoid and dislike strippers who act superior, who are snobs. One stripper commented about another: "She'll just have to learn she's no better than we are."

Newcomers are initiated into the business by being handed down practical advice. They are taught how to handle verbal insults while they perform. They are taught what to say if they spot a man masturbating and they don't dig it too much: "Put it away and save it for later" and "Do up your pants; I'm being paid, and you're not" are common methods of turning the guy off. Other tricks they learn are how to handle police by lying to them or "being nice to them when they're around"; the same holds true for any outsider. These protective tricks are taken for granted and are part of their normal daily behavior. It is normal to offer the following kind of advice to one another or a novice: "Think with your head, not with your pants . . . keep a cool head, or you'll get sucked under and never get out. They'll own you." Only most of them are in it for life regardless.

Sexual standards aren't generally imposed on one another. A person's sexual status is regarded as a private matter, nobody's concern but that particular individual's. As one girl put it: "Each to his own . . . they leave me alone, so I leave them alone . . . they know it if you're really straight, so they leave you alone usually . . . that's the way it is." Another girl said: "I only initiate a girl if she approaches me first, and most of them like it after, especially after doing a show." However, there are, of course, exceptions. For example, some straight strippers resent playing the same bill as a well-known lesbian and will try to get out of the job or else ask for a separate dressing room. Also, some lesbians disobey the norm and try to initiate an affair with a novice.

When strippers do make friends, they put themselves out for them because friends aren't easy to find in this world. If they hit it off, they will try to get each other jobs, teach each other routines, loan props and costumes, sometimes loan money for drinks, socialize in bars after work, go to parties together, protect each other from the police and other outsiders, visit each other at home, introduce each other to their men and go out in mixed groups. But perhaps most important, they will sit and listen to each other's problems with sympathy, because after all, one girl's troubles are those of every other.

Strippers don't downgrade comics but accept them as part of the show, though not too important a part. They joke around with them after work and go out for drinks with them. They also treat them as confidants, telling them all their troubles, hopes and dreams.

With respect to the master of ceremonies, strippers like to have him on their side, especially if they are having a fight with another girl. But the MC can also be the cause of friction. If he shows more attention to one stripper than another, the rejected one will feel jealous and malicious. For example, in one of the strip bars in Toronto, the MC always gave a more elaborate introduction to one stripper than to the other. He also joked more with her offstage. His favorite was black, the other white. One evening, the white stripper whispered across the table: "He always spends more time with her than me . . . . I don't know. I guess he just prefers niggers . . . . Oh, I guess that isn't nice, is it? Well, it's the truth anyway, isn't it?" She then began to laugh about her whispered confession of jealousy.

In essence, their everyday world is one of what to do next, after the show, before the next show, what to drink, where to drink it, when to go home, writing to one another, when they might see each other again—about the "old days of burlesque," how good they are onstage, about "14-year-old boys" (college students) who are still wet behind the ears, about owing the agent, a "bum," a fin, about an old friend accused by the police of this or that, in one case murder—and teasing each other about picking up other men or women and about who will pay for the drinks this time.

A stripper's persona can be thought of as a sexual extravaganza—a way of being and living in the world as a sexual creature, larger than life. It is for this reason they often appear onstage and off as caricatures of female sexuality. Perhaps the silicone injections most of them have had done to their breasts best illustrate this point. Their breasts are made so large that whether they want to be "in play" offstage or not, it would be difficult to disguise the nature of their work. This might be an additional reason for playing up, offstage, the artfulness of stripping until it takes on a socially significant meaning. However, the attention they pay to the body, to their costumes, facial expressions, makeup and so forth is all a part of a ritual they go through every day to help make the performance more of a show. It also makes it more unreal and impersonal. It is a kind of sexual circus.

This almost parodic quality in the face they turn to the world perhaps explains why one woman in my sample tried to deny what she did, and she said she was really a model. It also explains why they don't distance themselves from the occupation itself but rather try to redefine it so that it suits their bodies, so to speak. By endowing their overblown bodies with a useful social function, a sex extravaganza, they are saying they are moral bodies inhabited by moral people. Their "passing" technique, then, involves a new definition of sexual morality rather than an attempt to live up to the existing one.

All the skills they learn as strippers can be seen, in a sense, as working up to this new definition of sexual morality and sexual worth. It is the only stance they can take, which is why it is so strictly enforced among members of their own group.

Corporeal Ideology

What I am saying is that as their work is expressed in their bodies, so, too, is their ideology. The body becomes an object that every member of the audience is supposed to identify with and use in his own way. If it stimulates masturbation, that is perhaps not in keeping with the official norms governing the occasion, but it is still in line with the expressed function the strippers declare as being theirs.

Because strippers manifest a certain sameness in their self-presentations, they become almost indistinguishable from one another in the same ways that members of the audience become indistinguishable from one another to the strippers.

Their coping device, then, is to make the body moral in the same way they make the show and themselves moral, all being part of the same phenomenon and sharing in stigma. At the same time, it is to state that, other than having this extravagant body and sexual presence, they are normal, that is, no different than any other woman. To state this, as I discussed, is to conceal any kind of information about themselves that would give the lie to their self-presentation. Strippers are constantly playing this kind of show in a conscious way; it illustrates the complicated nature of destigmatizing processes and the complexities of those who have to work out a suitable identity.

Discussion Questions
1. What is "normal" sexual behavior and what is "perversion"?
2. Should college health centers distribute birth control information and supplies?
3. Is abortion a private or a public matter?
4. Should "victimless crimes" like prostitution and homosexuality concern the police?
5. What does attendance at a strip show imply about the members of the audience?

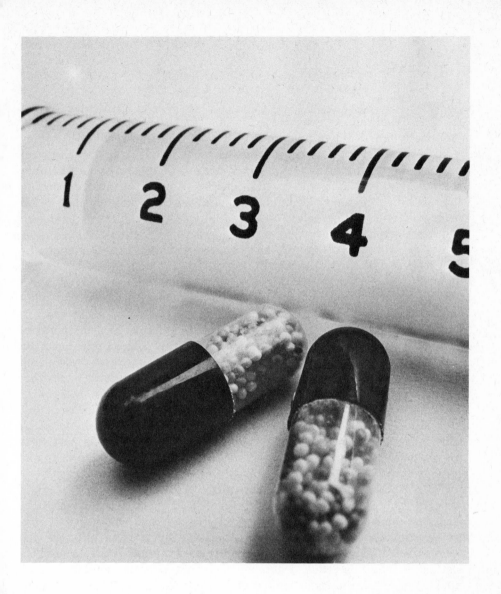

Chapter 9
Drugs
and Behavior

The definition of "drug" recently has become very limited and very emotionally laden. When one group of people hear the word "drug," they immediately think of a terrible substance that is wrecking the minds of children and destroying everything held dear by our society. With another group the word "drug" calls to mind visions of consciousness expansion along with exciting and pleasurable experiences. It is unlikely that either group of people will associate the word "drug" with aspirin or penicillin or other such substances that would have come to mind immediately about a decade ago. It is important to remember that a drug, as defined by the World Health Organization, is "any substance that, when taken into the living organism, may modify one or more of its functions." So defined, it includes aspirin and penicillin, marijuana and heroin, meat and potatoes, and alcohol and nicotine.

A drug, by itself, is neither good nor bad. What is of principle concern is whether the effect produced by the drug is desirable or undesirable; and it is clear that what is desired in some quarters is very much to be feared in others. In this chapter we will be dealing with drugs that are widely used in order to affect the psychological state of the individual, and are used in a self-prescribed manner. We will attempt to present this information in a factual manner rather than in a way that is colored by value judgment, since the ultimate judges of whether or not a particular drug effect is desirable must be the individual who is taking the drug and those people with whom he comes into contact.

The first paper in this chapter, by Dr. Dale C. Cameron, presents a series of factual statements about the effects of those drugs which have generated the most recent public interest. These include narcotics, barbiturates, amphetamines, hallucinogens, and marijuana. The physical and chemical effects of the drugs are described in very lucid detail. In order to best understand this article a number of definitions might well be kept in mind. First of all, the term "addiction" is not used since it is ambiguous and misleading. In its place the term "dependence" is used. Dependence can be either physical or psychological, and the specific characteristics of drug dependence will differ according to the type of drug being discussed. Physical dependence is what we ordinarily think of when the term "addiction" is used. It occurs when the individual organism adapts to the presence of the drug so that, if the drug is not present, a set of uncomfortable symptoms ensue. These symptoms constitute a "withdrawal syndrome," and the particular symptoms that characterize a withdrawal syndrome will differ from drug to drug. Psychological dependence does not involve these physical withdrawal symptoms but instead is associated with a feeling of satisfaction produced by the drug, such that continued drug use is required in order to produce psychological pleasure or to avoid psychological discomfort. It is possible for a drug to induce either physical dependence or psychological dependence or both. The term "tolerance," also used in the article, refers to a condition in which the same quantity of a drug will produce a lesser effect over time so that, in order to maintain the same effect, the individual will have to take increasingly larger dosages of the drug. Finally, it is important to keep in mind that Dr. Cameron is discussing typical effects produced by typical dosages of the drug in typical individuals. Any single person can have a unique reaction to a substance; in general, an individual's reaction will vary according to such things as the dosage that is taken, the situation in which it is taken, and the expectations that the user has about the drug. Thus different people can report different experiences with the same substance, and it is difficult to predict, for any single individual, how he is likely to respond to a drug.

Although we, in this country, have grown accustomed to the use of alcohol and have generally accepted it socially, many people consider alcohol a far greater menace to public health than any of the drugs that have become more notorious in recent years. It is true that alcohol is now a legal substance whereas most of the drugs described by Dr. Cameron, taken in a self-prescribed manner, are illegal, but that is a social complication independent of the chemical nature of the substances. Although it may be more socially acceptable, there is no reason to think of alcohol as being harmless nor to overlook the millions of people whose problem with alcohol constitutes a real danger to themselves and their loved ones. A major research program concerning the effects of alcohol and the patterns of alcohol usage is currently being conducted at George Washington University. The article by Barbara Ford describes many of the findings of this project. It is of particular note that careful distinctions are made among types of alcohol users, and it is clear that different types of users are quite different people and show quite different effects. This same recognition might be in order with drug users who all are considered, by some people, to be the same whether they smoke marijuana occasionally or inject heroin regularly.

Marijuana smoking makes the front pages of newspapers daily and provides a major concern in many quarters. This is true despite the fact that very little is known about the long-term effects of marijuana usage, and what is known about its short-term effects is not very frightening. The recent report of the commission appointed by President Nixon to study the effects of marijuana clearly recognized that marijuana smoking does not necessarily lead to the use of stronger drugs and that occasional short-term use appears to produce little effect either positive or negative. It also recognized that continued use of a more regular nature could be associated with undesirable symptoms such as loss of energy and motivation, that its use is most unwise when driving, and that a great deal of research remains to be done concerning whether or not there are any

long-term harmful effects. It is noteworthy both that the commission recommended the reduction of the criminal penalties typically associated
with marijuana and also that it did not recommend legalization of the
substance.

In light of the furor about marijuana, about which so little is known,
it is remarkable that so little attention is paid to nicotine, about which so
much is known. Again to refer to a governmental body, multiple reports
from the Surgeon General's office over the past decade have continually
associated smoking with a variety of life-threatening diseases. The association of nicotine with cancer is well known, and recent evidence has
associated smoking with heart disease and a number of pulmonary disorders such as emphysema and bronchitis. In addition to these potentially
lethal diseases, there are a number of other effects on health that are
less dramatic but also of concern.

In her article Amy Gross reviews a number of reasons that motivate
people to smoke and a number of programs that have been instituted to
help people who wish to break this very difficult habit. She gives some
helpful hints about day-to-day methods to approach the task of stopping
smoking that might be of use if you choose to attempt to break this habit.

The function of this review has not been to suggest that any drug
is better than another. Rather, the point is that every drug has some
effect. Whether or not the subjective effects are desirable is very much a
matter of individual choice. Whether or not the consequences of taking
the drug, which include physical, psychological, social, and legal possibilities, are worth the immediate desirability of the effect is also a matter of
individual choice. It is important that each individual recognize this,
weigh the alternatives, and then arrive at the choice that is most in his
own best interests.

Suggested Readings

Blum, Richard H. *Society and Drugs*. San Francisco: Jossey-Bass, 1969. Blum, Richard
   H. *Students and Drugs*. San Francisco: Jossey-Bass, 1969. A two-volume series
   about past and present patterns of drug use. The first volume is more historical
   in nature, providing a context for the discussion of contemporary patterns of
   usage. The second volume reports the results of current studies of local high
   school and college drug scenes.
Borgatta, Edgar F., and Evans, Robert R. *Smoking, Health and Behavior*. Chicago:
   Aldine, 1968. A collection of papers by social scientists and physicians concerning the relationship between smoking and health. Research is cited frequently and related to issues of public policy.
Nowlis, Helen H. *Drugs on the College Campus*. New York: Doubleday, 1969. A comprehensive summary of current information about the properties of various
   drugs and the nature and extent of their use on college campuses.

34. Facts about Drugs
Dale C. Cameron

"...the immediate psychic effect produced depends a good deal on the expectations and desires of the user."

Before there can be any understanding of drugs, it must be understood that there are a wide variety of drugs, and each one has a somewhat different pattern of effects. Dr. Cameron describes the major classes of drugs and the effects of each.

The meaning of the word "drug" differs very much depending upon the context in which the word is used. In this article we shall be dealing with drugs in the broadest possible meaning of the word. The WHO Expert Committee on Drug Dependence defined a drug as "any substance that, when taken into the living organism, may modify one or more of its functions."

Drugs of all sorts have long been used and their variety and number keep growing. However, it is primarily those on which a person may become dependent that interest us here. Drug dependence may be described as "a state, psychic and sometimes also physical, resulting from the interaction between a living organism and a drug, characterized by behavioural and other responses that always include a compulsion to take the drug on a continuous or periodic basis in order to experience its psychic effects, and sometimes to avoid the discomfort of its absence. A person may be dependent upon more than one drug."

Since the characteristics of dependence vary with the drug involved, it is important to use the term in specific reference to the type of drug.

Drugs of the morphine type (narcotics) are derived, in large part, from opium. Opium is the coagulated juice of the poppy plant *Papaver somniferum L.* which grows well in dry sunny places throughout the world. Opium contains a powerful painkiller and other medically useful drugs can be derived from this source. Its principal analgesic action is due to an alkaloid named morphine, after Morpheus, the Greek god of dreams. Morphine can be converted to codeine, a drug with both mild analgesic and cough suppressant actions. Heroin, an opiate readily made from morphine, and opium itself are widely used by narcotic-dependent persons.

A number of non-opiate, synthetic compounds also have narcotic and analgesic properties. Unfortunately, they all share with morphine and opium the capacity to produce dependence of the morphine type.

With narcotics generally, psychic dependence is strong and tends to develop early. The range and paradoxical nature of the effects are astonishing. Narcotics can have both euphoriant and sedative effects, give "relief" from pain and anxiety or "relief" from excessive passivity. Narcotics come as close to being a panacea as any drug yet found by providing different solutions for different people or even for the same person at different points in time. They are used to give "relief," to make someone feel better or just not to feel at all. However, physical dependence also develops early and its intensity roughly parallels the dosage taken. If you were to take ten mg. of morphine every four hours for about two weeks you would develop some physical dependence. Such dependence is an adaptive state of the body which requires *continued* taking of the drug to *prevent* the appearance of an illness or abstinence syndrome that is specific in its signs and symptoms for this group of drugs. Tolerance to narcotics also occurs rapidly, making it necessary to take increasing doses of the drug to achieve the same effect.

The withdrawal or abstinence syndrome, which with morphine or heroin reaches its peak in forty-eight to seventy-two hours after the last dose, is characterized by physical and mental stresses of many sorts ranging from anxiety, restlessness, perspiration, runny nose and eyes, to aches and pains, nausea and vomiting, cramps, weight loss and, in some rare and very extreme cases where no medical care is available, shock and death.

Drugs of the morphine type are most widely used in certain countries of the eastern Mediterranean and in Asia. Until the last ten to fifteen years, opium was generally the drug of choice in most of these areas. At that time, estimates of use ranged up to 6 percent of the total populations in some countries, but these estimates must be considered as very rough guides. In more recent years, there has apparently been a marked increase in the use of heroin instead of opium, especially by younger persons in these regions, though in some local areas opium remains the drug of choice. Because activities associated with the non-medical use of morphine-type drugs are now illegal in nearly all countries, it is very difficult to obtain good estimates on the prevalence and incidence of such use.

There is believed to be substantial use of opium in the hill areas where Thailand, Burma, Loas and China are in close proximity. Opium and morphine are used in Singapore, while heroin is the drug most taken in Hong Kong and the plains of Thailand. Very rough estimates suggest that users in this general region of the world might be measured in hundreds of thousands.

It has been suggested that there are 120,000 to 180,000 heroin users in the United States of America (1 in 1140 to 1700 persons). In the United Kingdom the number of heroin and other opioid users coming to the attention of the Home Office in 1969 was about 2300, or about 1 person in 24,500. The use of opioids in Europe remains on a small scale despite a recent sharp rise in some countries.

Sedative drugs enjoy a rising popularity as a means of coping with our present hectic way of life. In the past fifty years numerous barbituric acid derivatives have been developed. Some are short and intermediate acting, such as hexobarbital, others are long acting, such as phenobarbital. All are toxic. Those most self-administered by drug users are of the short and immediate acting types, for example, amobarbital, cyclobarbital, hexobarbital, pentobarbital, secobarbital. Certain, but not all, so-called tranquillizers also produce dependence of the barbiturate type. Among those that do are meprobamate, chlordiazepoxide and diazepam. They are used medically to relieve anxiety without producing as much sedation as barbiturates.

With all drugs of this type psychic dependence can be relatively strong. Persons taking these sedatives usually are seeking escape or oblivion, but in some cases sedatives may be taken as part of a drug spree, often in combination with other drugs. The symptoms and signs of chronic intoxication with barbiturates are similar to those seen in alcohol intoxication. Large doses produce lack of motor co-ordination, impairment of mental function and occasionally a toxic psychosis, coma and death. Physical dependence can be strong and usually develops when the daily intake reaches three to four times the usual therapeutic dose.

Tolerance does not develop as rapidly or uniformly as with narcotics. For example, there is little tolerance to the usual minimum lethal dose, so that those who self-administer substantial amounts of barbiturates are often unconsciously skating on the ragged edge of suicide.

The withdrawal syndrome begins twenty-four hours after the last dose and reaches its peak in two to three days. It is characterized by anxiety, tremor, weakness, distortion of visual perception, insomnia, and sometimes grand-mal convulsions and delirium similar to delirium tremens as seen in some cases during withdrawal from alcohol; a major psychotic episode may be provoked.

Alcohol produces psychic dependence of varying degrees from mild (alcohol is missed if not available) to moderate (more than occasional, inappropriate intoxication in a social setting, and often a secret source of supply) to strong (drinking more than is culturally approved, an obsession with the supply of alcohol, and serious interference with personal and social life).

Physical dependence develops slowly and only after fairly heavy consumption. Tolerance develops slowly and is far from complete, especially to doses sufficient to produce coma, and it may diminish to the point of unusual sensitivity in the later stages of alcoholism. Physical dependence and tolerance usually do not develop at social drinking levels.

The withdrawal syndrome is very similar to that of barbiturates and other sedatives. Both types are severe and may result in grand-mal convulsions and/or delirium. It is interesting to note that there is also partial cross-tolerance between alcohol and the barbiturates. That is one reason why barbiturates are relatively effective in controlling the withdrawal syndrome associated with alcohol dependence. These two forms of dependence are essentially a single type.

The moderate use of alcohol in its various beverage forms is not deviant behaviour in most countries of the world, although in certain countries in North Africa, the Middle East and the Indian-Pakistani subcontinent such use is considered so; but even in some of them the prevalence seems to be increasing. The immoderate use of alcohol is deviate behaviour in essentially all countries. It would appear that, of those who drink at all, a certain percentage do become dependent on alcohol. Estimates made some time between 1945 and 1963 on the rate of alcoholism per 100,000 persons in the population aged 20 or over in selected countries include the following: England and Wales—865 to 1100; Switzerland—2100 to 2700; Chile—3610 to 4150; various states of the United States—1500 to 7090; and France—5200 to 7300 (WHO Expert Committee on Mental Health, 1967). The highest figure is about 8.5 times that of the lowest and illustrates the variability in rates of alcoholism.

However, I want to relate these figures to those given earlier for drugs of the morphine type. In the UK, that figure was 1 in 24,500, as compared with 1 in 99 to 117 for alcoholism. The highest estimated rate of current narcotic use in the world is 1 in 45; the highest alcoholic rate is 1 in 13.7.

Drugs producing dependence of the *amphetamine* type are central nervous system stimulants. Medically, they are effective in treating narcolepsy and certain types of hyperactive behaviour in children. However, they are most widely used in medical practice as appetite suppressants. Not all drugs producing dependence of the amphetamine type are amphetamines. Other central nervous system stimulants such as methylphenidate and phenmetrazine are also involved.

This group of drugs produces mood elevation, elation and a sense of heightened awareness. It is these effects that are desired by certain persons and results in their psychic dependence. With large doses, such dependence is often rapid and strong. Tolerance, especially to low doses, is relatively slow to develop and irregular. It may, however, start to develop at usual therapeutic dose levels and can become very marked. When very large amounts are taken, tolerance develops rapidly. Doses several hundred times the therapeutic amount have been taken by highly tolerant persons. There is little, if any, physical dependence and there is thus no abstinence syndrome *per se*, but exhaustion and depression are frequently seen following cessation of intoxication. The visual distortions, hallucinations and sometimes psychotic episodes seen in amphetamine-dependent persons are initiated by intoxication, not withdrawal.

Drugs of the amphetamine type are used in deviant ways in a number of places in the world. One pattern involves the oral self-administration of relatively stable amounts ranging from one or two to several therapeutic doses daily or intermittently. Persons of all ages, especially those of middle age, appear to be concerned. A second pattern involves a rapid escalation over periods of one or two weeks to massive oral and often intravenous doses. Such deviant use is to be found primarily among late adolescents and young adults. One or both of these patterns of use have been identified in Canada, Japan, Sweden, the United Kingdom and the United States of America, among others. Such use in Japan and the United Kingdom has markedly decreased and the trend is said to be downward in Sweden, although deviant use of amphetamine-type drugs is beginning to appear in certain African, European, South American and other countries.

Cocaine, like the amphetamines, is a central nervous system stimulant and produces toxic and euphoriant effects similar to those of drugs producing dependence of the amphetamine type. It is not included among those drugs because, unlike them, it produces no tolerance.

Cocaine is derived from the leaves of the coca plant, which is indigenous to the Andean region of South America. Formerly used in medical practice as a potent local anaesthetic, it has largely been replaced by equally effective anaesthetics without dependence liability.

Cocaine produces very strong psychic dependence. The drug produces a sense of excitement, heightened and distorted awareness and hallucinations. There is no physical dependence, nor tolerance. However, since the drug is rapidly destroyed in the body, some cocaine-dependent persons take up to ten grams per day during "sprees." There is no withdrawal syndrome *per se*, but there is often marked exhaustion when the intoxication wears off.

The chewing of coca leaves is a very common practice in some localities of the Andean region of South America. Zapata-Ortiz, in 1970, estimated that 6,000,000 persons were regular users in Bolivia and Peru, the principal countries involved. This would mean that 1 in every 2.5 persons of all ages used coca to some extent. Certainly the chewing of coca leaves has a stimulating effect, but the degree of stimulation achieved is simply not to be compared to that resulting from the intravenous use of cocaine.

Many different preparations are derived from the plant *Cannabis sativa L.*, which is ubiquitous in its growth throughout the temperate to tropical zones of the world. These preparations, such as marihuana and hashish, can produce drug dependence of the *cannabis type*. Though still used in some traditional systems of medicine, cannabis has essentially no place in modern medicine.

As with other drugs, the effects of cannabis depend greatly on the amount taken. Cannabis preparations produce effects ranging from anxiety, mood elevation, elation, hilarity, distortions of sensory (particularly visual) perception and loss of inhibitions to delusions, paranoid ideas, depersonalization, agitation, confusion and sedation. These effects lead to a moderate-to-strong psychic dependence on the part of *some* experimenters and are apparently the basis for continued use on the part of heavy users. As with narcotics, the immediate psychic effect produced depends a good deal on the expectations and desires of the user. There is relatively little, if any, tolerance in man, little tendency to increase the dose, little, if any, physical dependence, and hence no regularly reported withdrawal syndrome. Recent reports, however, indicate the need for further studies of tolerance and physical dependence in man.

The use of cannabis in one or another of its several forms—bhang, ganja, charras, marihuana, maconha, kif and hashish, to mention but a few—is particularly widespread in those areas of the world where alcohol is least used. It is also relatively prevalent in some countries where alcohol is widely used. Alcohol is not widely used in India. In certain parts of that country the use of bhang, which is usually taken orally, is neither illegal nor socially unacceptable, while the availability of ganja, a stronger preparation, is controlled and the use of charras is prescribed. Ganja is usually more potent than bhang and marihuana; charras is a resinous material comparble to hashish which is more potent than other commonly used preparations. There is great variation in the potency of cannabis preparations, so that one sample of marihuana may be practically inert while another may be stronger than some samples of ganja or hashish. This, no doubt, accounts for some of the differing views expressed about the "effects of marihuana." The nature of cannabis preparations used varies widely, not only in the Indian-Pakistani subcontinent, but also in certain Middle Eastern, African and South American countries, and their use is gaining popularity in some North and South American and Western European countries.

Drugs of the *hallucinogen type* include lysergide (more popularly known as LSD), mescaline, psilocybin, and dimethyl tryptamine (known as DMT). Lysergide is a synthetic substance; it is readily made from lysergic acid which occurs in ergot, a parasitic fungus that grows on rye and other grains. Psilocybin occurs in certain mushrooms and mescaline in peyote, a form of cactus. Other hallucinogens such as DMT and STP are purely synthetic materials.

Aside from the very local use of hallucinogenic mushrooms and peyote in certain native religious ceremonies, these substances are used largely by those who have more than usual interest in artistic and intellectual pursuits, whether or not they excel in these fields, and by others for "kicks" (changes in sensory perception, development of hallucinations, etc.) and particularly for "expansion of consciousness" and "mystical insight." Such use is to be found primarily in developed countries of the West. Some seek insight into their own emotional problems. Those who *repeatedly* use these drugs in an attempt to achieve the described experience may be said to have psychic dependence. There is no physical dependence. However, tolerance develops rapidly and can be marked. There is cross-tolerance among at least the first four hallucinogens named. The sensations described, as well as the panic reactions and frank psychoses not infrequently produced, are manifestations of intoxication and not of withdrawal.

The use of dependence-producing drugs involves a complex interaction between the properties of the drug taken, the characteristics of the drug taker and his socio-cultural environment.

The capacity to induce psychic dependence is the only characteristic shared by all dependence-producing drugs. Not all persons who experiment with, or even use, these drugs develop psychic dependence. Some persons are more prone than others to develop such dependence, and some drugs are more liable than others to induce it. Psychic dependence may be said to exist when the use of dependence-producing drugs becomes an important life-organizing factor or a stereotyped response to a wide variety of internal and external stimuli. Drug-taking becomes an important life-organizing factor when substantial amounts of time and energy are devoted to obtaining, thinking about, using or discussing the drug or drugs in question; it is a stereotyped response when a person tends to deal with all problems and joys by taking drugs.

Among the more important motives that often appear to be associated with the use of drugs are (1) to escape from something, (2) to have a new, pleasurable or thrilling experience, (3) to achieve improved "understanding" or "insight," (4) to achieve a sense of belonging, and (5) to express independence and sometimes hostility.

In settings where a particular drug is socially acceptable, moderate use tends to be widespread. However, when large numbers of persons use a drug, and attitudes towards intoxication are lenient or ambivalent, a significant proportion of users tend to become dependent. Where the use of a drug is not culturally accepted, such individual use as does occur tends to be excessive though not widespread in the population. The deviant use of drugs often appears to be associated with rapid socio-economic change and may be related to a weakening of cultural controls as old patterns of living are replaced by new. Also, the extent and rapidity of mass communication and transportation now enables many persons in one part of the world to learn quickly of the doings of others far away. The sensational manner in which news of drug use and users is sometimes presented, rumours and misinformation about alleged benefits of such use may stimulate some persons to seek out and experiment with drugs. Looking at some of the so-called news reports on drugs, I am sometimes reminded of a perhaps apocryphal entrepreneur, active in the United States during the prohibition era, who marketed, at least temporarily, a packet containing sugar and a fruit flavour. The label read somewhat as follows: "Instructions: Use only for the preparation of syrup! Warning: Do *not* place in an earthenware container with yeast and cover with two gallons of water. To do so might result in the production of an alcoholic beverage, which is unlawful."

"...women who drink heavily are far likelier to drink for escape reasons than their male counterparts...."

Although there is a tendency to regard it as a beverage rather than a drug, alcohol probably produces serious consequences on a more widespread scale than any of the more publicized drugs of abuse. Ms. Ford reviews a number of patterns of drinking and some characteristics of different groups of drinkers.

The typical U.S. heavy drinker is: (a) a skinny derelict sobbing over a glass of whiskey, (b) a middle-aged executive gulping a secret "quick one" before a suburban party, (c) an aged spinster sipping gin in her rented room, (d) none of these. The correct answer? The last one. According to the most extensive survey ever made of American drinking practices, the *typical* heavy drinker is more likely to be that friendly young man in the next apartment than any of the stereotypes above.

The results of the survey, which was conducted by George Washington University during a few months in 1964 and 1965, were published this spring under the title *American Drinking Practices*. If you can wade through the statistics, the book presents some intriguing data on U.S. drinkers and non-drinkers. Two-thirds of the 2746 respondents in all parts of the country drink, it reveals, 53 percent of them at least once a month. But only 12 percent can be called heavy drinkers.

What is this hard-drinking 12 percent really like?

A composite picture of the typical heavy drinker as revealed by the respondents' own answers to a lengthy questionnaire indicates that he is likely to be a male under 45, married and a big city resident. Born in this country in an urban area, he is probably a high school graduate who works as a businessman, a semi-skilled worker or a service worker. He does not attend church regularly but he describes his religious affiliation most often as Catholic, or, if he is of Irish descent, liberal Protestant.

He gets along fairly well with his wife and family, has more friends than average and is no more neurotic or alienated than you or I. He seldom drinks alone and he prefers beer to wine or whiskey. His parents, his wife and his friends are likely to drink too, some of the friends "quite a bit." They do not frown on his drinking. He says he would miss drinking a lot, even though he experiences unfavorable effects from it. He maintains he used to drink more but he doesn't think of himself as a heavy drinker now.

An impulsive fellow, he is probably a heavy smoker and overweight.

What about women who drink heavily? They do exist—five percent compared to 21 percent for males—but while their traits, in general, are similar to those of their male counterparts, they do present a slightly different picture. Women heavy drinkers are more neurotic and alienated, lose their tempers more, and, for some reason, do not tend to be overweight.

The survey that elicited these portraits of the heavy drinker was directed by three researchers from George Washington University's Social Research Group: Dr. Don Cahalan, Dr. Ira H. Cisin and Miss Helen M. Crossley. "Sure, we drink," smiles Miss Crossley, a bubbly, plump, blonde woman as she eats an ice cream sundae during a recent interview. "We fired one guy who was a total abstainer and we caught him at it," adds Dr. Cahalan, a slim, gray-haired man who sips a glass of iced tea.

Categories of Drinkers

It is obviously a favorite joke. But Cahalan points out that even the interviewers used in the survey were drinkers because abstainers were found to obtain less honest answers from the respondents.

Their recently-published book, Cahalan goes on to explain, marks the half-way point in a 20-year program of drinking research being sponsored at GWU under grants from the National Institutes of Mental Health. At this stage of the research, he is concentrating on the heavy drinkers revealed by the survey, particularly a group that the survey refers to as "heavy escape" drinkers. This group, six percent of all respondents questioned (nine percent of all the drinkers), includes those whom Cahalan believes either are, or will probably become, "problem drinkers"—in more familiar terminology, alcoholics. Cahalan is now completing a second, follow-up survey that discusses drinking-related problems.

"We want to know what kind of behavior early in the game is predictive of problems later," he says. "We would expect that a person who does a number of atypical things is more likely to get in trouble."

In *American Drinking Practices,* the basic categories of drinkers are based on three factors: amount drunk per occasion, number of occasions and variability. The last is a combination of the amount usually drunk and the most ever drunk. Respondents are also scored on their consumption of three different kinds of alcoholic beverages: spirits (whiskey, gin, etc), beer and wine. What the GWU researchers end up with, after applying various complex statistical methods to their data, are five basic classifications: heavy, moderate, light, infrequent and abstainers.

A *typical* drinker in each category consumes alcohol in the following pattern:

- Heavy: either drinks every day, with at least five or more drinks on occasion, or drinks at least once a week, usually downing five or more drinks at a time.
- Moderate: drinks several times a month but usually takes no more than three or four drinks per occasion.

- Light: drinks at least once a month but keeps his consumption down to one or two drinks per occasion.
- Infrequent: drinks less than once a month.
- Abstainer: does not drink at all.

How do you get respondents to tell you how much they drink, particularly when the answers could be embarrassing? As Cahalan and Miss Crossley explain, the GWU questionnaire, the subject of which is described in vague terms ("what people do in their leisure time") begins with general questions. Alcohol is not even mentioned until Question No. 8. "People don't usually catch on until about the 20th question," says Miss Crossley. After alcohol is introduced, clever phrasing of questions leads respondents to believe that no matter how much or how often they drink, someone drinks more.

One crucial question in the survey covers reasons for drinking. Eleven such reasons are furnished, five so-called "escape" reasons, four "social" reasons and two "enjoyment" reasons. One escape reason, for instance, is "I drink when I want to forget everything." One social reason is, simply, "I drink to be sociable." One enjoyment reason is "I like the taste." Respondents who say at least two out of the five escape reasons are "fairly" or "very" important to them are arbitrarily classified as escape drinkers.

Twenty-nine percent of all the persons interviewed fell into the "escape" class but only six percent, as noted before, qualified as both escape drinkers and heavy drinkers. The GWU researchers offer some interesting insights into this small but significant group based on the heavy escape drinker's responses on the carefully-worded questionnaires.

Compared to the heavy social drinker, the data shows, the heavy escape drinker is not nearly as likely to be that friendly young man next door. Neurotic and alienated, the heavy escape drinker worries about everything: his drinking, his health, his goals, his occupation. He thinks the past year was not a good one for him, he claims "more than my share of problems" and his childhood, according to him, was unhappy. When depressed or nervous, he is much more likely not only to drink but to eat, smoke or take tranquilizers—all oral gratifications, as the GWU group notes.

Generally, the heavy-escape drinker tends to be older and of lower social status and income than other heavy drinkers. The group also includes an above average percentage of non-whites. Less gregarious than other heavy drinkers, the heavy-escape drinker is more likely to have parents or a spouse who drink. More parents, however, tend to disapprove of drinking.

Although slightly more men drinkers than women drinkers drink to escape (32 percent compared to 26 percent), women who drink heavily are far likelier to drink for escape reasons than their male counterparts (64 percent compared to 48 percent). The reasons, the GWU group suggests, lie in the American culture's lack of permissiveness towards women who drink heavily. A woman who dares to drink heavily is much more likely to be a non-conformist or to have problems —or simply to have more problems because she drinks heavily.

The GWU classification of basic types of drinkers runs into one particular snag, as the researchers are quick to admit. It fails to distinguish between the drinker who drinks often but lightly—one or two drinks—and the drinker who drinks less often but puts away half a dozen or more each time. The first kind of drinker is called the "spaced" drinker, the second the "massed" drinker.

In an appendix to *American Drinking Practices,* the authors suggest a new classification that takes massed and spaced drinking into account. When the new system is applied to the 1964–65 data, the indications are that the massed drinker has a lot more problems than the spaced drinker, even though they may end up consuming the same amount of alcohol at the end of the year. The massed drinker reports more often that someone—friend, family, spouse, employer, neighbor—tried to get him to drink less during the past year. Massed drinkers themselves worry more about their drinking.

Massed drinkers are also more likely to say they would miss drinking if they had to give it up, they get angrier oftener, they are more dependent on drinking to cope with problems, and they are more likely to have had hangovers during the past year. Massed drinkers report themselves less satisfied with life, too.

The study Dr. Cahalan is now completing on problem drinking follows up 80 percent of the respondents in the first survey. Three years have elapsed between the two surveys. To determine the prevalence of drinking-related problems in this group, Cahalan devised a list of 11 different kinds of problems, ranging in seriousness from trouble with the police to drinking to coping with stress. A respondent gets a high score if he has at least one problem in a severe form or three or more problems in a mild form.

Nine percent of all the drinkers questioned in this second survey do get a high score, a figure that corresponds exactly to the nine percent of all drinkers who were found to be heavy escape drinkers three years earlier. The new study confirms that more men than women and more persons under 50 have drinking problems, but it finds some new problem patterns among men and women. Men's drinking problems taper off only after age 70, but women's drinking problems decline much earlier—after 50. Men seem to have more problems in their 20s, while the danger age for women comes in their 30s and 40s—possibly because women start to drink later than men.

In his new study, Cahalan is trying to link problem drinking with other factors to see if he can come up with a short list of "clues" that might alert health workers to a possible future problem drinker. He lumps the factors he is investigating into six big categories: exposure, social ties, expectations, alienation, conformity and attitudes. At the present time, he and his GWU colleagues are still trying to develop statistically significant factors (usually called "independent variables"), but they have already come up with one and possibly two that seem to be definitely linked with problem drinking.

Can you guess which is the most significant of the six categories listed above? *Attitudes toward drinking.* The significance of this factor surprised the researchers a little, too. Cahalan says that the attitudes towards drinking measured in the first GWU survey constituted the best single measure to predict the drinking problems he found three years later.

Some other intriguing data revealed in the second survey:

• The second significant independent variable measured thus far is exposure to drinking, which includes permissiveness towards it.

- Men with high risk scores on all independent variables continue to have problems with drinking long after other drinkers taper off.
- There is a substantial turnover in heavy drinkers, about half of them drinking more and about half less.
- Among the major religions, Catholics have the most problem drinkers, Jews the fewest.
- Men of lower economic and social status have more drinking problems.
- The largest cities contain the most problem drinkers.

Cahalan emphasizes that both GWU studies, unlike most other studies of drinking, are based on samples of *household* populations. As such, they do not include institutionalized alcoholics. But what they do include, he believes, are the problem drinkers who risk becoming tomorrow's institutionalized drinkers. In a few years, the GWU researchers plan to follow up their sample to see which early-warning signals present in their first surveys have been followed by the development of the more serious consequences of problem drinking.

36. Smoking
Amy Gross

"Though the body may become nonaddicted after two weeks, the head stays hooked for months, some say years."

Nicotine, like alcohol, is not often considered by society to be a drug. But nicotine, like alcohol, is a drug that is widely used, abused, and has serious consequences for the individual and society. Ms. Gross not only describes some reasons for smoking, but, more important, describes some techniques for stopping smoking.

Smoker Personalities . . .
Dr. Silvan Tomkins, the man everyone quotes when they're getting down to smoking basics, was an addicted smoker and stopped, years ago, by going to movies for three days and nights. So he is comfortably empathetic—he knows the draws of a cigarette and the people who are drawn.

"There's no one smoker personality," he told us. "But there are kinds of people who tend to be one or another kind of smoker.

"*The Positive-Affect Smoker* is someone who's well in control of himself, smokes for enjoyment and in moderation—never more than three, four cigarettes a day, usually with a drink, or coffee, or after a meal. He's an exceptional human being, ordering his experience to get the maximum out of life. And his smoking isn't a real problem.

"*The Negative-Affect Smoker* uses a cigarette as a pacifier. He reaches for it when he's in trouble, and he's in trouble often enough so that he smokes quite a lot. He may go on to solve the problem, or he may smoke instead of attacking the problem. . . . He may be an overly dependent person. . . . He smokes erratically—enjoying a vacation, for example, he might not smoke at all. You can find what part of his life is most difficult by seeing where he smokes most—at the office, at home.

"*The Addictive Smoker* starts needing a cigarette the minute he's stamped one out. He craves cigarettes, panics at the thought of giving them up. The addict is usually a negative-affect smoker for whom the cigarette has become an end in itself, rather than a way out of trouble. Interestingly, neither the addict nor the negative smoker really enjoys smoking, just as the compulsive eater doesn't really enjoy eating—he doesn't eat slowly enough to taste the food, savor the experience. And part of both the negative-affect/addict patterns is habitual smoking—burning up cigarettes without being aware they're smoking."

. . . And How They Stop

"*A Time to Mourn:* The addict's suffering, when he stops, is real, and similar to the mourning experience. When a loved one dies, there's an idealization of what's been lost. So, with cigarettes, there's a magnification of the desire to smoke, and a magnification of the threat of suffering. It's extraordinary—it looks as though you won't be able to tolerate the deprivation, that it will just get worse and worse. It's a trial by fire, and the memory of it keeps you from backsliding—ex-addicts rarely return to cigarettes.

"*When a negative-affect smoker stops,* the suffering is more subdued, but he has difficulty. He doesn't think he can stop. He'll try—and stay off for a month or so—but will backslide easily when tension mounts.

"*The positive-affect smoker* only needs to be shown the health facts about smoking for him to stop. His smoking is driven not by suffering but by the promise of rewards. When he sees that the rewards are not what he thought, he renounces them. It's ironic: those who enjoy smoking most can easily give it up, and they're the ones who least need to stop."

What Kind of Smoker You Are

Say it's 11:00 P.M. and you're home, undressed for the evening, and you've just finished your last cigarette. What do you do?

(a) . . . Get dressed and find an open store.
(b) . . . Plan to get a pack first thing in the morning.
(c) . . . Think lightly that you'll pick up a pack sometime tomorrow.

If you've checked:

(a) you're probably an addicted smoker
(b) a negative-affect smoker
(c) a positive-affect smoker.

Who Smokes?

Psychologists pocketed away in universities and hospitals around the country are attempting to define The Smoker. They're not having very much luck. What's proved in Seattle is doubted in Gainesville, and statistical slivers of difference are fleshed out into published papers. Here, just to profile the direction of current research, a sweeping up of the slivers.

Smokers have been found to be more: extroverted, restless, impulsive, active, independent, open to new experience, defiant, rebellious, disobedient, thin, anxious . . .

than nonsmokers who've been found to: get better grades in school; have greater internal organization (meaning a more consistent sense of identity); be more religious—or at least be more likely to attend church regularly.

Cigarettes Work Three Ways

"They serve a social function—to bring you closer to other smokers. A cigarette is contagious, like a yawn. Sixty per cent of cigarettes are smoked with other smokers. The gestures, the exchange of lights, ash trays, packs are part of the forces that make a group cohesive. The social gesture of offering a cigarette, or a light, is an ice breaker—it works. Tomkins says Americans are inhibited: given the powerful jolt of alcohol, at a party, say, a cigarette follows logically as a step toward intimacy. . . .

"A role function—the gestures, the style of the smoking ritual, the choice of lighter, cigarette case, holder, the brand of cigarette—that's all part of self-concept. Actors use the fact and the style of smoking to build up a character. . . . We've asked college girls how they thought they looked when they smoked, and many indicated that they regarded smoking as part of the pattern of behavior of a sophisticated person, as making for an air of being busy, involved. . . .

"An emotional function—to stimulate or sedate, or simply for pleasure" (Dr. Bernard Mausner, Beaver College).

"Me and My Winstons . . . We Got a Real Good Thing . . ."

An illiterate ploy playing on one draw of a cigarette. Listen to these smokers, ex-smokers: "There's something so companionable about a cigarette" . . . "It's my constant friend" . . . "There's a tremendous loneliness when you stop."

"Cigarettes," says Dr. Tomkins, "offer a sedative kind of friendship."

"Compulsive Behavior—dealing with food, cigarettes, booze, whatever—is powerfully reinforcing. It alleviates anxiety, is a method of self-control, of adjusting feelings" (Jay Tooley, Jacksonville [Ill.] State Hospital).

" 'Orality' " is a fancy psychological term for deprivation," says Dr. Martin Jacobs of Boston U. School of Medicine. "We've found that addicted smokers share a sense of having been deprived as children, and a certain amount of bitterness for one or both of their parents. They're defensive—instead of a woe-is-me attitude, they've adopted a defiant, I-don't-need-you stance, an exaggerated self-reliance. And because they don't trust people, they've turned to objects for support. It's the same thing with people who overeat, overdrink, live on addictive pills, pile up possessions—they're all turning to substitutes for people.

"You just can't tell these smokers to stop on their own. You have to recognize the strength of the drive, the importance of cigarettes in their life. We're trying short-term group therapy—to teach them how to be non-smokers, to help them turn to other people instead of objects."

Fidget

"Smoking organizes a chain of small, continuous movements that's an acceptable outlet for tension. This chain, rather than anything in the smoke, may be the primary explanation for whatever calming effects smoking may have. And if that's true, then someone who wants to stop smoking might find it helpful to devise an alternate chain of movements" (Dr. Leo Srole, Columbia U. College of Physicians and Surgeons).

"One of the pleasures of smoking is the local irritating effect of nicotine, and the damage brought about by the heat of the smoke and some of its chemicals. The chronic bronchitis of a heavy smoker creates an 'itch' in his throat, which he interprets as a hunger for a cigarette and scratches with the hot nicotinized smoke from the next cigarette. If not scratched, the local irritation will disappear within a week or two" (Dr. Borje Ejrup, the New York Hospital Cornell Medical Center).

"The warm air, the stimulation of the lips—the pacifier effect—*that* may be what's calming about a cigarette" (Dr. Mausner).

"What's relaxing about a cigarette is not in the smoke but in the deep inhalation—it reproduces the mechanics of a sigh, which calms the nervous system, ventilates the lungs, forces out accumulated carbon dioxide, and stimulates the blood-flow to the heart" (Dr. Ejrup).

When a nonsmoker feels nervous or hungry, he thinks he's nervous or hungry. When a smoker feels nervous or hungry, he thinks he wants a cigarette.

The Cigarette as Smoke Screen

"The face," says Dr. Tomkins, "is the locus of emotional life." Rather than reflecting what's going on in the inner show, the face directs the show.

How: "Every emotion—terror, excitement, anger—has an instinctual cry that's sealed off first in the face. A stimulus produces an automatic change in breathing and a change in blood-flow to the face—hot in anger, cold in fear—which moves the nerve receptors in the face to a position of heightened sensitivity. The feedback from those now-extrasensitive receptors *is* the emotional experience. And anything that changes the set of the musculature of the mouth changes the feedback. Smoking substitutes a rhythmic, relaxed muscle pattern for a tense, angry, or anxious one. And it regulates breathing—deepens the shallow breaths of depressions, smooths the deep, irregular breathing of anger. These physical changes spare you the strain of trying to control and conceal the signs of negative emotion—and that, in and of itself, is a relief."

Hooked

"There's no question in my mind that smoking is a real pharmacological habit. I believe there's a physical dependence on nicotine, just like the dependence on heroin, but not as strong. Nicotine may operate as an amphetamine, to release certain substances from the brain that improve mood, and thereby reinforce the smoking behavior. The solution to the smoking problem isn't to isolate the nicotine: it's a poison and you can't market it, except in a white paper cylinder" (Dr. Murray Jarvik, Albert Einstein College of Medicine).

What nicotine does that you could get hung up on

Nicotine turns up:

- pulse rate (5–20 extra beats a minute)
- blood pressure
- intestinal motor activity
- circulation on skin
- relase of ready-to-go-to-work sugar; and it . . .
- stimulates central nervous system
- extends the dream stage of sleep.

Nicotine turns down:

- reflex response
- sensitivity to bitter taste/sugar/salt/touch
- sharpness of vision
- appetite
- absorption of food.

"The impulse to smoke is probably a chemical process. Since the desire subsides, usually, in one to two minutes, we can assume that the chemical of the impulse is destroyed and fades away if new impulses don't follow. If the smoker stops thinking about wanting a cigarette, the urge disappears, in a very short time" (Dr. Ejrup).

If you're thinking about stopping . . .

There's help to be had. The problems of helping people stop, and helping them stay stopped, are keeping a lot of other people busy. Some current answers . . .

Hypnosis is, for many, the most inviting answer. It seems to be a short cut to the level of motivation required to stop (one girl sat through a group hypnotherapy session just out of curiosity and hasn't smoked since). And it seems to reduce the withdrawal agonies. "The smoker can deal with his irritability, tension, anxiety better with hypnotherapy than with any other method," said Dr. William Nuland, president of the Society for Clinical and Experimental Hypnosis, who sees, he says, "the last resorters, the ones who've tried everything."

One of these last resorters, a self-described "oral-compulsive truly happy only when smoking, eating, and talking at the same time," made notes as she unlatched herself from two-pack-a-day smoking:

> "I've stopped before. Several times. Real nightmares . . . the thought of stopping again terrified me. Then, a couple of friends went through hypnosis and it sounded as though part of the constant conscious "no" work (whenever I stop smoking, my brain sets up an incessant and exhausting chant of "no, no, no, you may not have a cigarette, no . . .") would be shouldered by the unconscious, and also, as though I'd learn how to relax away the knottiness of nonsmoking.
>
> Dr. Nuland, a fatherly, family-doctor sort, asked half an hour's worth of questions (included: why did I smoke; why did I want to stop), assured me that the hypnotic state was like being *almost* asleep—i.e., I was not to worry about being sawed in half.
>
> Well, after my arm became weightless and rose off my leg, and we —Dr. Nuland and I—rode down a ten-flight escalator slanted in my head, I arrived at a velvety dark, warm-bath feeling. I was disturbed only by the conviction that I was cheating—that I was not really hypnotized, and I was playing along merely to be nice to Dr. Nuland. His voice was feeding me back my reasons for wanting to stop, leading me to imagine myself not smoking in different situations, telling me that when I'd want a cigarette, I'd breathe deeply and imagine myself as relaxed as I was at that moment (and that was v . . . . e . . . . rrr . . . . rr . . . . y . . . . r . . . . ee . . . . l . . . . a . . . . ah . . . . x . . . . e . . . . d . . . .).
>
> Afterward, I felt swimmingly loose, limp, and happy for about three hours. And I felt as though I'd been rewired. I'd note an urge for a cigarette and automatically I'd be breathing in great gulps of air. A total and amusing absence of free will—I didn't have a chance to resist the urge on my own—which lasted about a day. By the end of the week, it had occurred to me that I really loved smoking. I'd been talking to Dr. Nuland during the week, and I told him life was not easy. So a second session—a booster shot—was arranged with Dr. Peter Field, a psychologist associate of Dr. Nuland. . . . Today's the last of the first 14 killer days. I feel a flurry for a cigarette maybe three, four times a day, but I don't take it very seriously. And I am often aware of an itch at the bottom of my stomach, but that fades when something's absorbing me, and deep breathing helps, too. And I never want to smoke again. Never.

"Dr. Nuland's method," says Dr. Field, "stresses a high degree of individuation—fitting the smoker's motivation and experience to the hypnotherapy suggestions—and a high degree of maintenance. Patients have to call in, keep in touch. There may be a second or even a third session: the first to deal with the smoking, another to deal with withdrawal symptoms like tension, weight gain, perhaps a relapse. The fears of substitute symptoms, by the way, are greatly exaggerated—Dr. Nuland's found this to be very rare. . . . Hypnosis is quicker than any other method. And the personal component is stronger—the relationship between therapist and patient fortifies the nonsmoking."

To find a hypnotherapist: write to the Society for Clinical and Experimental Hypnosis, Inc., 353 W. 57th St., N.Y., N.Y. 10019; include stamped envelope.

Group withdrawal programs are for those who find competition spurring, team spirit heartening. How to find one: check local public-health service; or phone book for privately organized clinics, which go by names like Smokestoppers, Smoke Watchers, Society to Overcome Puffing (S.T.O.P.). This last will set up shop in companies and colleges. For info, write to Suite 9C, 777 United Nations Plaza, N.Y., N.Y. 10017. . . . The Five-Day Plan of the Seventh Day Adventists gentles you through the first five days of unsmoking.

Volunteer. . . . If you're at school, check the psych department to see if anyone's doing research in unsmoking, and offer your services as a guinea pig.

Drugs. . . . By which we mean everything from a kindly doctor's issuing you a threat (e.g., you'll lose all your teeth by the time you're 30 unless you stop) and a week's worth of mild tranquilizers, to the various nicotine-antagonistic drugs. What's being used primarily is one or another form of lobeline, a nicotine-like chemical that: a) answers some of the withdrawal need for nicotine, and b) makes smoking prohibitively unpleasant. Packaged into tablets, most research reviewers find it no more effective than placebos (which are often effective). . . . Dr. Ejrup injects massive doses of lobeline or a nicotine derivative during the first ten days of nonsmoking, and finds that his patients are "amazed" at the absence of withdrawal symptoms. . . . Dr. Jarvik's research suggests M.D.-prescribed amphetamines might be helpful. . . . The key to most drug treatment is probably the fact that a doctor is involved. You feel you're in authoritative hands; you feel a responsibility to him to "do well"; your suffering is minimal because he's told you it will be minimal.

Write away: a little book called "Learning to Live Without Cigarettes," for instance, is waiting to help. Every trick to help you stop, every reason why you should. A limited supply of complimentary-to-MLLE copies is on tap at: the Philadelphia Dept. of Health, Room 540, Municipal Services Bldg., Philadelphia, Pa. 19107. Or check with local bookshop (it's published by Doubleday). And/or write to American Cancer Society; they'll stuff your mailbox with brochures.

Behavioral therapists, working on the generally accepted principle that smoking is a piece of learned behavior, are trying to devise ways of helping people unlearn it.

"Find a highly probable behavior," suggests Jay Tooley (of the Center for Human Actualization at Jacksonville [Ill.] State Hospital), "like getting up from your desk at work, walking into your room at school, drinking coffee, and link it up with a reinforcing thought pattern. Make a contract with yourself, for instance, that before you can sip your coffee, you will think about some grisly aspect of smoking—the likelihood of emphysema, say—then about how much better you'll feel when you stop. Keep a chart of when you smoke, and how much—this self-monitoring calls attention to each cigarette and, in and of itself, tends to reduce smoking."

Stopping

"You can't be relaxed and anxious simultaneously. People can be conditioned to respond to an anxiety-provoking stimulus with a relaxation response rather than the previously conditioned and undesirable response" (Jay Tooley). SO— when the urge hits:

(1) smooth your brow with your fingers
(2) push down your shoulders
(3) breathe deeply, slowly.

How to Puff Your Way out of a Nicotine Fit

Press index finger against left nostril. Breathe in through right nostril to count of four. Hold breath to count of eight, then exhale. Reverse sides and repeat.

Panic measure: Quickly pull yourself up straight; put your index and third fingers against your almost-closed lips in holding-a-cigarette position; and breathe in deeply through your mouth, drawing the air all the way down deep to your abdomen. Exhale completely. Repeat until you're reconnected to reality.

Stretch . . . any way and every way in private. In public, though, simply breathe in while you lift rib cage and subtly move arms as if to touch elbows behind you; exhale, pushing shoulders down, stretching up neck.

If you feel the craving in your stomach . . .

(1) Drink something warm—that's like putting those tense muscles into hydrotherapy
(2) Rub your stomach, Buddha-like, to shake out the tension in muscles
(3) Breathe, yogalike. Sit up straight, arms relaxed in your lap. Exhale completely. Inhale through nose, using air to push abdomen out. Exhale, pulling in abdomen and holding breath for five to seven seconds. Repeat 10–15 times. Concentrate on moving only abdomen, not chest.

The Empty Mouth

When you stop smoking, you will interpret the absence of tobacco taste in your mouth as a signal to smoke. This is, obviously, a misinterpretation. Carry around a mouth spray, or some kind of breath freshener, or even a tiny tube of toothpaste, and spritz or dab tongue when the signal's emitted.

Before giving in and lighting up . . . isolate the craving. What exactly do you want in the cigarette? The ammonia? Carbon monoxide? Formaldehyde? Hydrocyanic acid (a component of gas-chamber gas)? Nitric acid (helps hydrochloric acid dissolve gold)? Tars (the glop used in labs to give rats and mice cancer)? Nicotine (one drop in blood would kill an adult)? Radioactive polonium?

Though the body may become nonaddicted after two weeks, the head stays hooked for months, some say years. Be prepared.

How Not to Suffer without . . .

The Prebreakfast Cigarette. Acclaimed by most addicted smokers as the kingpin cig of the day because "it wakes me up." Dr. Tomkins labels this baby a negative-affect cigarette, knows that for some people, waking up is a minor trauma: "They need the mild initial stimulation of a cigarete." Instead:

(1) first thing you do is devour a fresh orange or grapefruit—whole or juiced, fresh citrus fruits are instant wake-ups

(2) take your shower in the morning rather than at night

(3) stretch this way and that, up and down

(4) grab some deep breaths as you walk by an open window.

The First-Cup-of-Coffee Cigarette. First two weeks off smoking, skip coffee. If that's just too much deprivation, read A.M. newspaper while you sip. Or mete out breakfast so you've got something to nibble with coffee. Or change the way you take your coffee—add or subtract cream or sugar—or take tea, to shake up pattern punctuated by a cigarette. Or swig your coffee, and do something active with extra time. You're going to have a lot more energy and you'll need to siphon it off.

The After-a-Nice-Meal Cigarette. A pleasure smoke, a good reason to linger lazily. To be compensated for by *real* lazy lingering. Think of: just sitting there. Not fluttering or flicking, or burning away the taste of a meal. And while other people are inhaling hot smoke, you are inhaling cool air. . . . Try not to stuff yourself with food: a crammed tum belabors breathing, which will make you want a cigarette. Try, too, ignoring the potatoes during the meal so you can dessert during smoketime.

The With-a-Drink Cigarette. A tough one. The alcohol is a deinhibitor, says Dr. Tomkins, and whatever's been under tension comes out from under. That's likely to be an urge to smoke. Also, he says, the alcohol puffs up an overweening confidence that you can smoke Just One. Prepare yourself to withstand the assault on your iron will. Before you go to the drink-date, sit down somewhere alone and quiet and turn on Prevision: see yourself at the date, without a cigarette, breathing deeply, hands quiet. You're as serene and still as a cat. Imagine X offering you a cigarette; then see yourself easily refusing it, saying thanks but you've stopped. Prevision works—concentrate.

The Crowded-Room Cigarette. Parties are hell for unsmokers—the flow of drinks and people are enough to make admirably strong wills wilt. Many of the cigarettes craved here are probably negative-affect cigs. Crutches. You want not a smoke but a soothing, a supporting. Use Prevision to focus in on you moving easily about that crowded room, unburdened by a fuming cigarette, pack, and lighter, trying to keep your eyes clear of the smoke unfurling from the hands of all those nervous people who are smogging up the room.

Discussion Questions
1. Why do people use drugs?
2. How can people stop using drugs if they wish to?
3. Compare the personal and social consequences of using marijuana, nicotine, and alcohol.
4. If you decided to stop smoking, how could you do it?
5. What, other than chemical effect, determines how people respond to drugs?

Chapter 10
The Counter Culture

The term "counter culture" refers to the values and attitudes of a group of people who find themselves in sharp alienation from the values more commonly held in our society. These common values are seen as belonging to the establishment and are rejected by many young people. The counter culture does not refer to every adolescent who finds himself in opposition to his parents, but only to that group which feels that a sharp and radical revision of our society is necessary. There are some adult spokesmen for this group, including Herbert Marcuse, Norman Brown, Allen Ginsberg, Alan Watts, Timothy Leary, and Paul Goodman. However, while these adults often find themselves attracting attention because of their radical views, the heart of the counter culture is made up of young people.

It is rather easy to state some of the things that the counter culture is against and wishes to see abolished. Foremost among the rejected values is a technocracy that glorifies efficiency, production, and machinery at the expense of the human spirit. Hypocrisy is seen as the hallmark of communication among the over-thirty generation and is sharply rejected. Conservatism as it is expressed in politics, in dress, in openness to experience, and in life style is scorned. Many of the most familiar aspects of our culture are seen as unnecessary or harmful and would not survive the revolution of the counter culture.

The counter culture is not only a statement of alienation but is also a positive assertion of a new set of values. Honesty and openness are valued above all, and members of the counter culture strive to increase their experience and to reject false barriers. The revolution includes relatively minor issues such as dress and appearance and also major areas such as politics and social relations. The selection in another chapter of this book by Herbert Otto describing the development of communes is one example of a radical revision that would be espoused by the counter culture. Traditional patterns of the family and of living are rejected in favor of a more broadly based community.

While the counter culture is espoused by a radical and alienated group, it is possible to observe a number of ways in which the ideas and philosophy of this group have been incorporated into the establishment. This process, known as co-opting, occurs when some of the radical ideas of a minority group are taken over in adulterated form by the group in power, and by doing so much of the strength can be taken away from the radical movement. This can be seen in styles of dress, in hair styles, in popular music, and in many other areas. Something as simple as long hair, which used to be the sign of the alienated young, has now become the badge of the Madison Avenue executive. The music of the Beatles was once seen as very unorthodox, but it recently has become the dominant musical force of the past decade. As the ideas of the young are integrated by the older generation, it serves to invigorate the dominant culture, but it does so at the expense of any likelihood of real revolution.

The image of the counter culture presented in the mass media has generally been an unfavorable one. It is unusual for an antiwar parade to be covered on television without having the camera focus on a long-haired, bearded hippie type. Drugs are prominently discussed, and the general impression is given that the young are radical, non-conformist, and threatening to traditional values. The strength of the counter culture is very rarely presented, and the establishment only sees a picture of the seemingly more dangerous component of that group.

Since the traditional establishment media have not presented the counter culture in a fair way, an alternate channel of public expression known as the underground press has developed. Many magazines and papers have been published which serve as spokesmen for the young; and they probably present as one-sided and radical a position as the establishment media, although they do it in the opposite direction. The underground press is present in high school communities, college communities, and also in a number of nonacademic settings. The high school underground press is discussed by Diane Divoky, as she describes many of the issues that concern these papers and the attempts that often are made to suppress this channel of expression.

The underground press has given rise to a great many rumors and anecdotes about the exploitative attitudes of the establishment toward the counter culture. For every scare story about hippies there are similar stories told about "pigs." Some of the rumors from both sides probably have some degree of truth to them, while others probably are completely unfounded. The usual method of deciding on the truth of these stories is to see whether or not it agrees with one's own prejudice. Obviously this is not the best approach to determining the truth or falsity of an assertion. Behavioral science has provided us with a methodology that is useful in assessing the validity of many social assertions. The conflict between counter culture and establishment is an area ripe for investigation in this manner.

Dr. F. K. Heussenstamm reports a small field study in which one such conflict is explored. This study is not of perfect design, and she discusses ways in which the methodology might be improved upon. However, it is one of the rare attempts to substitute fact for fancy in an emotion-charged area. The area of investigation was the attitude of police officers toward advocates of the Black Panther position. While the establishment claims that policemen behave appropriately and only respond under extreme provocation, the counter-culture claims that their members are martyred and victimized. One small hypothesis generated from these concerns has to do with the fate of individuals who display bumper stickers declaring their allegiance to the Black Panther party. Dr. Heussenstamm's study clearly demonstrates the dangers inherent in displaying such stickers. Clearly this study only reflects upon this one hypothesis, and other hypotheses are as likely to be decided in favor of the establishment as of the counter culture. The important point is that the techniques of behavioral science can be employed, and it is possible to make clear tests of the hypotheses in question.

The usual academic establishment has proven to be a favorite target for the counter culture. The meaninglessness of academic competitiveness, of grading procedures, and of many required features of education have often been cited by the critics of academia. Education is often scorned, and the image of the disembodied intellect proceeding in a feelingless fashion and operating like a robot has been the butt of many counter-culture jokes.

The counter culture has an approach to education that serves as a substitute for traditional techniques. This is the encounter group; the goal of education through encounter is the heightening of feelings. One application of this approach is discussed in another chapter by Terry Borton. A danger of this approach is that the disembodied intellect will be replaced by the mindless discharge of emotion. Many books have been written about variations on the encounter-group theme. These are reviewed in the article by Henry S. Resnick, and in the review a good picture is given of many of the encounter techniques which are employed.

Encounter group has been called our greatest social invention by Dr. Carl R. Rogers, who is one of the foremost psychologists of our time. Dr. Rogers sees the encounter-group philosophy as giving rise to an individual who embodies a new set of values. This person is described in Rogers' paper as "The Person of Tomorrow," and that represents the clearest statement of the idealized member of the counter culture. Both negative aspects of our culture that are rejected and positive values that are endorsed are described in this paper. It is difficult to study this paper without coming away with a clearer view of the goals and values of the counter culture.

Suggested Readings

Howard, Jane. *Please Touch*. New York: Dell, 1971. The author's account of her personal experience with a variety of different approaches to encounter-group leadership. This is one of the books reviewed in the article by Resnick.

Mead, Margaret. *Culture and Commitment*. New York: Doubleday, 1970. The famous anthropologist's book discussing her views about the generation gap. The distinction between postfigurative, cofigurative, and prefigurative cultures, where respectively children learn from adults, both learn from peers, and adults learn from their children, is elaborated.

Rogers, Carl R. *On Becoming a Person*. Boston: Houghton Mifflin, 1961. A thoughtful series of papers by Rogers reflecting upon the human condition. A prime emphasis on the role of psychotherapy in enhancing the growth process.

Roszak, Theodore. *The Making of a Counter Culture*. New York: Doubleday, 1969. A description of the values of the counter culture and some of the primary influences on this subgroup. The book is positive in its endorsement of the values but retains a thoughtful and critical approach.

37. The Way It's Going to Be
Diane Divoky

"...the school used its power to suppress ideas."

If the mass media is controlled by spokesmen for the establishment, we can expect the counter culture to develop its own channels of expression. The underground press is an example of such a development. In this article Ms. Divoky describes some of the methods and concerns of the high school underground press.

The words of the school board were unimpeachable: "It is the aim of our high school to encourage students to freely express themselves, in writing or otherwise, as part of their educational program."

What they meant, in fact, was that the school board in suburban Long Beach, New York, would not allow students to distribute on school premises their fledgling independent newspaper, Frox. The thirteen staff members, supported by their parents, had made a formal written request to the school's principal. Their concessions were clear: "no obscenity," a promise "to publish views in opposition to our own," and a willingness "to accept a faculty adviser who is not a censor."

Backed by a new school board resolution that managed to come out squarely for both freedom of expression and full school control, the principal responded rapidly: "I feel compelled to refuse you the right to distribute Frox as you request and must advise you that any violation will lead to disciplinary procedures."

Bewildered by their inability to help the teen-agers come to a "reasonable, democratic compromise" with the traditionally liberal school administration, the parents have turned to lawyers. At the same time, the students find themselves in a drastically changed role. Youngsters who get good grades and lead school activities, they are suddenly rebels confronting the adults who control their education. They have become members of a growing minority of high school students who are coming into focus as "the new problem" in the nation's schoolhouse.

Yet the mood that is nurturing a network of nearly 500 "underground" high school papers, a national student-run press service to feed them, and the proliferation of independent high school unions and chapters of Students for a Democratic Society is being set by a kind of student the school finds difficult to label. This "new problem student" is most often not a classroom failure; frequently,

From Saturday Review, February 15, 1969. Copyright 1969 Saturday Review, Inc. Reprinted by permission.

he is black and from a poor family but not "disadvantaged." Sometimes, when his behavior approaches its most disruptive, he resembles a juvenile delinquent, and sometimes, too, he is simply a follower, pressured by the values and styles of the dominant peer group into acting without thinking.

These students, six-year-olds when John F. Kennedy became President, were the youngest witnesses to the high hopes for a more open society that came in the early Sixties—with its battles for civil rights and against poverty. In their short span of history, they have seen on television the assassinations and funerals of three national leaders who embodied these hopes. The war in Vietnam, beginning for them as nothing much more than another TV shoot-'em-up, has become a frightening reality as they approach draft age. Still vitally young themselves, they have watched the nation's shift from a youthful sense of unlimited expectations to the middle-aged habit of assessing and conserving old strengths and former gains.

Fed by the mass media, urged by parents and teachers to inquire, the students are sensitive to the larger world—and their limited role in it—as no generation before. For them, the student council that fulfills itself by planning dances, academic work that leads only to high College Board scores, and school newspapers that highlight class elections and football games are not only artificial, but inappropriate.

The underground press is, at first, an escape from the carefully delineated boundaries of school activity and opinion. Not surprisingly, therefore, the newest papers tend to be the most ambitious in scope, boldly taking on the great issues in the national arena. The first mimeographed issue of *Alternative* in Eugene, Oregon, was almost completely devoted to opposition to the Vietnam war. The *Strobe*, an amateurish sheet published in "Baltimore's liberated zone," attacks war, poverty, George Wallace, and the "pigs of Chicago." The Appleton (Wisconsin) *Post-Mortem*, edited by Fox Valley High School students "to challenge the myths and realities of their town and society," gets a bit closer to home by focusing on local police tactics.

In their open horror and bewilderment over the happenings in the society, the articles in these papers tend to emotional or moralistic generalizations, very serious but simple truths. They convey the teen-agers' sense of the outrages happening out there in the world, but also their inability—and lack of equipment —to come to grips with problems that are so vast, so complex, so distant from their own lives.

Society seems unable to let the young stay naive. The underground newspaper, dismissed as a potential educational tool by school administrators in spite of the student initiative and social concern it displays, teaches in another way. As they seek to express their opinions, the students discover that unlike their parents, their college counterparts, the man on the radio or the street corner, they have no right to express an opinion at all.

Last year, John Freeburg, a senior at rural South Kitsap High School outside of Seattle, Washington, began to edit and publish a mimeographed newspaper for students that reflected his own opposition to the Vietnam war, as well as to the adult Establishment's reaction to long hair. John himself was clean-cut in every sense of the word. The son of a commercial airlines pilot, a boy who spent summers working with diabetic children, he was a principal's dream: a consistent high honor student, one of three chosen by the faculty as "outstanding students," a student council representative, and ironically, regional winner of the Veterans' of Foreign Wars "What Democracy Means to Me" contest. Even in getting out his paper, he operated true to form, submitting articles to the school administration for approval before each issue.

In spite of this, three months before graduation John was suspended, and his parents' efforts to have him reinstated by the school board proved fruitless. The state Civil Liberties Union stepped in and obtained a court order for his reinstatement. An ACLU suit on his behalf for damages brought against the school district is still pending in the U.S. District Court. It claims that John's civil rights were violated; the district's counterclaim uses the traditionally unassailable argument that his activities were disruptive to school operation.

But even if his case should succeed—setting a precedent for the rights of high school students—John Freeburg has gone from idealism to skepticism about the "system" that found his exercise of freedom of the press an embarrassment to be eliminated in the face of pressures from right wing groups in the small community. His school said he was old enough to praise democracy publicly, but not to speak about its seamier aspects. Rather than practicing the ideals of freedom and tolerance it preached, the school used its power to suppress ideas. Something was terribly wrong, John decided, not just across the world in Vietnam, but in the institution that was supposed to educate him.

The staff of *Frox* is undergoing the same experience. Their crudely printed paper has worked almost painfully to link the relevant national issues to their own suburban community, to bring the big labels—"racism, imperialism, poverty"—home to Long Beach. Then they found their careful arrangements for distribution were canceled out by the refusal of the principal and the ambiguous educational rhetoric of the school board. Their own school has shown that, as Ira Glasser, associate director of the New York Civil Liberties Union, has stated: "In the classroom we teach freedom, but the organization is totalitarian. The kids learn that when the values of freedom and order conflict, freedom recedes." With what they're learning, the Long Beach students won't have to rely on clichés about freedom and repression. They now have their own gut-level issue, with all its complexities and subtleties. Unwittingly, the school system has given injustice the relevance the students themselves could not.

Once students begin to see the school as a bankrupt, manipulative bureaucracy—and themselves as its most vulnerable victims—the stage is set for the real student movement. The underground paper takes on a double role: to contradict the system that says students have no uncensored voice, and to talk with the authority of the insider about the follies of the institution and the ways it might be undermined or openly confronted. In the second issue of Ann Arbor (Michigan) High School's *Us*, the students explained what they learned from the furor produced by their first issue:

> The suppression we encountered was frightening. The savage in Huxley's *Brave New World* comments on our situation, saying to the Controller, "You got rid of them. Yes, that's just like you. Getting rid of everything unpleasant instead of learning to put up with it. Whether 'tis better in the mind to suffer the slings and arrows of outrageous fortune, or to take arms against a sea of troubles and by opposing end them. . . . But you don't do either. Neither suffer nor oppose. You just abolish the slings and arrows.

It's too easy." We fear the brave new world, we fear . . . "lobotomized" education, especially in this tremendous school. The issue which was created with this publication was not one of censorship of the *Optimist*. The school paper is possibly the best in the nation. Outside of administrative demands on space and content, we do not question its excellence. The existence of anti-distribution laws for student literature is the major objection. This is a violation of our constitutional rights. If this journalistic endeavor is a failure, it can easily be forgotten. But, if you or they force us to stop, we are all failures. Then, this school, city, and country, and the principles they supposedly represent are lies.

The more seasoned underground papers operate confidently on the understanding that change in the schools is their first order of business, and that national issues—the cry for law and order, teacher militancy—do affect their lives as students. At first glance, these papers are fun. They call themselves *The Pearl before the Swine*, *The Finger*, *Napalm*, *The Roach*, *The South Dakota Seditionist Monthly*, *Big Momma*, *The Philistine*, *The Bleeding Rose*, *Dormat Dwellers*, even *The New York Herald Tribune*. They are fresh, crazy, biased, irreverent in their view of the world, and often unexpectedly inventive in the way they present it. Albert Shanker, United Federation of Teachers president, becomes a great vulture, perched over the bodies of children. Samson Jones gets kicked out of Gaza Central High School for his long hair—and in a rage pulls the school down.

The more stylish ones are almost a new pop art form. Print runs around, over, and under stark drawings, viciously pointed cartoons, poignant photographs. Sometimes the word itself becomes the design. Dreamy poems are transposed on psychedelic drawings. Surrealistic obscene headlines fly out from the page. And often a picture stands by itself, telling the story rather than illustrating it. This is the work of McLuhan's generation.

The national focus for the underground is HIPS, the High School Independent Press Service (160 Claremont Avenue, New York, N.Y. 10027), which offers a weekly packet of news and illustrations of high school uprisings, busts, dress codes, discipline, and politics. Some sixty papers and 400 fans subscribe, at an often uncollected fee of $4 a month. "HIPS is very much in the revolutionary bag," a staffer admits. "I suppose we're just as bad as the *Times* in being biased. But underground papers are more interesting to read than the *Times*. They don't start with the usual 'who, where, when, what, why.' HIPS gets people to think. Gets them radicalized before they get into college. If that happens, chances are a fourth of them will never get to college."

One of the slickest papers HIPS services is the *New York High School Free Press*, which publishes 10,000 copies every three weeks (5 cents for students, 15 cents for teachers). It introduced itself last fall with a full-cover photo of a naked Negro baby girl holding the black flag of anarchy: "Ursula, seven months and already foxy as hell," the editors explained. A coupon form invites the reader to subscribe or, if he prefers, to curse and threaten the "hippie-commie-yippie-queer-pinkos" who print it. Another reader service is a directory of pertinent phone numbers: for prayers, demonstrations, birth control and abortion information, draft counseling, the FBI, and "nighttime companions"—the Girl-Scouts.

Yet silliness serves more serious purposes. The *Free Press*, with first-hand reports on national and school crises and interviews with prominent figures, is a sober attempt to reach radical and politically oriented students throughout the city. Its mix of serious radicalism and youthful gags, reflects its staff, a closely knit group of intense, quick-witted students, most of whom attend New York's highly selective Bronx High School of Science. In the living room of one of their homes, the students—a balance of whites and blacks—can go with breathtaking speed from typical teen-age roughhousing to political debate.

Reggie Lucas, the paper's fifteen-year-old music critic, talks about "breaking down the traditional teacher-student relationship" in the schools, so that by "interchanging roles, the teacher, as well as the student could learn." Everything the adult Establishment does, he explains politely, "is not just undesirable, but repugnant to us. The real hero today is the person who can mess up the society and pervert the youth."

Leader of the group is Howie Swerdloff, at seventeen a good-natured veteran of the underground press and racial student movement, who wrote last fall:

> The main thing that's taught us in school is how to be good niggers, obey the rules, dress in our uniforms, play the game, and NO DON'T BE UPPITY! Oh, we're trained for participating in the "democratic process"—we have our student governments—they can legislate about basketball games and other such meaningful topics. Don't mention the curriculum—THEY'LL tell us what to learn. Oh, we can express our complaints in the school newspaper—but the principal says what gets printed and don't embarrass the school's reputation.

Howie's immediate fight is with the school establishment; his long-range goal is to destroy the government he finds hopelessly oppressive through a world-wide people's revolution. His mother views his position with pride tempered by concern. When he was only fifteen, she recalls, she was first called into school about his activities. Finding Howie distributing antiwar leaflets across the street from the school, she began to apologize to the irate principal. Howie stopped her: "My lawyer said it's OK, Mother."

The Swerdloffs, liberals of another generation, are hopeful about the contributions their son and his friends will make to change the society, yet are appalled by the often violent reaction of the society to the youthful protests. "You wonder," Mrs. Swerdloff said, recalling the violence in Chicago during the Democratic convention. "You teach them such good values, and then when they go ahead and act on them, all this happens."

The underground high school press represents attitudes that have generated a variety of organizations bent on changing the school and the society. Their tactics range from polite dialogue to picketing to direct confrontation with the authorities. It is, nonetheless, difficult to categorize these groups, since their degree of militancy and their deviance from accepted student behavior depend a great deal on the response of school and community officials, the particular issues involved, and on the students themselves.

There is no one approach among the black separatist groups. New York City's High School Coalition, affiliated with the Black Panther party, spews vitriolic rhetoric in its newsletter and operates on a single dogma: the necessity of black liberation by any means possible. In contrast, the Modern Strivers, a group of young Negroes at Eastern High School in Washington, D.C., talks black power, but in the traditional American terms of self-help, hard work, and foundation funding.

The degree of flexibility within a community helps to determine the degree to which a group is regarded as a problem. In Berkeley, California, the liberal, interracial Youth Council, which has a poster of Black Panther leader Eldridge Cleaver in its office in city hall, received the support of city fathers even after its president was arrested for selling drugs. In Milwaukee, however, the beginnings of a student alliance, a rather apolitical group hoping for school reform, brought shocked cries from administrators, city officials, and the state's principals' association, who were ready to accuse "subversive" outside influences of stirring up the unrest.

The students are conscious of the variety within their ranks. The New York High School Student Union, an integrated, citywide group with semi-autonomous locals in 108 public and private schools, operates so flexibly that members at one school can be requesting more school dances while those at another can be out protesting the war. Its leaders tend to be disdainful of the doctrinaire approach of Students for a Democratic Society, and prefer to let their members "do their own thing."

Many groups, however, influenced by nearby college activity, have become SDS affiliates. Last year, eleven high schools in Seattle formed SDS chapters. In St. Louis, the citywide SDS group became large enough to be broken up into individual high school chapters. The Akron-based Ohio Union of High School Students, though not affiliated with SDS, has an adviser from the organization. National SDS headquarters has been overwhelmed by the flood of requests for literature from high school groups, and estimates an increase of about 800 percent over last year. To meet the demand, the SDS national council decided in October to hire a full-time secondary school coordinator.

The schoolmen, caught offguard by the new attitude, are now rushing to diagnose the problem and find solutions. The National Association of Secondary School Principals reports the findings of a national survey of student unrest in large and small school systems at its annual convention this month. A new NASSP handbook suggests ways to make the student council more meaningful. The organization's September 1968 bulletin was devoted to student unrest and included articles about its link with college militancy, possible reasons and solutions for the "coming revolt," and even one on what to do either before— or when—the legal showdown comes. ("The handwriting is on the wall; public school students will be protected in their constitutional rights," it said.)

Reaction to the new activism by schoolmen has been as varied as the kinds of students involved, their forms of dissent, and the responses of communities. A few school administrators regard the militancy as a potentially beneficial force, an often responsible if sometimes shrill demand for a more active role in school affairs. Just as the mass media and current events have taught the students something, so too they may have learned, really learned, what the schools' rhetoric says they should—to inquire critically.

Dr. Eugene Smoley, a high school principal in Montgomery County, Maryland, puts it this way: "The activists represent a real challenge educationally by questioning the foundations of the society. They're looking for ways to be helpful, pushing for a way for their actions to have some influence, pressing for more meaningful lives. The movement is a very positive thing, because it can only be compared with the apathy of an earlier time."

Many other schoolmen, however, dismiss the activism as a fad, claim that the high school students are only imitating their older brothers and sisters in college, or maintain that because students have always complained, all grievances are on the order of gripes about the cafeteria food.

The school administrator is, indeed, the man in the middle, caught between the community he serves and a whole new set of realities. Traditionally, the community—and the society—expect him to run a well ordered, efficient institution founded on a number of assumptions: Students are children, in both the legal and educational sense. They are pretty much alike—naïve and awkward as they grow. When they learn, they learn in school. The principal is legally responsible for the well-being of school children, and educationally responsible for what goes into their heads.

Although the legal fiction that students are children to be protected remains, much else has changed. Norman Solomon, honors senior and reporter for the county newspaper, who addresses the Montgomery County school board on the system's inputs and outputs and the "serious gap that presently exists between rhetoric and reality," cannot be dismissed as a charming child. The two Berkeley high school seniors who sit as full voting members on city committees know more about the operation of bureaucracy than any textbook could teach them. After his week in Chicago during the 1968 Democratic National Convention, Howie Swerdloff can tell his teachers a good deal about violence and police brutality in this nation.

To what extent can sophisticated adolescents be considered adults when they are still legally children? If the school is to educate, can it afford not to capitalize on the increasing awareness and concern of the students? Can the school be a public forum while maintaining its tight authoritarian patterns? If the school grants more freedom to students, is it opening itself up to irresponsible—as well as responsible—adolescent judgments? Can it find a place for its dissatisfied minority without threatening its more accepting, complacent majority?

The revolt itself testifies that students have been learning more than the schools have taught: from parents who are as well or better educated than teachers; from the mass media with which the school finds itself in competition; from actual participation in the politics and culture of the society. To accept this knowledge and experience means facing up to a set of complicated problems. To deny it is to deny the students themselves.

"...the voice of paranoia or reality."

There is much folklore about conflicts between the establishment and the counter culture. Folklore, no matter how compelling, cannot substitute for data. In this paper Dr. Heussenstamm describes a systematic attempt to explore the reality of one such conflict.

A series of violent, bloody encounters between police and Black Panther Party members punctuated the early summer days of 1969. Soon after, a group of black students I teach at California State College, Los Angeles, who were members of the Panther Party, began to complain of continuous harrassment by law enforcement officers. Among their many grievances, they complained about receiving so many traffic citations that some were in danger of losing their driving privileges. During one lengthy discussion, we realized that all of them drove automobiles with Panther Party signs glued to their bumpers. This is a report of a study that I undertook to assess the seriousness of their charges and to determine whether we were hearing the voice of paranoia or reality.

Recruitment advertising for subjects to participate in the research elicited 45 possible subjects from the student body. Careful screening thinned the ranks to 15—five black, five white, and five of Mexican descent. Each group included three males and two females. Although the college enrolls more than 20,000 students (largest minority group numbers on the west coast), it provides no residential facilities; all participants, of necessity then, traveled to campus daily on freeways or surface streets. The average round trip was roughly ten miles, but some drove as far as 18 miles. Eleven of the 15 had part-time jobs which involved driving to and from work after class as well.

All participants in the study had exemplary driving records, attested to by a sworn statement that each driver had received no "moving" traffic violations in the preceding twelve months. In addition, each promised to continue to drive in accordance with all in-force Department of Motor Vehicles regulations. Each student signed another statement, to the effect that he would do nothing to "attract the attention" of either police, sheriff's deputies or highway patrolmen —all of whom survey traffic in Los Angeles county. The participants declared that their cars, which ranged from a "flower child" hippie van to standard American makes of all types, had no defective equipment. Lights, horns, brakes and tires were duly inspected and pronounced satisfactory.

The appearance of the drivers was varied. There were three blacks with processed hair and two with exaggerated naturals, two white-shirt-and-necktie, straight caucasians and a shoulder-length-maned-hippie, and two mustache-and-sideburn-sporting Mexican-Americans. All wore typical campus dress, with the exception of the resident hippie and the militant blacks, who sometimes wore dashikis.

A fund of $500 was obtained from a private source to pay fines for any citations received by the driving pool and students were briefed on the purposes of the study. After a review of lawful operation of motor vehicles, all agreed on the seriousness of receiving excessive moving traffic violations. In California, four citations within a twelve-month period precipitates automatic examination of driving records, with a year of probation likely, or, depending on the seriousness of the offense, suspension of the driver's license for varying lengths of time. Probation or suspension is usually accompanied by commensurate increases in insurance premiums. Thus, the students knew they were accepting considerable personal jeopardy as a condition of involvement in the study.

Bumper stickers in lurid day-glo orange and black, depicting a menacing panther with large BLACK PANTHER lettering were attached to the rear bumper of each subject car and the study began. The first student received a ticket for making an "incorrect lane change" on the freeway less than two hours after heading home in the rush hour traffic. Five more tickets were received by others on the second day for "following too closely," "failing to yield the right of way," "driving too slowly in the high-speed lane of the freeway," "failure to make a proper signal before turning right at an intersection," and "failure to observe proper safety of pedestrians using a crosswalk." On day three, students were cited for "excessive speed," "making unsafe lane changes" and "driving erratically." And so it went every day.

One student was forced to drop out of the study by day four, because he had already received three citations. Three others reached what we had agreed was the maximum limit—three citations—within the first week. Altogether, the participants received 33 citations in 17 days, and the violations fund was exhausted.

Drivers reported that their encounters with the intercepting officers ranged from affable and "standard polite" to surly, accompanied by search of the vehicle. Five cars were thoroughly gone over and their drivers were shaken down. One white girl, a striking blonde and a member of a leading campus sorority, was questioned at length about her reasons for supporting the "criminal activity" of the Black Panther Party. This was the only time that an actual reference to the bumper stickers was made during any of the ticketings. Students, by prior agreement, made no effort to dissuade officers from giving citations, once the vehicle had been halted.

Pledges to Drive Safety

Students received citations equally, regardless of race or sex or ethnicity or personal appearance. Being in jeopardy made them "nervous" and "edgy" and they reported being very uncomfortable whenever they were in their automobiles. After the first few days, black students stopped saying "I told you so," and showed a sober, demoralized air of futility. Continuous pledges to safe driving were made daily, and all expressed increasing incredulity as the totals mounted. They paid their fines in person immediately after receiving a citation. One student received his second ticket on the way to pay his fine for the first one.

No student requested a court appearance to protest a citation, regardless of the circumstances surrounding a ticketing incident. When the investigator announced the end of the study on the eighteenth day, the remaining drivers expressed relief, and went straight to their cars to remove the stickers.

Some citations were undoubtedly deserved. How many, we cannot be sure. A tightly designed replication of this study would involve control of make and year of cars through the use of standard rented vehicles of low-intensity color. A driving pool of individuals who represented an equal number of both extreme-left and straight-looking appearance with matched age-range could be developed. Drivers could be assigned at random to pre-selected, alternate routes of a set length. Both left-wing and right-wing bumper stickers could also be attached at random after drivers were seated in their assigned vehicles and the doors sealed. In this way, no subject would know in advance whether he was driving around with "Black Panther Party" or "America Love It Or Leave It" on his auto. This would permit us to check actual driving behavior in a more reliable way. We might also wish to include a tape recorder in each car to preserve the dialogue at citation incidents.

No More Stickers

It is possible, of course, that the subjects' bias influenced his driving, making it less circumspect than usual. But it is statistically unlikely that this number of previously "safe" drivers could amass such a collection of tickets without assuming real bias by police against drivers with Black Panther bumper stickers.

The reactions of the traffic officers might have been influenced, and we hypothesize that they were, by the recent deaths of police in collision with Black Panther Party members. But whatever the provocation, unwarranted traffic citations are a clear violation of the civil rights of citizens, and cannot be tolerated. Unattended, the legitimate grievances of the black community against individuals who represent agencies of the dominant society contribute to the climate of hostility between the races at all levels, and predispose victims to acts of violent retaliation.

As a footnote to this study, I should mention that Black Panther bumper stickers are not seen in Los Angeles these days, although the party has considerable local strength. Apparently members discovered for themselves the danger of blatantly announcing their politics on their bumpers, and have long since removed the "incriminating" evidence.

"...lasting personal change happens slowly when it happens at all."

Many books have been written about nonverbal communications and the encounter-group movement in which such techniques flourish. Resnick reviews a number of those books and, in doing so, tells a great deal about what the movement can and cannot produce.

Leisured Americans have always had a weakness for costly regimens that promise to make them better than they are, and for the last several years the human potential-encounter group-"new therapies" movement has enjoyed increasing popularity as a means for putting people back "in touch" with themselves so that they can enjoy richer, more meaningful lives. So far no one has figured out exactly how many people have taken part in encounter groups, but Jane Howard gives us a rough idea in *Please Touch: A Guided Tour of the Human Potential Movement.* "A Bengal Indian I chanced to meet on a commuter train to Grand Central Station said oh yes, he'd been to several encounter groups," she writes. "My mother's cousin Chuck, near Los Angeles, said oh yes, he had thought of leading groups himself. A pair of bearded guitarists on a Caribbean beach said oh yes, they had hitchhiked most of the way down from New Hampshire to be in a twelve-day encounter. . . ." In other words, the group movement is *big.* For growing hordes of people, particularly Californians, group has become a way of life. And even the most conventionally turned-off man in the street has probably heard of the Esalen Institute in Big Sur, currently the world capital of psychic liberation.

Last spring the mountain came to Muhammed after all when Esalen staged a three-day "benefit" in a New York City hotel. The purpose was to raise money for scholarships, research, and development, and, in the faintly patronizing words of a brochure, "to give people on the East Coast a chance to sample, firsthand, the range of Esalen's programs." Although the National Training Laboratories of Bethel, Maine, which introduced group sensitivity-training in 1947, is actually the oldest of the several hundred growth and training centers that Esalen has come to symbolize, nowadays Esalen seems to be where it's all happening by dint of publicity alone. Therefore, despite the fact that most of the basic Esalen techniques are widely known and used in growth centers throughout the nation, several thousand New Yorkers were eager to experience for themselves (on a gut level, to be sure) what the mountain was all about.

It was the usual encounter-group crowd: largely white, middle-class, over-thirty-ish; often members of the "helping" professions; hip enough to know that the movement Esalen represents is supposed to be terribly groovy but not quite hip enough to be groovy without Esalen's help. Under the direction of such prominent movement leaders as Alan Watts, Bernard Gunther, William Schutz, Virginia Satir, and Ida Rolf, the benefit participants, who paid $75 for the full weekend's activities, went through some dozen or so workshops—in "Sensory Awakening," "Gestalt Awareness Training," and "Relaxation Techniques for Psychic Survival," to name a few. Divided into small groups and seated on the floors of the hotel's Grand Ballroom, Crystal Room, Palm Room, etc.—a far cry indeed from the oft-photographed seaside cliffs and virgin forests of Big Sur— the participants hugged each other, held hands, fantasied, breathed deeply, OM-ed, danced, laughed, and got in touch with everything from joy to sudden, perhaps painful, self-awareness. There was a high premium on nonverbalness, of course, and for those unaccustomed to touching (Esalen people tend to stand around in twos or threes with arms linked, rather like happy drunken roisterers) the weekend was, if nothing else, a profoundly sensual, even sexual experience —a kind of ultimate singles mixer.

In Janet Lederman's demonstration of "Gestalt Awareness as Applied to Children," for example, one exercise required the participants, who had ar-ranged themselves into pairs, to play alternately the roles of an autistic child and a teacher intent on drawing the child into communication. The "children" were asked to assume positions expressing intense withdrawal; the "teachers" could communicate with the children only nonverbally, using their bodies in any way possible; and five minutes later the teachers would move on to a new child. Naturally this activity encouraged a good deal of hit-and-run romance.

In fact, so much of the Esalen weekend consisted of mere flashes that, unless the participants were already well acquainted with the general goals of the human potential movement, they were probably misled as to what Esalen and the movement are really attempting to do. All but the most rigid skeptics are bound to be "turned-on" by the warm-up exercises with which leaders usually begin group sessions when the participants are strangers to each other —it's difficult not to unbend when one is directed to stare into a partner's eyes for a half-minute or introduce oneself by shaking legs—but these moments of brief intensity are not what the human potential movement, at its best, is get-ting at. "It took us a long time to debunk the whole Freudian crap," wrote the late Fritz Perls, one of the movement's founders, "and now we are entering a new and more dangerous phase. We are entering the phase of the turner-onners: turn on to instant cure, instant joy, instant sensory-awareness. We are entering the phase of the quacks and the con-men, who think if you get some break-through, you are cured. . . ."

Unfortunately, conducting groups can be an easy way to make a fast buck. Anyone who wants to proclaim himself a group leader can run groups whether he has had sufficient training or not—one simply has to find a dozen or more gullible takers. Although most of the Esalen staff have earned graduate degrees, the principal qualification even for a trained group leader is only a year or so of experience. Thus, it's difficult to separate the wheat from the chaff, and of the thousands of groups that meet regularly all over the United States there must be a sizable number in which the tacitly accepted goal is not growth, but thrills.

All encounter groups emphasize physical and nonverbal behavior, of course. Gestalt therapy deals with the whole person, not just what Perls called the "computer" operations of the intellect, and to some extent the human potential movement, like the counter-culture of which it is a part, is an overreaction to the basically cerebral, impersonal, joyless way of life that the mores and educational institutions of America perpetuate. In emphasizing the growth of the whole self and the importance of joy and intimacy, encounter groups are often sexual as well as sensual. There really is nude bathing and group massage in the hot sulphur springs at Esalen. But even at Esalen people cannot shed their former selves as easily as they remove their clothes. Much of the work in encounter groups—in ongoing groups especially, as opposed to weekend or five-day marathons—is grueling and painful. Ideally it produces insights that lead to growth—insights that happen, as they always have, in the head as well as the gut.

Jane Howard's first brush with the human potential movement occurred when she was working on a story about Esalen for *Life,* where she is a staff writer. She became so interested that eventually she took a year's leave of absence to do a book on the subject. Writing with admirable candor, she emerges in *Please Touch* as a rather conventional Midwestern WASP, her glamorous career notwithstanding, whom the movement gradually won over as a highly sympathetic observer if not a full-fledged convert. But, like Esalen's New York weekend, in her eagerness to convey glimpses of essenses, she betrays the movement's real goals. Her knowledge is thorough, but academic; even while she was experiencing various kinds of groups, she remained basically a reporter. And she tried to cover too broad a spectrum, taking part in what seem to have been several dozen groups and documenting at length fifteen or so.

The resulting "guided tour" is often delightful reading—some of it is first-rate satire; other parts are genuinely moving—but the over-all effect is relentlessly, annoyingly superficial. With one exception, even the in-depth accounts of various marathons have the hit-and-run air of Esalen's quickie-demonstrations. The exception is an eight-day "Advanced Personal Growth Laboratory," and it seems to be the only occasion in which the author really let all her barriers down, abandoned the role of reporter-participant, and surrendered herself to the experience.

Despite its basic flaws, *Please Touch* is the best comprehensive guide to the human potential movement available. Miss Howard has a capacity for gathering huge masses of facts and making sense of them with wit and style. The movement has become a vast and sprawling beast, almost impossible to define or describe except through endless firsthand accounts; but Miss Howard brings order to the confusion.

One chapter of the book describes the sort of people who join groups; another introduces the "circuit riders," the movement's peripatetic gurus; there is a chapter on group in schools and one that offers a concise history; other topics include the group movement in churches, techniques of fantasy and psychodrama, and the bioenergetics therapy of Alexander Lowen. At the end Miss Howard presents several recurrent criticisms of the movement and answers them, usually in the movement's favor. And throughout the book, of course, there are descriptions of actual groups—a dating group, a nude group, a couples group, a group for families, the Synanon "Stew," an interracial group, the crucial eight-day marathon, and a group for business executives.

One might well ask why, if Jane Howard became such an enthusiast, didn't she let herself get more involved in groups and write a more involving book? Why didn't she realize, for example, that even though she repeatedly depicts herself as moving from one experience to another without really putting down roots, the awareness hasn't served her in the creation of this book? Jane Howard's next book may go deeper than *Please Touch*; however, in her final chapter she offers a brief self-portrait and assessment of the changes she sees in herself—she dances more freely, but she is still emphatically "a child of the Gutenbergian print-freak heritage," still very much like what she was before— which can only remind the reader that lasting personal change happens slowly when it happens at all.

The human potential movement has already produced an enormous quantity of literature, and accounts of groups and marathons in the form of transcriptions from tape could have been predicted long ago. Even last year Fritz Perls's *Gestalt Therapy Verbatim* used the technique to illustrate Perls's own highly personal approach. It is odd and somewhat surprising, then, to discover that John Mann, chairman of the Department of Sociology at State University College in Geneseo, New York, a student of Jacob L. Moreno, the originator of psychodrama, and a frequent group leader himself, decided to present a two-day encounter, involving thirteen people, in a form that is primarily fictional.

Mann tells us in an explanatory "interlude with the author" that many of the incidents he describes in *Encounter*, whose narrative resembles the transcription of a tape but obviously isn't, actually happened in groups he has led, and that Richard, the leader in the book, mirrors himself. Nevertheless, Mann strains his technique far beyond conventional realism. At the beginning he presents, in parenthetical form, the thoughts and reactions of one of the most articulate members of the group, which provides a revealing but highly artificial commentary on the group's early hours together. Later we begin to realize that things are happening with a poetic logic and consistency unusual in real life. "The encounter weekend that has been described is probably more intense than those which are available generally," Mann explains. "This is partly the result of the written form." And the various participants speak in such stilted prose—more like the ultra-refined language of Ivy Compton-Burnett's novels than the barrages of obscenity and hip jargon one is likely to hear in actual encounter groups—that credibility suffers.

Yet the approach has certain advantages. Mann has a flair for poetic lyricism that produces a definite unity of tone and style—as he says himself, his own technique tends to focus on fantasy and role-playing—and the stilted speeches are almost balanced by passages of startling vividness. For example, following one episode, in which Richard directs the group to imagine a nude marathon, Ann, a man-hater and part-time Lesbian, gives this account:

I had a strange experience. It was really unpleasant. We were all here undressed, looking around and waiting to see what would happen next. Nobody wanted to make the first move. Then you suddenly reached up near your neck and started to unzip your skin. You had a zipper that went straight down the front. You took off your skin like a sweater. Underneath were blood vessels, muscles, fat, and various organs. Other people started doing the same thing. Then you started taking yourself apart. I remember when you reached in and took out your heart. You had all the various parts in front of you neatly arranged, and everyone was copying you. In the end we all sat there, a circle of upright grinning skeletons and Marcia asked you, "Is this a nude marathon?"

In another passage the group spins out a lengthy fantasy in which each member tells how it feels to be a stream, flowing from the mountains to the sea. This has the effect of a communal poem, and it would never have happened so perfectly in a real marathon.

The semifictional form allows Mann to create scenes, moreover, that the reader wouldn't be able to see if *Encounter* were a literal transcription of a tape-recorded group. In a moment of complete, if melodramatic, freedom Marcia, the original narrator and one of the group's strongest personalities, wanders nude in a nearby forest. At midnight on Saturday various members of the group encounter each other in the sauna of the house where the marathon is being held. And in another scene everyone goes out to the forest to enact a fantasy in which the Devil and an Angel of God vie for the allegiance of one of the women, portrayed as a religious fanatic. There is even an epilogue, in which the group meets again a month later at Marcia's apartment.

But in the long run the participants are stereotypes instead of real people, and the instances of larger-than-life vividness and poetry are not frequent enough or consistent enough to justify the technique. It might have worked in the hands of a skilled novelist or playwright, but more often than not *Encounter* is solemn and pretentious when it was clearly intended to be lyrical or poetic.

In direct contrast to *Encounter, Marathon 16* reports the experiences of a very real sixteen-hour group, involving five men, five women, a leader, and a nonparticipating writer-observer, that was organized specifically to be recorded in book form. This is the second collaborative effort of Martin Shepard, M.D., a New York psychiatrist who is on the board of directors of Anthos (an East Coast Esalen), and Marjorie Lee, a novelist, and the jacket copy announces with a palpable sense of pride that their first, *Games Analysts Play*, whose title tells all, won Dr. Shepard the distinction of being dropped as a member of the William Alanson White Institute. As one of the group members remarks toward the end of the marathon, Shepard is indeed gifted with a good deal of *chutzpah;* he dominates the gathering from beginning to end, and, probably to a greater extent than in most marathons, the group is a reflection of his own character.

All groups reflect the personalities of their leaders, of course. Although leaders of encounter groups often rely on a wide repertoire of conventional techniques and exercises, each leader's own personality is a far subtler, and more pervasive, element. It seems perfectly in keeping with Mann's general conception of the leader's role in *Encounter,* for example, that at one point Richard falls into an extended semi-coma, then later tells the group, "At first I thought that I should hurry back. Then I decided to go with the experience. Eventually it ended of its own accord." In *Gestalt Therapy Verbatim,* Fritz Perls appears to be a kind of Darryl Zanuck of the psyche, guiding his patients in and out of brief, psychodramatic epiphanies with cheery benevolence and consummate skill. Martin Shepard comes on like a drill sergeant, or perhaps a football coach, and consequently *Marathon 16* radiates aggression and competitiveness.

Considering that one purpose of encounter groups is to encourage spontaneity among the participants, Shepard has set up what seems an almost restrictively rigid structure for *Marathon 16*. Although he allows various episodes to happen whenever they will ("Little Prince's Freak-out," "Kari's Trip," "Bernard's Obnoxiousness," "Sarah's Loneliness"), he is naggingly insistent about offering direction—"I'd like you to think of something else now: the thing you're most ashamed of ..."; "Listen, we're going into the other room for this, where there's more space. I would like everybody to think about where they stand in terms of assertiveness and submissiveness ...": "What I'm going to do now is undress, and I want everybody else to undress also. ..." Ultimately the leader's role is a question of style—people often accused Fritz Perl's of being manipulative; nevertheless, he got results. But whereas Shepard's style may be effective in his office, in book form it becomes monotonous and obtrusive; *Marathon 16* often sounds like a contest in self-assertion. Mann creates obvious stereotypes with no depth at all, yet only a few of Shepard's quite genuine people are strong enough to come to life on the printed page—the odds are against them. (It should be noted, however, that, as participants in marathons often do, they all seem to love each other at the end.)

The market will probably bear many more books like *Encounter* and *Marathon 16*, for even the latter, despite its faults and its over-all monotonousness, is absorbing to read. There is, after all, a huge public for "true life confessions," and titles like these are only a more sophisticated version. Readers can even play the private game of deciding which marathons they liked best. The only danger is that once these books have served their basic educational purpose by illustrating the general principles of encounter groups, they will survive as little more than peepshows. The result, a real threat within the human potential movement itself, could easily be a growing imperviousness to intimacy, the exact opposite of what the movement's adherents hope to achieve.

Encounter and *Marathon 16* also raise questions about the appropriateness of presenting encounter groups in book form at all. The best medium to communicate a true sense of what groups are about, it would seem, is film. Indeed, several films of groups have already been made at Esalen, and are readily available. Esalen has also produced a number of tape recordings of groups (a radio station in Philadelphia even broadcasts groups live), and while these cannot be as vivid as filmed groups, which, in turn, would suffer in comparison with the real thing, they are probably better able than books to capture the feel of the phenomenon. In book form encounter groups, even more than playscripts, are merely a map of the territory.

Turning to an examination of *Body Language*, by Julius Fast, after the *sturm und drang* of three books that attempt to convey the emotional impact of the human potential movement in depth, is roughly akin to following a full performance of Wagner's Ring cycle with a rendition of "Frère Jacques." *Body Language* is a simple, and somewhat simple-minded, little book about the relatively new science of kinesics, the study of behavioral patterns of nonverbal communication. Kinesics, which recently rated a cover story in *The New York*

Times Magazine, is an important part of the human potential movement. But after reading *Body Language* one can only wonder what all the fuss is about.

Although he pays far too much homage to other people's studies and published papers, Fast does make some interesting points about the ways in which people's bodies communicate their feelings and needs. For instance, he talks about the human "territorial imperative" and cites experiments that show how often people subconsciously defend their own particular spheres. He also introduces yet another new science: "proxemics," the study of zones of territory and how we use them. Some readers will find entertaining Fast's numerous anecdotal case studies: for example, of Annie, who is a masochist, and her husband Ralph, a sadist, whose "delicate torture" consists solely in the "careful manipulation of his mask, by timing his body language," *i.e.,* by not smiling at the dinner table until poor Annie is ready to "die a thousand deaths." Fast has a ludicrous chapter about how a sexy stud named Mike uses his body language to "score" that ought to be reprinted in *Playboy* ("If you throw your quarry off balance . . . moving in for the kill becomes relatively easy."). In another chapter, entitled "Winking, Blinking, and Nods," the author discusses at length the various communicative powers of the eyes. And he even explains a newly invented body language "alphabet," which enables kinesicists to make a written record of body language in detail. They are welcome to it.

Fast's book is actually a crash course in sensitivity, and some people can probably benefit from reading it. Where else can one zero in on the real meaning of why Billy Graham points upwards when he talks about heaven and downwards when he talks about hell?

There will always be room in America for a good gimmick. But if we buy the myth of instant sensitivity and instant fulfillment of human potential, we'll only get what we deserve.

"He has a belief in his own potential and in his own direction."

In his image of the person of tomorrow, Dr. Rogers is describing an idealization of a member of the counter culture. As with any generalization, it applies only in some parts to some members of that group. It might be interesting to think, as you read, of how comfortable you would be in possessing each of the characteristics being described.

I am fascinated these days by what I am convinced is a most significant phenomenon. I am seeing a New Man emerging. I believe this New Man is the person of tomorrow. I want to talk about him.

I have seen him emerging, partially formed, from encounter groups, sensitivity training, so-called T-groups. I realize that for many years I saw facets of him emerging in the deep relationship of individual psychotherapy. I see him showing his face in the rapidly growing trend toward a humanistic and human psychology. I see him in the new type of student emerging on our campuses, and in campus unrest all over the world—Paris, Czechoslovakia, Japan, Columbia, Berkeley, San Francisco State, Harvard, and many other places. He is not all lovable, he is sometimes frightening, but he is emerging. I see him in the surge toward individualism and self-respect in our black population in and out of the ghettos, and in the racial unrest which runs like a fever through all our cities. I see elements of him in the philosophy of the "drop-outs" in our generation—the hippies, the "flower people." I see him, strangely enough, in the younger members of industrial management today. I catch what to my older eyes is a confusing glimpse of him in the musicians, the poets, the writers, the composers of this generation—I'll mention the Beatles, and you can add the others. I have a feeling that the mass media—especially television—have helped him to emerge, though on this I am not very clear. But I have named, I think, a number of the areas and trends which perhaps have caused the emergence, and certainly permit us to see, the qualities of this New Man.

Though I am excited and full of anticipation about this person of tomorrow, there are aspects of the situation which are very sobering. I believe the New Man has characteristics which run strongly counter to the orthodoxies, dogmas, forms, and creeds of the major western religious—Catholicism, Protestantism, Judaism. He does not fit at all into traditional industrial management and organization. He contradicts, in his person, almost every element of traditional schools, colleges, universities. He certainly is not suited to become a part of

Published and distributed by Sonoma State College, 1969. Reprinted by permission.

bureaucratic government. He doesn't fit well into the military. Since our culture has developed all these orthodoxies and forms of present-day life, we have to ask ourselves seriously if this New Man is simply a deviant misfit, or whether he is something more hopeful.

There is another reason for thinking deeply and soberly about him. He is almost the antithesis of the Puritan culture, with its strict beliefs and controls, which founded our country. He is very different from the person admired by the industrial revolution, with that person's ambition and productivity. He is deeply opposite to the Communist culture, with its controls on thought and behavior in the interest of the state. He in no way resembles the medieval man —the man of faith and force, of monasteries and Crusades. He would not be congenial with the man produced by the Roman Empire—the practical, disciplined man. He is also very alien to today's culture in the United States, which emphasises computerized technology, and the man in uniform—whether military, police, or government inspector.

If, then, he is new in so many ways, if he deviates so deeply from almost all of the gradually developed norms of the past and even the present, is he just a sport in the evolutionary line, soon to die out or be discarded? Personally I do not believe so. I believe he is a viable creature. I have the conviction that he is the person of tomorrow, and that perhaps he has a better chance of survival than we do. But this is only my own opinion.

I have talked about him at some length, but I have made no attempt to describe his attitudes, his characteristics, his convictions. I should like to do this very briefly. I would like to say that I know of no one individual to whom all of the following statements would apply. I am also keenly aware that I am describing a minority, probably a small minority, of our present-day populations, but I am convinced that it is a growing minority. What follows is a groping, uncertain characterization of what I see as the New Man. Some of his qualities are probably temporary ones, as he struggles to break free from the cocoon of his culture. I shall try to indicate these. Some, I believe, represent the process person he is becoming. Here then are some of his characteristics as I see them.

He has no use for sham, facade, or pretense, whether in interpersonal relationships, in education, in politics, in religion. He values authenticity. He will not put up with double talk. He hates statements such as these: "Cigarette smoking is a romantic, exciting, pleasurable, satisfying thing—(and of course it kills many through lung cancer)." Or, "we are following a noble pathway in protecting South Vietnam and living up to our commitments and treaties—(but in doing so we kill thousands of men, women and children, many of them completely innocent, others whose only crime is that they have a goal for their country different than ours)." He hates this kind of thing with a passion. He regards the current culture as almost completely hypocritical. I believe that this hatred for phonyness is perhaps the deepest mark of the New Man.

He is opposed to all highly structured, inflexible, institutions. He wants organizations to be fluid, changing, adaptive, and *human*. It will be clear from what follows how deep is his dislike for bureaucracy, rigidity, form for form's sake. He simply will not buy these qualities.

He finds educational institutions mostly irrelevant and futile so far as he is concerned. His unrest—in college and high school—arises out of a hundred specific issues, but none of these issues would be important if his school were truly meaningful for him. He sees traditional education as it is—the most rigid, outdated, incompetent institution in our culture.

He wants *his* learning to involve feelings, to involve the *living* of learnings, the *application* of relevant knowledge, a *meaning* in the here and now. Out of these elements he sometimes likes to become involved in a searching for new approximations to the truth, but the pursuit of knowledge purely for its own sake is not characteristic.

Religious institutions are perceived as definitely irrelevant and frequently damaging to human progress. This attitude toward religious institutions does not mean at all that he has no concern for life's mysteries or for the search for ethical and moral values. It seems, in fact, that this person of tomorrow is deeply concerned with living in a moral and ethical way, but the morals are new and shifting, the ethics are relative to the situation, and the one thing that is not tolerated is a discrepancy between verbal standards and the actual living of values.

He is seeking new forms of community, of closeness, of intimacy, of shared purpose. He is seeking new forms of communication in such a community— verbal and nonverbal, feelingful as well as intellectual. He recognizes that he will be living his transient life mostly in temporary relationships and that he must be able to establish closeness quickly. He must be able to leave these close relationships behind, without excessive conflict or mourning.

He has a distrust of marriage as an institution. A man-woman relationship has deep value for him only when it is a mutually enhancing, growing, flowing relationship. He has little regard for marriage as a ceremony, or for vows of permanence, which prove to be highly impermanent.

He is a searching person, without any neat answers. The only thing he is certain of is that he is uncertain. Sometimes he feels a nostalgic sadness in his uncertain world. He is sharply aware of the fact that he is only a speck of life on a small blue and white planet in an enormous universe. Is there a purpose in this universe? Or only the purpose he creates? He does not know the answer but he is willing to live with this anxious uncertainty.

There is a rhythm in his life between flow and stability, between changing-ness and structure, between anxiety and temporary security. Stability is only a brief period for the consolidation of learning before moving on to more change. He always exists in this rhythm of process.

He is an open person, open to himself, close to his own feelings. He is also open to and sensitive to the thoughts and feeling of others and to the objective realities of his world. He is a highly aware person.

He is able to communicate with himself much more freely than any previous man. The barriers of repression which shut off so much of man from himself are definitely lower than in preceding generations. Not only is he able to communicate with himself, he is also often able to express his feelings and thoughts to others, whether they are negative and confronting in nature, or positive and loving.

His likes and dislikes, his joys and his sorrows are passionate and are passionately expressed. He is vitally alive.

He is a spontaneous person, willing to risk newness, often willing to risk saying or doing the wild, the far-out thing. His adventuresomeness has an almost Elizabethan quality—*everything* is possible, *anything* can be tried.

Currently he likes to be "turned on"—by many kinds of experiences and by drugs. This dependence on drugs for a consciousness—expanding experience is often being left behind as he discovers that he prefers to be "turned on" by deep and fresh and vital interpersonal experiences, or by meditation.

Currently he often decides to obey those laws which he regards as just and to disobey those which he regards as unjust, taking the consequences of his actions. This is a new phenomenon. We have had a few Thoreaus but we have never had hundreds of people, young and old alike, willing to obey some laws and disobey others on the basis of their own personal moral judgment.

He is active—sometimes violently, intolerantly, and self-righteously active —in the causes in which he believes. Hence he arouses the most extreme and repressive antipathies in those who are frightened by change.

He can see no reason why educational organizations, urban areas, ghetto conditions, racial discrimination, unjust wars should be allowed to remain unchanged. He has a sustained idealism which is linked to his activism. He does not hope that things will be changed in 50 years; he intends to change them *now*.

He has a trust in his own experience and a profound *distrust* of all external authority. Neither pope nor judge nor scholar can convince him of anything which is not borne out by his own experience.

He has a belief in his own potential and in his own direction. This belief extends to his own dreams of the future and his intuitions of the present.

He can cooperate with others with great effectiveness in the pursuit of a goal which he is convinced is valid and meaningful. He never cooperates simply in order to conform or to be a "good fellow."

He has a disregard for material things and material rewards. While he has been accustomed to an affluent life and readily uses all kinds of material things, taking them for granted, he is quite unwilling to accept material rewards or material things if they mean that he must compromise his integrity in order to do so.

He likes to be close to elemental nature; to the sea, the sun, the snow; flowers, animals, and birds; to life, and growth, and death. He rides the waves on his surfboard; he sails the sea in a small craft; he lives with gorillas or lions; he soars down the mountain on his skis.

These are some of the qualities which I see in the New Man, in the man who is emerging as the person of tomorrow. He does not fit at all well into the world of the present. He will have a rough time trying to live in his own way. Yet, if he can retain the qualities I have listed so briefly, if he can create a culture which would nourish and nurture those qualities, then it may be that he holds a great deal of promise for all of us and for our future, In a world marked by incredibly rapid technological change, and by overwhelming psychological sham and pretense, we desperately need both his ability to live as a fluid process, and his uncompromising integrity.

Perhaps some of you in this audience will have resonated to my description because you see in yourself some of these same qualities emerging in you. To the extent that you are becoming this person of tomorrow and endeavoring to sharpen and refine his qualities in a constructive fashion, I wish you well. May you find many enduring satisfactions as you struggle to bring into being, within yourself and in your relationships with others, the best of this New Man.

Discussion Questions

1. What do we have to lose, or gain, by discouraging ideas which we find offensive?
2. How does contemporary popular music reflect the ideas and values of our culture?
3. In what ways would you wish to be like the person of tomorrow? In what ways would you not?
4. Is "turning on" a worthwhile goal in its own right? Or should it be a means toward an end?
5. How has the establishment changed and adopted some of the habits and values of the counter culture?
6. How could you use the techniques of the social sciences to obtain evidence that reflects on the truth or falsity of many of the stereotypes of either the establishment or the counter culture?